$155.00

REF
PR
85
.B688
suppl. xiii

D0824525

BRITISH WRITERS

BRITISH WRITERS

JAY PARINI
Editor

SUPPLEMENT XIII

CHARLES SCRIBNER'S SONS
A part of Gale, Cengage Learning

Colo. Christian Univ. Library
8787 W. Alameda Ave.
Lakewood, CO 80226

GALE
CENGAGE Learning

Detroit • New York • San Francisco • New Haven, Conn • Waterville, Maine • London

GALE
CENGAGE Learning

British Writers Supplement XIII

Project Editor
Michelle Kazensky

Copyeditors
Gretchen Gordon, Laura Myers, Linda Sanders

Proofreader
Susan Barnett, Tara Marion

Indexer
Wendy Allex

Permissions Researcher
Laura Myers

Permissions
Barb McNeil, Margaret Chamberlain-Gaston, Jacqueline Key

Composition Specialist
Tracey L. Matthews

Buyer
Rhonda A. Dover

Publisher
Frank Menchaca

Product Manager
Peg Bessette

© 2008 Charles Scribner's Sons, a part of Gale, Cengage Learning

For more information, contact
Gale
27500 Drake Rd.
Farmington Hills, MI 48331-3535
Or you can visit our Internet site at
gale.cengage.com

All RIGHTS RESERVED.
No part of this book may be reprinted or reproduced or utilized in any form or by any electronic, mechanical, or other means, now known or hereafter invented including photocopying and recording, or in any information storage or retrieval system, without permission in writing from Charles Scribner's Sons.

  For permission to use material from this product, submit your request via Web at http://www.gale-edit.com/permissions, or you may download our Permissions Request form and submit your request by fax or mail to:

The Permissions Department
Gale
27500 Drake Rd.
Farmington Hills, MI 48331-3535
Permissions Hotline:
248 699-8006 or 800 877-4253, ext. 8006
Fax: 248 699-8074 or 800 762-4058

  Since this pages cannot legibly accomodate all copyright notices, the acknowledgments constitute an extension of the copyright notice.

LIBRARY OF CONGRESS CATALOGING-IN-PUBLICATION DATA

British writers. Supplement XIII / Jay Parini, editor.
    p. cm.
Includes bibliographical references and index.
    ISBN-13: 978-0-684-31518-8 (alk. paper)
    ISBN-10: 0-684-31518-1 (alk. paper)
1. English literature--Bio-bibliography. 2. English literature--History and criticism. 3. Commonwealth literature (English)--Bio-bibliography.
4. Commonwealth literature (English)--History and criticism. 5. Authors, English--Biography. 6. Authors, Commonwealth--Biography. I. Parini, Jay.
    PR85.B688 Suppl. 13
    820.9--dc22   [B] 2007025420

Printed in the United States of America
2 3 4 5 6 7 15 14 13 12 11 10 09

Acknowledgments

Acknowledgment is gratefully made to those publishers and individuals who permitted the use of the following materials in copyright:

MONICA ALI. Boehmer, Elleke. From *Colonial and Postcolonial Literature*. Second Edition. Oxford University Press, 2005. Copyright © 2005. Reproduced by permission of Oxford University Press./ *Guardian,* June 17, 2003. Copyright 2003 Guardian Newspapers Limited. Reprinted by permission of Monica Ali and Aragi Inc./ Ashcroft, Bill, Gareth Griffiths, and Helen Tiffin. From *The Empire Writes Back.* Routledge, 1989. Copyright © 1989 Bill Ashcroft, Gareth Griffiths, and Helen Tiffin. All rights reserved. Reproduced by permission of the publisher.

JOHN BURNSIDE FILE. Burnside, John. From *Common Knowledge.* Martin Secker & Warburg Ltd, 1991. Copyright © John Burnside 1991. Reproduced by permission of Random House Group Limited./ From *Feast Days.* Martin Secker & Warburg Ltd, 1992. Copyright © John Burnside 1992. Reproduced by permission of Random House Group Limited./ From *The Myth of the Twin.* Cape Poetry, 1994. © John Burnside 1994. Reproduced by permission of Random House Group Limited./ *Scottish Studies Review 4,* v. 1, spring, 2003; Dosa, Attila, *Poetry and Other Realities: Scottish Poets in Conversation,* Rodopi, 2007. Reproduced by permission./ From *Swimming in the Flood.* Cape Poetry, 1995. © John Burnside 1995. Reproduced by permission of Random House Group Limited./ From *A Normal Skin.* Cape Poetry, 1997. © John Burnside 1997. Reproduced by permission of Random House Group Limited./ From *The Asylum Dance.* Cape Poetry, 2000. © John Burnside 2000. Reproduced by permission of Random House Group Limited./ From *The Hoop.* Carcanet Press, 1988. Copyright © 1988 John Burnside. All rights reserved. Reproduced by permission of Carcanet Press Limited./ From *The Light Trap.* Cape Poetry, 2002. Copyright © John Burnside 2002. Reproduced by permission of Random House Group Limited./ From *The Good Neighbour.* Cape Poetry, 2005. Copyright © John Burnside 2005. Reproduced by permission of Random House Group Limited./ From *Burning Elvis.* Jonathan Cape, 2000. Copyright © John Burnside 2000. Reproduced by permission of Random House Group Limited./ From *Common Knowledge.* Martin Secker & Warburg Ltd, 1991. Copyright © John Burnside 1991. Reproduced by permission of Random House Group Limited.

EDWARD CARPENTER. Forster, E.M. From *Maurice.* Copyright © 1971 by the trustees of the late E.M. Forster. Used by permission of W.W. Norton & Company, Inc./ Rowbotham, Sheila. From *Socialism and the New Life.* Pluto Press, 1977. Copyright © Pluto Press 1977. Reproduced by permission./ *Victorian Literature and Culture,* v. 32, 2004 for "Morris, Carpenter, Wilde, and the Political Aesthetics of Labor" by Ruth Livesey. Copyright © 2004 Cambridge University Press. Reproduced by permission of the publisher and author.

CIARAN CARSON Carson, Ciaran. From *The Star Factory.* Arcade Publishing, 1997. Copyright © 1997 by Ciaran Carson. All rights reserved. Courtesy of Arcade Publishing./ From *Belfast Confetti.* Wake Forest University Press, 1989. Copyright © Ciaran Carson 1989. All rights reserved. Reproduced by permission./ From *The New Estate.* Blackstaff Press, 1976. © Ciaran Carson 1976. All rights reserved. Reproduced by permission Wake Forest University Press./ From "Smithfield Market," in *The Irish for No.* Edited by Peter Fallon. Wake Forest University Press, 1987. © Ciaran Carson 1987. All rights reserved. Reproduced by permission./ From "Dresden," in *The Irish for No.* Edited by Peter Fallon. Wake Forest University Press, 1987. © Ciaran Carson 1987. All rights reserved. Reproduced by permission./ From "Belfast Confetti," in *The Irish for No.* Edited by Peter Fallon. Wake Forest University Press, 1987. © Ciaran Carson 1987. All rights reserved. Reproduced by permission./ *The Irish Review,* v. 8, spring, 1990. Copyright © The Irish Review 1989. Reproduced by permission./ From *First Language: Poems.* Wake Forest University Press, 1994. Copyright © Ciaran Carson 1994. All rights reserved. Reproduced by permission./ From *Opera Et Cetera.* Wake Forest University Press, 1996. Copyright © Ciaran Carson. All rights reserved. Reproduced by permission./ From *Last Night's Fun.* North Point Press, 1997. Copyright © 1996 by Ciaran Carson. All rights reserved. Reproduced by permission of North Point Press, a division of Farrar, Straus and Giroux, LLC./ From *The Twelfth of Never.* Gallery Books, 1998. © Ciaran Carson 1998. All rights reserved. Reproduced by permission of Wake Forest University Press./ From

ACKNOWLEDGMENTS

The Star Factory. Arcade Publishing, 1997. Copyright © 1997 by Ciaran Carson. All rights reserved. Courtesy of Arcade Publishing.

STEWART CONN. Conn, Stewart. From *Stolen Light.* Bloodaxe Books, 1995. Copyright © Stewart Conn 1995. All rights reserved. Reproduced by permission.

JOHN CORNFORD. Cornford, Frances. From *Mountains & Molehills.* Cambridge University Press, 1934. Reprinted with the permission of Cambridge University Press./ From "Cambridge Socialism," in *John Cornford: A Memoir.* Edited by Pat Sloan. Jonathan Cape, 1938. Reproduced by permission of Carcanet Press Limited./ From "Poems Written at Cambridge: Keep Culture Out of Cambridge," in *John Cornford: A Memoir.* Edited by Pat Sloan. Jonathan Cape, 1938. Reproduced by permission of Carcanet Press Limited./ Kiernan, Victor. From "Recollections," in *John Cornford: A Memoir.* Edited by Pat Sloan. Jonathan Cape, 1938. Reproduced by permission of Carcanet Press Limited./ From "Sad Poem," in *John Cornford: A Memoir.* Edited by Pat Sloan. Jonathan Cape, 1938. Reproduced by permission of Carcanet Press Limited./ Cornford, F. M. From "John as a Child," in *John Cornford: A Memoir.* Edited by Pat Sloan. Jonathan Cape, 1938. Reproduced by permission of Carcanet Press Limited./ From "The Struggle for Power in Western Europe," in *John Cornford: A Memoir.* Edited by Pat Sloan. Jonathan Cape, 1938. Reproduced by permission of Carcanet Press Limited./ From "Diary Letter from Aragon," in *John Cornford: A Memoir.* Edited by Pat Sloan. Jonathan Cape, 1938. Reproduced by permission of Carcanet Press Limited./ From "Poems Written in Spain," in *John Cornford: A Memoir.* Edited by Pat Sloan. Jonathan Cape, 1938. Reproduced by permission of Carcanet Press Limited./ Cornford, Christopher F. From "At School," in *John Cornford: A Memoir.* Edited by Pat Sloan. Jonathan Cape, 1938. Reproduced by permission of Carcanet Press Limited./ From "Letter to Frances Cornford" [June 1936] in *Understand the Weapon Understand the Wound.* Edited by Jonathan Galassi. Carcanet New Press, 1976. Copyright © Jonathan Galassi 1976. Reproduced by permission of Carcanet Press Limited./ From "Letter to His College Tutor, 4 Oct. 1936," in *Understand the Weapon Understand the Wound.* Edited by Jonathan Galassi. Carcanet New Press, 1976. Copyright © Jonathan Galassi 1976. Reproduced by permission of Carcanet Press Limited./ From "Letter to Margot Heinemann, 8 Dec. 1936," in *Understand the Weapon Understand the Wound.* Edited by Jonathan Galassi. Carcanet New Press, 1976. Copyright © Jonathan Galassi 1976. Reproduced by permission of Carcanet Press Limited./ From "Letters to Margot Heinemann, Autumn 1936, 21 Nov 1936," in *Understand the Weapon Understand the Wound.*

Edited by Jonathan Galassi. Carcanet New Press, 1976. Copyright © Jonathan Galassi 1976. Reproduced by permission of Carcanet Press Limited./ Bernard Knox, "Premature Anti-Fascist," *Abraham Lincoln Brigade Archives— Bill Susman Lecture Series,* 1998. Reproduced by permission./ From "Extracts from Letters, 1928-1933: Letter to His Mother, Stowe, 1930," in *John Cornford: A Memoir.* Edited by Pat Sloan. Jonathan Cape, 1938. Reproduced by permission of Carcanet Press Limited./ Bernard Knox, "Premature Anti-Fascist," *Abraham Lincoln Brigade Archives— Bill Susman Lecture Series,* 1998. Reproduced by permission./ Heinemann, Margot. From "Grieve in a New Way for New Losses," in *New Writing.* Edited by John Lehmann. Lawrence and Wishart, 1937. Reproduced by permission./ From "Poems Written at School," in *John Cornford: A Memoir.* Edited by Pat Sloan. Jonathan Cape, 1938. Reproduced by permission of Carcanet Press Limited./ From "Communism in the Universities," in *John Cornford: A Memoir.* Edited by Pat Sloan. Jonathan Cape, 1938. Reproduced by permission of Carcanet Press Limited.

JACKIE KAY. Kay, Jackie. From *Bessie Smith.* Absolute Press, 1997. © Jackie Kay 1997. Reproduced by permission.

JAMES MANGAN. Welch, Robert. From *A History of Verse Translation From the Irish 1789-1897.* Barnes & Noble Books, 1988. Copyright © 1988 by Robert Welch. All rights reserved. Reproduced by permission.

RUTH PITTER. Pitter, Ruth. From *Essays & Poems Presented to Lord David Cecil.* Constable, 1970. © 1970 by Ruth Pitter. Reproduced by permission of Constable & Robinson LTD.

PHILIP PULLMAN. *Sunday Telegraph,* January 27, 2002. Copyright © 2002 Sunday Telegraph. Reproduced by permission.

CRAIG RAINE. *The English Review,* April, 1991. Copyright 1991 Philip Allan Updates. Reproduced by permission./ From *The Onion, Memory.* Oxford University Press, 1978. © Craig Raine 1978. All rights reserved. Reproduced by permission./ *Helix,* 1984. © Poetry Helix, 1984. Reproduced by permission./ *The Malahat Review,* February, 1983. © The Malahat Review, 1983. All rights reserved. Reproduced by permission./ From *A Martian Sends a Postcard Home.* Oxford University Press, 1979. Reproduced by permission./. *Times Literary Supplement,* v. 1141, October 16-22, 1987. Copyright © 1987 by The Times Supplements Limited. Reproduced from The Times Literary Supplement by permission./ *Poetry Review,* v. 76, December, 1986. Reproduced by permission./ *New*

ACKNOWLEDGMENTS

York Review of Books, v. 42, March 23, 1995. Copyright © 1995 NYREV, Inc. Reprinted with permission from *The New York Review of Books./ The Sunday Herald,* July 16, 2000. COPYRIGHT 2000 SMG Newspapers Limited & SMG Sunday Newspapers Limited. Reproduced by permission of the author, Andrew Billen./ *The English Review,* April, 1991. Copyright 1991 Philip Allan Updates. Reproduced by permission.

DOROTHY RICHARDSON. Hanscombe, Gillian E. From *The Art of Life: Dorothy Richardson and the Development of Feminist Consciousness.* Ohio University Press, 1983. Copyright © 1982 by Gillian E. Hanscombe. Reproduced by permission.

MARY DARBY ROBINSON. Pascoe, Judith. From "Introduction," in *Mary Robinson: Selected Poems.* Edited by Judith Pascoe. Broadview Literary Texts, 2000. © 2000 Judith Pascoe. Reproduced by permission.

PETER SCUPHAM. Scupham, Peter. From *Collected Poems.* Carcanet Press, 2002. Copyright © Peter Scupham, 1975. Reproduced by permission of Carcanet Press Ltd./ From *Out Late.* Oxford University Press, 1986. Reproduced by permission of Carcanet Press Ltd./ From *The Air Show.* Oxford University Press, 1988. Reproduced by permission of Carcanet Press Ltd./ From *Night Watch.* Anvil Press Poetry, 1999. Copyright © Peter Scupham, 1999. Reproduced by permission./From *The Small Containers.* Phoenix Pamphlet Poets, 1972. Copyright © Peter Scupham, 1972. Reproduced by permission.

EDWARD UPWARD. Upward, Edward. From *The Coming Day and Other Stories.* Enitharmon Press, 2000. © Edward Upward 2000. Reproduced by permission./ From *The Railway Accident and Other Stories.* Penguin Books, 1972. Copyright © 1969 Edward Upward. Reproduced by permission./ From *Journey to the Border.* Enitharmon Press, 1994. © Edward Upward 1994. Reproduced by permission./ Upward, Edward and Christopher Isherwood. From *The Mortmere Stories.* Enitharmon Press, 1994. © Edward Upward 1994. © Don Bachardy 1994. Reproduced by permission./ From "A Marxist Interpretation of Literature," in *The Mind in Chains: Socialism and the Cultural Revolution.* Edited by C. Day Lewis. Frederick Muller Ltd., 1937. Reproduced by permission of The British Library./ From *The Spiral Ascent.* Heinemann,1969, 1977. © Edward Upward, 1969, 1977. Both reproduced by permission of The British Library./Upward, Edward and Christopher Isherwood. From *The Mortmere Stories.* Enitharmon Press, 1994. © Edward Upward 1994. © Don Bachardy 1994. Reproduced by permission./ From *The Night Walk and Other Stories.* Heinemann, 1987. © Edward Upward 1979, 1980, 1981, 1984, 1985, 1987. Reproduced by permission of The British Library./ From *An Unmentionable Man.* Enitharmon Press, 1994. © Edward Upward 1994. Reproduced by permission./ From *The Mortmere Stories.* Enitharmon Press, 1994. © Don Bachardy 1994. Reproduced by permission./ *London Magazine,* June, 1988; April/May, 1990 © *London Magazine,* 1988, 1990. Both reproduced by permission./ From *The Scenic Railway.* Enitharmon Press, 1997. © Edward Upward 1997. Reproduced by permission./ From *The Railway Accident and Other Stories.* Penguin Books, 1972. Copyright © 1969 Edward Upward. Reproduced by permission.

KEITH WATERHOUSE. Waterhouse, Keith. From *There is a Happy Land.* Michael Joseph, 1957. Reproduced by permission of Penguin Books, Ltd./ *The Guardian,* April 14, 2001. Copyright 2001 Guardian Newspapers Limited. Reproduced by permission of Guardian News Service, LTD./ From *Billy Liar.* Michael Joseph, 1959. Copyright © 1959 by Keith Waterhouse. Reproduced by permission of Penguin Books, Ltd./ From *Jeffrey Bernard is Unwell.* Samuel French, 1991. © 1991 by Keith Waterhouse Ltd. Reproduced by permission.

JOHN WYNDHAM. Wyndham, John. From *Sleepers of Mars.* Coronet Books, 1973. Copyright © 1938 by the Executors of John Beynon Harris. Reproduced by permission.

Contents

Introduction

"Reading a book is like rewriting it for yourself," said Angela Carter, the modern English novelist. There is a huge and complicated truth in that statement. As we read a novel or story, a poem or play, we imagine our own lives in relation to the lives unfolding before our eyes. Our past experiences influence how we see what is going on before us, on the page. This is one of the great delights of reading, but it remains one of its dangers as well. One can read too much of oneself into a text, thus altering the text in ways that obscure its vision.

Good criticism is useful in this regard, as it helps us to see how another reader sees a text. If the critic is an intelligent reader, and one who has read widely and therefore has a lot of cultural knowledge to bring to bear on the text, then all the better. One of our implicit goals in *British Writers* is to find and bring before readers a sequence of essays on interesting and important writers by readers of considerable breadth of understanding. These essays are meant as introductions, and they contain a good deal of biographical information that may be useful, but they are also quite sophisticated, in that the critics are asked to probe deeply.

British Writers was originally an off-shoot of a series of monographs that appeared between 1959 and 1972, the *Minnesota Pamphlets on American Writers*. These pamphlets were incisively written and informative, treating ninety-seven American writers in a format and style that attracted a devoted following of readers. The series proved invaluable to a generation of students and teachers, who could depend on these reliable and interesting critiques of major figures. The idea of reprinting these essays occurred to Charles Scribner, Jr., an innovative publisher during the middle decades of the twentieth century. The series appeared in four volumes entitled *American Writers: A Collection of Literary Biographies* (1974). *British Writers* itself began with a series of essays originally published by the British Council, and regular supplements have followed—this is

the thirteenth in the series. The goal of the supplements has been consistent with the original idea of the series: to provide clear, informative essays aimed at the general reader. These essays often rise to a high level of craft and critical vision, but they are meant to introduce a writer of some importance in the history of British or Anglophone literature, and to provide a sense of the scope and nature of the career under review.

The authors of these critical articles are mostly teachers and scholars. Most have published critical work in the field, and several are well-known writers of poetry or fiction as well as critics. As anyone glancing through this volume will see, they have been held to the highest standards of clear writing and sound scholarship. Jargon and theoretical musings have been discouraged, except when strictly relevant. Each of the essays concludes with a select bibliography of works by the author under discussion and secondary works that might be useful to those who wish to pursue the subject further. Supplement XIII is to a degree focused on contemporary or fairly modern writers, such as Monica Ali, John Burnside, Ciaran Carson, Stewart Conn, Jackie Kay, Ruth Pitter, Philip Pullman, Craig Raine, Peter Scupham, and John Wyndham, many of whom who have had little sustained attention from critics, although most are rather well known. They have all been written about in the review pages of newspapers and magazines, often at considerable length, and their work has acquired a substantial following, but their careers have yet to attract significant scholarship. That will certainly follow, but the essays included in this volume constitute a beginning of sorts, an attempt to map out the particular universe of each writer.

A number of classic writers from the distant past included here are Edward Carpenter, James Clarence Mangan, Dorothy Richardson, Mary Robinson, and William Thomas Stead—important authors from earlier centuries who, for one reason or another, had yet to be treated in this series.

INTRODUCTION

Some writers in this volume belong to the more recent past, such as John Cornford and Edward Upward. These are well-known figures in the literary world, major voices, and it is time they were added to the series.

As ever, our purpose in presenting these critical and biographical essays is to bring readers to the texts discussed, to give them useful information and critical hints that will assist them in the act of reading—this complicated process in which they discover themselves as well as the text before them.

—*JAY PARINI*

Chronology

CHRONOLOGY

1499   Amerigo Vespucci's first voyage to America
Erasmus' first visit to England

1503   Thomas Wyatt born

1505   John Colet appointed dean of St. Paul's: founds St. Paul's School

1509–1547   Reign of Henry VIII

1509   The king marries Catherine of Aragon

1511   Erasmus' *Praise of Folly* published

1513   Invasion by the Scots defeated at Flodden Field

1515   Wolsey appointed lord chancellor

1516   Sir Thomas More's *Utopia*

1517   Martin Luther's theses against indulgences published at Wittenberg
Henry Howard (earl of Surrey) born

1519   Charles V of Spain becomes Holy Roman Emperor

1519–1521   Magellan's voyage around the world

1525   Cardinal College, the forerunner of Christ Church, founded at Oxford

1526   Tyndale's English translation of the New Testament imported from Holland

1529   Fall of Cardinal Wolsey
Death of John Skelton

1529–1536   The "Reformation" Parliament

1531   Sir Thomas Elyot's *The Governour* published

1532   Thomas Cranmer appointed archbishop of Canterbury
Machiavelli's *The Prince*

1533   The king secretly marries Anne Boleyn
Cranmer pronounces the king's marriage with Catherine "against divine law"

1534   The Act of Supremacy constitutes the king as head of the Church of England

1535   Sir Thomas More executed
Thomas Cromwell appointed vicar general of the Church of England

1536   The Pilgrimage of Grace: risings against the king's religious, social, and economic reforms
Anne Boleyn executed
The king marries Jane Seymour

1537   The dissolution of the monasteries: confiscation of ecclesiastical properties and assets; increase in royal revenues
Jane Seymour dies

1538   First complete English Bible published and placed in all churches

1540   The king marries Anne of Cleves
Marriage dissolved
The king marries Catherine Howard
Fall and execution of Thomas Cromwell

1542   Catherine Howard executed
Death of Sir Thomas Wyatt

1543   The king marries Catherine Parr
Copernicus' *De revolutionibus orbium coelestium*

1546   Trinity College, Cambridge, refounded

1547   The earl of Surrey executed

1547–1553   Reign of Edward VI

1548–1552   Hall's *Chronicle*

1552   The second Book of Common Prayer

ca. 1552   Edmund Spenser born

1553   Lady Jane Grey proclaimed queen

1553–1558   Reign of Mary I (Mary Tudor)

ca. 1554   Births of Walter Raleigh, Richard Hooker, John Lyly, and Fulke Greville

1554   Lady Jane Grey executed
Mary I marries Philip II of Spain
Bandello's *Novelle*
Philip Sidney born

ca. 1556   George Peele born

1557   Tottel's *Miscellany*, including the poems of Wyatt and Surrey, published

ca. 1558   Thomas Kyd born

1558   Calais, the last English possession in France, is lost
Birth of Robert Greene
Mary I dies

1558–1603   Reign of Elizabeth I

1559   John Knox arrives in Scotland
Rebellion against the French regent

ca. 1559   George Chapman born

1561   Mary Queen of Scots (Mary Stuart) arrives in Edinburgh

CHRONOLOGY

Thomas Hoby's translation of Castiglione's *The Courtier Gorboduc*, the first English play in blank verse
Francis Bacon born

1562   Civil war in France
English expedition sent to support the Huguenots

1562–1568   Sir John Hawkins' voyages to Africa

1564   Births of Christopher Marlowe and William Shakespeare

1565   Mary Queen of Scots marries Lord Darnley

1566   William Painter's *Palace of Pleasure*, a miscellany of prose stories, the source of many dramatists' plots

1567   Darnley murdered at Kirk o'Field
Mary Queen of Scots marries the earl of Bothwell

1569   Rebellion of the English northern earls suppressed

1570   Roger Ascham's *The Schoolmaster*

1571   Defeat of the Turkish fleet at Lepanto

ca. 1572   Ben Jonson born

1572   St. Bartholomew's Day massacre
John Donne born

1574   The earl of Leicester's theater company formed

1576   The Theater, the first permanent theater building in London, opened
The first Blackfriars Theater opened with performances by the Children of St. Paul's
John Marston born

1576–1578   Martin Frobisher's voyages to Labrador and the northwest

1577–1580   Sir Francis Drake sails around the world

1577   Holinshed's *Chronicles of England, Scotlande, and Irelande*

1579   John Lyly's *Euphues: The Anatomy of Wit*
Thomas North's translation of *Plutarch's Lives*

1581   The Levant Company founded
Seneca's *Ten Tragedies* translated

1582   Richard Hakluyt's *Divers Voyages Touching the Discoverie of America*

1583   Philip Massinger born

1584–1585   Sir John Davis' first voyage to Greenland

1585   First English settlement in America, the "Lost Colony" comprising 108 men under Ralph Lane, founded at Roanoke Island, off the coast of North Carolina

1586   Kyd's *Spanish Tragedy*
Marlowe's *Tamburlaine*
William Camden's *Britannia*
The Babington conspiracy against Queen Elizabeth
Death of Sir Philip Sidney

1587   Mary Queen of Scots executed
Birth of Virginia Dare, first English child born in America, at Roanoke Island

1588   Defeat of the Spanish Armada
Marlowe's *Dr. Faustus*

1590   Spenser's *The Faerie Queen*, Cantos 1–3
Richard Brome born

1592   Outbreak of plague in London; the theaters closed
Henry King born

1593   Death of Christopher Marlowe

1594   The Lord Chamberlain's Men, the company to which Shakespeare belonged, founded
The Swan Theater opened
Death of Thomas Kyd

1595   Ralegh's expedition to Guiana
Sidney's *Apology for Poetry*

1596   The earl of Essex's expedition captures Cadiz
The second Blackfriars Theater opened

ca. 1597   Death of George Peele

1597   Bacon's first collection of *Essays*

1598   Jonson's *Every Man in His Humor*

1598–1600   Richard Hakluyt's *Principal Navigations, Voyages, Traffics, and Discoveries of the English Nation*

1599   The Globe Theater opened
Death of Edmund Spenser

1600   Death of Richard Hooker

1601   Rebellion and execution of the earl of Essex

1602   The East India Company founded
The Bodleian Library reopened at Oxford

1603–1625   Reign of James I

1603   John Florio's translation of Montaigne's *Essays*

CHRONOLOGY

CHRONOLOGY

ca. 1637 Thomas Traherne born
1637 Milton's "Lycidas"
Descartes's *Discours de la méthode*
King Charles's levy of ship money challenged in the courts by John Hampden
The introduction of the new English Book of Common Prayer strongly opposed in Scotland
Death of Ben Jonson
ca. 1638 Death of John Webster
1638 The Scots draw up a National Covenant to defend their religion
ca. 1639 Death of John Ford
1639 Parliament reassembled to raise taxes
Death of Thomas Carew
Charles Sedley born
1639–1640 The two Bishops' Wars with Scotland
1640 The Long Parliament assembled
The king's advisers, Archbishop Laud and the earl of Strafford, impeached
Aphra Behn born
Death of Philip Massinger
1641 Strafford executed
Acts passed abolishing extraparliamentary taxation, the king's extraordinary courts, and his power to order a dissolution without parliamentary consent
The Grand Remonstrance censuring royal policy passed by eleven votes
William Wycherley born
1642 Parliament submits the nineteen Propositions, which King Charles rejects as annihilating the royal power
The Civil War begins
The theaters close
Royalist victory at Edgehill; King Charles established at Oxford
Death of Sir John Suckling
1643 Parliament concludes the Solemn League and Covenant with the Scots
Louis XIV becomes king of France
Charles Sackville, earl of Dorset, born
1644 Parliamentary victory at Marston Moor

The New Model army raised
Milton's *Areopagitica*
1645 Parliamentary victory under Fairfax and Cromwell at Naseby
Fairfax captures Bristol
Archbishop Laud executed
1646 Fairfax besieges King Charles at Oxford
King Charles takes refuge in Scotland; end of the First Civil War
King Charles attempts negotiations with the Scots
Parliament's proposals sent to the king and rejected
1647 Conflict between Parliament and the army
A general council of the army established that discusses representational government within the army
The Agreement of the People drawn up by the Levelers; its proposals include manhood suffrage
King Charles concludes an agreement with the Scots
George Fox begins to preach
John Wilmot, earl of Rochester, born
1648 Cromwell dismisses the general council of the army
The Second Civil War begins
Fairfax defeats the Kentish royalists at Maidstone
Cromwell defeats the Scots at Preston
The Thirty Years' War ended by the treaty of Westphalia
Parliament purged by the army
1649–1660 Commonwealth
1649 King Charles I tried and executed
The monarchy and the House of Lords abolished
The Commonwealth proclaimed
Cromwell invades Ireland and defeats the royalist Catholic forces
Death of Richard Crashaw
1650 Cromwell defeats the Scots at Dunbar
1651 Charles II crowned king of the Scots, at Scone
Charles II invades England, is defeated at Worcester, escapes to France

CHRONOLOGY

Thomas Hobbes's *Leviathan*

1652 War with Holland
Death of Richard Brome

1653 The Rump Parliament dissolved by the army
A new Parliament and council of state nominated; Cromwell becomes Lord Protector
Walton's *The Compleat Angler*

1654 Peace concluded with Holland
War against Spain

1655 Parliament attempts to reduce the army and is dissolved
Rule of the major-generals

1656 Sir William Davenant produces *The Siege of Rhodes*, one of the first English operas

1657 Second Parliament of the Protectorate
Cromwell is offered and declines the throne
Death of Richard Lovelace

1658 Death of Oliver Cromwell
Richard Cromwell succeeds as Protector

1659 Conflict between Parliament and the army

1660 General Monck negotiates with Charles II
Charles II offers the conciliatory Declaration of Breda and accepts Parliament's invitation to return
Will's Coffee House established
Sir William Davenant and Thomas Killigrew licensed to set up two companies of players, the Duke of York's and the King's Servants, including actors and actresses
Pepys's *Diary* begun

1660–1685 Reign of Charles II

1661 Parliament passes the Act of Uniformity, enjoining the use of the Book of Common Prayer; many Puritan and dissenting clergy leave their livings
Anne Finch born

1662 Peace Treaty with Spain
King Charles II marries Catherine of Braganza
The Royal Society incorporated (founded in 1660)

1664 War against Holland
New Amsterdam captured and becomes New York
John Vanbrugh born

1665 The Great Plague
Newton discovers the binomial theorem and invents the integral and differential calculus, at Cambridge

1666 The Great Fire of London
Bunyan's *Grace Abounding*
London Gazette founded

1667 The Dutch fleet sails up the Medway and burns English ships
The war with Holland ended by the Treaty of Breda
Milton's *Paradise Lost*
Thomas Sprat's *History of the Royal Society*
Death of Abraham Cowley

1668 Sir Christopher Wren begins to rebuild St. Paul's Cathedral
Triple Alliance formed with Holland and Sweden against France
Dryden's *Essay of Dramatick Poesy*

1670 Alliance formed with France through the secret Treaty of Dover
Pascal's *Pensées*
The Hudson's Bay Company founded
William Congreve born

1671 Milton's *Samson Agonistes* and *Paradise Regained*

1672 War against Holland
Wycherley's *The Country Wife*
King Charles issues the Declaration of Indulgence, suspending penal laws against Nonconformists and Catholics

1673 Parliament passes the Test Act, making acceptance of the doctrines of the Church of England a condition for holding public office

1674 War with Holland ended by the Treaty of Westminster
Deaths of John Milton, Robert Herrick, and Thomas Traherne

1676 Etherege's *The Man of Mode*

1677 Baruch Spinoza's *Ethics*
Jean Racine's *Phèdre*

CHRONOLOGY

King Charles's niece, Mary, marries her cousin William of Orange

1678 Fabrication of the so-called popish plot by Titus Oates
Bunyan's *Pilgrim's Progress*
Dryden's *All for Love*
Death of Andrew Marvell
George Farquhar born

1679 Parliament passes the Habeas Corpus Act
Rochester's *A Satire Against Mankind*

1680 Death of John Wilmot, earl of Rochester

1681 Dryden's *Absalom and Achitophel* (Part 1)

1682 Dryden's *Absalom and Achitophel* (Part 2)
Thomas Otway's *Venice Preserv'd*
Philadelphia founded
Death of Sir Thomas Browne

1683 The Ashmolean Museum, the world's first public museum, opens at Oxford
Death of Izaak Walton

1685–1688 Reign of James II

1685 Rebellion and execution of James Scott, duke of Monmouth
John Gay born

1686 The first book of Newton's *PrincipiaDe motu corporum*, containing his theory of gravitationpresented to the Royal Society

1687 James II issues the Declaration of Indulgence
Dryden's *The Hind and the Panther*
Death of Edmund Waller

1688 James II reissues the Declaration of Indulgence, renewing freedom of worship and suspending the provisions of the Test Act
Acquittal of the seven bishops imprisoned for protesting against the Declaration
William of Orange lands at Torbay, Devon
James II takes refuge in France
Death of John Bunyan
Alexander Pope born

1689–1702 Reign of William III

1689 Parliament formulates the Declaration of Rights

William and Mary accept the Declaration and the crown
The Grand Alliance concluded between the Holy Roman Empire, England, Holland, and Spain
War declared against France
King William's War, 1689–1697 (the first of the French and Indian wars)
Samuel Richardson born

1690 James II lands in Ireland with French support, but is defeated at the battle of the Boyne
John Locke's *Essay Concerning Human Understanding*

1692 Salem witchcraft trials
Death of Sir George Etherege

ca. 1693 Eliza Haywood born

1694 George Fox's *Journal*
Voltaire (François Marie Arouet) born
Death of Mary II

1695 Congreve's *Love for Love*
Death of Henry Vaughan

1697 War with France ended by the Treaty of Ryswick
Vanbrugh's *The Relapse*

1698 Jeremy Collier's *A Short View of the Immorality and Profaneness of the English Stage*

1699 Fénelon's *Les Aventures de Télémaque*

1700 Congreve's *The Way of the World*
Defoe's *The True-Born Englishman*
Death of John Dryden
James Thomson born

1701 War of the Spanish Succession, 1701–1714 (Queen Anne's War in America, 1702–1713)
Death of Sir Charles Sedley

1702–1714 Reign of Queen Anne

1702 Clarendon's *History of the Rebellion* (1702–1704)
Defoe's *The Shortest Way with the Dissenters*

1703 Defoe is arrested, fined, and pilloried for writing *The Shortest Way*
Death of Samuel Pepys

1704 John Churchill, duke of Marlborough, and Prince Eugene of Savoy defeat the French at Blenheim
Capture of Gibraltar

CHRONOLOGY

Swift's *A Tale of a Tub* and *The Battle of the Books*
The Review founded (1704–1713)

1706 Farquhar's *The Recruiting Officer*
Deaths of John Evelyn and Charles Sackville, earl of Dorset

1707 Farquhar's *The Beaux' Stratagem*
Act of Union joining England and Scotland
Death of George Farquhar
Henry Fielding born

1709 The *Tatler* founded (1709–1711)
Nicholas Rowe's edition of Shakespeare
Samuel Johnson born
Marlborough defeats the French at Malplaquet
Charles XII of Sweden defeated at Poltava

1710 South Sea Company founded
First copyright act

1711 Swift's *The Conduct of the Allies*
The *Spectator* founded (1711–1712; 1714)
Marlborough dismissed
David Hume born

1712 Pope's *The Rape of the Lock* (Cantos 1–2)
Jean Jacques Rousseau born

1713 War with France ended by the Treaty of Utrecht
The *Guardian* founded
Swift becomes dean of St. Patrick's, Dublin
Addison's *Cato*
Laurence Sterne born

1714–1727 Reign of George I

1714 Pope's expended version of *The Rape of the Lock* (Cantos 1–5)

1715 The Jacobite rebellion in Scotland
Pope's translation of Homer's *Iliad* (1715–1720)
Death of Louis XIV

1716 Death of William Wycherley
Thomas Gray born

1717 Pope's *Eloisa to Abelard*
David Garrick born
Horace Walpole born

1718 Quadruple Alliance (Britain, France, the Netherlands, the German Empire) in war against Spain

1719 Defoe's *Robinson Crusoe*

Death of Joseph Addison

1720 Inoculation against smallpox introduced in Boston
War against Spain
The South Sea Bubble
Gilbert White born
Defoe's *Captain Singleton* and *Memoirs of a Cavalier*

1721 Tobias Smollett born
William Collins born

1722 Defoe's *Moll Flanders*, *Journal of the Plague Year*, and *Colonel Jack*

1724 Defoe's *Roxana*
Swift's *The Drapier's Letters*

1725 Pope's translation of Homer's *Odyssey* (1725–1726)

1726 Swift's *Gulliver's Travels*
Voltaire in England (1726–1729)
Death of Sir John Vanbrugh

1727–1760 Reign of George II

1728 Gay's *The Beggar's Opera*
Pope's *The Dunciad* (Books 1–2)
Oliver Goldsmith born

1729 Swift's *A Modest Proposal*
Edmund Burke born
Deaths of William Congreve and Sir Richard Steele

1731 Navigation improved by introduction of the quadrant
Pope's *Moral Essays* (1731–1735)
Death of Daniel Defoe
William Cowper born

1732 Death of John Gay

1733 Pope's *Essay on Man* (1733–1734)
Lewis Theobald's edition of Shakespeare

1734 Voltaire's *Lettres philosophiques*

1736 James Macpherson born

1737 Edward Gibbon born

1738 Johnson's *London*

1740 War of the Austrian Succession, 1740–1748 (King George's War in America, 1744–1748)
George Anson begins his circumnavigation of the world (1740–1744)
Frederick the Great becomes king of Prussia (1740–1786)
Richardson's *Pamela* (1740–1741)
James Boswell born

1742 Fielding's *Joseph Andrews*

CHRONOLOGY

Edward Young's *Night Thoughts* (1742–1745)

Pope's *The New Dunciad* (Book 4)

1744 Johnson's *Life of Mr. Richard Savage*

Death of Alexander Pope

1745 Second Jacobite rebellion, led by Charles Edward, the Young Pretender

Death of Jonathan Swift

1746 The Young Pretender defeated at Culloden

Collins' *Odes on Several Descriptive and Allegorical Subjects*

1747 Richardson's *Clarissa Harlowe* (1747–1748)

Franklin's experiments with electricity announced

Voltaire's *Essai sur les moeurs*

1748 War of the Austrian Succession ended by the Peace of Aix-la-Chapelle

Smollett's *Adventures of Roderick Random*

David Hume's *Enquiry Concerning Human Understanding*

Montesquieu's *L'Esprit des lois*

1749 Fielding's *Tom Jones*

Johnson's *The Vanity of Human Wishes*

Bolingbroke's *Idea of a Patriot King*

1750 The *Rambler* founded (1750–1752)

1751 Gray's *Elegy Written in a Country Churchyard*

Fielding's *Amelia*

Smollett's *Adventures of Peregrine Pickle*

Denis Diderot and Jean le Rond d'Alembert begin to publish the *Encyclopédie* (1751–1765)

Richard Brinsley Sheridan born

1752 Frances Burney and Thomas Chatterton born

1753 Richardson's *History of Sir Charles Grandison* (1753–1754)

Smollett's *The Adventures of Ferdinand Count Fathom*

1754 Hume's *History of England* (1754–1762)

Death of Henry Fielding

George Crabbe born

1755 Lisbon destroyed by earthquake

Fielding's *Journal of a Voyage to Lisbon* published posthumously

Johnson's *Dictionary of the English Language*

1756 The Seven Years' War against France, 1756–1763 (the French and Indian War in America, 1755–1760)

William Pitt the elder becomes prime minister

Johnson's proposal for an edition of Shakespeare

Death of Eliza Haywood

1757 Robert Clive wins the battle of Plassey, in India

Gray's "The Progress of Poesy" and "The Bard"

Burke's *Philosophical Enquiry into the Origin of Our Ideas of the Sublime and Beautiful*

Hume's *Natural History of Religion*

William Blake born

1758 The *Idler* founded (1758–1760)

Mary Darby Robinson born

1759 Capture of Quebec by General James Wolfe

Johnson's *History of Rasselas, Prince of Abyssinia*

Voltaire's *Candide*

The British Museum opens

Sterne's *The Life and Opinions of Tristram Shandy* (1759–1767)

Death of William Collins

Mary Wollstonecraft born

Robert Burns born

1760–1820 Reign of George III

1760 James Macpherson's *Fragments of Ancient Poetry Collected in the Highlands of Scotland*

William Beckford born

1761 Jean-Jacques Rousseau's *Julie, ou la nouvelle Héloïse*

Death of Samuel Richardson

1762 Rousseau's *Du Contrat social* and *Émile*

Catherine the Great becomes czarina of Russia (1762–1796)

1763 The Seven Years' War ended by the Peace of Paris

Smart's *A Song to David*

1764 James Hargreaves invents the spinning jenny

CHRONOLOGY

1765 Parliament passes the Stamp Act to tax the American colonies
Johnson's edition of Shakespeare
Walpole's *The Castle of Otranto*
Thomas Percy's *Reliques of Ancient English Poetry*
Blackstone's *Commentaries on the Laws of England* (1765–1769)

1766 The Stamp Act repealed
Swift's *Journal to Stella* first published in a collection of his letters
Goldsmith's *The Vicar of Wakefield*
Smollett's *Travels Through France and Italy*
Lessing's *Laokoon*
Rousseau in England (1766–1767)

1768 Sterne's *A Sentimental Journey Through France and Italy*
The Royal Academy founded by George III
First edition of the *Encyclopaedia Britannica*
Maria Edgeworth born
Death of Laurence Sterne

1769 David Garrick organizes the Shakespeare Jubilee at Stratford-upon-Avon
Sir Joshua Reynolds' *Discourses* (1769–1790)
Richard Arkwright invents the spinning water frame

1770 Boston Massacre
Burke's *Thoughts on the Cause of the Present Discontents*
Oliver Goldsmith's *The Deserted Village*
Death of Thomas Chatterton
William Wordsworth born
James Hogg born

1771 Arkwright's first spinning mill founded
Deaths of Thomas Gray and Tobias Smollett
Walter Scott born

1772 Samuel Taylor Coleridge born

1773 Boston Tea Party
Goldsmith's *She Stoops to Conquer*
Johann Wolfgang von Goethe's *Götz von Berlichingen*

1774 The first Continental Congress meets in Philadelphia
Goethe's *Sorrows of Young Werther*

Death of Oliver Goldsmith
Robert Southey born

1775 Burke's speech on American taxation
American War of Independence begins with the battles of Lexington and Concord
Samuel Johnson's *Journey to the Western Islands of Scotland*
Richard Brinsley Sheridan's *The Rivals* and *The Duenna*
Beaumarchais's *Le Barbier de Séville*
James Watt and Matthew Boulton begin building steam engines in England
Births of Jane Austen, Charles Lamb, Walter Savage Landor, and Matthew Lewis

1776 American Declaration of Independence
Edward Gibbon's *Decline and Fall of the Roman Empire* (1776–1788)
Adam Smith's *Inquiry into the Nature & Causes of the Wealth of Nations*
Thomas Paine's *Common Sense*
Death of David Hume

1777 Maurice Morgann's *Essay on the Dramatic Character of Sir John Falstaff*
Sheridan's *The School for Scandal* first performed (published 1780)
General Burgoyne surrenders at Saratoga

1778 The American colonies allied with France
Britain and France at war
Captain James Cook discovers Hawaii
Death of William Pitt, first earl of Chatham
Deaths of Jean Jacques Rousseau and Voltaire
William Hazlitt born

1779 Johnson's *Prefaces to the Works of the English Poets* (1779–1781); reissued in 1781 as *The Lives of the Most Eminent English Poets*
Sheridan's *The Critic*
Samuel Crompton invents the spinning mule

CHRONOLOGY

Death of David Garrick
1780 The Gordon Riots in London
Charles Robert Maturin born
1781 Charles Cornwallis surrenders at
Yorktown
Immanuel Kant's *Critique of Pure Reason*
Friedrich von Schiller's *Die Räuber*
1782 William Cowper's "The Journey of John Gilpin" published in the *Public Advertiser*
Choderlos de Laclos's *Les Liaisons dangereuses*
Rousseau's *Confessions* published posthumously
1783 American War of Independence ended by the Definitive Treaty of Peace, signed at Paris
William Blake's *Poetical Sketches*
George Crabbe's *The Village*
William Pitt the younger becomes prime minister
Henri Beyle (Stendhal) born
1784 Beaumarchais's *Le Mariage de Figaro* first performed (published 1785)
Death of Samuel Johnson
1785 Warren Hastings returns to England from India
James Boswell's *The Journey of a Tour of the Hebrides, with Samuel Johnson, LL.D.*
Cowper's *The Task*
Edmund Cartwright invents the power loom
Thomas De Quincey born
Thomas Love Peacock born
1786 William Beckford's *Vathek* published in English (originally written in French in 1782)
Robert Burns's *Poems Chiefly in the Scottish Dialect*
Wolfgang Amadeus Mozart's *The Marriage of Figaro*
Death of Frederick the Great
1787 The Committee for the Abolition of the Slave Trade founded in England
The Constitutional Convention meets at Philadelphia; the Constitution is signed

1788 The trial of Hastings begins on charges of corruption of the government in India
The Estates-General of France summoned
U.S. Constitution is ratified
George Washington elected president of the United States
Giovanni Casanova's *Histoire de ma fuite* (first manuscript of his memoirs)
The *Daily Universal Register* becomes the *Times* (London)
George Gordon, Lord Byron born
1789 The Estates-General meets at Versailles
The National Assembly (Assemblée Nationale) convened
The fall of the Bastille marks the beginning of the French Revolution
The National Assembly draws up the Declaration of Rights of Man and of the Citizen
First U.S. Congress meets in New York
Blake's *Songs of Innocence*
Jeremy Bentham's *Introduction to the Principles of Morals and Legislation* introduces the theory of utilitarianism
Gilbert White's *Natural History of Selborne*
1790 Congress sets permanent capital city site on the Potomac River
First U.S. Census
Burke's *Reflections on the Revolution in France*
Blake's *The Marriage of Heaven and Hell*
Edmund Malone's edition of Shakespeare
Wollstonecraft's *A Vindication of the Rights of Man*
Death of Benjamin Franklin
1791 French royal family's flight from Paris and capture at Varennes; imprisonment in the Tuileries
Bill of Rights is ratified
Paine's *The Rights of Man* (1791–1792)
Boswell's *The Life of Johnson*

CHRONOLOGY

Burns's *Tam o'Shanter*
The *Observer* founded

1792 The Prussians invade France and are repulsed at Valmy September massacres
The National Convention declares royalty abolished in France
Washington reelected president of the United States
New York Stock Exchange opens
Mary Wollstonecraft's *Vindication of the Rights of Woman*
William Bligh's voyage to the South Sea in H.M.S. *Bounty*
Percy Bysshe Shelley born

1793 Trial and execution of Louis XVI and Marie-Antoinette
France declares war against England
The Committee of Public Safety (Comité de Salut Public) established
Eli Whitney devises the cotton gin
William Godwin's *An Enquiry Concerning Political Justice*
Blake's *Visions of the Daughters of Albion and America*
Wordsworth's *An Evening Walk* and *Descriptive Sketches*
John Clare born

1794 Execution of Georges Danton and Maximilien de Robespierre
Paine's *The Age of Reason* (1794–1796)
Blake's *Songs of Experience*
Ann Radcliffe's *The Mysteries of Udolpho*
Death of Edward Gibbon

1795 The government of the Directory established (1795–1799)
Hastings acquitted
Landor's *Poems*
Death of James Boswell
John Keats born
Thomas Carlyle born

1796 Napoleon Bonaparte takes command in Italy
Matthew Lewis' *The Monk*
John Adams elected president of the United States
Death of Robert Burns

1797 The peace of Campo Formio: extinction of the Venetian Republic
XYZ Affair
Mutinies in the Royal Navy at Spithead and the Nore
Blake's *Vala, Or the Four Zoas* (first version)
Mary Shelley born
Deaths of Edmund Burke, Mary Wollstonecraft, and Horace Walpole

1798 Napoleon invades Egypt
Horatio Nelson wins the battle of the Nile
Wordsworth's and Coleridge's *Lyrical Ballads*
Landor's *Gebir*
Thomas Malthus' *Essay on the Principle of Population*

1799 Napoleon becomes first consul
Pitt introduces first income tax in Great Britain
Sheridan's *Pizarro*
Honoré de Balzac born
Thomas Hood born
Alexander Pushkin born

1800 Thomas Jefferson elected president of the United States
Alessandro Volta produces electricity from a cell
Library of Congress established
Death of William Cowper and **Mary Darby Robinson**
Thomas Babington Macaulay born

1801 First census taken in England

1802 The Treaty of Amiens marks the end of the French Revolutionary War
The *Edinburgh Review* founded
England's war with France renewed
The Louisiana Purchase
Robert Fulton propels a boat by steam power on the Seine
Birth of Thomas Lovell Beddoes
George Borrow and **James Clarence Mangan**

1804 Napoleon crowned emperor of the French
Jefferson reelected president of the United States
Blake's *Milton* (1804–1808) and *Jerusalem*

CHRONOLOGY

The Code Napoleon promulgated in France
Beethoven's *Eroica* Symphony
Schiller's *Wilhelm Tell*
Benjamin Disraeli born

1805 Napoleon plans the invasion of England
Battle of Trafalgar
Battle of Austerlitz
Beethoven's *Fidelio* first produced
Scott's *Lay of the Last Minstrel*

1806 Scott's *Marmion*
Death of William Pitt
Death of Charles James Fox
Elizabeth Barrett born

1807 France invades Portugal
Aaron Burr tried for treason and acquitted
Byron's *Hours of Idleness*
Charles and Mary Lamb's *Tales from Shakespeare*
Thomas Moore's *Irish Melodies*
Wordsworth's *Ode on the Intimations of Immortality*

1808 National uprising in Spain against the French invasion
The Peninsular War begins
James Madison elected president of the United States
Covent Garden theater burned down
Goethe's *Faust* (Part 1)
Beethoven's Fifth Symphony completed
Lamb's *Specimens of English Dramatic Poets*

1809 Drury Lane theater burned down and rebuilt
The *Quarterly Review* founded
Byron's *English Bards and Scotch Reviewers*
Byron sails for the Mediterranean
Goya's *Los Desastres de la guerra* (1809–1814)
Alfred Tennyson born
Edward Fitzgerald born

1810 Crabbe's *The Borough*
Scott's *The Lady of the Lake*
Elizabeth Gaskell born

1811–1820 Regency of George IV

1811 Luddite Riots begin
Coleridge's *Lectures on Shakespeare* (1811–1814)

Jane Austen's *Sense and Sensibility*
Shelley's *The Necessity of Atheism*
John Constable's *Dedham Vale*
William Makepeace Thackeray born

1812 Napoleon invades Russia; captures and retreats from Moscow
United States declares war against England
Henry Bell's steamship *Comet* is launched on the Clyde river
Madison reelected president of the United States
Byron's *Childe Harold* (Cantos 1–2)
The Brothers Grimm's *Fairy Tales* (1812–1815)
Hegel's *Science of Logic*
Robert Browning born
Charles Dickens born

1813 Wellington wins the battle of Vitoria and enters France
Jane Austen's *Pride and Prejudice*
Byron's *The Giaour* and *The Bride of Abydos*
Shelley's *Queen Mab*
Southey's *Life of Nelson*

1814 Napoleon abdicates and is exiled to Elba; Bourbon restoration with Louis XVIII
Treaty of Ghent ends the war between Britain and the United States
Jane Austen's *Mansfield Park*
Byron's *The Corsair* and *Lara*
Scott's *Waverley*
Wordsworth's *The Excursion*

1815 Napoleon returns to France (the Hundred Days); is defeated at Waterloo and exiled to St. Helena
U.S.S. *Fulton*, the first steam warship, built
Scott's *Guy Mannering*
Schlegel's *Lectures on Dramatic Art and Literature* translated
Wordsworth's *The White Doe of Rylstone*
Anthony Trollope born

1816 Byron leaves England permanently
The Elgin Marbles exhibited in the British Museum
James Monroe elected president of the United States
Jane Austen's *Emma*

CHRONOLOGY

Byron's *Childe Harold* (Canto 3)
Coleridge's *Christabel, Kubla Khan: A Vision, The Pains of Sleep*
Benjamin Constant's *Adolphe*
Goethe's *Italienische Reise*
Peacock's *Headlong Hall*
Scott's *The Antiquary*
Shelley's *Alastor*
Rossini's *Il Barbiere di Siviglia*
Death of Richard Brinsley Sheridan
Charlotte Brontë born

1817 *Blackwood's Edinburgh* magazine founded
Jane Austen's *Northanger Abbey* and *Persuasion*
Byron's *Manfred*
Coleridge's *Biographia Literaria*
Hazlitt's *The Characters of Shakespeare's Plays* and *The Round Table*
Keats's *Poems*
Peacock's *Melincourt*
David Ricardo's *Principles of Political Economy and Taxation*
Death of Jane Austen
Death of Mme de Staël
Branwell Brontë born
Henry David Thoreau born

1818 Byron's *Childe Harold* (Canto 4), and *Beppo*
Hazlitt's *Lectures on the English Poets*
Keats's *Endymion*
Peacock's *Nightmare Abbey*
Scott's *Rob Roy* and *The Heart of Mid-Lothian*
Mary Shelley's *Frankenstein*
Percy Shelley's *The Revolt of Islam*
Emily Brontë born
Karl Marx born
Ivan Sergeyevich Turgenev born

1819 The *Savannah* becomes the first steamship to cross the Atlantic (in 26 days)
Peterloo massacre in Manchester
Byron's *Don Juan* (1819–1824) and *Mazeppa*
Crabbe's *Tales of the Hall*
Géricault's *Raft of the Medusa*
Hazlitt's *Lectures on the English Comic Writers*

Arthur Schopenhauer's *Die Welt als Wille und Vorstellung (The World as Will and Idea)*
Scott's *The Bride of Lammermoor* and *A Legend of Montrose*
Shelley's *The Cenci*, "The Masque of Anarchy," and "Ode to the West Wind"
Wordsworth's *Peter Bell*
Queen Victoria born
George Eliot born

1820–1830 Reign of George IV
1820 Trial of Queen Caroline
Cato Street Conspiracy suppressed; Arthur Thistlewood hanged
Monroe reelected president of the United States
Missouri Compromise
The *London* magazine founded
Keats's *Lamia, Isabella, The Eve of St. Agnes, and Other Poems*
Hazlitt's *Lectures Chiefly on the Dramatic Literature of the Age of Elizabeth*
Charles Maturin's *Melmoth the Wanderer*
Scott's *Ivanhoe* and *The Monastery*
Shelley's *Prometheus Unbound*
Anne Brontë born

1821 Greek War of Independence begins
Liberia founded as a colony for freed slaves
Byron's *Cain, Marino Faliero, The Two Foscari*, and *Sardanapalus*
Hazlitt's *Table Talk* (1821–1822)
Scott's *Kenilworth*
Shelley's *Adonais* and *Epipsychidion*
Death of John Keats
Death of Napoleon
Charles Baudelaire born
Feodor Dostoyevsky born
Gustave Flaubert born

1822 The Massacres of Chios (Greeks rebel against Turkish rule)
Byron's *The Vision of Judgment*
De Quincey's *Confessions of an English Opium-Eater*
Peacock's *Maid Marian*
Scott's *Peveril of the Peak*
Shelley's *Hellas*

Death of Percy Bysshe Shelley

Matthew Arnold born

1823 Monroe Doctrine proclaimed

Byron's *The Age of Bronze* and *The Island*

Lamb's *Essays of Elia*

Scott's *Quentin Durward*

1824 The National Gallery opened in London

John Quincy Adams elected president of the United States

The *Westminster Review* founded

Beethoven's Ninth Symphony first performed

William (Wilkie) Collins born

James Hogg's *The Private Memoirs and Confessions of a Justified Sinner*

Landor's *Imaginary Conversations* (1824–1829)

Scott's *Redgauntlet*

Death of George Gordon, Lord Byron

1825 Inauguration of steam-powered passenger and freight service on the Stockton and Darlington railway

Bolivia and Brazil become independent Alessandro Manzoni's *I Promessi Sposi* (1825–1826)

1826 André-Marie Ampère's *Mémoire sur la théorie mathématique des phénomènes électrodynamiques*

James Fenimore Cooper's *The Last of the Mohicans*

Disraeli's *Vivian Grey* (1826–1827)

Scott's *Woodstock*

1827 The battle of Navarino ensures the independence of Greece

Josef Ressel obtains patent for the screw propeller for steamships

Heinrich Heine's *Buch der Lieder*

Death of William Blake

1828 Andrew Jackson elected president of the United States

Births of Henrik Ibsen, George Meredith, Margaret Oliphant, Dante Gabriel Rossetti, and Leo Tolstoy

1829 The Catholic Emancipation Act

Robert Peel establishes the metropolitan police force

Greek independence recognized by Turkey

Balzac begins *La Comédie humaine* (1829–1848)

Peacock's *The Misfortunes of Elphin*

J. M. W. Turner's *Ulysses Deriding Polyphemus*

1830–1837 Reign of William IV

1830 Charles X of France abdicates and is succeeded by Louis-Philippe

The Liverpool-Manchester railway opened

Tennyson's *Poems, Chiefly Lyrical*

Death of William Hazlitt

Christina Rossetti born

1831 Michael Faraday discovers electromagnetic induction

Charles Darwin's voyage on H.M.S. *Beagle* begins (1831–1836)

The Barbizon school of artists' first exhibition

Nat Turner slave revolt crushed in Virginia

Peacock's *Crotchet Castle*

Stendhal's *Le Rouge et le noir*

Edward Trelawny's *The Adventures of a Younger Son*

Isabella Bird born

1832 The first Reform Bill

Samuel Morse invents the telegraph

Jackson reelected president of the United States

Disraeli's *Contarini Fleming*

Goethe's *Faust* (Part 2)

Tennyson's *Poems, Chiefly Lyrical*, including "The Lotus-Eaters" and "The Lady of Shalott"

Death of Johann Wolfgang von Goethe

Death of Sir Walter Scott

Lewis Carroll born

1833 Robert Browning's *Pauline*

John Keble launches the Oxford Movement

American Anti-Slavery Society founded

Lamb's *Last Essays of Elia*

Carlyle's *Sartor Resartus* (1833–1834)

Pushkin's *Eugene Onegin*

Mendelssohn's *Italian Symphony* first performed

CHRONOLOGY

1834   Abolition of slavery in the British Empire
Louis Braille's alphabet for the blind
Balzac's *Le Père Goriot*
Nikolai Gogol's *Dead Souls* (Part 1, 1834–1842)
Death of Samuel Taylor Coleridge
Death of Charles Lamb
William Morris born

1835   Hans Christian Andersen's *Fairy Tales* (1st ser.)
Robert Browning's *Paracelsus*
Births of Samuel Butler and Mary Elizabeth Braddon
Alexis de Tocqueville's *De la Democratie en Amerique* (1835–1840)
Death of James Hogg

1836   Martin Van Buren elected president of the United States
Dickens' *Sketches by Boz* (1836–1837)
Landor's *Pericles and Aspasia*

1837–1901   Reign of Queen Victoria

1837   Carlyle's *The French Revolution*
Dickens' *Oliver Twist* (1837–1838) and *Pickwick Papers*
Disraeli's *Venetia* and *Henrietta Temple*

1838   Chartist movement in England
National Gallery in London opened
Elizabeth Barrett Browning's *The Seraphim and Other Poems*
Dickens' *Nicholas Nickleby* (1838–1839)

1839   Louis Daguerre perfects process for producing an image on a silver-coated copper plate Faraday's *Experimental Researches in Electricity* (1839–1855)
First Chartist riots
Opium War between Great Britain and China
Carlyle's *Chartism*

1840   Canadian Act of Union
Queen Victoria marries Prince Albert
Charles Barry begins construction of the Houses of Parliament (1840–1852)

William Henry Harrison elected president of the United States
Robert Browning's *Sordello*
Thomas Hardy born

1841   New Zealand proclaimed a British colony
James Clark Ross discovers the Antarctic continent
Punch founded
John Tyler succeeds to the presidency after the death of Harrison
Carlyle's *Heroes and Hero-Worship*
Dickens' *The Old Curiosity Shop*

1842   Chartist riots
Income tax revived in Great Britain
The Mines Act, forbidding work underground by women or by children under the age of ten
Charles Edward Mudie's Lending Library founded in London
Dickens visits America
Robert Browning's *Dramatic Lyrics*
Macaulay's *Lays of Ancient Rome*
Tennyson's *Poems*, including "Morte d'Arthur," "St. Simeon Stylites," and "Ulysses"
Wordsworth's *Poems*

1843   Marc Isambard Brunel's Thames tunnel opened
The Economist founded
Carlyle's *Past and Present*
Dickens' *A Christmas Carol*
John Stuart Mill's *Logic*
Macaulay's *Critical and Historical Essays*
John Ruskin's *Modern Painters* (1843–1860)

1844   Rochdale Society of Equitable Pioneers, one of the first consumers' cooperatives, founded by twenty-eight Lancashire weavers
James K. Polk elected president of the United States
Elizabeth Barrett Browning's *Poems*, including "The Cry of the Children"
Dickens' *Martin Chuzzlewit*
Disraeli's *Coningsby*
Turner's *Rain, Steam and Speed*
Edward Carpenter and Gerard Manley Hopkins born

CHRONOLOGY

1845 The great potato famine in Ireland
      begins (1845–1849)
      Disraeli's *Sybil*
1846 Repeal of the Corn Laws
      The *Daily News* founded (edited by
      Dickens the first three weeks)
      Standard-gauge railway introduced
      in Britain
      The Brontës' pseudonymous *Poems
      by Currer, Ellis and Action Bell*
      Lear's *Book of Nonsense*
1847 The Ten Hours Factory Act
      James Simpson uses chloroform as
      an anesthetic
      Anne Brontë's *Agnes Grey*
      Charlotte Brontë's *Jane Eyre*
      Emily Brontë's *Wuthering Heights*
      Bram Stoker and Flora Annie Steel
      born
      Tennyson's *The Princess*
1848 The year of revolutions in France,
      Germany, Italy, Hungary, Poland
      Marx and Engels issue *The Com-
      munist Manifesto*
      The Chartist Petition
      The Pre-Raphaelite Brotherhood
      founded
      Zachary Taylor elected president of
      the United States
      Anne Brontë's *The Tenant of Wild-
      fell Hall*
      Dickens' *Dombey and Son*
      Elizabeth Gaskell's *Mary Barton*
      Macaulay's *History of England*
      (1848–1861)
      Mill's *Principles of Political
      Economy*
      Thackeray's *Vanity Fair*
      Death of Emily Brontë
1849 Bedford College for women
      founded
      Arnold's *The Strayed Reveller*
      Charlotte Brontë's *Shirley*
      Ruskin's *The Seven Lamps of Archi-
      tecture*
      William Thomas Stead born
      Death of Anne Brontë, Thomas
      Lovell Beddoes and **James Clar-
      ence Mangan**
1850 The Public Libraries Act
      First submarine telegraph cable laid
      between Dover and Calais

      Millard Fillmore succeeds to the
      presidency after the death of Taylor
      Elizabeth Barrett Browning's *Son-
      nets from the Portuguese*
      Carlyle's *Latter-Day Pamphlets*
      Dickens' *Household Words* (1850–
      1859) and *David Copperfield*
      Charles Kingsley's *Alton Locke*
      The Pre-Raphaelites publish the
      Germ
      Tennyson's *In Memoriam*
      Thackeray's *The History of Penden-
      nis*
      Wordsworth's *The Prelude* is pub-
      lished posthumously
1851 The Great Exhibition opens at the
      Crystal Palace in Hyde Park
      Louis Napoleon seizes power in
      France
      Gold strike in Victoria incites Aus-
      tralian gold rush
      Elizabeth Gaskell's *Cranford*
      (1851–1853)
      Meredith's *Poems*
      Ruskin's *The Stones of Venice*
      (1851–1853)
1852 The Second Empire proclaimed
      with Napoleon III as emperor
      David Livingstone begins to ex-
      plore the Zambezi (1852–1856)
      Franklin Pierce elected president of
      the United States
      Arnold's *Empedocles on Etna*
      Thackeray's *The History of Henry
      Esmond, Esq.*
1853 Crimean War (1853–1856)
      Arnold's *Poems*, including "The
      Scholar Gypsy" and "Sohrab and
      Rustum"
      Charlotte Brontë's *Villette*
      Elizabeth Gaskell's *Crawford and
      Ruth*
1854 Frederick D. Maurice's Working
      Men's College founded in London
      with more than 130 pupils
      Battle of Balaklava
      Dickens' *Hard Times*
      James George Frazer born
      Theodor Mommsen's *History of
      Rome* (1854–1856)
      Tennyson's "The Charge of the
      Light Brigade"

CHRONOLOGY

Florence Nightingale in the Crimea
(1854–1856)
Oscar Wilde born

1855 David Livingstone discovers the
Victoria Falls
Robert Browning's *Men and Women*
Elizabeth Gaskell's *North and South*
Olive Schreiner born
Tennyson's *Maud*
Thackeray's *The Newcomes*
Trollope's *The Warden*
Death of Charlotte Brontë

1856 The Treaty of Paris ends the
Crimean War
Henry Bessemer's steel process
invented
James Buchanan elected president
of the United States
H. Rider Haggard born

1857 The Indian Mutiny begins; crushed
in 1858
The Matrimonial Causes Act
Charlotte Brontë's *The Professor*
Elizabeth Barrett Browning's *Aurora Leigh*
Dickens' *Little Dorritt*
Elizabeth Gaskell's *The Life of Charlotte Brontë*
Thomas Hughes's *Tom Brown's School Days*
Trollope's *Barchester Towers*

1858 Carlyle's *History of Frederick the Great* (1858–1865)
George Eliot's *Scenes of Clerical Life*
Morris' *The Defense of Guinevere*
Trollope's *Dr. Thorne*

1859 Charles Darwin's *The Origin of Species*
Dickens' *A Tale of Two Cities*
Arthur Conan Doyle born
George Eliot's *Adam Bede*
Fitzgerald's *The Rubaiyat of Omar Khayyám*
Meredith's *The Ordeal of Richard Feverel*
Mill's *On Liberty*
Samuel Smiles's *Self-Help*
Tennyson's *Idylls of the King*

1860 Abraham Lincoln elected president
of the United States

The *Cornhill* magazine founded
with Thackeray as editor
James M. Barrie born
William Wilkie Collins' *The Woman in White*
George Eliot's *The Mill on the Floss*

1861 American Civil War begins
Louis Pasteur presents the germ
theory of disease
Arnold's *Lectures on Translating Homer*
Dickens' *Great Expectations*
George Eliot's *Silas Marner*
Meredith's *Evan Harrington*
Francis Turner Palgrave's *The Golden Treasury*
Trollope's *Framley Parsonage*
Peacock's *Gryll Grange*
Death of Prince Albert

1862 George Eliot's *Romola*
Meredith's *Modern Love*
Christina Rossetti's *Goblin Market*
Ruskin's *Unto This Last*
Trollope's *Orley Farm*

1863 Thomas Huxley's *Man's Place in Nature*

1864 The Geneva Red Cross Convention
signed by twelve nations
Lincoln reelected president of the
United States
Robert Browning's *Dramatis Personae*
John Henry Newman's *Apologia pro vita sua*
Tennyson's *Enoch Arden*
Trollope's *The Small House at Allington*
Death of John Clare

1865 Assassination of Lincoln; Andrew
Johnson succeeds to the presidency
Arnold's *Essays in Criticism* (1st ser.)
Carroll's *Alice's Adventures in Wonderland*
Dickens' *Our Mutual Friend*
Meredith's *Rhoda Fleming*
A. C. Swinburne's *Atalanta in Calydon*

1866 First successful transatlantic telegraph cable laid
George Eliot's *Felix Holt, the Radical*

CHRONOLOGY

Elizabeth Gaskell's *Wives and Daughters*
Beatrix Potter born
Swinburne's *Poems and Ballads*

1867   The second Reform Bill
Arnold's *New Poems*
Bagehot's *The English Constitution*
Carlyle's *Shooting Niagara*
Marx's *Das Kapital* (vol. 1)
Trollope's *The Last Chronicle of Barset*
George William Russell (AE) born

1868   Gladstone becomes prime minister (1868–1874)
Johnson impeached by House of Representatives; acquitted by Senate
Ulysses S. Grant elected president of the United States
Robert Browning's *The Ring and the Book* (1868–1869)
Collins' *The Moonstone*

1869   The Suez Canal opened
Girton College, Cambridge, founded
Arnold's *Culture and Anarchy*
Mill's *The Subjection of Women*
Trollope's *Phineas Finn*

1870   The Elementary Education Act establishes schools under the aegis of local boards
Dickens' *Edwin Drood*
Disraeli's *Lothair*
Morris' *The Earthly Paradise*
Dante Gabriel Rossetti's *Poems*
Saki [Hector Hugh Munro] born

1871   Trade unions legalized
Newnham College, Cambridge, founded for women students
Carroll's *Through the Looking Glass*
Darwin's *The Descent of Man*
Meredith's *The Adventures of Harry Richmond*
Swinburne's *Songs Before Sunrise*
William H. Davies born

1872   Max Beerbohm born
Samuel Butler's *Erewhon*
George Eliot's *Middlemarch*
Grant reelected president of the United States
Hardy's *Under the Greenwood Tree*

1873   Arnold's *Literature and Dogma*
Mill's *Autobiography*
Pater's *Studies in the History of the Renaissance*
Trollope's *The Eustace Diamonds*
Dorothy Richardson born

1874   Disraeli becomes prime minister
Hardy's *Far from the Madding Crowd*
James Thomson's *The City of Dreadful Night*

1875   Britain buys Suez Canal shares
Trollope's *The Way We Live Now*
T. F. Powys born

1876   F. H. Bradley's *Ethical Studies*
George Eliot's *Daniel Deronda*
Henry James's *Roderick Hudson*
Meredith's *Beauchamp's Career*
Morris' *Sigurd the Volsung*
Trollope's *The Prime Minister*

1877   Rutherford B. Hayes elected president of the United States after Electoral Commission awards him disputed votes
Henry James's *The American*

1878   Electric street lighting introduced in London
Hardy's *The Return of the Native*
Swinburne's *Poems and Ballads* (2d ser.)
Births of A. E. Coppard and Edward Thomas

1879   Somerville College and Lady Margaret Hall opened at Oxford for women
The London telephone exchange built
Gladstone's Midlothian campaign (1879–1880)
Browning's *Dramatic Idyls*
Meredith's *The Egoist*

1880   Gladstone's second term as prime minister (1880–1885)
James A. Garfield elected president of the United States
Browning's *Dramatic Idyls Second Series*
Disraeli's *Endymion*
Radclyffe Hall born
Hardy's *The Trumpet-Major*
Lytton Strachey born

CHRONOLOGY

1881   Garfield assassinated; Chester A. Arthur succeeds to the presidency
Henry James's *The Portrait of a Lady* and *Washington Square*
D. G. Rossetti's *Ballads and Sonnets*
P. G. Wodehouse born
Death of George Borrow

1882   Triple Alliance formed between German empire, Austrian empire, and Italy
Leslie Stephen begins to edit the *Dictionary of National Biography*
Married Women's Property Act passed in Britain
Britain occupies Egypt and the Sudan

1883   Uprising of the Mahdi: Britain evacuates the Sudan
Royal College of Music opens
T. H. Green's *Ethics*
T. E. Hulme born
Stevenson's *Treasure Island*

1884   The Mahdi captures Omdurman: General Gordon appointed to command the garrison of Khartoum
Grover Cleveland elected president of the United States
The *Oxford English Dictionary* begins publishing
The Fabian Society founded
Hiram Maxim's recoil-operated machine gun invented

1885   The Mahdi captures Khartoum: General Gordon killed
Haggard's *King Solomon's Mines*
Marx's *Das Kapital* (vol. 2)
Meredith's *Diana of the Crossways*
Pater's *Marius the Epicurean*

1886   The Canadian Pacific Railway completed
Gold discovered in the Transvaal
Births of Frances Cornford, Ronald Firbank, and Charles Stansby Walter Williams
Henry James's *The Bostonians* and *The Princess Casamassima*
Stevenson's *The Strange Case of Dr. Jekyll and Mr. Hyde*

1887   Queen Victoria's Golden Jubilee
Rupert Brooke born
Haggard's *Allan Quatermain* and *She*
Hardy's *The Woodlanders*
Edwin Muir born

1888   Benjamin Harrison elected president of the United States
Henry James's *The Aspern Papers*
Kipling's *Plain Tales from the Hills*
T. E. Lawrence born

1889   Yeats's *The Wanderings of Oisin*
Death of Robert Browning

1890   Morris founds the Kelmscott Press
Agatha Christie born
Frazer's *The Golden Bough* (1st ed.)
Henry James's *The Tragic Muse*
Morris' *News From Nowhere*
Jean Rhys born

1891   Gissing's *New Grub Street*
Hardy's *Tess of the d'Urbervilles*
Wilde's *The Picture of Dorian Gray*

1892   Grover Cleveland elected president of the United States
Conan Doyle's *The Adventures of Sherlock Holmes*
Shaw's *Widower's Houses*
J. R. R. Tolkien born
Rebecca West and Hugh MacDiarmid born
Wilde's *Lady Windermere's Fan*

1893   Wilde's *A Woman of No Importance* and *Salomé*
Vera Brittain born

1894   Kipling's *The Jungle Book*
Moore's *Esther Waters*
Marx's *Das Kapital* (vol. 3)
Audrey Beardsley's *The Yellow Book* begins to appear quarterly
Shaw's *Arms and the Man*

1895   Trial and imprisonment of Oscar Wilde
William Ramsay announces discovery of helium
The National Trust founded
Conrad's *Almayer's Folly*
Hardy's *Jude the Obscure*
Wells's *The Time Machine*
Wilde's *The Importance of Being Earnest*
Yeats's *Poems*

CHRONOLOGY

1896   William McKinley elected president of the United States
Failure of the Jameson Raid on the Transvaal
Housman's *A Shropshire Lad*
Edmund Blunden born

1897   Queen Victoria's Diamond Jubilee
Conrad's *The Nigger of the Narcissus*
Havelock Ellis' *Studies in the Psychology of Sex* begins publication
Henry James's *The Spoils of Poynton* and *What Maisie Knew*
Kipling's *Captains Courageous*
Shaw's *Candida*
Stoker's *Dracula*
Wells's *The Invisible Man*
Death of Margaret Oliphant
Ruth Pitter born

1898   Kitchener defeats the Mahdist forces at Omdurman: the Sudan reoccupied
Hardy's *Wessex Poems*
Henry James's *The Turn of the Screw*
C. S. Lewis born
Shaw's *Caesar and Cleopatra* and *You Never Can Tell*
Alec Waugh born
Wells's *The War of the Worlds*
Wilde's *The Ballad of Reading Gaol*

1899   The Boer War begins
Elizabeth Bowen born
Noël Coward born
Elgar's *Enigma Variations*
Kipling's *Stalky and Co.*

1900   McKinley reelected president of the United States
British Labour party founded
Boxer Rebellion in China
Reginald A. Fessenden transmits speech by wireless
First Zeppelin trial flight
Max Planck presents his first paper on the quantum theory
Conrad's *Lord Jim*
Elgar's *The Dream of Gerontius*
Sigmund Freud's *The Interpretation of Dreams*
V. S. Pritchett born

   William Butler Yeats's *The Shadowy Waters*

1901–1910   Reign of King Edward VII
1901   William McKinley assassinated; Theodore Roosevelt succeeds to the presidency
First transatlantic wireless telegraph signal transmitted
Chekhov's *Three Sisters*
Freud's *Psychopathology of Everyday Life*
Rudyard Kipling's *Kim*
Thomas Mann's *Buddenbrooks*
Potter's *The Tale of Peter Rabbit*
Shaw's *Captain Brassbound's Conversion*
August Strindberg's *The Dance of Death*

1902   Barrie's *The Admirable Crichton*
Arnold Bennett's *Anna of the Five Towns*
Cézanne's *Le Lac D'Annecy*
Conrad's *Heart of Darkness*
Henry James's *The Wings of the Dove*
William James's *The Varieties of Religious Experience*
Kipling's *Just So Stories*
Maugham's *Mrs. Cradock*
Stevie Smith born
Times Literary Supplement begins publishing

1903   At its London congress the Russian Social Democratic Party divides into Mensheviks, led by Plekhanov, and Bolsheviks, led by Lenin
The treaty of Panama places the Canal Zone in U.S. hands for a nominal rent
Motor cars regulated in Britain to a 20-mile-per-hour limit
The Wright brothers make a successful flight in the United States
Burlington magazine founded
Samuel Butler's *The Way of All Flesh* published posthumously
Cyril Connolly born
George Gissing's *The Private Papers of Henry Ryecroft*
Thomas Hardy's *The Dynasts*
Henry James's *The Ambassadors*

CHRONOLOGY

Alan Paton born
Shaw's *Man and Superman*
Synge's *Riders to the Sea* produced
in Dublin
Yeats's *In the Seven Woods* and *On
Baile's Strand*
William Plomer and **Edward Up-
ward** and **John Wyndham** born

1904 Roosevelt elected president of the
United States
Russo-Japanese war (1904–1905)
Construction of the Panama Canal
begins
The ultraviolet lamp invented
The engineering firm of Rolls
Royce founded
Barrie's *Peter Pan* first performed
Births of Cecil Day Lewis and
Nancy Mitford
Chekhov's *The Cherry Orchard*
Conrad's *Nostromo*
Henry James's *The Golden Bowl*
Kipling's *Traffics and Discoveries*
Georges Rouault's *Head of a Tragic
Clown*
G. M. Trevelyan's *England Under
the Stuarts*
Puccini's *Madame Butterfly*
First Shaw-Granville Barker season
at the Royal Court Theatre
The Abbey Theatre founded in
Dublin
Death of Isabella Bird

1905 Russian sailors on the battleship
Potemkin mutiny
After riots and a general strike the
czar concedes demands by the
Duma for legislative powers, a
wider franchise, and civil liberties
Albert Einstein publishes his first
theory of relativity
The Austin Motor Company
founded
Bennett's *Tales of the Five Towns*
Claude Debussy's *La Mer*
E. M. Forster's *Where Angels Fear
to Tread*
Richard Strauss's *Salome*
H. G. Wells's *Kipps*
Oscar Wilde's *De Profundis*

Births of Norman Cameron, Henry
Green, and Mary Renault

1906 Liberals win a landslide victory in
the British general election
The Trades Disputes Act legitimizes
peaceful picketing in Britain
Captain Dreyfus rehabilitated in
France
J. J. Thomson begins research on
gamma rays
The U.S. Pure Food and Drug Act
passed
Churchill's *Lord Randolph
Churchill*
William Empson born
Galsworthy's *The Man of Property*
Kipling's *Puck of Pook's Hill*
Shaw's *The Doctor's Dilemma*
Yeats's *Poems* 1899–1905

1907 Exhibition of cubist paintings in
Paris
Henry Adams' *The Education of
Henry Adams*
Henri Bergson's *Creative Evolution*
Conrad's *The Secret Agent*
Births of Barbara Comyns, Daphne
du Maurier, and Christopher Fry
Forster's *The Longest Journey*
André Gide's *La Porte étroite*
Shaw's *John Bull's Other Island*
and *Major Barbara*
Synge's *The Playboy of the Western
World*
Trevelyan's *Garibaldi's Defence of
the Roman Republic*
Christopher Caudwell (Christopher
St. John Sprigg) born

1908 Herbert Asquith becomes prime
minister
David Lloyd George becomes chan-
cellor of the exchequer
William Howard Taft elected presi-
dent of the United States
The Young Turks seize power in
Istanbul
Henry Ford's Model T car produced
Bennett's *The Old Wives' Tale*
Pierre Bonnard's *Nude Against the
Light*
Georges Braque's *House at
L'Estaque*

Chesterton's *The Man Who Was Thursday*

Jacob Epstein's *Figures* erected in London

Forster's *A Room with a View*

Anatole France's *L'Ile des Pingouins*

Henri Matisse's *Bonheur de Vivre*

Elgar's First Symphony

Ford Madox Ford founds the *English Review*

1909 The Young Turks depose Sultan Abdul Hamid

The Anglo-Persian Oil Company formed

Louis Bleriot crosses the English Channel from France by monoplane

Admiral Robert Peary reaches the North Pole

Freud lectures at Clark University (Worcester, Mass.) on psychoanalysis

Serge Diaghilev's Ballets Russes opens in Paris

Galsworthy's *Strife*

Hardy's *Time's Laughingstocks*

Malcolm Lowry born

Claude Monet's *Water Lilies*

Stephen Spender born

Trevelyan's *Garibaldi and the Thousand*

Wells's *Tono-Bungay* first published (book form, 1909)

1910–1936 Reign of King George V

1910 The Liberals win the British general election

Marie Curie's *Treatise on Radiography*

Arthur Evans excavates Knossos

Edouard Manet and the first post-impressionist exhibition in London

Filippo Marinetti publishes "Manifesto of the Futurist Painters"

Norman Angell's *The Great Illusion*

Bennett's *Clayhanger*

Forster's *Howards End*

Galsworthy's *Justice* and *The Silver Box*

Kipling's *Rewards and Fairies*

Norman MacCaig born

Rimsky-Korsakov's *Le Coq d'or*

Stravinsky's *The Firebird*

Vaughan Williams' *A Sea Symphony*

Wells's *The History of Mr. Polly*

Wells's *The New Machiavelli* first published (in book form, 1911)

1911 Lloyd George introduces National Health Insurance Bill

Suffragette riots in Whitehall

Roald Amundsen reaches the South Pole

Bennett's *The Card*

Chagall's *Self Portrait with Seven Fingers*

Conrad's *Under Western Eyes*

D. H. Lawrence's *The White Peacock*

Katherine Mansfield's *In a German Pension*

Edward Marsh edits *Georgian Poetry*

Moore's *Hail and Farewell* (1911–1914)

Flann O'Brien born

Strauss's *Der Rosenkavalier*

Stravinsky's *Petrouchka*

Trevelyan's *Garibaldi and the Making of Italy*

Wells's *The New Machiavelli*

Mahler's *Das Lied von der Erde*

1912 Woodrow Wilson elected president of the United States

SS *Titanic* sinks on its maiden voyage

Five million Americans go to the movies daily; London has four hundred movie theaters

Second post-impressionist exhibition in London

Bennett's and Edward Knoblock's *Milestones*

Constantin Brancusi's *Maiastra*

Wassily Kandinsky's *Black Lines*

D. H. Lawrence's *The Trespasser*

Death of **William Thomas Stead**

1913 Second Balkan War begins

Henry Ford pioneers factory assembly technique through conveyor belts

Epstein's *Tomb of Oscar Wilde*

New York Armory Show introduces modern art to the world

Alain Fournier's *Le Grand Meaulnes*

CHRONOLOGY

Freud's *Totem and Tabu*
D. H. Lawrence's *Sons and Lovers*
Mann's *Death in Venice*
Proust's *Du Côté de chez Swann* (first volume of *À la recherche du temps perdu*, 1913–1922)
Barbara Pym born
Ravel's *Daphnis and Chloé*
R.S. Thomas born

1914 The Panama Canal opens (formal dedication on 12 July 1920)
Irish Home Rule Bill passed in the House of Commons
Archduke Franz Ferdinand assassinated at Sarajevo
World War I begins
Battles of the Marne, Masurian Lakes, and Falkland Islands
Joyce's *Dubliners*
Norman Nicholson born
Shaw's *Pygmalion* and *Androcles and the Lion*
Yeats's *Responsibilities*
Wyndham Lewis publishes *Blast* magazine and *The Vorticist Manifesto*
C. H. Sisson born and Patrick O'Brian

1915 The Dardanelles campaign begins
Britain and Germany begin naval and submarine blockades
The *Lusitania* is sunk
Hugo Junkers manufactures the first fighter aircraft
First Zeppelin raid in London
Brooke's *1914: Five Sonnets*
Norman Douglas' *Old Calabria*
D. W. Griffith's *The Birth of a Nation*
Gustav Holst's *The Planets*
D. H. Lawrence's *The Rainbow*
Wyndham Lewis's *The Crowd*
Maugham's *Of Human Bondage*
Pablo Picasso's *Harlequin*
Sibelius' Fifth Symphony
John Cornford and Denton Welch born

1916 Evacuation of Gallipoli and the Dardanelles
Battles of the Somme, Jutland, and Verdun
Britain introduces conscription

The Easter Rebellion in Dublin
Asquith resigns and David Lloyd George becomes prime minister
The Sykes-Picot agreement on the partition of Turkey
First military tanks used
Wilson reelected president president of the United States
Henri Barbusse's *Le Feu*
Griffith's *Intolerance*
Joyce's *Portrait of the Artist as a Young Man*
Jung's *Psychology of the Unconscious*
Moore's *The Brook Kerith*
Edith Sitwell edits *Wheels* (1916–1921)
Wells's *Mr. Britling Sees It Through*

1917 United States enters World War I
Czar Nicholas II abdicates
The Balfour Declaration on a Jewish national home in Palestine
The Bolshevik Revolution
Georges Clemenceau elected prime minister of France
Lenin appointed chief commissar; Trotsky appointed minister of foreign affairs
Conrad's *The Shadow-Line*
Douglas' *South Wind*
Eliot's *Prufrock and Other Observations*
Modigliani's *Nude with Necklace*
Sassoon's *The Old Huntsman*
Prokofiev's *Classical Symphony*
Yeats's *The Wild Swans at Coole*

1918 Wilson puts forward Fourteen Points for World Peace
Central Powers and Russia sign the Treaty of Brest-Litovsk
Execution of Czar Nicholas II and his family
Kaiser Wilhelm II abdicates
The Armistice signed
Women granted the vote at age thirty in Britain
Rupert Brooke's *Collected Poems*
Gerard Manley Hopkins' *Poems*
Joyce's *Exiles*
Lewis's *Tarr*
Sassoon's *Counter-Attack*

Oswald Spengler's *The Decline of the West*

Strachey's *Eminent Victorians*

Béla Bartók's *Bluebeard's Castle*

Charlie Chaplin's *Shoulder Arms*

1919 The Versailles Peace Treaty signed

J. W. Alcock and A. W. Brown make first transatlantic flight

Ross Smith flies from London to Australia

National Socialist party founded in Germany

Benito Mussolini founds the Fascist party in Italy

Sinn Fein Congress adopts declaration of independence in Dublin

Eamon De Valera elected president of Sinn Fein party

Communist Third International founded

Lady Astor elected first woman Member of Parliament

Prohibition in the United States

John Maynard Keynes's *The Economic Consequences of the Peace*

Eliot's *Poems*

Maugham's *The Moon and Sixpence*

Shaw's *Heartbreak House*

The Bauhaus school of design, building, and crafts founded by Walter Gropius

Amedeo Modigliani's *Self-Portrait*

1920 The League of Nations established

Warren G. Harding elected president of the United States

Senate votes against joining the League and rejects the Treaty of Versailles The Nineteenth Amendment gives women the right to vote

White Russian forces of Denikin and Kolchak defeated by the Bolsheviks

Karel apek's *R.U.R.*

Galsworthy's *In Chancery* and *The Skin Game*

Sinclair Lewis' *Main Street*

Katherine Mansfield's *Bliss*

Matisse's *Odalisques* (1920–1925)

Ezra Pound's *Hugh Selwyn Mauberly*

Paul Valéry's *Le Cimetière Marin*

Yeats's *Michael Robartes and the Dancer*

Edwin Morgan born

1921 Britain signs peace with Ireland

First medium-wave radio broadcast in the United States The British Broadcasting Corporation founded

Braque's *Still Life with Guitar*

Chaplin's *The Kid*

Aldous Huxley's *Crome Yellow*

Paul Klee's *The Fish*

D. H. Lawrence's *Women in Love*

John McTaggart's *The Nature of Existence* (vol. 1)

Moore's *Héloïse and Abélard*

Eugene O'Neill's *The Emperor Jones*

Luigi Pirandello's *Six Characters in Search of an Author*

Shaw's *Back to Methuselah*

Strachey's *Queen Victoria*

Births of George Mackay Brown and Brian Moore

1922 Lloyd George's Coalition government succeeded by Bonar Law's Conservative government

Benito Mussolini marches on Rome and forms a government

William Cosgrave elected president of the Irish Free State

The BBC begins broadcasting in London

Lord Carnarvon and Howard Carter discover Tutankhamen's tomb

The PEN club founded in London

The *Criterion* founded with T. S. Eliot as editor

Kingsley Amis born

Eliot's *The Waste Land*

A. E. Housman's *Last Poems*

Joyce's *Ulysses*

D. H. Lawrence's *Aaron's Rod* and *England, My England*

Sinclair Lewis's *Babbitt*

O'Neill's *Anna Christie*

Pirandello's *Henry IV*

Edith Sitwell's *Façade*

Virginia Woolf's *Jacob's Room*

Yeats's *The Trembling of the Veil*

Donald Davie born

1923 The Union of Soviet Socialist Republics established

CHRONOLOGY

French and Belgian troops occupy the Ruhr in consequence of Germany's failure to pay reparations
Mustafa Kemal (Ataturk) proclaims Turkey a republic and is elected president
Warren G. Harding dies; Calvin Coolidge becomes president
Stanley Baldwin succeeds Bonar Law as prime minister
Adolf Hitler's attempted coup in Munich fails
Time magazine begins publishing
E. N. da C. Andrade's *The Structure of the Atom*
Brendan Behan born
Bennett's *Riceyman Steps*
Churchill's *The World Crisis* (1923–1927)
J. E. Flecker's *Hassan* produced
Nadine Gordimer born
Paul Klee's *Magic Theatre*
Lawrence's *Kangaroo*
Rainer Maria Rilke's *Duino Elegies* and *Sonnets to Orpheus*
Sibelius' *Sixth Symphony*
Picasso's *Seated Woman*
William Walton's *Façade*
Elizabeth Jane Howard born

1924 Ramsay MacDonald forms first Labour government, loses general election, and is succeeded by Stanley Baldwin
Calvin Coolidge elected president of the United States
Noël Coward's *The Vortex*
Forster's *A Passage to India*
Mann's *The Magic Mountain*
Shaw's *St. Joan*
G. F. Dutton born

1925 Reza Khan becomes shah of Iran
First surrealist exhibition held in Paris
Alban Berg's *Wozzeck*
Chaplin's *The Gold Rush*
John Dos Passos' *Manhattan Transfer* Theodore Dreiser's *An American Tragedy*
Sergei Eisenstein's *Battleship Potemkin*
F. Scott Fitzgerald's *The Great Gatsby*

André Gide's *Les Faux Monnayeurs*
Hardy's *Human Shows and Far Phantasies*
Huxley's *Those Barren Leaves*
Kafka's *The Trial*
O'Casey's *Juno and the Paycock*
Virginia Woolf's *Mrs. Dalloway* and *The Common Reader*
Brancusi's *Bird in Space*
Shostakovich's *First Symphony*
Sibelius' *Tapiola*

1926 Ford's *A Man Could Stand Up*
Gide's *Si le grain ne meurt*
Hemingway's *The Sun also Rises*
Kafka's *The Castle*
D. H. Lawrence's *The Plumed Serpent* T. E. Lawrence's *Seven Pillars of Wisdom* privately circulated
Maugham's *The Casuarina Tree*
O'Casey's *The Plough and the Stars*
Puccini's *Turandot*
Jan Morris born

1927 General Chiang Kai-shek becomes prime minister in China Trotsky expelled by the Communist party as a deviationist; Stalin becomes leader of the party and dictator of the Soviet Union
Charles Lindbergh flies from New York to Paris
J. W. Dunne's *An Experiment with Time*
Freud's *Autobiography* translated into English
Albert Giacometti's *Observing Head*
Ernest Hemingway's *Men Without Women*
Fritz Lang's *Metropolis*
Wyndham Lewis' *Time and Western Man*
F. W. Murnau's *Sunrise*
Proust's *Le Temps retrouvé* posthumously published
Stravinsky's *Oedipus Rex*
Virginia Woolf's *To the Lighthouse*

1928 The Kellogg-Briand Pact, outlawing war and providing for peaceful settlement of disputes, signed in Paris by sixty-two nations, including the Soviet Union

Herbert Hoover elected president of the United States

Women's suffrage granted at age twenty-one in Britain

Alexander Fleming discovers penicillin

Bertolt Brecht and Kurt Weill's *The Three-Penny Opera*

Eisenstein's *October*

Huxley's *Point Counter Point*

Christopher Isherwood's *All the Conspirators*

D. H. Lawrence's *Lady Chatterley's Lover*

Wyndham Lewis' *The Childermass*

Matisse's *Seated Odalisque*

Munch's *Girl on a Sofa*

Shaw's *Intelligent Woman's Guide to Socialism*

Virginia Woolf's *Orlando*

Yeats's *The Tower*

Iain Chrichton Smith born

1929   The Labour party wins British general election Trotsky expelled from the Soviet Union

Museum of Modern Art opens in New York

Collapse of U.S. stock exchange begins world economic crisis

Robert Bridges's *The Testament of Beauty*

William Faulkner's *The Sound and the Fury*

Robert Graves's *Goodbye to All That*

Hemingway's *A Farewell to Arms*

Ernst Junger's *The Storm of Steel*

Hugo von Hoffmansthal's *Poems*

Henry Moore's *Reclining Figure*

J. B. Priestley's *The Good Companions*

Erich Maria Remarque's *All Quiet on the Western Front*

Shaw's *The Applecart*

R. C. Sheriff's *Journey's End*

Edith Sitwell's *Gold Coast Customs*

Thomas Wolfe's *Look Homeward, Angel*

Virginia Woolf's *A Room of One's Own*

Yeats's *The Winding Stair*

Second surrealist manifesto; Salvador Dali joins the surrealists

Epstein's *Night and Day*

Mondrian's *Composition with Yellow Blue*

Death of Edward Carpenter and Flora Annie Steel

Keith Waterhouse born

1930   Allied occupation of the Rhineland ends

Mohandas Gandhi opens civil disobedience campaign in India

The *Daily Worker*, journal of the British Communist party, begins publishing

J. W. Reppe makes artificial fabrics from an acetylene base

John Arden born

Auden's *Poems*

Coward's *Private Lives*

Eliot's *Ash Wednesday*

Wyndham Lewis's *The Apes of God*

Maugham's *Cakes and Ale*

Ezra Pound's *XXX Cantos*

Evelyn Waugh's *Vile Bodies*

Birth of Kamau (Edward) Brathwaite and Ruth Rendell

1931   The failure of the Credit Anstalt in Austria starts a financial collapse in Central Europe

Britain abandons the gold standard; the pound falls by twenty-five percent

Mutiny in the Royal Navy at Invergordon over pay cuts

Ramsay MacDonald resigns, splits the Cabinet, and is expelled by the Labour party; in the general election the National Government wins by a majority of five hundred seats

The Statute of Westminster defines dominion status

Ninette de Valois founds the Vic-Wells Ballet (eventually the Royal Ballet)

Coward's *Cavalcade*

Dali's The *Persistence of Memory*

John le Carré born

O'Neill's *Mourning Becomes Electra*

Anthony Powell's *Afternoon Men*
Antoine de Saint-Exupéry's *Vol de nuit*
Walton's *Belshazzar's Feast*
Virginia Woolf's *The Waves*
Caroline Blackwood born

1932 Franklin D. Roosevelt elected president of the United States
Paul von Hindenburg elected president of Germany; Franz von Papen elected chancellor
Sir Oswald Mosley founds British Union of Fascists The BBC takes over development of television from J. L. Baird's company
Basic English of 850 words designed as a prospective international language The Folger Library opens in Washington, D.C. The Shakespeare Memorial Theatre opens in Stratford-upon-Avon
Faulkner's *Light in August*
Huxley's *Brave New World*
F. R. Leavis' *New Bearings in English Poetry*
Boris Pasternak's *Second Birth*
Ravel's *Concerto for Left Hand*
Peter Redgrove born
Rouault's *Christ Mocked by Soldiers*
Waugh's *Black Mischief*
Yeats's *Words for Music Perhaps*

1933 Roosevelt inaugurates the New Deal
Hitler becomes chancellor of Germany The Reichstag set on fire
Hitler suspends civil liberties and freedom of the press; German trade unions suppressed
George Balanchine and Lincoln Kirstein found the School of American Ballet
Beryl Bainbridge born
Lowry's *Ultramarine*
André Malraux's *La Condition humaine*
Orwell's *Down and Out in Paris and London*
Gertrude Stein's *The Autobiography of Alice B. Toklas*
Peter Scupham and Anne Stevenson born

1934 The League Disarmament Conference ends in failure
The Soviet Union admitted to the League
Hitler becomes Führer
Civil war in Austria; Engelbert Dollfuss assassinated in attempted Nazi coup
Frédéric Joliot and Irene Joliot-Curie discover artificial (induced) radioactivity
Einstein's *My Philosophy*
Fitzgerald's *Tender Is the Night*
Graves's *I, Claudius* and *Claudius the God* Toynbee's *A Study of History* begins publication (1934–1954)
Waugh's *A Handful of Dust*
Births of Fleur Adcock, Alan Bennett, Christopher Wallace-Crabbe, and Alasdair Gray

1935 Grigori Zinoviev and other Soviet leaders convicted of treason
Stanley Baldwin becomes prime minister in National Government; National Government wins general election in Britain
Italy invades Abyssinia
Germany repudiates disarmament clauses of Treaty of Versailles
Germany reintroduces compulsory military service and outlaws the Jews
Robert Watson-Watt builds first practical radar equipment
Karl Jaspers' *Suffering and Existence*
Births of André Brink, Dennis Potter, Keith Roberts, and Jon Stallworthy
Ivy Compton-Burnett's *A House and Its Head*
Eliot's *Murder in the Cathedral*
Barbara Hepworth's *Three Forms*
George Gershwin's *Porgy and Bess*
Greene's *England Made Me*
Isherwood's *Mr. Norris Changes Trains*
Malraux's *Le Temps du mépris*
Yeats's *Dramatis Personae*
Klee's *Child Consecrated to Suffering*

CHRONOLOGY

Benedict Nicholson's *White Relief*
Edward VII accedes to the throne in January; abdicates in December

1936–1952 Reign of George VI

1936 German troops occupy the Rhineland
Ninety-nine percent of German electorate vote for Nazi candidates
The Popular Front wins general election in France; Léon Blum becomes prime minister
Roosevelt reelected president of the United States
The Popular Front wins general election in Spain
Spanish Civil War begins
Italian troops occupy Addis Ababa; Abyssinia annexed by Italy
BBC begins television service from Alexandra Palace
Auden's *Look, Stranger!*
Auden and Isherwood's *The Ascent of F-6*
A. J. Ayer's *Language, Truth and Logic*
Chaplin's *Modern Times*
Greene's *A Gun for Sale*
Huxley's *Eyeless in Gaza*
Keynes's *General Theory of Employment*
F. R. Leavis' *Revaluation*
Mondrian's *Composition in Red and Blue*
Dylan Thomas' *Twenty-five Poems*
Wells's *The Shape of Things to Come* filmed
Steward Conn and Reginald Hill born
Death of **John Cornford**

1937 Trial of Karl Radek and other Soviet leaders
Neville Chamberlain succeeds Stanley Baldwin as prime minister
China and Japan at war
Frank Whittle designs jet engine
Picasso's *Guernica*
Shostakovich's Fifth Symphony
Magritte's *La Reproduction interdite*
Hemingway's *To Have and Have Not*

Malraux's *L'Espoir*
Orwell's *The Road to Wigan Pier*
Priestley's *Time and the Conways*
Virginia Woolf's *The Years*
Emma Tennant born
Death of Christopher Caudwell (Christopher St. John Sprigg)

1938 Trial of Nikolai Bukharin and other Soviet political leaders
Austria occupied by German troops and declared part of the Reich
Hitler states his determination to annex Sudetenland from Czechoslovakia
Britain, France, Germany, and Italy sign the Munich agreement
German troops occupy Sudetenland
Edward Hulton founds *Picture Post*
Cyril Connolly's *Enemies of Promise*
du Maurier's *Rebecca*
Faulkner's *The Unvanquished*
Graham Greene's *Brighton Rock*
Hindemith's *Mathis der Maler*
Jean Renoir's *La Grande Illusion*
Jean-Paul Sartre's *La Nausée*
Yeats's *New Poems*
Anthony Asquith's *Pygmalion* and Walt Disney's *Snow White*
Ngg wa Thiong'o born

1939 German troops occupy Bohemia and Moravia; Czechoslovakia incorporated into Third Reich
Madrid surrenders to General Franco; the Spanish Civil War ends
Italy invades Albania
Spain joins Germany, Italy, and Japan in anti-Comintern Pact
Britain and France pledge support to Poland, Romania, and Greece
The Soviet Union proposes defensive alliance with Britain; British military mission visits Moscow
The Soviet Union and Germany sign nonaggression treaty, secretly providing for partition of Poland between them
Germany invades Poland; Britain, France, and Germany at war
The Soviet Union invades Finland
New York World's Fair opens

CHRONOLOGY

Eliot's *The Family Reunion*
Births of Ayi Kwei Armah, Seamus Heaney, Michael Longley and Robert Nye
Isherwood's *Good-bye to Berlin*
Joyce's *Finnegans Wake* (1922–1939)
MacNeice's *Autumn Journal*
Powell's *What's Become of Waring?*
Ayi Kwei Armah born

1940 Churchill becomes prime minister
Italy declares war on France, Britain, and Greece
General de Gaulle founds Free French Movement
The Battle of Britain and the bombing of London
Roosevelt reelected president of the United States for third term
Betjeman's *Old Lights for New Chancels*
Angela Carter born
Chaplin's *The Great Dictator*
Bruce Chatwin born
Death of William H. Davies
J. M. Coetzee born
Disney's *Fantasia*
Greene's *The Power and the Glory*
Hemingway's *For Whom the Bell Tolls*
C. P. Snow's *Strangers and Brothers* (retitled *George Passant* in 1970, when entire sequence of ten novels, published 1940–1970, was entitled *Strangers and Brothers*)

1941 German forces occupy Yugoslavia, Greece, and Crete, and invade the Soviet Union
Lend-Lease agreement between the United States and Britain
President Roosevelt and Winston Churchill sign the Atlantic Charter
Japanese forces attack Pearl Harbor; United States declares war on Japan, Germany, Italy; Britain on Japan
Auden's *New Year Letter*
James Burnham's *The Managerial Revolution*
F. Scott Fitzgerald's *The Last Tycoon*

Huxley's *Grey Eminence* Shostakovich's *Seventh Symphony* Tippett's *A Child of Our Time*
Orson Welles's *Citizen Kane*
Virginia Woolf's *Between the Acts*

1942 Japanese forces capture Singapore, Hong Kong, Bataan, Manila
German forces capture Tobruk
U.S. fleet defeats the Japanese in the Coral Sea, captures Guadalcanal
Battle of El Alamein
Allied forces land in French North Africa
Atom first split at University of Chicago
William Beveridge's *Social Insurance and Allied Services*
Albert Camus's *L'Étranger*
Joyce Cary's *To Be a Pilgrim*
Edith Sitwell's *Street Songs*
Waugh's *Put Out More Flags*
Births of Douglas Dunn, and Jonathan Raban

1943 German forces surrender at Stalingrad
German and Italian forces surrender in North Africa
Italy surrenders to Allies and declares war on Germany
Cairo conference between Roosevelt, Churchill, Chiang Kaishek Teheran conference between Roosevelt, Churchill, Stalin
Eliot's *Four Quartets*
Henry Moore's *Madonna and Child*
Sartre's *Les Mouches*
Vaughan Williams' *Fifth Symphony*
Peter Carey and David Malouf born

1944 Allied forces land in Normandy and southern France
Allied forces enter Rome
Attempted assassination of Hitler fails
Liberation of Paris
U.S. forces land in Philippines
German offensive in the Ardennes halted
Roosevelt reelected president of the United States for fourth term
Education Act passed in Britain

Pay-as-You-Earn income tax introduced

Beveridge's *Full Employment in a Free Society*

Cary's *The Horse's Mouth*

Huxley's *Time Must Have a Stop*

Maugham's *The Razor's Edge*

Sartre's *Huis Clos*

Edith Sitwell's *Green Song and Other Poems*

Graham Sutherland's *Christ on the Cross* Trevelyan's *English Social History*

Craig Raine and W. G. Sebald born

1945   British and Indian forces open offensive in Burma

Yalta conference between Roosevelt, Churchill, Stalin

Mussolini executed by Italian partisans

Roosevelt dies; Harry S. Truman becomes president

Hitler commits suicide; German forces surrender The Potsdam Peace Conference

The United Nations Charter ratified in San Francisco The Labour Party wins British General Election

Atomic bombs dropped on Hiroshima and Nagasaki

Surrender of Japanese forces ends World War II Trial of Nazi war criminals opens at Nuremberg

All-India Congress demands British withdrawal from India

De Gaulle elected president of French Provisional Government; resigns the next year

Betjeman's *New Bats in Old Belfries*

Britten's *Peter Grimes*

Orwell's *Animal Farm*

Russell's *History of Western Philosophy*

Sartre's *The Age of Reason*

Edith Sitwell's *The Song of the Cold*

Waugh's *Brideshead Revisited*

Births of Wendy Cope and Peter Reading

1946   Bills to nationalize railways, coal mines, and the Bank of England passed in Britain

Nuremberg Trials concluded

United Nations General Assembly meets in New York as its permanent headquarters The Arab Council inaugurated in Britain

Frederick Ashton's *Symphonic Variations*

Britten's *The Rape of Lucretia*

David Lean's *Great Expectations*

O'Neill's *The Iceman Cometh*

Roberto Rosselini's *Paisà*

Dylan Thomas' *Deaths and Entrances*

Philip Pullman born

1947   President Truman announces program of aid to Greece and Turkey and outlines the "Truman Doctrine"

Independence of India proclaimed; partition between India and Pakistan, and communal strife between Hindus and Moslems follows

General Marshall calls for a European recovery program

First supersonic air flight

Britain's first atomic pile at Harwell comes into operation

Edinburgh festival established

Discovery of the Dead Sea Scrolls in Palestine

Princess Elizabeth marries Philip Mountbatten, duke of Edinburgh

Auden's *Age of Anxiety*

Camus's *La Peste*

Chaplin's *Monsieur Verdoux*

Lowry's *Under the Volcano*

Priestley's *An Inspector Calls*

Edith Sitwell's *The Shadow of Cain*

Waugh's *Scott-King's Modern Europe*

Births of Dermot Healy, and Redmond O'Hanlon

1948   Gandhi assassinated

Czech Communist Party seizes power

CHRONOLOGY

Pan-European movement (1948–1958) begins with the formation of the permanent Organization for European Economic Cooperation (OEEC)
Berlin airlift begins as the Soviet Union halts road and rail traffic to the city
British mandate in Palestine ends; Israeli provisional government formed
Yugoslavia expelled from Soviet bloc
Columbia Records introduces the long-playing record Truman elected of the United States for second term
Greene's *The Heart of the Matter*
Huxley's *Ape and Essence*
Leavis' *The Great Tradition*
Pound's *Cantos*
Priestley's *The Linden Tree*
Waugh's *The Loved One*
Death of Denton Welch
Ciaran Carson born

1949   North Atlantic Treaty Organization established with headquarters in Brussels
Berlin blockade lifted
German Federal Republic recognized; capital established at Bonn
Konrad Adenauer becomes German chancellor
Mao Tse-tung becomes chairman of the People's Republic of China following Communist victory over the Nationalists
Peter Ackroyd born
Simone de Beauvoir's *The Second Sex*
Cary's *A Fearful Joy*
Arthur Miller's *Death of a Salesman*
Orwell's *Nineteen Eighty-four*

1950   Korean War breaks out
Nobel Prize for literature awarded to Bertrand Russell
R. H. S. Crossman's *The God That Failed* T. S. Eliot's *The Cocktail Party*
Fry's *Venus Observed*
Doris Lessing's *The Grass Is Singing*

C. S. Lewis' *The Chronicles of Narnia* (1950–1956)
Wyndham Lewis' *Rude Assignment*
George Orwell's *Shooting an Elephant*
Carol Reed's *The Third Man*
Dylan Thomas' *Twenty-six Poems*
Births of Sara Maitland, and A. N. Wilson

1951   Guy Burgess and Donald Maclean defect from Britain to the Soviet Union The Conservative party under Winston Churchill wins British general election The Festival of Britain celebrates both the centenary of the Crystal Palace Exhibition and British postwar recovery
Electric power is produced by atomic energy at Arcon, Idaho
W. H. Auden's *Nones*
Samuel Beckett's *Molloy* and *Malone Dies*
Benjamin Britten's *Billy Budd*
Greene's *The End of the Affair*
Akira Kurosawa's *Rashomon*
Wyndham Lewis' *Rotting Hill*
Anthony Powell's *A Question of Upbringing* (first volume of *A Dance to the Music of Time*, 1951–1975)
J. D. Salinger's *The Catcher in the Rye*
C. P. Snow's *The Masters*
Igor Stravinsky's *The Rake's Progress*
Peter Fallon born

1952–   Reign of Elizabeth II At Eniwetok Atoll the United States detonates the first hydrogen bomb The European Coal and Steel Community comes into being
Radiocarbon dating introduced to archaeology
Michael Ventris deciphers Linear B script
Dwight D. Eisenhower elected president of the United States
Beckett's *Waiting for Godot*
Charles Chaplin's *Limelight*
Ernest Hemingway's *The Old Man and the Sea*
Arthur Koestler's *Arrow in the Blue*

F. R. Leavis' *The Common Pursuit*
Lessing's *Martha Quest* (first volume of *The Children of Violence*, 1952–1965)
C. S. Lewis' *Mere Christianity*
Thomas' *Collected Poems*
Evelyn Waugh's *Men at Arms* (first volume of *Sword of Honour*, 1952–1961)
Angus Wilson's *Hemlock and After*
Births of Rohinton Mistry and Vikram Seth

1953   Constitution for a European political community drafted
Julius and Ethel Rosenberg executed for passing U.S. secrets to the Soviet Union
Cease-fire declared in Korea
Edmund Hillary and his Sherpa guide, Tenzing Norkay, scale Mt. Everest
Nobel Prize for literature awarded to Winston Churchill
General Mohammed Naguib proclaims Egypt a republic
Beckett's *Watt*
Joyce Cary's *Except the Lord*
Robert Graves's *Poems 1953*
Death of Norman Cameron

1954   First atomic submarine, *Nautilus,* is launched by the United States
Dien Bien Phu captured by the Vietminh
Geneva Conference ends French dominion over Indochina
U.S. Supreme Court declares racial segregation in schools unconstitutional
Nasser becomes president of Egypt
Nobel Prize for literature awarded to Ernest Hemingway
Kingsley Amis' *Lucky Jim*
John Betjeman's *A Few Late Chrysanthemums*
William Golding's *Lord of the Flies*
Christopher Isherwood's *The World in the Evening*
Koestler's *The Invisible Writing*
Iris Murdoch's *Under the Net*

C. P. Snow's *The New Men* Thomas' *Under Milk Wood* published posthumously
Births of Iain Banks, Louise De Bernières, Romesh Gunesekera, Kevin Hart, Alan Hollinghurst, and Hanif Kureishi

1955   Warsaw Pact signed
West Germany enters NATO as Allied occupation ends The Conservative party under Anthony Eden wins British general election
Cary's *Not Honour More*
Greene's *The Quiet American*
Philip Larkin's *The Less Deceived*
F. R. Leavis' *D. H. Lawrence, Novelist*
Vladimir Nabokov's *Lolita*
Patrick White's *The Tree of Man*
John Burnside and Patrick McCabe born

1956   Nasser's nationalization of the Suez Canal leads to Israeli, British, and French armed intervention
Uprising in Hungary suppressed by Soviet troops
Khrushchev denounces Stalin at Twentieth Communist Party Congress
Eisenhower reelected president of the United States
Anthony Burgess' *Time for a Tiger*
Golding's *Pincher Martin*
Murdoch's *Flight from the Enchanter*
John Osborne's *Look Back in Anger*
Snow's *Homecomings*
Edmund Wilson's *Anglo-Saxon Attitudes*
Janice Galloway and Philip Kerr born

1957   The Soviet Union launches the first artificial earth satellite, *Sputnik I*
Eden succeeded by Harold Macmillan
Suez Canal reopened
Eisenhower Doctrine formulated
Parliament receives the Wolfenden Report on Homosexuality and Prostitution

Nobel Prize for literature awarded
to Albert Camus
Beckett's *Endgame* and *All That
Fall*
Lawrence Durrell's *Justine* (first
volume of *The Alexandria Quartet*,
1957–1960) Ted Hughes's *The
Hawk in the Rain*
Murdoch's *The Sandcastle*
V. S. Naipaul's *The Mystic Masseur*
Eugene O'Neill's *Long Day's Jour-
ney into Night*
Osborne's *The Entertainer*
Muriel Spark's *The Comforters*
White's *Voss*
Death of **Dorothy Richardson**

1958 European Economic Community
established
Khrushchev succeeds Bulganin as
Soviet premier
Charles de Gaulle becomes head of
France's newly constituted Fifth
Republic The United Arab Republic
formed by Egypt and Syria The
United States sends troops into
Lebanon
First U.S. satellite, *Explorer 1,*
launched
Nobel Prize for literature awarded
to Boris Pasternak
Beckett's *Krapp's Last Tape*
John Kenneth Galbraith's *The Af-
fluent Society*
Greene's *Our Man in Havana*
Murdoch's *The Bell*
Pasternak's *Dr. Zhivago*
Snow's *The Conscience of the Rich*

1959 Fidel Castro assumes power in
Cuba
St. Lawrence Seaway opens
The European Free Trade Associa-
tion founded
Alaska and Hawaii become the
forty-ninth and fiftieth states
The Conservative party under
Harold Macmillan wins British
general election
Brendan Behan's *The Hostage*
Golding's *Free Fall*
Graves's *Collected Poems*
Koestler's *The Sleepwalkers*

Harold Pinter's *The Birthday Party*
Snow's *The Two Cultures and the
Scientific Revolution*
Spark's *Memento Mori*
Robert Crawford born

1960 South Africa bans the African Na-
tional Congress and Pan-African
Congress The Congo achieves inde-
pendence
John F. Kennedy elected president
of the United States
The U.S. bathyscaphe *Trieste* de-
scends to 35,800 feet
Publication of the unexpurgated
Lady Chatterley's Lover permitted
by court
Auden's *Hommage to Clio*
Betjeman's *Summoned by Bells*
Pinter's *The Caretaker*
Snow's *The Affair*
David Storey's *This Sporting Life*
Ian Rankin born

1961 South Africa leaves the British
Commonwealth
Sierra Leone and Tanganyika
achieve independence The Berlin
Wall erected The New English
Bible published
Beckett's *How It Is*
Greene's *A Burnt-Out Case*
Koestler's *The Lotus and the Robot*
Murdoch's *A Severed Head*
Naipaul's *A House for Mr Biswas*
Osborne's *Luther*
Spark's *The Prime of Miss Jean
Brodie*
White's *Riders in the Chariot*
Jackie Kay born

1962 John Glenn becomes first U.S.
astronaut to orbit earth The United
States launches the spacecraft *Mari-
ner* to explore Venus
Algeria achieves independence
Cuban missile crisis ends in with-
drawal of Soviet missiles from
Cuba
Adolf Eichmann executed in Israel
for Nazi war crimes
Second Vatican Council convened
by Pope John XXIII

CHRONOLOGY

Nobel Prize for literature awarded to John Steinbeck

Edward Albee's *Who's Afraid of Virginia Woolf?*

Beckett's *Happy Days*

Anthony Burgess' *A Clockwork Orange* and *The Wanting Seed*

Aldous Huxley's *Island*

Isherwood's *Down There on a Visit*

Lessing's *The Golden Notebook*

Nabokov's *Pale Fire*

Aleksandr Solzhenitsyn's *One Day in the Life of Ivan Denisovich*

1963   Britain, the United States, and the Soviet Union sign a test-ban treaty

Birth of Simon Armitage

Britain refused entry to the European Economic Community The Soviet Union puts into orbit the first woman astronaut, Valentina Tereshkova

Paul VI becomes pope

President Kennedy assassinated; Lyndon B. Johnson assumes office

Nobel Prize for literature awarded to George Seferis

Britten's *War Requiem*

John Fowles's *The Collector*

Murdoch's *The Unicorn*

Spark's *The Girls of Slender Means*

Storey's *Radcliffe*

John Updike's *The Centaur*

1964   Tonkin Gulf incident leads to retaliatory strikes by U.S. aircraft against North Vietnam

Greece and Turkey contend for control of Cyprus

Britain grants licenses to drill for oil in the North Sea The Shakespeare Quatercentenary celebrated

Lyndon Johnson elected president of the United States

The Labour party under Harold Wilson wins British general election

Nobel Prize for literature awarded to Jean-Paul Sartre

Saul Bellow's *Herzog*

Burgess' *Nothing Like the Sun*

Golding's *The Spire*

Isherwood's *A Single Man*

Stanley Kubrick's *Dr. Strangelove*

Larkin's *The Whitsun Weddings*

Naipaul's *An Area of Darkness*

Peter Shaffer's *The Royal Hunt of the Sun*

Snow's *Corridors of Power*

Alan Warner born

1965   The first U.S. combat forces land in Vietnam The U.S. spacecraft Mariner transmits photographs of Mars

British Petroleum Company finds oil in the North Sea

War breaks out between India and Pakistan

Rhodesia declares its independence

Ontario power failure blacks out the Canadian and U.S. east coasts

Nobel Prize for literature awarded to Mikhail Sholokhov

Robert Lowell's *For the Union Dead*

Norman Mailer's *An American Dream*

Osborne's *Inadmissible Evidence*

Pinter's *The Homecoming*

Spark's *The Mandelbaum Gate*

1966   The Labour party under Harold Wilson wins British general election The Archbishop of Canterbury visits Pope Paul VI

Florence, Italy, severely damaged by floods

Paris exhibition celebrates Picasso's eighty-fifth birthday

Fowles's *The Magus*

Greene's *The Comedians*

Osborne's *A Patriot for Me*

Paul Scott's *The Jewel in the Crown* (first volume of *The Raj Quartet*, 1966–1975)

White's *The Solid Mandala*

1967   Thurgood Marshall becomes first black U.S. Supreme Court justice

Six-Day War pits Israel against Egypt and Syria

Biafra's secession from Nigeria leads to civil war

Francis Chichester completes solo circumnavigation of the globe

Dr. Christiaan Barnard performs first heart transplant operation, in South Africa
China explodes its first hydrogen bomb
Golding's *The Pyramid*
Hughes's *Wodwo*
Isherwood's *A Meeting by the River*
Naipaul's *The Mimic Men*
Tom Stoppard's *Rosencrantz and Guildenstern Are Dead*
Orson Welles's *Chimes at Midnight*
Angus Wilson's *No Laughing Matter*

1968   Violent student protests erupt in France and West Germany
Warsaw Pact troops occupy Czechoslovakia
Violence in Northern Ireland causes Britain to send in troops Tet offensive by Communist forces launched against South Vietnam's cities Theater censorship ended in Britain
Robert Kennedy and Martin Luther King Jr. assassinated
Richard M. Nixon elected president of the United States
Booker Prize for fiction established
Durrell's *Tunc*
Graves's *Poems 1965–1968*
Osborne's *The Hotel in Amsterdam*
Snow's *The Sleep of Reason*
Solzhenitsyn's *The First Circle* and *Cancer Ward*
Spark's *The Public Image*
Monica Ali born

1969   Humans set foot on the moon for the first time when astronauts descend to its surface in a landing vehicle from the U.S. spacecraft *Apollo 11*
The Soviet unmanned spacecraft *Venus V* lands on Venus
Capital punishment abolished in Britain
Colonel Muammar Qaddafi seizes power in Libya
Solzhenitsyn expelled from the Soviet Union
Nobel Prize for literature awarded to Samuel Beckett

Carter's *The Magic Toyshop*
Fowles's *The French Lieutenant's Woman*
Storey's *The Contractor*
Death of **John Wyndham**

1970   Civil war in Nigeria ends with Biafra's surrender
U.S. planes bomb Cambodia The Conservative party under Edward Heath wins British general election
Nobel Prize for literature awarded to Aleksandr Solzhenitsyn
Durrell's *Nunquam*
Hughes's *Crow*
F. R. Leavis and Q. D. Leavis' *Dickens the Novelist*
Snow's *Last Things*
Spark's *The Driver's Seat*
Death of Vera Brittain

1971   Communist China given Nationalist China's UN seat
Decimal currency introduced to Britain
Indira Gandhi becomes India's prime minister
Nobel Prize for literature awarded to Heinrich Böll
Bond's *The Pope's Wedding*
Naipaul's *In a Free State*
Pinter's *Old Times*
Spark's *Not to Disturb*
Birth of Sarah Kane and Martin McDonagh

1972   The civil strife of "Bloody Sunday" causes Northern Ireland to come under the direct rule of Westminster
Nixon becomes the first U.S. president to visit Moscow and Beijing
The Watergate break-in precipitates scandal in the United States
Eleven Israeli athletes killed by terrorists at Munich Olympics
Nixon reelected president of the United States
Bond's *Lear*
Snow's *The Malcontents*
Stoppard's *Jumpers*

1973   Britain, Ireland, and Denmark enter European Economic Community
Egypt and Syria attack Israel in the Yom Kippur War

CHRONOLOGY

Energy crisis in Britain reduces production to a three-day week
Nobel Prize for literature awarded to Patrick White
Bond's *The Sea*
Greene's *The Honorary Consul*
Lessing's *The Summer Before the Dark*
Murdoch's *The Black Prince*
Shaffer's *Equus*
White's *The Eye of the Storm*
Death of William Plomer

1974 Miners strike in Britain
Greece's military junta overthrown
Emperor Haile Selassie of Ethiopia deposed
President Makarios of Cyprus replaced by military coup
Nixon resigns as U.S. president and is succeeded by Gerald R. Ford
Betjeman's *A Nip in the Air* Bond's *Bingo*
Durrell's *Monsieur* (first volume of *The Avignon Quintet*, 1974–1985)
Larkin's *The High Windows*
Solzhenitsyn's *The Gulag Archipelago*
Spark's *The Abbess of Crewe*
Death of Nancy Mitford
Death of Edmund Blunden

1975 The U.S. *Apollo* and Soviet *Soyuz* spacecrafts rendezvous in space
The Helsinki Accords on human rights signed
U.S. forces leave Vietnam
King Juan Carlos succeeds Franco as Spain's head of state
Nobel Prize for literature awarded to Eugenio Montale

1976 New U.S. copyright law goes into effect
Israeli commandos free hostages from hijacked plane at Entebbe, Uganda
British and French SST Concordes make first regularly scheduled commercial flights The United States celebrates its bicentennial
Jimmy Carter elected president of the United States

Byron and Shelley manuscripts discovered in Barclay's Bank, Pall Mall
Hughes's *Seasons' Songs*
Koestler's *The Thirteenth Tribe*
Scott's *Staying On*
Spark's *The Take-over*
White's *A Fringe of Leaves*

1977 Silver jubilee of Queen Elizabeth II celebrated
Egyptian president Anwar el-Sadat visits Israel
"Gang of Four" expelled from Chinese Communist party
First woman ordained in the U.S. Episcopal church
After twenty-nine years in power, Israel's Labour party is defeated by the Likud party
Fowles's *Daniel Martin*
Hughes's *Gaudete*

1978 Treaty between Israel and Egypt negotiated at Camp David
Pope John Paul I dies a month after his coronation and is succeeded by Karol Cardinal Wojtyla, who takes the name John Paul II
Former Italian premier Aldo Moro murdered by left-wing terrorists
Nobel Prize for literature awarded to Isaac Bashevis Singer
Greene's *The Human Factor*
Hughes's *Cave Birds*
Murdoch's *The Sea, The Sea*
Death of Hugh MacDiarmid

1979 The United States and China establish diplomatic relations
Ayatollah Khomeini takes power in Iran and his supporters hold U.S. embassy staff hostage in Teheran
Rhodesia becomes Zimbabwe
Earl Mountbatten assassinated The Soviet Union invades Afghanistan
The Conservative party under Margaret Thatcher wins British general election
Nobel Prize for literature awarded to Odysseus Elytis
Golding's *Darkness Visible*
Hughes's *Moortown*

CHRONOLOGY

Lessing's *Shikasta* (first volume of *Canopus in Argos, Archives*)
Naipaul's *A Bend in the River*
Spark's *Territorial Rights*
White's *The Twyborn Affair*

1980 Iran-Iraq war begins
Strikes in Gdansk give rise to the Solidarity movement
Mt. St. Helen's erupts in Washington State
British steelworkers strike for the first time since 1926
More than fifty nations boycott Moscow Olympics
Ronald Reagan elected president of the United States
Burgess's *Earthly Powers*
Golding's *Rites of Passage*
Shaffer's *Amadeus*
Storey's *A Prodigal Child*
Angus Wilson's *Setting the World on Fire*

1981 Greece admitted to the European Economic Community
Iran hostage crisis ends with release of U.S. embassy staff Twelve Labour MPs and nine peers found British Social Democratic party
Socialist party under François Mitterand wins French general election
Rupert Murdoch buys *The Times* of London Turkish gunman wounds Pope John Paul II in assassination attempt
U.S. gunman wounds President Reagan in assassination attempt
President Sadat of Egypt assassinated
Nobel Prize for literature awarded to Elias Canetti
Spark's *Loitering with Intent*

1982 Britain drives Argentina's invasion force out of the Falkland Islands
U.S. space shuttle makes first successful trip
Yuri Andropov becomes general secretary of the Central Committee of the Soviet Communist party
Israel invades Lebanon
First artificial heart implanted at Salt Lake City hospital

Bellow's *The Dean's December*
Greene's *Monsignor Quixote*

1983 South Korean airliner with 269 aboard shot down after straying into Soviet airspace
U.S. forces invade Grenada following left-wing coup
Widespread protests erupt over placement of nuclear missiles in Europe
The [00a3]1 coin comes into circulation in Britain
Australia wins the America's Cup
Nobel Prize for literature awarded to William Golding
Hughes's *River*
Murdoch's *The Philosopher's Pupil*

1984 Konstantin Chernenko becomes general secretary of the Central Committee of the Soviet Communist party
Prime Minister Indira Gandhi of India assassinated by Sikh bodyguards
Reagan reelected president of the United States
Toxic gas leak at Bhopal, India, plant kills 2,000
British miners go on strike
Irish Republican Army attempts to kill Prime Minister Thatcher with bomb detonated at a Brighton hotel
World Court holds against U.S. mining of Nicaraguan harbors
Golding's *The Paper Men*
Lessing's *The Diary of Jane Somers*
Spark's *The Only Problem*

1985 United States deploys cruise missiles in Europe
Mikhail Gorbachev becomes general secretary of the Soviet Communist party following death of Konstantin Chernenko
Riots break out in Handsworth district (Birmingham) and Brixton
Republic of Ireland gains consultative role in Northern Ireland
State of emergency is declared in South Africa

CHRONOLOGY

Nobel Prize for literature awarded to Claude Simon

A. N. Wilson's *Gentlemen in England* Lessing's *The Good Terrorist*

Murdoch's *The Good Apprentice*

Fowles's *A Maggot*

1986 U.S. space shuttle *Challenger* explodes

United States attacks Libya

Atomic power plant at Chernobyl destroyed in accident

Corazon Aquino becomes president of the Philippines

Giotto spacecraft encounters Comet Halley

Nobel Prize for literature awarded to Wole Soyinka

Final volume of *Oxford English Dictionary* supplement published

Amis's *The Old Devils*

Ishiguro's *An Artist of the Floating World*

A. N. Wilson's *Love Unknown*

Powell's *The Fisher King*

1987 Gorbachev begins reform of Communist party of the Soviet Union

Stock market collapses

Iran-contra affair reveals that Reagan administration used money from arms sales to Iran to fund Nicaraguan rebels

Palestinian uprising begins in Israeli-occupied territories

Nobel Prize for literature awarded to Joseph Brodsky

Golding's *Close Quarters*

Burgess's *Little Wilson and Big God*

Drabble's *The Radiant Way*

1988 Soviet Union begins withdrawing troops from Afghanistan

Iranian airliner shot down by U.S. Navy over Persian Gulf

War between Iran and Iraq ends

George Bush elected president of the United States

Pan American flight 103 destroyed over Lockerbie, Scotland

Nobel Prize for literature awarded to Naguib Mafouz

Greene's *The Captain and the Enemy*

Amis's *Difficulties with Girls*

Rushdie's *Satanic Verses*

1989 Ayatollah Khomeini pronounces death sentence on Salman Rushdie; Great Britain and Iran sever diplomatic relations

F. W. de Klerk becomes president of South Africa

Chinese government crushes student demonstration in Tiananmen Square

Communist regimes are weakened or abolished in Poland, Czechoslovakia, Hungary, East Germany, and Romania

Lithuania nullifies its inclusion in Soviet Union

Nobel Prize for literature awarded to José Cela

Second edition of *Oxford English Dictionary* published

Drabble's *A Natural Curiosity*

Murdoch's *The Message to the Planet*

Amis's *London Fields*

Ishiguro's *The Remains of the Day*

Death of Bruce Chatwin

1990 Communist monopoly ends in Bulgaria

Riots break out against community charge in England

First women ordained priests in Church of England

Civil war breaks out in Yugoslavia; Croatia and Slovenia declare independence

Bush and Gorbachev sign START agreement to reduce nuclear-weapons arsenals

President Jean-Baptiste Aristide overthrown by military in Haiti

Boris Yeltsin elected president of Russia

Dissolution of the Soviet Union

Nobel Prize for literature awarded to Nadine Gordimer

1992 U.N. Conference on Environment and Development (the "Earth Summit") meets in Rio de Janeiro

Prince and Princess of Wales separate

War in Bosnia-Herzegovina intensifies

CHRONOLOGY

Bill Clinton elected president of the United States in three-way race with Bush and independent candidate H. Ross Perot

Nobel Prize for literature awarded to Derek Walcott

Death of **Ruth Pitter**

1993 Czechoslovakia divides into the Czech Republic and Slovakia; playwright Vaclav Havel elected president of the Czech Republic

Britain ratifies Treaty on European Union (the "Maastricht Treaty")

U.S. troops provide humanitarian aid amid famine in Somalia

United States, Canada, and Mexico sign North American Free Trade Agreement

Nobel Prize for literature awarded to Toni Morrison

1994 Nelson Mandela elected president in South Africa's first post-apartheid election

Jean-Baptiste Aristide restored to presidency of Haiti

Clinton health care reforms rejected by Congress

Civil war in Rwanda

Republicans win control of both houses of Congress for first time in forty years

Prime Minister Albert Reynolds of Ireland meets with Gerry Adams, president of Sinn Fein

Nobel Prize for literature awarded to Kenzaburo Õe

Amis's *You Can't Do Both*

Naipaul's *A Way in the World*

Death of Dennis Potter

1995 Britain and Irish Republican Army engage in diplomatic talks

Barings Bank forced into bankruptcy as a result of a maverick bond trader's losses

United States restores full diplomatic relations with Vietnam

NATO initiates air strikes in Bosnia

Death of Stephen Spender

Israeli Prime Minister Yitzhak Rabin assassinated

Nobel Prize for literature awarded to Seamus Heaney

1996 IRA breaks cease-fire; Sein Fein representatives barred from Northern Ireland peace talks

Prince and Princess of Wales divorce

Cease-fire agreement in Chechnia; Russian forces begin to withdraw

Boris Yeltsin reelected president of Russia

Bill Clinton reelected president of the United States Nobel Prize for literature awarded to Wislawa Szymborska

Death of Caroline Blackwood

1996 British government destroys around 100,000 cows suspected of infection with Creutzfeldt-Jakob, or "mad cow" disease

1997 Diana, Princess of Wales, dies in an automobile accident

Unveiling of first fully-cloned adult animal, a sheep named Dolly

Booker McConnell Prize for fiction awarded to Arundhati Roy

1998 United States renews bombing of Bagdad, Iraq

Independent legislature and Parliaments return to Scotland and Wales

Booker McConnell Prize for fiction awarded to Ian McEwan

Nobel Prize for literature awarded to Jose Saramago

1999 King Hussein of Jordan dies

United Nations responds militarily to Serbian President Slobodan Milosevic's escalation of crisis in Kosovo

Booker McConnell Prize for fiction awarded to J. M. Coetzee

Nobel Prize for literature awarded to Günter Grass

Deaths of Ted Hughes, Brian Moore, and Iain Chrichton Smith

2000 Penelope Fitzgerald dies

J. K. Rowling's *Harry Potter and the Goblet of Fire* sells more than 300,000 copies in its first day

CHRONOLOGY

Oil blockades by fuel haulers protesting high oil taxes bring much of Britain to a standstill

Slobodan Milosevic loses Serbian general election to Vojislav Kostunica

Death of Scotland's First Minister, Donald Dewar

Nobel Prize for literature awarded to Gao Xingjian

Booker McConnell Prize for fiction awarded to Margaret Atwood

George W. Bush, son of former president George Bush, becomes president of the United States after Supreme Court halts recount of closest election in history

Death of former Canadian Prime Minister Pierre Elliot Trudeau Human Genome Project researchers announce that they have a complete map of the genetic code of a human chromosome

Vladimir Putin succeeds Boris Yeltsin as president of Russia

British Prime Minister Tony Blair's son Leo is born, making him the first child born to a sitting prime minister in 152 years

Death of Patrick O'Brian Keith Roberts and R.S. Thomas

2001   In Britain, the House of Lords passes legislation that legalizes the creation of cloned human embryos

British Prime Minister Tony Blair wins second term

Margaret Atwood's *The Blind Assassin* wins Booker McConnell Prize for fiction Kazuo Ishiguro's *When We Were Orphans*

Trezza Azzopardi's *The Hiding Place*

Terrorists attack World Trade Center and Pentagon with hijacked airplanes, resulting in the collapse of the World Trade Center towers and the deaths of thousands. Passengers of a third hijacked plane thwart hijackers, resulting in a crash landing in Pennsylvania. The attacks are thought to be organized by Osama bin Laden, the leader of an international terrorist network known as al Qaeda

Ian McEwan's *An Atonement*

Salman Rushdie's *Fury*

Peter Carey's *True History of the Kelly Gang*

Deaths of Eudora Welty and W. G. Sebald

2002   Former U.S. President Jimmy Carter awarded the Nobel Peace Prize

Europe experiences its worst floods in 100 years as floodwaters force thousands of people out of their homes

Wall Street Journal reporter Daniel Pearl kidnapped and killed in Karachi, Pakistan while researching a story about Pakistani militants and suspected shoe bomber Richard Reid. British-born Islamic militant Ahmad Omar Saeed Sheikh sentenced to death for the crime. Three accomplices receive life sentences.

Slobodan Milosevic goes on trial at the U.N. war crimes tribunal in The Hague on charges of masterminding ethnic cleansing in the former Yugoslavia.

CHRONOLOGY

Yann Martel's *Life of Pi* wins Booker McConnell Prize for fiction
Nobel Prize for literature awarded to Imre Kertész

2003   Ariel Sharon elected as Israeli prime minister
Venezuelan President Hugo Chavez forced to leave office after a nine week general strike calling for his resignation ends
U.S. presents to the United Nations its Iraq war rationale, citing its Weapons of Mass Destruction as imminent threat to world security
U.S. and Britain launch war against Iraq
Baghdad falls to U.S. troops
Official end to combat operations in Iraq is declared by the U.S.
Aung San Suu Kyi, Burmese opposition leader, placed under house arrest by military regime
NATO assumes control of peacekeeping force in Afghanistan
American troops capture Saddam Hussein J.K. Rowling's *Harry Potter and the Order of the Phoenix*, the fifth installment in the wildly popular series, hit the shelves and rocketed up the best-seller lists
Nobel Prize for literature awarded to J. M. Coetzee
Death of C. H. Sisson

2004   NATO admits seven new members—Bulgaria, Estonia, Latvia, Lithuania, Romania, Slovakia, and Slovenia
Terrorists bomb commuter trains in Spain—al–Qaeda claims responsibility Ten new states join the European Union, expanding it to twenty–five members states total
Muslim terrorists attack a school in Beslan, Russia, resulting in over 300 civilian deaths, many of them schoolchildren George W. Bush is re–elected president of the United States

Allegations of corruption in the election of Ukraine's Viktor Yanukovych result in the "Orange Revolution" and Parliament's decision to nullify the first election results—the secondary run–off election is closley monitored and favors Viktor Yushchenko for president
A massive 9.0 earthquake rocks the Indian Ocean, resulting in a catastrophic tsunami, devastating southern Asia and eastern Africa and killing tens of thousands of people
Alan Hollinghurst's *The Line of Beauty* wins Man Booker Prize for fiction

2005   Terrorists bomb three subway stations in London, killing 52 and injuring more than 700
Pope John Paul II dies, marking the end of an era for the Roman Catholic Church. He is succeeded by Pope Benedict XVI
Hurricane Katrina hits the U.S. Golf Coast, devastating cities in Louisianna and Mississippi, and killing over 1,000 people.
J.K. Rowling's *Harry Potter and the Half-Blood Prince* sells over 6.9 billion copies on the first day of release in the U.S. alone
Nobel Prize for literature awarded to Harold Pinter
Deaths of Saul Bellow and Arthur Miller

2006   Former Iraqi President Saddam Hussein is found guilty for crimes against humanity and is executed in Iraq
Ban Ki-moon elected the next UN secretary-general
International Astronomical Union rules that Pluto is no longer seen as a planet
Fleur Adcock wins the Queen's Gold Medal for Poetry
Kamau Brathwaite wins the Griffin Poetry Prize for *Born to Slow Horses*

List of Contributors

JONATHAN BAINES. Jonathan Baines is writing a doctoral thesis on the concept of 'obliquity' in the work of William Empson and Paul Muldoon at Hertford College, Oxford. With luck it will be complete before Volume XIII appears. Recently he put his research on ice in order to move to Poland, where he worked as a visiting lecturer at the University of Warsaw. He continues to divide his time between England and Poland. **Ciaran Carson**

FRED BILSON. Fred Bilson holds a Bachelor's in Philosophy and in English and a master's in science. He has lectured in English, Linguistics and Computer Studies and works as an advisor to students who have difficulty structuring their writing. **Keith Waterhouse; John Wyndham**

J. C. BITTENBENDER. J. C. Bittenbender, Ph. D., is an associate professor of English at Eastern University in St. Davids, Pennsylvania where he teaches twentieth-century British literature. He specializes in modern Scottish and Irish literature and has published articles on Robert Burns, James Kelman, and Robert Crawford. His other areas of academic interest include Bakhtinian theory and censorship studies. **John Burnside**

SANDIE BYRNE. Fellow in English at Balliol College, Oxford. Her publications include works on eighteenth and nineteenth-century fiction and twentieth-century poetry. **Monica Ali; Philip Pullman**

GERRY CAMBRIDGE. Gerry Cambridge is a Scots-Irish poet, editor and essayist. His collections of poetry include *Madame Fi Fi's Farewell* (Luath Press, 2003) and *Aves* (Essence Press, 2007), a book of prose poems about wild birds. He is the founding editor of the Scottish-American poetry magazine *The Dark Horse,* and a Royal Literary Fund Writing Fellow at the University of Edinburgh for 2006–2008, where he works in the Schools of Biological Sciences and Physics. His website is: www.gerrycambridge.com. **Stewart Conn**

ASHLEY CROSS. Ashley Cross is an Associate Professor of English at Manhattan College in the Bronx. She has published articles on the Shelleys and Mary Robinson in *ELH, Women's Writing* and *Studies in Romanticism.* **Mary Darby Robinson**

NIKOLAI ENDRES. Nikolai Endres, Ph.D. Comparative Literature from UNC Chapel Hill, is an assistant professor at Western Kentucky University. He teaches Great Books, classics, mythology, critical theory, and gay and lesbian studies. He has published on Plato, Petronius, Gustave Flaubert, Edward Carpenter, Oscar Wilde, André Gide, Mary Renault, and Gore Vidal. He is working on a study of Platonic love as a homoerotic code in gay novels, as well as an investigation of Petronius' *Nachleben* in modern literature. **Edward Carpenter**

PATRICK DENMAN FLANERY. Patrick Flanery has recently completed a doctoral thesis at St. Cross College, Oxford, on the publishing and adaptation histories of Evelyn Waugh's novels. He has published on Waugh and J. M. Coetzee, and has interests in contemporary British and American literature, institutions of literature, textual criticism, adaptation theory, and postcolonial and South African literatures. **Craig Raine**

MICHELE GEMELOS. Michele Gemelos received her Bachelor of Arts degree from Skidmore College. She has a Master of Philosophy in English from the University of Oxford, where she is completing doctoral work on British writing about New York City. As the current Wilkinson Junior Research Fellow at Worcester College (Oxford), she has also published works on Ford Madox Ford and transatlantic literary relations. **William Thomas Stead**

LIST OF CONTRIBUTORS

PATRICIA B. HEAMAN. Patricia Heaman is a Professor of English Emerita at Wilkes University, Wilkes-Barre, Pennsylvania, where she teaches courses in nineteenth and twentieth-century literature. She is the author of numerous articles and reviews, including essays on George Eliot, Elizabeth Gaskell, Flora Thompson, Mary Wollstonecraft, Flannery O'Connor, Katherine Mansfield, John Updike, and William Faulkner. **Dorothy Richardson**

GAIL LOW. Gail Low teaches contemporary literature in English at the University of Dundee and has research interests in the field of postcolonial book history. She is the author of *White Skins/ Black Masks: Representation and Colonialism* (Routledge, 1996) and the co-editor of *A Black British Canon?* (Palgrave, Macmillan 2006). She is presently writing a monograph, *Publishing Postcolonial: West African and Caribbean writing in Britain 1950–1968.* **Jackie Kay**

HELENA NELSON. Born Cheshire, England 1953. B.A. Honours University of York, 1974; M.A. in Eighteenth Century Literature, University of Manchester 1977. 1978–1988 freelance writer of short fiction. Since 1988, full-time lecturer in English & Communication Studies at The Adam Smith College, Scotland. Editor and originator of *HappenStance Press* and chapbook review magazine *Sphinx.* Poetry reviewer for a variety of UK magazines. Poetry collections include: *Mr & Mrs Philpott on Holiday at Auchterawe,* Kettillonia 2001, and *Starlight on Water* Rialto Press, England 2003. **Ruth Pitter**

ADRIAN PATERSON. Lecturer in English at Hertford College, Oxford, where he teaches nineteenth and twentieth-century literature. A graduate of Worcester College, Oxford, and Trinity College, Dublin, he has published widely on modernist and Irish writing, notably on W. B. Yeats, Joyce, and poetic tradition, and is the author of a forthcoming work entitled *Words For Music Perhaps,* a study of Yeats and music. **James Clarence Mangan**

NEIL POWELL. Neil Powell is a poet, biographer and critic. His books include six collections of poetry-*At the Edge* (1977), *A Season of Calm Weather* (1982), *True Colours* (1991), *The Stones on Thorpeness Beach* (1994), *Selected Poems* (1998) and *A Halfway House* (2004)-as well as *Carpenters of Light* (1979), *Roy Fuller: Writer and Society* (1995), *The Language of Jazz* (1997) and *George Crabbe: An English Life* (2004). He divides his time between the Waveney Valley and the Surrey Hills. **Peter Scupham**

ROBERT SULLIVAN. Robert Sullivan was born in Ireland and was educated at universities in England and the United States. He is the author of two books of criticism and numerous articles on literature. Sullivan has been the recipient of two Fulbright Awards and is currently Visiting Professor of Literature at the University of Mostar, Bosnia and Herzegovina. **John Cornford; Edward Upward**

BRITISH WRITERS

MONICA ALI

(1968—)

Sandie Byrne

MONICA ALI IS the daughter of a Bangladeshi man, Hatem Ali and an English woman, Joyce Ali, who met in Great Britain when Hatem was a student in the 1960s. When Hatem returned to Dhaka, the capital and largest city of Bangladesh (formerly East Pakistan) Joyce followed him and they were married, amid family hostility. Monica was born there on October 20, 1967, but when the civil war between East Pakistan and West Pakistan began in 1971, the family left for Britain and settled in the town of Bolton, in Lancashire.

Describing her early life in a short essay published in the *Guardian,* "Where I'm Coming From" (June 17, 2003), Ali writes of the family being prepared for Dhaka's "murderous nights." They slept fully clothed on the balcony of their apartment, with money concealed in her father's sock. If the knock on the door came, her father would climb over the rail into the branches of the mango tree in the orchard of the next building, an orphanage. Her mother would hand the children to Mr. Ali, and they would slip into the orphanage. Ali recalls that her father was summoned, with fifteen colleagues, to a meeting at the university where he worked. Her mother asked him not to go, and he stayed away. Of the eleven who went, none came back. Flights from Dhaka were canceled, and Mrs. Ali took her children to the airport every day for a fortnight, through terrified and terrifying crowds, not knowing whether they would be able to get away. When they did, Mr. Ali, as a government employee, had to remain.

Being safe "home" in Britain was not all that Mrs. Ali had hoped, however. There was no warm welcome but family disapproval, and "Tagore's golden Bengal [seemed] a teasing counterpoint to our drab northern milltown lives." Mrs. Ali wrote her husband to say that she wanted to come back

to Dhaka. Instead, he escaped into India and was allowed to join his wife: "a temporary situation."

Ali writes that her personal history and what she calls her internalized folklore tell her that life hangs by a thread. The experience of being between two worlds, and of the civil war, which she calls "the genocidal midwifery that delivered the Bangladeshi nation," lies behind her novel, but the novel is not an account of it. "My book does not trace my family history. It is not concerned with all that. And yet there is something there: difficult to define, but demanding—in my eyes, at least—recognition." About the frequently put question of how she can write about a community (the Bangladeshi community in the East End of London) when she is not part of it, she writes:

> I could set lines of inquiry about my book into two broad camps. Tell us about "them," is one. The tyranny of representation—the phrase is not mine but belongs, I think, to C. L. R. James—means that when I speak, my brown skin is the dominant signifier. The other reaction is rather different. What gives you the right to write about "us," when you're clearly one of "them"? ... How can I write about a community to which I do not truly belong? Perhaps, the answer is I can write about it because I do not truly belong. Growing up with an English mother and a Bengali father means never being an insider. Standing neither behind a closed door, nor in the thick of things, but rather in the shadow of the doorway, is a good place from which to observe. Good training, I feel, for life as a writer.

Although Mr. Ali had been an inspector of technical colleges in Dhaka, in Britain he found it difficult to get work; for some time the family ran a small shop before he earned a history degree and became a teacher for the Open University and her mother became a counselor. After having attended the private Bolton Girls' School, at age eighteen Ali entered Oxford, where she read politics, philosophy, and economics at Wadham College. After graduating she worked in the marketing departments of two publishing houses and in a design and branding agency before marrying her husband, a management consultant, and starting a family.

BRICK LANE *(2003)*

The original title of this novel was *Seven Seas and Thirteen Rivers,* a reference to the distance, geographical and cultural, between Britain and the protagonist's place of birth, as well as to the internal distance she travels. This was also the title under consideration for the U.S. edition of the novel. Had it been adopted for the U.K. edition, it is possible that the novel would have attracted less controversy but probable that it would have been marketed differently and possibly not have become a best-seller, since *Seven Seas and Thirteen Rivers* is likely to connote the Indian subcontinent for a reader and suggests the starting point of the story, while *Brick Lane* denotes the destination point and an area not only known to most British readers but much in the news, as the subject of television and film documentaries.

The geographical area "Brick Lane" from which the novel takes its title covers not just the main street of that name but also the side roads and surrounding streets of an East London area that for centuries has been home to waves of migrants. Huguenot, Russian, Irish, Polish, Indian, Pakistani, and other peoples have found a home there. The fact that the novel is named for such an area rather than for the central protagonist or a metaphor for a significant event of the plot suggests that it is not, or not only, a bildungsroman, or fictional biography but also a broader canvas that represents the life of a community. To an extent this is true, though initially the story focuses on the life of Nazneen, a Bangladeshi woman who is sent to Britain for an arranged marriage, and initially the only part of Brick Lane she knows is the inside of the flat where she lives. Even so, she comes to know a lot about her neighbors. The paper-thin walls of the flats reveal a whole narrative of coughs, flushings, bed-head bangings, television programs, and arguments, and there is also the "tattoo lady" for whom Nazneen would like to have a few English words of greeting, always sitting on a balcony in an opposite block, smoking and drinking from a can. As the story, and Nazneen, come out of the flat, we are introduced to the wider community of Brick Lane.

The story opens far from Brick Lane in a small village in the Mymensingh district of East Pakistan where Nazneen is born. Although her father is an overseer and better-off than most villagers, by western standards the family is poor. Her premature birth is inauspicious. First she is assumed to be stillborn, then takes a breath but seems sickly; later she will not feed. The ancient midwife suggests that she can be taken to a hospital, which would be expensive, or left to her fate, and her mother, Rupban, decrees: "we must not stand in the way of Fate. Whatever happens, I accept it. And my child must not waste any energy fighting against Fate. That way, she will be stronger" (p. 3). Life or death is to be accepted as God's will. The baby lives, and one of the novel's major motifs is immediately established: the acceptance versus the refusal of one's destiny, or the "destiny" that is in fact the imposition of others' will. Nazneen passively and submissively imbibes the culture of the assignment of fate and the approved way for Muslim Bangladeshi women to accept the role assigned to them. Her mother tells her to be still in her heart and mind, "to accept the Grace of God, to treat life with the same indifference with which it would treat her.... What could not be changed must be borne. And since nothing could be changed, everything had to be borne. This principle ruled her life" (p. 4). In contrast, Nazneen's beautiful sister, Hasina, "listened to no one" (p. 4). She rejects the destiny laid out for her and elopes with the nephew of the sawmill owner. Nazneen never sees her again. Rupban commits suicide for reasons never fully articulated, her sorrow too great to be borne and the cause of it, the operation of "fate," too great to be fought.

One day Nazneen's father, Hamid, asks her if she would like to see a photograph of the man he has arranged for her to marry in a month's time. As if compensating by her dutiful subservience for Hasina's disobedience, Nazneen shakes her head and simply says that she hopes she will be a good wife. But she catches a glimpse of the photograph. Her husband-to-be, Chanu, is a much older man with a face like a frog. Nazneen arrives in East London as his wife, knowing only two phrases of English: "sorry" and "thank you." These are indicative of the role she is to fulfill and the life she is expected to lead. Although she has had little formal schooling, Nazneen is perceptive and intelligent, but she has neither outlet nor stimulus. Dislocated from everyone she knew, alone for the first time, for years she is virtually confined to a tiny flat in a high-rise block. She performs the role of the dutiful wife, never criticizing her husband, even when he refuses to allow her to go to college to learn English. When he quotes to her from English literature and translates phrase by phrase, and when he pontificates on social issues on the basis of one Open University module in "Race, Ethnicity and Identity" from a degree course he will never finish, the reader quickly understands that Chanu is a well-meaning but self-deceived and pompous failure. He complains endlessly about the injustices meted out to him: allegedly lesser men are promoted over his head; unmerited parking tickets are issued to him; his qualifications are overlooked, his abilities undervalued. Nevertheless, Nazneen cares for him, for their son, Raqib, who dies as a small baby, and their two daughters, Shahana and Bibi, on their diminishing income. Marking the monotonous rhythm of her days, weeks, and months is the regular task of paring the corns and calluses from Chanu's feet.

Nazneen constantly worries about Hasina, wondering what she is doing and feeling that no good can ever come from kicking against fate. Then a letter arrives, and the reader sees Nazneen's life in Britain counterpointed by Hasina's in Bangladesh. Hasina had seemed to escape the path laid out for her of arranged marriage and servitude but has only escaped into the same pattern but with less stability and security. Her letters are naive, poignant, and touching. She describes the exploitation, abuse, and cruelty to which she is subjected without ever losing her generosity and optimism. Nazneen, in her husband's cramped and shoddy council flat with paper-thin walls and furniture that ranges from the heavily cumbersome to the gimcrack, is asked to recall the stories that began with a prince who lived "seven seas and thirteen rivers away" and is told that Hasina imagines her like that: far-removed, in deserved, exotic luxury (p. 19). The reader is forced to reassess; Nazneen's poverty is made to seem like wealth compared to Hasina's deprivation, but the reference to it as princely riches is deeply ironic.

Gradually Nazneen's life opens. She learns some English. She ventures into Brick Lane to shop. She meets other Bangladeshi women. Then the political life of the community begins to intrude on her domestic sphere. She attends meetings and takes an interest in antiracist movements. A local political activist, Karim, becomes her lover, and Nazneen is shocked to the core by her life seeming to take a course she has chosen rather than one that has been laid out for her. Though the young and handsome Karim brings Nazneen physical pleasure for the first time, it becomes clear that he is no more liberating or liberated than Chanu. Born in Britain, Karim is attuned to the rise of religious fundamentalism in Bangladesh. He wants to connect to the "real" Bangladesh and its "real" culture and sees Nazneen less as a unique individual whose personality he could love than as a pure, authentic version of the Pakistani "village girl," in contrast to the hybridized or assimilated women of London's Bangladeshi communities. Chanu, overheard by Nazneen a week after their wedding, had used the same words of her: a village girl, unspoiled, a good worker. He also added words that indicate that he has examined her as a commodity. She is not beautiful—forehead too broad, eyes too close together, hips rather narrow—but he sees no reason why she should not be able to bear children. She is right for her assigned role.

MONICA ALI

Nazneen's daughters are becoming such hybrids, in spite of their father's efforts. He insists that they wait on him, wear traditional dress, and recite from the work of the national poets Rabindranath Tagore and Kazi Nazrul Islam. The eldest daughter, Shahana, wants jeans, spills paint on her *kameez,* prefers baked beans to dal, and, furious that she is forbidden to speak English in the house, does not make the effort to improve her written Bengali. The youngest daughter, Bibi, more like her mother, is desperately and touchingly keen to please and feels the guilt of her sister's rebellions. Chanu's reaction to Shahana's intransigence is violent but also comic:

> [He] wore himself out with threats before launching a flogging with anything to hand. Newspaper, a rule, a notebook, a threadbare slipper, and once, disastrously, a banana skin. He never learned to select his instrument and he never thought to use his hand. An instrumentless flogging was a lapse of fatherly duty. He flogged enthusiastically but without talent. His energy went into the niyyah— the making of his intention—and here he was advanced and skilful, but the delivery let him down. [The *niyyah* is the intention to pray which is recited before prayer in Islam.]
>
> (p. 128)

Meanwhile, some of the British characters in the book are resisting what they see as an attempt to hybridize or efface their identity. Chanu is driven to near apoplexy by the delivery of a leaflet that represents contemporary fears of multiculturalism; warning people of the threat to British culture from, for example, the provision of lessons on Buddhism and Islam and acceptance of national dress and holidays in schools and the use of public money for the benefit of migrant communities. In response, Asian groups produce their own literature, and a campaign of leaflet and counter-leaflet ensues.

When unrest erupts into riot and threatens Shahana, Nazneen does not remain passive or accepting of fate but acts of her own volition, courageously venturing into the streets. Following this exercise of her own agency, Nazneen further amazes herself by standing up to Mrs. Islam, the local loanshark, and when Chanu decides to return to Bangladesh, Nazneen, who

would once have submissively followed, listens to her daughters' and her own desires. Even though she wants to be reunited with her sister and to cushion Hasina from the worst of her trials, Nazneen chooses to stay in Brick Lane, which has become the nearest thing she has to home.

There are a number of significant motifs in the novel. Food, its preparation and consumption, is important. For years Nazneen does all the preparation for the family's meals, dividing her day between cleaning and cooking, but she cannot bear to eat in Chanu's presence, often starving herself all day and then standing in front of the refrigerator at night, stuffing into her mouth anything in front of her. She is expected to cook and serve food when Chanu brings home a colleague or the man he admires, Dr. Azad, and Chanu gives explicit instructions about how this should be prepared; there should be large pieces of meat. During their early years together, Chanu buys the food, Nazneen walking a few paces behind him as he selects vegetables from the local shops. Later, as Nazneen becomes more confident and Chanu less exuberant, she goes marketing. After Nazneen's depression, alienation, and claustrophobia cause a kind of breakdown, the reader learns that Chanu can cook, and for a while he does and delights in it. When Nazneen recovers, however, they revert back to their accustomed roles.

Ice-skating is also of symbolic significance in the narrative, even though it does not appear more than a few times. The first reference is when Nazneen, encountering British television, is enraptured by the grace of a couple apparently dancing, flowing across the ground powered by some invisible force. She watches the female skater spin and stop, with a look of triumph: "you knew she had conquered everything: her body, the laws of nature, and the heart of the tight-suited man" (p. 20). Chanu tells her that this is ice-skating. She finds it again and is still entranced by the freedom of the skaters' movements, and when she comes across a photograph of an ice-skating partnership in a magazine, she fantasizes that she is part of the picture and has a vivid imaginary experience of traveling fast on

4

one foot across ice that smells of limes. Finally, at the end of the novel, the friends who have forged strong bonds by their mutual support though suffering, difficulty, and more recently, daring new enterprises, take Nazneen on a mystery trip. It is to an ice-skating rink. She protests that one cannot skate in a sari, but her friends tell her that she can. This is England; she can do anything.

When *Brick Lane* was first published, Ali was hailed as a new leading light of British Asian writing, a genre that now includes Zadie Smith (*White Teeth,* 2000), Hanif Kureishi (*The Buddha of Suburbia,* 1990, and *The Black Album,* 1995), Nadeem Aslam (*Maps for Lost Lovers,* 2004), and Gautam Malkani (*Londonstani,* 2006), among others. These novels represent contemporary British society as complex, multiethnic, multicultural, and hybridized. Such writing can be seen as postcolonial fiction in the larger sense in that it has been produced in the era during and after the effects of the imperial process, and in the more specialized sense in that it was produced in the time when some former subjugated and/or colonized countries have taken back their independence and are concerned with issues of ethnic (as well as gender, class, and individual) identity. Specifically, *Brick Lane* depicts a community of people upon whom colonization has had an effect, whose ethnic identity is modified by the society of the colonizers and reinforced by efforts of resistance to that modification.

Helen Tiffin points out in *The Empire Writes Back* that postcolonial cultures are inevitably hybridized. *Brick Lane* represents hybrid, multicultural cultures but also the resistance to these cultures.

Ali's novel is not a work of theory, so it does not interrogate colonial discourses and discursive practices overtly. Nor is it, like Chinua Achebe's *Things Fall Apart* (1958), a representation of a precolonial culture and the damage done to that culture by the colonists or, like Jean Rhys' *Wide Sargasso Sea* (1966), an example of a postcolonial "writing back" to a colonial text (Charlotte Brontë's *Jane Eyre,* 1847) by foregrounding and ventriloquizing the hitherto suppressed colonial subject. Rather, *Brick Lane* represents the already

hybridized subject between two worlds: brought up in Bangladesh in one hybridized culture and living in England in another. Rather than a novel about a Bangladeshi woman changed by contact with western society then, *Brick Lane* is a novel about being between and outside worlds. Nazneen, because her family is poor, because she is female, because she does not (at first) speak English, because she is confined, and because she is a migrant is "other" in many ways and between several worlds.

The pocket of Bangladeshi culture in this fictional Brick Lane is not and cannot be untouched by European or British culture. Dr. Azad and his wife eat frozen television dinners; Nazneen's eldest daughter wants denim jeans and western shampoo. When Chanu returns to Bangladesh, it is not to the unchanged home of his imagination. The process of hybridization is two-way, however. The Brick Lane restaurants serving Bangladeshi food are frequented by British people, and Nazneen and her friends are able to start a clothes-making and retailing business because British girls are buying *salwaar kameez* (long tunic and loose trousers) and other kinds of traditional dress, often in a form adapted to western taste.

Since precolonial "purity" of identity and culture can never be fully recovered, Karim's attempt to return to an unadulterated, originary Bangladeshi culture is misguided because the cultures of the Indian subcontinent have been hybridized, as have those of Britain. Among the dangers of calling for the defense of a colonized culture against the influence of a colonizer is that of homogenization of the colonized, with a consequent loss of emphasis on difference. Just as in *Brick Lane* and other postcolonial novels, the British are represented as failing to distinguish among Indian, Bangladeshi, Pakistani, and other groups, so in emphasizing solidarity and the necessity of preserving "the" culture, Karim loses sight of the diversity of Bangladeshi traditions and even opinions.

Ali wrote *Brick Lane* in English, in which she has said she is now more at home than her first language; the novel was first published by an English (London) publisher, and it has become the object of study for English literary criticism. From the point of view of a postcolonial critique, this is problematic. Bill Ashcroft, Griffiths, and Tiffin explain in *The Empire Writes Back* (1989) that it can be argued

> that the study of English and the growth of Empire proceeded from a single ideological climate and that the development of the one is intrinsically bound up with the development of the other, both at the level of simple utility (as propaganda for instance) and at the unconscious level, where it leads to the naturalizing of constructed values (e.g. civilization, humanity, etc.) which, conversely, established "savagery", "native", "primitive", as their antitheses and as the object of a reforming zeal.
>
> (p. 3)

Ashcroft, Griffiths, and Tiffin also point out that an important aspect of imperialist attitudes was enshrined in the formation of English Studies, the evaluation of that which was deemed central, and the devaluation of that which was considered peripheral, marginal, or uncanonical. They continue:

> when elements of the periphery and margin threatened the exclusive claims of the centre they were rapidly incorporated. This was a process, in Edward Said's terms of conscious affiliation proceeding under the guise of filiation (Said 1984), that is, a mimicry of the centre from a desire not only to be accepted but also to be adopted and absorbed. It caused those from the periphery to immerse themselves in the imported culture, denying their origins in an attempt to become "more English than the English."
>
> (pp. 3–4)

The authors cite the works of Henry James and T. S. Eliot as examples, but we can see in postcolonial fiction a number of representations of characters who attempt to be more English than the English, in Meera Syal's *Anita and Me* (1996, for example, as well as characters who emphasize their difference from the colonial "centre."

In a section applicable to *Brick Lane* as well as to the other novels mentioned here, Elleke Boehmer shows that postcolonial writers are appropriating the techniques and forms of colonial texts, cutting down to manageable size the vast unknown by the use of comfortingly familiar nomenclature and tropes.

> In their myriad narratives of journeying we see how postcolonial writers have managed, though a process of mass imaginative appropriation, to hijack one of the defining stories of imperial expansion: the traveller's tale, the voyage of mystery, to the heart of darkness. Tales of occupation and settlement plotted from the colonial centre to the colonies have been supplanted by journeys *from* the hinterland *to* the city—with the extra inflection of the final moment of homecoming and return.... Incorporating indigenous cultural material, defiant of western authority, the postcolonial quest seeks mastery not in the first instance over land or other peoples, but of history and self.
>
> (p. 192)

Nazneen journeys from a rural home to an alien city, and while neither she nor any member of her community comes to master it, she does attain a measure of mastery over her own identity and her own future. In following Nazneen's journey, Ali, like George Eliot, Elizabeth Gaskell, and other Victorian novelists, uses fiction set largely in the domestic sphere, the traditional arena for women, as a venue for the social-problem or "condition of England" novel.

ALENTEJO BLUE *(2006)*

The setting of *Brick Lane* is in a community largely composed of migrants to Britain and first- or second-generation settlers in Britain. Most of the characters in *Alentejo Blue* are native Portuguese, and the British characters, expatriates and tourists, are in a minority. Where *Brick Lane*'s Chanu and Nazneen have had to learn a new language and pick their way through an alien environment with few familiar landmarks, here the English, Germans, and other non-Portuguese are the outsiders. They are not precisely colonists, but neither are they assimilated into Portuguese culture. A British child who has lived in Portugal for most of his life asks: "Am I Portuguese now?" His father replies: "Don't be so bleeding soft" (p. 102). But the Portuguese believe that cultural imperialism is coming their way.

"What language do you think your grandchildren will speak?".... "English, my friend," Vasco informed him. "With an American accent."

(p. 86)

The novel is set in the fictional village of Mamarrosa in the Alentejo, one of the five regions of Portugal. Alentejo, which lies to the south-center of the country, can be translated as "beyond the Tagus." It is separated from the northern regions by the Tagus River and bordered to the far south by the popular tourist destination the Algarve. The blue of "Alentejo Blue" is one of the two colors used on door and window frames of the whitewashed Alentejo houses (the other is yellow), but it could also be the blues of the area's spectacular skies, which characters in the novel perceive from time to time, and it could suggest something more abstract, a rhapsody in blue, or "the blues," both the music and the mood. A character, Teresa, also wears the color at a crucial crossroads in her life: "She wore her black slingbacks and a white cotton dress with blue flowers that matched the paint that framed the door. Alentejo blue. There she was, in a picture, in a moment, setting out for the rest of her life" (p. 177).

Two epigraphs precede the novel, one from *Journey to Portugal* (1981) by the Portuguese novelist José Saramago (winner of the 1998 Nobel Prize for literature), and one from T. S. Eliot's *Ash Wednesday* (1930), a six-part poem recording spiritual struggle and spiritual progress toward faith. The first, "Villages are like people, we approach them slowly, a step at a time," suggests that the narrative will take us slowly through the elements of Alentejo, initially through its inhabitants, one by one, and later through their interaction as community. The second, beginning "Because I do not hope to turn again," introduces the themes of change and resistance to change that pervade the novel.

The narrative of *Brick Lane* is told in the third person and largely seen from the perspective of Nazneen, but *Alentejo Blue* is a multi-perspective, almost polyphonic novel. The narrative dips in and out of the thoughts and voices of young, middle-aged, and old men and women, Portuguese and foreign, who live in or are visiting the village or surrounding houses, through their thoughts and conversations filling in the story of their lives to the present of the narrative. It begins with João, an eighty-four-year-old farmer, who comes out of his house in the early morning to find his friend and beloved of sixty-seven years, Rui, hanging from a tree. João remembers their first meeting, as hungry seventeen-year-olds looking for work and their history as they come together, lose each other, and are reunited again, in a beautifully written and moving but understated section reminiscent of Annie Proulx's short story "Brokeback Mountain."

In *Brick Lane* characters mourn their separation from and try to re-create Bangladeshi culture, but there is little reference to the country's immediate history; as Ali has said, the suffering and violence of the civil war is present in the sense of the fragility of life and the vulnerability of characters, especially women. In *Alentejo Blue* history is present through the story of João and Rui. João's memories show us the dominance of the Catholic Church and the wealthy, landed minority; the revolution of 1927; the establishment of a communist opposition; the reallocation of land to cooperatives; the failure of the cooperatives and the landowners' repurchase of the land, cheaply; the rise of António de Oliveira Salazar, officially president of the Council of Ministers of Portugal from 1932 to 1968 but in effect a fascist dictator; the establishment of the New State; the brutality of Salazar's secret police (PIDE); the coup by the Movimento das Forças Armadas (Armed Forces Movement), which in 1974 deposed Salazar's fascist heir, Marcello Caetano. Through all the changes of regime, those who had no capital remained poor, and those, like Rui and João, who hired themselves out to work on the land remained poorest of all.

Other local people are introduced. Vasco, owner of Mamarrosa's most popular café, once worked in the United States and therefore considers himself to be more cosmopolitan, informed, and sophisticated than his fellows. Though he is one of the few local people in the novel to have traveled abroad, he is also one of those who resist change. The food he makes is traditional—his mother's pigs' ears and tails salad, for example—and he dreams of attracting tourists to his café by its "authentic" ambience and cooking. For him the present is frequently interrupted by memories of the past; his time working in the restaurants of Cape Cod and the American wife he lost in childbirth. Vasco's café provides a space in which many of the strands of the narrative briefly intersect. Most of the characters in the novel pass through, and a number of them spend a lot of time at the bar or tables that Vasco constantly wipes in imitation of American waiters, but with an unwashed, all-purpose cloth. Eduardo, Vasco's sparring partner and opponent in a long-standing feud, drops in regularly. The beautiful young Teresa arrives at the café in the pursuit of her second job, selling insurance on commission, which too often seems to turn into social work instead. When we meet her, she is dreaming of the time when she will surprise her mother with the money she hopes to make, and the moment when she will give her fiancé, the mechanic Antonio, the gift of her virginity before telling him that she will not marry him and that she is leaving Portugal to work as an au pair in London. Teresa wants to make the occasion romantic and perfect but finds Antonio's callow approach far from either. Sexual encounters in the novel are not described in detail, and we receive the impression that they are generally unsatisfactory. Teresa might be said to have the experience but miss the feeling, as she is partly stoned and partly past caring, in the wake of Antonio's blithe lack of empathy.

The young of Mamarrosa are involved in a more modern, urban life than their elders. Antonio and his friend Vincente talk of engines, oil leaks, and fan belts. Taking some supplies to João, Teresa reflects that she envies the simple life he follows; the modern clutter and distractions he is not bothered by. When her mobile phone rings, she puts it away as though it were something shameful. In spite of the connection she feels with João as he gives her a simple country meal, she is unaware either of his almost lifelong love for Rui or that Rui has taken his own life.

None of the Alentejo locals is wealthy; few who left to make their fortune have returned, and in a more humorous take on submission to the will of God or events than that of *Brick Lane,* we see a grandmother's (Vasco's) response to the fates of these exiles. When her elder son, Humberto, goes to the mines in Mozambique, she says, "He has answered a call"; when her youngest son, Henrique, goes to fight in Angola, she says: "It is the Lord's will." When she learns that Henrique will not be coming home, she says "What is meant to be, must be," and goes out to feed the pig. But when Vasco breaks a teapot, she beats him with a big wooden spoon and tells him that of course he could help it. Vasco reflects, "With teapots you are free to choose, in matters of life and death you are not" (p. 77). This grandmother is also an example of the older generation's resistance to change. When "Senhor Pinheiro" pays for two windows to be put into the house she cannot get used to it and has them boarded up. Vasco's mother, on the other hand, has told him this shaking her head "to show how far she herself had come into the light" (p. 88).

It is said that one son of the village is to come home. Marco Alfonso Rodrigues is coming, and his shadow falls over the community long before he arrives. Rumors spread: he is a fantastically successful businessman; he is in electronics; he is in dry cleaning; he has plans for the village; he is going to build a four-hundred-bed hotel; he is going to develop the area as a tourist resort; he is going to make a nature reserve. When he arrives, he is not at all as anyone expected. Reticent, enigmatic, and given to spare gnomic statements, he is a disappointment to his cousin Eduardo, and Harry Stanton, an English writer and habitué of the café, insists that he is a hippy, a woolly-thinking drifter, but he is a catalyst for change in a way people did not expect.

Stanton is stalled on a fictionalized life of the Romantic artist William Blake, which is ironic, as he seems to be the very antithesis of a Romantic visionary. He loses his illusions about his dream of building a perfect sanctuary where he will be able to write in comfort and peace about his mental excuses for not working and his promises to himself to start working, and about himself as a good man. At the end of the story, he is considering leaving Mamarrosa for that most westernized and Americanized of Eastern

European cities, Prague. Other non-Portuguese inhabitants of Mamarrosa include a British family, the Potts. The Potts are mother Chrissie; son Jay (named after the dope his father smokes), into whose respective perspectives the narrative voice dips at different times; daughter Ruby; and father Michael (known as "China," a nickname derived from his surname). China has fled to Portugal to escape some unspecified trouble in Britain and, long saturated in drink and permanently addled by drugs, seems both belligerent and emasculated.

The family is near rock bottom. They scrape the smallest of subsistence livings, which China spends on animals he fails to husband, vehicles he wrecks, marijuana, and drink. Ruby, profoundly deaf and speech-impaired, shoplifts and picks up older men and local youths, including Teresa's brother, in the cafés and bars of the town. Jay is love starved and has shouldered too many responsibilities too young. Chrissie seems hopeless and to have given up trying to run the squalid house and decrepit smallholding or care for the children. Stanton befriends Jay, who he perceives as a grubby, lonely waif in filthy, outgrown clothes and tries to be kind to Ruby. He sleeps with Chrissie but is aware that he has no feelings for her and is then seduced by or seduces Ruby. The family, dysfunctional but nonetheless with strong ties among its members, is blown apart when it emerges that Ruby is pregnant; they assume by Stanton, though it might be Francisco, a local youth. Stanton learns that neither of the Potts parents is as uncaring and detached as he believed. Each reacts in a different way: China, outraged at first, likes the idea of becoming a grandfather; Chrissie organizes an abortion, illegal in Portugal. She is then thrown out by China and threatened with prosecution for murder by the Portuguese state. She escapes the accusation because hospital records show that the fetus had died, and the family pulls itself back together. China gets work, and they are seen in Vasco's café *en famille* and cleaned up for the first time.

Among the transient visitors, Eileen, a middle-age British woman who has come to realize the size of the gulf that lies between she and her husband, Richard, provides another aspect of the novel's title. She reflects that the sky is the same blue as a bowl she had carefully cradled all the way home from Agadir, only to drop it the next day. Eileen fantasizes about running away from her mundane life to Alentejo, where, she reflects, she could be an eccentric but accepted foreigner, keeping bees, growing runner beans, and looking after donkeys. "I could ride into town on a donkey, barefoot on a donkey with a wicker shopping basket, and everyone would know me and say in a fond sort of way, ah, there she goes, the crazy Englishwoman" (p. 115). Eileen's section of the novel shows us the holiday in Alentejo and her life at home from her perspective and is narrated in the first person, representing her interior monologue. This provides details of the village and people its natives do not think to note as well as a window onto events, which is of course partial and biased but also intimate. While we inhabit Eileen's mind, we feel sympathy for her and perceive that she is far from the stupid, irrational person the carping Richard describes. She is acute and responsive and has a wry sense of humor. Like Ali, she is an observer neither in the thick of things nor behind a closed door. When she is in conversation with two other vacationers, a young engaged couple, Sophie and Huw, however, we understand that they see Eileen quite differently, as a clinging and rather ridiculous old lady.

Similarly, we follow Sophie and Huw through some days' sightseeing in the region and their return to Mamarrosa, first from his perspective then from hers. Though narrated in the third person, this section uses free indirect style as well as dialogue to give insights into both characters. They have agreed that while on holiday they will put aside the arrangements for their approaching wedding, but the stressful topic is never far from their thoughts and never far from becoming an argument. Both Huw and Sophie have their own hopes, dreams, doubts, epiphanies, and disappointments, and each is irrevocably locked out of the other's. Huw has no idea that in a chapel made of human bones Sophie is having a profoundly affecting experience and turns the moment into bathos; Sophie has no idea of the effect her dangerous driving has had on him. These sections of the novel inevitably invite comparisons with modernist fiction, in particular that of Virginia Woolf. The couple's reactions to Stanton are diametrically opposed: Huw thinks he would be an interesting man to have a drink with; Sophie detests and wants to avoid him. Their argument leads to a throwaway but unforgivable remark in the context of Sophie's episodes of depression— "You're crazy" (p. 251)—and inevitably they are forced to socialize with Stanton at the Mamarrosa festival.

Two of the main events of the novel are festivities, the first of which, the opening of an Internet café, brings together a number of villagers, and the second of which brings together both locals and incomers. The Internet café has taken over the premises of a frozen fish shop. At its grand opening, it has chairs, tables, and computers but no Internet connection, the kitchen is not fully functioning, and the ice cream it serves is redolent of the building's previous occupants. Later, a mother, Dona Linda, spends hours looking at a webcam view of a bench in the Canadian town of Little Rock, even when it is night in Canada and the screen is dark because her daughter has gone to a Canadian town called Little River; she hopes that the two are close together and that her daughter might just happen to walk along the road to sit on the bench. To contemporary British and American eyes, Mamarrosa is old-fashioned, but things have changed, and are in the process of further hybridization. The harvesting of cork and the growing of fruit and vegetables is being supplemented by the tourist trade; the television shows Brazilian soap operas; and traditional local dishes are supplemented by international cuisine.

Food is important in the story, as it was in *Brick Lane*. Who eats what, with whom, and how much is always significant, as is the care with which the food is prepared, whether it is local and traditional, and how good it is. The climax of the novel is set during the *festa de Mamarrosa* in November, when the villagers and visitors come together for music, dancing, and food. There is happiness and celebration, discord and fighting,

plans for the future and nostalgia for the past. Some characters behave with courtesy and consideration, others badly. Vasco overeats hugely, sampling all the dishes laid out—fried liver with chili, baked tripe, *cataplana* (a traditional seafood dish cooked in a domed, hinged pot), rice with seafood, green beans, broad beans, pork, clams, goose barnacles, spider crabs, melon, pineapple, plums, half a pear, bread, cake, a bottle of sweet sparkling wine—and when he and Eduardo clash, grapple, and spin about the room, he is terribly sick. The next day the pair continue their sparring, which turns out to be not unaffectionate, as usual. As João thinks, "Everything keeps changing but still it remains the same" (p. 275). Marco Alfonso Rodrigues is found to have left, without having made anyone rich, erected a hotel, founded a resort, or made much impact on the village at all. All he has left behind is a note that simply reads: "Peace." Eduardo avers that after all he was not the real Marco Alfonso Rodrigues but an impostor.

The novel ends in December, some time after the main events of the narrative, which took place in spring and early summer, with João telling the story of Marco to his pig, but cautioning her: "There's more than one way to look it," before beginning the story again.

The strands of *Alentejo Blue* never really coalesce, and the characters' personal histories do not mesh, except in brief collisions. Not even the more perceptive or empathic of the characters can fully know any of the others, and most do not try. This adds to the sense that the character vignettes and minor incidents are snapshots of an ongoing reality rather than the carefully crafted and neatly tied-up pattern of a novel. It also adds to the reader's sense that the novel is a snapshot and cross section of Alentejo past and present, like the palimpsest wall coverings of the British edition's dust jacket, rather than a linear history of events that happen to a few selected characters living there.

OTHER WRITING

Ali has written introductions to two twentieth-century novels, Graham Greene's *The End of the*

Affair (1951) and R. K. Narayan's *The Painter of Signs* (1976). One link between the two is that Greene and Narayan were friends, Greene helping Narayan to find a publisher for his first novel, *Swami and Friends,* and suggesting "R. K. Narayan" as a pen name more easily managed by westerners than his full name, Rasipuram Krishnaswami Ayyar Narayanaswami.

The End of the Affair concerns an adulterous relationship, but there its resemblance to *Brick Lane* ends. *The End of the Affair* is set in London during the Second World War, and the relationship, more peripheral in *Brick Lane,* is central, though second to the relationship that develops between the main characters and faith, or God. The adulterous woman, Sarah, wife of the civil service nonentity Henry, gives up her lover, a well-known writer, Maurice, as part of a pact with God to save his life, and she subsequently dies. Maurice, made bitter and cynical by what he believes is Sarah's betrayal, eventually comes to understand what she did and to believe that she was almost saintly. The novel ends with Maurice and Henry sharing a house. In *The End of the Affair* it is Catholicism revived by the promise to God that parts the central protagonists, while in *Brick Lane,* religious scruples make Nazneen an unwilling adulteress, but religion is also evoked by Karim and his followers as part of their embattled culture and thus of the campaign that brings him and Nazneen together.

The Painter of Signs is set in the fictional Indian town of Malgudi, the location of several of Narayan's novels, into which comes Daisy, a feminist less interested in marriage than in bringing Indian women the liberation of family planning. She commissions signs for the clinics she plans to establish from Raman (Ram), an educated and conscientious sign painter who, in pursuit of a life based on reason, logic, and routine, is equally determined to avoid marriage. Thrown together by Ram's need to visit each location in order to decide on the best possible style of sign, the two fall in love. To an extent, like *The End of the Affair, The Painter of Signs* is about a triangular relationship, among Daisy, Ram, and the aunt with whom Ram lives, but the

novel is as much about changing Indian society as it is about love or Daisy and Ram.

RECEPTION

Brick Lane was published to both popular and critical acclaim. The product of the determination Ali mentions in her autobiographical essay was two chapters of a novel, which she sent to a friend at Doubleday. She was immediately offered a two-book publishing contract. The still-unpublished typescript also earned her a place on the *Granta* Best Young Novelists list, and the magazine published an extract from the novel, "Dinner with Dr. Azad." This first novel, *Brick Lane,* was published the following year and won the British Book Awards Newcomer of the Year Award, the W. H. Smith People's Choice Book Award for 2003, Barnes & Noble's Discover Award for New Writers, and the Quality Paperback Book Club's New Voices Award. It was also short-listed for the Man Booker prize, the British Book Awards Literary Fiction Award, and the *Guardian* First Book Award. It has been translated into thirty languages.

After such a successful debut, anticipation of Ali's next work was bound to be intense, and there was much speculation in the British press about the likely theme, setting, and quality of the second novel. Many commented on the pressure on the "sophomore" novelist, and it seemed almost a foregone conclusion that the rapturous reception of the first novel would not be repeated. Reviews of *Alentejo Blue* have been mixed. The interlacing but not fully integrated stories have been found too elusive and unsatisfying, but described as also pleasingly suggestive and concentrated vignettes. (See, for example, Alex Clark's review in the *Observer* (May 21, 2006, p. 23.)

Most critics agreed that the characterization, in particular of Nazneen and Chanu, but also of other characters, such as the wonderfully comic but also menacing monster Mrs. Islam, is one of the greatest strengths of *Brick Lane,* but Ali's representation of Bangladeshi characters, and her characters' comments about recent Sylheti migrants (from the Sylhet district in northeastern

Bangladesh), also caused controversy. An organization called the Greater Sylhet Welfare and Development Council sent a letter to Ali's publishers alleging that the portrayal of Sylheti people was unbalanced and unfair and demanding corrections to statements made by the characters about overcrowding, working conditions, and other issues. The *Guardian* newspaper reported the accusations and demands, comparing them to the protests made against Salman Rushdie's *Satanic Verses* (1988) by those who felt that he had insulted the Islamic faith.

Later, members of the Brick Lane community in London accused Ali of promoting racial stereotypes and depicting the inhabitants of their area in an insulting manner. They held a protest meeting in Brick Lane and initiated a campaign against a planned film adaptation of the novel (produced by Alison Owen, with the working title *Seven Seas*) which forced the filmmakers, Ruby Films, to find alternative locations. The authors Germaine Greer and Salman Rushdie took opposing stances on the subject in the pages of the British press in July 2006, and the novelists Hari Kunzru and Lisa Appignanesi were reported (in the *Guardian* of July 31, 2006) as having added their voices to Rushdie's in support of Ali.

Selected Bibliography

WORKS OF MONICA ALI

NOVELS

Brick Lane. London: Doubleday, 2003; London: Black Swan, 2004; New York: Scribners, 2003.

Alentejo Blue. London: Doubleday, 2006; New York: Scribners, 2006.

SHORT FICTION AND EXTRACTS

"Dinner with Dr. Azad." (Extract from *Brick Lane.*) *Granta 81: Best of Young British Novelists 2003* (April 3, 2002

33–46). Reprinted in *Story-Wallah: Short Fiction from South Asian Writers.* Edited by Shyam Selvadurai. New York: Houghton Mifflin, 2005.

"Sundowners." (Extract from *Brick Lane.*) *New Yorker,* January 23 and 30, 2006.

OTHER WRITINGS

"Where I'm Coming From." *Guardian* (http://arts.guardian.co.uk/features/story.html). June 17, 2003. (Personal essay.)

Introduction to *The End of the Affair,* by Graham Greene. London: Vintage, 2004.

Introduction to *The Painter of Signs,* by R. K. Narayan. Harmondsworth, U.K.: Penguin, 2006.

CRITICAL AND BIOGRAPHICAL STUDIES

Ashcroft, Bill, Gareth Griffiths, and Helen Tiffin. *The Empire Writes Back: Theory and Practice in Post-colonial Literatures.* London: Routledge, 1989.

Clark, Alex. "Escape from Brick Lane." *Observer,* May 21, 2006, p. 23. (Review of *Alentejo Blue.*)

Griffiths, Gareth. "The Myth of Authenticity." In *The Post-colonial Studies Reader.* Edited by Bill Ashcroft, Gareth Griffiths, and Helen Tiffin. London: Routledge, 1995, pp. 237–241.

Boehmer, Elleke. *Colonial and Postcolonial Literature.* 2nd ed. Oxford: Oxford University Press, 2005.

Tiffin, Helen. "Post-colonial Literatures and Counter-discourse." In *The Post-colonial Studies Reader.* Edited by Bill Ashcroft, Gareth Griffiths, and Helen Tiffin. London: Routledge, 1995, pp. 95–98.

INTERVIEWS AND JOURNALISM

Lane, Harriet. "Ali's in Wonderland." *Observer* http://observer.guardian.co.uk/bookgroup/story/0,,991601,00.html). June 1, 2003. (Interview with Ali.)

Lea, Richard, and Paul Lewis. "Local Protests over Brick Lane Film." *Guardian Unlimited* (http://books.guardian.co.uk/news/articles.html). July 17, 2006.

Cacciottolo, Mario. "Brick Lane Protesters Hurt over 'Lies.'" BBC News (http://news.bbc.co.uk/2/hi/uk_news/5229872.stm). July 31, 2006.

JOHN BURNSIDE

(1955—)

J. C. Bittenbender

A PROLIFIC WRITER whose stature as a poet and novelist has been steadily growing since the appearance of his first collection of poetry in 1988, John Burnside provides a voice that engages with the mystical and the organic as he investigates notions of personal identity and those myths we employ as we negotiate our way around the natural world. In addition to his many published volumes of poetry, fiction, and memoir, he has established a voice as a contributor to well-known international publications such as the New Yorker, the Times Literary Supplement, the London Review of Books, and the Guardian, and his work has been included in a number of anthologies. He is a writer who displays a passionate commitment to ecological and environmental concerns and who interrogates and revisions the world so that readers may always view it in a vibrant and numinous fashion. His poetry exhibits a wonderful combination of botany, horticulture, and biochemistry, as well as existential philosophy. He also engages with voices from other cultures, and he shows a particular fondness for Spanish-language poets such as Octavio Paz, Federico García Lorca, and Jorge Guillén as well as American poets such as Wallace Stevens, Marianne Moore, and William Carlos Williams. Defiant of any form of label, especially those aligned with a nationalism of geopolitics, he explained in an interview with Attila Dósa how he would like to be classified: "I'm happy to call myself a green poet or an environmental poet or an ecological poet, but not a nature poet. I'm not a Scottish poet and I'm not a religious poet. These are not useful labels for me" (p. 18).

Named by the Poetry Book Society as one of the twenty New Generation poets in 1994, over the years Burnside has won numerous prizes and awards for his poetry and has contributed poems to a variety of anthologies and literary journals.

In addition to his poetic art, Burnside has written novels, short stories, and memoir in addition to stories for radio. He is a committed writer, environmentalist and ecologist—a poet who reveals the mysteries of the world in a highly unique fashion. In both poetry and prose he offers the reader lyrical visions of the everyday epiphanies that haunt our always local and provisional worlds.

Born in Dunfermline, Scotland, on March 19, 1955, Burnside spent part of his childhood living in Cowdenbeath, in the west of Fife, before moving with his family to Corby, an industrial town in the English Midlands. He was educated in Catholic schools in Scotland and England, and he later studied English and European languages at Cambridge College of Arts and Technology. For years he worked as an engineer in computer systems design, and he later worked as a freelance writer. For a time he was writer in residence at Dundee University.

EARLY POETRY

Burnside writes deeply felt poetry that considers the world we live in from a number of perspectives. In his early work in The Hoop (1988), Common Knowledge (1991), and Feast Days (1992), he announces a number of prevalent themes that in many ways contribute to his understanding of the beauties and flaws of perception. One of the ways in which Burnside seeks to view the world is through the construction of a notion of the self. His poems offer rich philosophical visions of ways in which we create ideas of our own identities through sensory impressions of the natural world, firmly held beliefs that are handed to us through tradition, memory, and religion, as well as our perceptions of other identities.

In Burnside's debut collection of poetry, *The Hoop*, which won a Scottish Arts Council Book Award, the poet announces many of the themes to define his poetry. However, the concept of definition is itself problematic for Burnside, as he tends to eschew the notion that we can describe the world and our position in it with any degree of certainty. This concern that we as readers defy an assumption of a set and understandable world becomes the leading trope in his early poetry and plays a part in the way he develops his later philosophies of absence, language, and silence. In this collection, Burnside explores the role of memory and silence as well. The "hoop" becomes a unifying image, taking its cues from uses in Celtic mythologies. Early on in his work, Burnside attempts to offer organic understandings of the natural world that challenge traditional interpretations. His poetry exhibits nature in a way that seeks to redefine the way in which we "read" the world. Many of his poems provide intricate visions of flora and fauna that engage with a human psychology, making use of nature as a coded world that allows us ways of gauging our own notions of self.

In the poem "Silence Is Possible," Burnside investigates the condition of finding silence and registering absence:

Silence is possible, and after dark
it almost happens: silence, like a glove,
the perfect fit you always hoped to find.

(p. 16)

The poem goes on to enumerate the ways in which an authentic experience of silence is always fraught with the intrusive noise of the outside world. The experience of silence, though, does finally become possible through considerations of sounds (or the lack of sounds) that are otherwise rejected or not traditionally recognized:

Silence is possible,
but you have been a listener for years
and what could you find but the hard quiet
of huddled swimmers in a riverbed

or the casual hush of abattoirs
after the thud of a bullet nobody heard.

(p. 16)

Silence, as a form of absence, becomes possible through the recognition of the presence of sound. This becomes a typical device of Burnside, whereby opposites are defined in terms of one another; silence through sound, absence through presence, and vice versa.

In "After Viking," Burnside takes the Viking missions to Mars and uses them as a metaphor for silence and new definition:

Our music is a bottle full of wasps
and aching seas
but silence is the choice we failed to make […]

(p. 26)

This poem and others contain the image of the 'hoop' as one that serves to define the circularity of existence and the repetitive ways in which we learn of the world: "but form is the sub-organic / hoop of the virus" (p. 26). In "Inside" it appears as follows:

[…] and night is best appreciated in this hoop of light
where dripping is and everybody knows
magic is somewhere else, where no one goes.

(p. 28)

Burnside's second collection, *Common Knowledge*, also won a Scottish Arts Council Book Award. In this work he continues his quest to redefine the concept of definition, and he relates this to the ability to see the world in new ways. Poems from this volume seem to show Burnside working through a definition of what "common knowledge" represents and how inadequate the terms are. Many poems reflect themes of vision and transformation. The first section, "Home," is an extended series of meditations on the concept of home and how one comes to understand that designation. Here the speaker seems to be creating a world. One world is imagined and the other takes shape more unconsciously, and Burnside is adept at recognizing the differences between those two ways of "knowing" the world:

And morning changes—
sometimes to the angel we expect

JOHN BURNSIDE

watching the tomb in a garden of blood and lilies,
sometimes to the notion of a Christ
we half-invent[...]

(p. 3)

In some ways this poem announces another theme of Burnside's, which is a questioning of how we understand the significance of religion or the symbols or characters that have always stood for particular ways of religious thinking. He presents a pagan/Christian world that always seeks to define itself in terms of new visions. His religion is not atheistic or agnostic by any means, but is more likely to be informed by a fresh way of reading the mythos of religion through senses that have been dulled by traditional narrative that depends upon certainty.

As one proceeds through the vignettes of "Home," one begins to see Burnside outlining only tentative foundations of what one might see as identity or a sense of self or the flesh of the imagined world. Along the way he creates new definitions for "common" things like home by asking the reader to consider "a wireless country". Another definition for home might be"...wetland whispers shriven from the air; / warm valves gloved in citrinous velvet dust like jars of myrrh" (p. 4). Any one of these rich descriptions might serve as an adequate response to the question "what is home?" And Burnside opens the possibilities for the uses of all forms of human experience to aid in creating working definitions for home that are always fluid and subject to reevaluation and reinterpretation.

Although Burnside is a poet of landscape, he is not what one might call a "geographical" poet. He often writes of Scottish and other British locations, but he does not make the named identities of these places the focus of his writing. Attention is not drawn to the political landscape of the space he describes, but rather the reader is led to understand a topography of place that is more universal. This is part of Burnside's concern with dismantling certainty and the many ways in which humans manufacture certainty through language, naming, and other methods of identity formation. Burnside's landscapes are rather locales that are organic and imagined. He draws attention to what is mythic and created in the

world and to how these visions are inextricably linked to the mind and the heart. The speaker of "Home" also considers how home is something that is defined in part by time: "The past keeps shifting around us / but each year the same milk-coloured spring returns..." (p. 7). Later, home becomes defined in an aural fashion:

and home a series of lucid echoes
between a sky inscribed with gulls and stars
and these strange or familiar houses
where love is perfected.

(p. 7)

Home might also be described in terms of the "order" of language:

Sometimes you linger days
upon a word,
a single, uncontaminated drop
of sound; for days
it trembles, liquid to the mind,
then falls:
mere denotation,
dimming in the undertow of language.

(p. 9)

There is something both beautiful yet threatening about the language in these lines. The reader waits for the moment of significance, yet the language takes us somewhere that is dangerous in its rigidity and certainty. Burnside seems to suggest that the certainty of an "end" will take us away from the freedom and beauty of the waiting moment.

The second part of *Common Knowledge* is a section titled "Annunciations," a meditative prose poem in which Burnside imagines angels, the traditional understanding of angels, the "assumption" of angels, and the concept of annunciation. "This is one version of the Annunciation, but there are others," the poet suggests(p. 19). Burnside exercises a kaleidoscopic approach to the Annunciation in the same way as he has offered a multitextured and varied approach to the definition of home in the first section. This theme of "revisioning" religious (and primarily Christian) imagery and ritual is an element of Burnside's project to enrich experience through deconstruction and reformulation.

In the book's final section, "Common Knowledge," Burnside returns to the themes of a pluralistic understanding of home and how a more fluid understanding of home might serve to define us in a less restrictive manner. In "The Forest of Beguilement" the speaker addresses the theme of "beguilement" and how one is often tricked by illusions offered by the surrounding world, which is constantly changing:

Nothing convinces;
distance makes for home
in all directions:
empty dovecotes, burning thatch and bees,
cupboards of sweet jams and bottled skins;
rainfalls are enchantments in the mere
of dawn, and nothing there
so naked, that it never held
a thread of sleek intent[...]

(p. 52)

For Burnside the state of being unconvinced is perhaps one to be embraced, as it argues for a way of seeing the world anew with each shift of the eyes. To see the extraordinary in the ordinary is the preferred state of "being" in this world, and Burnside's poems articulate a particular organic metaphysics of seeing that is exhilarating. In the final poem of the collection, "Domestic," the speaker paints an immediately recognizable scene of home, then shifts the reader's vision elsewhere:

If we think of the homes we have known,
Or stops between tunnels
When silence steps up to a train
Through frost-printed trees,
...
...
...
it barely shows.

(p. 62)

In the final lines, self-definition becomes as untenable a project as it ever has been. The "safety" of home as a place that serves to define us is a false feeling, but it is a feeling that is ultimately desirable. For Burnside's speakers, the unimagined self is the one that is imprisoned by false constructs offered up by language and other ways of rigidly reading the world. Ultimately we

"become what we seem," and that new form of common knowledge opens up vistas (p. 62).

Burnside's third collection of poems, *Feast Days*, won the Geoffrey Faber Memorial Prize in 1994. The poems in this collection continue to explore questions of language and naming. Here the poems speak even more directly to the mythologies and fictions that humans create in an attempt to make sense of the world. In the first poem, "Septuagesima," Burnside provides an epigraph from Jorge Guillén that translates, "Names. / Above, below, they cover the essence / of things" (p. 1). This is appropriate not only for the poem, which considers the silence of the world the day before Adam came to "name the animals," but also for Burnside's philosophy, which recognizes the problematic nature of naming that reduces and limits the potential of that which surrounds us in the world:

A day like this, perhaps:
a winter whiteness
haunting the creation,
as we are sometimes
haunted by the space
we fill, or by the forms
we might have known
before the names,
beyond the gloss of things.

(p. 1)

The haunting here seems to be an almost desired state, before things were nailed down by language. Something potential is lost by naming, a presence that is erased by the act of naming. The word "gloss" serves to suggest that names can only ever be an artificial and superficial way of understanding the world. The word also hints at the sense of a veneer that is brushed over the world by naming and that often seals it off from fruitful possibility.

In the sequence "Aphasia in Childhood," Burnside brings to light metaphysical questions of being and the nature of the soul and squarely opposes them to what is learned in the classroom through imposed forms of learning and naming. The word "aphasia," an inability to express, becomes a theme here that Burnside will develop elsewhere (especially in his 1997 novel, *The

JOHN BURNSIDE

Dumb House). In section two of the sequence, the speaker attempts to enumerate

The evidence of home: hairs in the paintwork; broken fingernails between the carpet and the skirting-board. Traces; fibres; the smell of rubber gloves.

(p. 4)

Trying to make sense of the world can often be compared to puzzling out a detective story, but the clues can be left lying around in the most common fashion. Here Burnside joins themes announced in earlier collections and attaches them to new considerations of memory and the ways in which humans are rendered inarticulate by standard ways of looking at the world. In section five the speaker remarks on a new geography that is confronting him as he sits on a train and gazes out at the world passing by: "I am traveling a country of windows[...]" (p. 7). He is cognizant of a "new map" that is in the head and the heart rather than one that is taught or learned as a traditional way of looking at the world.

In "Aeaea" and "Penelope," Burnside plays with two accepted Homeric myths. Aeaea, the home of the sorceress Circe, is used by Burnside to highlight the idea that all geographies are ultimately fictitious. The speaker of the poem becomes like Odysseus in a search for a home that is always mythic. Along the way, in typical Burnside fashion, he asks us to reconsider definitions for other concepts or sentiments that we may have mistakenly thought were already explained. Here, love is reexamined as the speaker considers

a house of looms where nobody can tell
if love is skill
or fear of being lost.

(p. 12)

Circe's mythic house of looms becomes a location fraught with the possibility for reconfiguring what we know of love. In "Penelope," the speaker talks of how Odysseus' wife lies awake at night listening to his stories about her "other selves: Calypso, Nausicaa," thus asking the reader to contemplate possible different geographies of "self" (p. 13).

"The Noli Me Tangere Incident" (Jesus' admonition to Mary Magdalene: "touch me not") is one of Burnside's many prose poems. Here the speaker seems to recount the moment of Mary's entrance to the cave where Jesus was placed after the Crucifixion. She finds him gone and the poem describes this discovery in terms of an absence that potentially makes the Resurrection to come a form of presence that can only be accomplished through defining the elements of what is absent. Mary considers the sensory experience of hearing others who are trying to make sense of the absence of Christ, and she weaves together an understanding that might only be tentatively given a name: "nothing you would mistake for resurrection" (p. 14). This theme of defining presence by way of absence is a recurring one in Burnside's work. He consistently attempts to find "something" in the midst of nothingness or to define something by what it is not, and this establishes him as one of the most deeply metaphysical and existential poets writing today.

One of the highlights of *Feast Days* is the sequence of prose poems titled "Urphänomen" (Johann Wolfgang von Goethe's word for basic, archetypal phenomena). These poems reinforce the idea of Burnside as an existential poet, and they also point to his fascination with the role memory plays in defining being and the world that surrounds the individual. In section five, the speaker speaks of "this illusion"(p. 27). What seems to be insignificant in the mind of the speaker creates whole worlds of meaning. There are "mementos" strewn throughout the poem: "Somewhere inside the house, in an old medicine bottle, or pressed between the pages of the family bible, a thread of seaweed or a single petal of frangipani is drying through years of late shows and annual statistics: the only evidence of my crime" (p. 27). These are small things that conjure worlds of memory and meaning, but this is not necessarily to be a sought thing, since Burnside points out "later a memory will form in my skin like a tumour." (p. 27). Memory for Burnside may not be relegated to something ethical. It is neither good nor bad, it simply is. Neither is memory something that is necessarily a product or process of thought; it is more likely to be a "felt" thing. His poetic treatment of memory renders it as something much more akin to the sense of touch. The concept of memory can too easily become trapped in a definition as well, as a cerebral abstraction. Burnside's poems illustrate his desire to overcome this limited way of interpreting memory.

In the final section of the sequence, Burnside returns to the theme of home and the problematic nature of defining the places one inhabits. Here the concept takes on existential importance, as Burnside writes: "I will sleep as I slept before, but something will be awake in the room: a part of myself reflected in the cold and the darkness, and something I do not resemble, which nevertheless fits me precisely, a form I have moulded from what I am not, like a carapace or a shell". Being and nothingness are expressed here, where the form of the self is created out of absence. Soon after this the speaker announces, "I will think myself home....". The myth of home becomes something that is understandable through the agency of thought and reflection. Memory becomes a part of the process of realizing the self. The section and the poem end with the following words: "where home is the house I imagined and never expected: a sudden renewal, the pleasure of being lost" (p. 31). There is a certain joy of uncertainty in not truly "knowing" oneself, in allowing a freedom of creation in forming an idea of oneself, a self that is fluid.

Later poems in the collection engage with the idea of the fairy story or folktale. Burnside examines the philosophy of the fairy story or folktale in order to continue his concern with deconstructing standard ways in which humans interrogate the world. In the ninth section of "Urphänomen" he writes: "And I will wake, like one of the taken escaped from a day in faery liftetimes ago[...]" (p. 31). Burnside considers the ways in which humans mix the world of the fictional and fantastic with the "real" life. In doing so he suggests ways in which we might all be escaped characters from some other grand narrative that is beyond our knowledge. In "A Tall Story," the idea of the "unreal" tale is expanded upon as the speaker recounts the story of a man who encounters a hovering owl at a moment

when his car stalls on the road. This seemingly insignificant moment takes on immense importance as it is crafted into an epic explanation for one's identity. It is a moment, however, that is treated with a wry skepticism by others who hear the story and construct another definition of mythology that frames it into a fiction:

That's when the owl flew down
and hovered about the stopped
bonnet of the Cambridge, barely touching.
So he said. We never quite believed,
and besides, it was hardly a story: it seems the bird
flickered for one chill instant at the glass
then left him, startled, as the engine turned
and he drove on, along the empty road,
like someone taken in a fairy tale
who breaks the spell and brings a stranger home.

(p. 33)

The stranger here becomes in a way the self that is search of some validation. The man encountering the owl is a different person for having experienced the bird. This is a quotidian experience that is now full of existential importance.

"Frog" continues the concept of creating a notion of self from the "fairy tale." Here

The prince beneath the skin
has come to rest[...]
To think I saw in him
another self:
the changeling I might have been
with luck, or daring.

(p. 34)

The possibilities of fictional others who help to frame identities becomes a guiding force in this poem, but by the end the necessity of fluidity is emphasized in an articulation of home as something that is not necessarily the safe and certain place that we have always imagined. By the end of the poem the reader is confronted by "the meagre sanctuary of home," a frail sense of safety (p. 35). Home becomes just a reassuring construct that offers no real continuity or solidity. This definition of home becomes an artificial construct that is in its essence less real than the "fairy tale" selves that we construct on a daily basis.

JOHN BURNSIDE

A NEW GENERATION POET

Burnside's fourth collection, *The Myth of the Twin*, was published in 1994 and was a Poetry Book Society recommendation. Around the time of this publication he was acknowledged as one of the twenty New Generation poets in Britain. As the title implies, this is another collection that engages with a philosophy of mythology, particularly a mythology of the self that often depends on an "other" for completion. The first poem in the collection, "Halloween," announces through the title that a concern with the poems will be considerations of how notions of the self are haunted by misreadings and by disguises that pose as identities in a world that is fraught with illusion: "I have peeled the bark from the tree / to smell its ghost" (p. 1).

Burnside plays with the concept of "twins" by writing two poems with the title "The Myth of the Twin," thus asking the reader either to compare them or to defy our tendency to read twins as mirror images. The first poem of that title explores the nature of definitions and the ways in which we read the world. The speaker imagines an "other" like himself who shares a common dream:

[...] out walking on the beach
I lifted a pebble and split it
open, like an apricot, to find
a live child hatched in the stone

(p. 3)

The collection as a whole investigates the idea of different selves occupying the same mind and body. In the second poem also titled "The Myth of the Twin," the notion of a duplicated self becomes more complex and tied to alternative ways of thinking about the world:

Say it moved when you moved:
a softness that rose in the ground
when you walked, or a give in your step,
the substance that Virgil saw
in the shadows under our feet

(p. 53)

Here the other becomes not a mirror image of the self but rather a way of experiencing the world that is more richly varied than what we are used to. The other becomes a way of recognizing possible alternative explanations for the world that surrounds us. Even the term "explanations" becomes something that is antiquated and fraught with the possibility of stagnant completion. As in previous poems, Burnside asks the reader to contemplate new definitions. The "it" of the "other," or the twin might be

[...] the way that a stumbling or sudden
rooting in authenticity is not
the revelation of a foreign place,
but emptiness, a stillness in the frost,
the silence that stands in the birchwoods, the common
  soul.

(p. 53)

The concept of "the twin" becomes something that Burnside wishes to demythologize and reinterpret in the same way that he has interrogated terms such as "home" and "naming." Anything that serves to artificially solidify our understanding of the world is anathema to Burnside, and the idea of the twin is something that might too easily suggest a replication that denies the freedom of identity. This is a theory that he will develop further in his novel *The Dumb House* (1996), in which twins play a significant role in the lead character Luke's investigations into language development and identity formation.

The remainder of the collection is filled with ghosts or seeming apparitions of an "other" that may or may not be the self of the speaker. There are a number of elegies for the poet's grandfather: "Avoirdupois," "Variations on a Theme of Wallace Stevens," "Grandfather," "A Photograph of My Grandfather, c. 1961," and "My Grandparents in 1963." In many ways the speaker of these poems seems to gain a sense of identity by reinhabiting the spaces left vacant by the grandfather who is now gone. In "Variations on a Theme of Wallace Stevens," the speaker conjures up a vision of a man (presumably the grandfather) raking in the yard:

[A] ghost in his smoke-coloured shirt
with his back to the house,
my double, from his looks: same age, same build,

19

the same clenched rage in his arms,
the same bright fear

(p. 4)

Toward the end of the poem, however, the speaker draws attention to the otherness of this perceived self in the grandfather. They are not one and the same, as the speaker speaks of

[...] missing what he sees, or thinks he sees:
the sudden night, the blur of wind and rain,
the shadow in the woods that matches him
with nothing that is, and the nothing that is not there.

(p. 4)

The existential ending to the poem highlights the condition in which others are never "twinned" with selves in the order of being but rather serve as potential alternative selves. The absence of nothing, the deprivation of presence at the end, becomes the result of a vision that may or may not be flawed and may or may not align itself with the vision of the speaker who has been lured into seeing himself in the man/grandfather. The poem suggests ways in which identity is often created by how humans view themselves in terms of others and attempt to recognize resemblances between themselves and others. This is all part of the mythology that Burnside deconstructs in his poems.

Intricately linked with notions of identity for Burnside are questions of language and how it operates to tell us who we are. A number of poems in *The Myth of the Twin* engage with a sense of lost language, specifically the Gaelic and Scots languages that have been diminished over the years in Scotland. The ways in which language shapes an identity is the theme of "The Dead," where the speaker summons up the ghosts of the past, "weavers and children, and women with songs in their heads," who are resurrected through their rebirth into language due to "[...]the promise that must be fulfilled / in the shaping of language" (p. 8). In "Learning Gaelic," the speaker links memory, "anamnesis," with a language that is now an "heirloom" (p. 9). The speaker "lacks" the words that he knows "have always existed":

a sound for the feel of a place,
for snowfalls that cover the roads
and little owls ascending through the trees,
a name for the gap between margins,
for siftings and scattered remains,
for rising at night, in the moments I share with the
    dead,
and making my place in their house, an echo, singing.

(p. 9)

The speaker grieves over a lost language, one that seems to live on through its absence. Here again, Burnside evokes a sense of presence through absence and he highlights how these ways of defining being and nothingness are susceptible to the process of myth. Language serves to define us in some way and so does the language that is decaying and nonexistent. By the end of the poem the speaker takes his or her place in the seeming order of language, but that place is always only a tentative location.

Three additional poems in the collection speak to the loss of Gaelic and a language that is effective in framing a sense of "true" identity. "Love Poem," "Dialect," and "The North" all serve to focus on language and the purposes of "naming." In "Love Poem," the speaker wonders what it would be like

To think in the old language;
to waken at dawn
on the borders of dunlin and tern

(p. 13)

A reconfiguring of the world might occur if one were to not just speak in the old language but to think in it as well. By the end of the poem the act of naming becomes something more than a way of making sense of the world. Instead there is an aesthetics of naming that serves some larger purpose than just explanation: "to name things for the beauty of the sounds: / *uisge; aran; oidhche; gealach; teine*" (water, bread, night, moon, fire) (p. 13). In "Dialect," the speaker may be referring either to Gaelic or to Scots when he writes:

There were different words for dust:
one for the powdered film
of shading on a closed room's
windowsills,

and one for the inch-thick
layer of talcum and fibre
under the bed

(p. 25)

However, even in this language (or dialect) there
is nothing to

[...] describe the vividness
of rain-dark fur and flesh that shaped and gloved
the body of a fox beside the road.

(p. 25)

Burnside suggests that, no matter what the language or dialect, the act of assigning words, of naming, can significantly alter the potential experience of the world. In a moment of existential lamentation, the speaker regrets that there is not a word for "...the presence still to come[...]" Words are ineffective at capturing the essence and spirit of a world of experience that is constantly in process. For Burnside, the action of felt responses to the world is an area beyond possibilities of a language that is often reductive and incomplete. His poems allow readers to "see" the world in new ways and in doing so to be cognizant of the absence of any truly complete and finalized vision.

This notion of the incompleteness of language is continued in "The North," where the "dying language" is at once Gaelic and Scots and the language of a historical moment that recedes with time (p. 26). The speaker talks of "a common usage" that might be employed for describing a journey home at a particular time of day when a host of other conditions are in place. History and a sense of passing time are nothing but constructions of language,

sidestreets where the dead are walking out
in twos and threes, sealed in a foreign tongue,
a grammar of old recipes and prayers
reserving names for things, when they are gone.

(p. 26)

The poem seems to suggest that memory both creates and preserves a dying world, and it may only do so through the agency of language and naming things.

In addition to demythologizing the world of perceived experience and the role that language fraudulently plays in constructing notions of home and identity, Burnside consistently returns to questioning and revisioning traditional religions (specifically Christianity) and the ways of seeing that have become particularly associated with them. In the *Myth of the Twin,* he crafts a number of poems to respond to Christian experience. "Hymn to the Virgin," "R. E.," "Conversions," and "Faith" are all poems about how religious experience is an attempt to define the world in a particular way. In "Hymn to the Virgin," the speaker begins the poem in church and ends up reflecting upon this experience as he or she walks along a canal "shoulder-deep in sedge and meadowsweet". The speaker seems to exchange the natural world for the world of the church, which is "spawn-dark, silent, threaded with deceit, / cradled in a curvature of wings" (p. 17). The poem seems less a rejection of the feelings associated with religion than a rejection of the particular venues in which one is traditionally expected to experience spirituality.

In *Swimming in the Flood* (1995), Burnside's poetry moves from more solitary meditations of an individual speaker to the assumed voices of other identities. Much like Robert Browning, Burnside populates these poems with the voices of characters who have committed terrible deeds or who seem to be societal outcasts in one way or another. In the sequence "Wrong," the reader confronts a voice of insanity, perhaps that of a serial killer, somone who has been "mutilated" by society and who in turn has become mad and homicidal. Here Burnside investigates the art of the voyeur, with poetry that deals with the idea of looking at others "in passing" or as through a screen and attempting to fashion some notion of self from those visions. In "Wrong" the speaker moves from carving what seems to be a jack-o'-lantern, but what very well may be someone's face, to killing small animals and eventually to news stories concerning the murder of a small child. The final scenes are voiced in stage directions, as if the speaker is directing a filmed version of the event:

[...] and I think of his family
leaning to touch the screen
and find him again

or taste what they knew all along
was waiting to happen:
that sweetness that feathers the tongue;
that sense of themselves
as seen, like the people in movies.

(p. 10)

Creating speakers who are outcasts and "villains" in a traditional sense is another method by which Burnside can offer alternative visions of the world that surrounds us. Burnside's characters demand more from readers than simply horror and disapproval. Instead, the reader is given a more complex and intimate glimpse into the psyches of the outcasts and the perspectives they may have on a world that typically labels things "normal" or "abnormal."

A dominant theme in this collection is that of water and of the flow of life that passes the seemingly casual viewer. In "Swimming in the Flood" and "A Swimming Lesson," Burnside utilizes the theme of water in order to represent a condition (drowning or being submersed in water) whereby one might view alternative understandings of the world. In "Swimming in the Flood," there is a newsreel that offers a vision of a flood that differs from the one that was experienced by the speaker both at the time of the flood and in his dream of it later. In "A Swimming Lesson," Burnside presents the story of a woman who seems to be searching for an identity. Her journey is recounted through a speaker who is her murderer and who documents the movement of her body downstream to where it is discovered by the police. As he traces her movements downstream he is also composing lines of poetry dedicated to her that are represented in italics in the text:

In my dream you are sitting out
at the edge of the water,
watching me wade towards you in the dark
[...]
[...]
[...]
In my dream I am lifting the eyes from your milky
  skull
and I'm placing these pebbles of glass in the empty
  sockets

to see if they'll quicken and heal in your salvaged
flesh.

(p. 26)

For Burnside in this collection, water, and the flow of water, seems to offer a new vision. One's self may be lost in the flood, but a newer self is born from the experience of seeing through the flow. The seeming brutality of a violent death is balanced by a fresher understanding of identity. This concept of reconceiving the world through alternate visions is more directly dealt with in "An Ordered World," where the speaker imagines a world that is slow to let go of traditional, logical ways of explaining things. The "they" of the poem could either be humans or aliens who are encountering a new world that cannot be explained through traditional "terrestrial" avenues:

They listened for the hiss of radio
and animals that lingered in the flesh,
the origin of things, the coming end,
a god's withdrawal, fading in the mind.

(p. 24)

Burnside's vision of the world as a very "local" entity is taken up in "Parousia," the final poem in the collection. Here the speaker reimagines the Second Coming of Christ, and he turns the event into a moment of introspection on the part of the speaker, who imagines his own complementary rebirth. What had been an event of cosmic proportions that occurred at a specific time and place is made more parochial and ubiquitous:

All resurrections are local:
footprints bleeding away
through marsh-grass and water,
a sound you can almost hear
of the flesh renewed
in the plashing of rain
or a quick trout
breaking the stream.

(p. 54)

Here again an epiphany is gained through the breaking of the flow, a fleeting recognition of the spirit of the self making its presence known in the larger order of space and time.

JOHN BURNSIDE

In *A Normal Skin* (1997), Burnside uses images of skin and flesh as ways of encountering different interpretations of the world, much in the way that he employed water and flow in *Swimming in the Flood*. Where in the previous volume, water became a lens through which to understand different perceptions of the self, here the reader is asked to decipher the ever-changing nature of the flesh and how it serves as another part of one's identity that needs to be constantly reread. In the title poem, "A Normal Skin," the speaker considers a neighbor who suffers from eczema and who late at night

[...]lies in the healing darkness, half-awake,
achieving a normal skin
by an effort of will.

(p. 1–2)

This description is all by way of comparison with the speaker's own skin as he talks to another (a wife?) of how his skin has been misperceived as being sensitive. The "renewal" of one's skin seems to Burnside to speak of the different selves that inhabit the shell we expose to the world, a shell that continually becomes altered by that very exposure.

As in his previous collections, Burnside here also exhibits his skill at weaving poem sequences that make full use of the guiding images that he wishes to explore. Themes such as home, identity, memory, mythology, and reinterpretations of the natural world become intertwined and are developed in a more complex fashion in the longer poems of *A Normal Skin*, poems such as "A Process of Separation" and "Epithalamium." In the first section of the sequence "A Process of Separation," titled "Echo Pit Road," the speaker says, "I can still feel the dead against my skin" (p. 6). References to flesh and skin abound in the sequence as a way of highlighting what seems to be the central question of the collection, "What exactly is 'a normal skin'?" The concept of the constant shedding of skin and renewing of the self is one that Burnside will also explore in his novels *The Locust Room* (2001) and *Living Nowhere* (2003). The notion of others inhabiting one's skin is present here as well, as in the section titled "Mandrake," where the speaker confronts what seems to be either a corpse or the mandrake plant that resembles a man:

Now he will rise again and wander home:
drawn from the earth, he takes on human form,
he peels me from the air, wraps me in blood,
steps into my flesh and walks away.

(p. 13)

In "Epithalamium," the sequence honors a marriage of two selves and how they negotiate the ever-shifting identity of home and one another. It is yet another Burnside poem of renewed vision.

Other poems in the collection, such as "The Man Who Was Answered by His Own Self," "The Blind," and "Vanishing Twin," engage with Burnside's abiding concern with identity, vision, and how to define otherness. The ghostly presence of selves that might be encountering alternative worlds is articulated in a haunting fashion in lines like the following from "The Man Who Was Answered by His Own Self":

I answer the phone and the dark world is quietly
present: my own voice
lush as the midsummer distance where towns dissolve,
their people back from church, adjusting the dials
on empty wirelesses and tuning in
to nothing, to their own selves, calling home.

(p. 19)

In "The Blind," the speaker imagines a group of blind children swimming in the local baths "attuned to one another through the play / of water and skin" (p. 23). Alternative forms of communication, such as touch, offer the knowledge of identity in what seems a more assured fashion than a vision that might be fraught with deception and disguise. Here Burnside uses skin as something that offers the potential of a different sort of recognition and definition.

Finally, in "Vanishing Twin," the speaker imagines a dead sister who shared the womb with him as a twin. The poem suggests she died at birth, but the speaker still senses her presence and he speaks of what they shared: "I remember the fields of grain / in my sister's dream" (p. 29). Speaker and sister become one, and at the end of the poem she seems to reach into the womb/tomb of life to rescue the speaker from his own "still"

birth of life that carries its own signs of passage
on the skin:

She bled away. But sometimes I wake in the dark
and feel her with me, breathing through the sheets,
or I turn in the shimmer of day
and catch her out:
my opposite, though still identical,
she's reaching down to haul me from a web
of birthmarks, age lines, scars beneath the skin.

(p. 29)

Burnside's seventh collection of poetry, *The Asylum Dance* (2000), won the Whitbread Poetry Award in 2000 and was short-listed for the Forward Poetry Prize and the T. S. Eliot Prize. In this volume he continues to exhibit his skills at writing the long poem or poem sequence. "Ports," "Settlements," "Fields," and "Roads" serve as foundations in the volume around which the other shorter lyrics take their bearings. Here Burnside's sense of "home," and more so the sense of "dwelling," takes command of the poetry once more. In "Ports," a sense of home as dwelling and sanctuary is investigated. In the section titled "Haven," the speaker attempts to describe this refined sense of home:

Our dwelling place:
                    the light above the firth
shipping forecasts
                    gossip
                         theorems
the choice of a single word to describe
the gun-metal grey of the sky

(p. 1)

Again, Burnside chooses to redefine home or to explain the concept of home in a way that allows for a variety of interpretations. In "Settlements," this notion is expanded to include the idea of "constructing" home. The process of home-making as an act of introspection is suggested by the following lines:

—there's more to the making of home than I ever
  expected:
a process of excavation, of finding

something in myself to set against
the chill of the other

(p. 26)

Home becomes a function of identity and self-definition in these lines, a place of location that is beyond the purely geographical. These poems display a more complex psychology of home that Burnside wishes to reveal.

In the collection's title poem, "The Asylum Dance," the speaker remembers the annual outing to the "asylum" with his mother to share in the annual dance with the patients. The ritual of the dance becomes a way of communicating with those who are inside the asylum, in a supposedly "other" world, and Burnside uses the poem to question notions of normality:

All afternoon we picnicked on the lawn
then danced in awkward couples to the hiss
of gramophones, as daylight turned to dusk;
a subtle exchange in the half-light; acts of grace:
townsfolk conferring the weight of a normal world,
homes in the suburbs, the brisk lives of men who can
  who sleep,
the practiced charm of women who believe,
who wake and forget what they dreamed, and go off
  to work,
and wish for nothing.

(p. 32)

The dance highlights the similarities between two worlds and asks the reader to revision the concept of "asylum," and interpretations of where we all live, in a world that cannot be simply defined.

Perhaps the richest poem in the collection is the sequence titled "The Hay Devil," where Burnside questions the logic of seeing the world, and defining home in a particular way. He offers rich insights into alternative ways of seeing (not defining) the world in which we live. From opening lines in which the speaker recognizes the desire to have "a named world" (p. 46), the poem moves to the point where a new understanding of home becomes evident:

Now I am back
and home is a different country:
eel-streams in the fields

JOHN BURNSIDE

                    the narrow woods
a calm between the hills
that might be rain.
Home is a reason
                    a word from a children's primer
the field I have crossed today
for the hundredth time:
the sway of the wind in my hands
and a pulse in my spine
and something in the distance
                              shoreline
                                    firth
a wreath of smoke above the paper mill

                                    (p. 50)

Lines from Wallace Stevens' "Thirteen Ways of
Looking at a Blackbird," serve as the epigraph to
Burnside's eighth collection of poetry, *The Light
Trap*. This sense of simultaneous correspondence
is echoed in the final lines of the concluding
poem in the collection, "A Theory of Everything":

for this is how the world
occurs: not piecemeal
but entire
and instantaneous
the way we happen:
woman
blackbird man

                                    (p. 83)

The collection as a whole, which was short-listed
for the T. S. Eliot Prize and for the Saltire Society
Scottish Book of the Year Award, is infused with
this idea of the simultaneity of existence, primarily the ways in which the "natural" world of
flora and fauna connects so seamlessly with the
human. Early poems from the first section titled
"Habitat," such as "Koi," "Taxonomy," "Deer,"
and "Animals," explore ways in which a notion
of self can be derived from close examination of
the natural world that surrounds us. The calling
for an existential reconsideration occurs in the
first line of "Koi," the opening poem of the collection: "The trick is to create a world / from
nothing"(p. 3). The notion of aligning a sense of
self with the natural world is then confirmed in
these lines from "Animals":

They say, if you dream an animal, it means
"the self"—that mess of memory and fear
that wants, remembers, understands, denies.

                                    (p. 19)

Poems from the second, middle section of the
volume explore the theme of the title, "the light
trap." As in any Burnside collection, the themes
to be examined are forecast in earlier poems or
even earlier volumes of poetry. Here the idea of
trapping or containing light is first contemplated
in "Harunobu: 'Catching Fireflies'" from the first
section of the volume. Harunobu was an
eighteenth-century Japanese printmaker, and his
print "A Young Couple Catching Fireflies at
Night on the Banks of a River" appears to be the
inspiration for this poem. In the poem the couple

[...] go out to the lake,
with nets and traps,
to capture light
and hold it in a box.

                                    (p. 13)

The speaker connects this experience with his
own very modern experiments at shining a
flashlight ("torch") into "a moonless sky" and
considering the eternal traveling of the light.
(This is a theme that Burnside approaches in fiction as well, for example in the short story
"Ether" in his 2000 collection, *Burning Elvis*. In
Burnside's 2003 novel, *Living Nowhere*, the
character Jan also considers the eternal continuity
of energy that occurs when one dies.) Capturing
light is both possible and impossible in the poems
that follow. The commanding implication of this
trope is the illumination of one's "self" and the
continuity of the self in others and in the world
at large.

   At the conclusion of "The Hay Devil" (from
The Asylum Dance), the speaker says

          as I never quite arrive
at absence
          which is presence somewhere else

                                    (p. 52)

In the poem "The Light Trap," Burnside similarly
defines darkness in terms of what it is not:

And this is how darkness works: an alchemy
of chalk and silver, all our memories
of other gardens, distance, moonlit streams,
transformed to something punctual and slight,
flickering in the trap[...]

(p. 24)

Burnside is a poet of alchemy (one critic has noted the repeated use of this term in his work) who relates, in epiphanic fashion, the magical conversions of the seemingly commonplace to the status of the miraculous. Here darkness is converted to light, and what has appeared to be the light of vision is only obscurity, if it is a light that is not organically derived from the natural world.

Later poems in the collection deal with questions of kinship and the poet's own family (his wife and son). In many of these poems Stevens' blackbird serves as a recurring image of continuity that seems to alight on one poem then moves along to settle on the branches of another. Some of the final poems, set mostly in Norway, reiterate Burnside's abiding interest in the constant reconfiguring of an interpretation of home and our traditional definitions of time. "History" is a post–September 11 poem in which the poet flies a kite with his son on the beach in St. Andrews, Scotland, on a troubled September day in 2001. Toward the end of the poem, the speaker switches from contemplating the turbulent skies of what seems to be a suddenly more widespread and radically altered "human" history to consider what he calls

and the quiet, local forms
of history: the fish lodged in the tide
beyond the sands;
                    the long insomnia
of ornamental carp in public parks

(p. 41)

The importance and privileging of the local and the ephemeral nature of the world we suspect we live in is brought home by the speaker of "Bleik," who talks of

a glimpse of something, not quite what we thought,
but just enough, that we can think of home

in this, the most provisional of worlds

(p. 62)

And the speaker in the final section of "After Lucretius," who talks of a "truth" that is "always local" (p. 77).

Burnside's 2005 collection of poetry, *The Good Neighbor,* was short-listed for the Forward Poetry Prize. This volume investigates relationships between people and further develops the poet's concern with how individual identity is formed through contact with others. As in previous collections, Burnside reveals an intent to demythologize a particular way of looking at the world. The mythology of "the neighbor," and in particular the literary mythology of Robert Frost's "good fences make good neighbors" (the line serves as an epigraph to the first section, titled "Here"), is the target of Burnside's poems in this collection, poems that look at the barriers (artificial or not) that seem to separate us from others and that examine how we take a bearing from others that serves to define our own existence. The opening poem, "Good Neighbors," asks the reader to imagine the neighbor:

Somewhere along this street, unknown to me,
behind a maze of apple trees and stars,
he rises in the small hours, finds a book
and settles at a window or a desk
to see the morning in, alone for once,
unnamed, unburdened, happy in himself.

(p. 3)

Then, toward the end of the poem, the neighbor, who has seemed like such a stranger all along, is transformed into an "other" that is more recognizable:

and when he lays his book down, checks the hour [...]
my one good neighbor sets himself aside,
and alters into someone I have known:
a passing stranger on the road to grief,
husband and father; rich man; poor man;
thief.

(p. 3)

The neighbor seems to transform into some notion of the self, or at least some form or image with which the speaker can identify. Two poems from late in the collection also attempt to

JOHN BURNSIDE

demythologize the myth of the neighbor as someone who is purely other than the self. In "Blood," the neighbor is a presence to be feared for one reason or another, and the poem investigates what it really is that separates us from each other in this world. A man, waking to what he thinks is a sound in his house, goes to investigate and meditates on what keeps us from more intimate contact with others:

and he'd think, as he slipped on his shirt
and hurried downstairs,
how little there is to divide us, one from the another:
a paper-thin wall, a hayfield, a huddle of trees,
the wide dark pressed to a window, the starry sky,
or the hope that a snowfall will come, like a friend
  through the yard,
and not the gunman in his hat and scarf,
blessing himself on the threshold
before he steps in.

(p. 73)

Here it is implied that we all fabricate stories or myths about the true nature of our neighbors and that those fictions serve to define our own sense of self-awareness. In essence, buying into the idea of the neighbor as someone completely separate and "alien" is simply another way of living with oneself. In "Good Fences," the speaker tells of a border crossing (most likely between the United States and Mexico) and considers the artificial nature of a concept such as "border." Here the speaker identifies that we are all "aliens" in a landscape that is always shifting and tentative:

Good fences make good neighbors, someone said.
I'm not convinced.
The neighbours here keep stealing through the wire,
cunning and bright as coyotes—and when we chance
upon them, we remember who we are:
resident aliens, foreigners, fair-weather friends
working from field guides and road maps, dreaming
  the land
or stopping from time to time, to write things down:
Green-tailed Towhee, Verdin, Desert Star.

(pp. 76–77)

In addition to deconstructing the myth of the neighbor, *The Good Neighbor* contains poems that return to familiar Burnside interests: inven-

tions and reinventions of home, definitions of presence through absence, and revisionings of the natural world, to name a few.

Burnside produces both mesmerizing and vibrantly troubling poetry. His *Selected Poems* was published by Jonathan Cape in 2006, and another collection, *Gift Songs*, followed in 2007.

FICTION AND MEMOIR

In addition to a prolific poetic output, Burnside has been successful with novels, short stories, and memoir. A fifth novel, *The Devil's Footprints*, is forthcoming. In their own way, each of these works serves to augment and expand upon themes that have populated his poetry: home, memory, the natural world, identity, absence, and seeing the world "new."

Burnside's first novel, *The Dumb House* (1997), is a gothic tale that recounts the story of Luke, a dark character, who is interested in language development and how it is affected when one is raised from infancy without social contact or exposure to sound. Luke has a quirky childhood, which includes an unhealthy obsession with his mother. In his spare time, as a youth, he collects animals and insects and performs horrific experiments upon them. As he grows older he becomes fascinated with the legend of Akbar the Great, who filled his palace with newborn children raised by mutes. Akbar's interest was to see how and if language would develop in the children, so as to gauge whether language is acquired or innate. The story fascinates Luke, who attempts to re-create this experiment in his own world. Taking in a homeless girl, he impregnates her, and when she dies shortly after having given birth to twins, he creates a laboratory of sorts in his basement where the twins live unexposed to any sound other than music that is piped into the room they inhabit (the subtitle of the novel is "A Chamber Story"). After a series of gruesome follow-up experiments, the novel ends with Luke reevaluating his methods and searching for new subjects in order to resume his inquiry.

A richly disturbing, psychological novel, *The Dumb House* gives Burnside a greater range, in prose, to consider themes that he had previously addressed in his poetry. The nature of the self and of identity, and how that identity is framed and structured through one's engagement in language, is a large part of the concern of the novel. What is also implicated is the nature of "twinning" and the necessity of an "other" in which to define oneself. The twins of *The Dumb House* find a mute comfort in one another, and they quickly find a loyalty in their silence that Luke, the narrator, finds threatening. Toward the end of the novel, Luke realizes that the twins have created their own kind of communication and that he is the one, the "scientist," who has become mute and unable to effectively communicate:

> They were complicit. Maybe that was the reason for their singing—they weren't conversing, as such, they were simply performing a ritual of confirmation, a celebration of their combined existence. The complicity that existed between them suggested a world that I was incapable of experiencing, and some of the pleasure of being in that world, part of their private joy, was predicated upon my exclusion. It was as if I was the one who could not speak; as if, for me, the world was nothing more than a jumble of meaningless and disquieting sensations— and it came to me, then, that I was the one who had been placed in the Dumb House.
>
> (p. 175)

The novel was a haunting debut and was immediately praised by critics for its dark and troubling beauty.

A second novel, *The Mercy Boys*, was published in 1999 and was a joint winner of the 1999 Encore Award. This narrative follows the lives of four men who live and drink their days away in a pub (The Mercy) in Dundee. The narrative follows each character individually as he negotiates a life that is fraught with frustration, anger, insecurity, and an overwhelming inability to love in any authentic manner. The moments of personal reflection offered by each of the characters represent Burnside's abiding interest in finding the ways one knows one's self, and his interest in how that knowledge ties in with personal understandings of what might represent "home." An often violent book, *The Mercy Boys* leaves each of the characters with tragic endings, but ones

that were prepared for them as the novel develops. Here Burnside investigates the relationships that form between men who are searching for personal narratives to explain their own particular ways of being in the world. This fascination with the fictions that men create for themselves, and the frustrations and obstacles they encounter in doing so, can be traced through most of Burnside's novels and in his 2006 memoir *A Lie About My Father*. In his 2003 interview with Attila Dósa, Burnside admitted to this quest on the part of his male protagonists: "Most of my stories are about young men who are suddenly faced with the fact that they'd been standing still and that they haven't been paying attention to the world around them and it's time to change" (pp. 21–22).

In 2000 Burnside published a collection of short stories titled *Burning Elvis*. In these stories Burnside continues to investigate the themes that concerned him in *The Dumb House, The Mercy Boys*, and in his volumes of poetry. Here characters either disappear or become invisible as they journey toward understanding the self and the relationship of the self to the larger world. At the beginning of the story "Burning Elvis," the narrator comments, "I don't know why I choose to remember one thing, rather than another. Maybe whatever it was that happened turned out to be the myth I needed—the myth or necessary lie, which comes to the same thing" (p. 3). In this story and in the final story in the collection, "Graceland," the myth of Elvis Presley and Graceland serves as a model for the lives of the characters in the stories, who seem to be searching for that colorful or aesthetic lie that will explain their own particular reason for being in the world. In "Burning Elvis," the character Lindy sees Elvis as someone whose myth is not so much about the person but about the way in which he became a necessary sacrifice (much in the same way that Lindy later becomes sacrificed through her murder by a jealous lover): "She said anyone who had really loved Elvis would have helped him, by making him see that he was the phoenix, and he had to be burned. People think the phoenix story is about how everything that dies is reborn from its own ashes, not the rebirth,

JOHN BURNSIDE

but the necessary burning" (p. 7).

The story collection abounds with ghosts, imagined twins, and fabrications about others who may or may not have existed yet and have some influence on the narrators and their lives. In "What I Know About Myself," a father crafts stories to convince his son that he is not his real father. The narrator then imagines a "real" father who will do all those things that real fathers do with their sons. In "The Invisible Husband," a character named Laura, disconnected from her husband, creates an alternative husband in her mind, a spouse who accompanies her deeper into her own madness of an alternative world. In "Kate's Garden," a husband walks out of his house one summer's afternoon and disappears. A newlywed husband also disappears on the night of his wedding in "The Wedding Ceilidh."

Doppelgangers, mysterious doubles or twins who help to both complete and complicate the identities of others are also featured in the stories of *Burning Elvis*. In "Decency," a man on vacation with his wife is confronted by another man who claims to have committed murders and wishes to pass on his killing instinct. In "Folie à Deux," the narrator and his "twin" commit a senseless murder and when one of them is taken away the other one suffers from the deprivation:

> When I do sleep, I almost always dream about Val. I had no idea of our state of being—our state of grace—had a textbook name. *Folie à deux* is what they call it—shared insanity, madness times two.... we were the two halves of something that, otherwise, would have been incomplete, and whenever I looked at him, I saw myself, perfectly reflected. Now they tell me it was a form of mania; they're saying he was inside my head all that time, and I wasn't thinking straight.
>
> (p. 122)

Here one is reminded of the Scotsman James Hogg's *Private Memoirs and Confessions of a Justified Sinner* (1824), in which the doubles of Robert Wringhim and Gil-Martin perform equally horrific crimes. (Scott Brewster argues, similarly, that Burnside's novel *The Locust Room* bears comparison with Hogg's novel in terms of otherness and the notion of the double.)

In Burnside's third novel, *The Locust Room* (2001), he sets the action primarily in Cambridge, where Burnside himself went to college. The early sections of the novel recount the story of a boy named Paul who is living in Cambridge in the early 1970s. Paul is on a quest for an understanding of self (like many of Burnside's other fictional protagonists) while negotiating a world that is full of fear and uncertainty. A parallel narrative that runs alongside Paul's quest is the story of a rapist who is terrorizing the Cambridge area. The narrative of Paul's experiences with his friends, roommates, and girlfriends is interspersed with sections in which the reader is given a glimpse inside the head of the rapist—as he diagnoses his relationship with the world that surrounds him and his association with a dark "other" who exists outside of himself. Paul takes a position as a caretaker of sorts at a college-sponsored "insect station," where he looks after locusts in a "locust room." Locusts, and the "room" they inhabit, becomes a metaphor for the different layers or "shells" of self that often get stripped away in the quest to locate a pure and authentic identity.

The later sections of the novel deal with Paul coming to terms with his father's death (in Scotland) and his return to Cambridge. Another essential element of the novel is Paul's interest in photography and his recognition of the ways in which photography allows one to see the world in a particular way. Photography becomes a form of magic for Paul:

> He wasn't sure when he had decided this, but at some point he had come to believe that photography was, or could be, this Orphic art form, the art that brought us back to the things themselves. Language was too difficult; it was too socialised. People would get lost in the words, in the possible semantics; it was too much of an invitation to the ego to write or to speak. What was needed was an essentially silent work. Better to simply connect with things in themselves, and to show the connection—a meaningless, almost involuntary communion with things as they happened to be; if anything could free things from their names, as Orpheus had done, it would be a certain form of photograph, a way of picturing

the world from which all invested meaning had been stripped away, a neutral, and so natural act.

(pp. 175–176)

The psychology of self and a self-awareness of that psychology is a commanding presence in the stories from *Burning Elvis* as well as in the narrative of *The Locust Room,* and it is a theme that one can trace from *The Dumb House* through *Living Nowhere*, Burnside's fourth novel, published in 2003. In this book Burnside investigates the self and how it tries to find a geographical position in the world. The first sections of the narrative are told through the eyes of a variety of characters who live in Corby, the industrial town in the English Midlands where Burnside lived for a while in his youth. Two of the characters, Jan and Francis, share a special relationship that is shattered when Jan is murdered by a band of town bullies. The remainder of the novel recounts the travels of Francis, who disappears after Jan's death in a search to understand the meaning of "home" and his own identity in the world. The later sections of the novel are told through letters that Francis writes to the dead Jan, in which he shares his experiences and his thoughts of what it was that made the two boys integral halves of a shared self.

In the novel Burnside offers wonderful descriptions of landscape and states of feeling that are described in a richly poetic prose. Burnside also uses the novel to further explore the mythology of "home" that has served as a theme in so much of his poetry. Although most of the reflections on home are provided by Francis, an early consideration of what home signifies is offered by Alina, Jan's sister: "People here were always talking about *home*, and they always meant some other place, somewhere in the past or the future, a place they had come from, a place they were going to" (p. 13). This definition of home seems to inform Francis' travels at some level, as he comes to believe that home is always in the future and is not really a place you can pinpoint on a map. He spends years traveling around Britain and the United States in an effort to escape both Corby and a sense of home as a completed location. At one point in the novel Francis is accused by his girlfriend of not wanting to live anywhere, and he replies:

"No," I said. "My trouble is that I want to live nowhere." ... I don't know if she understood what I meant; probably not. I don't think I understood it myself when I said it, but I've been thinking about it ever since: about what we mean when we talk about home, and belonging, and how this is a world where nobody should feel altogether at home, this is a world where no honest person can feel he belongs—or not altogether. In a world like this—not the real, wide world of grass and earthquakes and bullfinches, but this world, this human state—grief, and anger, and guilt for that matter, are only natural. Home, wherever and for however long we find it, is, by its very nature, provisional and tainted.

(p. 305)

By the end of the novel, Francis has reached some reconciliation with his past, but his understanding of home as a provisional identity that should always be reinterpreted seems close to the philosophy of home as invention and the necessary revisioning of the world that Burnside presents elsewhere in his work.

Burnside's 2006 memoir, *A Lie About My Father*, won the 2006 Saltire Society's Scottish Book of the Year Award.—This beautifully written and highly acclaimed work centers on the author's difficult relationship with his emotionally abusive and alcoholic father. Along the way, Burnside recounts a journey he takes in understanding his own sense of self as it is "mirrored" in the image of his father. The "lie" of the title becomes a way of considering individual lives and history itself as fabrications of self-identity. Early on in the memoir Burnside tells of how his father would construct stories of his genealogy, and it was only after his death that the son heard the story of how the father was a foundling, abandoned as a baby on the steps of a small house in West Fife, Scotland. Later, the father seems to want to deny the son his own existence by telling him of an older sister who died at birth and of how "he wished she had lived, and I had died instead" (p. 33). As the book proceeds, Burnside begins to bring together the images of the father and the son, contemplating in a very philosophical fashion the nature of the lie. The narrator/author imagines an "invented" father, the one who would have done all those things expected of a father. The addictive personality of the father is an inheritance that the son honestly acknowledges in this book, as Burnside gives the reader the horrifying yet beautifully drawn details of his own descent into drug addiction and mental illness. Burnside sees himself as an invention, and this allows him to bridge some kind of gap between himself and his father. The reader is left at the end of the work with an image of the potential father that Burnside would like to cultivate as something to pass along to his own son and as a way of circumventing or even deconstructing the power of the lie. He draws essential differences between ghosts and spirits as he contemplates what true artifact of one's life is worthy to pass along to the next generation:

> Maybe one of the things a father does, for his sons at least, is to let them see the difference between spirits and ghosts, to reveal for them the fabric of the invisible world. Ghosts can be dismissed, or they can be sent on their way, some Halloween night, with a kind word and a warm fire, but spirits are with us always, and it seems that the stories we tell are the only means we have to decide who or what they are, and how they might be accommodated.
>
> (p. 324)

The "lie" of the self becomes a commanding message of the memoir, and it fits in with Burnside's other interests in the myths we are constantly constructing as we fashion our world moment by moment.

ESSAYS AND ANTHOLOGIES

In addition to his poetry, fiction, and memoir writing, Burnside has contributed as an editor and essayist to a number of publications. As a serious environmentalist and poet he often writes about the intersections of ecology and poetry. With Maurice Riordan, he edited a collection of poems titled *Wild Reckoning: An Anthology Provoked By Rachel Carson's "Silent Spring,"* and he has written other appreciations of Rachel Carson. In his role as a poet of dissidence he has written *A Poet's Polemic: Otro Mundo Es Posible: Poetry, Dissidence and Reality TV* (2003) and contributed an essay to the collection *Strong Words: Modern Poets on Modern Poetry* (2000). He also served as editor (with Alec Finlay) of *Love for Love: An Anthology of Love Poems* (2000).

The rich variety of Burnside's work in poetry, fiction, memoir, and essay offers a continual sense of renewal to the reader. As he said in the interview with Dósa, "What I'm writing is always about healing: about healing the world or about trying to heal one's vision of the world" (p. 22). Whether it is the violence of his novelistic characters searching for knowledge of the self or the deconstructive activity of his poetry that dismantles the assumptions we have about the world that surrounds us, the disorder he articulates becomes therapeutic through his poetic voice. His lyricism in verse and prose offers a salve of new vision to eyes that may grow too accustomed to traditional viewpoints and states of knowing.

Selected Bibliography

WORKS OF JOHN BURNSIDE

POETRY

The Hoop. Manchester, U.K.: Carcanet, 1988.

Common Knowledge. London: Secker and Warburg, 1991.

Feast Days. London: Secker and Warburg, 1992.

The Myth of the Twin. London: Jonathan Cape, 1994.

Dream State: The New Scottish Poets. Edited by Donny O'Rourke. Edinburgh: Polygon, 1993. (Includes nine poems by Burnside).

Swimming in the Flood. London: Jonathan Cape, 1995.

Penguin Modern Poets 9. London: Penguin, 1996. (Contributor, with Robert Crawford and Kathleen Jamie.)

A Normal Skin. London: Jonathan Cape, 1997.

The Asylum Dance. London: Jonathan Cape, 2000.

The Light Trap. London: Jonathan Cape, 2001.

New British Poetry. Edited by Don Paterson and Charles Simic. St. Paul, Minn.: Graywolf Press, 2004. (Contributor.)

The Good Neighbor. London: Jonathan Cape, 2005.
Selected Poems. London: Jonathan Cape, 2006.
Gift Songs. London: Jonathan Cape, 2007.

FICTION AND MEMOIR

The Dumb House. London: Jonathan Cape, 1997.
The Mercy Boys. London: Jonathan Cape, 1999.
Burning Elvis. London: Jonathan Cape, 2000.
The Locust Room. London: Jonathan Cape, 2001.
Living Nowhere. London: Jonathan Cape, 2003.
A Lie About My Father. London: Cape, 2006.
The Devil's Footprints. London: Jonathan Cape, 2007.

ESSAYS AND EDITED VOLUMES

Love for Love: An Anthology of Love Poems. Edited with Alec Finlay. Edinburgh: Pocketbooks, 2000. ("Introduction," pp. 13–18)
"Strong Words." In *Strong Words: Modern Poets on Modern Poetry.* Edited by W. N. Herbert and Matthew Hollis. Tarset, U.K.: Bloodaxe, 2000.
"Reluctant Crusader." *Guardian,* May 18, 2002. (Essay on Rachel Carson).
A Poet's Polemic: Otro Mundo Es Posible: Poetry, Dissidence and Reality TV. Edinburgh: Scottish Book Trust, 2003.
Wild Reckoning: An Anthology Provoked By Rachel Carson's "Silent Spring." London: Calouste Gulbenkian Foundation, 2004 (Editor, with Maurice Riordan.)
Foreword. In *Betrayal,* by the Marquis de Sade. Translated by Andrew Brown. London: Hesperus Press, 2006.

RECORDINGS

John Burnside: Reading from His Poems. Poetry Archive, 2005.
The Poetry Quartets: 7. With other Scottish poets W. N. Herbert, Liz Lochhead, and Don Paterson. London: British Council and Bloodaxe Books, 2000.

CRITICAL AND BIOGRAPHICAL STUDIES

Andersson, Dag T. "'…Only the Other Versions of Myself': Images of the Other in the Poetry of John Burnside." *Chapman,* no. 96: 35–39 (2000).
Brewster, Scott. "Borderline Experience: Madness, Mimicry, and Scottish Gothic." *Gothic Studies* 7, no. 1: 79–86 (May 2005).
Forbes, Peter. "John Burnside." British Council on the Arts: Contemporary Writers (http://www.contemporarywriters.com).
Galbraith, Iain. "Eclipsing Binaries: Self and Other in John Burnside's Fiction." *études écossaises* 8 (2002): 147–164.

Howarth, Peter. "Teachers' Pages: John Burnside in *New Writing* 9 & 10: New Versions of Pastoral?" British Council: New Writing Anthology (http://newwriting.britishcouncil.org/usr/downloads/seanmatthewsnotes/nw9&10-burnside-notes.doc).
Hunter, Aislinn. "Aislinn Hunter Introducing John Burnside." *ARC: Canada's National Poetry Magazine,* April 2006 (http://www.arcpoetry.ca/greatscots/features/2006_04_aislinn-hunter-introducing-john-burnside.php).
Mcluckie, Craig. "A Poet's Polemic." in *The Literary Encyclopedia,* November 19, 2003 (http://www.litencyc.com).
Thwaite, Mark. "On John Burnside's 'Septuagesima.'" *Readysteadybook,* April 20, 2006 (http://www.readysteadybook.com/article.aspx?page=onseptuagesima).
Yoshikawa, Akiko. "*Living Nowhere.*" *Eigo Seinen/Rising Generation* 149, no. 3: 170 (June 2003).

BOOK REVIEWS

Baker, Phil. "Experiments in Quiet." *Times Literary Supplement,* May 23, 1997, p. 20. (Review of *The Dumb House.*)
Bedford, Martyn. "*The Locust Room.*" *New Statesman,* May 28, 2001, p. 57. (Review of *The Locust Room.*)
Birch, Carol. "Never, and Forever." *Times Literary Supplement,* april 7, 2006, p. 25. (Review of *A Lie About My Father.*)
Burt, Stephen. "They Found a Cardigan." *Times Literary Supplement,* February 2, 1996, p. 28. (Review of *Swimming In The Flood.*)
Carnell, Simon. "The Shiver in the Hedge." *Times Literary Supplement,* January 2, 1998, p. 21. (Review of *A Normal Skin.*)
Dooley, Tim. "Incomplete Memories." *Times Literary Supplement,* May 22, 1992, p. 31. (Review of *Common Knowledge* and *Feast Days.*)
Gould, Alan. "Poetry in the Matter-of-Fact." *Quadrant* 42, no. 5: 80 (May 1998). (Review of *Selected Poems.*)
Imlah, Mick. "A Connoisseur of Rain." *Times Literary Supplement,* May 7, 1999, p. 23. (Review of *The Mercy Boys.*)
Lichtig, Toby. "Invented Places." *Times Literary Supplement,* July 11, 2003, p. 23. (Review of *Living Nowhere.*)
Mcallister, Andrew. "Killing Off the King." *Times Literary Supplement,* June 23, 2000, p. 25. (Review of *Burning Elvis.*)
Mcinerney, Stephen. "Glimmering Substance." *Quadrant* 47, no. 3: 82–84 (March 2003). (Review of *The Light Trap.*)
Mantel, Hilary. "What He Could Bear." *London Review of Books,* March 9, 2006, pp. 3–7. (Review of *A Lie About My Father.*)
Miller, Karl. "Old Nick At Work." *Times Literary Supplement,* March 2, 2007, p. 22. (Review of *The Devil's Footprints.*)

Murray, Nicholas. "The Smell of Frost on the Linen." *Times Literary Supplement*, July 8, 1994, p. 8. (Review of *the Myth Of the Twin*.)

Robinson, Peter. "Painters of the Forth Bridge." *Times Literary Supplement*, june 13, 2003, p. 11. (Review of *The Light Trap*.)

Saynor, James. "Cottage of Horrors." *New York Times Book Review*, July 12, 1998. p. 17. (Review of *The Dumb House*.)

"Sentiment Without Sentimentality." *Economist,* September 6, 1997, pp. 19–20. (Review of *A Normal Skin*.)

Wardle, Sarah. "Homing Instinct." *Times Literary Supplement*, February 9, 2001, p. 25. (Review of *The Asylum Dance*.)

Wootten, William. "Away at Home." *Times Literary Supplement*, February 17, 2006, p. 30. (Review of *The Good Neighbor*.)

INTERVIEWS

Dósa, Attila. "Poets and Other Animals: An Interview with John Burnside." *Scottish Studies Review* 4, no. 1: 9–23 (spring 2003).

Herbert, W. N. "John Burnside: An Interview." in *Talking verse*. Edited by Robert Crawford, Henry Hart, David Kinloch, and Richard Price. St. Andrews, Scotland: verse, 1995.

"Interview: John Burnside on Three Annunciation Poems." in *New Writing 13*. Edited by Toby Litt and Ali Smith. London: British Council and Picador, 2005. (also available at http://newwriting.britishcouncil.org/all/themes/ ?theme=18).

Merritt, Stephanie. "Dad, I Could've Killed You." *Observer*, February 26, 2006. (Interview with Burnside, discussing *A Lie About My Father*.) (also available at http://books. guardian.co.uk/departments/biography/story.html.)

Patterson, Christina. "The Books Interview—John Burnside: Why Hard Men Need Tough Love." *Independent*, May 19, 2001 (http://www.findarticles.com/p/articles/ mi_qn4158/is_20010519/ai_n14397362).

Yates, Emma. "Five Minutes with John Burnside." *Guardian*, January 23, 2001 (http://books.guardian.co.uk/poetry/ features/0,907485,00.html). (Includes audio clips.)

EDWARD CARPENTER

(1844–1929)

Nikolai Endres

In his own time, Edward Carpenter was a celebrity. On his seventieth birthday in 1914, he received a congratulatory address signed by notables such as the feminist Annie Besant, the historian Goldsworthy Lowes Dickinson, the sexologists Havelock Ellis and Magnus Hirschfeld, the painter Roger Fry, the socialists Sidney and Beatrice Webb, the anarchist Peter Kropotkin, the philosopher Rabindranath Tagore, and the writers George Bernard Shaw, H. G. Wells, and W. B. Yeats. On his eightieth birthday, Carpenter received a message of greeting from all members of the British cabinet, including Labour prime minister Ramsay MacDonald. Shaw named Carpenter the "Noble Savage"; Leo Tolstoy wrote a laudatory preface to a Russian translation of one of Carpenter's works, calling him a worthy successor of Thomas Carlyle and John Ruskin; Mahatma Gandhi also held Carpenter in high esteem. Even royalty took notice of him: Carpenter visited Windsor Castle in response to a request from Princess Alexandra (later Queen Alexandra) to tutor Prince Albert Victor and the future King George V. (Carpenter respectfully declined the honor.) And an Edward Carpenter Community is committed to "caring, trusting, personal growth, sharing, creativity, and other principles and intention aimed at nurturing 'community'." His works are prolific, too.

Though his work largely has been forgotten in the decades since his death, Carpenter could be viewed today as a prophet of modernism, a crusader for gay rights, an untiring idealist, and a crucial influence on later writers.

LIFE AND LETTERS

Edward Carpenter was born in Brighton on August 29, 1844, to middle-class parents. He grew up in a world of privilege and complacency that he later came to despise. His father, Charles Carpenter, served as a naval commander, practiced as a lawyer, and drew on investments in British and American railways. As a young boy, Carpenter's father read the German idealists Immanuel Kant, Johann Gottlieb Fichte, and Georg Wilhelm Friedrich Hegel. When he died, he left his son a substantial inheritance that secured his independence. His mother, Sophia Wilson Carpenter, a strict Puritan who dismissed affection as bordering on sin, devotedly submitted to her husband and took care of the education of Carpenter and his six sisters and three brothers. Carpenter's schooling began at Brighton College, where he divided his attention between literature and mathematics and was influenced by the Broad Church's liberal doctrine.

When he was thirteen, his entire family moved to France for a year; Carpenter spent his free time playing in the park of Versailles. After graduation from high school, Carpenter traveled to Heidelberg, Germany for some months, where he improved his language skills and "heard [Robert Wilhelm Eberhard von] Bunsen and [Gustav Robert] Kirchhoff lecture on Physics and Chemistry" (*My Days and Dreams*, p. 45). In 1864, Carpenter enrolled at Cambridge and studied mathematics and English. During his third year, he won a prize for a literary essay. In 1868, after graduating tenth in the mathematical honors examination, he began a career as a lecturer at Trinity Hall and was ordained a deacon in 1870. He came into close contact with F. D. Maurice, the founder of Christian Socialism. Soon though, Carpenter realized the sham of organized religion:

The deadly Philistinism of a little provincial congregation; the tradesmen and shopkeepers in their sleek Sunday best; the petty vulgarities and hypocrisies; the discordant music of the choir; the ignoble scenes in the vestry and the resumed saintly expression on returning into the church; the hollow ring and the sour edge of the incumbent's voice; and the fatuous faces upturned to receive the communion at the altar steps—all these were worse, considerably worse, than the undisguised heathenism of the chapel performance.

(*My Days and Dreams*, p. 53)

After a physical breakdown in 1872, he resigned all his clerical duties, focusing on teaching and lecturing for the people. Moreover, Carpenter turned to Walt Whitman's inspirational poetry, eagerly listened to the music of Richard Wagner and Ludwig van Beethoven, fervently embraced Socialism, and joined the University Extension movement in Sheffield, England. This democratic movement, founded by James Stuart, had two purposes: to admit women to higher learning and to absorb remote areas of England to Cambridge. In 1873, Carpenter published his first volume of poetry, titled *Narcissus*, which practically fell flat. He also composed a drama, *Moses* (1875), which hardly fared better; a revised edition, entitled *The Promised Land* (1910), suffered the same fate. All these failures took a toll, according to his biographers Sheila Rowbotham and Jeffrey Weeks:

The North was not quite what he imagined. He found soot and provincial respectability, suffered indigestion from landladies' cooking and was hurtled about in what seemed like unending railways on his lecturing circuit. As he scrambled around on astronomy outings, peering at the murky stars through polluted industrial skies with his young lady students, he must have cast wry thoughts over the Atlantic.

(*Socialism and the New Life,* p. 36)

Carpenter traveled widely. In France, for example, he witnessed firsthand the horrors of the Paris Commune. In 1873, he took a vacation in Italy: "The remnants of Greek civilization that he found in Italy seemed a complete antithesis to the stifling ideologies of commercialism and Christianity" (Weeks, *Coming Out*, p. 69). In 1877, Carpenter crossed the Atlantic and immediately went to 431 Stevens Street, Camden, New Jersey, where he met Walt Whitman; both men were

enchanted by each other. An entire book, *Days with Walt Whitman* (1906), is devoted to this close encounter. Carpenter also visited Ralph Waldo Emerson, Oliver Wendell Holmes, and John Burroughs, and he threw a stone into Walden Pond, paying his tribute to Henry David Thoreau, whose *Walden* (1854) he first read enthusiastically in 1883. After the death of his parents in the 1880s, Carpenter settled down at his retreat Millthorpe, which became a shrine for all classes of society:

Architects, railway clerks, engine-drivers, signalmen, naval and military officers, Cambridge and Oxford dons, students, advanced women, suffragettes, professors and provision-merchants, came into touch in my little house and garden; parsons and positivists, printers and authors, scythesmiths and surgeons, bank managers and quarrymen, met with each other. Young colliers from the neighboring mines put on the boxing-gloves with springs of aristocracy; learned professors sat down to table with farm-lads.

(*My Days and Dreams*, p. 164)

There he composed his epic collection of lyric poems, *Towards Democracy* (1905) and received the illustrious crusaders of his day: William Morris, Havelock Ellis (and his wife, Edith), Olive Schreiner (famous for her 1883 novel *The Story of an African Farm*), Eleanor Marx (the daughter of Karl Marx), Henry and Kate Salt, Annie Besant, Goldworthy Lowes Dickinson, and other members of the Progressive Association, the Fellowship of the New Life, the Fabians, and the Social Democratic Federation (SDF). When Morris broke with the SDF and formed the Socialist League, which mingled politics with spirituality, Carpenter followed suit. Ruth Livesey explains Morris and Carpenter's common goal:

Both writers worked up against late nineteenth-century aestheticism in their belief that the increasing autonomy of art was a symptom of advanced capitalism: a condition that would be terminated by the revolution, but that in the meantime needed to be exposed as the sickness it was. Whilst both writers struggled with the aestheticism of their time they also attempted to theorize the likely form of creativity and aesthetic expression in the coming socialist era. Despite clear political differences,

Morris and Carpenter shared a vision of the subject under socialism. It was a vision in which the self achieved fullest expression, clearest realization—true manhood—as Morris put it, through communal labor. For Morris and Carpenter the masculine laboring body became an aesthetic site: the origin for the rebirth of the arts after the demise of capitalism.

(p. 603)

Carpenter also became friends with art critic and wrtier John Ruskin but distrusted his escapes into the Middle Ages, as Ruskin was more interested in literature and history rather than political change. In the middle of the 1880s, Carpenter read Karl Marx's *Capital* (1867) for the first time, but he had already been influenced by H. M. Hyndman's *England for All* (1881), which he discovered in 1883. Another seminal text Carpenter systematically studied was the *Bhagavad-Gita*, the Hindu sacred verses that present a dialogue between Krishna and the warrior Arjuna about a love that unites the finite and infinite. In 1890, Carpenter set out for India and Ceylon. His biographer Chushichi Tsuzuki notes that "his journey to the East was as much a tour of discovery of the new India that was rising as it was a pilgrimage to the holy temples of the ancient religion for reassurance and reinvigoration of his faith" (p. 107). When he returned from India in 1891, Carpenter met George Merrill, a working-class man raised in the slums of Sheffield. George became the love of his life:

I take thy gift, so gracious and sparkling-clear,
Thy naïve offering, as of a simple Nature-child,
Wondering, like one who sees a rose in winter bloom-
  ing, or cypress 'mid a wilderness of rocks; [...]
Come, son (since thou hast said it), out of all Shiráz
Háfiz salutes thee comrade. Let us go
A spell of life along the road together.
       Towards Democracy, pp. 336–337)

The two put into practice one of Carpenter's greatest political ideals, the love between two masculine men that would bridge class and create a truly democratic erotic universe.

Carpenter also met John Addington Symonds, the author of famous essays in defense of homosexuality such as "A Problem in Greek Ethics" (1873) and "A Problem in Modern Ethics" (1891) and a collaborator with Ellis on several studies in sexual inversion included in *Studies in the Psychology of Sex* (1897–1928). In 1895, when Oscar Wilde was sentenced to prison for gross indecency, Carpenter felt the chill of being an outcast, but he never tired in his crusade. Seven years later, Carpenter published *Ioläus: An Anthology of Friendship* (1902). In 1922, Carpenter and Merrill moved south to a villa on a hill in Guildford. After Merrill died in 1928, Carpenter was left an emotional wreck. He suffered a stroke and died at Guildford on June 28, 1929, interred in the same grave as the love of his life.

POETRY AND POLEMIC

Towards Democracy, first published in 1883 and revised several times until its complete edition in four parts in 1905, contains almost three hundred lyric poems arranged in four sections. Part 1 comprises the long prose poem "Towards Democracy" in seventy cantos, a compendium of Carpenter's views on politics, erotics, spiritualism, socialism, feminism, and mysticism. The recurrent terms "freedom," "equality," "sky," and "joy" permeate the poem, coupled with a biblical, prophetic ring. Carpenter travels the world to spread his gospel of democracy, while at the same time denouncing England for her social ills, yet there is hope: "I see a great land poised as in a dream—waiting for the word by which it may live again" (p. 55). He seeks comfort in Earth: "The sun, the moon and the stars, the grass, the water that flows round the earth, and the light air of heaven: / To You greeting. I too stand behind these and send you word across them" (p. 13). He envisions "a millennium on earth—a millennium not of riches, nor of mechanical facilities, nor of intellectual facilities, nor absolutely of immunity from disease, nor absolutely of immunity from pain; but a time when men and women all over the earth shall ascend and enter into relation with their bodies—shall attain freedom and joy" (pp. 14–15). He ridicules the four pillars of society—law, medicine, church, and commerce: "The magistrate sits on the bench, but he does not exercise judgment; the doctor dispenses medicine but has heard no tidings of what health

EDWARD CARPENTER

is; the parson opens his mouth, but no intelligible sound comes forth; the merchant distributes evils just the same as goods" (p. 47). At the end, Carpenter insistently asks "What is Freedom?" His answer is as simple as it can be, both Socratic and Christian:

I AM.
In the recluse, the thinker, the incurable and the drudge, I AM. I am the giver of Life, I am Happiness. I am in the good and evil, in the fortunate and the unfortunate, in the gifted and the incapable, alike; I am not one more than the other.

(p. 93)

Part 2, "Children of Freedom," develops his new-found treasure:

O Freedom, beautiful beyond compare, thy kingdom is established!
Thou with thy feet on earth, thy brow among the stars, for ages us thy children
I, thy child, singing daylong nightlong, sing of joy in thee.

(p. 97)

Carpenter worships the (male) body:

All these in his eyes who stood there, lusty with well knit loins, devouring bread and cheese—all these and something more:
Nature standing supreme and immensely indifferent in that man, yet condensed and prompt for decisive action:
True eyes, true interpreters, striking as a man wielding a sledge strikes, in whom long practice has ensured the absolute consent of all his muscles!
True eyes, true interpreters—of abounding gifts free givers—
Without wrigglings and contortions, without egotistic embarrassments, grimaces, innuendos,
Without constraint and without stint, free!

(p. 122)

Democracy, as much as a political concept, is for Carpenter an affair of the heart. As Andrew Elfenbein contends: "Whitman and Carpenter allowed men to claim for themselves a more permanent understanding of democracy than that offered by the actual extension of the franchise: to accept their vision was to have democracy at every moment, rather than for a brief interval

during election season" (p. 101). In "As a Woman of a Man," Carpenter surrenders himself to Democracy, the personification of beauty, love, strength, passion, sex:

As a woman of a man so I will learn of thee,
I will draw thee closer and closer,
I will drain thy lips and the secret things of thy body,
I will conceive by thee, Democracy.

(p. 142)

Two other poems stand out. "On an Atlantic Steamship" recollects a trip to the United States: multinational passengers, changing weather, and awe-inspiring scenery. "After Long Ages" intimates a journey to paradise; after orgasmic bliss—"The ecstatic deliverance, the bursting of the sac, the outrush and innumerable progeny!" (p. 207)—the soul achieves felicity:

Spread, O earth, with blue lines of distant hills—stretch for the feet of men and all creatures!
Sing, chant your hymns, O trees and winds and grass and immeasurable blue! [...]
Being filled with love, having completed our pilgrimage,
We also pass into peace and joy eternal.

(p. 211)

In part 3, "After Civilisation," Carpenter foretells the demise of civilization and paves the way for a better world.

Part 4, "Who Shall Command the Heart," assembles Carpenter's best pieces. "I Hear Thy Call" responds to the call of a mysterious being:

Take me, great Life—O take me, long-delaying,
Unloose these chains, unbind these clogs and fetters;
I hear thy call—so strange—Mysterious Being,
I hear thy call—I come.

(p. 306)

"I Hear Thy Call" pays tribute to Whitman's poem "Long I Thought that Knowledge Alone Would Suffice" (from Leaves of Grass, 1881):

I heed knowledge, and the grandeur of The States, and the example of heroes, no more,
I am indifferent to my own songs—I will go with him I love,
It is enough for us that we are together—We never separate again.

"As the Greeks Dreamed" revels in Greece's sensuality:

How the human body bathed in the sheen and wet,
  steeped in sun and air,
Moving near and nude among the elements,
Matches somehow and interprets the whole of Nature.

(p. 313)

"A Mightier than Mammon," in many ways Carpenter's program piece, expresses the potential for bridging class barriers: "They only speak a few words, and lo! underneath all the differences of class and speech, of muscle and manhood, their souls are knit together" (p. 322); remarkably, women are included in Carpenter's vision: "And here are two women, both doctors and mature in their profession, whose souls are knit in a curiously deep affection. / They share a practice in a large town, and live in the same house together, exchanging all that they command, of life and affection and experience" (p. 323); to arrive at such an ideal, Carpenter advises: "The sacredness of sex in freedom is taught in schools and churches; the ulcer of prostitution slowly disappears; the wasted love that flows in a morbid stream through the streets, or desiccates in grand mansions, runs once more into the channels of free devotion and life" (pp. 326–327).

Eve Sedgwick astutely notes: "Because he was a pioneer both of socialism and at the same time of the study of sexuality, he never confined his vision of *class* struggle to the (*male*) wage workplace, nor his vision of ideal *sexuality* to the (*bourgeois*) female-immobilizing one" (p. 214). "O Child of Uranus" invokes the German sexologist Karl Heinrich Ulrichs' famous self-description as *anima muliebris virili corpore inclusa* ("a woman's soul trapped in a man's body") but shows understanding for his plight:

I see thee where for centuries thou hast walked,
Lonely, the world of men
Saving, redeeming, drawing all to thee,
Yet outcast, slandered, pointed of the mob,
Misjudged and crucified.

(p. 332)

"One at a Time" sets out, among the world's millions of faces, to spot other lovers of comrades:

"The soldier's cap, the felon's crop, the bishop's mitre, / Under the eyelids of the peasant woman, beneath the burnous of the Arab chieftain," Carpenter's "gaydar" makes them all out: "by the first glance revealed— / I see, and know my own" (p. 332). Political problems, especially imperialism, Carpenter denounces in "Empire":

An empty House to hear the burden of the sorrows of
  India,
And Irish questions treated with derision.
O England, thou old hypocrite, thou sham, thou bully
  of weak nations whom thou were called to aid,
Thy day of ruin surely is near at hand,
Save for one thing—which scarcely may be hoped
  for— / Save that a heart of grace within thee rise
And stay the greed of gold—which else must slay
  thee.

(p. 374)

The whole system must be overhauled: "Ignorance breeds Fear, and Fear breeds Greed, and Greed that Wealth whose converse is Poverty— and these again breed Strife and Fear in endless circles," but a new dawn has formed on the horizon: "Experience [...] breeds Sympathy, and Sympathy Understanding, and Understanding Love; / And Love leads Helpfulness by the hand, to open the gates of Power unlimited" (p. 319). Finally, in "India, the Wisdom-Land," Carpenter anticipates his voyage to the East, a repository of knowledge:

Handed down, the sacred lore, from one to another,
  carefully guarded,
Beneath the outer conventional shows, beneath all the
  bonds of creed and race, gliding like a stream which
  nothing can detain [...]
The soul's true being—the cosmic vast emancipated
  life—Freedom, Equality—
The precious semen of Democracy.

(p. 356)

Oliver Buckton proposes that, in *Towards Democracy*, "Carpenter's poetic persona ... emerges from a complex array of sources, including Greek art, Whitmanesque poetics of desire, socialism, and Eastern mysticism" (p. 180). Havelock Ellis, much to Carpenter's delight, initially dismissed *Towards Democracy* as "Whitman and water" (quoted in Tsuzuki, p. 61), but later he came to appreciate it very much. Carpenter, however, realized that in order to effect change, poetry was not enough; polemic was needed.

SOCIETY AND SOCIALISM

In his autobiography, *My Days and Dreams,* Carpenter argues that the real value of the modern Socialist movement "has not lain so much in its actual constructive programme as (1) in the fact that it has provided a text for a searching criticism of the old society and of the lives of the rich, and (2) the fact that it has enshrined a most glowing and vital enthusiasm towards the realization of a new society" (p. 126). *England's Ideal, and Other Papers on Social Subjects*, which first appeared in 1887 and went through many subsequent editions, collects Carpenter's vision of a just society.

In "England's Ideal," Carpenter bemoans the state of affairs of his home country. England has degenerated to "a kind of human sink into which much flows but of which nothing ever comes—except an occasional putrid whiff of Charity and Patronage" (p. 5), because it has lost sight of the great traditions of Christianity, democracy, and honesty. In "Modern Money-Lending, and the Meaning of Dividends: A Tract for the Wealthy," Carpenter realizes that "Political Economy always begins with an island!" (p. 25), meaning it begins with the individual, then on the island of England, and also in the island's dealing with its colonies. Everything is governed by the twin "deities" supply and demand. Soon, though, the people will be demanding that the land and the equipment be put into their hands and thus directly reap the fruits of their labor. According to "Social Progress and Individual Effort," since man forms society and its institutions and laws, *he* needs to reform them; it cannot be science and intellect; competition then shall be superseded by equality. In "Desirable Mansions," Carpenter bemoans materialism: "I go into the houses of the rich. In the drawing-room I see chill weary faces, peaked features of ill-health; downstairs and in the kitchen I meet with rosy smiles, kissable cheeks, and hear sounds of song and laughter. What is this?" (p. 75). It is a prison,

a gilded cage. In "Simplification of Life," he proposes a domestic economy. In "Does It Pay?" Carpenter recounts how "none of my well-to-do friends asked whether the work I was doing was wanted, or whether it would be useful to the community, or a means of healthy life to those engaged in it, or whether it was *honest* and of a kind that could be carried on without interior defilement"; they always asked "Does it pay?" (p. 121). "Trade" shows how production is vitiated by gain and profit. "Private Property" emphasizes that legal ownership is harmful, while true ownership necessitates a living and human relationship to the object owned. In "The Enchanted Thicket," Carpenter concludes: "In every department, of morality, good taste, commonsense, private and public expediency, a change in the lives of the rich is called for" (p. 177).

Civilisation: Its Cause and Cure (1889) went through many new, revised, and enlarged editions, a total of sixteen. It carries a Whitmanesque epigraph: "The friendly and flowing savage, who is he? / Is he waiting for civilisation, or is he past it, and mastering it?" (p. 1). Carpenter proffers three goals of a new civilization: the realization of a new society, in touch with nature and without class domination; the realization of a new science, no longer linked to the brain but to real life; and the realization of a new morality, the vital unity between man and his fellow beings.

The title chapter proposes that civilization is a social, bodily, intellectual, and moral disease: the opposite of health, unity, integration, wholeness, cleanness, togetherness, oneness, and holiness. Man has turned his back on himself, on his mother earth, on his community, on his spirit, and on his god. He began to suspect his neighbors, guarding his possessions with fierce jealousy, hence the division of society into classes. Carpenter fearfully sees "vast epidemic trains over the face of the earth, plagues and fevers and lunacies and world-wide festering sores, followed by armies, ever growing, of doctors—they too with their retinues of books and bottles, vaccinations and vivisections, and grinning death's-heads in the rear—a mad crew, knowing not what they do" (p. 33). For the cure, Carpenter attempts a synthesis between communism and savagery or anarchy.

In "Modern Science: A Criticism," Carpenter argues that the true field of science is life, but that science has separated the logical and intellectual from the instinctive and emotional. In "The Science of the Future: A Forecast," Carpenter urges a practical application of scientific theories: "Do we not want to feel *more*, not less, in the presence of phenomena—to enter into a living relationship with the blue sky, and the incense-laden air, and the plants and the animals—nay, even with poisonous and hurtful things to have a keener *sense* of their hurtfulness?" (p. 109). According to "Defence of Criminals: A Criticism of Morality," laws can be grossly unjust: "the so-called vices and defects [...] are necessary elements of human life, elements without which the so-called vices could not exist [...] The evil consists not in the actions or passions themselves, but in the fact that they are inhumanely used" (pp. 144–145). As a result, morals as an absolute code of action need to be discarded. There is only one supreme law, derived from Jesus Christ: love your neighbor as you love yourself.

In "Exfoliation," Carpenter privileges Lamarckian internal and organic variation—a form of willed or purposive evolution fueled by desire rather than necessity—over Darwinian external and accidental growth or survival of the fittest: "Variation is a process by which change begins in the mental region, passes into the bodily region where it becomes organised, and finally is thrown off like a husk" (p. 172). In "Custom," Carpenter wonders to what extent customs are due to fitness in nature or otiose habit and concludes that customs, like morals, need to be shaken off. "A Rational and Humane Society" laments a mechanistic view of science that utterly neglects "nature"—both the natural world and human nature—and fails to combine sense, intellect, and soul. In "The New Morality," Carpenter surveys the moral teachings of St. Paul, Baruch Spinoza, Plato, Jesus of Nazareth, Leo Tolstoy, Friedrich Nietzsche, and even George Bernard Shaw, and recommends Indian thought: "The only essential evil was ignorance (*avidya*)—that is, the fact of

the being or creature not knowing or perceiving its emanation from, or kinship with, the One" (p. 219)

An appendix on the characteristics and customs of precivilized peoples rounds out the volume.

SEX AND SEXUALITY

In the 1890s, a diverse group of authors, clergymen, artists, educators, philosophers, and scientists set out to destigmatize homosexuality. Carpenter, together with John Addington Symonds and Havelock Ellis, stands in the forefront of law reform: "All three writers can, in their different ways, be identified with a rejection of Victorian utilitarianism, determinism and materialism," Jeffrey Weeks points out in his groundbreaking 1977 study *Coming Out* (p. 49). Carpenter published three books on homosexuality: *Love's Coming-of-Age* (1896; revised and enlarged through eleven editions to 1923), *The Intermediate Sex* (1908), and *Intermediate Types Among Primitive Folk* (1914).

The first tract, *Love's Coming-of-Age*, is named after the god of love, Eros or Cupid, who is usually depicted as a child that needs to come of age. The book originally collected three pamphlets published in 1894: "Sex-Love: And Its Place in Free Society," "Woman: And Her Place in a Free Society," and "Marriage in a Free Society." An additional essay, "Homogenic Love: And Its Place in a Free Society," which had been privately circulated, had to be excluded because of the Oscar Wilde trials and was not published (in revised version) until 1906 as "The Intermediate Sex." "Sex-Love" contends that the Industrial Revolution divorced sex from biological and natural desire, thus alienating men and women from their bodies. Another problem—here Carpenter is presenting a modern, Foucauldian argument—is that sex, especially in moral discourse, has become a "consciousness" rather than a "hunger," a manifestation of an "unclean" rather than "sacred" body: "The body itself is kept religiously covered, smothered away from the rush of the great purifying life of Nature, infected with dirt and disease, and a subject for prurient thought and exaggerated lust such as in its naked state it would never provoke" (1927, pp. 23–24).

Next, Carpenter turns to women, who are disempowered because of an obsolete feudal system. A woman is a "serf" to her master-husband, who clings like "ivy" to an "oak." A total revaluation is in order: "Not till our whole commercial system, with its barter and sale of human labor and human love for gain, is done away, and not till a whole new code of ideals and customs has come in, will women really be free" (1927, pp. 76–77). Carpenter is particularly concerned with three types of women—the "lady," the working woman, and the prostitute—and negotiates various solutions to their problems. In "Marriage," Carpenter's outlook on marriage is bleak and graphic, a life sentence: "The brief burst of their first satisfaction has been followed by satiety on the physical plane, then by mere vacuity of affection, then by boredom and nausea" (1927, p. 95). He makes four suggestions for improvement: furthering the self-dependence of women, promoting rational teaching of heart and head for youths of both sexes, breaking up marriage as a pettily exclusive and rigidly monogamous relationship, and abolishing the current law that binds people together for life. Finally, Carpenter waxes lyrical:

> Is it possible [...] that there really *is* a Free Society—in another and deeper sense than that hitherto suggested—a society to which we all in our inmost selves consciously or unconsciously belong—the Rose of Souls that Dante beheld in Paradise, whose every petal is an individual, and an individual only through its union with all the rest—the early Church's dream, of an eternal Fellowship in heaven and on earth—the Prototype of all the brotherhoods and communities that exist on this or any other planet; and that the innumerable selves of men, united in the one Self, members of it and of one another (like the members of the body) stand in eternal and glorious relationship bound indissolubly together?
>
> (1923, pp. 177–178)

The final edition of *Love's Coming-of-Age*, which appeared in 1923, adds two chapters from *The Drama of Love and Death* (1912): "The Beginnings of Love" and "Love's Ultimate Meaning." The first is a technical exposé of cell growth,

reproduction, and death. The second elaborates on the fatality of self-consciousness to love, for which Carpenter blames Christianity and commercialism. Notes on the early star and sex worships, primitive group marriage, jealousy, family, and preventive checks to population, and an appendix of quotations conclude the volume.

"Homogenic Love," the only apologetic and well-known work of the period about homosexuality, reviews the historical, literary, artistic, and medical evidence for homogenic love. Carpenter's readings include David and Jonathan, Achilles and Patroclus, Orestes and Pylades, Harmodius and Aristogiton, Theocritus, Sappho, Aeschylus, Sophocles, Plato, Catullus, Martial, Virgil, Persian poets, the medieval tale of Amis and Amile, literature from Renaissance Italy and Elizabethan England, writing by the German scholar Johann Joachim Winckelmann, and Alfred, Lord Tennyson's *In Memoriam* (1850): "It will be noticed that here we have some of the very greatest names in all literature concerned; and that their utterances on this subject equal if they do not surpass, in beauty, intensity, and humanity of sentiment, whatever has been written in praise of the other more ordinarily recognized love" (1927, p. 328). The Hebraic tradition has reduced love and sex to child breeding, but Carpenter disagrees:

> Without denying that sexual intimacies do exist; and while freely admitting that, in great cities, there are to be found associated with this form of attachment prostitution and other evils comparable with the evils associated with the ordinary sex-attachment; we may yet say that it would be a great error to suppose that the homogenic love takes as a rule the extreme form vulgarly supposed; and that it would also be a great error to overlook the fact that in a large number of instances the relation is not distinctively sexual at all, though it may be said to be physical in the sense of embrace and endearment.
>
> (1927, p. 330)

Carpenter conceived of homosexuals as a third sex: "urnings" or "uranians," derived from Greek *ouranos*, Pausanias' Heavenly (or "homogenic") Aphrodite in the *Symposium*. Like Plato, Carpenter reiterates the notion that homogenic love is superior to heterosexuality. As the critic Frank

Leib puts it: "Love between persons of the same sex is necessarily gratuitous; it has no obvious social or biological utility. For Victorians of every race and religion, this makes it evil. For Carpenter, as for Plato, the fact that it is humanly useless renders it morally divine" (p. 76). Then Carpenter surveys current theoretical research: Richard von Krafft-Ebing, Albert Moll, Paul Moreau, Cesare Lombroso, Karl Heinrich Ulrichs, Havelock Ellis, and John Addington Symonds. According to sexologists, homosexuality was congenital and therefore unchangeable: "Too much emphasis cannot be laid on the distinction between these born lovers of their own sex, and that class of persons, with whom they are so often confused, who out of mere carnal curiosity or extravagance of desire, or from the dearth of opportunities for a more normal satisfaction (as in schools, barracks, etc.) adopt some homosexual practices" (1927, p. 332). Second, the number of homosexuals is much higher than previously estimated. Third, the homosexual does not have his orientation written all over him. All in all, however, Carpenter is not impressed with medical research. His agenda is political: "we have solid work waiting to be done in the patient and life-long building up of new forms of society, new orders of thought, and new institutions of human solidarity—all of which in their genesis will meet with opposition, ridicule, hatred, and even violence" (1927, p. 344). First and foremost, the British law will have to be changed. The Code Napoleon in France and the Codice Principe in Italy, for example, tolerate sexual inversion.

The Intermediate Sex (1908; third edition, 1912) compiles Carpenter's writings on homosexuality: "The Intermediate Sex," "The Homogenic Attachment" (which duplicates "Homogenic Love" from the previous volume), "Affection in Education," and "The Place of the Uranian in Society," plus an introduction and an appendix of notes and quotations. Early on, Carpenter extols homosexuals: "with their extraordinary gift for, and experience in, affairs of the heart—from the double point of view, both of the man and of the woman—it is not difficult to see that these people have a special work to

do as reconcilers and interpreters of the two sexes to each other" (1912, p. 14). This is a striking image, contrary to the Victorian view of homosexuals as disruptive, freakish, and promiscuous. Carpenter then lists the stereotypes of the male invert:

> not particularly attractive, sometimes quite the reverse [...] a distinctly effeminate type, sentimental, lackadaisical, mincing in gait and manners, something of a chatterbox, skilful at the needle and in women's work, sometimes taking pleasure in dressing in woman's clothes; his figure not unfrequently betraying a tendency towards the feminine, large at the hips, supple, not muscular, the face wanting in hair, the voice inclining to be high-pitched, etc.; while his dwelling room is orderly in the extreme, even natty, and choice of decoration and perfume.
> (1912 p. 29)

Inverted women fare hardly better:

> a rather markedly aggressive person, of strong passions, masculine manners and movements, practical in the conduct of life, sensuous rather than sentimental in love, often untidy, and *outré* in attire; her figure muscular, her voice rather low in pitch; her dwelling-room decorated with sporting scenes, pistols, etc., and not without a suspicion of the fragrant weed in the atmosphere; while her love (generally to rather soft and feminine specimens of her own sex) is often a sort of furor.
> (1912, pp. 29–30)

Carpenter admits that these examples are extreme and rare and holds up some of history's most revered figures: Michelangelo, Shakespeare, Christopher Marlowe, Alexander the Great, Julius Caesar, Queen Christine of Sweden, and Sappho. In "Affection in Education," Carpenter surveys schoolboy friendships, modeled on Greek *paiderastia*:

> The younger boy looks on the other a hero, loves to be with him, thrills with pleasure at his words of praise or kindness, imitates, makes him his pattern and standards, learns exercises and games, contracts habits, or picks up information from him. The elder one, touched, becomes protector and helper; the unselfish side of his nature is drawn out, and he develops a real affection and tenderness toward the younger. He takes all sorts of trouble to initiate his

protégé in field sports or studies; is proud of the latter's success; and leads him on perhaps later to share his own ideals of life and thought and work.

(1912, p. 81)

Antiquity provided such models, but they are utterly lacking in modern schools, where "panic terror" of affection prevails. "The Place of the Uranian in Society" offers radical models for accommodating Uranian love and hits at excellence in the artistic, musical, and literary realms, even in the business world, military service, and politics or administration, but crucially in "affairs of the heart." Uranians hold out the mirror to infinity: "it is possible that the Uranian spirit may lead to something like a general enthusiasm of Humanity [...] which will one day transform the common life by substituting the bond of personal affection and compassion for the monetary, legal and other external ties which now control and confine society" (1912, pp. 108–109). In his 1995 study *A Road to Stonewall*, the critic Byrne Fone praises Carpenter for his "advocacy of a liberationist position concerning sexual difference" and compares his efforts to "current attempts to institute rainbow curricula, establish gay studies in universities, and pass civil rights legislation" (p. 155).

Intermediate Types Among Primitive Folk comprises two parts: "The Intermediate in the Service of Religion" (originally published as "On the Connection Between Homosexuality and Divination" in the *American Journal of Religious Psychology* and in the *Revue d'ethnographie et de sociologie*, 1911) and "The Intermediate as Warrior." Long before the heyday of anthropological investigation, Carpenter was interested in how homosexuality made its inroads into "normal" society. According to his logic, manly-active homosexuals became military leaders, while effeminate-passive homosexuals took up religious services. Carpenter turns to the prophet or priest, the wizard or witch. Why are many homosexuals so gifted? First, since the "intermediate" man or woman belongs to neither gender, he or she would be unsatisfied with traditional work activities and would thus create a niche; second, because he is "different" from the majority and subject to great scrutiny, he would begin to think,

dream, and discover; third, because the intermediate type combines characteristics and powers of both sexes, the emotional plus the practical, he is superior to his fellow men; fourth, the blending of masculine and feminine temperaments produces in some cases a great genius:

whether they prophesied downfall or disaster, or whether they urged their people onward to conquest and victory, or whether by acute combinations of observation and experience they caught at the healing properties of herbs or determined the starry influences on the seasons and the crops—[these geniuses] in almost all cases would acquire and did acquire a strange reputation for sanctity and divinity—arising partly out of the homosexual taboo, but also out of their real possession and command of a double-engine psychic power.

(pp. 62–63)

Naturally, then, Carpenter considers hermaphroditism among gods and mortals, especially in Hindu literature and art, Hebrew stories (since Eve was created out of Adam, was Adam a "man-woman," with a female soul trapped in a man's body?), Greek mythology, and even Egyptian and Norse traditions. He concludes that some of the greatest figures in myth and history—Apollo, Buddha, Osiris, Lord Byron, St. Francis, Jesus of Nazareth—beautifully reconciled masculine and feminine traits, the seat of their greatness. There have also been great "gay" warriors: Dorian Greeks, Japanese Samurai, and other Mohammedan peoples. As Joy Dixon remarks: "Carpenter was reversing contemporary valuations of the primitive and the feminine, both of which were being constructed by late Victorian anthropologists and ethnologists as repositories of the superstitious and irrational" (p. 413).

Three more of Carpenter's texts on sexuality deserve to be mentioned briefly. *Iöläus: An Anthology of Friendship* (1902), named after Hercules' beloved charioteer, is divided into five sections: "Friendship-Customs in the Pagan and Early World," "The Place of Friendship in Greek Life and Thought," "Poetry of Friendship Among Greeks and Romans," "Friendship in Early Christian and Mediaeval Times," and "The Renaissance and Modern Times." Carpenter collects the biblical love story of David and

Jonathan, Plato's *Symposium*, Persian homoerotic poetry, Shakespeare's sonnets, Tennyson's *In Memoriam*, the correspondence between the German composer Richard Wagner and King Ludwig II of Bavaria, and many other sources. Though hardly complimentary, the book's nickname "The Bugger's Bible" testifies to the anthology's wide appeal. In *Some Friends of Walt Whitman: A Study in Sex-Psychology* (1924), a paper delivered to the British Society for the Study of Sex Psychology, Carpenter quotes copiously from *Leaves of Grass* and lectures on Whitman's homo sexual passion; he also talks about John Addington Symonds infamous letter to Whitman, in which he wanted an answer to what *exactly* Whitman was depicting in his homoerotic poetry, a request that Whitman angrily dismissed as Symonds' "morbid inferences"—certain things obviously are better left unsaid and Symonds should have known better; Carpenter concludes with an exhortation to uncouple sex from procreation: "When two people love each other to that degree that they become in effect one person they take on [a] new character, and may almost be said to enter into a new order of existence" (p. 15). In *The Psychology of the Poet Shelley* (1925), Carpenter investigates how the "love-element" saturates all of Percy Bysshe Shelley's poetry, asks why Shelley largely ignores direct references to physical sex acts while at the same time tackling delicate issues such as incest and polygamy and applies Freudian psychology to Shelley. He exalts Shelley as a new type of human being that will save the world and rid it from the evils of "gold" (greed) and "blood" (war). And once again, Carpenter laments the vulgarity of sex: "in the present day Sex is ceasing to wield the glamour which once surrounded it"; the reason is simple and strikingly modern: "We know too much about it!" (p. 31).

ORIENT AND OCCIDENT

In addition to his contributions to gay culture, Carpenter's visits to the East proved crucial to the development of his worldview. "For Carpenter," suggests the political theorist Vincent Geoghegan, "the Indian empire involved the juxtaposition of two 'races' who could not comprehend each other—a modern, materialist, English governing class, and an ancient, spiritual subject population—each with their own pattern of virtues and vices, and seemingly incapable of living in harmony with each other" (p. 521). Copiously illustrated, *From Adam's Peak to Elephanta: Sketches in Ceylon and India* (1892) chronicles his trip to South Asia. Adam's Peak is a shrine at 7,400 feet that supposedly retained the footprint of Buddha; the caves of Elephanta feature a statute of Siva, who is depicted as half man, half woman, hence an ideal type of the intermediate sex. Carpenter traveled through the Suez Canal to Colombo, to the Buddhist Temple at Kandy, and to the Indian cities of Madras, Calcutta, Benares, Delhi, and Bombay. Particularly interesting are the chapters on Carpenter's meeting with a *gñâni*, an esoteric teacher of the South Indian school of Brahminism:

> here in this man it was of absorbing interest to feel one came in contact with the root-thought of all existence—the intense *consciousness* (not conviction merely) of the oneness of all life [...] After seeing Whitman, the amazing representative of the same spirit in all its voluminous modern unfoldment—seven years before—this visit to the Eastern sage was like going back to the pure lucid intensely transparent source of some mighty and turbulent stream.
>
> (*My Days and Dreams*, pp. 143–144)

The teaching method Carpenter describes differs from Socratic inquiry, for the *gñâni* does not prove anything and simply hands down orally delivered doctrines; the pupil is not supposed to ask questions. Eventually, man and woman will become emancipated: "all distinction of castes, classes, all sense of superiority or self-goodness—of right and wrong even—and the most absolute sense of Equality must prevail towards every one, and determination in its expression" (*From Adam's Peak*, p. 162). There are three conditions for the attainment of divine knowledge, or *gñânam*: the study of the sacred books, the help of a guru, and the verification of tradition through personal practice. Initiation consists of meeting a guru, the consciousness of Grace, the vision of Siva, and finding the "universe within." To become a *gñáni* one goes through previous stages: student, householder, *yogi* (from *yog*, "to join"), each with appropriate costume and rules. The objective of his spiritual quest is "*universal* or *cosmic* consciousness, in contradistinction to the individual or special bodily consciousness with which we are all familiar" (p. 156), the Hindu philosophy of *Sat-chit-ánanda Brahm*, the all-pervading and all-perceiving bliss. Then Carpenter gathers the outstanding tenets of his master's ideas: "Gentleness, forbearance towards all, abstention from giving pain, especially to the animals, the recognition of the divine spirit in every creature down to the lowest, the most absolute sense of equality and the most absolute candor, an undisturbed serene mind, free from anger, fear, or any excessive and tormenting desire" (p. 176). It was through this teacher that Carpenter received first-hand instruction in Eastern thought, which fascinated him all his life. Also, one purpose of *From Adam's Peak* was to disseminate Eastern Wisdom to his British readers. Surprisingly, though, some of the *gñáni*'s views were entirely unaffected by millennia of discoveries; for example, he believed in a geocentric universe. When Carpenter left his teacher, the *gñáni* "returned to that state of interior meditation and absorption in the contemplation of the world disclosed to the inner sense, which had apparently become his normal condition" (p. 151).

CREATION AND CONSCIOUSNESS

The Art of Creation: Essays on the Self and Its Powers (1904) attempts a synthesis of the Eastern and Western concepts of man's origins, from the *Upanishads*, Buddha, Lao-tzû, Plato, Jesus, St. Paul, Plotinus, Spinoza, Kant, George Berkeley, Georg Wilhelm Friedrich Hegel, Arthur Schopenhauer, and modern philosophers. It does not suffice to study the art of creation externally: "*we have to learn and to practise the art in ourselves.* So alone will it become vital and really intelligible to us" (p. viii, emphasis in original). What convinces us that there is an intelligent Self in our fellow man? "It is that he has a Will and Purpose, a *Character*, which, do what you will,

tends to push outwards towards Expression" (p. 28). Creation is a work of art, constantly renewing itself, giving meaning to outer form by expressing its inward treasures.

In "Matter and Consciousness," Carpenter defines knowledge, perception, and consciousness as messages of communication between various selves. "The Three Stages of Consciousness" describes the knower, the knowledge, and the thing known—still undifferentiated, differentiated, and eventually reconciled. This is Cosmic Consciousness, when subject and object are once again unified and man triumphantly returns to the Garden of Eden. In "The Self and its Affiliations," Carpenter explores race consciousness: man is not a separate being but someone who "stretches (through affiliation after affiliation) into the far 'backward and abysm of Time,' who through endless centuries has been seeking to express itself; nevertheless whose consciousness is *here and now* in its visible body, as well as in that agelong world-life" (p. 102). In "Platonic Ideas and Heredity," Carpenter evokes Platonic *anamnesis* (recollection). How, for example, do we share a sense of justice or truth or beauty? Plato believed in a world of Absolute Forms, beyond the reach of time and place; the soul initially had a knowledge of the Forms but lost it after birth; therefore, human beings only have a memory of them. According to "The Gods as Apparitions of the Race-Life," the gods represent the life of the race itself, and through them "we reach to *another and more extended order of consciousness*" (p. 126).

In "The Gods as Dwelling in the Physiological Centres," Carpenter explains how all the gods represent both distinct feelings and activities in the race (war, love, day, night) and centers of organic life in the human body (love, sleep, pugnacity). "The Devils and the Idols" points out how devils result from tyranny suffered by ourselves and inflicted on others; the gods of one age become the devils of another. In "Beauty and Duty," Carpenter attempts to reconcile art and morality into "Love." The chapter "Creation" posits a new awareness of the body, an undreamed world of possibilities: "the individual should conceive and know himself, not as a toy and chance product of his own bodily heredity, but as identified and continuous with the Eternal Self of which his body is a manifestation" (p. 208). "Transformation" describes how this process works, by retaining the mind in a constant state of emotions. At the end, Carpenter extols sublime consciousness: "It is seen by lovers in each other's eyes—the One, absolute and changeless, yet infinitely individuate and intelligent—the Supreme life and being; of which all actual existence and Creation is the descent and partial utterance in the realms of emotion and thought" (p. 222). An appendix contains essays on the Mayfly, on health, and on a meditation on an evening in spring.

RELIGION AND REFLECTION

At the root of *Pagan and Christian Creeds* (1920) lies Carpenter's vision of a "world religion." How did religion arise? Three approaches have been put forth: first, the god cult, tying creed to the movement of the sun and other planets that led to the invention of the Olympian gods dwelling in heaven; second, the magic cult, connecting religion with the changes of the seasons and the ensuing belief in earth spirits; third, the phallic cult, equating worship with the body and the force of sex. However, Carpenter suggests, the historical order of these explanations is probably exactly the reverse. Because of fear and *self*-consciousness, accompanied by taboos (based on faith, not reason), which were gradually rigified into customs and laws, religion evolved "from crass superstition, senseless and accidental, to rudimentary observation, and so to belief in Magic; thence to Animism and personification of nature-powers in more or less human form, as earth-divinities or sky-gods or embodiments of the tribe; and to placation of these powers by rites like Sacrifice and the Eucharist, which in their turn became the foundation of Morality" (p. 15). Indebted to James Frazer's *The Golden Bough* (first published in 1890), Carpenter traces the origin of (pagan) religion in terms of psychological development: from animal consciousness to self-consciousness to a hitherto unnamed new form of consciousness (later referred to as

"universal" or "cosmic" consciousness) that finds expression in the rites, prophesies, and mysteries of early religions and in the poetry, art, and literature of later civilizations. Harking back to William Blake's stages of innocence, experience, and higher innocence, Carpenter proposes: "When man arrives at the final consciousness in which the idea of such a self, superior or inferior or in any way antagonistic to others, ceases to operate, then he will return to his first and primal condition, and will cease to need *any* special religion or gods, knowing himself and his fellows to be divine and the origin and perfect fruition of all" (p. 99).

How did Christianity supersede paganism? Did the pagan gods flee away in dismay before the sign of the cross and at the sound of the name of Jesus? Hardly. In great detail, Carpenter takes into account solar myths and Christian festivals and finds that most pagan deities were born around Christmas Day (just after the winter solstice), were conceived by a virgin (a belief dating back to matriarchal societies and, perhaps, parthenogenesis), and saw the light of day in a stable or cave (the place of the sun's winter retirement and vegetation's annual cycle of death). A star in the East showed three wise men the way; a threatened massacre of the innocents resulted in an escape to faraway lands; the deities were called "light bringer," "savior," "deliverer," and the like; they were nailed to a tree or cross, descended into the underworld, and rose from the dead; they founded communions of saints and disciples; and they were commemorated by Eucharistic meals. The similarities to Christianity are obvious, to the wrath of the early church, which invented "the innocent theory that the Devil—in order to confound the Christians—had, *centuries before*, caused the pagans to adopt certain beliefs and practices!" (p. 25). The symbolism of the zodiac and of Easter yield the same conclusion: Lent coincided with the festivities at the beginning of spring and return of vegetation; around Easter Day, the people celebrated the sun crossing the equator; the twelve disciples corresponded to the signs of the zodiac (the traitor being the serpent and the scorpion); several days commemorated an assumption, ascension, and nativity of the virgin. After pondering why tribes named themselves after animals, on what principle they selected them, and the reason they made these animals, Carpenter concludes that the totem sacraments (a totem being an adoption of an animal as an emblem) form the basis of the holy communion of bread/body and wine/blood, and that the term "sacrifice" literally translates as "to render sacred." Turning to food and vegetation magic, Carpenter points out that the tree and the snake naturally embody male and female sexuality, whose combination proves especially potent.

Next, the Christian doctrines of sin and sacrifice, guilt and expiation, transfiguration and redemption, baptism and confirmation are paralleled in pagan rituals. The theory of intra-uterine blessedness draws attention to an ineradicable memory of a prenatal stage of harmony in the maternal womb. This is how Carpenter explains the pagan Virgil's Fourth Eclogue that celebrates the return of a virgin, the birth of a new child sent down from heaven, and the coming of a messiah—decades before the birth of Christ. (Of course, Hebrew *messiah* means "the anointed one," which translates into Greek *christos*.) It is through "sin," which Carpenter diffidently derives from "to sunder," that man became separated from this Eden. Finally, ritual dancing eventually developed into communal drama, thence the congregations of the "church."

What is unique to Christianity, Carpenter continues, is the sex taboo, although it originates with St. Paul, not Jesus. Generally, Christianity, in its genesis, differs in its insistence on a renunciation of the world and cultivation of a purely spiritual love, in its morality with a center shifted from the public duty to one's neighbor to a private relationship to God, and in a surprisingly democratic tendency that included, for example, women, weaklings, and outcasts. Finally, Carpenter asks whether Christ is a legendary or historically verifiable figure:

> Have there been in the course of human evolution certain, so to speak, *nodal* points or periods at which the psychologic currents ran together and condensed themselves for a new start; and has each such node or point of condensation been marked by the appearance of an actual and heroic man (or woman) who supplied a necessary impetus for the new departure, and gave his name to the resulting movement? *or* is it sufficient to suppose the automatic formation of such nodes or starting-points without the intervention of any special hero or genius, and to imagine that in each case the myth-making tendency of mankind *created* a legendary and inspiring figure and worshiped the same for a long period afterwards as a god?
>
> (pp. 217–218)

That is the big question, and even Carpenter cannot answer it, but he feels that it is more important to acknowledge that such hallowed figures *have* evolved over time. Carpenter concludes with the "exodus" of Christianity: "that Christianity can *continue* to hold the field of Religion in the Western World is neither probable nor desirable" (p. 257)—unless it acknowledges and affiliates itself to its parents and changes its name from Holy Roman Church to Holy Human Church. A trend toward ecumenism seems to vindicate Carpenter, while at the same time religious affiliation accounts for most of the major world conflicts in our time. An appendix on the teaching of the Upanishads terminates the volume.

LEGACY

Two years after Carpenter's death, Gilbert Beith edited the volume *Edward Carpenter: In Appreciation*, which collects twenty-eight essays written by his friends; most of them border on panegyric. Beith also appended a "Farewell Message Left by Edward Carpenter To Be Read over His Grave," written December 30, 1910: "do not think too much of the dead husk of your friend, or mourn too much over it; but send your thoughts out towards the real soul or self which has escaped—to reach it. For so, surely, you will cast a light of gladness upon his onward journey, and contribute your part towards the building of that kingdom of love which links our earth to heaven" (p. 246).

Carpenter's most crucial influence was on E. M. Forster. In 1913, while his mother was taking a cure at Harrogate, Forster paid a visit to

EDWARD CARPENTER

Millthorpe in order to see Carpenter: in his "Terminal Note" to his novel *Maurice*, Forster says of Carpenter: "He was a rebel appropriate to his age. He was sentimental and a little sacramental… . He was a socialist who ignored industrialism and a simple-lifer with an independent income and a Whitmannic poet whose nobility exceeded his strength and, finally, he was a believer in the Love of Comrades" (p. 217). At one point, Carpenter's lover touched Forster on his posterior: "It must have been on my second or third visit to the shrine that the spark was kindled and he and his comrade George Merrill combined to make a profound impression on me and to touch a creative spring" (p. 217). As a result, Forster came to recognize his own homosexuality and wrote *Maurice*, which he revised several times. (The novel, written in 1913–1914, because of its daring subject matter was not published until 1971, one year after Forster's death.) The original bucolic epilogue depicted a chance meeting in Yorkshire (the home of Carpenter) five years later between Maurice's sister Kitty and two itinerant woodsmen: Maurice and his lover Alec. But Carpenter's legacy is even more profound. The critic Robert Martin assesses that the first half of *Maurice* traces John Addington Symonds' version of homosexuality, a "superior" homosexuality that neglects the needs of the body; the second half depicts Maurice's "salvation" through Carpenter's ideas, for it includes sex and makes Maurice reject class. In addition to the description in *Maurice*, Forster included a portrait of Carpenter in his 1951 volume *Two Cheers for Democracy*.

Critics also make an argument for Carpenter's influence on a controversial British writer of the next generation, D. H. Lawrence. Lawrence mentioned Carpenter's name only once in a letter, and they never met in person, it seems. However, Lawrence grew up in the vicinity of Sheffield; his birthplace, Eastwood, was a mere thirty miles away from Millthorpe; and he had friends who owned Carpenter's books. The two writers published in the same journals (*New Age*, *English Review*, *Occult Review*). Emile Delavenay argues that Carpenter's writings on sex and sexuality hold the key to Lawrence's "emotion-

ally troubled youth" (p. 39), although Lawrence remained reticent about his familiarity with Carpenter's work—wisely so, in light of homophobic hysteria, literary censorship, and legal prosecution. Still, "the themes of love and sex, ethics and aesthetics, art and society, art and the fulfilment of the individual" are linked in their works (p. 190).

Another influence is on Radclyffe Hall's *The Well of Loneliness* (1928). Laura Doan suggests that Hall was informed by Carpenter's vision of the "intermediate sex" rather than Havelock Ellis' and Richard Krafft-Ebing's research (the latter's name is referenced in the book but only to be discounted). Doan asserts that Hall and other lesbians in this period consciously used sexology in their attempts at self-identification, as a positive alternative to characterizations of lesbian sexuality in terms of pathology, degeneration, and morbidity. Carpenter saw love as transcendent and redemptive rather than neurotic, while Ellis adhered to homosexuality as congenital. In the end, Doan says, "Carpenter's radical proposal that the homosexual constitution and sensibility signaled a new evolutionary stage allows Hall to imagine a new role for female intermediates, particularly with regard to Stephen [Stephen Gordon, the heroine of *The Well*] who is singularly poised to play a special part in the salvation of her people" (p. 166). From a Carpenterian perspective, *The Well of Loneliness* thus ends on a hopeful note.

The Harlem Renaissance writer Claude McKay was exposed to Carpenter's writing through Walter Jekyll, his mentor and patron in Jamaica. McKay's autobiography *Home to Harlem* (1928) critiques capitalism as instrumental in maintaining racial hierarchies and investigates gender roles in terms of their political significance: "McKay derived much of his political understanding of masculine identity from Carpenter's theorization of the relationship between gender identities and socioeconomic structures, and he used this theoretical framework for locating a powerful political interface between black proletarian life and what he saw as a homosexual social vanguard," asserts Michael Maiwald (p. 826). Moreover, as Adrian Caesar has shown, many of the war poets—Rupert Brooke, Siegfried Sassoon, Wilfred Owen, and Robert Graves—read Carpenter. Carpenter and Merrill (spelled Merril) also featured in two plays written by Noël Greig and Drew Griffiths for the London theater Gay Sweatshop: *As Time Goes By* (1977) and *The Dear Love of Comrades* (1979).

A special issue of the journal *Prose Studies* devoted to Carpenter was published as a book under the title *Edward Carpenter and Late Victorian Radicalism* (1990), edited by Tony Brown includes articles on Carpenter and utopianism and popularity; Carpenter's position in the British Socialist movement; Carpenter on feminism and Olive Schreiner; Carpenter's orientalism; and late-nineteenth-century realism. Especially pertinent is Beverly Thiele's assessment in "Coming-of-Age: Edward Carpenter on Sex and Reproduction," which explains Carpenter's uncritical acceptance of society's view of reproduction: "The dominance of a paradigm of biological evolution, his own life-long project to make sense of, and then justify, the homosexual experience, his close association with 'childless' women, and his class- and sex-based distance from working class women who had experienced childbirth, miscarriage and child-rearing, all contributed to the deletion of a culturally and humanly significant reproduction" (p. 123). Carpenter's works, mostly out of print, have been reissued by Gay Men's Press, thus far in two volumes, *Towards Democracy* (reissued in 1985) and *Edward Carpenter: Selected Writings. Volume 1: Sex* (1984, edited by David Fernbach and Noël Greig). In 2005, the U.S. publisher Kessinger, which digitally preserves rare books, reissued Carpenter's works in six volumes, adding to its series of numerous other reprints of books by Carpenter. Excerpts from Carpenter's writings on homosexuality appeared in a number of anthologies in the last decades of the twentieth century.

In a 1987 essay titled "Commanding the Heart: Edward Carpenter and Friends," Sheila Rowbotham provides a fitting coda to any overview of Carpenter's literary and cultural legacy: "Victorian values continue to find echoes in our own times. Through their midst steps a white bearded gentleman in a Walt Whitman hat murmuring about the needs of the body and the heart, checking nuclear fall-out leaves and inquiring whether—in the words of his socialist song—it is yet time for England to arise?" (p. 46).

Selected Bibliography

WORKS OF EDWARD CARPENTER

PRIMARY WORKS

Narcissus. London: H. S. King, 1873.

Moses. London: E. Moxon, 1875.

England's Ideal, and Other Papers on Social Subjects. London: Swan Sonnenschein, 1887; rev. ed., 1895.

Civilisation: Its Cause and Cure, and Other Essays. London: Swan Sonnenschein, 1889; enlarged ed., New York: Allen & Unwin, 1921.

From Adam's Peak to Elephanta: Sketches in Ceylon and India. London: Swan Sonnenschein, 1892.

Love's Coming-of-Age: A Series of Papers on the Relations of the Sexes. Manchester, U.K.: Labour Press, 1896; 12th ed., London: Allen & Unwin, 1923; repr., New York: Vanguard, 1927.

Angels' Wings: A Series of Essays on Art and Its Relation to Life. London: Swan Sonnenschein, 1898.

Ioläus: An Anthology of Friendship. London: Swan Sonnenschein, 1902.

The Art of Creation: Essays on the Self and Its Powers. London: George Allen, 1904.

Towards Democracy. London: Allen & Unwin, 1905; London: Gay Men's Press, 1985.

Days with Walt Whitman, with Some Notes on His Life and Work. London: George Allen, 1906.

The Intermediate Sex: A Study of Some Transitional Types of Men and Women. London: Swan Sonnenschein, 1908; 3rd ed., New York and London: George Allen, 1912.

Sketches from Life in Town and Country, and Some Verses. London: George Allen & Sons, 1908.

The Promised Land. London: Swan Sonnenschein, 1910 (Drama; a revised edition of *Moses*).

The Drama of Love and Death: A Study of Human Evolution and Transfiguration. London: George Allen, 1912.

Intermediate Types Among Primitive Folk: A Study in Social Evolution. London: George Allen, 1914.

EDWARD CARPENTER

The Healing of Nations, and the Hidden Sources of Their Strife. London: Allen & Unwin, 1915.

My Days and Dreams, Being Autobiographical Notes. London and New York: Allen & Unwin, 1916.

Pagan and Christian Creeds: Their Origin and Meaning. London and New York: Allen & Unwin, 1920.

Some Friends of Walt Whitman: A Study in Sex-Psychology. British Society for the Study of Sex Psychology, publication no. 13. London: J. E. Francis, 1924; Folcroft, Pa.: Folcroft Library Editions, 1969.

The Psychology of the Poet Shelley. With George Barnefield. London: Allen & Unwin, 1925.

Edward Carpenter: Selected Writings. Volume 1: Sex. Edited by David Fernbach and Noël Greig. London: Gay Men's Press, 1984.

REPRINTS IN ANTHOLOGIES

"Homogenic Love." In *Sexual Heretics: Male Homosexuality in English Literature from 1850 to 1900.* Edited by Brian Reade. London: Routledge & Kegan Paul, 1971.

The Penguin Book of Homosexual Verse. Edited by Stephen Coote. Harmondsworth, U.K.: Penguin, 1983. Excerpts from *Towards Democracy*

The Columbia Anthology of Gay Literature: Readings from Western Antiquity to the Present Day. Edited by Byrne R. S. Fone. New York: Columbia University Press, 1998. Excerpts from "Homogenic Love."

Nineteenth-Century Writings on Homosexuality: A Sourcebook. Edited by Chris White. London and New York: Routledge, 1999. Excerpts from "Homogenic Love" and *Some Friends of Walt Whitman* and *Towards Democracy.*

UNPUBLISHED PAPERS AND BIBLIOGRAPHIES

Brown, Tony. "Figuring in History: The Reputation of Edward Carpenter, 1883–1987. Annotated Secondary Bibliography, I & II." *English Literature in Transition* 32, nos. 1–2: 35–64, 170–210 (1989).

Endres, Nikolai. "Edward Carpenter." In *Reader's Guide to Lesbian and Gay Studies.* Edited by Timothy F. Murphy. Chicago: Fitzroy Dearborn, 2000. pp. 117-119.

Sheffield City Libraries. *Papers of Edward Carpenter, 1844–1929, from Sheffield Archives, Sheffield Libraries and Information Services: Part 1, Correspondence and Manuscripts; Part 2, Manuscripts, Cuttings, Pamphlets, and Selected Publications; a Listing and Guide to the Microfilm Edition.* Marlborough, U.K.: A. Matthew, 1994.

Sheffield Free Public Libraries. *A Bibliography of Edward Carpenter: A Catalogue of Books, Manuscripts, Letters, Etc., By and About Edward Carpenter in the Carpenter Collection in the Department of Local History of the Central Library, Sheffield, with Some Entries from Other Sources.* Sheffield, U.K.: Sheffield Free Public Libraries, 1949; Folcroft, Pa.: Folcroft Library Editions, 1974.

CRITICAL AND BIOGRAPHICAL STUDIES

BIOGRAPHY

Forster, E. M. *Maurice.* Harmondsworth, U.K.: Penguin, 1971.

Neild, Keith. "Edward Carpenter." In *Dictionary of Labour Biography.* Edited by Joyce M. Bellamy and John Saville London, 1974. Vol. 2, pp. 85–92.

Rowbotham, Sheila, and Jeffrey Weeks. *Socialism and the New Life: The Personal and Sexual Politics of Edward Carpenter and Havelock Ellis.* London: Pluto, 1977.

Tsuzuki, Chushichi. *Edward Carpenter, 1844–1929: Prophet of Human Fellowship.* Cambridge, U.K.: Cambridge University Press, 1980.

CRITICISM AND INTERPRETATION

Beith, Gilbert, ed. *Edward Carpenter: In Appreciation.* London: Allen & Unwin, 1931.

Bredbeck, Gregory W. "Queer Superstitions: Forster, Carpenter, and the Illusion of (Sexual) Identity." In *Queer Forster.* Edited by Robert K. Martin and George Piggford. Chicago: University of Chicago Press, 1997. pp. 29–58.

Bridgwater, Patrick. "Edward Carpenter and Nietzsche." In *German Studies at the Millennium.* Edited by Neil Thomas. Durham, U.K.: University of Durham, 1999. pp. 196–223.

Brown, Tony. "Edward Carpenter, Forster, and the Evolution of *A Room with a View.*" *English Literature in Transition* 30, no. 3: 279–300 (1987).

Brown, Tony, ed. *Edward Carpenter and Late Victorian Radicalism.* London: Cass, 1990.

Buckton, Oliver S. *Secret Selves: Confession and Same-Sex Desire in Victorian Autobiography.* Chapel Hill: University of North Carolina Press, 1998.

Caesar, Adrian. *Taking It Like a Man: Suffering, Sexuality, and the War Poets: Brooke, Sassoon, Owen, Graves.* Manchester, U.K.: Manchester University Press, 1993.

Cocks, H. G. *Nameless Offences: Homosexual Desire in the Nineteenth Century.* London: I. B. Tauris, 2003.

Cook, Matt. *London and the Culture of Homosexuality, 1885–1914.* Cambridge, U.K.: Cambridge University Press, 2003.

Copley, Antony. *A Spiritual Bloomsbury: Hinduism and Homosexuality in the Lives and Writings of Edward Carpenter, E. M. Forster, and Christopher Isherwood.* Lanham, Md.: Lexington, 2006.

d'Arch Smith, Timothy. *Love in Earnest: Some Notes on the Lives and Writings of English 'Uranian' Poets from 1889 to 1930.* London Routledge & Kegan Paul, 1970.

David, Hugh. *On Queer Street: A Social History of British Homosexuality 1895–1995.* London: HarperCollins, 1997.

Delavenay, Emile. *D. H. Lawrence and Edward Carpenter:*

A Study in Edwardian Transition. London: Heinemann, 1971.

Dixon, Joy. "Sexology and the Occult: Sexuality and Subjectivity in Theosophy's New Age." *Journal of the History of Sexuality* 7, no. 3: 409–433 (1997).

Doan, Laura. "The Outcast of One Age Is the Hero of Another: Radclyffe Hall, Edward Carpenter, and the Intermediate Sex." In *Palatable Poison: Critical Perspectives on "The Well of Loneliness."* Edited by Laura Doan and Jay Prosser. New York: Columbia University Press, 2001. pp. 162–178.

Elfenbein, Andrew. "Whitman, Democracy, and the English Clerisy." *Nineteenth-Century Literature* 56, no. 1: 76–104 (2001).

Fletcher, John. "Forster's Self-Erasure: *Maurice* and the Scene of Masculine Love." In *Sexual Sameness: Textual Differences in Lesbian and Gay Writing.* Edited by Joseph Bristow. London: Routledge, 1992. pp. 64–90.

Fone, Byrne, R. S. *A Road to Stonewall: Male Homosexuality and Homophobia in English and American Literature, 1750–1969.* New York: Twayne, 1995.

Geoghegan, Vincent. "Edward Carpenter's England Revisited." *History of Political Thought* 24, no. 3: 509–527 (2003).

Henderson, Linda Dalrymple. "Mysticism as the 'Tie That Binds': The Case of Edward Carpenter and Modernism." *Art Journal* 46: 29–37 (spring 1987).

Leib, Frank B. *Friendly Competitors, Fierce Companions: Men's Ways of Relating.* Cleveland, Ohio: Pilgrim Press, 1997.

Livesey, Ruth. "Morris, Carpenter, Wilde, and the Political Aesthetics of Labor." *Victorian Literature and Culture* 32, no. 2: 601–616 (2004).

Maiwald, Michael. "Race, Capitalism, and the Third-Sex Ideal: Claude McKay's *Home to Harlem* and the Legacy of Edward Carpenter." *Modern Fiction Studies* 48, no. 4: 825–857 (2002).

Martin, Robert K. "Edward Carpenter and the Double Structure of *Maurice.*" In *Literary Visions of Homosexuality.* Edited by Stuart Kellogg. New York: Haworth Press, 1983. pp. 35–46.

McCracken, Scott. "I Am the Lover and the Loved—I Have Lost and Found My Identity: Edward Carpenter and *Fin-de-Siècle* Masculinities." In *Signs of Masculinity: Men in Literature, 1700 to the Present.* Edited by Antony Rowland, Emma Liggins, and Eriks Uskalis. Amsterdam: Rodopi, 1998. pp. 139–161.

Pannapacker, William A. " 'The Bricklayer Shall Lay Me': Edward Carpenter, Walt Whitman, and Working-Class 'Comradeship.'" In *Mapping Male Sexuality: Nineteenth-Century England.* Edited by Jay Losey and William D. Brewer. Madison, N.J.: Fairleigh Dickinson University Press, 2000. pp. 277–298.

Pierson, Stanley. "Edward Carpenter, Prophet of a Socialist Millennium." *Victorian Studies* 13, no. 3: 301–318 (1970).

Rahman, Tariq. "The Alienated Prophet: The Relationship Between Edward Carpenter's Psyche and the Development of His Metaphysic." *Forum for Modern Language Studies* 23, no. 3: 193–209 (1987).

———. "Edward Carpenter and E. M. Forster." *Durham University Journal* 79, no. 1: 59–69 (1986).

———. "The Literary Treatment of Indian Themes in the Works of Edward Carpenter." *Durham University Journal* 80, no. 1: 77–81 (1987).

Rowbotham, Sheila. " 'Commanding the Heart': Edward Carpenter and Friends." *History Today* 37, no. 9: 41–46 (1987).

Sedgwick, Eve Kosofsky. *Between Men: English Literature and Male Homosocial Desire.* New York: Columbia University Press, 1985.

Simons, John. "Edward Carpenter, Whitman, and the Radical Aesthetic." In *Gender Roles and Sexuality in Victorian Literature.* Edited by Christopher Parker. Aldershot, U.K.: Scholar Press, 1995. pp. 115–127.

Weeks, Jeffrey. *Coming Out: Homosexual Politics in Britain from the Nineteenth Century to the Present.* London: Quartet, 1977.

Weir, Lorna. "Cosmic Consciousness and the Love of Comrades: Contacts between R. M. Bucke and Edward Carpenter." *Journal of Canadian Studies/Revue d'études canadiennes* 30, no. 2: 39–57 (1995).

CIARAN CARSON

(1948—)

Jonathan Baines

CIARAN CARSON IS a writer of astounding versatility. His reputation rests not so much on a single masterpiece—although several of his books, such as *The Irish for No*, (1987) and *The Star Factory*, (1997), certainly deserve such high praise—as on the great variety of his oeuvre, both within individual volumes and across generic boundaries. Over the last thirty years, he has produced seven major volumes of poetry, three books of verse in translation, two wonderfully idiosyncratic memoirs, and two highly unorthodox novels. His favorite subject is Belfast, Northern Ireland, the city where he has lived all his life, and of which he is now the undisputed, unofficial laureate. The visions of Belfast that Carson lays before the reader are so extraordinary that his achievement merits comparison with that of Dickens's London or Joyce's Dublin. Belfast, however, is by no means his only subject. The subtitle of *Last Night's Fun* (1996) gives a good indication of the breadth of his interests: it is declared to be a book "about music, food and time." Carson's enthusiasms are eclectic, but even the most unlikely ones become infectious in his handling of them. They include—to give the briefest selection—etymology, hagiography (the biography of the lives of saints), philately (stamp-collecting), traditional Irish music, the amber trade, the underground rivers of Belfast, and the perfect breakfast. His home ground is "honeycombed with oxymoron and diversion" and a place where "the tiny ancillary moments of your life assume an almost legendary status" (*The Star Factory*, p.70). His poems are often distinguished by an unusually long line, the most basic function of which is to keep as many elements in play as possible. Carson's work is in thrall to the overwhelming abundance of sense—impressions that the city makes available, and the maelstrom of associations they can induce; it is ignited by the possibility that the medium of literature might render both the welter of the quotidian and the ever-expanding "contents of the memory theatre" (p. 67) with a shocking immediacy. In accordance with its ambition to achieve immediacy, Carson's writing privileges music, orality, and the art of storytelling. He is a gifted flautist and singer. In a 1989 interview to mark the publication of his third book of poems, *Belfast Confetti*, he talks about his renunciation of poetry in favor of music:

> I got a job in the Arts Council about 1975...the job was concerned with traditional music, song and dance, so I started to get absorbed into that whole area of experience. After a year or two it struck me that poetry, or poems, were so remote by comparison. Removed, academic. Whereas with the music—you're right up against the stuff, it's hitting you from all sides, it's alive, here in front of your very eyes and ears, right now. That's a very attractive immediacy. It's not about withdrawing into your cell to compose these careful utterances about life.

> *(Interview with Rand Brandes, p. 81)*

Carson's remarkable creativity since his return to poetry, and the development of his unique prose style, have been marked by a desire to integrate his feeling for music with the "careful utterances" distinctive of literature. At its most extreme, this can involve an appreciation of language that as nearly as possible divorces words from any of their regular meanings. More generally, he brings the sensibility of a musician to bear on the long lines of his poems: his musical ear helps to keep the cacophony of his subject matter in check.

The figure of Carson's father represents another possibility for negotiating the chaos of Belfast, and assumes a massive importance in Carson's more recent work. William Carson—also known by his Irish name Liam Mac Carráin—provides two principal sources of inspiration for his son's writing. Firstly, he worked as a postman for many years, and his son transforms this unromantic profession into a powerful metaphor for successful communication. Secondly, Carson's father was an author in his own right, who in 1986 published "a slim compendium of anecdote and memoir" (*The Star Factory*, p. 76), written in Irish. His son offers three possible translations of its title: *Here, There, and There Again*, or *This, That, and The Other*, or *Miscellanae*. Sections of the book, translated into English, are incorporated into Carson's own prose. Carson develops his father's practice of digression—and of digressions within digressions—deftly handling narrative developments that threaten to spool away into nonsense; he also inherits the skill of keeping a firm hold on the audience's attention. His childhood memories of his father's storytelling also play a major role in his work. William Carson features as one of the main characters in the novel *Fishing for Amber*, and the novel is dedicated to his memory.

Carson is an important figure in what is often referred to as the "Ulster Renaissance": the great burgeoning of literary activity in Northern Ireland that began in the mid-1960s and continues to this day. The difficulty of seeing him as part of a clearly defined literary movement should, however, be recognized. Scholars are increasingly keen to consider him as one of a trio of Northern Irish poets alongside his contemporaries Medbh McGuckian and Paul Muldoon. This trio has been described as the second generation of the Ulster Renaissance, following hard on the heels of three poets who began to make themselves heard in the mid-1960s: Seamus Heaney, Michael Longley, and Derek Mahon. The schema is neat—although "generation" is hardly the right word to describe an age gap of roughly ten years but something of an oversimplification. Carson's independence is evidenced by the notoriously hostile and frequently cited review of Seamus Heaney's *North* (1975), accusing Heaney of being "the laureate of violence—a mythmaker, an anthropologist of ritual killing, an apologist for 'the situation,' in the last resort, a mystifier"

("Escaped From The Massacre?", p. 183). Carson's stringent position in this review—his insistence that poetry must not aestheticize violence—is certainly bound up with the fact that he stopped writing his own poetry around this time. With the publication of *The Irish for No* after this hiatus, he demonstrated that his work is truly *sui generis* or the only one of its kind, unique.

BIOGRAPHICAL OUTLINE

Like his books, Carson's biography revolves around Belfast, where he was born on October 9, 1948. He describes himself as "the little piggy who stayed at home" ("Revised Version," *Belfast Confetti*, p. 57). The Carson family lived in the Lower Falls in West Belfast, an area that was home to a large number of the city's Catholic minority; it would become one of the districts to suffer the most severely during the Troubles. Carson attended St Gall's Public Elementary School, and his route there and back was in part determined by the fact that, as the child of a Catholic family, it was dangerous for him to walk the streets of the neighboring Protestant district of the Shankill, another part of town that became synonymous with violence in the early 1970s:

> *Never go by Cupar Street*, my father would warn me, and I knew this was a necessary prohibition without asking why, for Cupar Street was one of those areas where the Falls and Shankill joined together as unhappy Siamese twin, one sporadically and mechanically beating the other round the head
> ("Revised Version," *Belfast Confetti*, p. 59)

Carson has described his childhood sense of being not only part of a religious minority, but also a linguistic one, as a result of his parents' decision to speak exclusively in Irish to their children. "My father and mother weren't native speakers," he explains, "but learned at classes when I suppose they were in their late teens or early twenties" (Brandes, p. 77). The title of his fourth book of poems, *First Language*, alludes to this formative experience, which also contributes to his considerable skills as a translator.

CIARAN CARSON

When Carson was "about seven", his family moved "to a semi-detached housing estate in Andersonstown" (*Last Night's Fun*, p. 79) on the western fringes of Belfast. At age nine or ten, he transcribed the lyrics of "The Old Colonial Boy" into a notebook, an event that he subsequently came to see as a possible point of departure for his career as a writer, his interest in traditional music, and in the figure of the scribe (*Last Night's Fun*, pp. 161–2). Carson went to St Mary's Christian Brothers Grammar School, where the pedagogical methods helped to shape his intense fascination with, and his intense suspicion of, systems of classification:

> We learned lists of Latin, French and Irish words, together with their proper conjugations and declensions, their voices, tenses and moods; we sang names, dates, places, populations; we got poems, songs and recitations off by heart. We were expected to enumerate and name the angels' hierarchies, and know the function of the sacred vessels and accessories.
>
> (*The Star Factory*, p. 212)

In many different ways, lists and "recitations off by heart" would become a feature of Carson's work, most horrifyingly in the prose—poem "Question Time," in which the speaker is beaten by strangers who appear to be IRA men, and only released after listing the streets of the Catholic neighborhood where he grew up.

Carson's writing life began in earnest at the age of fifteen or sixteen, partly as a result of reading T. S. Eliot and Gerard Manley Hopkins. The following year, he hitchhiked to Castleblaney for his first *fleadh* (festival of traditional music). Between 1967 and 1971, he was "an ostensible student" of Queen's University, Belfast, where he studied English Literature and formed an important friendship with Paul Muldoon:

> Muldoon was writing amazing poems when he was a mere boy. [...] I knew Paul very well, from when he arrived in Belfast at about the age of eighteen. We seemed to hit it off well together. He and I would get together very often, but we wouldn't necessarily talk about poetry, or why you write. On the odd occasion, he might show me a poem and

I'd read it and say "Aye," or, "I think it works" and he might say, "Aye, I think so myself", or whatever.
(Brandes, p. 79)

Carson's first pamphlet of poems, *The Insular Celts,* was published in 1973. Its best poems were included in his debut volume, *The New Estate,* published in 1976. In 1978, he issued a second pamphlet, entitled *The Lost Explorer*. Around this time he became disillusioned with literature: "I was dissatisfied with poetry for some time; compared to the urgency of traditional music, which was engaging my attention, poetry seemed a rather anal and furtive pursuit" (interview with Frank Ormsby, p. 7). For almost a decade he dedicated his creative energies exclusively to traditional Irish music, but returned to poetry with a fresh conviction in the mid-1980s. Since the publication of *The Irish for No* in 1987 he has been very prolific as a poet, novelist, and translator.

From his late twenties until the year of his fiftieth birthday—between "about 1975" (Brandes, p. 81) and 1998—Carson worked for the Arts Council of Northern Ireland, firstly as the Traditional Arts Officer, and from 1991 as the Literature / Traditional Arts Officer. He worked to foster young talent and helped to disburse the government purse. He has been a Professor at Queen's University Belfast, and the Director of the Seamus Heaney Centre for Poetry. In 1982 he married Deirdre Shannon, a fiddle-player, and they have had three children together. "Interestingly," Carson remarks in a wry aside tucked away in a footnote to *Last Night's Fun*, "the nice eccentric priest wrote my name as 'Casson', and so it is on our marriage certificate. So, formally, Deirdre Shannon and I are probably not married at all" (p. 182). This playful sense of the uncertainties attendant upon even the most sacred things is central to Carson's work.

EARLY POETRY: THE NEW ESTATE (1976) AND THE LOST EXPLORER (1978)

Of all his books, Carson's debut volume of poems is the one that most closely resembles the productions of his Northern Irish contemporaries.

It consists exclusively of lyric poems, thirty-three in total, the majority of which do not extend to a second page. They are arranged in a loose chronological sequence which runs from the medieval matter of the opening "The Scribe in the Woods" and the poems about Saint Ciaran, through to the contemporary setting of "Fishes in a Chinese Restaurant", and the "marble [T]oilet fixtures, the silence of water-beds" and the "book of poems you bought yesterday" that make their appearance in the title poem, which itself closes the volume. Although explicit autobiography is absent from *The New Estate*—the only one of Carson's books about which such a statement can be made—any reader of *The Star Factory* cannot help but identify the "new estate" with the Mooreland housing estate in West Belfast, where the Carson family took up residence in the mid-1950s. This estate is, however, as much metaphysical as an actual location, and the book as a whole, despite certain misgivings and ironies, argues for the existence of a fragile continuity between the medieval scribe and the contemporary poet, living amongst "washing [that] flutters like the swaying lines |Of a new verse" (p. 41).

The fragility of this tradition is underlined by the prevailing themes of isolation, withdrawal, and silence, which are handled delicately, rather than dramatically. The impersonality of the volume is enhanced by the inclusion of five translations: three adapted from Early Irish, one from Welsh, and one from the work of the Greek poet, George Seferis. With its debt to the quieter moments of Sylvia Plath's work, "The Moon Parlour" is a representative poem:

Still no sign; she has quietly forgone
Our invitation. Our host is downcast, he gestures
As if dusting glass.
We handle his expensive china reverently,
Seeking gentle dislocations. My watch ticks
Slowly; pock-marks drizzle on the window.
Our illumination mists upon the lawn outside.

(*The New Estate*, p. 34)

Typically, the characters in the poem, though suggestively sketched, remain obscure. Just as there is "no sign" of the expected guest, there is barely a sign by which we might recognize those who have invited her. The poem deals with "pock-marks" rather than identifying marks; the reader is forced to handle the poem "reverently" partly because there is very little to get to grips with. *The New Estate* boasts a whole series of "gentle dislocations" like this: its minimalism gravitates towards the "silence in the space between" the double-glazing of the poem "Moving In" (p. 29).

This "space" sets off the more solid virtues of the traditional crafts celebrated in "The Casting of the Bell" and "Interior with Weaver." The situation of the speaking voice of the latter poem is reminiscent of Heaney's sonnet "The Forge": it is the first, most benign, of Carson's allusions to the work of the older poet. "Interior with Weaver" and "The Forge" both place their central figures in the darkness of a rural building, with the speaker outside, looking in. Carson's "All we can see of him..." recalls Heaney's phrase "All I know is a door into the dark" (p. 10). That neither the blacksmith nor the weaver can be seen clearly allows for the possibility that their trades are receding into redundancy, and that the poems should be read as elegies, but in both cases there is an insistence on the tenacity of these forms of industry such that the darkness comes to represent the mystery of their preservation and, indeed, the preservation of a "mystery," in its archaic sense of "profession."

The New Estate also praises a more modern form of artistry in "Engraving from a Child's Encyclopaedia":

You can clearly see the etched lines on the plate,
how many hours of trouble went in making this

(p. 15)

Admiration for the execution of painstaking detail develops into a considerable theme later in Carson's career, culminating in the vivid treatment of the Golden Age of Dutch painting in the seventeenth century woven into the fabric of *Fishing for Amber*. In the context of *The New Estate,* the "etched lines" of the illustrations in the encyclopedia focus our attention on the six woodcuts that illustrate the volume. These are reproduced from *De Re Metallica* by Georgius Agricola, a seminal late medieval work examining metallurgy and sixteenth-century developments in mining in central Europe. Originally intended to help explain new building techniques, the illustrations provide a visual echo of the image of the new estate itself, and add an extra dimension to the book's tentative celebration of tradition.

Compared to the careful composition of *The New Estate,* the pamphlet *The Lost Explorer* is something of a jumble. With hindsight, the majority of its ten poems seem to include premonitions of Carson's decade-long poetic silence. They are preoccupied with passivity: if the explorer of the title knew where he or she was, then some decisive action could be taken. As it is, most of the poems remain in limbo. The irresolution in the pamphlet calls to mind great possibilities—anything could happen—but, because nothing yet has, the lyrics tend to run into painful and bathetic dead ends. The negativity is made all the more acute by the exotic settings of some of the poems. The speaker of "East of Cairo," for example, is a young traveler who reflects bitterly on the apparent failure of his trip of self-discovery. The poem ends, however, with an unexpectedly ethereal evocation of the Dalai Lama.

This swerve away from the brash despondency of the poem's opening recalls the "gentle dislocations" of *The New Estate* and makes "East of Cairo" one of the pamphlet's most successful poems.

The pamphlet's other notable inclusion, "The Patchwork Quilt," is exceptional in that it contains the seeds of themes and techniques that come to their fruition in *The Irish for No,* where the poem is reworked and extended as "Patchwork." Carson reveals for the first time his gift for committing spoken language to the page. The speaker describes in detail a quilt that has been twenty years in the making.

This heterogeneity looks forward to Carson's engagement with the city and with memory, and the everyday miracle of the quilt represents his ability to make the most chaotic material hang together.

THE IRISH FOR NO *(1987)* *AND* BELFAST CONFETTI *(1989)*

The Irish for No is a book of pivotal importance in Carson's career. It is a maverick performance that displays his use of the long line to full advantage for the first time, and its poems still retain their capacity to surprise. The volume's tremendous verve and inventiveness are a world away from the cautious lyrics of the 1970s. Its publication was not merely a watershed in Carson's own career, but in the literary culture of Northern Ireland. As the critic John Goodby has aptly put it: "The most radical transformation of the Northern Irish poetry scene of the late 1980s occurred with the reappearance of Ciaran Carson" (*Irish Poetry Since 1950,* p. 290). *Belfast Confetti,* appearing two years after *The Irish for No,* is very much its companion volume. Both books showcase Carson's arresting powers of observation. They have a documentary quality that unforgettably captures a city which, by the late 1980s, had suffered over twenty years of civil unrest. The poems square up to the cityscape: "Everything unstitched, unravelled—mouldy fabric, [R]usted heaps and bolts, electrical spare parts [...] as the charred beams hissed and flickered, I glimpsed a map of Belfast [I]n the ruins" (*The Irish for No,* "Smithfield Market," p. 37). Between them, *The Irish for No* and *Belfast Confetti* provide a map of a ruined city, and the very care with which they do so points to ways in which it might be rebuilt.

The title *The Irish for No* refers to the absence of single words for "yes" and "no" in the Irish language: agreement and disagreement are expressed instead by reiteration of the verb, with a negative attached if necessary. This feature of the language guarantees—or at least provides for—garrulity, and is therefore in keeping with the wildly digressive narrative poems that open and close the book. In between these two groups of longer poems we find sixteen lyrics that resemble misshapen sonnets, with lines that can stretch to more than twenty syllables, and in place of octet and sestet, a stanza of five lines followed by a four-line stanza. Each poem resembles a snapshot of the city, or a short film, with the emphasis on disintegration and transmogrification, frequently as a result of the Troubles, but also registering other upheavals distinctive of the 1980s, such as the redevelopment and reappropriation of urban sites. Carson returns again and again to hole-in-the-wall taxi operations—which might or might not be fronts for illegal activity—each of which are fitted up with "a wire grille and a voice-box uttering gobbledygook" ("Night Patrol," p. 34). This "voice-box" comes to represent the various strains of "gobbledygook" that noisily constitute the life of Belfast. The poems are alert to, and constantly question, the competing discourses that seek to control the way we read a city.

Carson exchanges the careful, limpid diction of *The New Estate* for a colloquial, idiomatic register. The first lines of *The Irish for No's* magnificent opening poem, "Dresden", take clichés and make them do the work of convincing us that we are in the presence of a fluid and engaging raconteur: something "is anybody's guess...But that's another story...At any rate...to tell you the truth" (p. 11). The speaker is also distinguished by his penchant for self-correction, another feature that enables the text to approach the condition of spoken language. The narrative typically proceeds by presenting us with a piece of information—"I stayed there once"—and then turning back on itself in order to qualify the original statement—"Or rather, I nearly stayed there once." As well as integrating the practice of storytelling with poetry, the inclusion of these on-the-hoof adjustments manifests an exploration of the workings of memory, another of Carson's obsessive themes. *The Irish for No* draws an extended comparison between memory and the city, both riddled with holes, and endeavors to establish, in the face of the violence of the Troubles, a fruitful relationship between the two.

False starts and ambiguities characterize Carson's narrative poems, which savour their "in-between-ness," their being "neither [O]ne thing nor the other" (*Belfast Confetti,* "Loaf," p. 15); his squashed sonnets favor a much sharper outline. They also deal in disconcerting clashes of register, accommodating, for example, the

lexicon of military jargon alongside spoken language:

A Saracen, Kremlin-2 mesh. Makrolon face-shields. Walkie-talkies. What is
My name? Where am I coming from? Where am I going? A fusillade of question-marks.
(*The Irish for No,* "Belfast Confetti", p. 31)

The juxtaposition of the direct, plaintive questions, which are simultaneously existential, banal, and threatening, alongside the outlandish nomenclature of the soldiers' hardware, creates a friction that is at the heart of Carson's poetry. The phrase "Belfast confetti" carries a similar charge, pulled in different directions by its connotations of harmony and festivity, and its colloquial meaning of the "ammunition&hellip:tried and tested by generations of rioters" *Belfast Confetti,* "Brick," 72), the handfuls of debris gleaned from the shattered city.

belfast confetti expands the blueprint of *the irish for no,* maintaining its tripartite arrangement—two suites of narrative poems, either side of a series of squashed sonnets—but interleaving prose meditations between the shorter poems, and versions of Japanese haikus between the longer ones. The book's structure is thus perfectly symmetrical, and invites comparisons between pieces that occupy corresponding positions in each of the book's halves, and further comparisons between pieces in *Belfast Confetti* and their opposite numbers in *The Irish for No.* This elaborate construction reproduces the labyrinthine nature of the city that the books celebrate: it also, appropriately enough, leads very often to apparent dead ends. The echo-chamber effect resembles the accident that occurs in the course of "The Queen's Gambit":

as someone spills a cup of tea on a discarded *irish news*
a minor item bleeds through from another page, blurring the main story
(p. 38)

this enshrines both carson's narrative method and his sense of the city as composed of multiple layers that all have their claim upon our attention, but are often only revealed by chance.

the inclusion of short prose pieces provides another means of investigating the sediment of memory and what we might term the contemporary archaeology of the city. the reduction of linguistic pressure that prose entails enables carson to take a more leisurely tour of the city:

at times it seems that every inch of belfast has been written-on, erased, and written-on again: messages, curses, political imperatives, but mostly names, or nicknames—Robbo, Mackers, Scoot, Fra— sometimes litanized obsessively on every brick of a gable wall, as high as the hand will reach, and sometimes higher, these snakes and ladders cancelling each other out in their bid to be remembered. *remember 1690. remember 1916. most of all, remember me. i was here.*

(*schoolboys and idlers of pompeii*, p. 52)

belfast is transformed into a palimpsest that both defies the reader and throws open the floodgates of interpretation. the graffiti "litanized obsessively" provides a counterpart to Carson's own cataloging—"Ireland's Entry, Elbow Lane, Weigh-House Lane, Back Lane, Stone-Cutter's Entry" ("Turn Again," p. 11)—and the observation that some of it is written "higher" than we could reach conjures up the possibility of some agency other than the human conspiring to create carson's visions of belfast.

FIRST LANGUAGE (1993) AND OPERA ET CETERA (1996)

the focus of *first language* is not trained so unrelentingly on the city. it is a book packed with allusions to the troubles, but—to a borrow a phrase from Carson's version of Arthur Rimbaud's "Le Bateau Ivre"—they are "slabbered with a monster's verbiage" (p. 36). The poems often put language first, in the sense that it can be difficult for the reader to get with any degree of confidence beyond the music of their language to a meaning that is capable of being stated simply. On the whole, the narratives of *The Irish for No* and *Belfast Confetti* can be readily followed: in fact, they compel the reader's attention. In contrast, the stories told in *First Language* often disintegrate altogether. The emphasis is on

the capacity of spoken language to tip over into a kind of babble, or a kind of Babel. The pun on "babble" and "Babel" is central to the book and is given greater prominence by the cartoonish painting of the Tower of Babel reproduced on its cover. *First Language* is not, however, solely concerned with the phenomenon—at once disconcerting and exhilarating—of language being gabbled and garbled. It also features several translations, or versions: three based on passages from Ovid's *Metamorphoses,* two poems "after" sonnets by Baudelaire, one "after" the Irish poet Seán Ó Ríordáin, and "Drunk Boat", the book's centerpiece, Carson's take on Rimbaud. These acts of translation indicate a faith in language as a bearer of significance, and the volume derives much of its power from the tension between this conviction and all the forms of "blah" ("All Souls," p. 40) that carson recreates with such panache.

the prevalence of "blah" is related to Carson's belief that nothing is ever forgotten absolutely. "On Not Remembering Some Lines Of A Song" dramatizes this axiom:

it's coming back in dribs and drabs, for nothing ever is forgotten: it's in there somewhere in the memory-bank, glimmering in binary notation.

(p. 27)

this apparently optimistic attitude is developed in a distressing direction: a direction inherent in the cold, science-fiction quality of the metaphor that renders human memory in "binary notation". In some respects it is comforting to believe that nothing gets completely forgotten: at the same time, however, it is an overwhelming and nightmarish possibility. The "memory-bank" has more sensations and information deposited within it than our waking consciousness can cope with: to remember everything can be a form of madness. *first language* captures the quality of this nightmare precisely.

one of carson's techniques for achieving this end is collage. the poem "Four Sonnets" is the most extended example of this method. With a different title, it would not be immediately obvious that the four sections are relatives of the sonnet: each consists of fourteen very long lines, unrhymed, and each set apart in its own stanza. Connections can be made with Carson's other work—"Put your ear to the street, and you will hear the underground streams of Belfast" (p. 22)—but they are eclipsed by the way the poem stubbornly disconnects one line from the next. Some motifs recur—clocks and puppets, for example—but there is no means of establishing a narrative; there is much reported speech, but no dialogue to be identified. Tantalizingly, aspects of the poem almost cohere, and many of the poem's images self-referentially stand for an idea of order that is just out of reach: "I was trying to tell the time when I swallowed a lemon pip from my sixth or seventh gin-and-tonic" (p. 25). Unable to put all these pieces together, we are thrown back to the possibility of reading the poem for the sound of its language.

The poem "Second Language" recounts a dream vision about Carson's earliest linguistic experiences, which include the apprehension of "Wordy whorls and braids and skeins and spiral helices" (p. 10). In this poem, the consciousness of the child is used to counteract the centripetal energies of language; in others, narrators reminiscent of the storytellers from Carson's earlier books go some way toward fulfilling this role. In *Opera Et Cetera,* the lyrics take their cue from "Four Sonnets" and become increasingly antagonistic to notions of explanation, legibility, and clarity. *Opera Et Cetera* is Carson's most surreal book. Whereas the translations in *First Language* counterpoint its more mercurial aspects, the versions of lyrics by the Romanian poet Stefan Augustin Doinas are quite in keeping with the other poems of *Opera Et Cetera.* The book alternates between forms of ecstasy and paranoia. The first of its four sections, "Letters From The Alphabet," is a series of twenty-four poems, each consisting of five long-lined couplets. Some of the letters are personified—we can imagine them as writing the "Letters" of the title and sending them to the reader—others are imagined as objects, or given multiple roles to play. The poems have one foot in Belfast, one in a bizarre fantasy, and their head in the clouds:

K is the leader of the empty orchestra of karaoke.
K is the conductor on the wrong bus that you took

today and landed you in yesterday
Where everything was skew. The rainbow colours
  were all out of kilter,
Like oil had leaked out all over the road from a
  dropped and broken philtre.
There, no one wanted to be recognised, and walked
  around in wrap-round Polaroids.

(*K*, p. 21)

Opera Et Cetera is enamored with things in disguise—and the odder the better, hence the "wrap-round Polaroids"—and with things that are "out of kilter." The Latin tags that provide the titles for the sequence "Et Cetera," for the reader with no Latin, come under both of these categories. "Jacta est alea"—"the die is cast"—dramatizes the volume's refusal to have any truck with common sense or dialogue:

We end up talking about talk. We stagger on the
  frontier.
    He is pro. I am con.
Siamese-like, drunken, inextricable, we wade
    into theRubicon.

(*Jacta est alea* p. 44)

The proverbial significance of crossing the Rubicon is turned on its head: Carson recasts the decisive moment preserved by the tag as the infinite postponement of decision. It is perhaps just possible to imagine this plunge into the Rubicon as a triumphant moment, but it is easier to see it as a kind of despair.

A number of fictional detectives are written into "Opera," the book's last section. Their presence is intended to bring home how unlikely it would be, even for a reader with the deductive powers of Sherlock Holmes, to straighten out the poem's ferociously tangled narrative. In one respect, "Opera" seems a perverse choice of title: the action of an opera, though it might very well be melodramatic or preposterous, is usually easily followed. Carson's "Opera" constantly hints at the presence of a legible narrative, but delights in throwing the reader off the scent: it deals in red herrings and perverse lexical choices. In another respect, however, the title "Opera" is appropriate: the narrative, or lack of it, often appears to be merely a vehicle for the raucous music of the poem's language. Formally, it mirrors "Letters From The Alphabet," with each of the twenty-four lyrics named after a term in radio operator's code—"Alpha," "Bravo," "Charlie," and so on. While the code is designed to reduce the possibility of confusion, with the words chosen expressly so that the receiver would be highly unlikely to mistake one for another, Carson's lyrics actively seek to maximize confusion. When using the code, it is helpful to discount the associations of the words, and to treat them as twenty-four counters, pointing only to their initial letters. "Opera" reintroduces these associations and incorporates further obscure and often seemingly arbitrary connections, sometimes prompted by concerns that are, as nearly as possible, solely textual or musical, entirely discounting the ordinary meanings of the words. "Kilo", for example, ostensibly concerns a "rendezvous"— one that has yet to occur—"in a Falls Road taxi." In its final line, as if from nowhere, Maigret appears:

Maigret blew a cloud of briar smoke and spoke: *Lo-Ki? Kilo? O.K.! K.O.!*

(p. 77)

The anagram "Lo-Ki" ironically echoes the word "low-key" from earlier in the poem: "low-key" is the last thing *Opera Et Cetera* aspires to be. The danger is that Maigret's "briar smoke" might choke the reader to death, or at least knock her out.

MEMOIRS: LAST NIGHT'S FUN *(1996) AND* THE STAR FACTORY *(1997)*

Both of Carson's memoirs have their genesis in earlier works. *Last Night's Fun* takes off from his irreverent, but informative, *Pocket Guide to Traditional Irish Music* (1986). It has at its heart Carson's long-standing love of the traditional music scene. Like the *Pocket Guide*, but on a larger scale, it features versions of stories, lyrics, poems, jokes, sleeve notes, extracts from essays and interviews with musicians. *The Star Factory* is similarly compendious—these works frequently have about them the feel of an almanac or a scrapbook—and has its origins in the prose vignettes of *Belfast Confetti*. It is Carson's great

hymn to Belfast, a vivid record of dream visions of the city, shuttling between the present moment of writing and the adventures of childhood, and touching on a whole host of other destinations, historical and imaginative, en route. While the chapters of *Last Night's Fun* are named after folk tunes, so that the contents-page constitutes a kind of set list upon which the memoir works virtuoso variations, most of the chapters in *The Star Factory* are named for a location in Belfast, either a street or a building, which makes the book resemble an unusual gazetteer. Carson's imagination is fired by a copy of the *Belfast Street Directory* for 1948, the year of his birth, and his own book transforms the notion of a dry and functional catalog, represented by the *Directory,* into a surreal love letter to the city.

It is slightly misleading to think of *Last Night's Fun* and *The Star Factory* simply as memoirs. They both eschew a chronological approach, preferring to surrender themselves to the promptings of memory, and happily skip back and forth across the decades. They also dispense with any ambition to be comprehensive. We might expect a memoir to try and account for everything of personal significance during a given period of time, but Carson's prose extravagantly flouts these expectations. This dovetails beautifully with the conception of traditional music developed in the *Pocket Guide* and *Last Night's Fun*. For Carson, "tradition" is not something monumental, but something always in process and always subject to change. The fun that the book has with personal pronouns helps to bring this observation home: the "I" reminiscing, often in the present tense, about a particular musical evening will at times give way to a "you," gently unfixing the idea that the reader and the narrator occupy fixed, final positions.

Last Night's Fun sumptuously recreates the atmosphere of a traditional music session in the corner of a pub, and relishes the banter of the musicians and the ritual of breakfast the following morning. Fondly recreating the fantastical pub talk that underpins the whole volume, Carson draws a comparison between the preparation of breakfast and the previous night's performance:

If traditional musicians are engaged with constant repetition and renewal, infinite fine-tunings and shades of rhythms, variations on the basic, cooks are even more so. ...The freshness of the egg, the weather, the altitude, the water, whether you add salt or not, and whether you start from cold or boiling: all these are important factors in what seems a simple operation.

(p. 15)

The idea of "variations on the basic" takes on a huge importance in *Last Night's Fun*. It is in such "variations" that music lives. The melody might be terrifically simple, its ingredients as unremarkable as an egg, but "it does not know the printed confines of the dotted crotcheted page" (p.160). *Last Night's Fun* celebrates performance and spontaneity. It is only in the context of performance that the "variations" can be appreciated: "The song must *be*. It must be sung right *now*, contemporaneously" (p. 160).

Carson's advocacy of performance is—at times with a dash of irony—reinforced by his habit of date-stamping his prose with a flourish: "As I write, it is two minutes to midnight on the twelfth of December 1994..." (p. 34). This practice self-consciously turns the act of writing into a performance and *The Star Factory* takes it to far greater lengths. Not only is Carson apt to take time out to tell us that, at the moment of writing, it is "7.15 p.m. on 8 April 1997" (p. 223), he also opens his narrative to moment-by-moment reports of its own creation. When uncertain of a detail pertaining to the bonfires he remembers from his childhood, he telephones his brother Pat for corroboration. Pat is unable to confirm or deny the veracity of the detail, but remembers some further details, that themselves become part of the narrative. Elsewhere, talking the reader through a calendar illustrated with Belfast photographs, Carson reaches November and "the defunct Brown Horse Bar," but cannot recall what stands in its place: "Annoyed by this lapse of memory, I jump into the car and drive down to where it was" (p. 94). Because it is as much about the process of remembering as it is about the memories themselves, *The Star Factory* is both a memoir and a diary. This hybridity is present in all life writing, but the degree of Carson's emphasis on the present is unusual and charm-

ingly effective. The reader shares a quiet wonder at the fact that the territory of *The Star Factory,* the province of memory, will always exceed any map made of it. As Carson writes after one of the book's many lavishly detailed catalogs: "these are *but some* of the objects I retrieved just now, perusing one adjacent drawer of the table under the machine on which I'm typing" (p. 68).

One of the haul of childhood memories recounted in *The Star Factory* concerns the family saying the rosary together during Carson's childhood. Here and elsewhere, he is silent on the subject of his current religious beliefs, but throughout *The Star Factory* there is a rich seam of religious metaphor, which gives weight to a wide variety of scenes and items. A bend in the river behind the Mooreland housing estate is shaded by a "clerestory of branches," beneath which it "was easy to imagine dim organ-music in this miniature cathedral" (p. 99); a copy of Henry Fielding's *Joseph Andrews* is imagined as a "pocket icon" (p. 225); a Singer sewing machine under its cover "looked like a small catafalque or tabernacle on an altar" (p. 139); cornershops are possessed of "chapel-vestibule gloom" (p. 181); and his father's bedtime story is compared to "Midnight Mass" (p. 142). The book's other striking recurrent metaphor is writing, or the alphabet: a goods-trains pulls a "hundred and something modules of giant linear script" (p. 89); elsewhere, "Co-ordinated, countless sentences of starlings flit and sway in baroque paragraphs across the darkening sky, as they compose exploded founts of type" (p. 237). The builders of a new estate are recast as authors:

Had their basic modules been alphabet bricks, I could have seen them building lapidary sentences and paragraphs, as the storeyed houses became emboldened by their hyphenated, skyward narrative, and entered the ongoing, fractious epic that is Belfast.

(p. 126)

Carson's extended metaphors ensure that, within this reimagining of the growing city, the alphabet bricks become infused with spilt religion. His meditation on the 1948 *Belfast Street Directory* leads him to reflect on "the cabalistic or magical implications of the alphabet" (p. 7); a few chapters later, he announces: "Sometimes I am in religious awe of the power of names" (p. 43). Reading *The Star Factory*, it is hard not to assent to these supranational convictions. The memoir's success lies in Carson's ability to persuade us of the force of the poetic logic that governs memory, and informs our relationships with the city, but without letting these "magical implications" multiply to the extent that they obscure, or undermine, the remarkable feats of self-revelation that make the book unique.

FICTION: FISHING FOR AMBER (2000) AND SHAMROCK TEA (2001)

Fishing for Amber reworks in prose the alphabeticizing of *Opera Et Cetera* on a grander scale. Its chapters run from "Antipodes" to "Zoetrope." Many of the titles qualify as exotic ("Helicon," "Io," "Jacinth"), but the rarefied atmosphere implicit in such choices is complicated by some abstract choices ("Whereabouts," "Ramification"), and deflated by some humorously banal ones ("Kipper," "Xerox"). Like the surreal poems of *Opera Et Cetera,* the chapters are wont to detach themselves from their titles. They usually include at least two distinct narratives, often only one of which will maintain some connection with the title. Furthermore, the title sometimes corresponds to a small detail in a given chapter, apparently with no broader relevance to the chapter as a whole. The relationship, therefore, between the abecedary on the contents page and the contents of the book is an extremely playful one, even more so than Carson's two memoirs. In fact, *Fishing for Amber* is the most playful of his books, and its tricksy titles are only part of the story.

Carson's debut novel announces itself not as a novel, but as "a long story," thus casually inventing a new genre. The book is actually a miscellany of over fifty short stories: the "long story" is, among other things, the story of how all these other stories found themselves between the covers of a single book. The shortest answer is that every chapter touches upon "amber." Carson positively revels in the fact that his choice of a single theme seems to have the effect of diversi-

fying rather than unifying his book. An historical account of the Teutonic Knights controlling the amber trade in the fifteenth century and a folktale in which some amber jewelry plays only a cameo role are given equal weight in the book's freewheeling, inclusive universe. This approach brings out an ambiguity in the title: *Fishing for Amber* is both a record of Carson's somewhat haphazard research into amber—his fishing trips in search of references to amber include a sublime evocation of New York Public Library—and a metaphor for the unusual reading experience that the novel provides. Within each chapter we fish both for amber and for its significance: a pursuit that can call for considerable reserves of readerly patience.

The short stories that make up the "long story" are drawn from a wide variety of sources. The sheer diversity of the materials powerfully resists summary, but some headway can be made by considering the book's different narrators. First, we have a narrator called Carson. The book encourages us to make no distinction between this narrator and the author. In the course of the book's action—that is, in the rare intervals when we are not listening to a story being told—Carson visits The Netherlands with his wife, goes to hear a series of stories performed by his father, and spends time in a pub on the shores of Lough Neagh, in Northern Ireland, with a Dutchman called Jan Both and a Polish sailor called Jarniewicz. These four men—Carson, Carson's father, Jan Both, and Jarniewicz—narrate most of the novel, but just as the chapters drift away from their titles, it is easy to forget who is telling which particular story. Stories spawn stories, and things that at first seem to be incidental repeatedly elbow aside what we had taken to be the dominant narrative. There is no reliable narrator to help to keep the others in check. To further complicate things, the identity of a particular narrator is sometimes only made apparent after the fact.

We only learn, for example, at the start of the following chapter that the contents of "Nemesis" have been spoken aloud by Carson for the pleasure and instruction of Jan Both. "Nemesis" opens with a reworking of a story from Ovid's

Metamorphoses that tells of the origin of amber. It is rendered in a stirring present tense, and often in headlines. This gives way to an extract from Pliny the Elder, scornfully providing a survey of explanations as to where amber comes from and ridiculing them one by one. Pliny is followed by a brief digression on some Chinese lore and customs regarding bees, with honey deemed to be a distant cousin of amber. Finally, we are presented with a Lithuanian folktale that identifies the source of amber in tears wept by a mermaid whose fisherman lover has been struck dead with a thunderbolt by her divine husband. This last narrative is by no means told for laughs, but rather delivered in good storybook fashion.

A précis of "Nemesis" provides a useful sense of the book's ardor for the miscellaneous and of the varying tones of voice in which its stories are told. They are held together less by the recurrence of amber than by a belief in the value of a story well told. Jarniewicz reminisces briefly about his father, who resembles Carson's father and in turn stands for an ideal. The allusion to Coleridge's "Kubla Khan" and "Rime of the Ancient Mariner" pinpoints the book's ambition: to gather stories that do not give up their meaning as a nut cracked reveals a nut, but rather come into their own in the act of being retold.

Shamrock Tea, like *Fishing for Amber,* is painstakingly divided into sections of equal length. The 101 chapters, each three pages long, call to mind *The Thousand and One Nights,* flagging once again Carson's love of narrative deferral. Every chapter is named after a color—with the exception of the last, entitled "Blank"—transforming the novel into a bizarre box of paints featuring everything from the fantastic ("Dragon's Blood") to the everyday ("Brick Red"). It is no exaggeration to state that many of the novel's scenes are truly bizarre. Unlike *Fishing for Amber,* there is a more-or-less conventional plot—not quite submerged by the energetic divagations into the lives and work of saints, philosophers, and artists—albeit a plot distinguished by its towering absurdity and total irresolution. In brief, the principal narrator is again called Carson, and was born in Belfast in the year of the author's birth. He tells the story

of his childhood: shortly after going away to boarding school, he was enlisted by a secret society called the Ancient Order of Hibernians to travel through time with two young companions to fifteenth-century Bruges. Their mission was to gather a sufficient quantity of the hallucinogenic known as shamrock tea to render the water supply of Belfast highly potent. The narcotic effect would be such, according to the Hibernians, that the citizens of Belfast would forget their differences and live in harmony.

One of the book's central conceits is that art provides an experience so intense as to utterly reorder one's consciousness. Within the frame of the novel, this point is made by the fact that a perfectly executed painting can provide access to another world. The Hibernians can, therefore, use Jan van Eyck's *Arnolfini Double Portrait* as a time-machine to put their plan into action. Similarly, aided by a little shamrock tea, Carson and his cousin Berenice inadvertently use a copy of van Eyck's painting as a portal to the Silent Valley dam, the very spot earmarked for the introduction of shamrock tea on a larger scale. Maeterlinck—the third child selected by the Hibernians for the mission—is held to be a particularly suitable choice because he has already paid a visit to fifteenth-century Ghent courtesy of a stained-glass window depicting the Angel Gabriel. Set down baldly like this, *Shamrock Tea* sounds preposterous, and it is. The plot is intended to have a comic dimension, but a more serious point is being made as well. The novel circles around a cluster of interconnected themes, all of which function as a metaphor for aesthetic experience: illness, convalescence, intoxication, flight, and time-travel. All these states of mind allow for a mode of perception that imbibing shamrock tea guarantees. The narrator's eccentric Uncle Celestine—who turns out to be a key Hibernian—articulates this condition, imagining a future in which the inhabitants of Belfast have had their tap water spiked:

> They will see the world as it really is, a world in which everything connects; where the Many is One, and the One is Many. There will be no division, for everything in the real world refers to something else, which leads to something else again, in a

CIARAN CARSON

never-ending hymn of praise. The world is an eternal story.

(p. 236)

Both of Carson's novels sponsor this mysticism, which once again echoes Coleridge, while ironically undermining it. The dream of "no division" remains a dream: the world is only "an eternal story" within Carson's fictional parameters.

RECENT POETRY: THE TWELFTH OF NEVER (1998) AND BREAKING NEWS (2003)

The Twelfth of Never has more in common with Carson's fiction than any other of his volumes of poetry. Like Fishing for Amber and Shamrock Tea, it operates according to a template. While the novels have chapters that are fastidiously kept to the same length, The Twelfth of Never is a sequence of seventy-seven near-sonnets, composed of twelve syllable lines, alexandrines, rather than the standard iambic pentameters. That each line should be augmented by two syllables often produces echoes of ballad meter. This effect is sometimes made more insistent by the placement of a caesura, or by rhetorical repetition:

There's muskets in the thatch, and pikestaffs in the hay,
And shot in butter barrels buried in the bog,
Extrapolated powder in the tin for tay;
And everything is wrapped in blue-as-gunsmoke fog.

(Lord Gregory, p. 47)

These balladic tendencies complement the numerous elements of Irish folk songs and ballads that are worked into the book, and constitute one of the major thematic strands running through the sequence. The interweaving of several incongruous strands offers another point of contact with Carson's fiction. Many of the poems are inspired by a trip Carson took to Japan in 1998; others have their genesis in Carson's reading about Napoleon's campaigns. Another major source of material is the 1798 rebellion of the United Irishmen. The book thus has something in com-

mon with Carson's experience of Japan: "Tokyo amazed me: ultra-modern on the surface; but go down an alleyway, enter a doorway, and you come across another world." (Mitsuko Ohno, p. 19).

All these ingredients make for a disorienting reading experience, but it is one which we are prepared for: from the off:

This is the land of the green rose and the lion lily,
Ruled by Zeno's eternal tortoises and hares,
Where everything is metaphor and simile:
Somnambulists, we stumble through this paradise
From time to time, like words repeated in our prayers,
Or storytellers who convince themselves that truths
are lies.

(Tib's Eve, p. 13)

The Twelfth of Never situates itself in a dream state, a parallel history conjured not least by the book's title. The epigraph, from Brewer's Dictionary of Phrase and Fable, explains that Saint Tib's Eve is celebrated "neither before Christmas Day nor after it" (p. 12). Carson chooses the twelfth in order that his "paradise" might offer some sort of imaginative alternative to July 12, the day on which Orangemen take to the streets of Northern Ireland to hold their annual marches; it also suggests Twelfth Night festivities and hence the notion of an epiphany, the moment at which the eternal enters into the mundane. The book is a mosaic of disparate fantasies—some ethereal, some violent—that has as its finale Carson's whole cast of characters ascending a "long ladder propped against the gates of Heaven" ("Envoy," p. 89). The individual scenes are vivid, unlike the intense confusion of Opera Et Cetera, but the net effect is hallucinatory and kaleidoscopic.

Carson's most recent book of poems, Breaking News, marks a startling departure. His long lines are pared back to units so short they resemble newspaper headlines. Some of the poems they form are composed of fewer words than can be found in individual lines in Carson's previous volumes. On these drastically reduced canvases, many of his preoccupations are reduced to their bare bones:

everyone is watching everybody
in the grey light
of surveillance

(*Blink*, p. 24)

The sensation of being watched—the "British Army [h]elicopter [p]oised" ("Home," p. 12) over the city casts a long shadow over the volume—seems to have determined the very form of the poems. One line gives way to the next with a rapidity that bespeaks paranoia. In the short poems that take up most of the book, Carson dispenses entirely with punctuation. This decision also images anxiety: it is as if the author is reluctant to loiter long enough to arrange the commas and periods. At any rate, the poems' building blocks are stark enough to determine their own syntax. Lots of them describe a similar trajectory, and it is the trajectory of breaking news. "Horse at Balaklava, 1854" is a good example: it describes the slaughter of a horse in the Crimean War, presenting us "one minute" with the horse in rude health, and "the next" with its flesh being torn by a shell. These temporal indications are all the more forceful because they occupy stanzas of their own, although the fact that the poem's longest stanza runs to seven words—"flowing mane [t]he picture of life"—means that the lyric is forceful from start to finish. Another key line that is given its own stanza is the single word "remark," offered as an imperative. This sequence—"one minute," "the next", "remark"—is characteristic of the volume, and the violent death of the warhorse and a bomb detonating in Belfast are described in the same unblinking manner (p. 18).

The book's title is broken into two poems: "Breaking" and "News." Together they present a car bomb in terms of "one minute" and "the next." The phrase "breaking news" corresponds to the ambition of the poems, their desire to break "news" open and make available to the reader that which the language of newspaper reports tends to muffle and distort. In "News," this goal finds an exact typographical equivalent when the "*Belfast Telegraph*" sign above a newsstand becomes, after the explosion, "*fast rap*" (p. 17). The news is, quite literally, broken up. One problem that the book comes up against is that in its concentration upon single incidents, there is no possibility of sustained narrative. This difficulty is addressed by placing alongside the brief, costive, broken lyrics, a series of poems dedicated to the first modern war correspondent, William Howard Russell, known in his own day as Balaclava Russell for his reports for *The Times* on the Crimean War, and later as Bull Run Russell as a result of his coverage of the American Civil War. Carson's poems are remakes of Russell's dispatches: "in many instances I have taken his words *verbatim*, or have changed them only slightly to accommodate rhyme and rhythm"(" *Notes*," p. 74). In contrast to the poems in the mold of "News," the poems inspired by Russell are packed to bursting with material detail: "What debris a ruined empire [l]eaves behind it!" ("Sedan," p. 71). *Breaking News* attacks the thorny question of the appropriate way to write about conflict by approaching it from two utterly different angles. In doing so, the volume seeks to break the hold that the media can have over our imaginations, and provides an alternative insight.

CONCLUSION

Carson's voice is an important one in the context of the "Ulster Renaissance," and more generally in contemporary Anglophone literature. It is to be hoped that his work will not be eclipsed by the substantial reputations of his compatriots Seamus Heaney and Paul Muldoon. His portrayals of Belfast are indispensable because they are neither disfigured by partisan zeal, nor have they been cowed by the monstrosity of the situation into an attitude of fence-sitting, or the repetition of platitudes. His various enterprises as a translator also deserve recognition and attention, not least the extraordinary, and extraordinarily ambitious, rendering of Dante's *Inferno*, in terza rima throughout, which was published in 2003. Carson thrives on the exactions of large-scale formal challenges. The linguistic precision with which he undertakes them is matched, paradoxically, by the intense attraction of everything that exceeds formal limitations. His multifaceted celebration of "the ongoing, fractious epic that is Belfast" (SF, p. 126) always gives due emphasis to that adjective "ongoing." He is a poet of the provisional, the digressive, the oblique—a list that, not insignificantly, could go on. His poetry teaches us to be suspicious of all overly pat conclusions: not a lesson that is learned in a hurry.

Selected Bibliography

WORKS OF CIARAN CARSON

The Insular Celts. Belfast: Ulsterman Publications, 1973.

"Escaped From The Massacre?" a review of Seamus Heaney's *North. The Honest Ulsterman* 50, Winter 1975, pp. 183–186.

The New Estate. Belfast: Blackstaff Press, 1976.

The Lost Explorer. Belfast: Ulsterman Publications, 1978.

The Pocket Guide to Irish Traditional Music. Belfast: Appletree Press, 1986.

The Irish for No. Dublin: Gallery Press, 1987.

Belfast Confetti. Oldcastle: Gallery Press, 1989.

First Language. Loughcrew: Gallery Press, 1993.

Last Night's Fun. London: Jonathan Cape, 1996.

Opera Et Cetera. Newcastle upon Tyne: Bloodaxe Books, 1996.

The Star Factory. London: Granta, 1997.

The Alexandrine Plan: versions of sonnets by Baudelaire, Mallarmé, and Rimbaud. Oldcastle, County Meath: Gallery Press, 1998.

The Twelfth of Never. Oldcastle, County Meath: Gallery Press, 1998.

Fishing for Amber. London: Granta, 1999.

The Ballad of HMS Belfast: A Compendium of Belfast Poems. London: Picador, 1999.

Shamrock Tea. London: Granta, 2001.

The Inferno of Dante Alighieri: A New Translation. London: Granta, 2002.

Breaking News. Oldcastle, Co. Meath: Gallery Press, 2003.

The Midnight Court: a new translation of Cúirt an Mhéan Oíche by Brian Merriman. Oldcastle, Co. Meath, Ireland: Gallery Press, 2005.

CRITICAL AND BIOGRAPHICAL STUDIES

Brandes, Rand, "Ciaran Carson," an interview held in Madden's Bar, Belfast, 8 August 1989. *The Irish Review* 8, Spring 1990, pp. 77-90.

Clark, Heather, *The Ulster Renaissance: Poetry in Belfast 1962–1972.* Oxford: Oxford University Press, 2006.

Corcoran, Neil, *Poets of Modern Ireland: Text, Context, Intertext.* Cardiff: Univeristy of Wales Press, 1999.

Gillis, Alan, and Aaron Kelly, eds., *The Cities of Belfast.* Dublin: Four Courts Press, 2003.

Goodby, John, *Irish Poetry Since 1950.* Manchester: Manchester University Press, 2000.

Ohno, Mitsuko, "Hokusai, Basho, Zen and More: Japanese Influences on Irish Poets." *Jornal of Irish Studies* (IASIL–JAPAN), 17: 15–31 (2000).

MacDonald, Peter, *Mistaken Identities: Poetry and Northern Ireland.* Oxford: Clarendon Press, 1997.

McCracken, Kathleen, "Ciaran Carson: Unravelling the Conditional, Mapping the Provisional," in Michael Kenneally, ed., *Poetry in Contemporary Irish Literature.* Gerrards Cross: Colin Smythe, pp. 356–72.

Murphy, Shane, "Sonnets, Centos and Long Lines: Muldoon, Paulin, McGuckian and Carson," in Matthew Campbell, ed., *The Cambridge Companion to Contemporary Irish Literature.* Cambridge: Cambridge University Press, 2003, pp. 189–208.

Ormsby, Frank, "Ciaran Carson," an interview. *Linen Hall Review* 8:1: 5–8 (April 1991).

STEWART CONN

(1936—)

Gerry Cambridge

STEWART CONN IS one of contemporary Scotland's most respected poets, a figure widely admired for the integrity of his vision and the unshowy authenticity of his poetic voice. A modest, unassuming, and socially compassionate man, in a poetic career spanning almost forty years he has fretted at major themes: love, the responsibilities of the individual, mortality, and the temporal transcendence to be found in art, in particular the visual arts, as witness his love for the impressionists and Renaissance classicists. He is a grave and yet unforbidding poet, with an engaging human warmth, wry awareness, and acceptance of human foibles along with an acute awareness of social strata. His work is underpinned by a strong and yet not evangelical humanist stance, which allies it with that of Scottish contemporaries such as Douglas Dunn, yet it is salted and grained by the wholly individual timbre of his own voice. The attentive reader of his poetry will gain a strong impression of numerous aspects of contemporary Scotland, both rural and urban, since the 1960s, yet cast too in a historical perspective. While Conn is fundamentally a lyric poet, the work contains a strong documentary strand that gives a reassuring dependability to the poet's vision.

LIFE

Stewart Conn was born on November 5, 1936, in Glasgow's Hillhead district, in what is now the prosperous West End of the city, in a top flat in Cranworth Street during a period when Conn's father was minister of a local church of Scotland. The poet would later recount revisiting where he was born and finding the name on the flat's doorplate was "R. C. Risk: [my father]'d have enjoyed that" (*Distances,* p. 56). It is an anecdote that hints tellingly at the Church of Scotland's ambivalent relationship with Roman Catholicism in Scotland yet is left tantalizingly unexplicated. The poet trusts his—presumably Scottish—audience to implicitly understand these ambivalences.

The poet's parents in some respects were representative of the contrasts and conflicts in his own background experience, in particular the famous divide between Scotland's two major cities, Glasgow and Edinburgh. His father, John Cochrane Murdoch Conn, was from Glasgow. His mother, Jessie Conn (née Stewart) was an Edinburgh woman whom Conn later remembered affectionately as having to some degree, through the marriage to his father, been exiled from her Edinburgh roots. Social mores and expectations of different Scottish regions feature frequently in the poet's awarenesses.

The family, including a sister born in 1939—a second sister would arrive in 1943—moved to Kilmarnock in Ayrshire, then a relatively prosperous industrial town, when Conn was "almost six" (*Distances,* p. 55). Even today, Ayrshire, the birthplace of one of Conn's great literary forebears, Robert Burns, retains its bracing and somewhat rebarbative air. In Kilmarnock, Conn's father was minister of St. Marnock's, a central charge largely affiliated with a working-class base; the poet's early background was modest yet comfortable. Conn was, in the Scots expression, a "child of the manse," a situation to which the poet responded by becoming largely agnostic. To his credit, Conn senior, a scholarly and ecumenically progressive man, never tried to coerce his son into joining his church, though his gifts as an orator and giver of sermons Conn later credited with possibly encouraging in him the seed of an interest in literature. The young Conn attended Kilmarnock Academy, both at primary and secondary levels, amusingly describing himself and his fellow pupils as "snobby wee bastards" (Cambridge, p. 30) in red blazers and red caps, at times set upon by the rougher youths from further up the Kilmarnock valley. "Our wee caps started rolling down the Kilmarnock Water like rowan berries" (p. 30).

The young Conn had little affection for Kilmarnock itself, but his father came out of farming stock; his relatives owned two farms on nearby Craigie Hill, some three miles from the town's outskirts. Conn has compared this in a modest way to his equivalent of Edwin Muir's Edenic childhood on Orkney: visits on Sundays and during holidays to the farms, Harelaw (the "Hill of the Hare" in Scots) and High Landcraig, excited and engaged him, peopled as they were by a host of characters of almost biblical vividness and pervaded by the spirit of Robert Burns. It was a way of life and setting later to be commemorated and celebrated in the poet's early poems and credited with giving him—in its matter-of-factness regarding the poetry of Burns as something as everyday as grass—a distrust of ivory-tower elitism and an ambivalence about the role of the "poet" in general, a tension often seen in his verse. In the town's Dick Institute Library and Museum as a teenager Conn discovered to his surprise contemporary Scottish poetry, and he wrote his first poems in the institution's reading room. At age eighteen he became infatuated for a time by the work of Dylan Thomas, as carried away by that poet's orotund sonorities as he was baffled by their meanings.

The poet attended Glasgow University in 1954, where he took English, French, and history, but left voluntarily at the end of his first year, concerned that his creative faculties would be swamped by his critical ones. He served two years, to 1957, in National Service, mainly as a personnel clerk at RAF Swinderby, in Lincolnshire, dismayed by the flatness of the surrounding landscape. By 1958, at the age of twenty-two, he had joined the BBC in Glasgow as a studio manager—the beginning of a long and distinguished career with this major organization, which saw Conn latterly, via work as a drama producer, as the head of radio drama. In this position he made the acquaintance of many of the Scottish writers of the times, including eminent Scottish poets such as George Mackay Brown, Douglas Dunn, Edwin Morgan, Alasdair Maclean, and, especially important to him on a personal level, Iain Crichton Smith. He was also in a position to commission plays and other features from such writers and did so with his characteristic scrupulous generosity.

In 1960 Conn had met his wife-to-be, Judith Ann Clarke, the "Judy" of his many book dedications, a cheerful and vivacious woman of Protestant Irish background who was working in Glasgow on attachment from the BBC in London. The couple married in 1963 in Bangor Abbey, County Down, Ireland, and have remained happily married since. Judy Conn's personality often seems to have been a source of great support and comfort to the poet. She is the subject of a number of his more affecting poems and, one suspects, the muse for many of them, giving his poems about mortality, love, and art's limited but vital capacity to console a notable edge and poignance. Also in 1963, Conn won a Gregory Award—the foremost acknowledgment in Britain for a young poet of promise—via a panel comprising the critics Herbert Reid, Bonamy Dobree, and Howard Sergeant.

Conn and his family—two sons, Arthur and Ian, had been born in, respectively, 1973 and 1975—remained in Glasgow until 1977, years in which the poet not only consolidated his career as a playwright and radio producer but also established a considerable reputation as one of the most interesting of contemporary Scottish poets, with three collections from the reputable English publisher Hutchinson to his credit: *Stoats in the Sunlight* (1968), *An Ear to the Ground* (1972), and *Under the Ice* (1978). These volumes confirmed him as a writer of individual lyricism and voice, *An Ear to the Ground* being the book "choice" of the British Poetry Society for 1972. Meanwhile, the increasing frailty of his father—he died in 1974—resulted in a new group of poems concerned with the quandary of facing up to a parent's mortality and of Conn's relationship to him.

Conn and his family relocated to Edinburgh in 1977 as part of a BBC Radio resettlement, taking up residence in a comfortable flat in the city's new town. In 1983 he was awarded a Thyne scholarship, the most prestigious offered by the English Speaking Union Scotland to enable writers to travel abroad to study and research their own particular vocations. The distinction doubly pleased him for its acknowledgment of his avocation as a writer as opposed to his day job in radio drama. The poet visited South Africa for two months, a trip that produced a new range of South African poems as well as opening his sensibility to the bewildering harshnesses of apartheid. *In the Kibble Palace: New and Selected Poems* followed in 1987. By 1992, though, dismayed by increasing bureaucracy at the BBC, Conn had opted for early retirement from the organization in order to devote himself to writing, concentrating both on poetry and plays. The ensuing decade saw not only the death of his mother, Jessie, in 1993—she had outlived her husband by nineteen years—but the publication of four volumes of poetry. The year 2002 marked a substantial development in the poet's career, coinciding usefully with his dwindling output as a playwright: in May, Conn was appointed for three years as Edinburgh's first "Makar," or poet laureate, a largely titular but prestigious appointment carrying a minor remuneration but which helped, nonetheless, to validate him—a man frequently modest to a fault regarding his poetry—as a poet. Concretely the appointment helped him to raise the public profile of poetry in the Scottish capital and produce work for his 2005 collection *Ghosts at Cockcrow,* as well as garnering invitations for him to attend poetry conferences in central Europe: in Zagreb, Croatia (2004), Tetovo, Macedonia (2005), and Vilnius, Lithuania (2006), occasions that gave this socially aware poet new insight into recent European history. In 2006 the poet was chosen to receive the Iain Crichton Smith Award for services to literature, administered by the Institute of Contemporary Scotland.

STOATS IN THE SUNLIGHT

This essay will concern itself with Conn as poet, his dramatic work having been usefully covered in *British and Irish Dramatists Since World War II,* in the Dictionary of Literary Biography series. Though Conn's earliest poetry appeared in two pamphlets, *The Chinese Tower,* a poem sequence set in France, and *Thunder in the Air,* published by the Scot Duncan Glen's culturally vital Akros Press, his first full collection was a hardcover, its contents divided into two sections. Section 1 comprises mainly poems about his Scottish experience—farm and landscape—and the second ranges through history, often in the form of dramatic monologues spoken by various personae. Strongly influenced by poets such as Ted Hughes—in 1968 the presiding eminence in British poetry—whose first book had been called *The Hawk in the Rain*—and by the Scottish poet Norman MacCaig, *Stoats* is an at times mannered if solid performance. Many of its poems resoundingly rhyme, and the volume opens with the anthology piece "Todd," about the biblical patriarch of Conn's childhood experiences who was to form the subject matter of a number of the farming poems. White-haired, horse-devoted, from a fundamentalist religious background unassailed by doubt, Todd is a representative of a vanishing way of life, a pattern that was breaking up in Conn's childhood—though pockets of it remained in Ayrshire as late as the 1970s—and is now wholly gone. The poem's popularity as an anthology piece is understandable: it is readily comprehensible, written in quatrains rhyming *abba,* and neatly and elegantly constructed. The irony is strong. The middle section of the piece recounts anecdotally the man's devotion to Clydesdale horses, and the closure visualizes him, wryly, transformed into a horse himself; a transformation that in its whimsy distances the narrator from fundamentalist absolutes as well as making an ironic point about the true objects of Todd's devotion.

Seven of the opening section's sixteen poems appear to deal with Conn's early farm experience: "Todd," "The Orchard," "Harelaw," "Ayrshire Farm," "Afternoon," "Craigie Hill," and "Ferret." They are pieces with a strong documentary underpinning, often solidly retrospective: in interview Conn has quoted approvingly the statement by the American poet Dabney Stuart that he began to write poetry when he began to remember. Some, such as "Ferret" or "Craigie Hill," which is about encountering stoats (an ermine in its sleek brown summer coat), are pure reminiscence; others, such as "Harelaw" and "Ayrshire Farm," contrast the altering and relatively squalid present with the settled and, it is implied, more vigorous and genuine past. The poet revisits old haunts only to find the farm sold, the landscape changed. In general the poems are strongest in technique when Conn uses assonance rather than full rhyme.

If Hughes often appeared to be interested in violence as an absolute, Conn's scrutiny of it has a sort of fascinated horror. The second section of *Stoats in the Sunlight* has no shortage of brutality, with the poet very aware of precariousness, of facing "up to the particular," of the nature of "margins," in a twelve-line poem of that title, which are "the nature / Of the charmed lives we bear." (p. 51) The poet has a finely tuned awareness of that good fortune, yet is far from blind to the horror around, as this section makes clear: "Vanities" (pp. 41–45) expounds religious and medieval cruelties, and the section opens and closes respectively with "Flight" (p. 33) and "Ambush," (p. 60) poems in which the temporal and geographical circumstances remain unexplained but in which the speakers are fleeing some conflict. The book's closing image, referring back intriguingly to the earlier stoat poem, is of "eight men," "like stoats in the sunlight," "fastened through the throat to trees (p. 60)."

Conn's first book was a significant debut, showing its influences in the way of many first books, but elucidating some of his major preoccupations: the attempt for decency in a brutal world, a nervy awareness of vulnerability, and a clear-eyed facing up to physical horror. In later books he would leave the explication of pure violence, influenced by Hughes, well behind. It was with his second book that he can be said to have found his characteristic voice.

AN EAR TO THE GROUND

It is a voice that appears hardly to have changed since. In *An Ear to the Ground,* from a technical standpoint Conn largely left behind the sometimes clanging full rhymes that had marred some of the pieces in his first volume; in their place he employed assonance, with full rhyme only for particular emphasis, and an individuality of rhythm that supplants the straitjacketing metric of pieces such as "Harelaw." The book is in three sections, opening with "Kilchrenan," a poem in unrhymed couplets dealing obliquely with the Highland Clearances—which saw large parts of the land cleared of crofters by Scottish landowners to make way for sheep—and providing a social context for the volume's uneasy title. Section 1 contains fine poems continuing Conn's preoccupation with his early farm experience in "On Craigie Hill," "Forebears," and "Farm Funeral." These have a more subdued and elegiac air than related poems in the first book and all seem solidly dependable in texture and emotional veracity. They are less celebration than commemoration. "It is hard to look / Back with any sense of belonging" Conn writes in "On Craigie Hill," as if all that had happened since—he was by this time working with BBC Radio in Glasgow—had distanced him. These pieces are notable for their lack of sentimentality and their concrete details. In the last of them, "Farm Funeral," which also closes the first section, the funeral is that of Todd Cochrane, Conn's great-uncle.

A neat combination of assonance and internal rhyme helps bind the closure in the technical equivalent of the old man's composure to the end: "he" rhymes with the first syllable of "even," and that, with the second syllable of "Craigie," helps couple him with the named locality; "laced" and "place" help confirm the sartorial details they describe. Even in death a ceremonious rectitude is observed with an energy opposite and equivalent to that of "the roisterer" with whom he is compared.

Among other interesting pieces, in "Journeying North" the poet is on a train, returning from London after viewing a Réne Magritte exhibition at the Tate Gallery. He contrasts his uneasy impressions of some of the paintings on display with his fears—which are of a different order—as he heads heads north on the train. He imagines his wife setting the table for a meal and eating, with it all implies of the animal need to survive and the potential brutality thereof, is intriguingly coupled and contrasted with the delicate image of a former wedding. Nearing Gretna, traditionally a venue in which young couples get married, the poem's narrator hears anvils strike. Conn's is a poem of new marriage which contrasts effectively the relatively theoretical disturbances of art with those of actuality, manifested in the forbidding power of those "heavy anvils." The poem prefigures pieces in the book's closing section. Additionally section 1 includes two fine related poems, the first of which, "Crippled Aunt," has the baffled narrator examining the aunt's constancy of fundamentalist faith in the face of her disability and the traffic accident that caused it. Beautifully written in five-line stanzas, nominally rhyming *abbaa,* the poem intriguingly approaches and distances itself from this rhyme scheme in a way illustrative of the aunt's faith and the narrator's doubt. The opening stanza, a vignette detailing the aunt's constancy in church, has full "a" rhymes on "glance," "trance," and "dance"; the central three stanzas, which notate the narrator's bafflement at the aunt's faith, in general move farther from this underpinning rhyme scheme.

The closure's full rhyme returns to the aunt's faith: the technical closure mimics her faith's absolutism. The other piece, "Summer Afternoon," features a great-aunt of the poet, though some details of the poem Conn has said are invented. The poem recounts how the old lady is taken indoors from the garden when rain begins.

Conn's willingness to engage with grievous subject matter has always been one of his poetry's strong points. Technically, too, here the line break splitting "poor" from "Creature" makes the center line of the closing stanza a complete semantic unit that can be read as commenting on the poverty of the love felt by the narrator as much as of that love borne him by the old lady in earlier and happier times. Conn is a scrupulous exploiter of line ends, a technique perhaps learned from a master, the Scottish poet W. S. Graham.

Of the book's remaining two sections, the strongest is the third—the second section comprises a single sequence, "The Predators," which is a sort of travelogue detailing historical and religious violence, yet with no rooted connection to Conn's other work. In section 3 a significant poem, "Tremors," from which the volume's title is taken, evokes the sense of foreboding found from this point on through much of Conn's poetry. It recounts a childhood memory of laying an ear to the track of a railway line to hear the train approaching, then pressing oneself into the verge while the great machine roars past. The poem is a grave mapping of the inevitability of dissolution, difficulty, and death. While it is entirely unmetaphorical in its particulars, its whole setting and atmosphere is a metaphor, and it convinces primarily because of the plain veracity of the style. Allied to this piece, which is central to the section and to much of Conn's later work, are a poem about visiting his parents, "Family Visit," two about his aging father, "To My Father" and "Reiteration," and a sequence of three marriage poems that close the volume. The family poems contrast difficult immediate realities involving aging parents with a happier and more vivacious past; they detail readily identifiable experience in crisply crafted stanzas.

The enjambment between "great" and "Rainbarrels" again shows Conn's adroitness with line ends: the closure is also an elegy for a more illustrious age, an impression confirmed by the now "pocked marble" of the bridge and the slant rhyme of "sludge" with this formerly impressive structure. The poet's parents too, in their relationship to a grander past, seem emblematic of a faded glory in his mind.

The volume closes with three poems about marriage, two of which, "At Coruisk" and the closing poem, "Marriage a Mountain Ridge," Conn reprinted in his later *Selected* volumes. Both broadly use mountain imagery as symbolic of the emotional landscapes of a marriage; the closing poem, in its four sections of attenuated couplets emphasizing precariousness, notates "the dark couloirs" (p57) of a shared life. Emotional precariousness, a sense of foreboding, and relationship within marriage would be themes Conn would develop in his next volume, *Under the Ice.*

STEWART CONN

UNDER THE ICE

A frequent motif through this volume is ice, and being trapped under ice—a symbol for the despair of the terminally ill (such as Conn's father), for the condition of mortality, and for repressed states of mind. Conn also here proved himself a poet of the uncertainties and difficulties of marriage as well as its grace. While he deals with distinctly uncheery subject matter, Conn's making art from despair is profoundly reassuring. The volume opens with the book's title poem, and the narrator's "waltzing" on its surface; here ice provides, paradoxically, support as well as separation. It is a poem poised in ambiguity, imagining "Raeburn's skating parson," in the famous Scottish painting attributed to Henry Raeburn, ostensibly of his friend the Reverend Robert Walker and known as *The Skating Minister,* believed to date from the last decade of the eighteenth century. Conn wonders whether the figure—who is depicted confidently skating with his chest thrust out while gazing blithely ahead of him, into space—was a man of God truly, or simply presenting a decorous front.

Immediately following "Kitchen Maid" is "Visiting Hour," which has the narrator standing by his father's hospital bedside, helpless in the face of his final illness. The first stanza of this poem, which has two eight-line stanzas, recounts Conn's childhood memory of his father smashing the ice on a garden pond to release its five goldfish to swim freely—in one reading, they could symbolize the five members of the Conn family. The second stanza switches to the altered circumstances, beginning: "Since then …" and ending with its grievous image of helplessness. Each stanza hermetically seals off its content: the first, of action and saving possibility; the second, of despair. Other strong poems about Conn's aging parents here are "Reawakening," about his father, and "Afternoon Visit," one of the rare poems about Conn's mother. Written in muscular quatrains to a rhyming template *abab,* the stanzas slip in and out of the certainties of full rhyme. It is a poem that fairly bristles with the tension of an adult's despair in the face of his parent's increasing disability.

The tensions of an ordinary domestic situation, experienced by thousands of people every day, are powerfully conveyed. The closing image of men fighting through an elemental chaos is resonant and it is part of Conn's skill that it seems not at all arbitrary. He conveys expertly the powerful choreography of feeling below an everyday domestic surface. One also notes the poet's increased technical skill: here, full rhyme strengthens meaning rather than directs or falsifies it, and that "tense," poised as at the edge of a cliff at the middle stanza's end, helps in its judicious placement to emphasize the narrator's frame of mind.

Another strong feature of the volume is a series of poems charting Conn's developing relationship within his marriage. These include, as well as "Kitchen Maid," "Arrivals," "In the Kibble Palace," "Aquarium," "Last Christmas," "Removal," and "Along the Terrace," poems that mingle love, affection, doubt, and fear for the future. The four-part "Arrivals" has him greeting his wife at the airport after her visit to Ulster, then reminiscing about happy times spent together in Europe and driving back through a grimly urban Glasgow together.

This gives a sense of some of Conn's best work: unironic emotion, plain language, and honesty, set down in convincing rhythms with astute slant rhymes. It is a style and voice uniquely identifiable as his, and the best of it transcends the personal circumstances of its making to achieve a wider relevance, as in the stanza quoted. Technically Conn seemed by now wholly comfortable with his forms, having achieved a distinctive rhythmical free verse that, in its assonances and regular stanzas, also profited from his work's earlier formality. His verse has all the strength of the single, suffering individual responding honestly to his contemporary experience and setting it down as authentically as possible. An example is the brief vignette "Along the Terrace," a poem of marital uncertainty that begins "Drinks, along the terrace," which echoes the clinking of glasses via the comma after the opening noun. In a series of rapid transitions, each of which brings an observed situation closer to the narrator, it moves deftly from this one-line description, to three lines about the disintegration of "another marriage," to a brief doubting question about the relationship of the narrator and his wife, and ends with immediate proximity

While there are other flavors and themes in the volume, it is the poems of familial and marital relationships that remain with the reader. *Under the Ice* marked Conn's final appearance under the Hutchinson imprint. It would be nine years till his next book appeared.

IN THE KIBBLE PALACE: NEW AND SELECTED POEMS

This volume was published by Bloodaxe Books, located in the north of England and Conn's publisher ever since. The "Kibble Palace" of the book's title is, perhaps symbolically, a large ornamental glass house set in Glasgow's Botanic Gardens—a place of emotional importance for Conn both in his early childhood and later, from 1958 when he settled in Glasgow. The new volume is in three sections: broadly speaking, section 1 contains the farm poems and pieces on early childhood; section 2 contains poems of Conn's marriage and adult life, including the pieces about his parents; and the third and closing section, containing poems written between 1978 and 1986, has a distinctly autumnal feel and finds the poet pondering the onset of middle age. Section 2 finishes with "Removal," originally the penultimate poem in *Under the Ice*. It is typical Conn in its concerns and has the narrator pondering miscellaneous mementoes of happy experiences stored in an attic and re-encountered before a removal. Conn sees clearly the cost of happiness, which, eventually, is its opposite: "Each memory, as it clarifies," is "happy / Yet packed with pain" (p. 74). In this context, the verb "packed" carries a powerful charge, meaning both packed away with its concomitant pain and crammed with it to bursting.

"Removal" sets the stage neatly for the opening poem of section 3, "Moving In," in which, newly moved to Edinburgh, the couple featured in the poem cling to one another in bed and "prepare for a long winter" (p. 76). A poem about his son's birthday contrasts the happiness of the

child, newly five, with "another murderous / dawn," in which the world "prises itself apart" (p. 78), and there is a fine poem, "Before Dark," dedicated to Conn's contemporary Douglas Dunn. Conn's poem contrasts the student population of the West End of Glasgow and its confidence with the poet's middle-age uncertainty and awareness that, all too soon, he and his wife may be no more than a memory to his sons, as his own parents are now to him. Against these erosions he pits, as at the conclusion of a four-part poem, "Recovery," written after his friend and fellow poet Iain Crichton Smith's recovery from a mental breakdown, "those massive forces, / endurance and love" (p. 99). While Conn contrasts against mortality the love for his wife in a delicate lyric, "Cherry Tree, In December," in which the unseasonally blossoming tree acts as a metaphor for the resurgence or confirmation of love within marriage, the section is not the cheeriest of reads. One might well feel that there is more to be said for existence than the catalog of despair that, to some extent, Conn presents in the book's final section, and it may well be that the poet himself came to feel similarly. At any rate, by the time of his next volume, *The Luncheon of the Boating Party*, the poet had left the BBC and committed himself to a freelancing life and, complementarily, seems to have found in a new series of poems about art the transformation of despair to a hard-won radiance.

THE LUNCHEON OF THE BOATING PARTY

In a sense this volume is built around its five-section title poem, based on Renoir's famous painting of 1880–1881, when the artist had just turned forty. It was painted at Chatou outside Paris on the banks of the Seine, at the Maison Fournaise, one of Renoir's favorite haunts. Conn had encountered the original painting at an exhibition in London's Hayward Gallery in the summer of 1988. The effect on the poet had been immediate: "I was utterly bowled over by it," he said in an interview. "I remember it was as though torrents of light came out of it" (Cambridge, p. 35). While in earlier work Conn had often featured pictorial art, contrasting its relative timelessness with mortal life, "The Luncheon of the Boating Party" functions as a wonderful two-way mirror, with the mirror's glass the equivalent of the poem's text and, on one side of the mirror, the painting itself and, on the other, the human characters and situations from which the painting came. The poem is about mortality, transience, beauty, art, yet it also has a Chekhovian air and vivacity. Written throughout in five-line stanzas, its first four sections are monologues by characters delineated in the painting. They are, in order of appearance, Alphonse Fournaise Junior, the son of the proprietor of the Maison Fournaise; Baron Raoul Barbier, a former mayor of Saigon and a noted bon vivant; an "Unknown Man," the fourteenth figure in the picture, visible only in profile against the dark-jacketed Charles Ephrussi, an art historian and editor of the *Gazette des beaux-arts;* and finally, Madame Renoir, Aline Charigot at the time of the painting, later Renoir's wife. The poem finishes with Renoir himself speaking as a mortally ill old man, reminiscing about the painting and about his life.

The painting and Renoir himself seem to have been the perfect objective correlative for Conn's middle-aged and nonjudgmental awareness of human foibles, his desire for the transcendence of despair and grief through praise, and for his dramatist's ability to project himself into other voices. The characters speak in voices and attitudes variously puzzled, quirky, humorous, envious, vain, condescending, and aware of condescension; the poet also manages to provide background detail about the painting's provenance as well as paradoxical asides about art itself. This wittily juxtaposes the paradox of the illusion of art with the speaker's social awareness. There is cross-referencing too, as in the second section, when Baron Barbier comments on how Alphonse was almost painted out of the finished piece, then painted in again, wearing his white singlet.

The aesthetic distancing of the artist is deftly conveyed. The ghost of ambiguity around "purely," which can mean in this context either "only" or "in a pure state" comments intriguingly on the mystery of art. Read one way this implies

that the essences of the sitters, their pure being, are concentrated in the final work of art.

In the final stanza of section 3—spoken by the "Unknown Man," whose lack of identity conveys a great sense of mystery and of the curious final anonymity of all of us, judged on a cosmic or geological scale—the closure is beautifully resonant.

The adjective "magical" here, in a context so adjectivally plain, carries its full weight and serves to evoke not only the whole spirit of a sunlit French afternoon with the shimmer of light under awnings, among wine and food, but the mystery of transience, of art that attempts to transcend transience, and of the sheer astonishment of life as it is shown us by its brevity. The speaker's description of the Baron Barbier being, possibly, "from another planet" points up the distance between individuals of different backgrounds, for it is plain from his down-to-earth tone that the "Unknown Man" knows little of the rarefied world of art.

The sequence closes with two sections spoken respectively by Madame Renoir and by Renoir himself, Madame Renoir before her death recalling details of the poem being painted, and Renoir as an old man who has outlived his wife and is waiting for death. He responds to his critics by emphasizing his "dream of harmony, not anarchy" (p. 55), in a moving closure of a powerful sequence. "The Luncheon" is probably Conn's most complete statement, and it sits as the centerpiece of the volume much as its subject would in a gallery; the book's other poems, to some extent, read like smaller works that add to the sequence's central focus. Included in the book's second section with the "Luncheon" are numerous French travelogue poems, often attractive but appearing generally slighter in comparison with the impressive title poem with which they are juxtaposed.

The book's opening section shows Conn revisiting, not wholly successfully, earlier Ayrshire landscapes in two pieces—"Family Tree," later slightly rewritten and reformatted for his new *Selected Poems,* and "Craggy Country." In this section, too, is a biographical poem, one of a number in his oeuvre, about the Paisley ornithologist Alexander Wilson, who moved to America and was a contemporary of John James Audubon; there are two likable sequences of poems set on Skye, full of local color in a context of the narrator's increasing awareness of his aging; and a slight encomium to the Greenock poet W. S. Graham, marred by the inaccuracy of having barn owls that "flutter / and whoo." (Owls are silent in flight, and it is the tawny owl that makes the call phonetically described as "whoo"; barn owls' calls are different.)

The strongest poems in the opening section are those that engage Conn's central concerns, elucidated powerfully in the title poem, of love and transience. Among them is "Burial Mound," a complex love poem in which the "Mound" of the title is Maeshowe in Orkney, a neolithic chambered cairn dating from around 2750 B.C.E. Access to it is by a low, narrow passage that is so positioned that it admits the light fully into its interior annually only on December 21, the winter solstice, when, just before sunset, it illuminates the far wall of the inner chamber. The inside of the chamber has carved runic inscriptions by Vikings who ransacked the tomb sometime in the twelfth century for the grave goods stored there. The poet recounts being shown the interior by a terse guide with a torch "flitting" across the walls, an acutely chosen verb in which light itself is shown as being as frail, as temporal, and as capable of flying off as a bird.

This is a complex closure that bears close reading. While a reader could take the "lie" as decidedly ambiguous, it seems in this context to have its principal meaning. The closure is a frail affirmation against the entrance of that "invader," a frailty shown in that "At least we are together," while the alliterations on "lie," "least," "love," and "live" further act as a frail defense against dissolution. Yet the "live" can be read doubly, not only as in "alive" but "live" as in an electric cable, with all that that implies of dangers. (Conn has never been an easy love poet: he understands the difficulties of love as well as its blessings.) The couple is doomed because, although together, the two are mortal, as symbolized by the chilling comparison of their room to the burial mound of the first four stanzas. Technically the lines have

all of Conn's habitual astuteness in their assonances; yet for all that, their register is no more than that of plain speech.

The Luncheon of the Boating Party marked the beginning of Conn's attempt to be reconciled to mortality in his art. In the place of the at times bitter and bemused questioning of the earlier work, increasingly there is praise and an awareness of what one elegy calls "unendurable radiance" (p. 42).

IN THE BLOOD

In the Blood, the blurb announced, marked a return to Conn's "Ayrshire roots," though privately, much later the poet admitted this was the volume he was least satisfied with. There is always a danger of sentimentality when a mature poet revisits earlier material or memories already explored. The reader suspects that the poet is running out of fresh material. Conn's return to Ayrshire did produce interesting pieces, collected here in the book's opening section, but his emphasis on blood ties to a particular soil seemed somewhat forced and the poet privately acknowledged an uncharacteristic desire to be poetically "fashionable" behind some pieces in the book. The volume begins lightheartedly, however, with the ironically titled "Kilmarnock Edition"—usually the fabulously rare edition of Burns's poems printed in Kilmarnock by John Wilson in 1786 but here a childhood volume of Burns's poems "presented by Kilmarnock Burns Club," turned up during a house move, and from which the young Conn had recited Burns's verse for school audiences. The adult poet's memory of his studied childhood performances is charming in its self-mockery.

It is a light poem with a serious point to make, restating Burns's criterion of goodness. Though this criterion can be read as heartwarmingly sentimental, it can also seem deeply ironic in its irreconcilable aims, for often the happiness of some is directly dependent on the unhappiness of others.

Conn's background in drama is behind this depiction of his histrionic younger self, and a Scots word such as "laldie"—still in common speech and meaning, in conjunction with "give it," to act with vigorous enthusiasm—add vernacular energy and amusement. Interestingly Conn never reprinted the poem in his later *Selected,* nor another delicate lyric, "Castles," which in three quatrains sets four Ayrshire castles in their complicated historical context.

Here all the vibrant complexity of the past is simplified and clarified to schoolhouses and, ultimately, colors. Unlike elsewhere, Conn lets the image and the aesthetic strategy speak for itself. It is a plain, luminous closure, acknowledging territoriality and the simplification of the past in the present; the rhythmical dance of the proper nouns and their colors give the closure the simplified ironic air of a nursery rhyme. By contrast, a long piece such as "Terra Firma," which immediately precedes "Castles," for all its solid documentary delineation of the poet's early life in Kilmarnock, like a number of other poems in this selection can seem like rhythmical prose set down in lines. A weakness of the work at times is in Conn's insistence on drawing out a moral for the reader, thus diminishing the imaginative contract between reader and author; additionally, one can feel suspicious of a poem having too many designs on our response to it. At times, curiously, one wants poetry and its poet not to care what its reader thinks of it, with the same indifference, say, as a big day of elemental weather or a mountain; as with a little poem such as "Castles," one wants it simply to be fully itself, with a devil-may-care vivacity.

The opening section also contains a lively and—in their focus on childhood and ordinary detail—strangely reassuring series of vignettes, "Early Days," and a successful lyric, "Country Dance," a rhythmically lively depiction of stook building in the labor-intensive agriculture of the earlier twentieth century.

Of the book's remaining two sections, section 2 seems the strongest. It opens with the adroitly constructed "Jawbone Walk," deftly written in unrhymed triplets. The poem records and comments wryly upon an encounter with a quirky down-and-out who possesses a prehistoric perspective on the Edinburgh environment of the area known as The Meadows. The poem alternates cannily between description and the tramp's monologue on the passing scene.

The closing image is allowed to speak for itself, conjoining both these prehistoric creatures and the immortal desire to stave off death represented by the hospital outbuildings. Extinct, the mastodons live on in all their prehistoric lumbering magnificence in the hospital metaphor. They are "looming," that is, in this context, "approaching," not only in the sense of growing larger as he approaches them but in time too for all of us.

"Inheritance," immediately following, is a strong, completely contemporary poem demonstrating the plain-speaking gravitas Conn can achieve with a big subject that transcends the simply personal by linking it to larger concerns.

Enjambments from line to line and stanza to stanza set up a processional tone. The poem was written in the aftermath of the infamous Jamie Bulger case, in which a two-year-old toddler, James Bulger, was abducted from a Liverpool shopping mall on February 12, 1993, by two ten—year—old boys and later brutally murdered. For a time anxious parents took to fastening their toddlers to them by the wrist when out in public.

Among the other strong poems in the volume were "Losing Touch," a five-part sequence depicting the final days of Conn's mother, and a fine elegy, "Presence," for a former employee of the Scottish Arts Council, Deirdre Keaney, killed in a car accident. Concisely written in three three-line stanzas, the first four lines acknowledge sadness, but the poem closes with a recognition of the numinous as sensed in the slow dimming of an evening sky to an afterglow framed against the Border hills in which the dead woman seems "both present, and absent" (p. 48).

AT THE AVIARY

In 1984 Conn had visited South Africa on a Thyne travel scholarship awarded by the English Speaking Union. A second visit followed in 1993 when he was asked to judge the Amstel South African Playwriting Competition. *At the Aviary* is a thirty-two-page near-pamphlet, with a spine, which gathers twenty-three poems written after these visits. Travelogue poetry is a strong feature of Conn's oeuvre. The pieces here are part travelogue, part depictions of landscape and a culture that tie in with some of Conn's central concerns: his unsettling awareness of class differences and factions that has been part of his sensibility from the beginning. The pieces in the earlier part of the volume seem most successful if one reads them purely as impressions on a sensitive humane man of the jarring discordances in apartheid, though they remain, finally, impressionistic, perhaps with the exception of a slender poem written in four quatrains, "House Guest," in which the narrator lets himself into where he is staying and, puzzled by a clicking sound, finally tracks its source—a caged hamster.

The image is left to speak for itself without extrapolation. As an image of the self-imprisonment inherent in white "supremacy," it is powerful. Of course, plain speaking without resort to images can also be a sure aesthetic strategy, but it requires a greater authority of voice and rhythm to achieve. It also avoids the potential misreading of an imagistic aesthetic and ensures that one's words cannot be misinterpreted: one thinks in this context of some politicians' wishful misreadings of Robert Frost's "Mending Wall" as indicating his approval of metaphorical wall building and, therefore, validating their own. At his best Conn outwits such misreadings, though it may come at the cost of pleasing aesthetic ambiguities. He is a remarkably moral poet in what seems his desire to be read plainly.

At the Aviary finishes with a brief group of poems on African fauna and flora, which to a degree contrast the lively vibrancy of the country's natural history with its human complexities. The best of the poet's work, however, remains that which is closest to his known landscapes and preoccupations, and the range of his achievement would be seen fully in his next volume, *Stolen Light,* a selected poems of distinction.

STOLEN LIGHT: SELECTED POEMS

While *Stolen Light* added little to Conn's oeuvre with the exception of a small number of more recent poems and a group of poems uncollected from his early pamphlets, and although it mainly preserves the original chronology of the pieces, the volume does offer a chance to see the poet in the round. A substantial 192-page paperback, in seven sections (Conn has frequently seemed a careful orderer of poems in his collections), it shows him to be a fine lyric poet, yet socially aware and responsible, whose work seems full of many of the colors and tensions and pleasures of contemporary Scotland. The poems have nonetheless a reassuring dependability of tone, and if at times their impression of earnestness seems over-solemn, that is the cost of their seriousness, of Conn's willingness to face up to grievous circumstance and make order from sorrow. The new *Selected* also adds interesting new poems such as "Faces," a four-section piece which, though its two middle sections may be weaker, it opens with a memorable image of faces of young travelers on a train.

Conn's transposition of actual experience into an artistic comparison links back to *The Luncheon of the Boating Party;* the comparison is fresh, apt, and memorable. At the section's end he sees the young people reclaiming backpacks and crossing "the leafy platform / to the Rowardennan bus" (p. 178). The elevation of the artistic comparison juxtaposed with the rustling organic leafiness of that platform and the saving ordinariness of "the Rowardennan bus"—Rowardennan being the site for a youth hostel on the banks of Loch Lomond—are pleasing. The final section of the poem has the narrator buying a somber spirit mask, the view seen through its eye sockets "alarmingly similar to my own" (p. 179). The poet was looking toward age. His next collection, *Ghosts at Cockcrow,* which appeared when the poet was sixty-eight, would have a new, autumnal note.

GHOSTS AT COCKCROW

Not only is this book overshadowed by transience—an awareness that has been his, after all, since the beginning—but also there appears the beginning of reconciliation to it, as well as a sharper awareness of his own aging. The book takes its title from a quote about the passing generations by G. M. Trevelyan, about how the present and its people become the past, "one generation vanishing after another, gone as utterly as we ourselves shall shortly be gone like ghosts at cockcrow" (p. 51). The book brings together a number of his dominant themes: transience, the attempt at transcendence of mortal pain through art, his early Kilmarnock background, and ideological violence.

Added to this, however, is a new focus on Edinburgh, the city his family had lived in since 1977, yet given added weight by Conn's appointment in May 2002 as the city's first Makar—a mediaeval Scots word for a poet, or "maker"—a largely titular appointment that appears to have given the poet a fresh impetus and a renewed sense of responsibility toward poetry's civic function in an Edinburgh context. The second of the book's five sections mainly comprises a group of poems set in the city, the opening piece, Heirloom, announcing that Conn's maternal grandfather owned a licensed grocer's on the High Street: a very Scottish claiming of one's right to Edinburgh subject matter. The first eight of the twelve subsequent poems deal manifestly with Edinburgh subject matter or are set recognizably in the city while embracing other themes, as in Autumn Walk, which amusingly recounts Conn, invested with a cloak of invisibility by his advancing age, overhearing the frank sexual conversation of two young female students discussing young men, or in an attractive poem, Coastlines, in which the narrator rises from bed before his wife and visits Leith Harbour and its anchored ships, part of the famous tall ships race, imagining, at the poem's close, a breeze filling the full-rigged sails.

It is with a similar optimism that the collection opens, in "Realm of Possibility," in which the poet's study, covered with dropcloths for a plasterers' visit, becomes a place of creative anticipation, leading to the first section's preoccupation at times with art and its transcendences, though placing among this, perhaps ironically, poems such as "Kosovo," a series of eight vignettes of the Balkan conflict that focus on its effect on individuals. It is a mark of Conn's skill that the reader does not feel that material to which the poet has no right as subject matter is being appropriated, though at times he points the moral perhaps too clearly, as at the end of the section "The Inheritors," two couplets about the contemporary reciprocation for historical violence, a section he feels compelled to close by emphasizing the biblical quotation about an eye for an eye. "Young Huntsman with Falcon," based upon the volume's cover image from the Musee du Petit Palais, Avignon, makes explicit the love prevalent in making art that is implicit in "The Luncheon of the Boating Party," though one of the section's most affecting pieces, "Ministrations," achieves a dignified and grave plain speaking. It contrasts the ghosts of childhood or superstition with maturity's white-vestured apparitions.

The poem's reversal of the trope of ghostliness at the poem's close is neatly achieved, and the trim, terse three-line stanzas—though one or two could be deleted without losing anything essential—descend down the page like the speaker's awareness of the process of dissolution. The closure's single end-stopped line is apt, understated, yet weighty in its import and therefore all the more convincing for its understatement.

Section 3 is the title sequence, a travelogue, though Conn's positioning it centrally indicates the import he places upon it. Travelogues, however, only become more than that in a poetic context when they ally themselves with a writer's central concerns; while "Ghosts at Cockcrow" is not wholly uninteresting for its details, there is little sense of its writing being essential to the poet, or of its incidentals marrying with his central subject matters. Even a brief piece such as "Ministrations" seems more central. Its incidentalness is a criticism that can be leveled far less at section 4, "Roull of Corstorphin," a sequence based upon the mention of this obscure Edinburgh poet in William Dunbar's magnificent 1505 elegy "Lament for the Makars." Part documentary, part dramatic monologue spoken by the imagined Roull, a figure who at times seems to bear comparison with Conn himself, the sequence, in thirteen sections, is most interesting both for this intersection between Conn's voice and the imagined Roull's and for its documentary underpinning. It has something of a ceremonial, dutiful air, appropriate considering Conn's position at the time as Edinburgh Makar, but which may seem to some readers to derive from that sense of civic responsibility rather than from his own pure impulse. Poetry is fundamentally anarchic, unlikely to come at one's bidding, and seldom thrives on a sense of duty. Its unbiddability, of course, is a huge part of its force. The poet seems on more secure ground with the volume's closing section, which brings together a number of familiar Conn subjects: there are pleasing praise poems to his wife, including a light, witty piece, "My Lady," which subverts the idea of the praise-lavished muse by letting her complain in the final line about the narrator's neglect, in this torrent of praise, of his domestic duties: "Why not add my Lady of the Binbag to the list?" (p. 81). There is a fine revisiting of a Kilmarnock memory of the mystique of a locally famous cricket ball lobbed into the crowd and mysteriously vanishing thereafter.

The wonderful sudden acceleration of movement here across the closing lines, the local vernacular name of "Killie" for Kilmarnock, and the full rhymes at closure evoke all of the excitement of childhood in a context intimate and local, enacting via the final rhymes that stillness they describe.

The collection closes with the comical, anecdotal, and poignant "The Actor's Farewell," in which the speaker recounts his playing in *Hamlet,* most usually as the ghost of Hamlet's father, and lastly "Angel with Lute," spoken by an angel on a fresco—a metaphor for the creativity of art—which has outlasted, with some minor deterioration, centuries, owing to the care with which the painter "prepared his pigments." It is a resonant poem about love, about artistic care, and about the practice of art.

This captures some of the best of Conn: plain speech, unmetaphorical, imbued with great warmth that outwits sentimentality and conveys an insight into the processes of the making of art as well as a faith in its ability, however temporarily, to transcend worldly brutality. In that paradox of art the angel survives while its creator dies. It represents the love implicit in artistic devotion, symbolized by that secret kiss that sustains and grants this angel, centuries later, a voice.

Conn is a considerable poet of praise, though he has arrived at this position via a difficult charting of emotion. His work has an affectionate but by no means sentimental integrity. While there are numerous negligible poems among his output, and he can at times seem to overproduce simply for the sake of it—he is a writer in love with the act of making poetry, which may well lead him on occasion into writing when he has little new to say—the best of the work is soundly made and full of a caritas that does not preclude honesty. It is an oeuvre for which it is possible to feel considerable warmth; humane, human-scaled, it never forgets that the suffering or joyous or otherwise experiencing individual is at its heart. It most brings to mind Auden's observation that in our time writing a poem is a political act, emphasizing as it does the stubborn presence of individuality against those forces that would flatten or otherwise make uniform individual sensibilities. Conn has to date produced a body of work wholly distinctive in tone, and the best of it is of wide relevance: a thoroughly responsible poetry that often improves with renewed acquaintance.

Selected Bibliography

WORKS OF STEWART CONN

POETRY AND ESSAY/MEMOIR

The Chinese Tower. Edinburgh: MacDonald, 1967.

Thunder in the Air. Preston: Akros, 1967.

Stoats in the Sunlight. London: Hutchinson, 1968.

Ambush and Other Poems. New York: Macmillan, 1970. (U.S. version of *Stoats in the Sunlight*).

An Ear to the Ground. London: Hutchinson, 1972.

Under the Ice. London: Hutchinson, 1978.

In the Kibble Palace: New and Selected Poems. Newcastle upon Tyne, U.K.: Bloodaxe, 1987.

The Luncheon of the Boating Party. Newcastle upon Tyne,

STEWART CONN

U.K.: Bloodaxe, 1992.

At the Aviary. Plumstead, South Africa: Snailpress, 1995.

In the Blood. Newcastle upon Tyne, U.K.: Bloodaxe, 1995.

Stolen Light: Selected Poems. Newcastle upon Tyne, U.K.: Bloodaxe, 1999.

Distances: A Personal Evocation of People and Places. Dalkeith, U.K.: Scottish Cultural Press, 2001.

Ghosts at Cockcrow. Tarset, U.K.: Bloodaxe, 2005.

PLAYS

The Burning. London: Calder & Boyars, 1973.

The Aquarium, The Man in the Green Muffler, and I Didn't Always Live Here. London: Calder & Boyars, 1976.

Thistlewood. Todmorden, U.K.: Woodhouse, 1979.

Hugh Miller. Callender, U.K.: Diehard, 2002.

UNCOLLECTED PROSE

"A Tale of Two Cities." *Scottish Review* 18:3–8 (May 1980).

"Ways of Losing: The Radio Work of Iain Crichton Smith." In *Iain Crichton Smith: Critical Essays.* Edited by Colin Nicholson. Edinburgh: Edinburgh University Press, 1992. pp. 26–36.

"A Sense of Belonging." In *Spirits of the Age: Scottish Self Portraits.* Edited by Paul Henderson Scott. Edinburgh: Saltire Society, 2005. pp. 165–172.

EDITED WORKS

New Poems: A PEN Anthology of Contemporary Poetry. London: Hutchinson, 1974.

The Ice Horses: The Second Shore Poets Anthology. With Ian McDonough. Edinburgh: Scottish Cultural Press, 1996.

100 Favourite Scottish Poems. Edinburgh: Luath Press, 2006.

CRITICAL AND BIOGRAPHICAL STUDIES

Abse, Dannie. "Stewart Conn." In *Corgi Modern Poets in Focus 3.* Edited by Dannie Abse. London: Corgi Books, 1971. pp. 113–120.

Aitchison, James. "A Note on 'Angel with Lute.'" *Dark Horse* 19:44-45 (winter 2006–2007).

Brown, Ian. "Stewart Conn." In *British and Irish Dramatists Since World War II. Dictionary of Literary Biography* 233. Third series. Edited by John Bull. Detroit and London: Gale Group, 2001. pp. 77–83.

Crichton Smith, Iain. "The Poetry of Stewart Conn." In *Toward the Human.* Loanhead, Midlothian, U.K.: Macdonald, 1986. pp. 159–166.

Dunn, Douglas. "Stewart Conn in the Seventies." *Dark Horse* 19:46–49 (winter 2006–2007).

Macrae, Alasdair D. F. "Conn Amore." *Dark Horse* 19:50–55 (winter 2006–2007).

Scott, Alexander. "Stewart Conn's 'Todd.'" *Akros,* pp. 52–53 (October 1983).

INTERVIEWS

Brown, Ian. "Cultural Centrality and Dominance: The Creative Writer's View—Conversations between Scottish Poets/Playwrights and Ian Brown." *Interface* 3:17–67 (summer 1984).

Cambridge, Gerry. "Proximities and Distances: Stewart Conn in Conversation." *Dark Horse* 19:28–42 (winter 2006–2007).

Wright, Allen. "A Writer Demands to Work." *Scotsman,* p. 13 (July 29, 1992).

JOHN CORNFORD

(1915–1936)

Robert Sullivan

JOHN CORNFORD WAS born in Cambridge, England, on December 27, 1915. His father, F. M. Cornford, was Professor of Classics at Trinity College, Cambridge, and his mother Frances, granddaughter of Charles Darwin, was a minor poet beginning to make a reputation for herself by the time of John's birth. He joined a sister, Helena, who was born two years before him, and they were joined by a brother, Christopher, two years later. Another brother, Hugh, was born in 1921, and finally another sister, Clare, in 1924. Rupert John Cornford (to give him his full name) was killed fighting on the Cordoba front in the Spanish Civil War on December 27, 1936 (his twenty-first birthday) or in the early hours of the following morning. His body was never recovered.

John Cornford demonstrated a remarkable precociousness in the many endeavors that he undertook as a young man, yet such a prodigious talent was perhaps predictable given the intellectual milieu into which he was born. His father was a graduate of Trinity College (as was his clergyman father before him), where he took a "double-first" in the Classical Tripos examinations. Apart from his other publications, F. M. Cornford's translation of Plato's *The Republic* was for decades the standard text for university students. He married Frances Crofts Darwin in 1909. Her father (Charles Darwin's son) was also called Francis, leading a family friend to suggest a Christmas play entitled "The Importance of Being Frank"! The Darwins were an established family in Cambridge. Frances's father was a botanist and Fellow of Christ's College and his daughter, the aspiring poet, grew up in a liberal and culturally advantaged environment, a tradition that she continued when she set up house at Conduit Head with her new husband. She met another fledgling poet, Rupert Brooke, when he came up to Cambridge in 1906 and they became close friends. When Brooke died of blood poisoning on his way to the Gallipoli campaign in early 1915, the Cornfords decided to name their second child Rupert John in honor of their dead friend. The name Rupert was not to stick, however, and even if it had outlasted John's childhood he would not have felt comfortable with it in later years, scorning as he did the kind of romantic pastoral poetry practiced by Brooke and other Georgian poets, including his mother.

Indeed, it was only a matter of time before John was "lecturing" his mother on the decadence of the tradition within which she wrote, urging her to adopt a more "realistic" and contemporary aesthetic. His predilection for realism was foreshadowed in his childhood when, according to an anecdote remembered by his father, John's mother read him *The Little Mermaid,* one of her favorite childhood books: "Is the bottom of the sea *really* like that?" John asked. When his mother replied in the negative, he responded: "Then I think it's rather silly" (Sloan, *John Cornford: A Memoir,* p. 22). In this memoir, his father describes John as "a large placid baby with very dark eyes and skin and thick black hair" (p. 17), a complexion that was to remain with him for the rest of his life. The few pictures that we have of John in his maturity suggest that he would have made a natural Heathcliff in any production of *Wuthering Heights,* and the dramatic looks were to become an index of the energetic and volatile will within. His brother, Christopher, writes of his school days that "the most remarkable, the main thing about John, was his terrific rate of development, his burning energy.... 'Forging ahead' is a well-worn expression, but it is the best I can think of to describe his life. Trying to know him was like standing on a railway embankment and trying to grab an express train" (p. 29). This boundless energy would go through various transformations, from John's childhood enthusiasm for sports (especially cricket), a precocious immersion in the writing and critiquing of poetry, to eventually a total absorption in left-wing politics.

That he should turn to poetry early in his life was, of course, not coincidental given his mother's interests. However, an early intimacy with his mother was not to last as John began to take a more hurtful stance toward her. This stance manifested itself in his sometimes less than just critique of the poems she sent him while he was at Stowe, his public school. He was keen on the "new" poetry, especially that of T. S. Eliot, Robert Graves, and W. H. Auden. It seemed to him that his mother's poetry belonged to a previous age, a decadent tradition that lacked the impact of felt experience. In 1930, still not fifteen years old, he wrote his mother:

> Here are your two poems. I don't like either of them as much as the previous short one: though I think that in both of them you are getting much closer than in any of your earlier poems...to a live language...I wonder, how much of your poetry is shaped by tradition: are the poems that you write really your most important experiences? or has your view of poetry been so much moulded by the traditional view that the more important experiences are too repressed to occur in poem-form at all?

> (Sloan, p. 68)

In another letter, he responds: "I have just finished reading the 'Tapestry Song,' which I did not like in the very least. I did not think it one-tenth as good as the 'Autumn Fantasia,' which I nearly liked" (Sloan, p. 70). The following few stanzas from "The Tapestry Song" are sufficient to illustrate how the young, modernist-leaning Cornford could not even "nearly" like such an example of perfunctory pastoral from a dying tradition:

O here is Paradise for me
With white Does bounding
And here the fair immortal Tree
With various fruits abounding.
* * *
O sweeter, sweeter, every one
Than mead the Gods have drunk,

And all are for the Shepherd's Son
Who leans against the trunk.
(Frances Cornford, *Collected Poems*, p. 60)

It seems almost as if Mrs. Cornford wanted to entice her critically acute son into such negative criticism, because she wrote much better poetry than the above example and could have sent him poems of a more modern texture, poems such as "To a Fat Lady Seen From the Train," or "The Watch."

The gap between the poetic aesthetic of mother and son is illustrated by John's notebook, which he compiled during 1931, the year his mother was sending him some of her verses. He entered in this a series of ironic poems complete with a title and epigraph from Roy Campbell, a former pupil at Stowe who was to support Franco during the Spanish Civil War. The entry in the notebook is set out as follows:

A Slab of Tripe
Poems 1931
John Cornford.

And the epigraph thus:

Between the marble and the metal
I hear their reedy voices pipe.
Where the blue burnished angels settle
Like flies upon a slab of tripe.
(Cornford Archive, Wren Library, Cambridge)

The ironic gap between the pastoral piping of the "reedy voices" and the utterly arresting modern simile of the last line sets the tone for many of these poems that the fifteen-year-old John Cornford wrote in 1931. As well as a jaundiced look at human progress, one senses in these poems the young Cornford groping his way toward a sociological, if not socialist, critique of modern life:

The clink of empty glasses in dim bars
Hoot of the foghorn bawling out to sea,
The klaxoning of twenty million cars,
Is this thy chosen music,
liberty?
(Cornford Archive, Wren Library, Cambridge)

In another example titled "Machine" ("Man conquered nature; then I conquered man"), he writes of man's enslavement to industrial processes, until eventually he becomes buried by mechanization. "Garret," the longest of this set of poems, is in quatrain form and is the most insistent portrayal of modern squalor and alienation, relating as it does the sleepless night of a suffering working-class man. The following two stanzas give the flavor and, coincidentally, the influence of Eliot, who, the young poet was reading at this time:

Aroused, at length he staggered from his bed,
Tormented by his night of useless pain,
Then clapped his cool hands to his burning head
To ease the angry drumming in his brain.
Then fumbled in a drawer for shirts and braces,
In the dim squalor of the city room,
While from the street below a sea of faces
Tossed ever onwards, upturned through the gloom.
(Cornford Archive)

If the example given above bears the marks of his reading of Eliot, the stanza below from another poem written at Stowe suggests how Auden's influence is present as well. Indeed, these representative lines betray a peculiar fusion of Eliot's allegorical land laid waste and the conspiratorial healer-leader of Auden's early poems, a fusion that hallmarked many of Cornford's poems at this stage:

Turn back. There is no more peace in this landscape.
Heap up the stubble as fuel for an angry mind
That else will burn what it was lighted to warm.
No peace for you here, no more oneness with earth,
And that is not to be recovered. Turn back.
* * *
Shall the eye which saw the land in order
Be blinded by the light which fails without it?
Or will you, at the head of the pass on your alone
  journey,
Looking back over the green land stretched out
  beneath you,
Where farms are lighted at evening and smoke goes
  up straight,
Turn downwards back into that quiet valley?
(Sloan, pp. 60–61)

John's English teacher at Stowe recognized the affinity between his brilliant young pupil's work and that of the young author of *Poems* (1930) and he sent Auden a sample of John's poetry.

Auden responded with some avuncular advice, suggesting that the young poet adopt stricter verse forms in his compositions.

Throughout 1932, John was anxious to leave Stowe and he wrote to his parents (mainly his mother) on different occasions to allow him to do so. Although only sixteen, he had outgrown his school and felt that there was not much more to be learned there. Part of his dilemma was that John had already won a major scholarship to Trinity College, Cambridge, but he could not accept it for at least another year. This would mean "wasting" his time at Stowe when he felt that he could be out in the world gaining other valuable experiences. Allied to this was the fact that he had become acutely aware of the current political and economic situation, of the dramatic rise in unemployment and the concomitant hardship endured by the British working class. He began to read Marx: "I have bought myself a *Kapital* and a good deal of commentary on it...Also *The Communist Manifesto,* with which I am a little disappointed, though part of it was an extremely remarkable prophesy" (Sloan, pp. 44–45). Poetry was pushed further and further into the margins of John's life as he threw himself, with all his notable gusto, into the realm of political analysis. To one correspondent he apologized for letters that were like manifestoes, and in another to his liberally—oriented parents he is sorry for "addressing [them] like a public meeting" (Sloan, p. 46). In yet another letter to them he wrote, "I don't think of communism as inevitable, like measles, or the war, or the present crisis, but as *necessary*" (Sloan, p. 47).

The historical circumstances in which the politically astute John Cornford found himself during his final term at Stowe in 1932 became more and more acute. His letters were almost exclusively concerned with the contemporary political situation. In one letter, he lectured his mother on the hunger marchers (she had asked if John felt the marchers were "really" hungry), in another he argued for a more abrupt form of revolution rather than the gradualist Fabianism to which his parents subscribed; and in yet another on the mutual exclusiveness of communism and pacifism. Regardless of whether his mother could bridge the gap between her well-meaning liberalism and her son's ever-increasing commitment to revolutionary politics, she did agree to let him leave Stowe at the end of 1932, no doubt hoping that John would return to the family home while waiting to take up his fellowship at Cambridge. Her son had other ideas. In the autumn of 1932, he wrote to his mother that he was looking forward to living alone and he made plans to study at The London School of Economics, an institution founded by the Fabians, which while not as "revolutionary" as John might have wished, was gaining a reputation for student radicalism. Fortuitously, perhaps, the rooms he moved into just off Red Lion Square shared the same street with the well-known Parton Street Bookshop, a center for young left-wing radicals. He had now successfully broken free not only of parental control, but also the *loco parentis* of Stowe, and he immediately threw himself into student politics with all the boundless energy for which he was known.

This flurry of activity in political matters, rather than academic studies, continued to worry his mother, so that John had at times to write and reassure her that his "practical" activities (his work for the Labour Research Department, for example) formed part of his education. However, despite these letters of explanation and reassurance, Mrs. Cornford was still anxious enough about her son's well-being and the intensity of his commitment to persuade him to take a short family holiday in the south of France. When he returned to London, around Easter, 1933, he wrote to his mother to say that the "South of France was well worth it, though not perfectly successful" (Sloan, p. 87).

The trip had certainly been far from "perfectly successful" if it was meant to distract John from the fervency of his activities in London. His commitment only became more resolute. Most significantly, his new life dictated that he break off a romantic attachment he had had over the past few years with his cousin Elizabeth. In a letter dated April 24, 1933, a week or so after he had returned from France (it is very possible that Elizabeth was there as well), he wrote to his friend and confidant Tristan Jones that he had

had to "break with Elisabeth" and he thinks this will be "for good" (Sloan, p. 88). The "break with the past" that John speaks of in this letter was deepened further when, shortly after making this statement, he was eating at The Nanking Chinese restaurant in Soho—a favorite meeting place for radical students—and was introduced to an attractive young woman. She was Ray (Rachel) Peters, a working-class woman from the depressed area of Wales. Ray was a few years older than John and a member of the Communist Party. She and John bonded almost immediately and soon after Ray moved in with him at his Parton Street lodgings.

John Cornford officially joined the Communist Party of Great Britain (he had been a member for some time of the Communist Youth League) on March 17, 1933. By the summer of that year he had broken free from most aspects of his bourgeois background. He engaged himself in various kinds of Party work, carried out multiple trades-union related tasks for the Labour Research Department, and had established both social and emotional ties to the working class. All the components of his new life during the six months or so he spent in London, he would take with him to Trinity College, Cambridge, in October. He was just seventeen-years-old.

CAMBRIDGE

Shortly after his arrival at Trinity College, John became involved with student politics with all his well-known vigor. He worked tirelessly to establish the communist faction within the socialist student movement. In "Communism in the Universities," a reflective essay he wrote in 1936, John examined the situation of those students he and others were trying to convert. The growth of communism, he argues, could no longer be considered "a phenomenon that can be dismissed as an outburst of transient youthful enthusiasm" (Sloan, p. 157). Most students, he wrote, do not confront hardships of the working class, but "a medical student comes up against the fact, for example, that hundreds of children suffer every year from rickets, which is an unnecessary and preventable disease [brought about by] poverty."

He goes on to give more concrete examples: "People with Firsts [top class honors degrees] who, a few years ago, turned up their noses at teaching jobs are now glad enough to get a job in a secondary school...I have known one case of a graduate with first class honours in Zoology with a job as a rat catcher at 30 s[hillings] a week" (Sloan, pp. 159–160).

Near the beginning of this essay, John outlined several of the successes of the student socialist movement, particularly the demonstration on "Remembrance Day," November 11, 1933, and the welcoming of the Hunger Marchers in 1934. And there were other successes for the "Cornford Socialists." They "put tremendous energy into a campaign to receive the North-east Coast contingent [of the Hunger Marchers] on its way to London" (Sloan, p. 103), and staged "a very successful" demonstration against Oswald Mosley's British Union of Fascists, "ending with a speech by John, very excited, on the fountain in the market-place and a fine...drinking and singing party" (Sloan, p. 109).

Despite his hectic schedule organizing meetings, demonstrations, and proselytizing on behalf of the Communist group within the university socialist movement—while also studying for a history degree—John found the time to write several articles. In one piece, "The Class Front of Modern Art," published in *The Student Vanguard,* December, 1933 (he had published a similar article, "Art and the Class Struggle" in the same periodical in May 1933), John condemned what he diagnosed as the bourgeois artist's separation of art and life, the reactionary premise of the artist as an impartial observer. Like many young men who moved from an interest in poetry to an active role in socialist causes (Christopher Caudwell is a paradigmatic example), the young Cornford no doubt felt himself forced to examine the "bourgeois art" that he once practiced through the lens of his new perspective.

This task of bringing his poetic endeavors into line with his proletarian activity is evidenced by the few poems he wrote during this period at Cambridge. Primarily, they bear the scars of a struggle between a persona that wishes to speak collectively on behalf of a cause, and the rem-

nants of an individual lyrical impulse that must be suppressed or renounced. One of these poems, "Keep Culture Out of Cambridge," a sonnet that satirizes the feigned and ultimately superficial positions taken by modernist poets and artists, can also be read as a document that records John Cornford's own renunciation of his previous poetic proclivities and the adoption of a persona that utilizes the collective "we" that speaks for the Party. Alluding to Eliot's poem "Whispers of Immortality," and adopting Eliot's images of sterility, it begins: "Wind from the dead land, hollow men, /Webster's skull and Eliot's pen," and goes on to catalo some of the modernist "tricks" John Cornford and his contemporaries "once thought smart." The poem concludes with the following lines:

There's none of these fashions have come to stay,
And there's nobody here got time to play,
All we've brought are our party cards
Which are no bloody good for your bloody charades.

(Sloan, p. 171)

These lines mark a collective "we" or "us" that sets itself in an adversarial relation to "them" or "you," a poetic strategy that is a constant feature in John's poetry at this time. There is as well in these poems the shared subject matter of a necessary pain, or "hurt" ("hurt" is a ubiquitous term), if the old life is to be shed and the new communist life brought into being. One of the poems begins "Shall spring bring remembrance, a raw wound smarting? /Say rather for us fine weather for hurting, /For there's no parting curse we fear/ Here we break for good with the old way of living." The stanzas continue thus:

Best cut out all the talk of renewing
And the wordy philosophies of destroying—
Easiest far to tell them straight
We don't do this for fun, and joking apart,
We mean what we say, and don't care if we hurt,
For there's plenty to do, and no time to wait.

(Sloan, p. 169)

The collective "we" of the poem, "Who know the future holds pain and anger," are willing to forgo popularity to "Throw pepper in the eyes of the policeman's horses," and "Seduce from allegiance His Majesties forces," all to further the cause of seeing "The old world in a new light." The poem culminates in the grand gesture, the rhetorical flourish:

Now the crazy structure of the old world's reeling,
They can see with their own eyes its pitprops falling,
Whether they like it, or whether they don't.
Though they lie to themselves so as not to discover
That their game is up, that their day is over,
They can't be deaf to our shout, "RED FRONT!"
(Sloan, pp. 169–171)

John Cornford had written better poetry than this as a schoolboy, and, as we shall see, he would write better poetry again in Spain, a poetry in which the collective and the personal, the "we" and the "I," are in a heartfelt dialectical tension.

Another poem of this Cambridge period, "As Our Might Lessens," with its epigraph from the Anglo-Saxon epic "The Battle of Maldon," is in a similar vein. In the struggle to shape history and capture the future, "action" must supplant introspection, even if this means suffering through a "senseless-seeming pain" in order to usher in the new life. The second section of the poem begins:

No abstraction of the brain
Will counteract the pain.
The living thought must put on flesh and blood.
Action intervenes, revealing
New ways of love, new ways of feeling,
Gives nerve and bone and muscle to the word.

It is "action," the Marxian "praxis," that will ensure "new ways of living" and, like the Anglo-Saxon warriors at Maldon, the "soldiers" who fight this fight must be resolute, their "sinews hard as metal" (Sloan, pp. 173–75).

It seems evident in these poems that John Cornford was attempting to forge a plain style that would allow him to express his newfound weltanschauung and had he survived Spain we must wonder what kind of poet, if any, he would have become. It is important to remind ourselves that he had barely turned twenty when he was writing these poems in Cambridge and was—apart from his many political activities—negotiating the space between adolescence and adulthood, from schoolboy-student to socialist leader.

In his contribution to the Sloan memorial volume, Victor Kiernan, John's close friend at the time, presented the portrait of a dedicated communist, but also of a very young man with anarcho-romantic ideas. This manifested itself in various ways, not the least of which was his reaction against the restrictions, particularly the sartorial regimen, required of him at Stowe, his public school, and later at Cambridge. Victor Kiernan remembered him cutting somewhat of a ragged figure as he strode across Great Court (Trinity's main quadrangle), or walked along the Cloister by New Court as he made his way to the library. His academic gown, required dress for all undergraduates, had reached such a state of dishevelment that "the Procters declared him academically nude" and Kiernan was obliged to supply him with "an old gown of [his] own" (Sloan, p. 115). John's college rooms between Bishop's Hostel and New Court were Spartan, featuring light bulbs as nude as his gown. It was there, in the "long room" that Kiernan would sometimes visit John, once witnessing him "use a bread-knife to clean his fingernails with complete naturalness" (Sloan, p. 115). His reputation and eccentric behavior caused him to be lampooned in *Trinity Review,* the College magazine. At one point, Kiernan compared his general demeanor to that of Lenin's: "he followed Lenin in his complete contempt for all useless sentiment and psychological weakness". Once, Kiernan asked John, "what single thing in the universe gave him most satisfaction, and he answered, after thinking for a minute, 'the existence of the Communist International'" (Sloan, p. 120). Like a lot of charismatic leaders (it is no coincidence that Kiernan should compare him to Lenin), John's personality had its "ruthless" edge as well as its caring one. Kiernan remarked on a discernible "mixture of sensitiveness and roughness in him," (Sloan, p. 118) that ranged from his being genuinely moved by the music of Sibelius, to expressing an admiration for Béla Kun, who was forced to machine-gun "five thousand prisoners during a forced retreat in the Russian Civil War: [John] told it not in a spirit of sadism, but of appreciation of an act of political necessity firmly carried out" (Sloan, p. 122).

This necessary ruthlessness, what Kiernan above terms as a "contempt for all useless sentiment and psychological weakness," could enter into personal relations as well as political matters, and at times it is figured in the imagery of some of his poems. In "Sad Poem," written on the occasion of John's ending his relationship with Ray Peters, the controlling imagery is one of indispensable pain and hurting. The first stanza explores what their love had been, how it is now "gone," and the fact that they have "loved each other too long to try to be kind." The second stanza expresses the need for the requisite surgery if the cancer of deceit is not to fester:

Though parting's as cruel as
the surgeon's knife,
It's better than the ingrown canker, the rotten leaf.
All that I know is I have got to leave.
There's new life fighting in me to get at the air,
And I can't stop its mouth with the rags of old love.
Clean wounds are easiest to bear.

(Sloan, p. 168)

It was not long before John met a new love, a love that he took with him to Spain and which was to last the rest of his short life. According to a short memoir Margot Heinemann contributed to the archive in the Wren Library, she met John on a picket line outside a bus garage in Cambridge in 1934. Like him, she was upper-middle class, educated at Rodean, one of the most prestigious girls' public schools in England, and had taken a "double first" in English at Newnham College, Cambridge. She had published in the *Cambridge Review,* and was a member of the Communist Party. Like John, she also worked for the Labour Research Department, her specialty being the coal-mining industry and trades union organization. Once they had met, John and Margot tried to see as much as possible of one another, but this was not easy given John's studentship and other work in Cambridge, and Margot's work as a teacher in Birmingham. At one point John applied for a part-time tutorship at the Birmingham branch of the Worker's Education Association so that he might spend more time with Margot, but despite a strong reference from his history tutor at Trinity, he was turned down. On one visit to Birmingham he participated in a

trades union demonstration distributing leaflets outside a factory and he was arrested. During the Christmas vacation of 1935, he and Margot and other friends were able to spend a peaceful time at a country retreat owned by some friends of John's parents, but, inevitably, they had to go their separate ways, she to Birmingham and he back to Cambridge.

On the way back to Cambridge, John had to travel via Cardiff, Wales, in order to attend a University Labour Federation conference, at which he was elected Vice-President. Among his papers there is a poem dated "Cardiff, 3.1.36," with the ironic title "A Happy New Year," in which he expresses his loneliness at having just left Margot. He may have had in mind, consciously or not, his erstwhile hero Auden's reflective poem of the same title. As with other of John's poems, this three-stanza poem contemplates loss and hurt, as well as the concomitant necessity for a resilient attitude to combat such pain. The last line of the second quatrain turns the poem from a litany of loss toward a recognition of the need for human endurance; the speaker is after all, not a "statue" but a "man." The poem is short enough to quote in its entirety:

All last night we lay so close,
All completeness of the heart
The restless future will efface;
Tomorrow night we sleep apart.

The eyeless shutter clamping out,
Dear, the certainty of your touch,
All the warmth and all the light;
O don't think, it hurts too much.

Though your nerves are frozen numb,
Your sorrow will not make time stop,
You're not a statue but a man;
O don't grieve, it doesn't help.

(Cornford Archive)

Although John would go to Birmingham to visit Margot as often as he could, it would not be until Easter of 1936 that they would have another extended time together, visiting John's Cambridge friend Michael Straight, whose parents had converted Dartington Hall, Devon, into the well-known progressive school of that name. When they parted they had hoped to have another extended time together, traveling to France that summer when John had finished his degree and Margot was free from teaching. As we shall see, historical events prevented this excursion.

The fact that John spent so much of his time on political work did not preclude attention to his studies; indeed, the Communist Party insisted that student members do particularly well. Victor Kiernan saw John "on most mornings sitting concentratedly over a book in the college reading-room," and when he was able to look at John's notebooks after his death they showed that "he had worked as thoroughly for his Tripos as at politics" (Sloan, pp. 117–18). When he received his results in June, 1936, he wrote to his mother saying that he "wasn't surprised by the first [class honors], but quite a lot by the distinction." He goes on to tell her about his winning the Earl of Derby Research Scholarship, which would allow him to pursue research on "the social roots of the Elizabethan poets" (Galassi, *Understand the Weapon*, p. 170).

The holiday in France that he and Margot had planned after his examinations was at first postponed, then abandoned, when John heard of the uprising in Spain that had taken place on July 18, 1936. He was very interested in the events taking place in Barcelona, a city that was on the verge of becoming a workers' state. Margot Heinemann, in a note in the Cornford archive explained that "he went to Spain...with a press card hoping to report what was going on[,] not intending to join up at all... expecting the fighting to last only a few days." He and a Cambridge associate arrived in Dieppe, France, on August 6 and were in Barcelona two days later. The possibility that he might yet join Margot in France was set aside when John became embroiled in what became known as "the last great cause," the Spanish Republic's fight against the Fascist uprising led by Generalissimo Francisco Franco.

SPAIN

John Cornford arrived in Barcelona on August 8, 1936. His decision to go was made impulsively and his family seemed not to be aware of it. His brother Christopher, with whom he was fairly close, remembered being with him earlier that summer at the Cambridge Boating Sheds, then a short time later he heard that John had gone to Spain. Like many left-leaning intellectuals, John was aware of the political situation in Spain. In his 1934 essay, "The Coming Struggle for Power," he remarked on the recent "Anarchist workers' putsch in Spain" and on how the Spanish Communist Party had "converted it from a senseless terroristic putsch into a serious political struggle of the working class" (Sloan, pp. 141–42). By the time of his arrival in Barcelona, the workers in the form of militia committees were firmly in control, if "control" is the proper term. John, well versed in the theory of revolution, would now "understand physically what the dictatorship of the proletariat means" (Sloan, p. 198).

After what was no doubt an exhilarating two days imbibing the heady atmosphere of revolutionary Barcelona, John was anxious to see the war firsthand. He left on August 11 with the Austrian-born journalist Franz Borkenau, whose book, *The Spanish Cockpit*, records the political background and early months of the war. John noted in his diary many of his impressions on this trip to the front, impressions that he would later try to organize in a long letter to Margot Heinemann, and later still in his essay, "The Situation in Catalonia." John did not return to Barcelona with Borkenau, but instead enlisted in the P.O.U.M. (Partido Obrero de Unificación Marxista) militia.

The letter that he wrote to Margot Heinemann during those early days at the front ("Diary Letter From Aragon" in the Sloan memorial volume) enables us to get a sense of his movements and feelings during these few weeks. Although the letter is somewhat rambling and chronologically confusing, his thoughts and observations reveal a pattern of oscillation between the objective and the subjective, between his observations on the tactical and political events at the front and the fears and insecurities of John Cornford. In fact, this seemingly random letter concerns itself with the same dialectic of personal reflection and historical necessity as that of his well-known poem "Full Moon at Tierz: Before the Storming of Huesca" which was written during this period.

In the very first paragraph of the letter he asks himself: "why am I here?" As if subjecting himself to self-analysis, he goes on to tell Margot that she would know "the political reasons," the objective historical events that led him to this lonely hillside in Aragon. But, he tells her, there are subjective reasons as well (Sloan, p. 195).

Whatever the components of the personal element were, John now had plenty of time to reflect on them. The two terms that punctuate the early part of his Aragon letter are "loneliness" and "boredom," and this state was compounded by the fact that he could not communicate with any of his comrades because he could speak neither French nor Spanish. He remembers his first Sunday at the front, August 16, 1936, and how he could hear the "slow and mournful" bells of the church in Perdiguera, a village held by the fascists. He reflects: "I don't know why, but that depressed me as much as anything ever has" (p. 195). Then in a seemingly random juxtaposition, but one that perhaps betrays the logic of the unconscious, he reports that he had a dream: "One of the toughest people when I was small at school was the captain of rugger, an oaf called D——, I was in the same dormitory and terrified of him. I hadn't thought of him in years, but last night I dreamt extremely vividly about having a fight with him and holding my own" (Sloan, pp. 196–97). The "mournful bells" of Perdiguera no doubt brought back memories of bells that might have chimed in John's childhood with all their feelings of loneliness and insecurity, but the dream helped him dispel, or at least assuage, any doubts he might have when he faced combat.

After expressing his desire for some English cigarettes and English tea, he explains that he is to go into action soon near Huesca. On the night of September 1, 1936, there was a full moon and it must have been this night, or the next, that he turned the pages of his Cambridge diary to the blank pages devoted to October and penciled in the stanzas of "Full Moon at Tierz: Before the Storming of Huesca." The poem begins by describing the past as a prehistoric time when "a glacier, gripped the mountain wall,/ And time was inches." The second section moves through "Time present," to the here and now of Huesca

where "the fool moon/ Throws shadows clear as daylight's…" as "the barren hills of Aragon/ Announce [their] testing has begun." The "testing" of which the poem speaks is both a collective one (the "we" of the poem) and a personal one, that of the nerve of John Cornford:

Though Communism was my waking time,
Always before the lights of home
Shone clear and steady and full in view—
Here, if you fall, there's help for you—
Now with my Party, I stand quite alone.

Then let my private battle with my nerves,
The fear of pain whose pain survives,
The love that tears me by the roots,
The loneliness that claws my guts,
Fuse in the welded front out fight preserves.

(Sloan, p. 243)

This section of the poem echoes many of the "private" fears and anxieties that John had expressed in the Aragon letter. The fourth and final section pans out camera-like from the personal to the collective and political once more, this time focusing on the historical course of socialism and its importance for "the workers of all the world." Here the moon that shines on the plain around Huesca is the same moon that shines over Germany, England, and Wales, and it serves to symbolize the common fight throughout Europe "For Communism and for liberty":

Now the same night falls over Germany
And the impartial beauty of the stars
Lights from the unfeeling sky
Oranienburg and freedom's crooked scars.
We can do nothing to ease that pain
But prove the agony was not in vain.

England is silent under the same moon,
From Clydeside to the gutted pits of Wales.
The innocent mask conceals that soon
Here, too, our freedom's swaying in the scales.
O understand before too late
Freedom was never held without a fight.

(Sloan, p. 244)

Sometime during the attacks in the first weeks of September John found the time to write another poem, a short love lyric that appears in his diary immediately below the last stanza of "Full Moon at Tierz." A kind of last testament, the poem originally had no title and was published in *New Writing IV* (autumn 1937) under the generic title "Poem." Eventually, in the Sloan memorial volume, the lyric was given the title "To Margot Heinemann," in acknowledgement of its intended recipient. It is one of the most evocative love poems in the English tradition. Its deceptively simple sentiments are rendered in the most fundamental diction, yet the poem evokes a powerful response:

Heart of the heartless world,
Dear heart, the thought of you
Is the pain at my side,
The shadow that chills my view.

The wind rises in the evening,
Reminds that autumn is near.
I am afraid to lose you,
I am afraid of my fear.

On the last mile to Huesca,
The last fence for our pride,
Think so kindly, dear, that I
Sense you at my side.

And if bad luck should lay my strength
Into the shallow grave,
Remember all the good you can;
Don't forget my love.

(Sloan, p. 246–47)

It is extraordinary that even in this most personal of poems that John Cornford (consciously or not) could not help but incorporate the Marxist doctrine that had by now become part of his sensibility. It is in Marx's "Contribution to the Critique of Hegel's Philosophy of Right" that we will find the origin of John's metaphor: "Religion is the sigh of the oppressed creature, the heart of a heartless world, just as it is the spirit of spirit-less conditions" (Kamenka, p. 115). Communism and his love for Margot Heinemann become fused in this poem, a fusion that would afford John Cornford the spiritual sustenance he needed at the time.

Around the second week of September, John became ill with a stomach complaint that he had suffered from before, only this time it was much more severe. It became evident that he would have to be hospitalized and he was taken first to the makeshift hospital at Lerida, and when he was strong enough to be moved, back to

Barcelona. Whether or not he suggested it himself when he visited the offices of the Anti-Fascist Militias, or the proposition was put to him, it was decided that he should return to England on a propaganda mission. His passport shows a "Salida" (exit) stamp at Port Bou on September 14, 1936, and he was back in England by the September 16. It might have been on this trip or shortly after his arrival that John penned the last poem he ever wrote. It was thought for some time (understandably, given the sentimental romanticism of the implications) that "To Margot Heinemann" was John's last poem, but there is sufficient evidence to suggest that the much more cynical and ironically detached "A Letter From Aragon" was written either in the hospital or shortly after he had left for England. This free-verse poem with its deeply ironic refrain "This is a quiet sector of a quiet front," expresses in the most understated manner how matter—of—fact human suffering is in war. The description of " [They] buried Ruiz in a new pine coffin," in a shroud that "was too small and his washed feet stuck out," while the "stink of his corpse" comes through the "clean pine boards," is summarized in the Anglo-Saxon-like simplicity of "Death was not dignified." The poem then moves into the biographical realm when John recalls his recent time in the hospital:

In the clean hospital bed my eyes were so heavy
Sleep easily blotted out one ugly picture,
A wounded militiaman moaning on a stretcher,
Now out of danger, but still crying for water,
Strong against death, but unprepared for such pain.
This on a quiet front.

(p. 245–246)

The last words of the poem are given over to the exhortation of an "Anarchist worker," who admonishes the young English volunteer to "Tell the workers of England/ This was a war not of our own making," and, by implication, to enlist all the aid that can be mustered for this just cause. (Sloan, pp. 245–46). This was exactly the mission John Cornford undertook over the next three weeks while on leave in England.

Immediately upon his arrival, John set about the task of recruiting a group of volunteers that would return with him to Spain, and, hopefully, form the nucleus of a British militia unit. His experiences on the Aragon front had convinced him that a great deal more discipline and tactical expertise was needed, and he hoped his group might provide it. He had little time for personal affairs, although he did see his father in Cambridge, was able to meet with Margot, and visited Michael Straight again at Dartington. His brother Christopher saw him fleetingly: "He was back on leave, and I saw him for one evening in London: he was dressed in old flannels and the rope-soled shoes of the Spanish worker; his face was yellow with the effects of jaundice and a long journey...We walked together, as so often before, down the King's Road, he talking and I listening. People in the street watched us curiously. Then we parted, John still too excited to sleep; and that was the last time I ever saw him" (Sloan, pp. 58–59).

John called upon some of his communist friends from Cambridge and other universities for his recruiting "campaign," but other volunteers were signed up merely by chance. One of the group, Sam Russell, a University of London postgraduate in archeological studies, met John in the office of Harry Pollitt when he went to the Communist headquarters in King Street, London. Another was Bernard Knox, a contemporary from St. John's College, Cambridge. Before they set out for Paris, Bernard went with John to visit the latter's father in Cambridge, on which occasion Professor Cornford gave John the pistol that he bought for himself during the First World I. John's mother was ill and away from the family home, which meant that she never got to say goodbye to her son. Despite his hurried schedule—he was also writing his essay, "The Situation in Catalonia," during this period—he had time to visit his old friend Michael Straight at Dartington Hall around the 24 or 25 of September. They had hoped that Margot Heinemann would go as well but she was busy with her teaching in Birmingham. It was on this visit that the last photograph was taken of John Cornford, a portrait that appears as frontispiece for the Sloan memorial volume. It shows him striking a rather belligerent pose in a pair of well-worn trousers and jacket, a cigarette in his right hand and his left fist slightly raised and clenched. The group was to leave for France on October 6, and on October 4, John took the time to write to his College Tutor at Trinity College: "I am writing this letter to resign my scholarships.... I should like to take this opportunity of thanking you, and through you other Fellows of the College...for the tremendous personal kindness and interest you have always shown me, even though you must have looked with disfavour on many of my activities" (Galassi, p. 182).

As John's passport verifies, the volunteers arrived in Dieppe on October 6 and then made their way to Paris. One of the group, John Sommerfield, was soon to write *Volunteer in Spain* (1937), which is dedicated to John Cornford, and it is of inestimable value as it documents in some detail John's demeanor and exploits during his second stint in Spain. Sommerfield records that they had not been in Paris very long when they knew that John's idea for a small British unit would have to be abandoned. They found themselves in a hotel in the Bellville area of Paris with volunteers from France, Germany, Poland, Italy, and Belgium, all of whom left together by train for Marseilles and eventually boarded a ship for Alicante in Spain. The ship sailed through the night without running lights and the next morning entered the harbor at Alicante under the scrutiny of foreign ships that were enforcing the Non-Intervention agreement. Sommerfield remembers their disembarkation: "And we marched along the quay singing the 'International' with a new and joyous feeling. Then we were in the town and the streets were filling with crowds who sang with us, saluting with raised clenched fists and shouting" (Sommerfield, p. 17). They were then taken by train to Albacete, where all the new volunteers received their basic training, arriving cold and exhausted at four in the morning. After his experience on the Aragon front, when he had endured long periods of inactivity and boredom, John had told his group to be sure and pack reading matter. He had brought a volume of Marx's *Das Kapital*, a volume of Shakespeare's tragedies (no doubt a remnant of his erstwhile research proposal into the social roots of Elizabethan literature), and a pocket chess set.

When their weapons eventually arrived, the rifles turned out to be of World War I. vintage and the machine guns were ancient St. Etiennes that may have dated back to the Franco-Prussian war of 1870. It was with this antique weaponry that John and his group set out for Madrid on November 6, 1936. Sommerfield remembers their exhaustion after eleven hours in the lorry and how they thawed out over coffee: "John took off his great overcoat. How we had laughed at him in the hot days as he had trailed about in that monstrous coat…that reached down almost to his heels. With that, an ammunition belt strapped around him, rifle slung on one shoulder and blanket across the other, his high cheek-bones, sculptured almost Mongol face, he looked like something in a bad picture of the retreat from Moscow." (Sommerfield, p. 53).

They reached the outskirts of Madrid on November 7 (the anniversary of the Bolshevik Revolution, as their political commissar reminded them) and next day took part in the historic march of the first—officially called the XIth—International Brigade, lugging their fairly useless, but excessively heavy, St. Etienne machine guns. John Sommerfield had the feeling that theirs was less a triumphant entry than a desperate hope. Some locals thought that the city might fall by the weekend. Eventually, John's group arrived at the not quite completed Ciudad Universitaria (University City) which formed part of the frontline holding back the fascist advance. On this front, the forces fought from building to building, sometimes from academic department to academic department, classroom to classroom. John's group held the Filosofia y Letras (Philosophy and Letters) faculty, where they took up positions facing the enemy-held buildings dominated by the Hospital Clinico, in which the Moorish snipers held a superior hilltop position. Their section was allocated a lecture room on the top floor and Sommerfield remembers the delight of the group when they found they had clean toilets and showers with shining white tiled walls. He and John availed themselves of the facilities the very first night of their arrival, but their delight was short-lived when they found the

water was cold. More importantly, they had been issued a number of modern Lewis machine guns and it wasn't long before they had an opportunity to test them against the enemy.

From time to time, the unit was ordered to leave the Philosophy building and take up advanced positions in the surrounding terrain. It was during these brisk days and fiercely cold nights that John's "greatcoat" was the envy of his comrades, and his little pocket chess set got much use. Sommerfield remembers that they played games that were frequently interrupted because of enemy action. Their hardships in the area surrounding the university were bad enough, but to make matters worse, when they got back to University City, some of the buildings had been taken by the fascists and had to be recaptured. Despite the relative comfort of the Philosophy and Letters building, it was, in Bernard Knox's words, "no rest cure." They had to contend with snipers who fired constantly through the open windows. They improvised by constructing barricades from the numerous books from the faculty library. Knox recalls particularly a sturdy "encyclopedia of Hindu mythology and religion. We later discovered, after hearing bullets smack into the books, that the average penetration was to about page 350…" (Knox, "Premature Anti-Fascist"). Not all the books in the library were put to this use. Sommerfield found a set of Everyman Classics and remembers one particularly cold morning when he discovered "De Quincey's Lake poets and rolled [himself] up in a carpet and read voraciously [but] twice [he] had to leave his book to shoot at the Falangists who popped out like rabbits when the shells burst" (Sommerfield, p. 146). It was in such a situation that John Cornford might have killed his first enemy. He wrote to Margot: "The afternoon of the second day I think I killed a Fascist. Fifteen or sixteen of them were running from a bombardment. I and two Frenchmen were firing from our barricades with sights at 900. We got one and both said it was I that hit him, though I couldn't be sure" (Galassi, p. 188).

Daily life in the Philosophy and Letters building was a bizarre mixture of domesticity and extreme danger. Sommerfield recalls how, after they had built their barricades with "volumes of Indian metaphysics and early nineteenth-century German philosophy," they spread carpets on the floor, "found a clock and a barometer and hung them on the wall; some tourist 'Come to Sunny Spain' posters were found, and one put up as a mockery to the climate" (Sommerfield, p. 146). It was in the middle of such camaraderie that suddenly a shell burst into their quarters through the wall where the Sunny Spain poster had been. Sommerfield was on the last chapter of the Lake Poets, having read all afternoon, when he heard an "appalling crash and looked up and the room was thick with dust and smoke" (Sommerfield, p. 146). John Cornford received a head wound that he didn't treat as seriously as it deserved and Bernard Knox remembers that "for the next week or so, he wore a white bandage round the top of his head that made him look, from a distance, like a Moorish trooper" (Knox). The shell was from one of their own anti-aircraft guns deployed to keep the Fascist planes at bay.

Shortly after this incident, John and his group were given a short leave in the city of Madrid proper, where Knox remembers drinking numerous "cafés con leche" and going to the movies to see a Russian film. This respite did not last very long, however, and soon they were put on alert again and transported to the northwest front, on the Escorial road, near the village of Boadilla del Monte. With his head still bandaged in "Moorish style," John was elected to lead the section in this offensive. Bernard Knox would never forget this advance because it nearly cost him his life. Their orders were to cover the infantry attack, to retreat with their machine guns, and to hold the main road into the village. They withdrew by sections, one section covering the other's retreat. As Knox's group withdrew dragging the heavy machine guns, he felt "a shocking blow and a burning pain through [his] neck and right shoulder and fell to the ground on [his] back with blood spurting up like a fountain." He goes on: "John came back, with David, our Oxford man who had been a medical student. I heard him say: 'I can't do anything with that' and John bent down and said, 'God bless you, Bernard' and left. They had to go; they had to set up the gun

and cover the withdrawal of other crew" (Knox).

Miraculously, Bernard Knox did not die and made it back to his machine-gun section, much to the astonishment of his comrades. While Knox was in the Brigade hospital set up in the Palace Hotel in Madrid, John went to see him. He and the few survivors from the original group were on their way to join what was to become the British Battalion being formed at the training ground in Madrigueras near Albacete. Many new recruits, including Christopher Caudwell, who left England on December 11, were being trained here. Ralph Fox, novelist and communist intellectual, was also there at this time, serving as political commissar. It was proposed that John Cornford remain at the base to help train new recruits rather than going to fight at the Cordoba front, but he turned down this proposal, preferring instead to remain with his comrades. With the only four remaining comrades from the original group of twenty-one who were not dead or wounded, John set out on or about Christmas Day, 1936, for the little town of Andujar, where he detrained and prepared for the assault on Lopera, which was held by the fascists. This would be John Cornford's last battle.

This attack was criminally mishandled by the French commander, Major Lasalle; so much so that, shortly after the campaign, he was tried and shot as a fascist sympathizer and possible spy. The support that Lasalle had promised to Number One Company, John's company, never arrived, and despite many brave attempts to take and hold a ridge that became known as the "English Crest," they were decimated by Fascist airplanes, artillery, and machine-gun fire. During the final retreat, they had to leave the dead and wounded behind. John Cornford's body was among those never recovered. Given the chaos of the attack and the retreat, it is impossible to be certain exactly how John died. There have been many accounts, many noting his bravery, although his friend Michael Straight had heard rumors that he might have been shot mistakenly by his own side. The most intriguing account comes in the shape of a letter from Maurice Levine to John's brother Christopher and dated March 16, 1975. This handwritten letter, among the "Cornford Papers" in the Wren Library, gives the following account: The First British Company was ordered to withdraw from the crest of a hill "after heavy losses." On regrouping it was discovered that Ralph Fox had been left behind, wounded. Levine states that John Cornford went "back to the crest to help his comrade...It was either the 26 or 27 of December." If this account is accurate, it would mean that two of the most promising English intellectuals of the epoch may have died together.

John had written to Margot Heinemann more than once about the possibility of his being killed and not seeing her again. While still at training camp, he wrote, ominously: "It will be a matter of weeks before I get to the front, [and] then a short life but a merry one" (Galassi, p. 184). After a detailed account of the group's activities on the Madrid front, he closes another letter on a more positive note: "I felt very depressed when I wrote this. Now I've eaten and am for the moment in a building. I feel fine. Warm. I'll get back to you, love, don't worry. God bless you" (Galassi, p. 186). In most likely the last letter he had a chance to write, dated "8th December, '36," he ended the letter with the following: "Well, one day the war will end—I'd give it till June or July, and then if I'm alive I'm coming back to you. I think about you often, but there's nothing I can do but say again, be happy, darling. And I'll see you again one day. Bless you, John" (Galassi, p. 189).

Such a reunion was not to be, and Margot expressed her grief in a poem, "Grieve in a New Way for New Losses," published in the Autumn number of *New Writing,* 1937. The title and the refrain "All this is not more than we can deal with," expresses both the regret and defiant attitude that informs the elegy. The first stanza represents the general tone of the poem:

And after the first sense, "He will not come again"
Fearing still the images of corruption,
To think he lies out there, and changes
In the process of the earth from what I knew,
Decays and even there in the grave, shut close
In the dark, away from me, speechless and cold,

Is in no way left the same that I have known.

(Lehmann, p. 60)

Perhaps the final, more buoyant, words on John's death should be provided by his old comrade-in-arms, John Sommerfield. The epitaph-like conclusion to his memoir of the war suggests that the body may decay, but the spirit that John Cornford epitomized will never die: "I did not see him dead. I can only remember him alive and laughing, strong, resolute, and reliable.... To me he is the type and symbol of the youth of today whose conscious task is to change the world...." Cornford and others like him who were killed "represent something that cannot be killed, and their deaths will only be in vain if we fail to carry on the struggle in which they fell" (Sommerfield, p. 155).

Selected Bibliography

WORKS OF JOHN CORNFORD

BIBLIOGRAPHIES and ARCHIVAL MATERIAL
There is no comprehensive bibliography of Cornford's writings, but much of it is listed in Galassi and Sloan, details of which are given below. John Cornford's papers, among which there remains some unpublished material, are housed with his father's (F.M Cornford) in the Wren Library, Trinity College, Cambridge.

CRITICAL AND BIOGRAPHICAL STUDIES
Borkenau, Franz. *The Spanish Cockpit.* Ann Arbor: University of Michigan Press, 1963 (First published 1937).

Carpenter, Humphrey. *W. H. Auden: A Biography.* Boston: Houghton Mifflin, 1981.

Cornford, Frances. *Collected Poems.* London: The Cresset Press, 1955.

Cortada, James W. *Historical Dictionary of the Spanish Civil War.* Westport, Ct.: Greenwood Press, 1982.

Galassi, Jonathan. *Understand the Weapon: Understand the Wound.* Manchester: Carcanet Press, 1976.

Hobsbaum, Philip. "Frances Cornford." *British Writers Supplement VIII.* Farmington Hills, Michigan: Charles

Scribner's Sons, 2003.

Kamenka, Eugene, ed. *The Portable Karl Marx*. New York: Viking Penguin Books, 1983.

Knox, Bernard. "Premature Anti-Fascist." Abraham Lincoln Brigade Archives—Bill Susman Lecture Series. New York University, 1998. Online edition: http://www.alba-valb. org/lectures/1998_knox_bernard.html.

Lehmann, John, ed. *New Writing IV* (Autumn, 1937). London: Lawrence and Wishart, 1937.

Mendelson, Edward, ed. *The English Auden*. London, Boston: Faber and Faber, 1986.

Orwell, George. *Homage to Catalonia*. New York: Harcourt, Brace, 1952.

Sloan, Pat, ed. *John Cornford: A Memoir*. Dunfermline, Fife: Borderline Press, 1978. (first pub. 1938.)

Sommerfield, John. *Volunteer in Spain*. New York: Alfred A. Knopf, 1937.

Stansky, Peter, and William Abrahams. *Journey to the Frontier*. London: Constable, 1966.

Sullivan, Robert. *Christopher Caudwell*. London: Croom Helm, 1987.

JACKIE KAY

(1961—)

Gail Low

JACKIE KAY IS one of the best-loved contemporary poets in Britain today; she is equally at home as a dramatist and as a writer of fiction for adults and children. Her work is notable for its use of the personal and autobiographical as a springboard for writing, and it was with her first book of poetry, *The Adoption Papers,* a 1991 collection that explored crucial experiences in her own life, that she came into prominence. An overriding concern in her work has been the subject of identity, whether it be cultural, racial, or sexual identity, and always Kay has sought to underline the fluidity of those identifications. She is black and openly gay but is also wary of such labeling. Her 1998 novel, *Trumpet,* and her brilliant 1997 biography of Bessie Smith both reflect her keen appreciation and utilization of jazz musical forms. Her work offers a feminized landscape that is preoccupied with and focused on women, from petty domestic details to a world of women loving women. While she is ambivalent about the land of her birth, her writing is nonetheless grounded in Scotland; she has an excellent ear for cadences of speech, regional accents, and dialect, and these qualities come through in character studies brought vividly to life through her use of dramatic monologues.

LIFE AND WORK

Jackie Kay was born in 1961 in Edinburgh. Her Scottish mother and Nigerian father met at a dance; her father returned to Nigeria during Kay's mother's pregnancy and she was placed in an Edinburgh home for adoption. Kay was adopted at five months and raised in the northern suburbs of Glasgow. Her adoptive parents, whom she considers her "real" parents, are both white. Apart from her brother, who was also adopted,

Kay as a child did not come across another black person. Yet by virtue of her mixed-race parentage, Kay was always singled out as different; despite being brought up in a loving and stable home, she was frequently subject to racial abuse. The uncertainties of identity that arise from being adopted, of being black and hence deemed not Scottish, are addressed again and again in her work.

In interviews, Kay has spoken of how writing provided her with an imaginative "sanctuary" at an early age; it offered her a way to cope with anger and tension. Racial abuse, identity, and the terrain of childhood as a fraught emotional and imaginative space are themes in much of her writing for both adults and children; the battleground of the playground or the betrayal of adults and school friends forms the dramatic scenario of her fiction for younger readers, such as *Strawgirl* (2002), and are central to poems such as "Black Bottom," "Compound Fracture," and "Names" that appear in *The Adoption Papers.* Kay's adoptive parents were communists and activists, and she was brought along to antinuclear and antiapartheid protests and to peace marches. Her engagement with issues of social justice is evident from her early verse, and especially in the poetic sequence "Severe Gale 8," included in *The Adoption Papers,* which takes among its subjects the National Health Service, the poll tax, and urban homelessness. Her parents' influences have also contributed to a keen appreciation of musical and performative forms; her sensitivity to rhythm, choral repetition, and incantation links her to Scottish ballads, folk songs, and the traditions of publicly recited verse, as well as to African American jazz and blues, which her father, a jazz and blues enthusiast, encouraged.

From the age of eleven to sixteen, she attended the Royal Scottish Academy of Music and Drama with the hope of training as an actress. At sixteen, she met the Scottish writer Alasdair Gray, who had been given some of Kay's youthful work; he was impressed with her talents and gave her confidence to think of herself as a writer. She was already beginning to identify herself as lesbian. Kay read English at the University of Stirling and graduated in 1983. After university, she moved to London and worked in various jobs, including as a housecleaner and a hospital porter, while still writing. Tired of always having to assert her identity as black and Scottish, the move south from Scotland was motivated by a desire to be part of a multicultural environment. In 1985, she was asked by the Theatre of Black Women to write a short play; *The Meeting Place* was read that same year at the Gay Sweatshop Times Ten Festival. Redrafted and rewritten as *Chiaroscuro*, the play premiered at Soho Polytechnic in 1986 and later toured various arts festival circuits and community centers. *Chiaroscuro* takes on the subject of racial and sexual identities through its exploration of two women's sexual relationship and the reaction of their friends to their coming out; in the same context, the play addresses racism, homophobia, and the invisibility of lesbianism.

Her next play, *Twice Over,* written for Gay Sweatshop, was the gay theater group's first play by a black writer. After premiering at the Drill Hall in 1988, *Twice Over* was taken on a successful tour both in Britain and in the United States. The production of the play was undertaken during a time in British politics that saw the enactment in law of a bill, popularly called Clause 28, specifically prohibiting the promotion of homosexuality or materials with the intention of promoting homosexuality.

After Kay gave birth to a son, Matthew, in 1988, she remained in England. The need for a more positive and accepting environment for both herself and her son reinforced her decision not to return to Scotland to live. She remarked in an interview (p. 34), "I love the country, but I don't know if the country loves me." From 1989 to 1991 she held the appointed position of writer in residence at the London borough of Hammersmith.

Her first collection of poetry, *The Adoption Papers,* was published in 1991. The collection's long semiautobiographical title poem marked a coming of age in Kay's career as a poet and the volume garnered much critical acclaim. "The Adoption Papers" explores the nature and experience of maternity: the desire to be a mother and to have a mother, as well as the experience of relinquishing motherhood. It enacts the overwhelming desire for maternity by a mother and daughter, the trauma of separation, loss, regret, and the difficulties of a child coming to terms with rejection. The collection as a whole established her credentials as a poet with a gift for creating drama through poetry. It received many literary prizes, including a Saltire Society Scottish First Book of the Year Award and a commendation from the judges of the prestigious Forward Poetry Prize. The British Broadcasting Corporation's well-received radio broadcast of an adaptation of the title poem in 1990 further raised her profile as a writer. Kay moved to Manchester with her son to live with the equally well-known Scottish-born poet Carol Ann Duffy. This personal relationship was also the basis of a formidable poetic partnership, which lasted throughout the 1990s.

Kay's poetic documentary *Twice Through the Heart* was broadcast in 1992 as part of the BBC's *Words on Film* television series, which sought to involve a poet in the process of filmmaking. The series aimed at bringing a heightened awareness of language, rhythm, and metaphor to the subject matter of documentary filmmaking. Kay's took as her subject matter the story of Amelia Rossiter, who killed her husband after years of domestic violence. The film was a pointed intervention in debates about domestic violence and, in particular, in the official accounts of the telling of Rossiter's story. Some of these poems were collected in *Other Lovers,* Kay's second volume of poetry, published in 1993. *Other Lovers* also includes a powerful sequence of poems about the blues and about Bessie Smith, a longtime icon for Kay. The volume showcases Kay's flair for creating dramatic lyric and highlights what would be a long-standing preoccupation with identity and the nature of love. In many of the poems in the collection, one's sense of oneself is shown to be bound up with the important relationships that one has with others, or with the cessation of those relationships. In other poems, such as "Colouring In" and "The Crossing," Kay reflects on the significance of place and space to identity, a connection that is severed or sustained through time; poems with such concerns often return to an event prior in time to capture a luminous mood or emotion. A sense of loss pervades a cluster of these poems, creating an elegiac mood in the volume as a whole. Yet love is not simply romance but can turn to hate and violence. In ending the collection with the Rossiter poems on domestic violence, Kay reminds her readers that love is not merely a soft subject but also a complex and contradictory one. *Other Lovers* won the Somerset Maugham Award offered by the British Society of Authors while *Twice Through the Heart* was rewritten as an English National Opera libretto by Mark Anthony Turnage.

While working on the poems that would go into her third collection of verse, *Off Colour* (1998), Kay was approached to write a biography of Bessie Smith for the Outlines series of biographies by Absolute Press. The series, launched in 1997, aimed to address the way in which homosexuality informs the work and lives of influential gay and lesbian artists; the volumes were meant to be written in an entertaining and insightful manner. *Bessie Smith,* published in 1997, provided an accessible introduction to the blues singer that did not dodge questions about her private life; significantly, it also addressed the ways in which Smith .was important to Kay's own life as an artist. In writing the biography of the legendary blues singer, Kay's narrator is allowed to reflect on her own racial, sexual, and cultural identity. *Bessie Smith* is narrated in hybrid styles, voices, and modes: a biographer's knowledgeable but intimate account of her subject, a historian's rendering of blues tradition, a writer's heightened enactment of the drama of Smith's life, and a writer's personal revelations about her own life. Fantasy or dramatic sequences reenacting events in Smith's life, and spoken in her own voice, are juxtaposed with more critical

considerations, reminiscences by friends, or scholarly quotes. Fragments of songs are woven into the story of Smith's life; with the deliberate use of syntactical repetition, chorus, and rhetorical questions, the oral and performative antiphonal traditions of blues music are also reproduced in the actual narration of Smith's story. *Bessie Smith* is a tour de force, mixing fact and fiction, biography and creative writing.

Poems in the 1998 volume *Off Colour,* Kay's third collection of poetry, take for their subject matter sickness and disease, and they extend such concerns from the personal to the social, considering, for instance how an individual society may be physically ill and how society may be said to be "off color" in its prejudicial enactment of color (racism). There are explicit indictments of racism in a sequence of poems including "Crown and Country," "Teeth," "Race, Racist, Racism," and "Hottentot Venus"; poems also address the creation of borderlines marking differences between individuals and communities. *Off Colour* received a Poetry Book Society commendation and was short-listed for the T. S. Eliot Prize.

Kay's first novel, *Trumpet,* was also published in 1998 and was a critical triumph, winning the *Guardian* Fiction Prize and the Author's Club First Novel Award. The plot is loosely based on the story of Billy Tipton, a successful jazz musician who lived as a man, married and divorced a succession of women, and also "fathered" sons, but who after his death was revealed to be a woman. Kay's story of the transgendered jazz trumpeter, Joss Moody, is woven out of a number of voices: that of his wife, his adopted son, and a host of minor characters such as his elderly mother, a doctor, a cleaner, a journalist, a coroner, and a fellow musician. The novel has often been likened to a piece of jazz music, with a central solo and side improvisations by others who contribute to the story of Moody and his effect on their lives. Kay's recasting of the Tipton story moves the tale away from its voyeuristic and sensationalist potential toward a moving love story told by a grieving widow, her son, and his friends and acquaintances. *Trumpet* looks at the gap between the label and the person labeled, between gender and sexual identity, and explores the nature of love.

Kay was appointed North East Literary Fellow at the Universities of Newcastle upon Tyne and Durham in 2001, a creative and academic fellowship offered to established writers, a post she held till 2003. She has always taken an active role in teaching and promoting poetry, and in 2002, she was elected as a fellow to the Royal Society of Literature, the same year that her story collection *Why Don't You Stop Talking* appeared. Adroit in the art of dramatic monologues composed in verse, Kay demonstrated in her first collection of short stories how successfully she is also able to work a monologue in prose. Half of the stories are composed by first-person narrators who pour out the drama of their lives in words. The collection highlights Kay's affinity for detailing the pattern of women's lives in ordinary domestic situations such as shopping, preparing dinner, feeding the baby, visiting sick relations, or looking after one's children. Yet these ordinary stories are also extraordinary in their expression of the hysteria, loneliness, passion, and madness of the lives of characters going about their usual routines. The domestic is rendered a surreal space in stories such as "The Woman with a Knife and Fork Disorder," "Why Don't You Stop Talking," and "Shell." Many of Kay's stories are about characters who are lonely, who are desirous of establishing connections with others, or who love too obsessively. Yet if many of the stories are bleak, they are not humorless; the portrayal of a woman's jealousy at her partner's love affair with her baby in "Big Milk," for example, is handled with comic flair. In "Shell," the teenager's self-absorption renders him immune to the shock of his mother's transformation into a tortoise; the teenager's own wants are all he is interested in. The transforming power of love, and the affirmation of life and self that comes to couples in these relationships, lift the darkness in the collection.

In 2003, Kay received the Cholmondeley Award for Poets from the Society of Authors. In 2004, after the end of her North East arts fellowship, Kay joined the teaching staff at the University of Newcastle in a department that boasts an array of established writers teaching poetry. Her fourth collection of poetry, *Life Mask,* published in 2005, focuses on subjects and themes that have inspired much of Kay's poetic oeuvre: love gained or lost, identity, and transformation. *Life Mask* mines the rich seam of metaphors that accrue to the various guises of self that one wears to face the outside world. Her second collection of short stories, *Wish I Was Here,* was published in 2006. *Why Don't You Stop Talking* had showcased Kay's affinity for dramatic monologues and her ear for vernacular speech, expression, and rhythms, and the collection as a whole was also testament to Kay's poetic gifts in diction and in the painterly creation of tone and mood. *Wish I Was Here* furthers Kay's preoccupation with love: lost and unrequited, and as a result, spawning emotions that are obsessive and all-consuming. Falling out of love, the breakup of long-term relationships and the breakdown and exposure of one's sense of self that is a consequence of such breaks is the focus of attention. In all of these situations, she illuminates the ways in which identity is intimately bound up with others. In many ways, despite the last story of the collection, *Wish I Was Here* marks a preoccupation with age and aging, and Kay has spoke of this collection as a "mid life" book. In 2006, she was awarded an MBE (Member of the Order of the British Empire) for her services to literature.

THE NATURE OF BLOOD: ADOPTION AND IDENTITY PAPERS

"The Adoption Papers" addresses the nature of kinship: kinship as both affiliation and filiation. It explores femininity through the socio biological roles offered to women, as mothers and daughters, and looks specifically at the emotional and cultural expectations made of women, and their responses, in the occupation of those roles. "The Adoption Papers" is at once a moving personal story with which readers can empathize and also a story of what it is like to be a woman. The poem is narrated by three voices, that of a daughter, of her adoptive mother, and of her birth mother—each kept dramatically and typographically distinct (using different fonts— and all three voices are woven together as if they were parts in a choral ensemble. The poem's three sections are dated chronologically. The poem as a whole covers birth, adoption, childhood, and adulthood, when the adoptive daughter initiates the process of tracing her birth mother. "The Adoption Papers" is a story of origins and of birth, with adoption, the discovery of one's adoption, and the discovery of one's biological mother as primal scenes. In a moving section titled "The Telling Part," the conversation between adoptive mother and child, re-created between the adopted child and friends, over a "mammy" who "bot me oot a shop," who "says I was a luvly baby," and who "says she's no really ma mammy," leads one to see the struggles that the adoptive mother goes through to do the right thing by telling her daughter that she is not related by blood. Yet the adoptive mother's insistence that "she's my child," in response to the whispering campaign that adoption is "not like having your child though is it," is also testament to how nurture is not simply about nature. Two vivid dream sequences in the poem express the complexities of the triangular relationship: the haunting of "a baby Lazarus" who suckles nightly at her biological mother's breast despite being buried in the garden, and the adoptive mother's dream of the kidnapping of her baby by the biological mother. The fantasy sequence detailing the imaginary meeting of biological mother and child conveys acutely and sensitively their awkward expectance of kinship. The poem ends with an acceptance, not a fear, of kinship, but brooks no easy resolution.

A concern with identity has figured large in most of Kay's writing. Part of this preoccupation, Kay admits, seems to stem from being adopted, an experience whose legacy is to license the invention of different personas and families that one might claim kinship from. This play with different selves results in a conception of identity that rejects implications of some true, essential, and unchanging "me" that is untouched by parenting, upbringing, environment, or one's interaction with others; the adopted Colman Moody remarks, in *Trumpet,* that as William Dunsmore he would not only have smiled or

walked a little differently, he would be a "completely different man" (p. 57).

Kay's concern with identity also extends to race and culture, the external labels that condition and shape one's notion of self, and the gap that often extends between those names and labels and one own sense of who one is. In "Black Bottom," a poem midway through *The Adoption Papers,* the adopted child's visage leads to name-calling by both teachers and fellow students. The narrator of the poem, transported back in time, relives the moment when she is goaded into hitting a boy who calls her "Sambo" and "Dirty Darkie," and the shame that she feels is brought on by a teacher's racist presumption that as a black girl she should have rhythm.

The question of "what is in my blood?" has wider resonances because, of course, the narrator is a black child brought up by white mother. Her adoptive mother finds it difficult to soothe her child precisely because she cannot say that she has experienced racism.

"Black Bottom" interweaves the experience of racial abuse by the child with the biological mother's allusion to the feelings brought on by her lover, "the colour of peat," whom she sees in the face of her newborn infant, "as if he was there/ in that glass cot looking back through her." "Black Bottom" also holds out other forms of affiliation; the child identifies with figures across the Atlantic, such as the civil rights activist Angela Davis. In Kay's account of influential personages from her own childhood, she also includes the African National Congress antiapartheid politician, Nelson Mandela; the boxer Cassius Clay; and the musicians Count Basie, Duke Ellington, and Bessie Smith.

A BLACK ATLANTIC: BESSIE SMITH, BLUES, AND SEXUALITY

In the introduction to *Bessie Smith,* Kay records that growing up in a white neighborhood where no one looked like her produced a disjunction between what she looked like and what she saw in the mirror. She remarks, "My own face in the mirror was not the face I had in my head." Bessie Smith was to produce "the shock of my own reflection [that] came with the blues" (p. 13). With Bessie Smith came the challenge to think about her own skin color and what it signified. As Kay remarks in her conclusion to Smith's biography, she will "always associate the dawning of [her]...own realization of being black with the blues" (p. 138). Kay's account of her childhood encounter with Smith is framed in terms of mirroring: in her 1998 interview with Maya Jaggi she observes, "I looked at her and saw some reflection of myself." As a child, Kay would sing Smith's songs in front of a mirror, using her hairbrush as a microphone and mimicking the way Smith sang. She would compare Smith's looks with her own and think, "Maybe my great great grandmother was a blues singer" (p. 14). Later this reflection gained more political and cultural overtones; Smith signified a connectedness that emerges from a shared cultural history, "a common bond" of the history of racism, a "sharing of blood" through the performance of song.

The notion of a black Atlantic culture and heritage has been championed by cultural critics such as Paul Gilroy, who have argued that the music of jazz, ragtime, blues, and gospel records the history of slavery and of racism; its permutations of loss and longing echo the trauma of the breakup of families under slavery. Yet Gilroy, in his 1993 study *The Black Atlantic,* argues that such a legacy is not one of passive inheritance but rather is an active and contemporary act of invention and recreation; people of color in present times signify on these practices in order to keep alive the identity and history of a black Atlantic expressive culture. Kay's restaging of the blues falls within this cultural paradigm. "Even the Trees" in *Other Lovers* is written in the light of the Billie Holiday song "Strange Fruit"; the scene it conjures up is of a laborer who is tied to a tree and whipped. In contrast to the trees, who are mute witnesses, part of "the congregation of silence," humans with their songs recall the moment of violence and violation, and in doing so bear witness to those atrocities. A woman's memory, "a blue song in the beat of her heart,"

is why we remember certain things and not others;
the sound of the base, the sound of the whip, the strange
strangled wind, bruises floating through light air;[...]
Everything that's happened once could happen again.

In "The Right Season," blues trails are compared to "travelling on the underground railroad." Another poem, "In the Pullman," imagines Bessie and the narrator heading for the South and reflecting on the region's history of slavery, racism, and segregation; together they are driving "without moving" to "this big sadness hanging from the pawpaw tree."

Smith is an iconic figure for Kay, an imaginary friend, a lover, a "paragon of virtue," and an alter ego by which Kay can construct her identity as black woman. But Smith also represents the flowering of desire and sexuality; her life story is that of a strong, "libidinous, raunchy, fearless blueswoman" who lived her life as she pleased and did what she wanted despite the difficulties of her love life and the economies forced upon her at the start and end of her life. Kay's account of Smith focuses on her sexuality—the relationships with men *and* women that she was drawn to. The account is not salacious but celebratory in its libertarianism. Tongue in cheek, and with one eye on stereotypes and melodramatic fantasies about lesbian excesses, Kay dramatizes Ma Rainey's alleged entrapment and grooming of a young Smith.

Although Smith's relationship with Ruby Walker was not sexual in real life, writing in the voice of Smith, Kay's narrator is allowed to revel in the seduction of her longtime companion. In poems such as "The Red Graveyard," a poem from *Other Lovers* that appears at the start of *Bessie Smith,* Smith's sensuality and sexuality are "stones that open in the night like flowers"; Smith's music calls for a similar response on the part of her listeners; the young Kay caresses the wallpaper, "bumping flower into flower," picking up Smith's album cover her fingers "are all over her face. / Her black face. Her magnificent black face" (pp. 7–8). But the story of Smith's relationship with women, from Ruby Walker to the women in her show, is a continuum of female friendship, comradeship, and desire. Kay's biography of Smith allows her to narrate a full expression of sexual desire, not only homosexual but also heterosexual, for Smith did have relationships with men. Her songs signal a complexity of response; Smith's blues songs also inscribe a sexual political battlefield in which men "destroy and ruin women," a repetitive story of loss and pain in which women should no longer tolerate their mistreatment.

In addition to Smith's songs and the use of quotes from scholarly, critical, and biographical material, Kay's imaginative and dramatic reenactments add to the diverse quality of voices and genres contained within the text. Most distinctive, however, is the way *Bessie Smith* acknowledges the folk and the oral in a record of Smith's life. Kay recounts legendary stories people have told about Smith, and she argues that the variations that arise in the circulation of these stories reflect Smith's status as a folk hero to those storytellers. If it is sometimes difficult to tell fact from fiction—for example, in the different accounts of an incident in which Smith knocked down Carl van Vechten's wife at a party during the Harlem Renaissance, or the stories of Smith's "violent, drunken bawdiness" (p. 110)—variation is integral to what Smith represents for a people whose culture is based on the passing on of these stories.

The oral and spoken dimensions of *Bessie Smith* are perhaps the most intriguing aspects of Kay's narration. Kay's biography deliberately reproduces the pattern of repetition with variation that characterizes jazz and the antiphonal qualities of blues music; for example, in reflecting on Smith's relationship with her husband Jack Gee, she asks a series of rhetorical questions that essentially repeat the central puzzle of his "enormous hold over her." The narration invites responses, and then concludes with detailing what Smith did to please Gee.

Did she believed he loved her because he pawned his watch? Did she love him because he pawned his watch? What was it about Jack Gee that made Bessie stick with him for so long? She was not faithful to him, but she was obsessed with him. She did everything to try and make him happy. She

bought him an expensive watch. She bought him expensive cars...

(p. 47)

The almost identical syntactic structure of the sentences, the tactical and multiple use of similar phrases, is a rhetorical strategy of song and performances, employed often for emphasis, reminders, and calls for agreement. Thus, for example, when Kay describes Walker's idolization of Smith, she observes, "She loved the way she looked; the way she sang; the way she drank; the way she partied; the way she cussed; the way she fought; the way she danced; the way she spent money. Ruby loved everything about Bessie."(p. 85) The decision to incorporate a specifically oral dimension into the narration of *Bessie Smith* is an homage to the power of the blues and to the blues singer herself; as Kay remarks, "repetition is the secret of the blues" for it enables one to experience anew the "same truth over and over again."(p. 139)

TRUMPET: *PERFORMING IDENTITY*

Trumpet, written alongside *Bessie Smith*, exemplifies Kay's translation of the spirit of jazz and blues improvisation into fictional form. The real-life inspiration for the story, Billy Tipton, was himself a jazz pianist and saxophonist. Kay has remarked that what touched her about his story was a comment made by his adopted son, who thought of Tipton as a father even after he was revealed to be a woman. Tipton's extraordinary story of transgendered passing is thus, at once, also ordinary, when played out in the everyday domestic and familiar roles he occupied as friend, father, and husband. The challenge posed to Kay was how to stay true to the spirit of Tipton's story: the acceptance of his identity—of who Tipton chose to be—by his adopted son. *Trumpet* begins its story on the occasion of the death of Joss Moody, a transgendered black trumpeter. The shock of Moody's unveiling as a woman is imparted through the reactions of the doctor, the coroner, the unsuspecting son and fellow musician, and the cynical journalist who attempts to write Moody's story as sensationalist fodder. In many ways, the journalist and investigative reporter, Sophie, could be the reader's surrogate in the story, insofar as the spectacle and drama of the masquerade, the skill of Moody's evasion, and the puzzle of his duping are all areas of fascination. What stymies the gratification of such voyeuristic pleasures in *Trumpet* is that Moody's story is told by his widow. Millicent (Millie) Moody's tale is one of quotidian family dramas: her acceptance of Moody's desires; her anguished grieving of and respect for her dead husband; her refusal to be cast as the duped woman normalizes the extraordinary story of Moody's passing. As Millie explains, "No matter how hard I try, I can't see him as anything other than him, my Joss, my husband. It has always been that way since the first day he told me" (p. 35). Furthermore, Moody's story as told by his son, Colman, is a study less of Moody's deception and more of the psychology of a son coming to terms with his own identity and the passing of his father. Despite Colman's feelings of anger, of betrayal, and of failing to measure up to his father, the father-son relationship is not nullified in his narrative; the son admits that despite everything, "he'll always be a daddy to me" (p. 259). *Trumpet* ends with Colman as custodian of his father's letters, photographs, records, and documents, a role that suggests Moody's trust and his belief that his son would honor his tale. In a reversal of roles, Colman as custodian and narrator is given the role of the originator; his father writes to him from the past, "I will be your son now in a strange way. You will be my father telling or not telling my story.... The present is just a loop stitch" (p. 277).

In alluding to the present as a "loop stitch," Kay characterizes the temporal structure of the novel for her readers and makes a case for the transcendence of love. The novel begins with the death of Moody; linear time moves forward through the unfolding of events consequent to the discovery of his secret—including his wife and son's attempts to come to terms with his death and to turn the corner on their mourning. Linear chronology is also at least implicit in Colman and Sophie's attempts to reconstruct Moody's past, through letters and interviews. Yet, time in the novel, and the characters' experi-

ence of time, is not linear. In the various narratives of the characters who have known Moody, we are continually taken back in time; for example, in Moody's wife's narration of their courtship, her revelation of his secret, their wedding celebrations, and the adoption of their son, Colman, are woven into the narrative time of present grief. As with Colman's narration, these events are less memories and more a *reliving* of the past; time does not erode the vividness of the moment; many of these events are narrated in the present tense. Moody's letter to his son, read at the end of the novel, is a voice from the past, alluding to the arrival of Moody's father in Scotland at the turn of the century. The letter, an invitation to Colman to take up the reins of the narration, to reconstruct Moody's story, is an appeal framed for the future.

While linearity may be one of the central characteristics of music, there is also a sense in which music, in its use of motifs—or jazz, in its improvisations—disrupts the forward momentum of time. *Trumpet*'s main narrator is Millie Moody, with her son, Colman, contributing the other voice. Minor roles are played by the officials who oversee the registration of Moody's death, by his elderly mother, by a fellow musician, and by acquaintances. Each produces a different version of Moody, inflected by their contact with the man and what he means to them. In this, the form of the novel echoes jazz. Kay has commented on how the structure of the novel adds to the fluidity of its subject and subject matter; Moody's life and death are made to play differently though the "improvisations" by others, and in this way readers are made aware of different Moodys and of how Moody's identity is continually being reinvented through narrative. The various fabrications of Moody's persona pose the question: how is one to decide on who is the true or real Moody?

This is one of the most important questions *Trumpet* asks: whether identity is "being," a "real me" behind all the different versions of selves experiencing and experienced by others, or whether identity is, to some extent, a "process," a performance or a fabrication. Joss Moody's life story is tale of a man who has invented himself.

It is a story of a man who creates his identity through the selves that he staged for others, because that identity was truer to *who* he was than *what* he was. Joss Moody's careful imitation of masculinity, such as his use of bandages to disguise his breasts, his elaborate rituals of dressing and shaving, and his studied walk, all point toward reading masculinity not as a fact but as a construct. The novel seems to suggest that if the fact of his sex is the "pure and simple" answer to who Moody was, then such facts represent a travesty of his life and of all his friends and relations' experiences of him. Rather, the novel seems to assert that there should be no rigid line drawn between Moody's sex and his sexual identity; the former should not be able to determine all of the expressions of the latter.

Kay finds a potent metaphor for that border country between reality and appearance— between "being" and "process," between "essence and performance"—in jazz. At the novel's literal center, in a chapter titled "Music," sandwiched between investigative reporter and inquiring son, is a short chapter entirely devoted to Moody's playing of the trumpet. It depicts the trumpeter's transformation by his music; when Moody is carried away by his performance on the trumpet, he "loses his sex, his race, his memory" and is stripped of all until he is "barely human" (p. 131). In these moments, Moody is "naked"; the music is "naked jazz," "never lying," and "telling it like it is" (p. 132). But these moments are not unlike an epiphany, moments of musical ecstasy in a space beyond time. Moody, performing his music, quite literally experiences his own birth, his childhood as Josephine, his death, and his final send-off at the hands of the undertaker. His trumpet takes him beyond even his own birth to the story of his father, to the history of slavery and to Africa, and finally to a space beyond race and sex. "Nothing weighs him down. Not the past or future" (p. 136). For Kay, the performance describes simply a "space of possibility"; it enables, simultaneously, loss and discovery of self, memory and forgetfulness, traveling back in time and moving forward.

BLACK AND SCOTTISH

As much as *Trumpet* is about jazz, the book's characters and landscape are very much grounded in Scotland. The urban landscape of Glasgow, with its dance halls, is the setting for Moody's courtship of Millie; and Torr, the Scottish coastal village where Millie finds refuge after her ordeal, provides the novel with some of its most evocative passages. Moody himself is said to have clung to his Scottish identity, chastising his son for losing his Scottish accent, even when the music he plays and the icons of his musical pantheon are resolutely transatlantic. Kay's poetry and short fiction are likewise steeped in the landscape of Scotland, where place is imbued with emotional significance; for example, in the poetry collection *Life Mask*, "Glen Strathfarrar" is an elegaic "stock-still beauty" and suffused with the memory of past love; "High Land" is a wild night of passion when it is "hard to remember...who was who when the wind was coming in." In "What Ever," in the story collection *Wish I Was Here,* the shingle beach with its little tern is both a physical and mental space that Ina McEwans retreats to when she feels emotionally battered; her memories are of "the bright-yellow beak on a white beach, the sky, bruised and darkening as she walked, to a plum colour" (p. 103). At times, Kay's use of the landscape turns on a poetic metaphor; a restful stillness in "How to get away with Suicide" in *Wish I Was Here* is described as "the silence that pads across a loch on a wintry, misty morning with its webbed feet" (p. 43), while in the poem "Colouring In, " "the early evening light skipping across" the Fintry hills is "like a wee girl with a big rope, / the faraway rhyme of a song you used to know, the empty yellow stretch of land."

Kay's use of song and dialect also grounds her work in a Scottish space. In the poem "Watching People Sing," from *Other Lovers*, the narrator describes a social gathering in which her parents and their friends are invited to sing and to *"Gie it laldy"* (to do it with gusto). The narrator's relative youthfulness allows her to be part of the occasion, serving food and drinks, but distant enough to look at the "party social" from the outside. What she does see—and envy—is the community that is created around the songs that are sung. While more popular songs are on offer at the gathering, it is the folk songs that seem to call forth the hidden lives and feelings of singers and their audience.

Songs are not only the occasion for poetry; they are sometimes employed in the structure and form of the verse. Kay harnesses the forms of folk songs, ballads, and skipping songs in, for example, *Life Mask*'s "Old Aberdeen" and "Spoons" and *Off Colour*'s "The Broon's Bairn's Black."

Scottish words such as "pokey hats" (for ice cream cones), "teuchter" (derogatory for highlander or rural Scots), or "glaikit" (stupid or silly) appear alongside standard English in the poems. Kay has a remarkable ear for cadences of speech and regional dialect, and she puts this facility to good use in dramatic monologues written entirely in Scottish dialect, such as "A Guid Scots Death," or in the invented Broonspeak of the hilarious Broon poems, based on the much-loved characters of the Scottish D. C. Thompson comics of the same name. In the conversation between the child and her friends in "The Adoption Papers," the use of dialect lends a solidity to the adoptive child's voice that roots her to a Glaswegian space, and it adds a wryly comic tone to her anxieties about her status.

In other poems, language is explicitly linked to cultural identity, where to be Scottish is resolutely not to be English. In "Old Tongue" from *Life's Mask*, Kay mines the rich tradition of humor and musicality in Scots accent and dialect in sentences such as "*shut yer geggie or I'll gie you the malkie!*" but the poem also achieves a wider point about conformity to the dominant language. The speaker bemoans the loss of her "dour soor Scottish tongue," her "sing-songy" speech; having been "forced south," her old words "buried themselves," making her "mother's blood boil"; they are the "wrong sound" in her mouth.

If Scotland is associated in Kay's work with fulsome memories of lost childhood innocence, she is also quite vocal about how the country of her birth has excluded her on account of race.

Kay's childhood was not all rosy; many of her poems recall the racist nicknames leveled at her, the casual cruelty of the playground mirroring that of the adult world. In an interview with Libby Brooks for the *Guardian* in 2002, she tells a comic story of an encounter with a Glaswegian woman in a London pub who, when Kay divulges her roots, hoots with derision and calls her a "foreign-looking bugger!" Given Kay's strong Glaswegian accent, it is difficult to mistake where she is from but, as she remarks ruefully, some Scottish people won't actually hear her voice because they are too busy "seeing" her face. In the poem "So you think I Am a Mule?" (*Feminist Review*, p. 80) the speaker's response to a question about her origins is to say that she is from Glasgow and Fife. This information, however, is dismissed with the retort, "Ah, but you're not pure" (p. 80). The narrator of "In My Country" (from *Other Lovers*), circled by another woman as if she were "superstition; / or the worst dregs of her imagination," is interrogated with words that "spliced into bars / of an old wheel"—with the question, "*Where do you come from?*" The narrator, however, stands her ground; her vision is more complex than the version of a homogenized tartan Scotland that her interrogator has on offer: "Here," she replies. "Here. These parts."

Kay's Scottishness, evident through her work in its preoccupation with language, song, and place, is heightened by her public performances of her poetry; she reads in an unambiguous Glaswegian accent. But her writing identity strives to exceed the conservative bounds of what is signified by Scottishness; her own literary identity (and heritage) is a complex one involving many border crossings. Kay argues for a border trafficking that allows freedom of movement betwixt and between. As the narrator declares in "Kail and Callaloo" (from *Charting the Journey*), one can be "Celtic-Afro-Caribbean / in answer to the 'origin' question." Joss Moody's trumpeter is proud of his Scottish roots *and* his African American musical traditions, and he is both woman and man. In "Pride" (from *Off Colour*), the narrator's exchange with an Ibo man on the train offers the temptation of suggesting an exclusive kinship between the speaker and the

Nigerian. His ethnic exclusivity is comparable to that of "a MacLachlan, a MacDonnell, a MacLeod," the "quality of being certain" to the exclusion of other tribes or clans save that of your own; he acknowledges others only when they mirror himself. Such security of kinship may be seductive, but it is also an illusion; the Ibo man disappears at the end of the poem to leave the narrator with her reflection in the dark train window.

HOME AND UNHOMELY

Kay's short stories in *Why Don't You Stop Talking* and *Wish I Was Here* exhibit a fascination with the gray areas in which one identity shades into another, and one world meets with another. Both volumes contain stories of hybrid worlds where the human and the animal coincide, and where the domestic and familiar are made strange and "extraordinary." In stories such as "Shell" or "My Daughter the Fox," characters are both human and feral; in the former, a character's depression and gradual mental retreat and her growing distance from the everyday world she inhabits is rendered literal in the shell she grows around her. In the latter story, the narrator gives birth to a fox; her daughter's inhuman form elicits fear and bewilderment from family and friends, leading to both daughter and mother's exclusion from the human world. There are, however, advantages to living in a hybrid world. Her daughter's instincts and behavior call forth aspects of the mother that she has herself suppressed, making her more self-aware. In the final tale of *Why Don't You Stop Talking,* "In Between Talking About the Elephant," the difficulty of dealing with illness, pain, and death between longtime lovers is overcome through the story that each tells the other. Both the sick woman and her lover are interlocutors in a dialogue about the attributes of elephants and rituals within elephant herds; they use their talk of elephants to communicate deeply held emotions and feelings. The story's narrator observes in the dying moments of her lover's life, "There is nothing I can do. Only the elephant can help.... We would never have said the things we say to each other were it not for the enormous elephant" (p. 237). In these stories, Kay mines the animalistic and the feral for all their metaphoric value; the vixen is sleek, feminine, and powerful; the tortoise fearful and retiring; the elephant strangely human, while the shark in "Shark! Shark!" allows Kay to convey a man's fear of his mortality.

Many of Kay's stories occur within feminized spaces and describe domestic routines such as cooking, shopping, child minding, watching television, talking, exercising, or going to bed. These rituals are what anchor her figures to the familiar everyday world that they, women especially, occupy. Yet these small localized worlds are turned inside out in her stories; Kay's characters are often neurotic, lonely, suicidal, self-harming, or drifting into insanity. What is normal and homely appears to be a trick of perspective that results from an adherence to routine. In "Timing," found in *Why Don't You Stop Talking,* the narrator's ritual daily excursion to the park enables a degree of friendliness in her interactions with the people she meets along the way; there is a grandmother and granddaughter, an old man who walks a dog, and a man who feeds the geese. Yet this presumption of familiarity is illusory, because all parties involved avoid any kind of meaningful exchange. If the goose man were to speak to the narrator, she would walk in another direction; if the narrator followed the grandmother and her charge, she would be suspected of stalking. The story's one real attempt to communicate is met with a stony stare, as if the speaker were "stark, raving mad" (p.63).

Kay told Brooks in the *Guardian* interview of her fascination with the domestic "wee world," which, she argues, can "reveal its own violence" and its "own war," and many of her short stories exhibit these qualities. The title story of the collection *Why Don't You Stop Talking,* for example, begins with a shopping expedition in which a woman takes exception to another's disparaging looks at the items the woman has put into her shopping cart. This leads to a verbal confrontation. A further sequence of hostile exchanges typifies her journey home: she rebukes a man who "jumps" his turn in line to obtain money from an automatic teller, and she intervenes in an angry exchange between a mother and child. Yet, in all these interactions, the woman comes off the poorer. What starts off as a portrait of a strong woman turns into its opposite. It transpires that the woman is lonely; her attempts to appear friendly, to begin a conversation on the elevator or on the underground train, are rebuffed. A quite ordinary tale then begins to unravel, to terminate in its shock conclusion; the woman's tongue, treated literally as an object with an autonomous life of its own, is punished by taking a razor to it. "The pain feels deserved," the woman concludes grimly, as blood gushes from the wound (p. 50).

In a companion story of gradual disintegration, Kay looks at how what is regular and "homely" can be rendered as "unhomely." In "The Woman with a Fork and Knife Disorder," the story's protagonist, Irene, is a single mother who seems to take pride in keeping an orderly house and kitchen. She notices an open drawer, a misplaced knife and spoon, and, later still, a cluster of knives, forks, and spoons all out of place. As she increasingly finds cutlery in places where it is not supposed to be, the disorder threatens to overwhelm her peace of mind, as the pieces are transformed into menacing objects. She begins to imagine cutting her body with her sharp knives; "if she could just mark herself, one creative cleave with the carving knife," she thinks, then there would be both relief and excitement (p. 101). Irene's obsession with knives and forks seems to stem from her former husband's attempts at achieving upward mobility away from his working-class background; Irene feels out of place when she is taken to fancy restaurants—"the sight of all the cutlery made her anxious" (p. 105). She sees her distorted image reflected in a spoon, and she feels trapped and claustrophobic. Paradoxically, it is her depression that enables her most clear-sighted vision, her understanding that "her whole street was full of sadness, hidden behind the curtains" of domestic routines and neighborly privacy (p. 99). In the story's shock-

ing ending, Irene's mental deterioration culminates in a picnic at the park, where as she watches the Canada geese, she quite properly and daintily carves and eats the turf in front of her.

Kay's landscapes and preoccupations are very female ones, from an interest in women's lives and loves, to the domestic spaces they inhabit, to the sensuality of loving women. Her poetic imagery is oriented toward women's bodies, toward exploring the feminized spaces of the confessional, personal, and autobiographical, although some of her dramatic monologues, such as "Making a Movie" and "Married Women," are laced with irony and unselfconscious self-exposure. Many of her most memorable characters are, in the main, although not without exception, lonely and living on the edge of insanity and despair. Locked into the prison house of their own stories, they sit in a solipsistic narrative cell of their own, sometimes through no fault of their own. What saves them from such entrapment, in stories such as "In Between Talking About the Elephant" and "Physics and Chemistry" in *Why Don't You Stop Talking.* and "The Mirrored Twins" in *Wish I was Here,* is the transforming power of love, of finding another person who speaks one's language.

Selected Bibliography

WORKS OF JACKIE KAY

POETRY

A Dangerous Knowing: Four Black Women Poets. London: Sheba, 1984.

The Adoption Papers. Newcastle upon Tyne, U.K.: Bloodaxe, 1991.

Twice Through the Heart: A Dramatic Scene for Mezzo Soprano and Sixteen Players to a Text by Jackie Kay. With Mark-Anthony Turnage. English National Opera premiere, 1991. London: Schott, 1997.

Other Lovers. Newcastle upon Tyne, U.K.: Bloodaxe, 1993.

Penguin Modern Poets 8. London: Penguin, 1996. (Contributor, with Merle Collins and Grace Nichols.)

Off Colour. Newcastle upon Tyne, U.K.: Bloodaxe, 1998.
Life Mask. Newcastle upon Tyne: Bloodaxe, 2005.

FICTION
Trumpet. London: Picador, 1998.
Why Don't You Stop Talking. London: Picador, 2002.
Wish I Was Here. London: Picador, 2006.

CHILDREN'S WRITING
Two's Company. London: Blackie Children's, 1992.
Three Has Gone. London: Blackie Children's, 1994.
The Frog Who Dreamed She Was an Opera Singer. London: Bloomsbury Children's, 1999.
Strawgirl. London: Macmillan Children's, 2002.

OTHER WORK
Many Voices, One Chant: Black Feminist Perspectives. In *Feminist Review* 17: 80 (autumn 1984
Chiaroscuro. In *Lesbian Plays.* Edited by Jill Davis. London: Methuen, 1987.
Charting the Journey: Writings by Black and Third World Women Writers. Edited with Shabnam Grewal, Liliane Landor, Gail Lewis and Pratibha Parmar. London: Sheba Feminist Press, 1988.
Twice Over. In *Gay Sweatshop: Four Plays and a Company.* Edited by Philip Osment. London: Methuen, 1989.
Bessie Smith. Bath: Absolute Press, 1997.

CRITICAL AND BIOGRAPHICAL STUDIES

Anderson, Linda. "Autobiographical Travesties: The Nostalgic Self in Queer Writing." In *Territories of Desire in Queer Culture.* Edited by David Alderson and Linda Anderson. Manchester, U.K.: Manchester University Press, 2000. Pp. 68–81.

Dowson, Jane, and Alice Entwistle. *A History of Twentieth-Century British Women's Poetry.* Cambridge, U.K.: Cambridge University Press, 2005.

Halberstam, Judith. "Telling Tales: Brandon Teena, Billy Tipton, and Transgender Biography." *Passing: Identity and Interpretation in Sexuality, Race, and Religion.* Edited by Maria Carla Sanchez and Linda Schlossberg. New York: New York University Press, 2001. Pp. 13–37.

Rice, Alan. "'Heroes Across the Sea'": Black and White British Fascination with African Americans in the Contemporary Black British Fiction of Caryl Phillips and Jackie Kay." In *Blackening Europe: The African American Presence.* Edited by Heike Raphael-Hernandez. London and New York: Routledge, 2003. Pp. 217–231.

Severin, Laura. "Distant Resonances: Contemporary Scottish Women Poets and African-American Music." *Mosaic: A Journal for the Interdisciplinary Study of Literature* 39, no. 1:45–59 (2006).

———. *Poetry off the Page: Twentieth-Century British Women Poets in Performance.* Aldershot, U.K.: Ashgate, 2004.

Williams, Patrick. "Significant Corporeality: Bodies and Identities in Jackie Kay's Fiction." *Write Black, Write British: From Post Colonial to Black British Literature.* Edited by Kadija Sesay. Hertford, U.K.: Hansib, 2005. Pp. 41–55.

INTERVIEWS

"An Interview with Jackie Kay." *Poetry Archive* (http://www.poetryarchive.org/poetryarchive/singleInterview.do?interviewId=6580).

Brooks, Libby. "Don't Tell Me Who I Am." *Guardian,* January 12, 2002, p. 34.

Dyer, Richard. "Jackie Kay with Richard Dyer." In *Writing Across Worlds: Contemporary Writers Talk.* Edited by Susheila Nasta. London and New York: Routledge, 2004. Pp. 235–249.

Granelli, Seraphina. "On Matters of the Heart: Jackie Kay on Love." *Libertas.co.uk.* (http://www.libertas.co.uk/interviews.asp).

Jaggi, Maya. "The *Guardian* Fiction Prize: Race and All That Jazz." *Guardian,* December 5, 1998, p. 10.

Severin, Laura. "Interview with Jackie Kay." *Free Verse* (spring 2002). (Also available at http://english.chass.ncsu.edu/freeverse/Archives/Spring_2002/interviews/J_Kay.html.)

Sprackland, Jean. "The Poetryclass Interview: Jackie Kay." *Poetryclass* (http://www.poetryclass.net/inter2.htm).

Stuart, Andrea. "Books: Performing Writers: Jackie Kay." *The Independent,* August 8, 1998, p. 7.

JAMES CLARENCE MANGAN

(1803–1849)

Adrian Paterson

JAMES CLARENCE MANGAN, poet, translator, and sometime literary hoaxer, was the greatest Irish poet writing in English before W. B. Yeats (1865–1939). James Joyce, affirming this assessment, called him "one of the most inspired poets of any country ever to make use of the lyric form" (p. 130). He is remembered today, if at all, as the composer of one or two strange original lyrics and a handful of peculiarly powerful versions from the Irish into English. More than this, however, Mangan was a prolific translator of German poetry, an idiosyncratic prose stylist, and an exceptional manipulator of *all* verse forms, both in terms of metrical ingenuity and through the layers of framing and attribution that make up his texts' peculiar place in the world. Exhibiting a constant relish for excess, his poetry oscillates between plangent sorrow and whimsical self-consciousness, frequently departing wildly from its sources and fathering itself upon real or imagined authors from Germany, Persia, and Arabia. Mangan has thus left a collection of "translations" that are creations unique in the language, and at least one poem, "Dark Rosaleen," that has retained an almost supernatural force.

"People have called him a singular man, but he is rather a plural one—a Proteus" (*Collected Works of James Clarence Mangan: Prose* [hereafter referred to as *Prose*], vol. 2, p. 224). So Mangan described himself; and while the intensity of his poetry is instantly recognizable, the multiplication of his adopted voices is bewildering. National polemicist, hack writer, literary schizophrenic, comic lyrist, poète maudit, lovelorn melancholic, musician in verse; all these partial truths finally glance off him. Thus Mangan sits uncomfortably in a late-Romantic tradition. He sounds essentially eighteenth century in his attachment to the puns, trickery, and self-referential wit of Jonathan Swift and Laurence Sterne; squarely nineteenth century in his cultivation of a maudlin and introspective poetic persona and in the way he couples his muse with a burgeoning national consciousness; seemingly modern in that he was a urban poet, split up into fragmentary selves; and, even, postmodern in his absorbing literary game-playing, labyrinthine misattributions, and his constant mischievous attention to the paratextual surrounds of his periodical contributions.

Less predictable than his Dublin-born precursor Thomas Moore, who shared his ability to produce both satire and sentiment, his most pronounced literary debt is to Lord Byron, and Joyce compared him to Edgar Allan Poe in verbal virtuosity: "he might have written a treatise on the poetical art for he is more cunning in his use of the musical echo than is Poe," (p. 58). Roughly coinciding with the advent of the Union between the Kingdoms of Ireland and Great Britain (1800) and the end of the Irish potato famine, his unsteady life has often been supposed to shadow that period of disillusionment in Irish history. But Mangan's sorrows were not his nation's, and he was an infinitely superior versifier to the polemical poetasters of the nationalist "Young Ireland" movement, contributors to the weekly anti-Union newspaper of the 1840s, the *Nation;* as a translator of Irish he has no rival but the sweeter, more sedate Edward Walsh. Like Joyce, Yeats responded to Mangan with baffled admiration, but came to feel that behind his literary masks Mangan "had not thought out or felt out a way of looking at the world peculiar to himself" (*Letters,* vol. 4, p. 38). Nevertheless he included more of

Mangan's poems in his *A Book of Irish Verse* (1895) than those of any other poet. It is hard to disagree with his judgment.

As Yeats stressed, Mangan was a city poet, the product of attic rooms, public houses, streets, and the offices of copy clerks and antiquarians, evading in the fevered production of words the paralysis Joyce later found endemic in Dublin. So there is less contradiction than might be imagined in saying that in literary terms he was a traveler, a wayfarer, an internationalist in verse. Mangan was an imaginative trader, an importer of stolen literary goods, and an exporter of tapestries of astonishing manufacture. The loom on which he stretched his exotic (and synthetic) yarn was the periodical press; soaked in print, he produced articles rather than books, translations rather than self-seeded creations. Writing prose of surrealist mischief, if sometimes of uneven quality, this worked best when undermining his own poems, which are still best absorbed in this context. His translations follow an Irish tradition recounted by John Millington Synge in *The Aran Islands* (1907), that "a translation is no translation…unless it will give you the music of a poem along with the words of it" (p. 128), except that Mangan often improvises his own music upon hints from his originals, or abandons them entirely to produce poems that have the name and flavor of translations, but are entirely fabrications. "A translator," Mangan wrote, "in grappling with his original should be possessed by a feeling akin to that which animates the matador in his contests with the bull" (*Prose,* vol. 1, p. 161); and few translations left his pen without an increase in emotional temperature, sonic precocity, and a slain original. We expect poets to pay attention to sound: it is their job. But for Mangan words were things with audible weight, and poems asymmetric structures built in sound. At times Mangan was redundantly and rapidly productive; and there is a sense that, catching fire from an idea of oral performance, as well as of translation, the best of his poems are struck at such a temperature that the red-hot iron has not yet hardened into prosodic inflexibility and cool textual stability.

LIFE AND WORK

The man we know as James Clarence Mangan was not born with that name. Nor was he born when he claimed. Such elusiveness is characteristic, but these are the least of the problems facing his biographer. Chief among these is Mangan's fragment of *Autobiography* (collected in *Prose,* vol. 2), whose exaggeratedly severe account of his youth reads like a spiritual confession, and an eccentric notice appearing posthumously as part of his own series of "Sketches and Reminiscences of Irish Writers" (collected in *Prose,* vol. 2) for the *Irishman* newspaper, in which the poet himself must have had a hand. If we add to that the misleading self-revelation of his poetry, a bewildering array of pseudonyms that complicate the attribution of his work, and otherwise limited and speculative information, we can see why critics have responded by creating a succession of mythologies to fill a hollow vessel. What follows tries not to cast his poems as actors in his biography, and not to create anew the myth of "poor Mangan," suffering for Ireland or for his art, but to concentrate instead on what we know about his writing life.

Baptized plain James Mangan on 2 May 1803, the poet was probably the second of four sons (an elder brother dying young) from the marriage of Catherine Smith, of a prosperous grazier family, to James Mangan of Limerick, of whom little is known but that he was reputedly a "hedge-school teacher," one of that class of unofficial traveling scholars of rural Ireland whose arcane language learning was as notable as it was erratic. His son, in a sense, was to perpetuate this tradition. Mangan's early years were spent at a grocery shop on Fishamble Street, a once-respectable-enough commercial street in the Liberties of Dublin (that is, beyond the old city walls) near the tolling bells of Christ Church Cathedral. From here the young Mangan could walk to his first Jesuit school and, from 1813, to the newly built Catholic church of Saints Michael and John, where Mangan, like Joyce after him at Clongowes, served for a time as an altar boy. In eight years of formal education he attended four small schools of a dimly acceptable character, where he attached himself to languages, learning French well enough, and Latin, Italian, and Spanish to varying extents. How he acquired the German of so many of his translations, the only language after English in which he was really at home, retains an air of *unheimlich* mystery, and one has to assume not only a real flair for the language but the intense affinity of the self-taught linguist.

His father, not unlike Joyce's, seems to have fallen victim to drink and improvident business dealings that precipitated a social descent, the Mangans moving to a house on nearby Chancery Lane that the poet characterized as "one of the dismallest domiciles perhaps to be met with in the most forlorn recesses of any city in Europe" (*Prose*, vol. 2, p. 231). His description of these "two wretched rooms, or rather holes, at the rear of a tottering old fragment of a house" reflects what would be a continuing need for privacy, but perhaps it owed as much to the atmosphere of his early reading, which included the gothic extravagances of Anne Radcliffe and "Monk" Lewis alongside the poetry of Samuel Taylor Coleridge, Percy Bysshe Shelley, and Byron, who remained a favorite. These provided the dominant landscape of much of his later poetry: "in my boyhood," he wrote, "I was haunted by an indescribable feeling of something terrible" (p. 226). Whatever the truth in his insistence of neglect and unrivaled poverty, his response was in reading: "I sought refuge in books and solitude; and days would pass during which my father seemed neither to know nor care whether I were living or dead" (p. 229). What *is* certain about the family situation is that Mangan at fifteen was forced to go out to work and was apprenticed to a scriveners, where endless legal transactions fashioned a handwriting elaborately ornate but somehow appropriately secondhand. Certainly spending long days copying other people's words was bound to fuel a need to write something for himself, but no doubt it also contributed to the ease with which he slipped under the skin of other writers, appropriating their hand or signature even in works of his own.

On the other hand, spending most of the day wedged in a darkened Dickensian office with only a sulphurous fire for ventilation must have done little for his health, and according to his own account, he was only well when he determined to take exercise, which was not often. If not quite broken by this sedentary trade he became prone to illness, was hospitalized for fever, and began that obsessive scrutiny of his own physical well-being which became linked in his mind with mental and spiritual dissipation. It is typical that his name for this condition, "hypochondriasis," is the title of a poem whose comic tone and denouement (in which the complaining hypochondriac suddenly dies) seems to work against a simple biographical identification with its author.

In his last year at school, Mangan had been introduced to the art of writing puzzle poems for almanacs, and there seems little doubt that he lived for the composition of these rhymed anagrams, rebuses, and "enigmas" that, by demanding answers of the reader, fulfilled the function of a highly literary crossword. Despite later characterizing his fellow workers as monstrous, it was at his office that he fell into a community of like-minded contributors, and in a few years he had placed dozens of these pieces under several pseudonyms and become familiar with the games and proddings of a literary coterie that prized wit and ingenuity in rhyme above lyricism and sincerity—and, significantly, in which readers were also writers, conducting concocted arguments in print, as well as in local taverns. Mangan always wrote best when indulged by fellow enthusiasts, and he became immersed in print, the cultural pastime of a city unceremoniously deposed, following the Act of Union, from its status as the empire's second city. The Dublin of Mangan's youth was unreal: a pre-Union fervor of construction had played itself out, and the city was left contemplating the ghostly Palladian facades of empty institutions squatting amid an ingrained medieval geography. Perhaps accordingly Mangan's imaginative landscape, even in its rural incursions, tended to dwell upon scenes of ruined or depopulated buildings.

As his apprenticeship ended in 1826, so the almanacs went into decline, and Mangan's contributions to magazines for the next few years dried up as, it appears, he concentrated on his German. Accepting a position at a gloomy solicitor's office in Merrion Square, he was off work for a season, and may at this point have fallen calamitously in love with an unknown woman who, he later hinted, encouraged and then slighted him. Yeats, a devotee of the idea of the Romantic poet doomed in love, made attempts to identify her, but Mangan was no less affected by the death in October 1832 of a young student, Catherine Hayes, whom he had been tutoring in German and French, and to whom he had a strong attachment. In January 1831 Mangan's name had appeared on a list of law clerks calling for a meeting to petition Parliament for the repeal of the Union, a drive that following Daniel O'Connell's achievement of Catholic emancipation in 1829 became the preoccupation of nationalist opinion in Ireland. While Mangan convolutedly remarked in an long early letter that "you know, now, well, that I know very well that you know remarkably well that I know nothing whatever about Politics" (*Prose*, vol. 2, p. 241), this was undermined by his subsequent satirical-philosophical musings, although he maintained an evident cynical detachment. Mangan became involved with the Comet Club, a hotheaded pro-Repeal and virulently anti-tithe grouping of young literary firebrands, and began contributing oddly humorous verse and prose to their magazine the *Comet* and subsequently to the *Dublin Satirist*. Before long he was appearing in print for the first time as "J. C. M.," and then as "Clarence," revealing the assumption of his most persistent pseudonym. The name he most likely plundered from Maria Edgeworth's 1801 novel *Belinda*, whose melodramatic protagonist Clarence Hervey, like Mangan, identified himself with the "false, fleeting, perjured Clarence" of Shakespeare's *Richard III*. The following passage from *Belinda* might give us an idea why this pen name, which became ingrained, so enticed Mangan: Clarence, writes Edgeworth,

> had early been flattered with the idea that he was a man of genius; and he imagined, that, as such, he was entitled to be imprudent, wild, and eccentric. He affected singularity, in order to establish his

claims to genius.... His chameleon character seemed to vary in different lights, and in different situations, in which he happened to be placed. He could be all things to all men—and to all women.

(p. 14)

Evidently Mangan divined in "Clarence" a suitably schizophrenic literary persona.

Without abandoning other pseudonyms, Mangan also began to appear as "Clarence" in periodicals of a rather different tenor, producing original poems and German translations for the *Dublin Penny Journal,* a publication of genuine intellectual pretension associated with the energetic scholars John O'Donovan and George Petrie. From 1834 he contributed to that organ of conservative unionism, the *Dublin University Magazine,* alongside some of the most talented authors and scholars of the day, such as Samuel Ferguson, whose reviews of James Hardiman's *Irish Minstrelsy* (1831) Mangan was later to plunder for his own poetry. For the *Dublin University Magazine* he began his monumental but unsigned series "Anthologia Germanica" (January 1835), and "Literae Orientales" (September 1837), which encouched in a sharp prose commentary those colorful if treacherous verse translations from the German that established his reputation, and saw many of his most important poems in print. For the first time perhaps he was properly paid for his contributions, and with his regular income, while still supporting his dependent brothers and sisters, he was able to indulge in the pleasures of a professional writer, socializing in taverns with the novelist William Carleton and purchasing obscure titles from booksellers around the city. His reading was esoteric, delving into music theory, his favorite science of phrenology, and the supernatural visions of Emmanuel Swedenborg, all of which gave him matter for poetry. Some of the most resonant descriptions of the poet observe him propped at the city's bookstalls and libraries, his physical body symbolically shriveled to the stature of his umbrella and "all his soul...in a book" (Mitchel, p. 13). On publication Mangan had read Thomas De Quincey's *Confessions of an English Opium-Eater* (1822), and Charles Robert Maturin's *Melmoth the Wanderer* (1820), cultivating an early interest in narratives of literary and spiritual dissolution that were to influence his own, and indeed he extemporized a translation on Honoré de Balzac's continuation of *Melmoth,* "The Man in the Cloak" (1838). More than once encountering the Reverend Maturin near his home, Mangan had followed him through the city; and pursuing an enigmatic literary man in a cloak around the streets of Dublin seems an emblematic occupation for a man who never left the country of his birth but in imagination, and rarely left the claustrophobic embrace of the city.

Determining, however, to leave his job as printer's scrivener, in 1838 Mangan took a position under Petrie's direction at the Ordnance Survey Office, and he worked there for the next three years as a copyist. The survey sought to encompass such a broad range of material under the heading topographical, from music to manners, that if the project were not so earnestly and doggedly pursued, one would have to characterize it as lunatic ambition. In Petrie's office the past became a living thing, and centuries lay as lightly upon one another as dust, Latin and Gaelic annals underlying maps and archaeological reports of field workers. It was here that Mangan was first persuaded to make translations of some Irish poems, although the experiment was short-lived and none were to follow for a number of years.

There are signs in the vagaries of Mangan's attendance and habits that drink was beginning to get the better of him, and the use of opium, something Mangan strenuously denied, was becoming more than a painkiller. He certainly showed a literary awareness of the drug in composing the quixotic prose meditation "Sixty Drops of Laudanum" for the *Dublin University Magazine.* Moreover, judging from the accounts of his contemporaries, there seems little doubt that Mangan suffered from something close to manic depression, an affliction he described as "moral insanity," that left him oscillating, as he said, between the poles of enthusiasm and despair. One has to be careful, however, not to give credence to everything that was said about him, and it is all too easy to slip into a depiction

of the poet spending his life wallowing in the depths of suffering, as his later frenzied destitution casts a shadow over his earlier condition. Still, as he approached his late thirties, those letters extant from the period are peppered at once with optimistic schemes for future projects, jocular but real requests for payment, and, in what he called more "anti-philosophical" or "anti-poetic" modes of thought, his declared intentions of abandoning literature. Thus although he was accurately described in 1839 by Charles Gavan Duffy as "one of the most accomplished and popular writers for the *University Magazine*" (quoted in Shannon-Mangan, p. 188), under new editorship the magazine was accepting from him a noticeably reduced input. Duffy, a thrusting newspaper editor and future chronicler of "Young Ireland," and to whom Mangan related the story of a failed marriage proposal to a girl of fifteen, provided him with space on the pages of the Belfast *Vindicator,* and Mangan, in no mood, he said, for political articles, supplied him with damp squibs and meandering sketches featuring "The Man in the Cloak" that ponder tantalizingly in mockery of German metaphysics the question of identity and its masks.

In Ireland the political situation was changing. O'Connell's return from the Westminster Parliament and the inauguration of his widely attended rallies, known as "monster meetings," provided a political focus for the kind of cultural nationalism that magazines like the *Dublin University Magazine,* in some respects inadvertently, had fostered. When Duffy, Thomas Davis, and John Dillon in October 1842 inaugurated the *Nation,* a pro-Repeal weekly newspaper with an aim of producing a literature "racy of the soil," Mangan appeared prominently on the prospectus and in the first issue, but very seldom after this until 1846. Although still in contact with Duffy, he appeared out of sympathy with the "frothy speeches" (*Prose,* vol. 2, p. 256) in the journal, which nonetheless introduced writers like Edward Walsh and Dennis Florence MacCarthy to a wider public, and to Mangan; if the poetry was not always of this standard, Duffy and, prolifically, Davis toiling to little effect, it had the excuse that much of it was meant to be set to music, and

Davis's ambition had created the *expectation* of a literature that would plunder Irish myth, language, music, and above all history in the service of a national ideal.

By this time, the scholarly Ordnance Survey had been wound down, and Petrie had found Mangan solitary employment as a cataloging clerk for Trinity College Library, where Mangan at least had the opportunity to bury himself in books. In September 1843 the poet's father died, and while this could have been a relief, he was left with unresolved feelings of guilt and a renewed sense of responsibility for his family. By the end of the following year he was nursing his sick mother and unable to work, though he later returned to half-time employment at the library. It was probably evident that Mangan was in need of some assistance, and Duffy and Davis agitated, in both London and Dublin, for the publication of his *German Anthology: A Series of Translations from the Most Popular of the German Poets,* which, sponsored by Duffy, came out in midsummer of 1845, it was well reviewed and then forgotten. It was the only book of poems Mangan ever saw published, and made him perhaps £25. In an acutely self-scrutinizing letter perhaps intended to provide the basis for a biographical notice, he spoke of "the misery of my own mind—my natural tendency to loneliness, poetry, and self-analysis" and "that evil habit [no doubt alcohol] which has since proved so ruinous to me" (*Prose*, vol. 2, p. 277)—but nonetheless his poetic yield was rising, and in the previous two years he had manufactured some astonishing spurious translations such as "The Caramanian Exile" and "The Wayfaring Tree," attributed to Turkish and German authors.

With the death of Thomas Davis in September 1845, the impetus had sapped from the activities of what was by now known as "Young Ireland." But Duffy's recruitment to the paper of John Mitchel, firebrand solicitor and soon-to-be committed political rebel, reenergized the cause and the contributors to the *Nation.* Inspired by him, and by the enthusiasm of the young nationalist curate of his boyhood church, Father C. P. Meehan, at whose rooms Mangan became a frequent visitor, reading and reciting his poetry to an appreciative audience, in 1846 Mangan embarked on an *annus mirabilis* of poetic production, comparable in intensity if not in subtlety with John Keats's 1819. This renaissance, which occasioned some of his most pungent poems improvised upon Irish originals, such as "O'Hussey's Ode to the Maguire" and "Dark Rosaleen," was also evidently inspired by immediate events. Following the blight of the potato crop in 1845, famine had begun to take a chilling hold upon Ireland, and with genuine feeling Mangan girded himself for poetical expression that could at times be nakedly political, as in "The Sorrows of Innisfail," where Geoffrey Keating's original is overwritten with contemporary revolutionary feeling. If Mitchel is to be believed, as people continued their daily lives an air of unreality once more hung about the city, which remained for some time insulated against the famine's effects: the *Nation* was one of the few journals to carry a distressing diary of "The State of the Country" on its pages. Mangan's was the perfect voice to fill this vacuum: the city insider speaking as it were from outside, from the past, conducting ghostly voices at a heightened emotional pitch and articulating the contradictions of Dublin to itself, as indeed he had done all his life. Not that Mangan gave himself entirely over to nationalist polemic; a series conceived as "Echoes of Foreign Song" was intended for another book of translations in the *Nation* publisher James Duffy's "Library of Ireland" series; the book never appeared, but its demise left him with copious material for the "Lays of Many Lands" articles that he produced for the *Dublin University Magazine* until his death.

Following the death of his mother in late 1846 Mangan's last years represented a decline. With his brother he clung to the family home, but they were eventually forced to leave and find a series of cheaper lodgings. Dismissed from Trinity Library, and with no other employment, Mangan kept up a punishing workload of new poems and translations, later even writing in public houses (pubs), which gave him pen and paper *gratis.* First to Duffy, and then to Mitchel, Mangan addressed documents cast in the personal language of his abstinence vows, pledging himself religiously to the national cause. Duffy declined to publish, but the increasingly radical Mitchel, who had split with Duffy to found his own paper, the *United Irishman,* felt no such unease, and he quickly made Mangan's letter public. His timing was unfortunate, as just a few weeks later, in May 1848, the periodical was suppressed and Mitchel convicted and sentenced to exile, from where he was to produce his notorious *Jail Journal* (1854) and a posthumous edition of Mangan's verse largely made up of his German poems (1859). This left Mangan exposed politically and personally, and following the abortive insurrection of Young Irelanders in July 1848 many of his associates were in prison, in exile, or in hiding, while his older friends appeared unable to help, hamstrung by Mangan's unwillingness to accept charity and inability to stop drinking. His letters make for harrowing reading: newly tormented by religious guilt, they are a procession of renewed resolutions and pathetic but proud applications for money. It was around this time that Mangan began to achieve notoriety as a strange figure about the Dublin streets, complete with dilapidated cloak and umbrella, and it is striking how many of his contemporaries left descriptions of him as wraithlike or ghostlike, as if risen from the dead, images that were to color his later reputation.

He was still, however, able to work prodigiously, and working directly from the impromptu oral translations of the publisher John O'Daly was composing songs from the Irish; contributing poems and a series entitled "Sketches of Irish Writers" to a new journal, the *Irishman;* and to the end writing for the *Dublin University Magazine,* which seems never to have questioned his political leanings. Lacking funds and permanent housing, in April 1849 he succumbed to one of many cholera epidemics that flooded the city. Apparently recovering, but with years of weakened health behind him, Mangan was taken to the Meath hospital in Camden Street, and he died on 20 June. His doctor, the philologist Whitley Stokes, summoned the painter Frederick William Burton, who made a haunting chalk sketch of the dead poet with hollowed cheek and flowing hair. That same day O'Daly and Mangan's *The Poets*

and Poetry of Munster was sent to the press; the book appeared later the same year. Three years later, in 1852, his eccentric collaboration with O'Daly and John O'Donovan on a translation of Aenghus O'Daly's *The Tribes of Ireland* was published, and editions and memoirs followed from Mitchel, Meehan, and Duffy.

LITERARY APPRENTICESHIP

Little attention has been paid to Mangan's early poems, which is surprising, as they are not quite as marginal as the periodical culture they memorialize. In them we can glimpse, as in a glass darkly, the beginnings of Mangan's plural poetic identities. Essentially they disclose two things: first, the irresistible attraction sound had for Mangan, together with a characteristic inventiveness with rhyme and meter; and second, a strangely amplified sense of the demands of his form. These are poems aware of their place in a printed world, referring frequently to their own circumstance and manufacture: to the poet's writing table—and, as he usually features as a somewhat dissolute character, to the pen, ink, cigars, and brandy that help him write—to the columns of the magazine, to other contributors, and back upon themselves, as in his "Eight Stanzas," which farcically fulfils the expectations of its title—"The stanza halting here, I had best toss off another, // That being a good way to push through a Poem" (*Selected Poems* [hereafter cited as *SP*], 2003, p. 5). Even the much-maligned puzzle poems and enigmas placed in the popular almanacs are not exterior to his talent: Mangan, under a series of wild pseudonyms, kept up the fiction that all his readers were equally poets and developed a habit of directly addressing them, as "Bards of Hibernia" or "Bards of this Beautiful Isle." This had the effect of puncturing the inflated rhetoric that had built up around Irish poetry in English and turning the expectation of communal sorrow that was such a part of Thomas Moore's *Irish Melodies* (1807–1834) into a knowing acknowledgment of exhausted inspiration, as in "Hail to Thee, Bard!" (from *The Collected Works of James Clarence Mangan: Poems,* hereafter cited as *Poems*):

Give me your pity, then, ye Bards sublime
And let it flow in copious stanzas of rhyme
Weep each line, or I shall weep myself

(vol. 1, p. 21)

Extravagant melancholy is so often expressed only to be withdrawn: "And tears, say half a dozen, or seven, fell from me" ("Yesterday Afternoon, O'erpowered," *SP*, p. 9). While it is customary to detect the insertion of genuine personal feeling in Mangan's verse (the answers to his enigmas tended to be things like "Despair," or "Silence"), the poems themselves become waylaid by a fondness for puns or double rhymes. In these early almanacs appeared Mangan's first poems with national subjects, but with riddling solutions like "Emmet" or "Ireland" they too played havoc with sincerity, and an acute ear for poetic ventriloquism nearly tips even his "straighter" verses into self-parody. Mangan's early work displays such exuberance in plunging headlong into a vocabulary distended by the sublime, or bent underneath the weight of national sentiment, that the line between candor and cliché becomes smudged. This is a young man, as Yeats said of Joyce's early poems "practising his instrument, taking pleasure in the mere handling of the stops" (*Letters*, vol. 3, p. 282)—refining a technique that leaves nothing unsayable in sound, and poetry fizzing with energy and a discernible restlessness.

Mangan's ability to write poems for a *purpose,* whether as a puzzle, an announcement, or, soon, even as a translation, became early on a peculiar forte. This left him with a mastery of the occasional poem, but also a need always to play with the margins of his remit and confound formal expectations. Above all, he demanded of his poems that they conduct a dialogue with their surrounds, a habit that became inseparable from his poetic method. The Mangan poem without *some* interaction with the printed page of which it is a part, whether through an enigmatic epigraph or prose introduction, the interpolation of notes, or some typographic wizardry—or else by an infusion of whimsical or maudlin self-consciousness in the poem itself—is a rare bird.

Mangan's contributions to the *Comet* and the humorous magazines of the 1830s continued in this extravagant vein: he had inherited and exaggerated Byron's versatility with the bathetic timing of rhymes and with shifting tone. Even in those poems in which the feeling is sustained, traditionally seen as his finest, the poetic voice retains an insistent self-reflexiveness—

All is as gorgeous and as grand
As the creation wherewith teems
The poet's haunted brain amid his noonday dreams

(p. 19)

he muses in "Life Is the Desert and the Solitude" and a continued metrical virtuosity. This can be a distraction, but it can also provide a halting dramatic expressiveness, as in "The One Mystery," a poem Yeats called "all but the saddest of his songs" (*Uncollected Prose,* p. 115):

The flood of life runs dark—dark clouds
    Make lampless night around its shore:
The dead, where are they? In their shrouds—
    Man knows no more!

(*SP,* p. 16)

Flood is a common trope in Mangan's writing, and a redundance of liquid spills over into his verses, mimicking their extremes of emotion and the movement of the lines themselves. We can see this as part of an apocalyptically inclined imagination: as he remembered, for instance, "accounts of earthquakes, inundations and tempests; and narratives of 'moving accidents by flood and field,' possessed a charm for me which I could neither resist nor explain" (*Prose*, vol. 2, p. 236), and increasingly ghoulish visions of graves and the dead pile up in his poems. But the power of these particular lines lies, as so often, not in meaning but in cadence, and their anguished repetitions and broken punctuation, and final tolling syllables, are hyperbolically affecting.

Probably the best example of Mangan's uncomfortably self-unraveling poetry is "Verses to a Friend: On His Playing a Particular Melody Which Excited the Author to Tears," which for sixty-three lines maintains an unbroken, if comically severe, melancholy that only begins to disintegrate as the poet considers and rejects his metaphors as inadequate to the expression of such pain: "My drooping heart can no where borrow /

Language to paint its awful sorrow!" (*SP,* p. 14). The poem thereupon disintegrates into pure sound, a peculiar humming which is then "translated" for us in assiduously consonant lines that, as Mangan claimed, "I have a right to pique myself on, for the whole compass of English poetry exhibits nothing like them" (*Prose,* vol. 2, p. 247):

Tal lara, lara lal—tal lara, lara, lara!
D'ye want this Englished now? Then, here, you
  sumph, it is:
When men behold old mould rolled cold around my
  mound, all crowned with grass, alas!
Mankind, though blind, will find my mind was kind,
resigned, refined—but shrined like gas, in glass!
(SP, p. 14)

The reader's first feeling on encountering these sonic pyrotechnics must be bewilderment, and indeed the uncertainty of tone is fatally injurious to the effect. Still, the lines contain many qualities typical of Mangan: a direct address to the reader, a preoccupation with translation, a morbid prefiguring of the poet's grave, an apparently overwhelming melancholy, but most of all a sheer delight in patterns of sound, all of which constituted the ingredients of his more assured later poetry. There is a sense that Mangan was waiting for a subject to lift his alternately maudlin and quizzical verse into true poetry. Unquestionably in translation he found his métier.

OVERSETTINGS FROM THE GERMAN

The overwhelming majority of Mangan's writings go under the name of translation, and most of these have a German original behind them. Mangan was a self-taught Germanist, coming to the art of translation late, and at one remove, probably with literal English versions between him and his sources. Versification rather than literal rendering would always be his priority. The translations of Johann Wolfgang von Goethe and Friedrich von Schiller he began to supply to the Dublin papers from 1830 were relatively reticent compared with his later extravagances, but they do display an ear for unusual sound. Mangan concentrated his attentions on the recent

German poets of the early nineteenth century: not much of the rest, he claimed, was worthy of the translator's ink. But the inauguration of his unsigned articles of "Anthologia Germanica" in the *Dublin University Magazine* heralded a new sophistication in his manipulation both of translations and the prose that always accompanied them, from loose adaptations to the creation of entirely new poems. We might ask why Mangan spent so much time in German, and why he felt such an overwhelming identification with the language that he felt able to depart so radically from his sources and to forge a new order of "oversettings" (from the German *übersetzung*), finally even composing original poems as if they were translations.

The most convincing answer to both questions lies in sound. Not so much that Mangan felt an affinity with the distinctive noises of German, although this must have played a part. More that the idea of the sublime, as conceived in both Germany and England, had begun to privilege the terrifying and inassimilable resources of sound above any but the most vast and shrouded vistas—as Mangan mischievously put it "the Misty is...but a loftier species of the Sublime" (*Prose,* vol. 1, p. 105). This was almost as true of Coleridge and Shelley as it was of Goethe and Schiller; and must have added a philosophical basis to what was evidently an existing predilection for auditory imagery and effects. As an example we can take Mangan's revised version of Schiller's lengthy "The Lay of the Bell," which appeared in the *Dublin University Magazine* for February 1835. In Mangan's hands the poem essentially represents an opportunity for the manipulation of different kinds of sound, as the different bells pertaining to the different stages of life—wedding bell, funeral bell, and so on—cast their different tones over the separate sections of the poem, in a manner Poe was to follow in his cacophonous "The Bells." Mangan took the hint from Schiller's original, in which "though the metre incessantly varies as the subject ranges the variations are always in accordance with the finest principles of harmony" (*Prose,* vol. 1, p. 73), but he drove the conception much further than expected, producing not only chimes and clangs but also an orchestral range of overwhelming aural possibilities. We have the evidence of his prose and countless poems that Mangan did find the tolling of a bell particularly ominous. "The Marvellous Bell" is just one of many poems in which a constant knelling terrifically reminds us of coming death, and "Pompeii," typically contemplating a ruined cityscape, wonders whether in the "prodigies of sound" of thunder, flood, and earthquake "is there not a Voice which peals alike / To all from these" in a bell-like intimation of Judgment (*SP*, p. 268). There is perhaps nothing remarkable in hearing the passing of time and thus the pricking of conscience in the tolling of a bell: the interest is that Mangan fastens upon that part of a poem traditionally supposed least susceptible to translation, its sound, and makes it the dominant note of his poetry. In a long footnote to the poem, admitting that German is often noted for its double rhymes, Mangan denies there are fewer such terminations in English, and he takes it as a personal challenge to prove the resources of the language, inundating his poetry with double and treble rhymes, internal echoes, consonantal assonance, and an instinctive flair for unusual rhythmic patterning. In so often choosing to *describe* sound, whether sweet or sublime, and it was usually the latter, Mangan was able to overset his relish for sonic variation onto his subject and allow his poems as it were to describe themselves, matter and manner coinciding.

What this meant was that fidelity in translation was not a matter of attention to meaning but of sonic *transposition*. His free version of "The Fisherman" took Goethe's opening line "Das Wasser rauscht', das Wasser schwoll" and transposed it as "The waters rush, the waters roll," an affinity of rhyme more than meaning (*SP*, p. 56). Nor was he above changing the name of the central figure in his translation of a ballad by Friedrich Rückert: Mangan's "The Ride Round the Parapet" features "the Lady Eleanora von Alleyne," to provide an aural echo of "alone" and increased scope for rhyming. However, his versions ransacking the resources of English to effect the *replacement* of sonic properties, Mangan soon set himself free from the tethers of direct

imitation of German sounds and began creating poems much longer or much shorter than his sources, with meters and sound patterning that "improved" on the original and had little reference to the rhythm or meaning of his source. His defense was to posit the inferiority of the whole of the German tongue as compared to English, making it the translator's duty "to make up…the discrepancies and hollowness of the former language, by the fullness and rotundity of the latter" (*Prose,* vol. 2, p. 202). Elsewhere in his columns, though, he claimed the equality of all languages and argued instead the worthlessness of his source texts, saying that German poetry was "not merely obscure, but in the positive sense of the phrase unintelligible…it is the perfection of magnificent inanity" (*Prose,* vol. 1, p. 83). So to paraphrase, travesty, or disguise—all words he used to describe translation—could only improve on near-meaningless originals. Individual authors were translated only to be remorselessly criticized: Ludwig Tieck, he said, produced "maudlin drivel," Friedrich Gottlieb Klopstock "feeble phraseology," Gottfried August Bürger "platitude"; yet at the same time Mangan was candidly confessing that "we grow every day fonder and fonder of the German Muse" (*Prose,* vol. 1, p. 105–107).

It has taken some time for scholars to realize how integral to Mangan's poems and translations is the prose that surrounds them. His original articles were relatively inaccessible, and even now the Irish Academic Press edition of Mangan's *Collected Works* (published in a total of six volumes between 1996 and 2002) keeps apart prose and poetry. But all his poetical translations were only part of this eccentric inquisition into the origins and nature of languages, and the essence and value of originality, that strikes us as very modern, conducted as it is via clandestine sallies of sometimes antagonistic prose and verse in an august scholarly journal. His pronouncements on translation are temporary, distorting the poems they frame and in turn distorted by them: and read as a whole they are gloriously rich in contradiction. Mangan praises a liberal 1835 translation of *Faust* by his friend John Anster, for instance, for the incredible reason that he has translated that part of the mind of Goethe which was unknown to Goethe...He is a hundred times more Goethian than Goethe himself. He sees through his author, as through glass, but corrects all the distortions produced by the refraction of the substance though which he looks....—he is, in short, *the real author of* "Faust."

(*Prose,* vol. 2, p. 201)

This dizzying logic is in its surface plausibility and trickery almost Borgesian: "El original es infiel a la traducción" (the original is unfaithful to the translation), Jorge Luis Borges remarks of William Beckford's *Vathek,* after Samuel Henley's version of 1786 (*Obras completas,* p. 730). It gestures toward the notion that there is a source-Goethe, an Ur-Goethe, to which all other Goethes are indebted, but outrageously proposes that we might find him not by attention to his words but through a kind of translator's clairvoyance. Such occult reasoning justifies colossal liberties and cloaks Mangan's practice in another veil, finally delivering us helpless into the hands of the translator, who within his dominion is all-powerful. His dominion, however, might extend further than we imagine.

One explanation for Mangan's attachment to German was that reflections on the nature of translation had played a significant part in the revival of that literature from beneath the shadow of French and English. Mangan also had before him the examples of Coleridge, who had steeped himself in German thought, and De Quincey, who had, he said, "traced [Coleridge] through German literature, poetry and philosophy," according to Grevel Lindop in his 1981 biography of De Quincey, *The Opium-Eater.* In September 1834, De Quincey provoked a literary scandal by accusing the recently deceased Coleridge at once of genius and "barefaced plagiarism": Coleridge, De Quincey claimed, had not only denied plucking hints for his poems from German sources but also lifted long passages of his 1817 *Biographia Literaria* unattributed from the German philosopher Friedrich Wilhelm Joseph von Schelling. Questions of authenticity were thus swirling around such German borrowings; and to assume Coleridge's mantle of genius and plagiarist must have been for Mangan a tempting proposition. Only four months later, in January 1835, he

inaugurated his "Anthologia Germanica," beginning with a consideration of the merits of Goethe and Schiller. Mangan gives Schiller more concerted praise for his transcendent power and individuality but claims he "lacks the playful vein, the versatility, the Protean, Voltairean faculty of metamorphosis and self-multiplication possessed by Goethe" (*Prose,* vol. 1, p. 67). If from time to time Mangan aspired to be a Schiller, he was much closer to this conception of Goethe, and surely was here describing himself. It is no surprise then that before long Mangan had graduated to oversettings that bore only the merest trace of their original, or poems capriciously dubbed "the antithesis of plagiarism": "he has been also overmuch addicted to a practice...of fathering upon other writers the offspring of his own brain...I cannot commend it. A man may have a right to offer his property to others, but nothing can justify him in forcing it upon them" (*Prose,* vol. 2, p. 224). It became quite usual for Mangan to reverse Coleridge and smuggle his *own* poems into his articles by attributing them to real authors whose canon he could thereby helpfully enlarge, or even to foist them upon spurious German authors such as "Dreschler" or "Selber" ("Himself"). So his "Twenty Golden Years Ago" (1840), spoken as if by a reminiscent German poet:

O, the rain, the weary, dreary rain,
   How it plashes on the window-sill!
Night, I guess too, must be on the wane,
   Strass and Gass around are grown so still.
Here I sit, with coffee in my cup—
   Ah! 'twas rarely I beheld it flow
In the taverns where I loved to sup
      Twenty golden years ago!

(*SP,* p. 123)

This first stanza from one of Mangan's best and strangest poems is, extraordinarily, leavened with German words as if it were only half-translated from a German original. The Teutonic atmosphere thus created is of course entirely contrived, in part to allow room for a dig or two at the excesses of *Sturm und Drang* Romanticism, as the poet's tears are said to fall as fast as "High-Dutch floods, that Reason cannot dam," and his sorrow is compared with the (genuine) poet Justinus Kerner: "I have a deal more to wail about than Kerner has!" It is hard to say there is no genuine regret lurking in the poem's insistent rhythm, but we are left in little doubt this is a literary melancholy:

Though you find me, as I near my goal,
　Sentimentalising like Rousseau,
O! I had a grand Byronian soul
　　Twenty golden years ago!

(SP, p. 124)

The final irony is that the poet, this "tortured torturer of reluctant rhymes," is regretting the ebbing of his poetic inspiration as compared to "Deutschland's bardlings," whereas "in song / I could once beat all of them by chalks"—yet although given to another, the poem's weird inventiveness surreptitiously announces the *flourishing* of its author's muse. Nothing remains stable in these pseudo-German poems: already linguistically unsettled, they are upturned completely by the mischievous suggestions of the framing prose.

"LITERAE ORIENTALES"

The Orient was a place Mangan necessarily approached circuitously; recalling that "Goethe appears to have been skilled in the languages of the East" (*Prose,* vol. 1, p. 94), he peered through the lens of German scholarship, and those poems still clinging to authentic sources Mangan manufactured from German translations of eastern poetry. Still, he was never at pains to dissuade the reader that he was steeped in the original languages, whether Turkish, Persian, or Arabic, referring to the ellipses in manuscripts and indulging in the transliteration of more or less fraudulent fragments of eastern tongues. "It has been said that he has translated from fourteen languages; but he himself has assured me that he understands only eight," Mangan says of himself in the dissembling "Sketches of Irish Writers" and adds, for the wary reader, a caution: "he has translated from many besides that he does not understand" (*Prose,* vol. 2, pp. 223–224). This was quite true: however in his versions, borrowings, and inventions from oriental languages,

mostly serialized in the *Dublin University Magazine* as "Literae Orientales," Mangan's poetry takes flight, and he becomes that protean, ghostly figure he had long threatened to be.

Mangan's fascination for the East had begun early: like many of his generation, he was consumed by the folktales collected as *Arabian Nights,* and characters from these stories told by the legendary Scheherazade surface without warning in his prose, as he imagines glimpsing the dark magician Maugraby in the pubs of Dublin and streets of Vienna. Following the poetic incursions of Byron's *The Giaour* (1813) and Thomas Moore's *Lalla Rookh* (1817), Mangan was immersed in the oriental enthusiasms of his day, devouring English and German guidebooks and finding himself seduced by the sinister appeal of the Orient promulgated in gothic fiction from Beckford's *Vathek* (subtitled *An Arabian Tale* in the English edition of 1786) onward. Mangan's Orient then was not real, but a literary locality; a shadowy place, as he freely admits, existing in the mind and thus susceptible to whatever shaping we, or the author, might choose to put on it: "Alas! wanting that which we have not, cannot have, never shall have, we mould that which we really have into an ill-defined counterfeit of that which we want; and then casting a veil over it, we contemplate the creature of our own fancy" (*Prose,* vol. 1, pp. 129–130). While not quite anticipating the postcolonial theory of Edward Said, this is a remarkable admission of imaginative appropriation and sounds as if Mangan was allowing his disingenuous instincts free reign. Here his trademark pitch of lachrymose despair could be exercised using different props and different poets. That biographies of obscure authors with interesting names made up a good deal of oriental literary history was a glorious opportunity for mystification, and far from clearing up the difficulties Mangan created instead a sea of shape-shifting author-figures to whom he can attribute both sentiment and authorship.

So his translations progress from versified sayings, sonic fireworks, and casual additions to existing poems, as when he prints the last, rather Ozymandian stanza of the nostalgic "Time of the

Roses" in capitals because "in the MS of Nas-mi's Anthology this stanza is written in large and gorgeous characters" (*Poems,* vol. 1, p. 418)—needless to say, a whimsical invention His more extravagant creations were flagged by meaningful proprietorial cautions—"our translations shall be our own and our own only" (*Prose,* vol. 1, p. 142)—and an increasing instinct for typographic trickery, printing "wine" and "raki" upside down in "Song for Coffee-Drinkers," with an accompanying note admonishing us not to suspect the poems' authenticity. One or two poems stand out, notably "The Time of Barmecides," whose first line was translated back into spurious syllabic "Arabian." One stanza only will have to serve as a sample from a poem that works, as so often, by accumulated repetition and variation of the refrain:

I see rich Bagdad once agen,
  With turrets of Moorish mold,
And the Khalif's twice five hundred men,
  Whose binishes flamed with gold;
I call up many a gorgeous show
  Which the Pall of Oblivion hides—
All passed like snow, long, long ago,
  With the Time of the Barmecides;
All passed like snow, long, long ago,
With the Time of the Barmecides!

(*SP,* p. 119)

This is a poem in the tradition of Coleridge's "Kubla Khan," except from the point of view of an allegedly *Eastern* poet whose vision is fading. Like "Kubla Khan," it takes fire from the story of its mysterious creation—although depending on which version we read this fabrication is more or less suspicious, as its "translator" admits; and, from the strangeness of its vocabulary, which Mangan helpfully explains in gnomic notes ("binishes" are cavalry-cloaks, "Barmecides" Arabian nobles, both presumably included for their unnerving sound). Familiar, he said, with his own characteristic form of alternate prose and verse, the Orient was evidently also a source for new and interesting words, and, as here, for evocative proper nouns. Mangan's time at the Ordnance Survey had concentrated his ear on the unusual sounds and unlikely derivations of names, a predilection flaunted here that would

find consummation in his Irish poems.

Mangan mounts these meaningless reverberant names in giddying combinations, reminding us that following an exaggeratedly euphonic poem called "Ghazel and Song," Mangan had reprimanded the unwary: "if you have *read* this, reader, go over it again, we will thank you, and *sing* it" (*Poems,* vol. 2, p. 363). Probably the most convincing admission his autobiographical fragment contained was that "in my earlier years I was passionately fond of declaiming—not for my auditory but for myself. I loved to indulge in solitary rhapsodies—and if intruded on upon these occasions I was made very unhappy" (*Prose,* vol. 2, p. 230). The effect of such lonely rhythmical exertions can be felt in poems like "The Caramanian Exile," whose repetitions of the name "Karaman" over eight stanzas invoke a kind of orality that lifts the poem off the page into the realm of chant:

But Life at worst must end ere long,
        Karaman!
Azreel avengeth every wrong,
        Karaman! O, Karaman!
Of late my thoughts rove more among
Thy fields;— foreshadowing fancies throng
My mind, and texts of bodeful song,
        Karaman!
Azreel is terrible and strong,
        Karaman!
His lightning-sword smites all ere long,
        Karaman! O,Karaman!

(*SP,* pp. 181–182)

"One is not often electrified by such bursts of passion and feeling in Ottoman poetry," comments Mangan, critic of his own poem (*Prose,* vol. 2, p. 108). All the same his columns claimed that the energy of "compound epithets and sonorous polysyllables make us but indifferent amends" for the absence of the "irradiating light of Imagination" (*Prose,* vol. 2, p. 2). While this was so if the poems inclined too far toward bathos—as in, arguably, "The Wail and Warning of the Three Khalendars," where the necessity to find rhymes for Bosphorus ("The Bosphorus, the Bosphorus! / For life has lost its gloss for us!") mocks perhaps too openly the idea that what we are reading is a translation—an idea of oral, even musical performance still exerts a powerful tow on the reader or listener that helps compensate for a lack of imaginative complexity. This last ballad, said Mangan, would "thrill through the very soul of the listener" if only it were "sung to the vibratory music of the lute" (*Prose,* vol. 2, p. 108), and a notion of Eastern ejaculation and ritual chanting was conclusively brought into his poetry.

To what degree Mangan uses the Orient as a place where national ambitions could be eloquently but safely discharged has long been in question. In truth, he did not, at first, approach the Orient in this way: his opening article wonders at the peculiarity of national feeling ("nationality is not always rationality") and insists that the mind "repudiates every country on the map," though tending to incline "rather Eastward than Northward" (*Prose,* vol. 1, p. 129). But in "The Caramanian Exile" the violence Mangan allows into the poem can no longer help but stir thoughts of a struggle closer to home, particularly when he calls on the folklorist William Wilde to undertake a history of Caramania's bloody resistance against invasion. Unquestionably by the time he conceived the chilling "Siberia" (1846), an idea of Ireland was in his mind, but, typically, rather than featuring the exile's displacement *from* a lost green isle of plenty, Mangan envisioned a displacement *to* a wasteland of hunger, death, and silence:

In Siberia's wastes
    The Ice-wind's breath
Woundeth like the toothèd steel.
Lost Siberia doth reveal
    Only blight and death.
...
Therefore, in those wastes
    None curse the Czar.
Each man's tongue is cloven by
The North Blast, who heweth nigh
    With sharp scimitar.

                                        (*SP,* pp. 234–235)

Though many have seen a personal desolation in these lines, Siberia, far from the grandeur and exclamations of oriental exoticism, leads the poet to adopt a tone of terse northern fatalism, and it emerges as a potent symbol for post-famine Ireland, in a poem that eloquently addresses political silence as well as cultural desolation. Mangan's oriental impersonations and his eschatological imagination had equipped him with the tools to describe the crisis, and by the time of his "Song of the Albanian" (1847) his Eastern laments were quite evidently treating the worsening conditions of the famine, as "The stricken Dead lie without barrows / By roadsides, black and bare!" (*SP,* p. 271). Conversely those poems explicitly addressing Ireland often took on an Eastern visionary or prophetic cast, and the late poem "The Famine" unusually attributes the suffering not to British intransigence but to the prophesied coming of an Eastern cloud over the land: "Even as the dread Simoon of Araby / Sweeps o'er the desert through the pathless air" (*SP* p. 334). As Joyce remarked, "whether the song is of Ireland or Istambol [*sic*] it has the same refrain" (p. 57). In imagination Ireland and Orient could themselves be overset.

PERVERSIONS FROM THE IRISH

In mapping the Orient onto Ireland, Mangan knowingly joined a long and factitious tradition believing the Milesians, an ancient race of Ireland, were descended from Persians, Phoenicians, or other assorted Easterners: "according to [the Irish antiquarian Charles] Vallancey every Irishman is an Arab" (*Prose,* vol. 2, p. 7). Content to follow specious scholarship, by now Mangan was happily translating from the languages of East and West with little knowledge of either. But if his sideways attitude to the Irish language never quite faded, what he called his "perversions from the Irish" have since been much admired, and unquestionably they include some of his finest poems. His first ventures were attempted only in 1840 at the urging of George Petrie and were truly an Ordnance Survey production in all respects. Mangan worked, as for many of his later poems, from his colleague Eugene O'Curry's literal translations and produced versifications for Petrie's *Irish Penny Journal* prefaced by introductions from the polymath scholar. The most distinctive of these, "The

JAMES CLARENCE MANGAN

Woman of Three Cows" and "An Elegy on the Tironian and Tirconnellian Princes Buried at Rome," make an odd pairing, but Mangan reproduced the satiric voice of the former perfectly and gave to his lengthened lines an added disdainful gait, adding characteristic double rhymes and the odd ejaculation lifted directly from the Irish. It introduced readers to a different caste of Irish poetry, and if he produced it with his usual facility Mangan took it very seriously, quizzing Duffy as to why he omitted three stanzas on its republication in the Belfast *Vindicator*. What he called his "*transmagnifican-bandancial* elegy" (*Prose*, vol. 2, p. 275) is, however, an astonishing eighteen-stanza construction of a funeral wail that never was, the poem undertaking to describe the unearthly sound that would have arisen from Ireland had both princes been buried at home. Such a sonic invitation was perfect for Mangan, and drawing on the topographical resources of the survey, he mined Irish place names for every last ore, massing familiar and less-familiar syllables into a cumulative naming force unequaled in Ireland until Yeats. The poet takes a tangible pleasure in resurrecting the longed-for lament in the sonic explosions of Irish words like *keen* and *rann*, producing a lament sung not, as Yeats would have it, to sweeten Ireland's wrong, but to indulge in it, noisily:

O, had they fallen on Criffan's plain,
　There would not be a town or clan
　　From shore to sea,
But would with shrieks bewail the Slain,
　Or chant aloud the exulting *rann*
　　Of jubilee!

(*SP*, p. 133)

We should remember that these poems, with a long-lined Yeatsian-sounding "Kathleen ny Houlahan," popularized by inclusion in Duffy's best-selling *The Ballad Poetry of Ireland* (1845), represented only a teaspoonful amid the mounds of translations and original poetry Mangan had produced to this point. In November 1844, notes the biographer Ellen Shannon-Mangan, Duffy felt obliged publicly to call for Mangan's assistance with the national project:

How we wish the author of "The Barmecides" would lend his help to an Irish ballad history! His power of making his verses racy of the soil cannot be doubted by any one who reads his "Paraphrase of Kathleen ny Houlihan" and "Elegy on the Princes."

(p. 276)

The attempt to recruit Mangan, initially yielding little fruit, finally spurred him to a series of unashamedly political poems for the *Nation*. These had far more energy and metrical variation than the average nationalist poem, while their sometimes astonishing violence is leavened, again, by a self-referential attention to their published housing. Yeats, though, had it about right when he opined in *A Book of Irish Verse* that Mangan "is usually classed with the Young Ireland poets, because he contributed to their periodicals and shared their political views; but his style was formed before their movement began" (p. xvi). Of course, the Young Irelanders had styled themselves after the Young Germanists, and Mangan could place German poems to national freedom without hiccup in the *Nation;* so between Mangan's different enthusiasms and styles there was no necessary disjunction. Nonetheless, in the same month (July 1846) as penning the eerie *aisling* poem "A Vision of Connaught in the Thirteenth Century," Mangan produced a serene vision of Ireland in "The Lovely Land"; the comical squib of "Ibrahim Pacha and Wellington"; a translation of a German ballad of lost love called "The Miller's Daughter"; and the idiosyncratic "An Invitation," which, addressed to "Friends of Freedom," takes Joycean pleasure in the names of rivers from around the globe, from the "daedal Amazon" to "glorious Ohio!" (*Poetry*, vol. 3, p. 197). Such heterogeneity did not make his poems any less distinctive, but it did make them unpredictable: sometimes the only constant was the same attention to "prodigies of sound."

Beyond national ambition Mangan had plainly become absorbed in the rhythms of his Irish translations, working always from literal versions in English but often attempting to reproduce "the same irregular metre as the original" or improvise his own (*Prose*, vol. 2, p. 281). Irish poems, Mangan found, very often had a self-referential element, and when they did not, he provided one: his "Lament over the Ruins of the Abbey of Teach Molaga," sketching a moonlit picture of architectural desolation, not only laments the silence caused by the tyranny of "brutal England's power," but an additional final stanza reverses it. The poet greets the silence of the poem's end with his own silence, but is overcome by the irrepressible noise of nature:

I turned away, as toward my grave,
And, all my dark way homeward by the Atlantic's
  verge,
Resounded in mine ears like to a dirge
The roaring of the wave.

(SP, p. 250)

Such framing envoys were common to both the oriental and the Irish poems Mangan worked from, and became a distinctive feature of his own style.

Probably Mangan's finest achievement working from the Irish was the impassioned love song "Dark Rosaleen." Mangan took from James Hardiman's *Irish Minstrelsy* the suggestion that the original poem "Róisín Dubh" ("the Black Rose") was an allegorical ballad addressed to Ireland, ignoring Samuel Ferguson's insistence that the song was simply written by a priest in love. He also would have noted Hardiman's reiteration of Vallancey's questionable contention that such allegory had an ancient Eastern cast: "No nation," says Hardiman, quoting Charles Vallancey, "is more fond of allegory than the Irish. Their ancient poets were celebrated for their *Meimeadh* or allegorical poems. No other language than the Arabic has a word of this signification, viz. Mamma, a verse of occult mysterious meaning" (vol. 1, p. 351).

One can imagine Mangan leaping upon this suggestion and quite deliberately producing a national Irish poem of ritual Eastern resonance. To see how Mangan transformed his sources, we might briefly examine the English versions of the ballad that he plundered. The second stanza of Samuel Ferguson's translation (reprinted in Robert Welch, 1988) read like this:

The course is long over which I brought you from
  yesterday to this day—
Over mountains I went with her, and under sails across
  the sea:
The Erne I passed at a bound, though great the flood,
And there was music of strings on each side of me
  and my Roisin dubh.

(p. 114)

Thomas Furlong in Hardiman's *Irish Minstrelsy* had unsurprisingly converted the "music of strings" into that ever-present symbol of Irish national identity, the harp, translating the passage thus:

Long, long with
my dearest, thro' strange scenes I've gone
O'er mountains and broad valleys I have still toil'd
  on;
O'er the Erne I have sail'd as the rough gales blew,
While the harp pour'd its music for my Roisin Dubh.

(p. 255)

Mangan's version by contrast preserves some of the nationalist implications of this harp music but removes all trace of its merely conventional symbolism. Substituting instead a musically patterned system of words, his stanza is elaborated and prolonged, quickened into intensity:

Over hills, and through dales,
  Have I roamed for your sake;
All yesterday I sailed with sails
  On river and on lake.
The Erne…at its highest flood,
  I dashed across unseen,
For there was lightning in my blood,
  My Dark Rosaleen!
  My own Rosaleen!
Oh! there was lightning in my blood,
Red lightning lightened through my blood,
  My Dark Rosaleen!

(SP, p. 237)

Hidden unseen, the self-sacrifice of the poem's rebel persona is in becoming almost bodily possessed, galvanized by his own rhetoric—subsumed, like Mangan himself, into the fabric of his poem. These anguished repetitions and variations of bloods and lightnings have nothing to do with the "music" of the source, which is entirely eliminated, but everything to do with an occult musical imperative, creating a dizzying, mounting incantation improvised upon and completely overwhelming the original's musical hint. Mangan's early experiments in pure sound and self-consuming ventriloquism had prepared the skill needed to produce this kind of passage: Yeats almost seemed to be describing its power when he said that for Mangan at his best "the words flowed like electric flashes" (*Uncollected Prose*, p. 118). Ironically, under the stern gaze of his publisher O'Daly, for his collection *The Poets and Poetry of Munster* (1849) Mangan's fidelity to the actual rhythms and cadences of the Irish parallel texts, and more pertinently to the music printed alongside his poems, produced very little of his finest work. Closer to their Irish source, the two further versions of "Roísín Dubh" have their intensity muted; under pressure to make his verse actually (or very nearly) singable to the music it accompanied, Mangan in rhythmic inflexibility lost something of the distinctive note of his own poetry.

In all his poems, whether from Irish, German, or other sources, Mangan was consumed by sound, and thus also by poetry's hidden origins, how it comes into being. Hence his fascination with translation: his poetic facility could not survive being tethered, but before his best work could be generated, he needed an external structure, or merely the *sense* of a poem already somewhere in existence, from which hint he could create pieces of astounding originality. Originality to the end was his obsession and his burden: "it is," he wrote, "the error of poets that they consider themselves bound to be at all hazards original. They are ignorant that the value of originality is to be tested by the character of the originality" (*Prose*, vol. 1, p. 160). Finally, the character of Mangan's originality was prodigious: in the vagaries and ventriloquism of translation and pseudo-translation he discovered his plural self. As he says in "The Nameless One," always "his soul was mated with song"

With song which alway, sublime or vapid,
　Flowed like a rill in the morning-beam,
Perchance not deep, but intense and rapid—
　　A mountain stream.

　　　　　　　　　　　　　　(*SP*, p. 352)

When this autobiographical poem, perhaps his last, was published in October 1849 with the fiction that

... Old and hoary
　At thirty-nine, from Despair and Woe,
He lives

　　　　　　　　　　　　　　(*SP*, p. 353)

it was wrong on all counts: he was much older than thirty-nine, and no longer living, a disingenuous but revelatory and contradictory figure to the end.

Selected Bibliography

WORKS OF JAMES CLARENCE MANGAN

Mangan's poetry and prose chiefly appeared in numerous periodicals throughout his lifetime: the only books to which he had direct input appear below under "Contemporary Editions," followed by the modern-day *Collected Works* and some important selected editions that have shaped his reputation. His poetry and prose is most easily available in the selected editions published by the Irish Academic Press in 2003 and 2004—but to see poetry and prose in interaction, see Sean Ryder's 2004 edition.

CONTEMPORARY EDITIONS

Anthologia Germanica. German Anthology: A Series of Translation from the Most Popular of the German Poets. 2 vols. Dublin: William Curry, 1845; London: Longmans, Brown, 1845.

The Poets and Poetry of Munster: A Selection of Irish Songs by the Poets of the Last Century. As translator, with biographical sketches of the authors by John O'Daly. Dublin: John O'Daly, 1849.

The Tribes of Ireland: A Satire. By Aenghus O'Daly, with translations by Mangan, and other text contributed by John O'Donovan. Dublin: John O'Daly, 1852.

COLLECTED WORKS

The Collected Works of James Clarence Mangan: Poems. 4 vols. Edited by Jacques Chuto, Rudolf Patrick Holzapfel,

Ellen Shannon-Mangan, et al. Dublin: Irish Academic Press, 1996–1999.

The Collected Works of James Clarence Mangan: Prose. 2 vols. Edited by Jacques Chuto, Peter Van de Kamp, Augustine Martin, and Ellen Shannon-Mangan. Dublin: Irish Academic Press, 2002.

SELECTIONS

Poems by James Clarence Mangan. Edited by John Mitchel. New York: P. M. Haverty, 1859.

The Poets and Poetry of Munster. Edited by C. P. Meehan. 3d ed. Dublin: J. Duffy, 1885; Poole, U.K.: Woodstock, 1997.

A Book of Irish Verse. Edited by W. B. Yeats. London: Methuen, 1895 *Poems of James Clarence Mangan.* Edited by D. J. O'Donoghue. Dublin: O'Donoghue, 1903; London: A. H. Bullen, 1903.

Selected Poems of James Clarence Mangan. Edited by Jacques Chuto, Rudolf Patrick Holzapfel, Peter van de Kamp, and Ellen Shannon-Mangan. Dublin: Irish Academic Press, 2003.

Selected Prose of James Clarence Mangan. Edited by Jacques Chuto, Peter van de Kamp, and Ellen Shannon-Mangan. Dublin: Irish Academic Press, 2004.

James Clarence Mangan: Selected Writings. Edited by Sean Ryder. Dublin: University College Dublin Press, 2004.

MANUSCRIPT MATERIALS

Significant but limited collections of Mangan's letters and papers are held at the Royal Irish Academy, which holds the music manuscript book of Mangan's *Autobiography,* and at the National Library of Ireland. Most manuscripts of interest relating to Mangan's biography are available in the holdings for John O'Donovan, Charles Gavan Duffy, and John McCall at the National Library of Ireland,

with a few stray papers lodged, fittingly, in other libraries around Dublin, including that of Trinity College.

CRITICAL, BIBLIOGRAPHICAL, AND BIOGRAPHICAL STUDIES

Chuto, Jacques. *James Clarence Mangan: A Bibliography.* Dublin: Irish Academic Press, 1999.

Joyce, James. "James Clarence Mangan (1902)" and "James Clarence Mangan (1907)." In *Occasional Critical and Political Writings.* Edited by Kevin Barry. Oxford, U.K.: Oxford University Press, 2000.

Lloyd, David. *Nationalism and Minor Literature: James Clarence Mangan and the Emergence of Irish Cultural Nationalism.* Berkeley: University of California Press, 1987.

MacCarthy, Anne. *James Clarence Mangan, Edward Walsh, and Nineteenth-Century Irish Literature in English.* Lewiston, N.Y.: Edwin Mellen, 2000.

Shannon-Mangan, Ellen. *James Clarence Mangan: A Biography.* Dublin: Irish Academic Press, 1995.

Welch, Robert. *A History of Verse Translation from the Irish, 1789–1897.* Irish Literary Studies 24. Gerrards Cross, U.K.: Colin Smythe, 1988.

———. *Irish Poetry from Moore to Yeats.* Irish Literary Studies 5. Gerrards Cross, U.K.: Colin Smythe, 1980.

Yeats, W. B. "Clarence Mangan" [1887] and "Clarence Mangan's Love Affair" [1891]. In his *Uncollected Prose.* Vol. 1. Edited by John P. Frayne. New York: Columbia University Press, 1970. (Articles written about Mangan for *United Ireland.*)

———. *The Collected Letters of W. B. Yeats.* General editor, John Kelly. Vol. 3, *1901–1904,* and vol. 4, *1905–1907.* Oxford, U.K.: Oxford University Press, 1994, 2003.

———. Introduction. *A Book of Irish Verse.* London: Methuen, 1895.

RUTH PITTER

(1897–1992)

Helena Nelson

RICHARD CHURCH BELIEVED that Ruth Pitter's work would endure. In 1969 he said it was "non-fashionable, like all permanent things such as bread, and water, and a well-made table." By 1991, a year before Pitter's death, Jonathan Barker's entry in *Contemporary Poets* told another story. Conceding that she had been praised over the years by "an impressive range of readers" he pointed out that "today her work is largely unread" and hoped the 1990 Enitharmon edition of Pitter's *Collected Poems* would correct the balance. However, even today the mention of Ruth Pitter's name may evoke blank faces. It is a puzzling phenomenon. Pitter left a substantial body of individual and interesting verse (most of which is still in print); she was the first woman to win the Queen's Gold Medal for Poetry in the UK; she was praised in America, had highly influential literary friends; and yet she has never attained the status in "the canon" that might have been expected. The 1985 *Oxford Companion to English Literature* does not even list her (though most of her literary correspondents and friends are snugly housed between its covers). What went wrong?

EARLY SUCCESS

Ruth Pitter was born on November 7, 1897 in the London suburb of Ilford, the first child of two primary school teachers. A younger sister and brother would follow in due course. The background was not a wealthy one; Pitter's mother had to return to teaching after the birth of her third child to make ends meet. However, it was a home where poetry was valued and encouraged. While it would have been no surprise for children at that time to receive "pocket money" in exchange for household chores, in the Pitter household they were paid to learn poems by heart, "a penny to sixpence a poem according to length" (Russell, *Ruth Pitter: Homage to a Poet*, p. 20). This early practice ensured a stock of remembered verse that Pitter could still recall at will in her nineties.

Though the family lived in the city they made regular trips to the nearest wild countryside, Hainault Forest. Long rural walks were a feature of Pitter's early life and soon the family started to rent a run-down cottage in the forest, which they visited as a kind of home away from home. It was a place that would feature again and again in the poet's adult poems, a mental territory connected directly with both spiritual faith and poetic inspiration.

So much of Pitter's poetry has rural associations that it is easy to forget she was originally a city child. She later recalled the occasion of the first poem she ever wrote (at the age of five): "suddenly there came into my mind, overwhelmingly, an image of something we had seen on one of our walks—a desolate and abandoned place. It was the first thing that ever gave me a poetic sensation. My eyes filled with tears of a strange new kind. Seizing my stump of blue pencil and a bit of torn paper I began in painful capitals: "The old mill stands with broken shaft—" This early fragment suggests that even then iambic rhythms had gone deep. The child continued to write poems and withstood a certain amount of teasing both at home and at school as a result.

However, the young poet also had significant encouragement. When she was thirteen years old her father (whom she later described as an "agnostic Fabian") took her to see A. R. Orage, editor of *The New Age,* a socialist weekly. The paper had a small circulation but was publishing interesting new writers, many of whom went on to establish considerable reputations: it pioneered the avant-garde too, from Vorticism to Imagism. And it published young Ruth Pitter, who belonged to neither movement. Her firmly traditional verse forms started to appear regularly in the pages of the magazine.

Meanwhile, the teenage poet was studying at Coborn School in Bow, an old Christian charity school with a strong emphasis on good manners. Although she was something of a prodigy in poetic terms, in other school matters she did not do particularly well. Her younger sister, Olive, won an allowance in the County Scholarship examination, which meant she went to the County High School, and later took a degree in the London School of Economics. Ruth did not do well enough to manage this. Again, this road not taken—in academic terms—was significant to her. In later years, recalling a lunch with C. S. Lewis and Hugo Dyson at Magdalen College, Oxford, she made reference to her "chronic Jude-the-Obscure syndrome," a sense that she was "ignorant" compared to others.

In fact her secondary education served her remarkably well. After reading her early poems few people would conclude that she received anything less than a full classical upbringing. At Coborn, she learned Latin and from the start associated that "dead" language with poetry. She recalls this in her essay "The Art of Reading in Ignorance," found in *Essays and Poems presented to Lord David Cecil:*

> How it came about that I found a small selection from Horace's Odes on my school desk, when as yet I could hardly decline *mensa,* I do not know. Could it have been that the thoughtful, cultivated little woman who taught us could have decided that it was now or never for me? However, that may have been, there I was with the Ode to Faunus…The Ode is in Sapphics, easy for ignorance to scan; what is more, it can be sung to the tune of *"Parlez-moi d'amour,"* which it fits to perfection. It was the time and the place and the loved one together.
>
> (p. 198)

Metrical patterns—not least sapphics—would remain central in most of her later writing.

At the age of seventeen, Pitter was in the Intermediate Arts class, accruing learning but unlikely to go to university without the scholar-

ship needed to make this financially possible. However, everything changed with the start of World War I. She left school and took a clerical job in the War Office, from which she quickly switched to the more domestic role of making tea for the staff of about fifty.

PITTER AS CRAFTSWOMAN

Before long Pitter was drawn toward a more artistic role in life. She was, after all, the product of a family with arts and literary interests (her sister Olive would go on to become a novelist; her brother Geoffrey an architect and part-time painter). In 1916, she left the War Office and moved to Walberswick in rural Suffolk. Here she became an assistant (and effectively apprentice) to an artist couple who trained her to make simple decorated furniture; they also provided her accommodation. She enjoyed working with her hands but she was also still writing poems and developing intellectually. A. R. Orage, for example, who embraced all the radical ideas of his time in the pages of *The New Age,* introduced her to Ernest Jones's book on Freud, which affected her deeply. She met, and continued to correspond with, Eric Blair who (writing as "George Orwell") would go on to become one of the best-known novelists of his day.

When the war ended Pitter's employers moved to London and she went with them. She managed to save enough money to rent two rooms over their workshop, bought furniture, and acquired a little more independence. By this time, her poetry had attracted attention from one of Orage's readers, Hilaire Belloc. Belloc was a poet himself, as well as a prolific writer of many other art forms: novels, essays, reviews, biographies, and travel books. He was depressed by the current state of poetry and saw her as a shining hope for the future. In 1920 he paid for Pitter's *First Poems* to be published. The world did not share Belloc's enthusiasm. As he himself later put it, the publication "fell dead."

Pitter continued to work as an artisan, painting and decorating household goods; she also continued to write poems using traditional forms. But significant changes were underway: a few years previously, in 1915, Ezra Pound's *Catholic Anthology* had included a poem called "The Love Song of J. Alfred Prufrock" by an unknown new writer, T. S. Eliot. Eliot, Pound, the Imagists— these were just a few of the radical new influences that dominated British poetic culture in the third decade of the century. Innovation was the name of the game.

By this time, Pitter was in her twenties, the age when most young women form relationships of one kind or another. However, following World War I, women vastly outnumbered men. This may have been one reason why Ruth Pitter did not marry. Instead she maintained her dedication to poetry as a central vocation. In 1927 (the year after her father died) Belloc funded a more ambitious volume of Pitter's work, *First and Second Poems*. It was a substantial volume, with a spirited preface by Belloc in which he argued that Pitter's verse represented "an exceptional reappearance of the classical spirit amongst us." He also roundly criticized the current state of affairs in British poetry: "Now that all standards have gone and that society is but a dust, every reader must judge for himself." This time the book must have met with a reasonable reception because it was issued in the United States by Doubleday Doran three years later.

However, it is not always an advantage to be championed. Belloc's high praise for Pitter's "classical spirit" was unlikely to find favor with the contemporary movement that later became known as "Modernism." A battle of modes was going on. Belloc was not on the winning side and perhaps partly as a result, neither was Pitter. There is no published record of her thinking at this time. However, she was now thirty; she had not married; she had not become a highly acclaimed poet; her father (who had encouraged her early writing) was gone.

SETTING UP IN BUSINESS

In 1930 there was a significant change. Pitter had formed a friendship with Kathleen O'Hara, a fellow worker ten years her senior. The two women had an opportunity to buy a small business producing the kind of craft artifact they knew

well. Pitter was nervous about the idea but O'Hara (known as "K") encouraged her. They pooled their savings, bought the firm of Deane and Forester, and finally took over the whole building where the business was housed, giving up their separate flats to share accommodation. After six months, the business began to do quite well. K took care of buying, customer care, and work allocation. Ruth continued craft work and did the financial accounts. Soon they were employing a number of workers—women managers in a period when this was unusual. Meanwhile, Pitter's mother retired from teaching and bought a cottage in Felstead in Essex, providing a country retreat. The cottage had a large vinery where Ruth, who loved gardening, taught herself to grow, train, and prune vines. She was also working on her most ambitious poem to date, *Persephone in Hades,* a narrative extending over forty pages which was published privately in a limited edition of 100 copies (and never subsequently reprinted).

Poetry may have been central in Ruth Pitter's life but her work had made little impression on contemporary culture. However, in 1933 Alida Monro's new anthology, *Recent Poetry 1923–1933,* included two Pitter poems, which brought her more attention. For the first time, she breached traditional form with "Digdog," a poem which, according to Herbert Palmer in his *Post-Victorian Poetry* (1938), caused her to be grouped "among the more baffling of the modernists," an idea long lost by 1991, when Jonathan Barker was to remark that "on a first reading her poems seem to behave as though modernism never happened." Pitter was undoubtedly influenced by current poetic trends even though formally metrical writing remained her "norm." She was mingling with contemporary writers; she attended Poets' Club dinners and the connection with Alida Monro of the Poetry Bookshop must have brought her into contact with a wide range of poets. In 1934 (the same year her first publisher, A. R. Orage, died) she had a collection accepted by Cresset Press (publisher of D.H. Lawrence, Graham Greene, and Sylvia Townsend Warner). *A Mad Lady's Garland* received considerable critical acclaim. It was again prefaced by Belloc (with an additional foreword by John Masefield in the American edition); it was also publicly praised by the Irish poet George Russell (A.E.) and Walter de la Mare. The contents comprised a strange mixture of irrepressible pastiche, inspired satire, and emotive lyrical verse. Had Pitter ceased publishing at this point, her literary "image" would have been very different from what later emerged. She was moving into her late thirties—no longer a young poet.

WAR APPROACHES

Only two years later, a second collection appeared from Cresset Press, *A Trophy of Arms: Poems 1926–1935*. This book was very different from its predecessor, sober and formal in tone, employing a variety of traditional forms for traditional purposes. This time a preface was provided (somewhat fulsomely) by James Stephens. Again, the introduction may have done more harm than good. Stephens suggested "the Bad poet" was "superabundant in all anthologies of verse." Ruth Pitter, however, was to be regarded as "a pure poet...perhaps the purest poet of our day." He regarded her as second only to Yeats. Perhaps he did not take into account the contemporary reaction against archaic forms and inversions. In some poems Pitter used a plain and direct lyric style: in others she wrote in such a way as to be regarded as truly "Georgian" in the pejorative sense. Nonetheless, the volume won the Hawthornden Prize and attracted the attention of Lord David Cecil, literary biographer and academic. He sent a letter of appreciation, the beginning of a lifelong correspondence.

Meanwhile, the country was moving toward another war. Pitter's fifth book of poems, *The Spirit Watches*, was published in 1939, the same year World War II commenced. By this stage Pitter and Kathleen O'Hara were employing a dozen staff in their craft business but most of these immediately left to take up war work, and the commercial traveler on whom they relied for orders also left them. It became very difficult to continue trading. The poet and broadcaster John Arlott remembered visiting her during a blackout and listening to her in the dark as she talked about the impossibility of a great poet having a sense of humor. Perhaps she was thinking about her forthcoming collection, *The Rude Potato,* an almost entirely comic volume.

In 1940, the war took a bleak turn. France fell to Germany. Ruth and K made the decision to move from the artists' quarter of Chelsea to the industrial south side of the Thames, giving up their own business to support the war effort. They became office workers in a munitions factory and Pitter also did a weekly evening shift in a machine shop. Both women were living through their second major war.

In fact, it seems to have been a black period of Pitter's life on both public and private fronts, judging by poems from this period. John Arlott was deeply moved when Pitter read him her lyric "But For Lust," which agonizes over a friendship marred by sexual desire. Also written around this time, "Lament for One's Self" seems to refer to the same affectionate relationship, one that went badly wrong. Pitter was in her early forties: she must have had to face the fact that marriage and children were things that were not going to happen for her.

CRISIS OF FAITH

Some time in the early 1940s, Pitter experienced a dark night of the soul. It was a day in March when a man had fallen down the factory lift-shaft; the weather was bleak and wild. She paused on her way back across Battersea Bridge (all lights were blacked out because of the war) and leaned "over the parapet" thinking "Like this I cannot go on. I must find somebody or something. Like this I cannot go on."

Shortly afterward, she started to listen to the religious broadcasts of C. S. Lewis (whose *Screwtape Letters* had already impressed her). Lewis's lively approach to Christianity impressed her deeply and seemed the answer to a prayer. She later described his work in "The God" as "the joy of my life." Faith in God was the "something" she had been looking for, a natural orientation for a poet whose work, from the very start, had celebrated "the god who passeth all" (*First Poems,* 1990, p. 153).

RUTH PITTER

The year 1945 finally saw the end of hostilities but Ruth and K did not take up business as before. By this time K was nearing sixty and new tax regulations made everything more complicated. Ruth decided to work from home, creating hand-painted fiberglass trays, often patterned with flowers or vegetables. She painted freehand, using cellulose paints and a mercury-vapor lamp, both of which would feature in later poems. And of course she continued to develop as a writer. The poet Roy Fuller saw *The Bridge* (1945) as the first volume in which she spoke "systematically" in "a true voice—observation and thought without the glaze of false "poetry." It was a bleak collection, though: the last line of the concluding poem, "Sinking," was "Cease then your striving, sink and go down." A more cheerful sign was the publication of *Pitter on Cats* in 1946, another volume of humorous or whimsical poems, in which two of the cat poems from the earlier *A Mad Lady's Garland* were re-collected.

At about this time, Pitter began corresponding with C. S. Lewis, and then met him in person. After the visit (a successful one) she sent him more of her books, specifically *The Spirit Watches, The Bridge,* and *A Mad Lady's Garland.* Interestingly, she told him she thought the latter volume "my best & most original," and she was keen for him to see something more recent than *A Trophy of Arms.* In August 1946, though, she wrote to her friend Nettie Palmer: "he doesn't like the "Garland," and I can only hope he will never discover the 'Rude Potato.'" Lewis was to become one of her main correspondents but it was clear from the start where his preferences lay: he fully understood and praised those poems which focused on faith and affirmation, and he seemed to like an exalted tone. He praised, for example, lines like "Then Alleluia all my gashes cry" from "A Solemn Meditation." He begged her not to be "taken in by the silly idea that by simply mentioning dull or sordid facts in sub-poetical rhythms you can make a poem." This may have made the accommodation between her serious and experimentally comic "sides" more difficult.

Within two years Pitter was confirmed as a member of the Church of England, writing to

Nettie Palmer that she "was driven to it by the pull of C. S. Lewis and the push of misery." In 1950, a substantial volume of her selected poems appeared. *Urania* contained most of the contents of *A Trophy of Arms, The Spirit Watches,* and *The Bridge,* but none of her light verse.

MOVE TO THE COUNTRY

Pitter had always fervently loved gardening, even while living in London. Her mother's house in Felstead (the cottage with the vine) had provided a much-loved retreat; but in 1952 the cottage was sold. Ruth and K decided to sell their London property and move into the country, purchasing a house with a very large garden in Long Crendon, Buckinghamshire. Here Pitter was able to indulge her love of gardening to its fullest and also to take part in village life. Some happy years followed, though this was not her most productive time as a poet. In 1953 (the year Belloc died) *The Ermine* was published: barely sixty-two pages of poems from a ten-year period. The friendship with C. S. Lewis, which had been so important to her, met an immoveable barrier in the person of Joy Gresham, the woman whom the apparently confirmed bachelor would surprise the world by marrying.

Further recognition for poetry was on the horizon, though: in 1954 there was a Heinemann Foundation Award and then even more impressively in 1955, the Queen's Gold Medal for Poetry. At the age of fifty-seven, Ruth Pitter put on her new pink hat and best dark suit, climbed into the village taxi, and was driven nearly fifty miles to Buckingham Palace, where the Queen presented the medal and talked to her for ten minutes. Pitter was extremely proud.

Her newfound celebrity brought opportunities in the public eye. She took part in a number of radio and TV broadcasts, forming a warm friendship with poet and radio producer Arthur Wolseley Russell, who was to become one of her main correspondents. Her regular appearances on the BBC television program, *The Brains Trust,* made her widely admired, albeit more as personality than poet. For a year, she also contributed weekly articles to the popular magazine *Woman.* However, she seemed to have stopped writing poems: according to Arthur Russell she "told friends that she was a fulfilled artist and her task was complete" (p. 34).

In 1960, a letter arrived from the U.S. poet Carolyn Kizer, editor of *Poetry Northwest*. She had been introduced to Pitter's poetry through Theodore Roethke, who "worshipped her work." Now it was Kizer's hope to devote an issue of the magazine to the British poet—had she any new work she could contribute? Pitter responded with seven poems: unusual pieces, skilled and interesting work representing undoubted new development. They were published in the magazine with tributes from Stanley Kunitz, Thom Gunn, and John Holmes. In 1966, these seven poems would form the backbone of the collection *Still by Choice,* which only included twenty-six poems but received Poetry Book Society commendation.

In 1968, now in her early seventies, Pitter published *Poems 1926–1966* (appearing in the United States as *Collected Poems*). This was a substantial volume, including most of the poems published since *A Trophy of Arms*—both serious and humorous texts appearing between the same covers—the sort of volume expected from a mature poet coming to the end of her career, and perhaps the end of her life. A festschrift volume was organized by Arthur Russell in her honor. *Ruth Pitter: Homage to a Poet* appeared in 1969 containing tributes from poets such as Kathleen Raine, Elizabeth Jennings, Patrick Kavanagh, John Betjeman, John Wain, Edward Lucie-Smith, Robert Conquest, Roy Fuller, Richard Church, James Kirkup, Thom Gunn, John Arlott, Derek Parker, Robin Skelton, Carolyn Kizer, Stanley Kunitz, and so forth. They were poets who, in the main, represented the reflective mainstream of British verse.

To set Pitter's work in context, it is perhaps worth remembering that four years previously a volume called *Ariel* had been published, the posthumous second collection of a little-known poet named Sylvia Plath. Plath, not Pitter, would be the female writer to wield real influence over the next generation. Pitter had reached her high point with the 1968 collection of poems. From

now on she would be regarded (if read at all) as a member of the "old guard." Nevertheless, she lived for twenty-three years after the festschrift was published, in which time she was awarded the highest award of the Royal Society of Literature, the Companion of Literature, in 1974. In 1975 she published a new volume of poems, *End of Drought,* a book that mingled both humorous and serious work. But it did not bring her much glory.

DEPRESSION AND DECLINE

In the 1970s, K fell victim to a lingering illness that eventually took her life. The loss had a grievous effect on her life-long friend and companion. Pitter, who had formerly played an active role in village life, withdrew into the house, living as a recluse. Her essential shopping was done by a part-time gardener: she herself was rarely seen, only glimpsed at the window wearing an old dressing gown. Many readers must have assumed she was dead. There were no television appearances now, no interviews in poetry magazines, no critical biographies, no successful imitators. The award of CBE (Commander of the British Empire) in 1979 must have seemed hollow, since the "Commander" herself was actually leading an entirely isolated existence.

In 1984, when Pitter was eighty-seven, alive but mainly forgotten, she was sought out and befriended by a newcomer to Long Crendon—Muriel Dickinson. Together with her son, the composer Peter Dickinson, this new friend began the work of reintroducing the world to an apparently forgotten poet. Pitter was interviewed on BBC radio in 1987 at the age of ninety, and in the same year a limited edition of hitherto uncollected poems was printed—*A Heaven to Find.* The main body of her work was out of print though, and thanks to Muriel Dickinson's energy and interest, this was remedied by the 1990 Enitharmon volume of *Collected Poems,* introduced by Elizabeth Jennings. This did rally some attention, reminding a reading public and some fellow poets that Pitter was still very much alive, though she had become completely blind and rarely went out. Poet Anne Ridler (also a former friend and correspondent of C. S. Lewis) visited Pitter in her nineties and was delighted by that "rich and humorous" conversation which had won her such a following on the BBC *Brains Trust* program decades earlier. Her memory was as good as ever too: she could recite Horace in Latin, as well as "declaim with gusto her cat poem Quorum Porum." In 1992, at the age of ninety-six, she died.

THE ENDURING LEGACY

There is no doubt that Ruth Pitter was an extraordinary woman, a good and intelligent friend, and a wonderful letter writer. But what of Church's claim in 1969 that her work was that of "a superb craftsman," work which would "endure"? Poetic immortality is an uncertain affair. It depends on a continuing appreciative readership; and that readership in turn depends on availability of texts and on attention being drawn authoritatively to them. Despite the fact that two of Pitter's valued correspondents and admirers (Lord David Cecil and C. S. Lewis) were Professors of Literature in England's oldest universities, neither made a marked contribution to academic championship of her work. In fact, Pitter has rarely been the subject of sustained academic interest in her own country. Serious examination of her writing has recently been led by Don W. King, editor of the *Christian Scholar's Review* and Professor of English at Montreat College, North Carolina. King's work on C. S. Lewis led him to an interest in Pitter, especially in her development as a Christian poet. He is her first critical biographer. It seems a double irony that it took a U.S.-based editor (Carolyn Kizer) to bring Pitter back into public notice as poet in 1960. It is true that her work is, as Richard Church put it, "non-fashionable," but that is equally true of poets who have won considerably more academic interest. Could it be that Pitter acquired a wide popular readership with her humorous verse, while alienating the more literary reader? Did she commit the cardinal crime of being too accessible? Or was it just that her serious poems, drawing on mainstream English poetic tradition, failed to impinge on an academic readership at-

tuned to novelty and "movements?"

It remains difficult to estimate Pitter's achievement fairly. The collected volumes printed in the 1990s present a curious mixture to a new reader— some poems work beautifully, with a plain, clear voice which would command attention in any era. Others present ornate diction to a modern ear; even when they are partially successful they can easily alienate. The alternating sets of comic and serious verse (the poems tend to appear in the *Collected* in order of volume publication) are perplexing. In 1960, Stanley Kunitz remarked very accurately on Ruth Pitter's "perilous triumphs:" her perfectly achieved lyrics are set beside poems that teeter on the edge of archaic construction or tone.

How then to approach the labyrinth of her work? The *Collected Poems* (though not complete) are extremely substantial—well over 250 poems—some of them certainly flawed. Kunitz's term "perilous triumphs" is useful. The best thread to guide the reader through is Pitter's own description of her poetic aim (cited by Naomi Lewis in *Ruth Pitter: Homage to a Poet*): "I have tended...on the one hand to experiment, and on the other to strive towards an ideal of simplicity." Such simplicity is best accomplished "when the syllabic metre happens to fit the ordinary speech rhythm without distortion, so that it might be a child speaking, and yet it is poetry." Pitter's finest poems are those which did just that, and this golden thread in her work can be traced from her earliest work onward.

HIGH PERFECTION IN SIMPLICITY

In later life, Ruth Pitter dissociated herself from her early published work: "I produced little that I now think worth keeping until about the age of thirty." But *First & Second Poems* should not have been so easily dismissed from her collected work. Had Pitter published nothing else there would at least have been evidence of a poet exceptionally accomplished (from an early age) in the use of traditional form. Early Pitter demonstrates metrical skill across a wide range of stanzaic patterns. The influence of the poems she learned in childhood from Palgrave's *Golden*

Treasury (first published in 1897, the year of her birth) is clearly evident. Diction, however, is Victorian or earlier. Aphrodite's hair "stealeth down her alabaster sides." The old second person singular (thou) is used in preference to "you." The verse is spattered with exclamations such as "fie" and "nay" and "yea", not to mention "heigh ho"—terms that would have been considered archaic by many even in 1927. Exclamation marks proliferate, and abstract nouns are often capitalized ("cruel Care and starveling Penury"). There is frequent use of rhetorical questions, plenty of inversion ("Kind is the earth's breast") and negative imperative ("Think not upon us, lady")—a construction that would linger ominously in later work. And of course, there are many references to rural scenes, fays, fairies and elfin aspects.

Easy, therefore, to dismiss this as so much early rambling, but that would be—to use a well-tested English metaphor—throwing the baby out with the bathwater. A closer look reveals much of interest. The first poem ("The Swan," 1913) is a strong firm lyric, a confidently drawn visual scene depicting the swan as symbol of the human spirit. "Harmony,''" written in 1912 and found in *First and Second Poems*, is also a key poem. It is about the difficult relationship between artless spontaneity and art:

I heard a child upon an instrument
Make broken melody,
And sighed for all the glory that might be
Could that clear soul with cunning art be blent:
But never man did see
So high perfection in simplicity,
And my hope went.

(p. 21)

Use of form is subtle here: "broken melody" features on a short "broken" line. The first three lines are expressed simply while the fourth provides unexpected contrast with its marked alliteration and archaic "blent." The expression itself exemplifies that "cunning art" which mars the "clear soul" (simplicity). The poem ends starkly, simply, summing up Pitter's lifelong aim— "high perfection in simplicity." Even at this stage she knew how hard this would be to achieve.

These early poems show a poet for whom solitude was important; a person who felt her own "soul" as a mysterious presence almost separate from herself. Equally, the idea of the "holy thorn" (often a Christian symbol) is important in these early poems, though the concept of "holiness" is mingled with spells and fairy magic. There is a somewhat romanticized attraction to death, yet in some poems the pathos speaks truly. In "The Maid's Burial," for example, Pitter uses a simple stanzaic form and mainly simple language to set a scene:

No flower hath shed the sheath;
    The wood is all brown.
When you have passed the heath,
    Then lay her down.

(p. 61)

With the exception of the first line of that stanza, here is clear evidence of plain diction combined with simple, fluid movement of line and phrase. It seems likely that this was not the poetic feature for which Pitter was praised—by Belloc or others—but it was certainly at work and it was effective. "A Tree in Heaven" gives the thorn tree a heavenly immanence in a simply expressed and thought-provoking poem which certainly should have been "saved" for a collected works. The poet describes her dream vision of a tree "like to a Thorn:"

She had forgotten how to be
    A banner of the marching Spring;
She had put off her sorcery
    With winter and with burgeoning.

She was no more a Thorn, and yet
    Her fairness was her fairness still;
In a valley she was set
    And looked up to the quiet Hill.

(p. 109)

It is clear that Pitter had visionary experience as a child, something which later earned her the epithet "mystical." Here that visionary quality is in its early manifestation and at its most potent when expressed plainly. Although Pitter was brought up in a family that was only nominally Christian, plainly she thought in spiritual terms from the start, and her spiritual quest and her poetry were connected.

Whatever the absolute value of *First and Second Poems,* there are certainly pieces which should not have disappeared into obscurity. "The Burial" is one of the best. The simple phrasing and expression, masking a deeper perplexity, is worthy of Thomas Hardy:

"When we have buried her, made her unseen
  We will lie down and weep;
Our part is done; we have found her a green
  Quiet place wherein to sleep."

It was the mystery and the dark way
  That made them weep so sore;
They knew not whether she were grave or gay
  Or peaceful, or no more.

(p. 180)

The challenge, therefore, is one of filtering through the prominently elaborate, mannered texts to find the calm, clear voice that would eventually represent essential Pitter. But it is there.

First and Second Poems was followed by the ambitious, forty page narrative poem, *Persephone in Hades—reserved for private circulation.* Not a single fragment found its way into her later collected volumes and she herself seems to have relegated it to obscurity. This is regrettable. Not only is the form (partly Miltonic blank verse, partly a more unusually metered eleven syllable line) interesting, but also the story itself. Pitter uses Persephone as a symbol of immortality—the goddess who died and came back to life. The poem is about the triumph of love over death, the triumph of the spirit. Perhaps most interestingly of all, Persephone is presented as not unlike Christ: "Well mayest thou sing, / That to the lees hast drunk the dreadful cup / Of death, and found the elixir of life." Hades himself (Aidoneus in this poem) is more beautiful than sun or moon, "For utter wisdom from that forehead shone, / Knowledge of every dark and hidden thing." Persephone's union with him is the marriage of death and life, male and female, joy and despair—paradoxical polarities that would continue to haunt Pitter's poems. When Persephone returns to earth, the mortal inhabitants flock to see her and it is Persephone's role to teach them. It is a narrative in which Pitter explores death and renewal, using Greek myth to recreate an in-

tensely female spiritual vision, something far from the Christian story she later espoused. Surely this poem (which at its simplest level tells a dramatic story with delightful energy) would at least have been of interest to feminist critics. But it does not seem to have been noticed: printed in a limited edition of only 100 copies, it has apparently gone down to the underworld of the library stacks and has not (yet) been allowed to return.

A MAD LADY?

Devotees of Ruth Pitter's *First and Second Poems* could not possibly have predicted its successor. No wonder the garland belonged to a "mad" lady (perhaps a reference to Ophelia, or just to her own playful extravagances). Belloc provided another preface to this collection but his turn of phrase suggests he found it more difficult this time, even though he himself was well known for his comic verse. Pitter had, he said, "done the best thing that a poet can do, or indeed any writer—and that is, to challenge variety." John Masefield's introduction, which followed Belloc's words in the American edition, was warmer. "It would be unjust to call her poems satires," he observed, "for her judgments are merciful and her methods merry." He found her original in style and approach: "The work is distinct, its thought has a sharp edge or boundary, and a flavour of its own."

Today, the critical opinions of neither Belloc nor Masefield carry huge weight. Perhaps Pitter's name, connected with theirs, has gathered a certain dustiness—because *A Mad Lady's Garland* should still be regarded as a significant publication. It bursts with energy and merriment. Its drawback for a contemporary reader may be that part of the pleasure requires some knowledge of the poetic forms imitated. "Resurgam," for example, in twenty-two Spenserian stanzas, tells the sad story of a heretical caterpillar visited by a butterfly while feeding on a purple cabbage. The butterfly ("Imago") reveals the truth that "Death lies not in your coffin-chrysalid;" there is a future in the skies (p. 20). The caterpillar, profoundly moved by this visitation, pours his tale "into the tender ears / Of the new hatched" with the result that the young caterpillars become so fixated with visions of their immortal future that they forget to eat and simply sit staring at the sky(p. 22). Soon the caterpillar-narrator is denounced as a "windy purple fake" (p. 23). A fight ensues; the narrator is evicted and his acolytes experience a variety of regrettable fates. It is an extremely funny poem, mocking the influence of both religion and poetry. One caterpillar leaps off the tree, believing he can fly, and breaks his neck. Another displays Shelleyan tendencies:

with gesture antic
Anon his little claspers to the sky
Stretched in despair; then leaping corybantic
Cried with a crazy shriek Behold I fly!
Then sank to earth, and at each spiracle did sigh.

(*A Mad Lady's Garland*, p. 25)

The caterpillar-narrator is consumed with guilt at what he has done to "green intellect, which could not reach / So lofty theme." In a penultimate twist, the narrator fears that "fell Ichneumon" has laid eggs in him and "made a Poet, full of sickly lust; / Too delicate to do as others must." This is not even the last laugh: Pitter accomplishes an ironic climax when the protagonist finds peace: he dreams of an elderly man (recognizable as Socrates) who calls him "fellow worm" and reveals that he too was cast out for influencing the young and died in prison (pp. 26–27). He leaves the caterpillar, however, with a final consolation:

But there are heavens beyond heavens; these
Be but the ghostly Shadows of the Images.

(p. 27)

"Resurgam" is a fine piece of writing, a magnificently comic poem. However, it requires a fairly sophisticated reader—someone who will recognize and enjoy the Spenserian form, pick up the Platonic references, the dangers of poetry, and the mock-rhetoric. And it is interesting to see Pitter mocking the "high style" that she herself certainly practices elsewhere—but this time in order to create a magnificent bathos. The confidently playful voice at the heart of this poem should not be forgotten when reading any of Pit-

ter's work. She was exhilarated by the use of form, rose to the challenge magnificently, and yet was intensely aware of the dangers. "Digdog," the surreal "modernist" piece, imitates a dog rooting in a packing case, throwing out non-syntactical phrases like straw—yet even here Pitter (comparing herself with a dog) mocks herself:

sit on your tail and weep for there is nothing
nothing but dust and darkness
but strawdirt chaffdust smellillusion ALAS.

(p. 34)

It is easy to see the serious comment beneath the comic form, just as it is easy in this collection to see that Pitter was very much aware of contemporary poetic trends. In "Cockroach" for example, the cockroach observes:

Moderns? oh yeah, you call yourself moderns?
Well, I've been as modern as you
Any time these many million years.

(*A Mad Lady's Garland*, p. 68)

In fact, Pitter's own views are variously expressed in this collection by minor creatures: a kitten, an earwig, a church mouse, a flea. It was her habit to identify with the humbler parts of creation. *A Mad Lady's Garland* was a far cry from her earlier writing—although "Fowls Celestial and Terrestrial" did verge on the edge of the style she had mocked elsewhere. However, this was the poem Masefield praised; so, later, did her friend, Lord David Cecil. Praise can be dangerous to poets.

A TROPHY OF ARMS: POEMS 1926–1935

A Trophy of Arms, published two years later, clearly included poems written at the same time as (or earlier than) *A Mad Lady's Garland.* However, it presented a very different Ruth Pitter, perhaps one easier in many ways to understand—and perhaps one all too easy to overlook. This was the thirties. The dominant UK influences were very firmly non-Georgian: names such as W. H. Auden, Louis MacNeice, David

RUTH PITTER

Gascoyne, William Empson, Rex Warner, Stephen Spender and, T. S. Eliot, and it was easy to see that poetry was regarded as a mainly male preserve. As late as 1964, Robin Skelton's anthology *Poetry of the Thirties* included only one woman—Anne Ridler. Though Skelton contributed to Pitter's festschrift in 1969, he does not seem to have found her worthy of mention only a few years earlier. Why? The sixth poem in *A Trophy of Arms,* "The Comet," may help explain. It begins:

O still withhold thyself, be not possessed:
Hyperbola, the dread uncharted line,
Debase not into orbit; still make shine
Portentous rays or arrowy unrest
Among the earthy planets.

> (p. 7)

The style here is archaic; the repeated negative imperatives are mannered. It clearly presents as a throwback—nicely constructed formal verse, belonging to a former era, even though in a companion poem ("Dear Perfection") Pitter clearly longs for that "dear simplicity" which shames "the sum of my devices." Fortunately there are poems in this collection which confidently achieve that stated desire. In "Buried Treasure," for example, Pitter uses rhyming tetrameter couplets to rehearse the puzzle of "the twin-stemmed Paradox," the source of "truth." It is a perfect marriage of form and thought, one of Pitter's finest poems. The language is not conversational, but neither is it falsely rhetorical, and the poem is visionary, like much of Pitter's best work:

Truth I sought, and truth I found,
Wandering enchanted ground
Where among the dusty rocks
Grows the twin-stemmed Paradox,
Throwing from the single root
Sable flower and golden fruit.
There I watched till I could tell
Where her midnight shadow fell,
And delved a diamond from the sand
Too heavy for my human hand.
Hold me not false that cannot bring

Nor show to you the magic thing:
Under the dual I divine
The one, but cannot make it mine.

> (*A Trophy of Arms,* p. 37)

The aural pun in "dual" is brilliant: the shining heart of the poem. The poet is reaching for a complex idea here, a reconciliation of opposites—perhaps good and evil, or perhaps life and death, as in *Persephone in Hades.* The poem achieves "simplicity" and defies poetic "devices," in a metaphysical mode worthy of George Herbert. Pitter does not manage this in all her poems.

Her recurring weakness is overwrought expression; this asserts itself so strongly in poems like "The Comet," "Gentle Joy," and "Help, Good Shepherd," (and even the much-praised "A Solemn Meditation") that it can serve to drown out quieter but stronger poems such as "Buried Treasure," "The Paradox," "The Bad Girl," "Thought Against Drought," and "Sudden Heaven." The last of these is of particular interest because it recalls that visionary experience associated with Hainault Forest, a vision every bit as strong for Ruth Pitter as the "celestial light" recalled by William Wordsworth in his celebrated 1807 "Ode." Most of this poem (the ending lets it down slightly) achieves the kind of complex simplicity she was looking for:

All was as it had ever been—
The worn familiar book,
The oak beyond the hawthorn seen,
The misty woodland's look:

The starling perched upon the tree
With his long tress of straw—
When suddenly heaven blazed on me,
And suddenly I saw:

Saw all as it would ever be,
In bliss too great to tell;
For ever safe, for ever free,
All bright with miracle...

> (*A Trophy of Arms,* p. 51)

A further point of interest in *A Trophy of Arms* is the increased use of unrhymed sapphics (as in the lovely "Of Silence and the Air"). The last

141

line of the sapphic stanza, which comprises dactyl plus trochee ("flee to her mountain," "of the eternal"), seems to have particularly pleased her ear at the end of a line: it features in the eleven syllable lines of *Persephone in Hades* and in later unrhymed experimental verse forms it also recurs. *A Trophy of Arms* won the Hawthornden Award, one of Britain's oldest literary prizes. Pitter was ready with her next collection, *The Spirit Watches,* within three years.

THE SPIRIT WATCHES

There were significant changes in style in the new volume: the archaic "thou" was banished at last; mannered inversions were much reduced (though not eradicated); several poems achieved perfection in simplicity. Interestingly, the title poem (not the strongest, but not her weakest piece of writing either) was not included later in the selected volume, *Urania,* nor in *Poems 1926—1966.* On the whole, it's a strong collection. "The Hut" and "Time's Fool" recall the cottage in Hainault with its "damp bed, with the beetle's tap in the head-board heard,/ The dim bit of mirror, three inches of comb" (*Collected Poems 1990,* p. 101). "An Old Woman Speaks of the Moon" shows new confidence in a simple, long, conversational line, bringing the celestial and the ordinary into unforced harmony.

There is significantly wider use of plain language and simple forms in poems such as "A Natural Sorrow," "The Spring," "The Bush-Baby," and "The Bird in the Tree." The last of these is an important poem for Pitter: it records intense desire for the clarity of vision she had as a child.

The capitalization is not mere stylistic indulgence this time; it signifies the objects as eternal symbols. It may be argued that Pitter's habit of "milking" a poignant moment in the last two lines with an apostrophic "O" is a weakness. Perhaps here, where she speaks with such fervency, it may be permitted.

The most perfect poem in the volume though is "If You Came," which in its restrained simplicity cannot be faulted. It is a lyric which should live as long as poetry itself survives. Again, it draws on Pitter's woodland memories in a way that combines reality and metaphor, a poem about longing that goes unsatisfied. The poet addresses a person in direct terms, though the setting is metaphorical: "If you came to my secret glade," says the poet, "I would wash your feet." She would give the last of her bread—even her bed. The words are not overtly sexual, yet the poem has much to say about sexual longing.

The more complex "Bloweth Where it Listeth" is another poem that represents Pitter's unique voice and personality. The imagery is strangely surreal. The poet's spirit flies over the countryside until it comes to a lonely cottage where a poor soul is ironing. The disembodied spirit expects to find sorrow but sorrow is not there. Instead the lonely woman is treasuring the glimpse of a bird nesting near the house. The phrasing is ambiguous—both sparrow and observer love the eggs. The woman is filled with tenderness. The end of the poem is most curious of all. The poet's ghost, the spirit that came to bless the lonely woman, instead leaves enriched by her:

At this point in her life, Pitter had not formally embraced the Christian faith (though the title of this poem is a Biblical quotation) but there is little doubt that a strong sense of spiritual life continuously informed her work: this can be termed "mystical" or "pantheistic." Whatever it was, she began with it and it did not leave her.

THE RUDE POTATO

The next Pitter publication was the one she hoped C. S. Lewis would never come across, *The Rude Potato.* It is mainly light, comic verse, mischievously put together. The title poem celebrates Jimmy who finds the rudest potato he has ever met. Such "shamelessness" has this potato (no doubt due to its similarity to parts of the male body) that he takes it to the local pub where free drinks are offered on the strength of it.

Who but Pitter could celebrate on the one hand the life of the immortal soul and on the other natural lewdness? There is no doubt that she loved the comic spirit as much as anything else in poetry. Unlike *A Mad Lady's Garland,* no literary background is needed to savor the jokes in this collection, or to note her expert ear for natural speech rhythms. "The Weed" is a lengthy dramatic monologue, in cockney dialect, from a weed eulogizing its dead mother—a kind of verse obituary and something of a tour de force. The whole volume is illustrated with line drawings, a combination of verbal and visual lightness that must have recommended it to a general, as well as literary, readership. It did not, however, find favor with Pitter's American publisher, who was anecdotally reported as saying: "For fifteen years I've been building you up as a dedicated spirit, and now look what you've done!" In truth, there is no absolute division between Pitter's light verse and her more serious mode. In this collection, "The Morals of Pruning," "For Us All" and "The Bay-Tree" could have found a worthy place in any of her books. Above all, it is worth remembering that much of this inspired comic work was produced at a time of Pitter's life that was anything but amusing. "The Rude Potato" appeared during the war years. *The Bridge,* her next collection of poems, also emerged from this difficult period.

CROSSING THE BRIDGE

When K and Ruth literally crossed Battersea Bridge in London to take up war work it was also a symbolic step, and this is clearly indicated in the title poem of her 1945 collection, *The Bridge.* Roy Fuller correctly identified the strength of the writing here, though a couple of weaker poems still employ a "grand" tone. "Wherefore Lament," for example (written during an attack on London in 1940), returned to dramatic alliteration and archaic phrasing: "Whatever woe thou weepest, it must end..." It was not included in the later *Collected Poems.* But there are many consistently strong poems— for example, the unrhymed "The Swan Bathing" where the familiar trochaic foot at the end of each line lends a kind of metrical echo, though the main meter is irregular. Similar line endings are used in the lengthy "The Cygnet," as well as deliberate repetition of key words inside and at

the ends of lines. This works most completely, perhaps, in "The Bridge," where the combination of rhythm and repetition lends aching pathos.

Just under a fifth of the poems in the collection are unrhymed, evidence of ongoing experiment with the "vessel" that would form a poem. Some of the best work, however, still uses that simple rhyming tetrameter which seems to work so effortlessly for Pitter. "The Lost Tribe," for example, rivals the earlier "If You Came" in its plain and emotive longing:

How long, how long must I regret?
I never found my people yet;
I go about, but cannot find
The blood-relations of the mind.

Through my little sphere I range,
And though I wither do not change;
Must not change a jot, lest they
Should not know me on my way.

Sometimes I think when I am dead
They will come about my bed,
For my people well do know
When to come and when to go.

I know not why I am alone,
Nor where my wandering tribe is gone,
But be they few, or be they far,
Would I were where my people are!

(p. 178)

This is a poet who never belonged to a "school"—in both personal and poetic terms she felt alone. Yet she was determined to hold to her own method: "And though I wither do not change; / Must not change..." That "must" drives home the certainty. This is also the collection which included "But For Lust" (the poem that so impressed John Arlott during the war). This is a remarkable piece of writing, too, especially if we place it in its time context, for although lust today seems more of a deadly virtue than a sin, it was not so in London in 1940, and Pitter had not found a loving relationship in which sexual and spiritual love could combine.

Though Pitter would never be a confessional writer, there is clear personal import in many of the poems in this collection. Central to her craving is still tenderness for the unlovely, the broken, and the ruined place. Pitter identifies herself most completely with "The Small Plant" in the poem with that title. Her painter's eye combines with her poet's ear to celebrate both natural mystery and the imperative of her own art.

AFTER THE WAR

At this time, it is likely that Ruth Pitter was writing both comic and serious verse with equal attention and in almost equal quantity. In 1947 *Pitter on Cats* was published. Two of the cat poems from *A Mad Lady's Garland* appeared here together with eleven newer pieces. There is much of charm here, especially for cat lovers, but it is less individual than *The Rude Potato* and it certainly does not achieve the varied heights of the *Garland*. The book did not find an American publisher. It was followed in 1950 by *Urania,* a selected edition reproducing almost all of the three preceding serious volumes. Though the contents are not formally divided by reference to source, they mainly follow the original order, with the odd exception of "The Bridge:" this piece is included in the set of poems drawn from *A Trophy of Arms*. The same grouping persisted into the 1966 *Collected* (this again follows the original order without indicating sources), perhaps in error. However, it is mistakenly grouped in the 1991 and 1996 Enitharmon volumes, too, even though it was the title poem of its own collection.

Two more slim volumes would appear before the first *Collected* but Pitter's prolific phase was over. In 1953 *The Ermine* was the first serious new collection for eight years. It does not match its predecessor, *The Bridge,* in strength although Don W. King sees it as "the only one of her books that, at least in some ways, tells a story." He traces a movement of faith in *The Ermine,* from the uncertain "neophyte" who sees and feels something but "must not speak," through memories of childhood and on to "Five Dreams and a Vision" at the end, which culminates in a statement of Christian faith:

O well is me, and happy shall I be!
Look! He is there. Look on Him. That is He.
(*Collected Poems 1990*, p. 238)

The best poems, however, are not necessarily the visionary dreams at the end (though these are undoubtedly interesting) but four apparently simpler (and less obviously ambitious) pieces— "The Ermine," "Hen Under Bay Tree," "The Tuft of Violets," and "The Tree at Dawn." "The Ermine" echoes the rhyming tetrameter couplets of "The Buried Treasure" with equal success. It is a poem which operates as a single metaphor

The "sable spot" on the ermine reflects sin, the "black" which the poet must also learn to wear. "The Tuft of Violets" and "The Tree at Dawn" again return to Pitter's sense of the celestial in nature. The latter is a true gardener's poem, and though not comical, it turns on a highly individual view of the world, a way of seeing things that is entirely peculiar to its author. Her vision, simultaneously earthly and heavenly, includes "pale-blue velvet cabbages" and "pink sweet-peas," and it fades as the sun rises:

The god leaps up, the day is here,
The heat pours from the sky:
The tree is commonplace and dear,
And I am only I.

(p. 212)

The mystery in the "commonplace" was Ruth Pitter's native territory. When her expression drew on what she would later describe as "the legal tender and common currency of language" she had come into her own. This is equally well seen in "Hen Under Bay-Tree." Again, this poem could sit comfortably in either serious or comic mode, though the hen herself is accorded indisputable dignity. She has "stolen from the social pen" to "noblest solitude," the state Pitter herself rated so highly, but there's an affectionate tongue—in—cheek tone here. She sits beneath a "magical" tree, "resolved to rear a private brood." Like the sparrow which "hugged" her eggs, the hen is proud&,dash;"She keeps love's vigil glorious." She is a bird of faith and "The plant of honour is her house." This is not a grand poem, nor apparently a work of great art. And yet it is: the simplicity is deceptive, and the concept of honor is neither light nor easy to interpret. However, it is central in Ruth Pitter's poetry.

THE LAST YEARS

Thirteen years elapsed between *The Ermine* and *Still by Choice,* the latter an even slighter volume of only thirty—five pages. However, quantity is not the same as quality. There are many good poems here and every sign that Pitter can mingle the comic and the serious successfully in one volume. "The Heart's Desire is Full of Sleep" is a beautiful and intensely personal poem, once again expressing poignant regret. It stands with the best of her work. She classes herself with the "true emperors of desire" who continue to seek for the unattainable.

Poems such as "Moths and Mercury-Vapor Lamp" and "Exercise in the Pathetic Fallacy" exploit very different imagery, as does "Sweet Other Flesh." Here the diction is plain enough but the concept is challenging, a reminder that Pitter (though some of her best poems are expressed simply) is a poet of fine intelligence. Again "Sweet Other Flesh" could only have been authored by this poet. It rehearses the idea that the mind can step into "other flesh"—but by "flesh" Pitter means any life—form. It is a provocatively mysterious piece, in which the reader is reminded of Pitter's painter's eye, tracing the intimate detail of a small plant.

Sexual connotations are delicately evoked: the mind is allowed "to feed" on "Chaste palaces within a seed" before being dismissed. Pitter's artistry brings the reader into intimate connection with the flowers she herself studied so closely, both as painter and gardener. "Morning Glory" is one of the poems Kathleen Raine wished she had written; she envied the exactness of eye with which Pitter describes this beautiful flower, and once again the verse rehearses that mysterious connection between mind and body

In the same volume, "A Dream" was termed by Roy Fuller "one of the poet's most successful raids on the incommunicable," as indeed it is. There are no weak poems in the set, with the possible exception of "Who Knows?" and even this piece is not so much weak as occasional with

the occasion lost. Although Pitter was not writing in quantity, the poems that emerged at this time are of a high caliber. All the old mannerisms are gone: a plain style is used to express even the most complex ideas.

Another nine years would occur before *End of Drought,* a late collection but not a lame one. Its forty—seven pages included both lighthearted verse and a couple of strong descriptive poems— "So Good of Their Kind" for example, which describes slugs mating with a clarity to rival D. H. Lawrence at his best, and "So I Thought She Must Have Been Forgiven," another compelling dream poem.

A Heaven to Find (printed only in a limited edition) was the final fragile gathering which affirmed Pitter's faith in "absolute good" and the "pull of God." It included the delightfully comic "Potting Shed Tutti—Frutti," a couple of interesting fragments, and some previously unpublished poems. Of these, "Cricket Match, 1908" was written when the poet was only eleven years old. She may have dismissed her first three poetry publications, but here she restored a gleeful poem which preceded them. Perhaps it was the best proof of all that she had completed a circle which began and ended in playful simplicity:

O ye greedy! Now forsake the lime juice and cakes
Which may disable with their sudden aches!
(*Collected Poems 1990,* p. 291)

READING THE RIDDLE

What of readers coming to Ruth Pitter's work for the first time today? How can she be placed among the poets of her century? She was certainly no modernist, but neither was she a slave to tradition: she experimented in a wide range of verse forms. In her preface to *Poems 1926–1966* she discussed her consistent purpose as a poet, namely "to capture and express some of the secret meanings which haunt life and language: the silent music, the dance in stillness, the hints and echoes and messages of which everything is full." She saw how "life, bursting with its secret, sits hugging itself until we have read the riddle." Poems, according to Pitter, should begin and end in mystery, although their structure should be "clothed in the legal tender and common currency of language; perhaps the simpler the better, so that the crowning wonder, if it comes, may emerge clear of hocus-pocus." Throughout her poetic development, it is possible to trace a continuous development toward simplicity of expression used to support intensely complex thought. Indeed, that type of deceptive simplicity may in itself lead to the underrating of a poet.

But Pitter was also unusual in the way she applied her skill with equal dedication to both serious and comic verse. In the *1926–1966* preface, she refers to three spirits: "beatitude," "anguish," and finally "the spirit of comedy, refusing to be exterminated or left behind." She conjectures about the possibility of a comic work "as majestic as our loftiest tragedies." It was regrettable that her two "sides" were not allowed to mingle freely in her books in the uninhibited way they frequented her own consciousness. The collected volumes mainly group the poems in "light" and "serious" sets. In fact, they must have been written side by side—and some fall squarely in the middle, defying classification. There is scope for a good selected volume that would allow a new reader to see her extraordinary range with its constant interplay among beatitude, anguish, and comedy.

Ruth Pitter saw a vision of the sublime in the everyday, the celestial in the commonplace, the holy in the humorous—and she lived the same vision. A passionately dedicated woman, she celebrated the concept of honor, in an era when that idea was rare; she extolled (and exemplified) the virtues of tenderness, kindness and humility; she achieved some intensely beautiful lyrics as a result of a lifetime's practice in the art of poetry. She was a very good poet. She deserves to be better known.

Selected Bibliography

WORKS OF RUTH PITTER

POETRY

First Poems. London: Cecil Palmer, 1920. (Private printing funded by Hilaire Belloc.)

First and Second Poems. London: Sheed & Ward, 1927. New York: Doubleday Doran, 1930.

Persephone in Hades. France, Gers: A Sauriac, 1931. (A forty-page poem privately printed, an edition of 100 copies, now extremely hard to find.)

A Mad Lady's Garland. London: Cresset Press, 1934. New York: Macmillan, 1935. (Preface by Hilaire Belloc; also by John Masefield in the American edition.)

A Trophy of Arms: Poems 1926–1935. London: Cresset Press, 1936. New York, Macmillan, 1936. (Preface by James Stephens.)

The Spirit Watches. London: Cresset Press, 1939. New York, Macmillan, 1940.

The Rude Potato. London: Cresset Press, 1941. (Illustrated with line drawings by Roger Furse.)

The Bridge: Poems 1939–1944. London: Cresset Press, 1945; New York, Macmillan, 1946.

Pitter on Cats. London: Cresset Press, 1947.

Urania. (A substantial selection from *A Trophy of Arms, The Spirit Watches,* and *The Bridge*, with illustrated title page by Joan Hassall.) London: Cresset Press, 1950.

The Ermine: Poems 1942–1952. London, Cresset Press, 1953.

Poetry Northwest, Vol 1, No. 3 (1960). (Issue partly devoted to Ruth Pitter with fifteen of her poems and appreciations by Carolyn Kizer, Stanley Kunitz, Thom Gunn, and John Holmes).

Still by Choice. London: Cresset Press, 1966.

Poems 1926–1966. London: Barrie & Rockcliff/The Cresset Press, 1968. Published in New York by Macmillan as *Collected Poems* in 1969. (Preface by Pitter herself, giving an overview of her purpose and method: particularly interesting for her views on the importance of comedy.)

End of Drought. London: Barrie & Jenkins, 1975.

A Heaven to Find. London: Enitharmon Press, 1987. (Limited edition of 200 copies; a selection of previously unpublished poems and fragments written between 1908 and 1976.)

Collected Poems (1990). Petersfield: Enitharmon Press, 1990. (Introduced by Elizabeth Jennings)

Collected Poems. London: Enitharmon Press, 1996. (A revised version of *Collected Poems (1990)*)

PROSE

"The Art of Reading in Ignorance" in *Essays and Poems presented to Lord David Cecil.* Edited by W. W. Robson. London: Constable & Company, 1970.

CRITICAL AND BIOGRAPHICAL STUDIES

Barker, Jonathan. *Contemporary Poets: Ruth Pitter.* Chicago and London: Saint James Press, 1990.

Church, Richard. *Contemporary Poets: Ruth Pitter.* Chicago and London: Saint James Press, 1975.

King, Don W. *Ruth Pitter Project Web Page* including biographical sketch and photos of Pitter at *www.montreat. edu/dking/Ruth%20Pitter/RuthPitterProject.htm* as well as links to essays dealing with Pitter's correspondence, her friendship with C. S. Lewis, and her development as a Christian poet.

King, Don W. "The Religious Poetry of Ruth Pitter," *Christianity and Literature 54* (Summer 2005): 521–562.

King, Don W. *C. S.Lewis, Poet. The Legacy of His Poetic Impulse*. Kent, Ohio and London: The Kent State University Press, 2001.

King, Don W. (forthcoming) *Hunting the Unicorn: A Critical Biography of Ruth Pitter*. Kent, Ohio and London: The Kent State University Press, 2008 (estimated date).

Palmer, Herbert. "Post-Victorian Poetry." London: J. M. Dent & Sons Ltd, 1938.

Arthur Russell, ed. *Ruth Pitter: Homage to a Poet*. London: Rapp and Whiting, 1969. With an introduction by Lord David Cecil. (Includes a biographical essay by Arthur Russell as well as twenty-seven essays/appreciations by authors/poets, etc.)

PHILIP PULLMAN

(1946—)

Sandie Byrne

PHILIP PULLMAN IS the doyen of the crossover novel—fiction published for young adults that also appeals to older readers. Although he has been writing for publication since the early 1970s and has been a well-respected children's author since the 1980s, he attained international best-seller status only in 1995, with the publication of the first volume in the trilogy known as *His Dark Materials*. The series has brought him adulation, honors, stage and screen adaptation, and accusations of being a corruptive and dangerous influence.

LIFE

Philip Pullman was born Philip Nicholas Outram in Norwich, in Norfolk, near the eastern coast of England, on 19 October 1946, to Audrey Evelyn (Merrifield) and Alfred Outram. When Philip was six years old, he and his younger brother, Francis, were taken to Southern Rhodesia (now Zimbabwe), where his father, who was a pilot in the Royal Air Force, had been posted. The family returned to England when Alfred Outram's tour of duty in the RAF ended, but he was later posted to Kenya during the Mau Mau fighting and was killed in a plane crash. Audrey Outram took up a post at the British Broadcasting Corporation in London, and her two sons were sent to live with their grandparents in the rectory of the village of Drayton, in Norfolk, of which Pullman's grandfather was parish priest. Following their mother's remarriage to another RAF pilot, John Pullman, Pullman and his brother were taken to Australia, but the family returned when he was ten, first to London, then to Llanbedr in North Wales. Here the family was increased by the birth of a half-brother and half-sister, and later by the arrival of a stepbrother, from his stepfather's first marriage.

Pullman has written that, as a young child, he saw his parents as glamorous but somewhat remote figures: his mother a sophisticated beauty and his father a heroic but frequently absent fighter. As an adult, he discovered aspects of his father's character and of his parents' life together that caused him to revisit and rewrite his memories of his early years.

Pullman was an avid reader and storyteller from a young age. In Australia he discovered superhero comics, and in Wales he was inspired and encouraged by a teacher, Enid Jones, to whom he still sends copies of his books. After reading English language and literature, which he disliked, at Exeter College, Oxford, Pullman worked in a shop before, at the age of twenty-five, becoming a teacher. He taught in a number of middle schools (for pupils between the ages of nine and thirteen) in Oxford, then became a tutor of trainee teachers at Westminster College, also in Oxford, remaining in the post for eight years and combining it with writing before becoming a full-time author. He married Judith Speller in 1970. For a number of years he famously wrote in a cluttered and dusty shed in the garden of the family home on the outskirts of Oxford, but after the success of *His Dark Materials,* he moved to a seventeenth-century farmhouse in an Oxfordshire village, where he has a study in which he writes and makes things in wood and metal.

WRITING CAREER AND NARRATIVE STYLE

Pullman usually declines to discuss his first book, *The Haunted Storm* (1972), which was written for adults, regarding it as an apprentice piece. His second, *Galatea*, also for adults, was published in 1978, and his first book for children, *Count Karlstein,* was published in 1982 (reprinted in 1991 with illustrations by Patrice Aggs; later editions have illustrations by Diana Bryan). He has published approximately twenty books, for which he has been awarded prizes including the Carnegie Medal, the *Guardian* Children's Book Award, the Nestlé Smarties Book Prize, the Astrid Lindgren Award, the *Publishers Weekly* Best Book of the Year Award, and the Whitbread Book of the Year Award (in 2000, for *The Amber Spyglass,* the third book in the trilogy *His Dark Materials*). The latter was the first time that prize had gone to a work of young adult fiction (although the book was read by many adults).

Pullman characteristically writes using an omniscient, anonymous first-person narrator, but he gives the perspective of the central protagonist or protagonists of each episode. Although the narrative voice does seem to be a personality, it is never intrusive. When it offers information, this is usually based on the perceptions and interpretations of the central character, although the narration does not become free indirect style. In *Northern Lights* (1995), for example, the heroine, Lyra, peering from her hiding place behind a chair, watches the Master of Jordan College (an institution based on Exeter College, Oxford) donning his academic gown, and the narrative voice observes: "The Master had been a powerful man, but he was well over seventy now, and his movements were stiff and slow" (pp. 5–6). Similarly, when Lyra sees the college Steward at work, the narrative voice informs us: "he smoothed his hair over his ears with both palms and said something to his dæmon. He was a servant, so she was a dog; but a superior servant, so a superior dog. In fact, she had the form of a red setter" (p. 7).

Pullman is sparing with adjectives and even more so with figurative language, usually reserving symbol and metaphor for objects or entities that have symbolic value in their respective worlds, rather than for description. The ancient and decrepit figure of the Authority, who dissolves into the air near the end of the third book of *His Dark Materials,* is described through simile; he is as light as paper. This suggests that the Authority's weight—the weight of authority—is that of the books, codes, rules, rituals, and canons of the church.

Pullman's descriptions are usually straightforward; when he describes a character or place he often employs the most simple and obvious adjectives, but the effect is of clarity rather than cliché. The opening sentence of the 1986 volume *The Ruby in the Smoke*—the first in the "Sally Lockhart" trilogy of adventures—employs the pathetic fallacy, "On a cold, fretful afternoon in early October"; but these are rare in the novel, and the heroine is introduced simply as "a young girl" getting out of a hansom cab, who is "a person of sixteen or so—alone, and uncommonly pretty. She was slender and pale, in mourning, with a black bonnet under which she tucked a straying twist of blond hair which the wind had teased loose. She had unusually dark brown eyes for one so fair" (p. 3). The *prosopopaeia* of "teased," personifiying the wind, almost passes unnoticed, and the rest of the description is entirely prosaic. Simile is also used with restraint, as when a young boy appears "like the solidification of all the grime in the city air" (p. 4).

Pullman is a master of the cliff-hanger and of the deferred explanation. A strategy in *The Butterfly Tattoo* (originally published in 1992 as *The White Mercedes*) is to tell the reader what is going to happen from the first line, but to defer revealing how and when. In *The Subtle Knife* (1997), the second book of the trilogy *His Dark Materials,* scenes cut between the various protagonists, often at moments of danger or high tension. The first book in the trilogy ends as the heroine is about to cross from one world to another, and the second ends with the hero's discovery that she has been abducted.

Though not lapidary, Pullman's language is evocative and vivid, and flexible enough to deliver a fast pace, suspense, tension, harrowing emotion, excoriating satire, and poignant, painful, and joyful occasions. It is also often humorous, irreverent, and even boisterously operatic, particularly in *Count Karlstein,* which has elements of both gothic and farce.

Though Pullman's supremely imagined worlds contain talking bears, branch-flying witches, shamanic magic, and diamond-skeletoned, seed-pod-wheel-riding creatures with horns and a trunk, the writing is realist; the narratives are orderly and plausible and obey their own internal logic. Within Pullman's realist mode, however, there is often metafiction; a number of his stories are about storytelling. *Clockwork; or, All Wound Up* (1997), for example, is a story-within-a-story about a storyteller who may have sold his soul in exchange for an ending to his story and an apprentice clock-maker who may have sold his soul in exchange for a feature of the story. In *The Amber Spyglass,* the heroine's storytelling gift entrances the Harpies who rule the afterlife, and it ultimately determines the fate of inhabitants of many worlds.

Though best known for his other-worlds series, Pullman also writes fiction set in our own world and time. He has been unafraid of controversy or of denying his readers a cozy fix of sentiment in either kind of writing. The fiancé of his heroine Sally Lockhart, and a major character in her adventures, is killed in *The Shadow in the North* (first published in 1986 as *The Shadow in the Plate*). His young-adult novel *The Butterfly Tattoo* is a tragedy that tackles issues of abuse and whose young hero kills the beautiful girl with whom in the opening section he falls in love. *The Broken Bridge* (1990) is written from the point of view (though in the third person) of a person Pullman can never have been, a young girl of mixed race. The third novel of the trilogy *His Dark Materials, The Amber Spyglass,* denies its two main protagonists, and therefore its readers, the fully happy ending they have striven for.

Pullman learned the craft of drama by writing plays for his middle-school pupils to perform, and in the early 1990s he published two plays based on fiction classics. *Frankenstein* (1990) is a sympathetic portrayal of the monster of Mary Shelley's novel, and *Sherlock Holmes and the Limehouse Horror* (1992) is both an affectionate parody of Arthur Conan Doyle's great and eccentric detective and a convincing entry in the Holmes canon.

HISTORICAL FICTION

A series of books featuring a heroine named Sally Lockhart describes the adventures of a young woman who is very unlike her Victorian contemporaries' ideal of femininity. Orphaned Sally has little formal education in the usual subjects, but she can ride like the wind, handle a gun, and plan a campaign, and she is a feminist. The first Sally Lockhart story, *The Ruby in the Smoke,* is set in 1872, when Sally is about sixteen years old and has recently lost her father, who apparently drowned in a shipwreck in the South China Sea. Trying to piece together fragmentary clues, Sally asks her father's employees if they know the significance of "The Seven Blessings." On hearing the phrase, one of them falls dead at her feet. Sally becomes embroiled in the opium trade and the search for a ruby of fabulous value, and in the process comes to understand the value of her own detecting skills. Her second adventure, *The Shadow in the North,* is set six years later, in 1878. Sally has set up her own business, and is a well-respected financial consultant, but it seems that she has given one client bad advice: to invest her money in the Anglo-Baltic shipping company, whose ships mysteriously disappear, sink, or are impounded with mystifying regularity. With the assistance of her allies Fred and Jim, Sally Lockhart investigates. The third adventure, *The Tiger in the Well* (1991), opens nearly two years after the death of Sally's fiancé, Frederick Garland—Fred, whom we first met in *The Ruby in the Smoke*—on a settled domestic scene in the Twickenham house where Sally now lives with her daughter, Harriet. Then a stranger arrives to serve "divorce" papers on the unmarried Sally, papers that ostensibly prove the existence of Sally's living husband and Harriet's father. Sally's history has been rewritten, and she must become invisible in order to work out how she can reclaim it.

The Tin Princess (1994) also has a young female protagonist and is set in nineteenth-century England, but here the central heroine is a multilingual young woman named Rebecca Winter, known as Becky. Hired to be a German tutor to the cockney Miss Bevan, Becky discovers that her pupil is in fact the wife of a prince. Becky and her new friend become caught up in the politics of Razkavia, a mountainous country in central Europe, where they face more than political machinations. The opening of *The Tin*

Princess nods at two earlier novels, Daphne du Maurier's *Rebecca* (1938), in the name of the heroine, and Jane Austen's *Emma* (1816) in the syntax of the first sentence: "Rebecca Winter, gifted, cheerful and poor, had lived sixteen years without seeing a bomb go off" (p. 1).

Though the Sally Lockhart series is set in the nineteenth century, the independent, intelligent, and active Sally is a good role model for any twenty-first-century teenager, and the evocation of grimy, foggy, seedy Victorian London slums and the Victorian underworld is excellent. Television adaptations of the first two Sally Lockhart stories have been filmed by the BBC.

In the mid-1990s Pullman also wrote two historical novels for younger readers featuring "The New Cut Gang": *Thunderbolt's Waxwork* (1994) and *The Gas-fitters' Ball* (1995), like the Sally Lockhart novels, are set in the Victorian period, but in a disreputable part of South London, Lambeth. Where the Sally Lockhart novels resemble the mysteries of Charles Dickens, the New Cut Gang stories resemble Dickens at his most picaresque. The stories follow the adventures of the New Cut Gang: Benny Kaminsky, Thunderbolt Dobney, and their friends Bridie, Sharky Bob, and the Perretti twins, Angela and Zerlina, a group that ranges in age from six to thirteen. In *Thunderbolt's Waxwork,* the gang members have made a waxwork of their friend Dippy and are trying to find a way of having it exhibited at the Waxworks Museum, but people keep trying to steal it. When Thunderbolt's dad is arrested, the gang becomes involved in a counterfeit-money caper that requires them to outwit the criminals and the police. In *The Gas-fitters' Ball,* the gang helps to restore ten thousand pounds sterling's worth of stolen silver to the Worshipful Company of Gas-fitters, and also acts as a matchmaker for a friend.

FAIRY TALES AND ILLUSTRATED STORIES

Pullman's Web site describes his shorter, nonrealist fiction for young people as "fairy tales," possibly because they tend to lack the moral complexity and ambiguity of the longer works, they have characters more clearly delineated as good or bad, and they finish with loose ends tied up and just desserts distributed. A number are adaptations and developments of plays he wrote for his pupils during his time as a schoolteacher. Most of his stories for younger children have been published or reprinted with illustrations.

Spring-Heeled Jack, first published in 1989, was reprinted in 1991 with illustrations by David Mostyn—pen drawings that suggest both Victorian engravings and modern comic books. It is the story of three orphans, two brothers and a sister, who are helped by a hero who dresses up as the devil to terrify criminals. *The Firework-Maker's Daughter* (1995), illustrated by Nick Harris (and by S. Saelig Gallagher for the first U.S. edition in 1999), has the atmosphere of a Far Eastern fable. It is the story of Lila, a girl who wants to follow her father into the profession of firework-maker but who first has to undertake a perilous journey and face the terrible Fire-Fiend. *The Wonderful Story of Aladdin and the Enchanted Lamp* (1993) was illustrated by David Wyatt, and in later editions by Sophy Williams. *Clockwork; or, All Wound Up* (1996) was illustrated by Peter Bailey; the first U.S. edition appeared in 1996 with illustrations by Leonid Gore. *Mossycoat* (1998) is a variant of the Cinderella story, illustrated by Peter Bailey. *I Was a Rat! or, The Red Slippers* (1999), illustrated by Peter Bailey, tells the story of a young boy dressed in a ragged page's uniform who turns up on the doorstep of an old, childless couple, unable at first to say much more than "I was a rat!" Is he telling the truth or acting a part? Sane or mad? The reader has to work it out, from a narrative studded with references to classic fairy tales. *I Was a Rat!* has been adapted for the stage and performed at the Edinburgh Fringe Festival; the first U.S. edition appeared in 2000 with illustrations by Kevin Hawkes. A more straightforward retelling of a familiar story is *Puss in Boots: The Adventures of That Most Enterprising Feline* (2000), illustrated by Ian Beck, but it has wonderful original touches in the shape of new characters, plot twists, and comedy. *The Scarecrow and His Servant* (2004), illustrated by Peter Bailey, is the story of a scarecrow brought to life by a bolt of lightning and of his faithful, quick-witted servant, Jack.

CONTEMPORARY FICTION: THE BROKEN BRIDGE (1990)

The Broken Bridge transfers Pullman's experience of being a well-traveled English boy in North Wales into the experiences of a mixed-race teenaged girl in a small village in the same area. Ginny is the daughter of a white man and a Haitian woman who, she has always known, died soon after she was born. But, like Philip Pullman, she has knowledge thrust on her that forces her to rewrite the history of her life and family. In the summer of her sixteenth birthday, she hears of the existence of a half-brother, who is about to come to make her close-knit duo a threesome. Then she learns some even more startling information, about her mother. The affinity that Ginny believed she had with her mother, through the creativity and the French language they shared, seems broken, but—again, like Pullman—she finds that her love of art and of the countryside changes her life in other ways. Gradually, she mends the broken bridges and reconnects her past and her present.

The White Mercedes, which appeared in 1992, since 1998 has been published under the title Butterfly Tattoo. Partly set, like His Dark Materials, in Oxford, The Butterfly Tattoo follows a character from the dirtier, rougher side of the city into the side inhabited by the gilded youth of the university. From the novel's opening sentence we learn that the protagonist, the likeable-seeming Chris, is about to meet a girl whom he will kill. Chris Marshall is seventeen years old and avoiding home, and his mother's new lover, as much as possible. He takes a casual job helping to set up the entertainment for an Oxford college summer ball, where he meets and falls for a girl, Jenny, whose seeming cheerfulness covers a dark past. Jenny proves as elusive as she is beautiful. In his subsequent anguished search for her, Chris learns the consequences of choosing the wrong person to trust. On his website, Pullman says of this novel, "The Butterfly Tattoo is a tragedy. I wanted to write a love story in which believable characters in a modern setting could encounter love and death in a realistic way."

HIS DARK MATERIALS

The best known of Pullman's work is the best-selling sequence of novels collectively titled His Dark Materials, a trilogy that comprises Northern Lights (1995; titled The Golden Compass in the United States), The Subtle Knife (1997), and The Amber Spyglass (2000). His Dark Materials has been adapted for the stage (performed at the Royal National Theatre in London in 2003), and in fall 2006, New Line Cinema was in production on a film version of the first book of the trilogy featuring Daniel Craig (as the character Lord Asriel) and Nicole Kidman (as Mrs. Coulter). Another volume related to the trilogy, Lyra's Oxford (2003), contains the short story "Lyra and the Birds," together with additional materials such as a map of the alternative Oxford that the Dark Materials protagonist inhabits. Pullman has suggested that he is working on another installment in the series, provisionally titled "The Book of Dust," which may not be a conventional sequel to The Amber Spyglass but rather a companion volume that includes short stories about some of the secondary characters of the series.

Northern Lights was initially published by Scholastic, a publishing house associated with children's and young adult fiction, but the book became an early example of the phenomenon known as "crossover" fiction; fiction that is successful with both older and younger readers, and each of the subsequent volumes has been likewise acclaimed by adult readers as well as children.

The title of the series is taken from book 2 of John Milton's Paradise Lost (1667): "his dark materials" are the threatening confusion of untamed elements from which God made the world we know and from which he could make others. This sets the epic character of the series, which explores the nature of matter, the universe, consciousness, understanding, and God, as well as interrogating ideas about religion, sin, authority, loyalty, and love. The series also has an ecological theme. It contrasts worlds in which technology has been developed thoughtlessly, and to the detriment of the environment, with worlds in which natural or low-tech rather than wasteful and damaging high-tech methods are used.

In *Paradise Lost,* Milton represents the "fruit" of man's first disobedience to God's will, and Pullman similarly depicts a revolt against a religious authority, a choice made by a young woman, and the acquisition of forbidden knowledge. The church of Lyra's world, like Christian churches of our own, depicts Eve as culpable, as the agent through which innocence was lost and sin entered the world. In Pullman's work, however, the young woman who is to be a second Eve, Lyra, is a heroine, and her act of disobedience against the church is the beginning of her world's emancipation. In the course of the series, we learn that other worlds have had an Eve, and that in each case the "Fall" she brings about is the development of self-awareness and the thirst for knowledge. This Fall is not a fall from grace and into sin, but something natural and normal, the development of a human being from child to adolescent to adult and from innocence and ignorance to experience.

Perhaps as influential as Milton for the series is the visionary poet William Blake. Blake produced two sets of illustrations for *Paradise Lost* and wrote a long poem, "Milton" (1804), which he planned to comprise twelve books, like *Paradise Lost,* but which was actually published in two. The poem criticizes Milton's view of Christianity and his privileging of reason over imagination, and spirit over body, but also depicts him as a savior who returns to the world a hundred years after the death of his body in order to slay Urizen, Blake's symbol of repressive reason and authority. Like Blake's written and pictorial art, Pullman's fiction expresses a profound mistrust of authority, particularly authority that is self-proclaimed and maintained through tyranny. In Lyra's world, a powerful church has used the carrot-and-stick of Heaven and Hell to impose obedience and has kept a stranglehold on scientific and technological knowledge, suppressing potentially subversive ideas in order to maintain ignorance rather than innocence. The God of that world (and others),

known as "the Authority," is an ancient, bearded old man, inaccessible and darkly inscrutable, who has become a figurehead for the exercise of earthly powers. The opponent of the Authority (and of his regent, Metatron) and thus a "Satan" figure (though for much of the trilogy he doesn't fully understand the nature of the God and religion of his world) is Lyra's father, Lord Asriel, whose biblical name echoes one of Blake's symbolic rebel angel-type figures. Lord Asriel seeks to destroy this God and the earthly powers that wield power in his name. One message of the series is that humankind must grow up and, in an Oedipal revolt against the father figure it has set above itself, become independent and self-governing, not blindly following religious laws but establishing a true code of morality. Humanity must no longer allow belief in a life hereafter to prevent humankind from truly living this life.

Another influence cited by Pullman is an 1810 essay by the German Romantic Heinrich von Kleist, titled "On the Marionette Theatre, which appeared in translation in the *Times Literary Supplement* in 1978. Kleist dramatizes a debate that Pullman explores throughout *His Dark Materials*: the loss of innocence and the acquisition of self-consciousness. (Readers interested in this source can find the essay, in English translation by Idris Parry, at the *Southern Cross Review* website, www.southerncrossreview.org.)

His Dark Materials is set in a number of different worlds, including our own. (Pullman produced illustrations for the chapter headings of the first two volumes of the trilogy, as well as small pictures as running heads for the second volume, to indicate which world the main characters are in at the time.) Lyra's home world is like our own but with significant differences. The Reformation has happened, and the dominant religion is broadly Calvinist but there is still an Inquisition and still a Pope, and his rule is worldwide. The Enlightenment has not taken hold, and the church maintains control over the progress of knowledge. What we know as science and technology are branches of "experimental theology," and any theories that contradict authorized knowledge are deemed heretical and suppressed. The West has not yet explored the rest of the world; in addition to ordinary humans, the population of the world includes witches and talking bears; and, most significant of all, every human has a dæmon. Although they have separate bodies, one animal and one human, the dæmon and its human partner have a bond that, until the church's experiments prove successful, seems indissoluble. They are two halves of one being that share feelings and sometimes thoughts, and the dæmon's actions may be outward signs of the inner state of its human. Until the human reaches adolescence, the dæmon's form is not fixed. It can change at will, or in response to, for example, alarm. Lyra's dæmon, Pantalaimon, or Pan, often takes the form of an ermine when he is relaxed or asleep; but he also becomes a mouse, when he needs to hide; a bird, when he and Lyra need to find something; a moth, when they need to spy on a conversation; and a wildcat, when he needs to fight. As the human partner reaches puberty, his or her dæmon begins to favor one form more and more often, and when the human reaches full adulthood, the dæmon ceases to change at all. Most human males have a female dæmon and most females a male. When the human dies, the dæmon vanishes. And, as the church discovers, severance of the bond between human and dæmon usually results in death from shock or a living death for both partners.

The first book of the trilogy, *Northern Lights* (published in the United States as *The Golden Compass*), introduces us to the young protagonist Lyra Belacqua. At twelve years old, Lyra remembers nothing of her life before she was brought to live in Jordan College, a men-only college of an alternative Oxford, by the man she knows only as her uncle Lord Asriel. Though she has a few lessons from the fellows of Jordan, Lyra's upbringing has largely been in the hands of the college servants, and she is more interested in playing with her best friend, Roger, a kitchen boy, on the roofs and in the crypts and cellars, and in other forbidden places, than she is in acquiring the social graces and intellectual attainments the college has to offer. Outside the college, she leads a gang of vagabonds about the streets and waterways of the city. She is uncouth, unkempt, and ignorant; she fights, boasts, and

tells lies; but she is also intuitive, dauntless, a brave leader, and a loyal friend.

The autocratic Lord Asriel arrives at Jordan one evening to report on the findings of recent expeditions to the far north. Lyra and Pan, hiding after some unsanctioned exploration of their own, witness an attempt to poison Asriel, warn him, and are allowed to stay on to do a little more spying. Lyra hears that Asriel is about to go north again, ostensibly to continue the exploration but in fact, she suspects, for another, mysterious purpose. She also hears of the existence of something called Dust, a kind of matter that accumulates around sentient, self-aware beings and is first seen on human skulls from thirty thousand to forty thousand years ago. She learns that the church is extremely interested in Dust, but Asriel leaves without telling her any more.

After Asriel is gone, Lyra returns to her usual pursuits. Stories are circulating the city about children vanishing, and it is rumored that they are being abducted by so-called Gobblers. When Roger disappears, Lyra determines that she will rescue him. Meanwhile, she is introduced to the glamorous Mrs. Coulter—a highly respected lay associate of the church, who is the widow of an eminent politician—and told that she is to live with her in the future. Before Lyra leaves Jordan College, the Master gives her a gift, an alethiometer (the "golden compass" of the U.S. title), a truth-telling instrument that at this stage Lyra cannot read. Her new life is luxurious, but when she learns that Mrs. Coulter works for the General Oblation Board (an oblation is an offering)—the "Gobblers" who have been stealing children—Lyra runs away. She is rescued by an old friend from Oxford, a "gyptian" (water gypsy). While aboard one of the gyptians' boats, Lyra learns her real history. She is the child of Lord Asriel and Mrs. Coulter, hidden since babyhood on Asriel's orders.

Lyra has been learning that she instinctively knows how to use the alethiometer, and when the gyptians decide to go north to search for the missing children, they allow her to go with them. At this point, Lyra's adventures really begin. Among other fabulous creatures, Lyra meets and befriends Iorek Byrnison, the king of the great armored bears who live in polar regions, and she is granted help by Serafina Pekkala, the queen of a powerful witch clan. She is captured by Samoyed hunters, who sell her to a place called the Experimental Station, where she finds a lot of other children who have been kidnapped or sold, including Roger. At the station, the church is investigating Dust; the church associates Dust with the loss of childhood and innocence, and therefore with sin, and is looking for a way to sever the Dustless children from their dæmons in a process called intercision. The process has a side effect, however; the resulting fission releases an enormous amount of energy. Mrs. Coulter arrives just as Lyra and Pan, plotting escape, are caught spying and are about to be intercised, and she saves them. Lyra organizes a breakout just as Iorek and the witches arrive in advance of the gyptians. Eventually Lyra and Roger find Lyra's father, guarded by armored bears under orders from Mrs. Coulter. Asriel believes that their world is just one among many and that if he can go to the other world he has glimpsed, he will be able to learn the secret of Dust. The climax of the story takes place as Asriel proves his theory and another world appears in the northern lights at the North Pole. But to effect the crossing, Asriel has had to generate energy, and he does so by intercising, and killing, Roger. Asriel crosses into the new world, and Lyra follows him.

Northern Lights, like Pullman's earlier fiction, is threaded with intertextual references. Michael Chabon points out details that reflect the novels of Vladimir Nabokov, for instance in the way a zeppelin features in the story (see "Dust and Dæmons," in Glen Yeffeth, ed., *Navigating the Golden Compass,* p. 5). In a webchat on BBC Radio 4, Pullman explained that the inspiration for the alethiometer "was partly the emblem books of the Renaissance and partly the memory theatre as described in a wonderful book by Frances Yates called *The Art of Memory.*" Another possible source, however, could be the geomantic compass on display at the Pitt Rivers Museum in Oxford, a place in our "real" Oxford, which Lyra visits in *Northern Lights.*

The Subtle Knife, the second volume of *His Dark Materials,* opens in our own world, apparently on a family whose problems are on a more ordinary and domestic scale than those of Lyra and Lord Asriel. Twelve-year-old Will Parry has been looking after his mother ever since the disappearance of his father during an expedition, which has left her nervous and insecure. But as she becomes increasingly paranoid and deluded, Will discovers that her persecution complex is not delusion after all. Someone is out to get them, or at least to get hold of something in their possession: John Parry's letters from his last expedition. When men break into the house, Will finds a safe haven for his mother and sets out to carry the letters as far away as he can. This turns out to be farther than he expected. In the suburb of North Oxford, an encounter with a cat leads him to something like a hole cut into the air, and the hole leads to another world. At first, Will seems to be the only inhabitant of the new world, although it clearly has been inhabited, and recently. The streets, shops, cafés, and houses show signs of recent occupancy, but they are deserted. Then he meets a grubby, disheveled girl with an animal that changes shape from a big cat to a stoat to butterfly. The girl is Lyra.

Will and Lyra are in Cittàgazze, a world infested by Specters, misty creatures that emanate from the Abyss and that flock to adults and suck the spirit out of them. Lyra has lost her father and the world to which he crossed in the fog of the world-bridge Asriel created. Now she is looking for scholars who can tell her about Dust. Will offers to take her into his world, where she can find scholars she would think of as theologians and he as scientists, and he can make inquiries about the disappearance of his father. Together, they go through the window to Will's world, where Lyra meets a scholar, Dr. Mary Malone, a former nun and a physicist who has been studying dark matter—Lyra's Dust. Dr. Malone tells Lyra that Dust is actually shadow particles—particles of consciousness. Shadow particles cluster around any products of human workmanship or thought, and they first appear on ancient skulls from some thirty thousand to forty thousand years ago. With Lyra's help, Dr. Malone finds a way to communicate with the shadow matter/Dust, or with what call themselves structures and complexifications of shadow-matter—angels. Malone learns that they have played a part in human evolution, and that she herself has a part to play in Lyra's adventure, the part of "the serpent."

While the protagonists are in Will's world, Lyra's alethiometer is stolen by the evil Sir Charles Latrum, who promises to return it if Will and Lyra will bring him something from Cittàgazze: a special knife. Back in Cittàgazze, Will is attacked and badly wounded—the knife severs two fingers of his hand. But he wins the fight, and thus becomes the unwilling bearer of the subtle knife, a blade that can cut through anything, even the fabric of worlds. Using the knife, Lyra and Will cut through to Sir Charles' house, where Lyra remembers that she has seen Sir Charles before, at Mrs. Coulter's house. He is Lord Boreal from her own world, and he is being visited by Mrs. Coulter. They steal back the alethiometer and barely make it back to Cittàgazze, where they are ambushed by the remaining children and only escape with the arrival of the witches, who have finally caught up with them. As they make their way out of Cittàgazze, Dr. Malone steps through the window, out of the Oxford of her world, and sets out to find Lyra.

On their journey the witches learn that Lord Asriel has built a fortress in which he is mustering forces from many worlds ready to wage war on the Authority, and Mrs. Coulter learns that her daughter "will be the mother—she will be life—mother—she will disobey—she will [be] Eve! Mother of All!" (Scholastic, 1998, p. 328) During a desperate fight, Will at last meets his father, only to lose him almost immediately to a witch's arrow. Before he is killed, John Parry tells Will that he must join Lord Asriel, because he carries the only weapon that can defeat the tyrant, the Authority. Will returns to the camp set up by his traveling companions, where he finds two entities of the kind who had communicated with Dr. Malone, angels, who now want to lead Will to the fulfillment of his task. But the witches who had been guarding Lyra have been attacked by Specters, and Lyra is gone. The novel ends with Will too miserably dazed to move.

In contrast to Lyra, Will is not a ragamuffin but a clean, tidy, well-brought-up, and polite boy. He is not a natural liar or deceiver, nor does he have Lyra's interest in the limelight of leadership; he has learned to be inconspicuous. As Lyra takes on a weight of responsibility, so Will learns that he cannot always do the best possible thing for all possible parties, and that neither good nor evil is necessarily clear-cut.

The Amber Spyglass, the third volume in *His Dark Materials,* opens on Lyra in a drugged sleep, hidden in a cave in a remote part of her own world, and guarded by her mother, Mrs. Coulter. Lyra dreams of Roger, whom she had inadvertently betrayed to his death, and she vows to find him. With the help of one of the angels, Will tracks down Mrs. Coulter, and they free Lyra, while the other angel warns Lord Asriel that the Authority has retired to the Clouded Mountain and resigned daily power to a powerful regent, Metatron. Allies of Asriel go to join forces with Lyra and Will, but Lyra insists that she must find Roger before anything else. She takes her companions on a journey no living person has made before, to the world of the dead—and to do so she must leave Pan behind and go on as a half-person.

Meanwhile, Dr. Malone has stepped into another world, the world of the mulefa (always spelled with a lowercase *m*), a peaceful community that lives in harmony with the environment. The trees on which mulefa society depends are dying, however. Having constructed the amber spyglass of the title, which enables her to see Dust, Dr. Malone learns that the trees are dying because Dust is moving out of the mulefa world, and out of other worlds, too. The Consistorial Court of Discipline of the church of Lyra's world learns that Lyra is to be a second Eve who will be tempted to disobedience. Should she give in to temptation, then (in an echo from George Herbert's poem "Love (III)"), "Dust and sin will triumph" (Scholastic 2000, p. 71). It sends an assassin, Father Gomez, to find and kill Lyra, and he arrives in the mulefa world.

Lyra, Will, and their companions find the world of the dead nothing like the Heaven promised by the various churches of the different worlds. It is a bleak, cold, gray place guarded by vicious Harpies who prey upon the secret weaknesses and vulnerable points of their charges. The Authority who put the Harpies in charge has given them to power to see the worst in everyone, and for hundreds of thousands of years they have fed on cruelty, meanness, and deceit. When Lyra tries to lie her way out, the Harpies fly at her, and she is badly hurt, but when she tells true stories, the Harpies are entranced. A bargain is struck. The Harpies will have the right to demand that everyone who comes to the land of the dead tells the story of his or her life, and in return, if the story is true, and the person has truly lived their life, the Harpies will escort them out of the world of the dead and through a window to a living world above. If anyone, other than an infant, has not truly lived, or lies, or holds anything back, the Harpies have the right to refuse to guide them. So the Harpies, Lyra, and Will lead the numberless dead through dark caverns and treacherous paths bordering the Abyss, up to the living worlds, where the dead will dissipate into the air, and the living can join the fight against the church and Metatron.

In Lyra's world, the church leaders have modified the intercision process to harness the latent energy and make it into a bomb that can be detonated remotely from one world to another. They use a lock of Lyra's hair stolen from Mrs. Coulter to direct the explosion to the world she currently inhabits. Thanks to the knowledge of one of the dead, the explosion misses Lyra, but it destroys a section of the narrow pathway, and she falls. Only the intervention of the leading Harpy saves her from the Abyss. The procession reaches the end, and Will cuts an opening into a living world. The ghosts stream out to become part of the matter of the universe, apart from Lyra's loyal allies, who join the fight.

At the last moment, Mrs. Coulter joins forces with Lord Asriel to save their daughter and together they drag Metatron into the Abyss. Will and Lyra find the Authority, a feeble, demented, ancient creature who is dissolved by the breath of air when he is released from the crystal litter in which he has been imprisoned. During the fight, Will and Lyra find that they are beginning

to be affected by the Specters; they are moving toward adulthood, and Dust is beginning to be attracted to them. Lyra is reunited with Pan, and Will with his dæmon, Kirjava, who in this world is visible. To protect them all from Specters, Will cuts through to another world, where they stay to rest and recover. It is the mulefa world, and here they find Mary and learn of her discovery.

The now almost adult children are beginning to realize that their feeling for one another is more than friendship. Dr. Malone fulfills her function as serpent and tempter in that the story she tells Lyra of the love of her life awakens in Lyra knowledge of the nature of her true feelings for Will. The two consummate their love as Father Gomez finds them, but he has been followed by an angel, who kills him. Mary has learned that the flow of Dust had turned when the subtle knife was made. The windows the knife has opened have allowed Specters into the worlds and have made Dust flow out of them and into the Abyss. Will and Lyra have reversed the flow for the mulefa world, but the knife has been used to make many windows between many worlds.

Will must close the windows. Since neither Will nor Lyra can remain for long in each other's world, they will be parted forever. There is momentary hope in that Dust is renewable; generated by knowledge and understanding; if enough people in each world continued to learn and gain wisdom, it might be enough to compensate for one open window. But that window must be reserved for the dead, or they will be forever trapped below. This is Lyra's temptation. If she chooses love, she condemns humanity to a grisly everlasting unlife. Will and Lyra make the decision, and part; Will returns to our world, where Dr. Malone will help him and his mother, and Lyra returns to Jordan College, and later school, in her own world. They agree that every year for as long as they live, at noon on Midsummer's Day, they will go to a place that exists in both worlds, a bench under a tree in the Botanic Gardens, and know that the other is near. The Kingdom of Heaven has been destroyed. Now it is time to build the Republic.

Three years after *The Amber Spyglass* brought a close to the initial trilogy of *His Dark Materials,* Pullman produced a curious volume, with engravings by John Lawrence, that revisited the world of the story's heroine. The introduction to *Lyra's Oxford* tells the reader that the book contains a story and several other things. These "might be connected with the story, or they might not; they might be connected to other stories that haven't appeared yet. It's not easy to tell" (p. ii). The other things are an annotated map of Lyra's Oxford (inserted between pages 16 and 17), a postcard sent to a friend, Angela Borman, by Dr. Malone soon after she left her religious order to work in Oxford (pages 51–52), a page from a guidebook to Oxford published by the City Museum, which lists a number of the locations of the story (pages 31–32), and a brochure for a cruise to the Levant on the liner SS *Zenobia* (pages 53–55). The itinerary is marked, the date of the ship's arrival in Smyrna, Monday, May 11, is ringed, and a line from the ring leads to a note: "Café Antalya, Süleiman Square, 11 a.m."

The introduction tells us that such things, cut adrift from the people for whom they once had a use, trace the line of a story in the same way that an ionizing particle in a bubble chamber traces the line of a path taken by something that cannot be seen. "That path is a story, of course" (p. iii). Dr. Malone would have been familiar with the way in which scientists work out the "story" of a particle from the trace it leaves, but, the introduction suggests, she might not have expected when she sent the postcard that it would trace part of a story that had not yet happened. "Perhaps some particles move backwards in time; perhaps the future affects the past in some way we don't understand; or perhaps the universe is simply more aware than we are. There are many things we haven't yet learned how to read," the introduction says. "The story in this book is partly about that very process" (p. iii).

The front of the card has four small black-and-white photographs of rather ordinary places, which seem odd choices to advertise a city as rich in architectural treasures as Oxford. It would make a very prosaic and even dull postcard, to all but readers of *His Dark Materials*. The locations are: a wooden bench that could be the place in the Botanic Gardens at which Lyra and Will have agreed to "meet" every Midsummer; the science building in which Dr. Mary Malone had her lab; the front garden of a house in Norham Gardens with a low wall topped by a hedge, where Lyra hid and was picked up by Sir Charles Latrum, who then stole her alethiometer; and the suburban street with a row of hornbeam trees in which Will discovered the window to Citàgazze.

The story traced in *Lyra's Oxford,* "Lyra and the Birds," is set two years after the end of *The Amber Spyglass,* in Oxford, where Lyra is a student at St. Sophia's. Lyra and Pan rescue a dæmon in the shape of a swallow, or house marten, that is being mobbed by a flock of starlings, and they learn that it has been sent by its witch. The witch's message is that they must help the dæmon to find a man called Sebastian Makepeace, somewhere in Jericho, a suburb of the city. The dæmon explains the behavior of the starlings and other birds they encounter, which all try to attack it, as being due to the sickness it carries, a malady that leads to the death of the human without the death of the dæmon. This raises Lyra and Pan's sympathy, and they track down Makepeace, whom they discover to be an alchemist. Lyra's suspicions are roused, however, and she tricks the dæmon into revealing that he already knows where the house is. A mad witch leaps out of the house and at Lyra in a murderous lunge, but another bird, a swan, launches itself at her, and the witch is killed. Sebastian Makepeace explains that he had been the witch's lover. Their son fought on the side of Asriel and against the side taken by his mother in the war against the Authority, and he was killed by one of his mother's arrows. The witch blamed both Makepeace and Lyra, and so had devised a plot to kill them both.

Safely back in St. Sophia's, Lyra and Pan realize that the behavior of the birds they had interpreted as aggressive was, in fact, protective of them. They listen to a nightingale and realize that the song has meaning even though they cannot understand it: "'Things don't mean things as simply as that,' Lyra said, uncertainly. 'Do they? Not like *mensa* means table. They mean all kinds of things, mixed up.' 'But it feels like it,' Pan said. 'It feels as if the whole city's looking after us. So what we feel is part of the meaning, isn't it?'" (p. 48).

CRITICAL RESPONSE

His Dark Materials has been compared to J. R. R. Tolkien's *The Lord of the Rings* (1954–1955) and C. S. Lewis' *Chronicles of Narnia* (1950–1956) in terms of imaginative range and power, although of course it is far removed from the Anglo-Saxon and Norse mythology and etymology of the former and the muscular Christianity of the latter. In a 2002 interview with the *Daily Telegraph,* Pullman expressed surprise at the comparison. "I think Lewis was a remarkable man. But when it came to the Narnia books, I think he was actually dangerous because those books celebrate death. As an end-of-term treat the children are killed: that to me is disgusting" (p. 26). The series has been denounced by church groups. After Pullman was awarded the Whitbread Book of the Year prize, the journalist Peter Hitchens, writing for the *Mail on Sunday,* suggested in a piece titled "This Is the Most Dangerous Author in Britain" that Pullman's agenda in writing the trilogy was to dethrone C. S. Lewis and provide an alternative and antidote to the Narnia stories, in novels that "proclaim the death of God to the young" (p. 63).

In the *Daily Telegraph* interview, Pullman responded to this kind of accusation by reminding readers that "the story [*His Dark Materials*] celebrates love, courage, an imaginative engagement with the world, tolerance, open-mindedness, courtesy. And it criticises cold-heartedness, fanaticism, cruelty, intolerance. Who could argue with that? Even *The Catholic Herald* will find something to agree with in there." Of the suggestion that he is an atheist, he said, furthermore:

Atheism suggests a degree of certainty that I'm not quite willing to accede to. I suppose technically you'd have to put me down as an agnostic. But if there is a God and he is as the Christians describe him, then he deserves to be put down and rebelled against. As you look back over the history of the Christian church, it's a record of terrible infamy and cruelty and persecution and tyranny. How they have the bloody nerve to go on "Thought for the Day" and tell us all to be good when, given the slightest chance, they'd be hanging the rest of us and flogging the homosexuals and persecuting the witches.

(*Daily Telegraph*)

The Archbishop of Canterbury, Rowan Williams, surprised many when he praised the adaptation of *His Dark Materials* that was performed in 2003 at the London Royal National Theatre, and he and Pullman participated in a live conversation at the theater in March 2004, discussing the part of religion in art and education. In that conversation, Pullman elaborated on the creation myth he envisaged for the series. He explained that there was no "creator," but that there was matter, which gradually became conscious of itself and developed Dust. The first figure to condense from matter was the Authority, and the angels that followed believed that he was the creator. The war in Heaven came when some angels no longer believed that, and from that challenge came the temptation and Fall.

Selected Bibliography

WORKS OF PHILIP PULLMAN

FIRST EDITIONS

The Haunted Storm. London: New English Library, 1972.

Galatea. London: Victor Gollancz, 1978.

Using "The Oxford Junior Dictionary': A Book of Exercises and Games. Oxford: Oxford University Press, 1979.

Count Karlstein; or, The Ride of the Demon Huntsman. London: Chatto and Windus, 1982.

The Ruby in the Smoke. Oxford: Oxford University Press, 1985.

The Shadow in the Plate. Oxford: Oxford University Press, 1986. Reissued as *The Shadow in the North.* Harmondsworth, U.K.: Penguin, in association with Oxford University Press, 1988.

How To Be Cool. London: Heinemann, .

Spring-Heeled Jack: A Story of Bravery and Evil. London: Doubleday, 1989.

Frankenstein. Oxford: Oxford University Press, 1990. (Dramatic adaptation.)

The Broken Bridge. London: Macmillan, 1990.

The Tiger in the Well. London: Viking, 1991.

Sherlock Holmes and the Limehouse Horror. Walton-on-Thames, U.K.: Nelson, 1992. (Drama.)

The White Mercedes. London: Pan Macmillan, 1992. Reissued as *The Butterfly Tattoo.* London: Macmillan Children's, 1998.

Thunderbolt's Waxwork. London: Viking, 1994.

The Tin Princess. London: Puffin, 1994.

The Firework-Maker's Daughter. London: Doubleday, 1995.

The Gas-fitters' Ball. London: Viking, 1995.

Northern Lights. London: Scholastic, . (Published in the United States as *The Golden Compass.*)

The Wonderful Story of Aladdin and the Enchanted Lamp. London: Scholastic, 1995.

Clockwork; or, All Wound Up. London: Corgi Yearling, 1997.

The Subtle Knife. London: Scholastic, 1997.

Mossycoat. London: Scholastic, 1998.

I Was a Rat! or, The Scarlet Slippers. London: Doubleday, 1999.

The Amber Spyglass. London: Scholastic, 2000.

Puss in Boots: The Adventures of That Most Enterprising Feline. London: Doubleday, 2000.

His Dark Materials. London: Scholastic, 2001. (Trilogy collecting *Northern Lights, The Subtle Knife,* and *The Amber Spyglass.*)

Lyra's Oxford. Oxford: David Fickling Books, 2003.

The Scarecrow and His Servant. London: Doubleday, 2004.

CRITICAL AND BIOGRAPHICAL STUDIES

Colbert, David. *The Magical Worlds of Philip Pullman.* New York: Berkley, 2006.

Gribbin, Mary, and John Gribbin. *The Science of Philip Pullman's "His Dark Materials."* New York: Knopf, 2005.

Lenz, Millicent, and Carole Scott, eds. *"His Dark Materials" Illuminated: Critical Essays on Philip Pullman's Trilogy.* Detroit: Wayne State University Press, 2005.

Squires, Claire. *Philip Pullman's "His Dark Materials" Trilogy: A Reader's Guide.* Continuum Contemporaries. London: Continuum, 2003.

Watkins, Tony. *Dark Matter: Shedding Light on Philip Pullman's Trilogy "His Dark Materials."* Downer's Grove, Ill.: Intervarsity Press, 2006.

Yeffeth, Glen, ed. *Navigating the Golden Compass: Religion, Science, and Dæmonology in Philip Pullman's "His Dark Materials."* Dallas, Texas: Benbella, 2005.

INTERVIEWS AND REVIEWS

BBC Radio 4 Arts and Drama. "*His Dark Materials*: Philip Pullman Webchat" (http://www.bbc.co.uk/radio4/arts/hisdarkmaterials/pullman_webchat.shtml).

Butler, Robert, moderator. "The 'Dark Materials' Debate: Life, God, the Universe" (http://www.telegraph.co.uk/arts/main.jhtml?xml=/arts/2004/03/17/bodark17.xml), March 17, 2004. (Transcript of a moderated conversation between Philip Pullman and the Archbishop of Canterbury, Rowan Williams.)

Hedblad, Alan, ed. "Philip Pullman." In *Something About the Author.* Vol. 71. Farmington Hills, Mich.: Gale, 1993.

Hitchens, Peter. "This Is the Most Dangerous Author in Britain." *Mail on Sunday,* January 27, 2002, p. 23.

"I Am of the Devil's Party." *Daily Telegraph,* January 29, 2002; also available at http://www.telegraph.co.uk/arts/main.jhtml?xml=/arts/2002/01/29/bopull27.xml. (Interview.)

Pullman, Philip. The author maintains an active website at http://www.philip-pullman.com that provides details of his publications and their background, and also includes a monthly newsletter in which he discusses educational and ecological as well as personal and literary matters.

Wagner, Erica. Review of *His Dark Materials. Times,* 18 October 18, 2000, pp. T2, T12.

CRAIG RAINE

(1944—)

Patrick Denman Flanery

IN HIS 1997 essay "A Criticism of Life," English poet Craig Raine asserts: "In my naïve, untheoretical, writerly way, I believe in language" (*In Defence*, p. 1). This subtle polemicism, with its oblique criticism of academic literary theory and self-location in a writerly tradition of "naïve" belief in language, informs much of Raine's poetic and critical output over the past three decades.

Craig Anthony Raine was born on December 3, 1944 in Bishop Auckland, Co. Durham, in the north of England, to Norman Edward and Olive Marie Raine. Raine notes that his father worked on the railways, and mastered many additional trades, though he was really a boxer. His father began fighting from the age of seven and turned professional when he was sixteen. Norman lost while fighting for the feather-weight title of Great Britain and returned to amateur status, twice fighting for England: once, in 1937, he beat German Olympic champion Otto Kästner. In 1940, while serving in the Royal Air Force, Norman Raine was injured in an explosion—in what the family thinks was a Glasgow munitions factory—and, as a result, became permanently disabled with epilepsy. After the war, Norman became a spiritualist and began working as a faith-healer after curing Raine's brother's polio.

Raine notes that his mother, Olive, wanted her children to do well—alluding to the iconic maternal characters in the novels of D. H. Lawrence, also a working-class writer from the north of England, as well as to Lawrence's own mother, who Raine describes as terrifically ambitious for her children. Raine contends that Olive "could see that education was a way to move socially" (Carey 1991, p. 14). As a result of Olive's influence, Raine and his brother did not attend the local state school, but were scholarship boys at Barnard Castle School, an independent boarding school. Though his mother was Catholic and Raine was raised in the Catholic church, he claims that he wasn't a religious boy, but was tremendously keen on ceremonial aspect of church. This kind of aesthetic detail occurs in some of his poetry.

Raine remembers reading T. S. Eliot's *Four Quartets* when he was sixteen, and though he acknowledges that he did not entirely understand Eliot's poetry then, he recognized that it *was* poetry and difficult to understand. Reading Eliot prompted him to begin writing his own juvenile poems, which he describes as reams of nonsense. Raine submitted two of these poems to Philip Toynbee at the *Observer,* who rejected them, explaining that they weren't very good. Raine's English master at school urged Raine to stop using the first person pronoun in his poetry. As a result, Raine says, he continues to find it difficult to use 'I' and recognizes that in his first collection, *The Onion, Memory,* he does not feature as a character, something he believes to be uncharacteristic of most first collections.

After leaving Barnard Castle School, Raine was admitted to Exeter College, Oxford, where he earned a B.A. in English and a B.Phil in Nineteenth-Century and Twentieth-Century Studies. During his undergraduate years, Raine says that he hardly wrote any poems, instead working on bad short stories. He began research towards a doctorate on Coleridge's philosophy but ultimately abandoned the degree, claiming that he was bored by the idea.

Raine held various temporary lectureships in English at Exeter College, Lincoln College, and Christ Church, Oxford between the years of 1971 and 1979. He was literary editor of the *New Review* in 1977 and 1978, and editor of the literary review *Quarto* in 1979 and 1980. Following a stint as the *New Statesman*'s poetry editor (during 1981), he became poetry editor at Faber and Faber for a decade, a post also once held by T.S. Eliot. In 1991, Raine was appointed to a Fellowship at New College, Oxford.

Although known as the originator of Britain's "Martian poetry" movement (of which Christopher Reid was the other chief exponent), much of Raine's work has taken as its subject, or been informed by, his domestic life, as well as the histories of his own and his wife's families. Since 1972, Raine has been married to English academic Ann Pasternak Slater (b. 1944), a lecturer at the University of Oxford and fellow of St. Anne's College. Pasternak Slater is the daughter of Lydia Pasternak Slater (biochemist, poet, and translator) and psychiatrist Eliot Trevor Oakeshott Slater, CBE, as well as the niece of Boris Pasternak. Raine and Pasternak Slater have a daughter, Nina Raine, a stage director and playwright, and three sons, including Moses Raine, who is also a playwright.

THE ONION, MEMORY *(1978)*

Raine's first collection of poetry immediately signaled his intention to force British poetry in a new direction. Though clearly influenced by his interest in T.S. Eliot (as well as the poets Robert Lowell, Elizabeth Bishop, and Gerard Manley Hopkins), novelists James Joyce, Rudyard Kipling, Vladimir Nabokov, and Saul Bellow are amongst Raine's most intriguing influences. Chief amongst these is Joyce, who, Raine describes as the writer he most admires.

He credits the acquisition of eyeglasses when he was a student with transforming "familiar fuzzy objects" into "unfamiliar and very sharp" things. Additionally, he claims that "having children" required that he "develop a microscopic eye and a microscopic ear [...] a sensitivity'; once developed, he says, "this attention to small things [...] never really leaves you" (Carey 1991, p. 16). The combination of these two qualities—the defamiliarization of the ordinary, and a hypersensitive attention to detail—informs the aesthetic impulses underlying the largest part of his creative work.

Gavin Ewart, reviewing *The Onion, Memory* in the *Times Literary Supplement,* noted that "there are qualities of thought and control" in the first collection which would have been beyond a younger writer, and "metaphor and simile" are the chief formal techniques at work (Ewart p. 728). Ewart argues, however, that only an educated audience would 'appreciate' Raine's "cleverness". His references, allusions, and language are frequently obscure, or at least require a willingness on the part of the reader to investigate the unknown. Raine's is not "popular" poetry of the John Betjeman variety, and his influence on British poetry over the past three decades is significant.

Divided into six sections, "Yellow Pages", "The Significance of Nothing", "All the Inventory of Flesh", "Pre-Raphaelite Paintings", "Rhyming Cufflinks", and "Anno Domini" (a ten poem cycle paralleling the life of Christ with the life of an English faith healer, modelled on Raine's father), *The Onion, Memory* contains some of Raine's best-known poems. In the first section, "The Butcher" alerts the reader to Raine's radically playful technique, and his dedication to entirely original images. The butcher offers "thin coiled coral necklaces of mince" and "heart lamé-ed from the fridge, a leg of pork/like a nasty bouquet, pound notes printed with blood" (*Onion* p. 2). Raine explains that in writing the "Yellow Pages" section, he was influenced by Picasso's cubist style.

Of "The Butcher," Raine argues that he very carefully describes the man, and by careful he means full of care: it's a tender, teasing poem— the way you tease someone you like'. His reflection of this empirical evidence means that, in Raine's view, he is being faithful to his own observations. The poem's origins, however, are clearly rooted in Raine's interest in Joyce, whose ability to "describe ordinary things and make them terrifically interesting" "completely galvanised" Raine as a student (Carey 1991, p. 18). He has referred many times to the scene in *Ulysses* in which Leopold Bloom 'goes into

Dlugacz's butcher's shop and buys a kidney'; Joyce writes 'nearly a page about the paper being torn, the greaseproof paper wrapping the moist gland, taking the money, the money being read, trickled into the till.' Raine felt that if Joyce could accomplish so much 'with something as ordinary as that, then the whole material of life' would be 'available to [the poet].' Raine's preoccupation with the quotidian is a response to what he sees—or saw in the late 1970s—as the phenomenon of English poetry in particular being 'shrunk into a corner' so that only 'landscape and the weather' were considered suitable subjects (Carey 1991, p. 18).

In "An Enquiry into Two Inches of Ivory", from the second section of *The Onion, Memory,* Raine's preoccupation with defamiliarizing the everyday comes to the fore:

We live in the great indoors:
the vacuum cleaner grazes
over the carpet, lowing,
its udder a swollen wobble...

(*Onion,* p. 10).

The inventive zoomorphism—a vacuum cleaner as grazing cow—opens the world, and the most banal aspects of modern life, to a potentially limitless field of linguistic and allusive play. A lightbulb is an "electric pear" which "ripens" with light, while light switches are "flat-faced/ barn-owls." These, Raine tells us, are all "Daily things. Objects / in the museum of ordinary art" (*Onion,* p. 10).

The ellipsis at the end of the poem's first stanza signals what Raine describes as aposiopesis, the sudden breaking off of speech, which signifies both the artificiality of the poetic form and Raine's tendency to allow ambiguity to function as a creatively destabilizing force in his work, or as David G. Williams suggests, this kind of "ending" means "that no neat summarising closure has been made", and, when such ellipses appear at the end of Raine's poems, as they often do, "the concerns of the poem will continue to resonate unresolved after the formal ending of the poem" (Williams, p. 456).

This new brand of "Martian" poetry, a term borrowed from Raine's second collection, is not without its convinced detractors. Andrew Waterman argues that "[t]he false-naivety inherent in the Martian procedures of defamiliarisation sentimentalises experience at the expense of true emotion', and is "useless for engagement with the moral life that such poetry mostly renounces anyway", while the style "reduces poetry to a parlour game, poems to strings of little visual riddles to be cracked and left emptied shells." Any such formulaic poetry, Waterman argues, can only "aspire to survive as a footnote to literary history" (Waterman, p. 46). Waterman compares Martianism with the early twentieth-century Georgian movement, which also considered its role "as revitalising English poetry, offering something new and unconventional" but which, in his view, only managed "to coordinate the aspirations of a younger generation anxious to make its distinctive mark" (Waterman, p. 47). It is clear that Waterman regards the achievements of Martianism as similarly self-interested.

Waterman contends that Martianism "operates an adaptable formula comprised of two connected tricks": one, "to discover visual likeness between things disparate in kind and context, with a claim thus to supply fresh perception purged of habitual associations," and two, "a more extreme variant" of this, "wherein, by affectation of alien's-eye untutored incomprehension of earthly matters, metaphor enacts inability to make normal sense of commonplace phenomena" (Waterman, p. 43). Dismissively, Waterman suggests that this style is merely "cribbed" from Anglo-Saxon riddles, and accuses Raine and Christopher Reid both of failing "significantly [to] illuminate human experience or enact human vision" (Waterman, p. 44).

Michael Hulse, however, has suggested that the "mixed reception from the Establishment" which greeted Raine's work—and Martianism more generally—was, in part, the result of "a good many poets of less vigorous imagination" feeling "threatened by poetry which so obviously fulfils Aristotle's prescription for genius—that it should possess the gift of making easy metaphoric connection' (Hulse 1983, p. 21). Of "[t]he quick sharp thrusts of [Raine's] couplets and the riddle-maker's precision of his images", Hulse says these "guarantee an agreeable aftertaste": "no one has seen quite as Raine has seen, no one has written as he has written, nor has anyone thought of his indelible images: the secret is his uniqueness" (Hulse 1983, pp. 21–2).

A MARTIAN SENDS A POSTCARD HOME *(1979)*

Raine has described his second collection as sombre and witty, two qualities which, to him, do not seem to be in conflict with each other, although his assessment of conflicting views of, and conflicting linguistic approaches to, describing the world is perhaps more illuminating. In an interview with John Carey, he asserts:

> there's a sort of standard way of looking at things – Oxford and Cambridge, BBC, Foreign Office, MPs—there's clearly an official version of life, which expresses itself in official language, and what interests me is the anonymous. Partly because I come out of the anonymous myself, and I know what vivid humus it is. [...] It's not good enough to say, look, this is an interesting geranium. You actually want the gravel at the bottom and the shards and then the Irish peat or whatever—everything. And there's something about the official record which is edited, abbreviated, censored—and I'm absolutely against censorship. [...] You have to admit what's going on in your head
>
> (Carey 1991, p. 15)

The collection as a whole is informed by an epigraph from James Joyce that describes, in illuminating terms, the very ordinary business of taking a train journey, signaling to the reader that what follows—Raine's poems—will similarly look upon the ordinary from a fresh perspective. "A Martian Sends a Postcard Home," the title poem in the collection, radically destabilizes the reader's expectations. Assuming that the speaking persona is a Martian—either literally or figuratively—the reader's job is to decode the elaborate defamiliarizing metaphors:

> Caxtons are mechanical birds with many wings
> and some are treasured for their markings—
> they cause the eyes to melt
> or the body to shriek without pain.
> I have never seen one fly, but
> sometimes they perch on the hand
>
> (*Martian,* p. 1)

One first has to know that, Caxton, refers to William Caxton, who died in 1492, and was the first English printer. Thus, in this context, "Caxtons" refers to books, "many wings" are pages, and like exotic birds, some books "are treasured" for their bindings, illustrations, and beauty of design, as well as for their contents, stories or poetry or whatever else, which have the power to make one's eyes "melt" or body "shriek"—from emotion in response to the book, rather than physical pain. Elsewhere in the poem, with the conceit firmly established, the Martian explains that "Rain is when the earth is television. / It has the property of making colours darker" and a "Model T"—or a car—"is a room with the lock inside—/ a key is turned to free the world / / for movement" (*Martian* p. 1). The Martian finds that "time is tied to the wrist / or kept in a box, ticking with impatience", while a telephone is "a haunted apparatus" that "sleeps" and, referring to the dial tone, "snores when you pick it up." A trip to the toilet means going "to a punishment room / / with water but nothing to eat", where adults "lock the door and suffer the noises / / alone [...] and everyone's pain has a different smell" (*Martian,* p. 2).

Charles Forceville rather unconvincingly complains of the "degree of arbitrariness" necessary "in selecting the phenomena with which the Martian is acquainted, and those with which he is not," and is worried by what he regards as "inconsistencies" suggestive of "a lack of internal coherence": "the poet has not consistently shown the world from the Martian's point of view" (Forceville, p. 104–5). As Michael Hulse notes, critics "unsympathetic" to the aims of Martian poetry ask "so what?" of this kind of metaphoric playfulness: "The charge against the poets is that their image-making zest and energy constitute shallowness and lack of human feeling." Hulse insists, however, that such charges fail to acknowledge Raine's appropriate "aesthetic context," one in which his images 'recreate (not describe) the object-subject, in which case they give us […] a Rilkean sense of penetration; or they serve as illustrative amplification in the delineation of situation, scene, or even narrative' (Hulse 1983, p. 26).

'Laying a Lawn', dedicated to British novelist Ian McEwan, a friend and contemporary of Raine's, returns to the rich imagery of books as material objects, describing rolls of sod as "crumbling tomes" which the speaker carries "two at a time from the stack", to "lay them open on the ground,"

> like the wordless books
> my daughter lugs about unread
> or tramples underfoot. I stamp
> the simple text of grass
> with woodwormed brogues

(Martian, p. 26)

The poem ends with an unflinching description of his young daughter, "the thin charcoal crucifix / her legs and buttocks make […] her little cunt's neat button-hole, / and the navel's wrinkled pip" (pp. 26–27). Andrew Waterman dismisses this as a "procedure [which] trails jarring conceptual incongruities" (Waterman, p. 45), while Charles Forceville argues that the speaker is "suppress-[ing] thoughts of his daughter's future suffering," as signified by the crucifix imagery (Forceville, p. 113). The speaker asserts that his and his daughter's "bodies are immortal in their ignorance" and concludes ambiguously that "neither one of us can read / this Domesday Book" *(Martian, p. 27)*. Forceville notes that "Domesday Book" refers both to William I's 1086 census in England, as well as "an Old English poem" called "Doomsday" (Forceville, p. 114), mingling the teleological with the ordinary intimacy of gardening.

"In the Dark' recounts a story about a teenage girl who lies "about her age" and has an encounter with a "young Coldstream guard": "Laid out on the grass, / her shrivelled tights, the wings / / of her nylon bra. Virgins" *(Martian, p. 29)*. "Six

months later," she finds herself pregnant, and takes an overdose of aspirin: "God danced on his cross / at the foot her bed / / like Nijinsky having a heart attack…". Michael Hulse describes this as "the finest poem" of the second collection, and while he acknowledges that there is nothing "original" in the story itself, he credits Raine with an exceptionally rendered "felicity that conjures forth every essential element in the narrative in a handful of precisely-chosen words," as well as with realizing that "such images speak for themselves", requiring no "overt moralizing"—something Raine's poetry conspicuously resists (Hulse 1983, p. 26).

The title poem in *A Martian Sends a Postcard Home* won the Prudence Farmer Award in 1978 for the best poem appearing in *The New Statesman,* and "Laying a Lawn" was joint winner of the same prize in 1980. "Flying to Belfast, 1977" and "Mother Dressmaking" won first prizes in the Cheltenham Festival of Literature, 1977 and 1978 respectively, while the collection as a whole won the Southern Arts Literature Prize in 1979.

Reviewing the collection in the *Times Literary Supplement* in 1980, John Bayley argues that, like Donne, Raine creates "popular and highly individualized versions of poetry's most ancient device for turning the unforgiving facts of existence to favour and to prettiness—the riddle", and credits him with having "far too tight a grip of things to need to display feeling," praising the "exoticism" of his "[m]anipulation of comparisons and verbal echoes" (Bayley 1980, p. 5).

RICH (1984)

Raine's third full-length collection, *Rich,* includes an extended prose narrative, "A Silver Plate," which recounts some of the experiences of his childhood and the history of his parents. An epigraph from Saul Bellow's *The Adventures of Augie March* both suggests the extent of the American novelist's influence on Raine's work, as well as rationalizes, as Bellow says, why a writer tells you more about the people who formed him than of the writer himself. During his childhood, Raine says that his father made no money out of faith-healing and the family was poor, living off Norman's pension from the war. Nonetheless, since his father was unemployed, Raine's he was always present, and one might trace the narrative impulse in Raine's verse to his father's talents as a story teller, with a large list of boxing stories. Olive's sewing supplemented the family's income, while his father and uncle performed a double act in concert parties— though these were curtailed by the constant threat of Norman's epileptic fits. Because of the familiarity of these fits Raine does not remember being frightened by them as a child, although his father would sometimes scream, while trying to smash his head on the floor. Olive, meanwhile, suffered from anaemia and depression sewing into the early hours of the morning.

Raine describes his home town as "a typical, ugly small town in the north of England"; Olive 'had social pretensions, looking down on their neighbors—as a result, the Raines weren't popular', and their middle-class neighbors disliked them. Raine admits that he and his brother behaved poorly thanks to their father's unflinching support of his sons against any claims levelled against them as children. Once, Raine attempted to have a birthday party like other children, but in the end only one boy came, without a present, and did nothing but eat.

Raine's was not a literary childhood: there were no books in the home where he lived; his father read popular cowboy stories but stopped when Olive ridiculed him for wasting time. Radio, instead, was the chief form of entertainment, and his mother made the family listen to the Christmas broadcast to the Commonwealth give by the Queen every year—an affectation which Raine links to her sense that her family had fallen from the middle class. His father, however, was not afraid to stand up for the family and as a disabled ex-serviceman, demanded a house. He got one a week later— the prefab Raine lived in until he was eleven.

Apart from the radio, the other chief entertainment of Raine's childhood was the cinema, and he recalls seeing Mario Lanza in *The Great Caruso,* and Jack Palance in *Attila the Hun* and *Apache.* After *Rich,* the influence of cinema, and cinematic techniques, becomes more apparent in

Raine's work. (See *The Electrification of the Soviet Union* and *History: The Home Movie* below). When he was nine, he joined the library and began reading two adventure stories a day for two years. Raine confesses that the most important book in his possession was not a book at all, but a serial comic-book version of Robert Louis Stevenson's novel *Kidnapped,* the pages of which he had torn from the back of a comic book he read at the time called the *Topper.* Once he had all the pages for *Kidnapped,* his mother sewed them together and he spent most of his childhood with the resulting book.

David Bromwich contends that there was some indication as early as *The Onion, Memory* that Raine was, in part, a confessional poet—"in certain respects his work was modelled on Lowell's and Plath's," though he "affected to be affectless" (Bromwich, p. 1193). Bromwich traces the influence of Robert Lowell's *Life Studies* on "A Silver Plate," although he credits Raine with a "much less mannered" prose style, "calm, disciplined and free of cliché."

"A Silver Plate" is book-ended by the sections "Rich" and "Poor," the poems of which tend largely to conform to Raine's established aesthetic, though there is some evidence of a growing preoccupation with the larger sweep of European history in the twentieth century, while in the first section the poems "An Attempt at Jealousy", "Pornography", "Arsehole", and "Gauguin" begin to indicate the extent to which Raine's work is intent on disturbing any anachronistic illusions that poetry need conform to a demure or polite idiom. As Raine himself has argued, 'It's all the inadmissable [sic] stuff that […] it's important to get into poetry, all the inadmissable [sic] evidence, all the evidence against yourself' (Carey 1991, p. 16).

THE ELECTRIFICATION OF THE SOVIET UNION
(1986)

In 1986, Raine's libretto for an opera composed by Nigel Osborne was published by Faber and Faber. Based on *The Last Summer,* Boris Pasternak's semi-autobiographical novella, and Pasternak's poem "Spectorsky", the opera is organized into two Acts and an Epilogue. In his "Production Note" for the libretto, Raine asserts that the adaptation was "conceived not as drama, but as poetic film," and each scene, if staged, calls for the projection of filmed sequences as a scenic backdrop.

John Bayley, assessing Raine's libretto in *Poetry Review,* explains that "Lenin is said to have remarked that Electrification + Soviets = Communism" (Bayley 1986, p. 11). Set in the winter of 1916 in Ousolie, Russia, with flashbacks to May and June 1914 and an epilogue in the early 1920s, the action of Raine's libretto centers around Serezha Spectorsky, a poet (and Pasternak alter ego), his sister, Natasha, and his relationship with a wealthy bourgeois family, the Frestlns. Bayley notes the "echoes of 'spectre' and 'spectator'"" in Spectorsky's name, which "gives its own meaning to the piece" (Bayley 1986, p. 11). Throughout the opera, the figure of Pasternak sits at a table on stage, writing the action that is taking place in front of the audience. The result, Ian Gregson argues, is that "three authors are in conversation with each other—one implied (Raine) one dramatised (Pasternak) and one prospective (Serezha)," so that the opera's "central theme" is Serezha's "prospectiveness" as an author, showing "how authors assimilate the voices of others" (Gregson, p. 141).

Serezha, who has failed the medical examination for military service, arrives in Ousolie after a three-day train journey. He tells Natasha that he is haunted by the wounded soldiers he has seen, but recognizes that he is only fitted for the trade of the useless intellectual. At Natasha's dacha, or country house, she receives a phone call (a sign of electrification which surprises Serezha) from Lemokh, a menacing student and symbol of the imminent revolution. Natasha tells her brother that Lemokh is coming for dinner and warns Serezha that Lemokh is practical and not a dreamer like Serezha.

This seems to spur Serezha's memory of 1914, when he worked as private tutor to the Frestln family, who are assumed by other characters to be Jewish. During the flashback, Serezha is infatuated with the family's governess, Anna Arild, who is in mourning for her dead husband and despises the Frestlns because they treat her like a chambermaid. Serezha comes to the Frestlns defense, but Anna is implacable.

Serezha encourages Anna to confide in him, and during a trip to a lake in the countryside, she tells him about her dead husband; Serezha tries to kiss her, but she slaps him and leaves.

Act Two, remaining in Serezha's flashback to 1914, begins with him visiting a prostitute, Sashka, with whom he is in love. Shortly after Serezha leaves Sashka's flat, police arrive to arrest her in the middle of the night. Meanwhile, Anna threatens to leave the Frestlns when their son, Harry, falls ill, and Mrs. Frestln begs her to stay. When Serezha returns to their house, he finds the Frestlns gone, and Anna sick in bed, hot with fever. He asks her to marry him, but while he is busy writing, she sneaks out of the house with her suitcase. Act Two ends with a return to 1916 and Natasha introducing Lemokh to Serezha, who refuses to shake his hand.

In the Epilogue, Serezha returns, after the Revolution, to the Frestlns' house where he finds Anna, now a fearsome party official, overseeing the dismantling of the property; she explains that the Frestlns were traitors to the state and, as such, their property must be confiscated. Serezha protests that they were his friends and Anna says, menacingly, that evidence is incriminating. She tells him to leave, promising to destroy the album containing the pictures. Serezha departs, but Lemokh, who is making an inventory of the Frestlns' belongings, takes the album from Anna before she has the opportunity to destroy it.

In a review of the Glyndebourne Touring Opera production in October 1987, Christopher Wintle describes it as "curiously underachieved" and he notes Raine's rebuttal, in his preface to the published libretto, of W. H. Auden's view that a good libretto places its characters in situations which are too tragic or fantastic for words, and his attempt to "redeem poetic drama for our time." Wintle identifies Raine's effort as "firmly in a Russian operatic tradition stemming from [Aleksandr Sergeyevich] Dargomizhsky," the nineteenth-century Russian nationalist composer, among whose works was an adaptation of Pushkin's play *The Stone Guest.* Wintle notes that

Pasternak's *The Last Summer* was "itself a loose conglomeration of episodes (though its title still seems more appropriate than Raine's Lenin-inspired replacement)" and charges Raine with clinging "too faithfully to the profusion of character and incident" of Pasternak's story "without fleshing out the main action sufficiently", with the result that, as performed, "the narrative is incomprehensible without reference, not merely to the libretto, but to the novella as well." Wintle suggests that Raine's libretto is "so terse that it might flourish better without music," but that it remains notable for "the very delightful and poignant quality of the lyrics" (Wintle, p. 1141).

John Bayley has expressed more fulsome praise for Raine's text, asserting that his "poetry here is so good, so superbly forceful and complete" that he finds it difficult "to imagine any music which would not diminish it" Bayley thought it the best poetry Raine then had written, "as good as the best of [W.H.] Auden in the same vein' though "completely itself, wholly original" (Bayley 1986, p. 11). Bayley sees in Raine's formal and stylistic technique a concern with "the poetic temperament of the young Pasternak", and intriguingly notes that Raine's octosyllabic line "comes most naturally to Russian, and is used by Pasternak himself" as well as by Pushkin "whose marvellous little dramatic compositions [...] like *Rusalka*, have a decided affinity with some of Raine's best effects" (Bayley 1986, p. 12). Bayley contends that *The Electrification of the Soviet Union* "hangs together with absolute precision" and as a "poetic drama [...] is complete and perfect" (Bayley 1986, p. 12).

In an interview conducted at the time of the libretto's publication, Raine argued that the formal constraints of opera negate the possibility of using "difficult metaphors that people would have to puzzle over"—the very kinds of metaphors which characterized his work up to this point. Moreover, he thought it necessary "to write songs in character", and since "most of [the] songs" in the opera were "written for people who would naturally express themselves simply" he chose "a rhetoric of plainness." The exception is Serezha Spectorsky, who, as "a poet [...] can borrow [Raine's] style" with the addition of "turbulence and an adolescent eloquence" suitable for the character's age—qualities which Raine regards as "slightly comical", and intended to "undercut" Serezha (Forbes, p. 10).

'1953', A VERSION OF RACINE'S ANDROMAQUE *(1990)*

In 1987, British theater and opera director Jonathan Miller commissioned Raine to translate seventeenth-century French playwright Jean Racine's version of the Greek tragedy (itself adapted from a version of the story by Euripides), intended for production at London's Old Vic theatre in 1988. Raine reports that "Miller wanted a clean, modern translation," one that eliminated the "thees" and "thous'"" of other translations. He attempted "about one act of straight translation into rhyming octosyllabics," the same form he had used for *The Electrification of the Soviet Union,* but found himself "bored"; he also "wanted to use [his] own language, [his] own contemporary speech" (Carey 1991, p. 18), and "realized that Miller's simple request was impossible" because Racine's idiom and imagery was so firmly rooted in the seventeenth century. Any attempt to render it in English would result in "an idiom which is neither contemporary nor anything approaching Racine's poetic diction, either in its genuine reach or in its artificiality." "The solution," Raine decided, "was to update the entire piece in order to use contemporary English fearlessly." As a translator, he says he felt the "need to create space for [himself] as a writer" because "there is a sort of egotism of the imagination," and, with translation, the translator has to "shove the other writer to one side". "Miller disagreed", however, and used a "more literal translation" by Eric Korn.

Raine's "free version" is set "in a fictitious 1953," hence the quotation marks around the date in the title, signifying a 1953 in which Britain has surrendered to the Axis powers, and World War II continues on the Russian front (*In Defence* pp. 24–5). Ultimately, Raine's adaptation was broadcast on BBC Radio 3 in 1990, and staged by Glasgow Citizens' Theatre in 1991, and by

London's Almeida Theatre in 1996, in a production directed by British playwright Patrick Marber.

As Guy Snaith suggests, in Raine's version London stands for Racine's Troy, Rome for Epirus, Nazi Germany for Greece (Snaith 1996, p. 15). Winston Churchill has died by inhaling his own vomit while passed out drunk, and Benito Mussolini has been succeeded by his son, Vittorio (Pyrrhus), who is in love with Annette LeSkye (Andromaque), the Jewish widow of English aristocrat Hector LeSkye (who Vittorio killed). In Rome, Annette and her son, Angus, claimant to the English throne, are both being held prisoner by Vittorio, who has promised to marry his mistress, German Princess Ira (Hermione), as a means of reinforcing the weakening Italo-German alliance. The play's action is triggered by the arrival of Princess Ira's cousin, Count Klaus Maria von Orestes, who is unrequitedly in love with her. Von Orestes demands that Vittorio turn over Angus LeSkye to Germany so that he can be exterminated because he is half-Jewish. Vittorio resists von Orestes, but gives Annette an ultimatum: unless she agrees to marry Vittorio, he will give Angus to the Germans. At first, Annette refuses, but eventually sees that she must consent, although she plans to kill herself after the marriage when Angus's safety is assured. Princess Ira, however, learning of Vittorio's plan to marry Annette, orders von Orestes to kill Vittorio, determined that no one should have him if she cannot. Thus, von Orestes kills Vittorio after his wedding to Annette LeSkye, and Princess Ira subsequently commits suicide.

Ian Gregson argues that *"1953"*, along with Raine's libretto for *The Electrification of the Soviet Union,* is a natural outgrowth of the poet's interest in "the juxtaposition of viewpoints," as "the clashing of points of view can be given theatrical form" and the dramatic form "averts" the "dangers" of a "claustropobic and distortive" "lyric selfhood" (Gregson, p. 130). Gregson argues that "the dramatic world" of Raine's version of Racine's play "is in dialogue with several other dramatic worlds—with Racine's *Andromaque',* as well as with the real history of World War II and the post-war period, with the result that "the premise" of Raine's version "can only be fully understood in the perspectives of the past and of other possible versions of the present" (Gregson, p. 130).

Snaith notes that Raine's version follows the structure of Racine's, with five acts, and scenes which "follow the order" of the original, although Raine does not adhere to "principles of French scenic division" (Snaith 1991, p. 144). Snaith, however, is unconvinced by Raine's directorial intrusions in the stage directions, including details of "cigarettes, evening gowns and shagreen compacts", which he feels suggest "Hollywood melodrama," a kind of "tinselly vulgarity" which infuses the drama with "a spurious glamour" (Snaith 1991, p. 145). Nevertheless, the Racinian theme of unrequited love is still intact in Raine's version and "[c]ruelty and suffering" remain the chief elements of characterisation, while Raine's formal technique foregrounds the characters' "sexuality, viciousness and desperation" (Snaith 1991, p. 146-48).

HISTORY: THE HOME MOVIE *(1994)*

A novel in verse, blending and fictionalizing the histories of Raine's own family with that of his wife, *History: The Home Movie* takes Europe in the twentieth century as its canvas and tracks the lives of the Pasternaks in their migrations from Russia to Germany to England, and the Raines from the north of England to Oxford. As Raine explains in his essay "Aristotle," the book "is partly about the Pasternaks, my wife's famous relations, and partly about my own much more ordinary family," although Raine does not consider the Raines in the least ordinary (*In Defence,* p. 514).

Dense with personal signification, which often slips into opacity, the poem is effectively a sequence of images or moments whose narrative purpose is not always clear. The book is less a linear narrative with a discernible plot than an imagistic series of snapshots, or, indeed, *home movies* (with the fractured, collage-like quality suggested by the term) of various moments in the lives of the Raines and Pasternaks.

Beginning with "1905: A Dacha by the Black Sea," Raine imagines his wife's grandparents, Rosalia and Leonid Pasternak, at home with their children. The intimacies of domestic life are immediately juxtaposed against the century's threat of impending conflict. The speaking persona of this first poem appears to shift between Raine's own objective narration and that of Leonid, an accomplished painter.

This immediately establishes the larger concerns of the book—the personal versus the "historical"—and suggests that Raine occupies a position analogous to Leonid's: a poet-as-painter of the story which will unfold, brooding and forensic in its detail, concerned with beauty but also with the banal specificities of everyday life, the inevitable "turds" of living which can be transformed into a work of art, and the filth of the twentieth century.

Amongst the more memorable and affecting sections of the novel is "1934: Answer the Telephone," in which Boris Pasternak, Leonid's son, receives a phone call from Stalin, to ask him if the poet Osip Mandelstam, who wrote a satirical attack on the Soviet leader, is a genius.

Nonetheless, despite his jealousy Boris confirms that Mandelstam *is* a genius, and only then does he realize that Stalin is asking not because he wishes to honor Mandelstam, but because he wants to know if he can safely *eliminate* the poet. In crediting him with genius, Boris saves the other poet's life, although not his liberty. As John Bayley argues of Raine's treatment of this well-known conversation, "it pungently makes the point that all poets cannot help being more interested in their own reputations than in those of their fellows,' while simultaneously being 'fascinated and seduced in the presence of power" (Bayley 1995, p. 54).

Elsewhere, in "1935: Who was Bismarck?", Raine imagines his wife's father, Eliot, a psychiatrist with eugenicist sympathies, on the verge of marrying Boris's sister, Lydia Pasternak. Eliot reflects on Germany's then recently established anti-Semitic laws stating that full Jews and half Jews must marry full Jews only and acknowledges Lydia's Jewishness.

Later we learn of Eliot's infidelities, and ultimately see, in "1971: Constance", the family journey—and history itself—coming full circle, with Lydia's daughter's visit to Russia in 1971, and her meeting with Osip Mandelstam's widow, Nadezhda. Once again, the intimate personal detail reverberates against the reader's knowledge of the historical events which precede and inform it.

While the book clearly has considerable personal significance for Raine himself, and is remarkably ambitious in its scope, there is little narrative coherence, and it is often difficult to know with any certainty what is happening, or even which of the many "characters" outlined in the family tree at the front of the book features in a given section. Rather than struggling to follow the impressionist narrative line, readers should see the book as an evocative sequence of images which demonstrate Raine's astute eye for the illuminating detail.

Critical reception of the work has been decidedly mixed. Michael Hofman, reviewing Raine's *Collected Poems* in *The Observer,* ungenerously dismisses *History* (included in full in the volume) as "a litany of insignificant and overspecified detail, sexual activity and laboured italics in between the now routine similes," characterized by "reductive and soulless commentary" (Hofman, online). John Bayley is less dismissive in his 1995 review, although his earlier enthusiasm for Raine is clearly dampened. He argues, correctly, that *History* belongs not to "poetic modernism", but to "postmodernism, where everything goes, provided it makes an impact on cue, and in the surprised moment." Of Raine's "home movie" trope, Bayley claims that the poet's "projector reels on erratically, careless of whether the picture makes sense or not"; what matters is that readers "register" the work's "vividness in their gasps or laughs or sniggers." He worries, however, that the result is "very repetitive and physical," and that the "novelty [...] soon begins to wear off," in spite of the obvious "authority" of the work—which he locates in its originality of form and intent. What most worries Bayley is what he perceives as the limitations of Martianism as a style, arguing that "when there

CRAIG RAINE

is no point" underlying the trick of defamiliarizing the familiar, then "this verbal nose-picking can become as wearisome for the reader as the mechanical rhythm of the home movie itself", so that it becomes little more than "a clever machine" (Bayley 1995, p. 54).

CLAY. WHEREABOUTS UNKNOWN *(1996)*

Raine explains on the cover copy of the Penguin edition of his most recent full collection that the poems in *Clay. Whereabouts Unknown* "were written in the decade" he spent working on *History: The Home Movie,* a period in which "two sons were born, one of whom sparked off" the seven-part poem "The Prophetic Book" first published in Poland in 1986. Raine describes "The Prophetic Book" as an expression "of sustained wonder at the world—its limitless, offhand beatitudes, its mysteries and its bleak brevities". Alongside the birth of two sons, the decade also saw the deaths of "many loved friends," including his wife's parents, and an "old love," Kitty Mrosovsky, who later became the subject of his 1999 poem *A la recherche du temps perdu..* The British Penguin edition is illustrated with a photograph of the artwork *Etude d'Expression,* 1900—a work made of clay, its whereabouts unknown.

"The Prophetic Book," first published in 1988 in Lódz, Poland, in a large-format limited edition with linocut illustrations by Krzysztof Wawrzyniak, with a parallel translation by Polish poet Jerzy Jarniewicz, moves through seven discrete narrative territories. The poem begins with a section titled *The Prophetic Book,* in which the speaker promises the world to his audience— implicitly, perhaps, the son Raine mentions in the blurb.

After the vast canvas of *History,* it initially appears that Raine has returned to the more intimate territory of his earlier work—the turban suggesting segmented fruit, suspensory bandages for ball baskets, "the lemon squeezer" representing the plastic shields which cover urinal drains in Britain. *Sheol,* the second section, however, returns to the kinds of historical concerns that featured in Raine's epic; its speaking persona is a

woman in a Nazi concentration camp, with a newborn baby. In his notes at the back of the volume, Raine explains that the content of *Sheol* is mostly taken from the testimony of Ruth Elias, a survivor of Dr. Josef Mengele's Birkenau who participated in the mock-trial at Jerusalemin 1985. Raine was unable to forget the testimony he heard on the BBC's "International Assignment." The third section, *Limbo,* places itself in Oxford, and, through a meditation on aging, laments the death of a friend.

The fourth section, *Shaman,* is informed by Raine's wide reading on shamanism, but appears to be rooted in his own boyhood experience of Roman Catholicism. The speaker has a shaman-like vision, in which he could see his dead sister, who died at the age of three, before he was ever born. He then moves on to more elaborately imagine being his parents.

The fifth section, *Paradise,* is more abstract, apparently addressed to a lover, or perhaps his wife. The sixth section, *A Chest of Drawers,* is a further meditation on death, prompted by the death of a friend's mother. *Coda,* the four-line final section sounds a hopeful, if, suitably for Raine, understated note of death and forgiveness.

Collectively, the seven sections of 'The Prophetic Book' seem to suggest, as Raine's own blurb does, a growing preoccupation with mortality, but also with the life cycle more generally, and human cruelty, isolation, and the great mysteriousness of family constellations, as well as a continued emphasis on the juxtaposition of intimate domestic moments against the sweep of history, though in this instance, history, as represented by *Sheol,* is kept discrete from the more personal intimacies of the other six sections—an unsettling reminder, perhaps, of humanity's remarkable talent for atrocity.

A LA RECHERCHE DU TEMPS PERDU *(1999)*

Raine's most recent volume of verse borrows its title from Marcel Proust's epic multi-volume semi-autobiographical novel of remembrance, though Raine's poem is defiantly seven-hundred lines in length—forty-one pages in its slim Picador edition. First published in the inaugural edition of Raine's own tri-quarterly literary journal, *Areté* (and, under the title "The Way it Was", in the short-lived American periodical *Talk Magazine*), the poem was received with both admiration and outrage. Its off-rhymed couplets are addressed to a dead lover widely recognized as the former academic, novelist, and translator Catherine "Kitty" Mrosovsky. Raine met Mrosovsky in 1967, and they dated for several years. Although unnamed in the poem at the request of her family—Mrosovsky died from an AIDS-related illness in 1995—there is no mystery about the identity of the poem's subject.

Raine does not flinch from describing the intimacies of his relationship with Mrosovsky and the poem functions both as confession and elegy. The jacket blurb on the Picador edition insists that "[b]ecause it takes commemoration seriously," the poem "extends the boundaries of the elegy" by attempting "to restore the lost person—in all her beauty, her difficulty, her charm, her formidable complexity, her sexuality, in all her reality." Sexuality and reality are chief amongst the poem's narrative and aesthetic concerns and, as such, have been the focus of hostile criticism. Beginning with Mrosovsky's cremation in London, the speaker laments the dead lover's absence. Appropriately, the intimate details of the relationship, which unfold over the length of the poem, sustain the promise of irritation and insolubility, even when recalling the occasion when Mrosovsky revealed that she had AIDS.

The colloquial language of the piece works both to situate the poem in a specifically British geographic and social context (Mrosovsky is presented as a kind of upper-middle class bohemian) and to ground her sexual affairs in the quotidian, even the routine. Answering charges of racism for his use of the term "black boys" in the poem, Raine insists that, for him, the term "black" is neutral and, far from functioning satirically, he argues that the phrase was the most economical way of conveying the information (Billen p. 7).

Rather than wallowing in any lurid imagining of the nature of his past lover's affairs with other men, the speaker is haunted by the very fact of Mrosovsky's promiscuity, so that at the funeral he was unable to cry. The juxtaposition of his understandable worries about his own health, with references to twentieth-century Czech poet Miroslav Holub and nineteenth-century English critic and artist John Ruskin, suggests a collision of aesthetic with more mortal concerns. Recalling Mrosovksy writing on an occasion, Raines writes of the density of signification that reinforces Mrosovsky's cosmopolitan social position (via the Sheaffer pen), but also sexualizes the whole of her person in the same moment that it fuses a memory of her alive with the unshakeable reality of her death. Sex, in this case, is conflated with death.

With direct references to several living writers, the social and literary context of the poem's narrative space is determinedly specific. The speaker accuses Mrosovsky of being "a literary snob" and specific references to Martin Amis, Julian Barnes, and Ian McEwan are set in contrast with the dead Mrosovky's translation of Gustave Flaubert's "foie gras text" *La Tentation de Saint Antoine* (*The Temptation of Saint Anthony*)—her drafts of which he had "gagged at"—and publication in 1985 of a novel, *Hydra,* "which was 'ambitious' and unreadable" even to the speaker, who suspected he "might have a walk-on part." Nonetheless, the speaker realizes that his ex-lover's literary efforts were comparatively 'trivial," because, by then, Mrosovsky knew that she had AIDS, her "ex-, the black bisexual" having "died in the States."

As if to explain (or perhaps defend) the title of the poem, the speaker records that Proust's novel was Mrosovsky's "favourite book", the fourth volume, *Sodome et Gomorrhe,* kept in the bathroom, "beside the loo." This might be read as a wry anticipation of critical hostility to the poem, as if Raine's own borrowing of the title of Proust's masterpiece for a work so spare and unapologetically naked in its physical descriptions had also sullied great art.

Writing in *The Guardian*, novelist Lucretia Stewart vaguely describes *A la recherche du temps perdu* as "pretty yucky," identifying this aesthetic undesirability as the reason why writers like Amis, McEwan, and Barnes have championed Raine (Stewart, online). Stewart compares the physical detail of Raine's poem with the work of English painter Lucian Freud, arguing that it provides "the kind of physical detail" that one would prefer not to have, and that the work belongs to the "[s]chool of ultra-realism," exploring not only AIDS but "genital herpes, eczema, athlete's foot and a cold." (Equally, one might trace the influence of hyper-realist Australian sculptor Ron Mueck, whom Raine admires.) Although acknowledging that some "will praise" the "frankness and honesty" of the poem, Stewart criticises Raine for "laddish arrogance," which she spuriously locates not only in the poem itself, "but in the fact of the writing" of the poem, the very act of *choosing* to write about a dead lover, the result of which, she charges, is the objectification of Mrosovsky.

Several months after Stewart's article appeared, Andrew Billen interviewed Raine for Glasgow's *Sunday Herald*. Seeking to clarify the circumstances of the poem's composition—as well as the nature of his relationship with Mrosovsky—Raine explains that he felt "a sort of responsibility" to remember the individual, who, "apart from [his] wife' was "the single most important person in [his] life" and "a great educational force". Raine describes himself when he first met Mrosovsky as being "a benighted provincial" while she was a "wonderful, cosmopolitan person who'd lived all over the world and was full of style and beauty and panache." The poem was an attempt "to be true to the relationship" and, he asserts, was not "written for moral simpletons" who

> want me to say that what I felt at the funeral was grief. What I felt at the funeral was grief and worry. My favourite bit of literature— the bit I would stand by—is John Donne on prayer. He says how difficult it is to pray because there are so many things on your mind. You are trying to speak to God but you are thinking about what happened yesterday, what's going to happen tomorrow and the piece of straw

> under your knee. It seems to me this is what great literature is. I'm not saying I write great literature, but the aim is also to include the piece of straw under the knee
>
> (Billen p. 7).

Raine once argued that a limited array of "certain emotions" such as "sadness" and "love" tend to be what the average readers of poetry are expected "to feel," or indeed to expect from the poetry they read. These, however, Raine regards as "a miserable choice of all the emotions one feels." In his later poetry, he clearly works to acknowledge and incorporate a wider range of human feeling, from the extreme to the banal— emotions like "anger, boredom, chilliness" which are so often excluded from poetry, and which necessarily feature in his project to accommodate and demand from poetry as a form "an absolute pursuit of the truth" (Carey 1991, p. 16).

THE POET AS CRITIC

Alongside his creative output, Raine has produced a considerable body of criticism, collected in two large volumes, *Haydn and the Valve Trumpet* (1986), and *In Defence of T.S. Eliot* (2000), as well as the critical monograph *T.S. Eliot* (2006). In 1999, Raine founded the literary journal *Areté: The Arts Tri-Quarterly,* establishing a unique arena for sharp and often unforgiving attacks on academic, critical, or artistic laxity, shoddiness, or outright failure, as well as a venue for the publication of new poetry, drama, fiction, and reportage. *Areté* has published work from an impressively eclectic group of writers including Ian McEwan, Martin Amis, Patrick Marber, Harold Pinter, William Boyd, Frederic Raphael, Wendy Cope, Peter Ho Davies, Timothy Garton Ash, Julian Barnes, Christopher Logue, David Lodge, Simon Armitage, David Hare, Ronald Harwood, and Tom Stoppard.

In a 1995 afterword to Vladimir Nabokov's novel *Lolita*, Raine wrote that Nabokov "is often described as a master of English," although Raine considers this "an accolade too bland to mean very much." Rather, he argues, with typical metaphoric panache, Nabokov was "a valet of English—constantly attentive to the nap of his high quality material, tweaking here, arranging there, burnishing every button, leaving nothing to chance, devoted to every detail. *Conscious*" (*Lolita* p. 330). It is a commonplace that a writer's criticism often illuminates his or her own work as much as the other writer's, and with Raine that is frequently the case. In both his poetry and criticism, he devotes himself to the minute detail, leaving nothing to chance, conscious both of the weight of English literary history and achievement that informs his own now sizeable achievement, as well as his place within it.

Selected Bibliography

WORKS OF CRAIG RAINE

POETRY

The Onion, Memory (Oxford: Oxford University Press, 1978)

A Martian Sends a Postcard Home (Oxford: Oxford University Press, 1979).

A Free Translation (Edinburgh: The Salamander Press, 1981).

Rich (London: Faber and Faber, 1984).

The Prophetic Book, trans. Jerzy Jarniewicz, illus. Krzysztof Wawrzyniak (Lódz, Poland: Correspondance des Arts II, 1989).

History: The Home Movie (London: Penguin Books, 1994).

Clay. Whereabouts Unknown (London: Penguin Books, 1996).

Collected Poems 1978–1999 (London: Picador, 2000).

A la recherche du temps perdu (London, Basingstoke & Oxford: Picador, 2000).

WORKS FOR THE STAGE

The Electrification of the Soviet Union (London: Faber and Faber, 1986).

"1953" A Version of Racine's Andromaque (London: Faber and Faber, 1990).

CRITICISM

"An Old Fashioned Radical: Richard Ellmann and Craig Raine on James Joyce", *Times Literary Supplement* 4114,

5 February 1982, 136.

"Introduction," in Kipling, Rudyard, *A Choice of Kipling's Prose,* selected by Craig Raine (London: Faber and Faber, 1987), 1-33.

William Golding (London: Book Trust in conjunction with the British Council, 1988).

"Introduction," in Chekhov, Anton, *My Life and Other Stories,* trans. Constance Garnett (London: Everyman's Library, 1992), vii-xx.

"Introduction," James Joyce, *Ulysses* (1922), (London: Everyman's Library, 1992), vii-xxv.

"Introduction," Lawrence, D.H., *Collected Stories* (London: Everyman's Library, 1994).

"Afterword," in Nabokov, Vladimir, *Laughter in the Dark,* (1938), (London: Penguin, 1998), 189-99.

Haydn & The Valve Trumpet (London: Faber and Faber, 1990).

"Afterword," in Nabokov, Vladimir, *Lolita,* (1959) (1995; London: Penguin Books, (2000), 319-31.

In Defence of T.S. Eliot (London: Picador, 2000).

T. S. Eliot (Oxford: Oxford University Press, 2006).

MISCELLANEOUS

1985 Anthology: The Observer & Ronald Duncan Foundation International Poetry Competition, selected by Amy Clampitt, Anne Stevenson, Craig Raine (London: Arvon Foundation, 1987).

Kipling, Rudyard, *Selected Poetry,* ed. Craig Raine (London: Penguin, 1992).

Pasternak, Evgeny, *Boris Pasternak, The Tragic Years 1930-1960,* trans. Michael Duncan, poetry trans. by Craig Raine and Ann Pasternak Slater (London: Collins Harvill, 1990).

Raine, Craig, *A Reader's Companion to "History: The Home Movie"* (New York: Doubleday, 1994).

—— "Lunching for literature - Craig Raine on the Magazine Diet that has him losing pounds", *New Statesman,* 17 January 2000, 43–4 [on *Areté*].

CRITICAL AND BIOGRAPHICAL STUDIES

Bayley, John, "Making it Strange", *Times Literary Supplement,* 4 January 1980, 5 [Review of *A Martian Sends a Postcard Home*].

—— ";Zhivaya Zhizn", *Poetry Review* 76/4, December 1986, 11-12 [Review of *The Electrification of the Soviet Union*].

—— "A Moment's Truth", *New York Review of Books* 42/5, 23 March 1995, 54 [Review of *History: The Home Movie*].

Benfey, Christopher, "Family Values", *The New Republic* 211/15, 10 October 1994, 47.

Billen, Andrew, "Poetry, Emotion", *The Sunday Herald,* 16 July 2000, 7.

Binyon, T.J., "Kipling, the blush-making prophet", *Times Literary Supplement,* 5 June 1987, 608 [Review of *A Choice of Kipling's Prose*].

Birkerts, Sven, "Craig Raine's "In the Kalahari Desert'"", *Ploughshares* 13/4, 1987, 154ndash;61.

Bromwich, David, "Tricks and treats", *Times Literary Supplement,* 19 October 1984, 1193 [Review of *Rich*].

Carey, John, *Craig Raine* (London: Book Trust in conjunction with the British Council, 1988).

—— "Face to Face. A conversation between Craig Raine and John Carey", *The English Review* 1/4, April 1991, 18.

Cunningham, Valentine, "Martian Poetry", *European English Messenger* 1/2, Spring 1992, 4ndash;8.

Delgado, Violeta, 'Anonymous Deaths: A Reading of Derek Mahon's 'A Refusal to Mourn' and Craig Raine's 'In the Mortuary,'" *Miscelánea: A Journal of English and American Studies* 18, 1997, 55ndash;67.

Eckle, Elfriede, *Die poetische Darstellung veränderter visueller Wahrnehmung im Zeitalter der Technik: eine komparatistische Analyse von Bildern aus Gedichten des englischen Lyrikers Craig Raine* (Berlin: Logos, 1999).

Ewart, Gavin, "References Back", *Times Literary Supplement,* 30 June 1978, 728 [review of *The Onion, Memory*].

Forbes, Peter, "A Martian at Glyndebourne", *Poetry Review* 76/4, December 1986, 7ndash;11 [Interview with Craig Raine].

Forceville, Charles, "Craig Raine's Poetry of Perception: Imagery in *A Martian Sends a Postcard Home*", *Dutch Quarterly Review of Anglo-American Letters* 15/2, 1985, 102ndash;15.

Gregson, Ian, "But Who Is Speaking?: 'Novelisation' in the Poetry of Craig Raine, *English* 41/170, Summer 1992, 127ndash;47.

Gunn, Thom, *Thom Gunn & Craig Raine* [sound recording] (London: Faber and Faber, 1983).

Haffenden, John, *Viewpoints. Poets in Conversation with John Haffenden* (London: Faber and Faber, 1981).

Haya, Kenichi, "Craig Raine", *Oberon: Magazine for the Study of English and American Literature* 46, 1983, 73ndash;89.

Hayes, Max Hunter, *"At a slight angle to the universe:" Martianism and cultural deracination in the works of Martin Amis, Craig Raine and Christopher Reid, 1977-1984,* Thesis (Ph. D.), University of Southern Mississippi, 2003.

Heaney, Seamus, "The Glamour of Craig Raine," *Ploughshares* 13/4, 1987, 162ndash;66.

Hermans, Theo, "Craig Raine: Het oog van de marsbewoner," *Nieuw Vlaams Tijdschrift* 36/1, January-February 1983, 1–20.

Hofman, Michael, "Raine, Raine, go away&," *the observer,* 3 december 2002, online: http://books.guardian.co.uk/reviews/poetry/0,,405948,00.html.

hulse, michael, "Alms for Every Beggared Sense: Craig Raine's Aesthetic in Context", *Critical Quarterly* 23/4, 1981 Winter, 13ndash;21.

—— The Dialectic of the Image: Notes on the Poetry of Craig Raine and Christopher Reid', *Malahat Review* 64, February 1983, 20ndash;27.

—— "Craig Raine & Co.: Martians and Story-tellers", *The Antigonish Review* 59, Autumn 1984, 21ndash;30.

—— "Craig Raine", in Sherry, Vincent B., Jr. (ed.), *Poets of Great Britain and Ireland since 1960,* Vol. II (Ann Arbor, MI: Gale, 1985), 454–59.

—— "Sitting on Craig Raine"s Ars Poetica', *European English Messenger* 1/2, Spring 1992, 9–11.

Jarniewicz, Jerzy, *The uses of the commonplace in contemporary British poetry: Larkin, Dunn and Raine* (Lódz : Wydawnictwo Uniwersytetu Lódzkiego, 1994).

Karr, Mary, "An Interview with Craig Raine', *Ploughshares* 13/4, 1987, 138–48.

Kermode, Frank, "*History: The Home Movie*" [Review], *The London Review of Books* 16/18, 22 September 1994, 3.

Kerrigan, John, "Notes from the Home Front: Contemporary British Poetry", *Essays in Criticism* LIV/2, April 2004, 103–27.

Levi, Peter, "*History: The Home Movie*" [Review], *The Spectator* 273/8670, 10 September 1994, 32.

Lux, Thomas, "On Craig Raine", *Ploughshares* 13/4, 1987, 149–53.

Mangan, Gerald, "*A la recherche du temps perdu*" [Review], *Times Literary Supplement* 5085, 2000, 3.

Moody, A.D., "Telling It Like It's Not: Ted Hughes and Craig Raine", *Yearbook of English Studies* 17, 1987, 166–78.

O'Brien, Sean, "*Clay. Whereabouts Unknown*" [Review], *Times Literary Supplement* 4866, 1996, 3.

Osborne, John, "The Incredulous Eye: Craig Raine and Post-Modernist Aesthetics", *Stone Ferry Review* 2, 1978, 51–65.

Porter, Andrew, "*Electrification of the Soviet Union*" [Review], *Times Literary Supplement* 5181, 2002, 18.

Rawson, Claude, "Punch Lines", *Times Literary Supplement,* 15-21 June 1990, 627 [review of *Haydn and the Valve Trumpet*].

Robinson, Alan, "Theatre of Trope: Craig Raine and Christopher Reid" in *Instabilities in Contemporary British Poetry* (Basingstoke and London: Macmillan Press Ltd., 1988), 16–48.

Sauerberg, Lars Ole, "Repositioning Narrative: The Late-Twentieth-Century Verse Novels of Vikram Seth, Derek Walcott, Craig Raine, Anthony Burgess, and Bernadine Evaristo" *Orbis Litterarum* 59/6, 2004, 439–64.

Snaith, Guy, "Andromache, Annette and *Andromaque*: A Look at two recent translations", *Seventeenth-Century French Studies* 13, 1991, 139–52.

—— "1953: An *Andromaque* for Our Times", *French Studies Bulletin. A Quarterly Supplement* 59, Summer 1996, 15–16.

Stewart, Lucretia, "Verse Confessions", *The Guardian,* 25 November 1999, online: http://books.guardian.co.uk/departments/poetry/story/0,6000,107687,00.html.

Tanner, Michael, "Arts – Opera: *The Electrification of the Soviet Union*; *Xerxes*", *The Spectator,* 16 November 2002, 69.

Waterman, Andrew, "Martian Invasion", *Helix* 17, 1984, 42–8.

Williams, David G., "Elizabeth Bishop and the 'Martian' Poetry of Craig Raine and Christopher Reid", *English Studies: A Journal of English Language and Literature* 78/5, September 1997, 451–58.

Wintle, Christopher, "Pre-revolutionary problems", *Times Literary Supplement,* 16–22 October 1987, 1141 [Review of *The Electrification of the Soviet Union*].

DOROTHY RICHARDSON

(1873–1957)

Patricia B. Heaman

DOROTHY RICHARDSON WAS in the vanguard of a generation of British women whose lives, by choice or necessity, differed sharply from those of their Victorian predecessors. She discovered that breaking with the traditions she was expected to inherit launched her on an exciting and liberating venture that marked an extraordinary change in women's lives and consciousness. Like Virginia Woolf (1882–1941) and Katherine Mansfield (1888–1923), who followed in directions Richardson had mapped, she learned that these newly created female lives required new literary forms and methods to express the experiences she and other women felt compelled to record in fiction, autobiography, essays, and criticism. Richardson thus paved the way for the development of a new aesthetic, a new narrative, and a new critical perspective that helped to shape the emergence of modernism in the early twentieth century.

In 1912 Richardson began her lifelong undertaking: writing the multivolume sequence novel *Pilgrimage,* in which she gave aesthetic form to the life she had created. The first volume, *Pointed Roofs,* was quickly recognized as a work of modernist innovation that broke with conventional realism to pursue a new direction in fiction by defining reality as the subjective apprehension of the world from a highly individualized perspective, rather than as detailed objective observation and reproduction of the external world. As the psychological novel and techniques that came to be labeled "stream of consciousness" became staples of modernism, Richardson's work was revisited and reassessed by feminist critics who found in her life and work an early critique of gender assumptions. Further, since the late twentieth century *Pilgrimage* has been studied as a work challenging boundaries that have traditionally defined fiction and autobiography as distinctly separate genres.

Although she began her literary career relatively late, Richardson depended on her writing to provide a bare livelihood most of her life. Her periodical publications include reviews, essays, articles, columns, sketches, and short stories. In addition, she earned money as a proofreader, copy editor, and translator. She hoped that such work would allow her to devote whatever time was left to *Pilgrimage,* composed in thirteen of what Richardson called "chapter-volumes" over a period of more than thirty years, comprising two thousand pages covering twenty years from 1893 to 1912 and including more than six hundred characters. *Pilgrimage* begins with the journey of Richardson's surrogate, seventeen-year-old Miriam Henderson, to a German girls' school where she has secured a position as a pupil-teacher and stops just short of the point at which Miriam begins writing the story of her life. Like better-known novels of the early twentieth century, such as D. H. Lawrence's *Sons and Lovers* (1913), James Joyce's *A Portrait of the Artist as a Young Man* (1915), and Marcel Proust's *à la recherche du temps perdu* (1913–1927), *Pilgrimage* uses the conventions of the bildungsroman and the *Künstlerroman* to connect the development of the liberated individual life with innovative artistic creation.

EARLY LIFE, 1873–1891

Dorothy Miller Richardson, born on May 17, 1873, in the town of Abingdon, in Berkshire, was the third of four daughters of Charles and Mary Miller Taylor Richardson. Charles, who hoped his third child would be a long-awaited son, worked as a grocer in the prosperous wine and provision business built by his father, but he aspired to leading a gentleman's life of cultured leisure. When his father died in 1874 Charles sold the family's thriving business, invested the proceeds, and set about living his dream. He had prepared for his rise in social status by rejecting his Dissenting roots and joining the Church of England, represented by the elegantly beautiful St. Helen's Church in Abingdon, recalled by Richardson in "What's in a Name," a reminiscent sketch she published in 1924, and by moving his family to a large house with a walled garden in Albert Park, a fashionable new area of the town.

While Charles pursued his gentleman's life by attending lectures at Oxford and in London, entertaining lavishly as a patron of the arts, and joining the British Association for the Advancement of Science, he expected his wife Mary, who had been brought up simply in a large Somerset family, to organize and manage the household according to precise rules he established as befitting the family's social standing. Her respect for her husband's authority and her desire to please meant remolding her carefree nature and assuming a role she had little relish for. Over time her sense of inadequacy and unworthiness led to serious mental health problems.

Charles, a strict and domineering Victorian paterfamilias, retained Dorothy's respect and love through his intelligence and confident self-assurance. He indulged his family by providing luxuries in keeping with its status, including a nurse, a governess, private schools, and an annual railway excursion to the seashore at Dawlish in Devon, which stood out in Richardson's memory as a high point in the idyllic life of her early years.

The exalted joy of a happy childhood is directly recorded in sketches written relatively late in Richardson's career. In "Beginnings," an autobiographical sketch written in 1933, she describes Berkshire as "a vast garden, flowers, bees and sunlight, a three-in-one, at once enchantment and a benevolent conspiracy of awareness turned towards a small being to whom they first, and they alone, brought the sense of existing" (*Journey to Paradise,* pp. 110–111). This memory of garden, flowers, bees, and summer sunlight becomes a touchstone moment of perfect bliss

recalled several times in the course of *Pilgrimage.* "Journey to Paradise," another autobiographical sketch, records the trip to Dawlish, where "I tasted the deepest of my joy" (*Journey,* p. 124).

Recovery of this primeval joy of childhood, manifested in intense awareness of her existence through connection with the natural world and usually represented in images of garden, sea, or sky, becomes the goal of Richardson's personal pilgrimage and of *Pilgrimage* itself. Throughout the work, Wordsworthian "spots of time"—in which her protagonist achieves an ecstatic awareness of the enduring "reality" of the present moment that redeems the mundane existence of ordinary life—have their source in the childhood experiences Richardson describes in her autobiographical sketches.

The paradise of childhood came to an end when Richardson was eight years old and her father moved the family to a "hired house with alien furniture" (Fromm, 1977, p. 12) in Worthing on the Sussex coast, a move probably undertaken for the sake of economy as well as for Mary Richardson's health. They remained there for two years before financial recovery made possible a move in 1883 to a luxurious brick home in the southwest London suburb of Putney, where once again Dorothy and her sisters lived a life of privilege, enjoying dances, tennis, croquet, and boating. "Beginnings" tells of this move to "a spacious suburban house whose garden restored a lost eternity" as a recovery of joy after the "heartbreak" (pp. 111–112) of two years in Worthing.

Following a year of what Richardson dismissed as "female education" (Fromm, 1977, p. 14) provided by a governess, Dorothy and her youngest sister, Jessie, were sent to Miss Sandell's School, later the Southwest London College for Girls, for the only formal education she received. There she studied French, German, literature, science, mathematics, Scripture, history, logic, and psychology. Her study of languages provided the basis for skills she later developed as a translator.

Between 1888 and 1890 the daughters became aware of deepening family problems: their mother's depression was worsening and their father's finances were strained. In 1890 Richardson described leaving her school as "heartbreak…. From this pain, only the relief of the writing of words, preferably rhymed, could bring relief" (*Journey*, p. 112). When it became apparent that the Richardson sisters would not be able to rely on their father's financial support, Dorothy responded to an advertisement in the *Times* for a pupil-teacher and accepted a position before informing her family. In 1891, at age seventeen, she left home for Hanover, a Prussian province now a part of northern Germany, marking the beginning of her independence and the time she would later choose as the starting point of *Pilgrimage*.

BREAKING AWAY, 1891–1895: POINTED ROOFS *(1915)*, BACKWATER *(1916)*, AND HONEYCOMB *(1917)*

Gloria Glikin Fromm first noted in her 1963 article "Dorothy M. Richardson: The Personal "Pilgrimage"" the extent to which *Pilgrimage* reprises Richardson's own life story. Because Richardson had been reluctant to reveal biographical information during her lifetime, *Pilgrimage* was initially received as a work of pure fiction, and its autobiographical dimension was not widely recognized until after her death in 1957. Fromm's article, her biography of Richardson, and subsequent scholarship have demonstrated that the life and work yield mutual illumination; it is therefore useful to discuss the two in tandem rather than to separate a chronology of events in Richardson's life from a discussion of similar events recorded in *Pilgrimage*.

Richardson began *Pointed Roofs,* the first chapter-volume of *Pilgrimage,* with the first steps her protagonist, Miriam Henderson, took in the early 1890s toward personal and economic independence and the exploration of selfhood. The pattern of *Pilgrimage* as a quest narrative that moves its protagonist toward the annihilation of time and internal conflict to recover joy and unity through the power of the imagination becomes apparent to readers only as the author/protagonist realizes that the disruptions and fragmentation of life are transformed by a purposeful, imaginative exploration of consciousness. The pattern emerges in *March Moonlight,* the incomplete, posthumously published chapter-volume with which *Pilgrimage* ends, when Miriam contemplates writing her story in the autumn of 1912—the year in which Richardson began *Pointed Roofs*. Thus *Pilgrimage* traces the development of the protagonist from the point of establishing independent selfhood to the discovery of her vocation as a writer.

Richardson's break with narrative conventions is implicit in her break with the authority of the past. The parallels between assuming responsibility for her own life and finding a new way of expressing her experience indicate the extent to which she came to see her life, her protagonist, and her art as an integrated, experimental work in progress. As Gillian E. Hanscombe has noted, "For the woman writer of this period, and especially for Richardson, the pressure to modify gender-typical attitudes and the need to integrate the role of the artist and the role of woman are specific problems to be resolved, both in the practice of art and the conduct of living" (*The Art of Life,* p. 25).

Published in 1915, when Richardson was forty-two years old, *Pointed Roofs* is, as George Thompson has demonstrated (*Reader's Guide,* p. 17), set in a time frame from early March to late July 1893 (corresponding to Richardson's life in 1891) at Fräulein Lily Pabst's school, where Miriam Henderson is a pupil-teacher. The method of subjective narration Richardson discovered allows Miriam to contemplate issues central to a young woman's life as a new century approaches. Miriam considers how both her background and European cultural attitudes have shaped gender roles, tries to sort out her feelings about men and marriage, and recognizes and accepts her own difference from other girls her age. She compares the education of German girls at Fräulein Pabst's, which is aimed at preparing young women for marriage, with her own English education. Miriam's path toward her vocation is suggested when she remembers the day the vice-principal at her school asked what the girls would most like to do in life and she expressed her desire to write a book.

Pointed Roofs shows Miriam's suspicion of men who invoke traditional gender roles and expect her to accept the prevailing view of male superiority. Although she is flattered and attracted when Pastor Lahmann, the French master, singles her out for special notice, she recoils from his assumptions about male-female relationships. Her instinctive response is to visualize the stereotypical scene his words evoke and to reject him and his ambitions.

Miriam's reaction to Pastor Lahmann anticipates her later wariness in relationships with men who cast her in female roles that suit their assumptions.

Pointed Roofs also introduces Miriam's susceptibility to a type of fragile, radiant, seemingly vulnerable feminine beauty in her response to a student at the school. This fascination forecasts Miriam's attraction in later volumes to women whose emotional appeal threatens her independence.

Pointed Roofs thus introduces themes woven throughout *Pilgrimage* while it accustoms the reader to the free indirect style that will unfold Miriam Henderson's journey of self-discovery. The chapter-volume ends with many loose threads. It is not clear whether Miriam regards her venture as a success or a failure. Perhaps more important than resolution is the impression created by Richardson's use of the cinematic technique of a fixed camera and a moving scene to represent this stage of Miriam's development. The final scene suggests that Miriam has achieved stable ground as the world of Germany and Fräulein Pabst seem to move away from her.

When Richardson returned from Hanover in 1891 she found conditions at home little changed: her father, despite his ongoing financial woes, remained self-assured and domineering; her mother's mental suffering and religious despair deepened; and her sisters were doing what they could to assure their own futures. Her eldest sister, Kate, and her youngest sister, Jessie, were both planning to marry, and Richie, the second sister, had taken a position as governess with a

Wiltshire family. Within a few months Dorothy took a teaching position at Edgeworth House, a girls' boarding school in Finsbury Park in north London, where she stayed for about a year and a half.

When Charles Richardson was declared bankrupt in 1893, a public auction disposed of what remained of the family's household possessions. Kate's fiancé turned over a small house he owned to the family rent-free in the hope of providing a fresh start, but by then there was little chance for recovery of either the family's solvency or its spirits. In 1895 Kate and Jessie married and Dorothy left Edgeworth House to become a governess for a wealthy suburban family. Mrs. Richardson's depression now required close attention, and in November, hopeful that a change would improve her condition, the family arranged for her to spend time at the seaside in Hastings and for Dorothy, who had left her position as a governess, to accompany her.

Dorothy attended Mary Richardson constantly and suffered with her as she struggled with anguished sleeplessness, feelings of worthlessness, and belief in her imminent damnation. One morning, when her mother appeared to be resting, Dorothy left their lodgings for a walk to seek some relief from her own torment. When she returned, she found that her mother had killed herself by cutting her throat with a kitchen knife.

Backwater, covering a period from August 1893 to December 1894, and *Honeycomb,* set in 1895 (Thompson, *Reader's Guide,* p. 17), correspond to events in Richardson's life during approximately the same time. In these chapter-volumes Miriam attempts to find a place in traditional occupations for young women of her class and education, first as a teacher and then as a governess. They explore Miriam's conflict between her attachment to the comfort and security of her middle-class roots and her desire for freedom.

Backwater continues the pilgrimage motif with a journey by tram Miriam takes with her mother for an interview at Wordsworth House, a North London girls' school. She accepts a position but returns home for a few months before her duties commence. The time at home contrasts the life she must leave, with its round of friends and social activities culminating in a dance given by Mr. Henderson, with the life of limited freedom and resources she finds at Wordsworth House. There Miriam feels her family's financial stress sharply, regretting that she can accept only token treats provided by other teachers for their common table. Despite her success with her pupils, Miriam is repulsed by the harsh accent and the materialist values of the North London class whose children she teaches, and she finds her work tiring and finally stultifying. Her privileged past fades, and her uncertain future, which will require further training if she is to continue teaching, stretches before her.

Honeycomb continues the pilgrimage as Miriam travels by train and private brougham to Newlands, the country estate of the Corries, where she is on trial as governess to the children of a wealthy family with a busy social life. Miriam is hopeful as she embarks on her new venture. She is cheered by Mrs. Corrie's welcome to the luxurious home, revels in the beautifully appointed room provided for her, savors the abundant fine food, and wonders at the light responsibilities for teaching the tractable children. In this protected atmosphere of leisure and comfort, she feels detached from the life she has left.

Miriam's impressions of this easeful world fade as she discovers the emptiness and superficiality of the women in the Corries' circle, as well as the insincerity and ultimately the callousness of the men. When she realizes that her views as a woman and an employee are not taken seriously, she feels breifly that she has left Newlands for ever.

The last section of *Honeycomb*, after Miriam's return home for her sisters' weddings, reflects the fragmented style of modernist fiction as scenes shift in time and place without transitions. At one point, as Miriam is playing the piano for her mother, she becomes aware of Mrs. Henderson's desperation. In the final chapter Richardson describes the downward spiral of events that lead to Mrs. Henderson's suicide at the seaside but omits the scene of Miriam's horrifying discovery. Only her response is recorded in a final scene that reveals the hell she has entered.

LONDON, 1896–1904: THE TUNNEL (1919), *INTERIM* (1919), *DEADLOCK* (1921), *REVOLVING LIGHTS* (1923), AND *THE TRAP* (1925)

After her mother's death, Richardson's grief and guilt immobilized her, and the family conferred on what could be done for her. It turned out that J. H. Badcock, a family connection, needed a secretary/receptionist/assistant for the dental practice he and two associates had in Harley Street in London's West End.

Thus in 1896, at the age of twenty-three, Dorothy Richardson joined the growing population of London's "new women," many from middle-class backgrounds, who could not or would not remain dependent on their families nor accept the limited freedom of teachers or governesses. She became part of a new female labor force, many in clerical positions supporting male professionals, single women who lived frugally on their one-pound-a-week salaries but had rooms of their own—albeit in cramped and stuffy attic spaces—that ensured the freedom at last to answer to no one. Richardson fell in love with London, with its diversity and cosmopolitanism, and with the opportunities it afforded her to explore her intellectual and emotional life. It was a love affair that lasted for the rest of her life, to be rivaled only by her later attachment to Cornwall.

When Richardson began her work in Harley Street, Badcock befriended her, chatting with her during the workday about theater and art and taking her with him sometimes to lectures and meetings of the Japan Society. His friendship opened a new intellectual world to her, and Richardson soon began to explore London on her own, establishing relationships with new and old friends and investigating the range of social and political movements that characterized the turn of the new century. She discovered anarchists,

unionists, suffragists, vegetarians, antivivisection-
ists, socialists, simple-lifers, and free-love
advocates. Having established herself in an attic
room at number 7, Endsleigh Street, on the edge
of Bloomsbury, she walked several miles to Harley Street and back each day. The social poles of
Bloomsbury and Harley Street deepened her
conflicting needs for both freedom and security:
as she explored the fringes of bohemian life in
Bloomsbury and the East End, she kept in touch
with conventional bourgeois life in Harley Street
and the West End.

Richardson soon reconnected with Amy Catherine Robbins, a former school friend who had
recently married her science teacher at London
University, a young writer named H. G. Wells.
She invited Richardson to meet her husband at
their home in Heatherlea in Surrey. The visit
began a relationship that started as fascination
with a man as confident and self-assured as her
father. Wells introduced her to the literary world
during weekends she spent at Heatherlea and later
at Spade House, the residence he built in Kent.
She enjoyed the challenge of intellectual debate
with him about ideas and books. Eventually their
relationship developed into an affair that resulted
in Richardson's pregnancy and a miscarriage.
Although Wells is not always favorably portrayed
as Hypo Wilson in *Pilgrimage,* he never objected
to Richardson's representation. Their friendship
survived the tumult of the complicated relationship and lasted until Wells's death in 1946.

Richardson's intellectual curiosity led her to
pursue self-education as well as new experiences.
She spent hours in the Reading Room of the British Museum, attended lectures, and cultivated
friendships with immigrants like Benjamin Grad,
a well-educated Russian Jew who lived in her
rooming house and to whom she agreed to give
English lessons. They explored London together,
and while she helped him with language and
social customs, he introduced her to a world of
politics, philosophy, and literature she had not
previously known. Her relationship with Grad
hovered in an unresolved area between friendship
and romance for years.

The Tunnel, arguably the best of the London
chapter-volumes, and *Interim* parallel Richard-

son's early years in London. Miriam moves into
Mrs. Bailey's rooming house on Tansley Street.
One of her first acts on moving in is to remove
the bars from the window of her room, letting in
the view of the sky, the sound of the bells of St.
Pancras, and the smell of London air freshened
by trees in the Bloomsbury squares.

Richardson pays homage to the realist tradition
in her detailed description of Miriam's typical
workday in chapter 3 of *The Tunnel.* She is
responsible for correspondence, appointments,
ushering patients to and from the treatment
rooms, cleaning up after each patient, sterilizing
and polishing instruments, bookkeeping, and
keeping drawers supplied. Despite her realization
that modern professionalism creates a need for
untrained support—usually by women—Miriam
gladly spends her weekdays at the Wimpole
Street offices and her evenings at Mrs. Bailey's.

As she becomes accustomed to her routine,
Miriam befriends Mag and Jan, young women in
clerical positions, and often spends evenings and
Sundays with them. To Miriam, Mag and Jan
epitomize new women: they wear knickers,
smoke, ride bicycles, have no particular respect
for their employers, and enjoy their freedom.
They make her realize that she is straddling two
worlds.

The characters described in *The Tunnel* and
Interim—Mrs. Bailey with her family and lodg-
ers; Mr. Hancock and his associates; Mag and
Jan; the Wilsons; Eleanor Dear, the tubercular
nurse who manipulates people through her
helplessness; Dr. Densley, the hardworking and
dedicated physician—all represent the many
worlds of a later Dickensian London that Miriam
embraces. Her openness to experience—her
delight in attending theater performances managed on her salary; her joy in the freedom of
riding a bicycle; her reflective concentration as
she attends a lecture on Dante; her sense of
adventure in entering a nightclub for the first
time—makes these volumes the most absorbing
in the loosely woven narrative of *Pilgrimage.*

The next three London chapter-volumes, *Deadlock, Revolving Lights,* and *The Trap,* covering
the period from 1900 to 1904, describe a matur-
ing, reflective Miriam searching for her place in

an ever-widening social sphere. Her work becomes routine, and some of the glow of freedom fades. Notably Richardson's free indirect style drifts into first person as Miriam becomes increasingly self-absorbed. Miriam's changed mood is reflected on her return to London after a holiday knowing that the holiday has had changed nothing. As her youthful enthusiasm falters, Miriam's essential loneliness in the bustling city becomes apparent. Her need for connection competes with her need for privacy in her developing relationships with Michael Shatov, Hypo Wilson, and the socialist movement.

In *Deadlock,* Michael Shatov, a Russian Jewish immigrant, revives Miriam's interest in life and offers an escape from isolation through love. As a language tutor to Shatov, Miriam quickly learns that he is much better educated than she is, and after their first lesson she realizes that they had been students together. Their conversations develop into intellectual companionship indispensable to both of them. As their friendship blossoms into love, Miriam feels the key to recovering unity and joy had been love all along. She believes that if she were to lose her connection to Michael, she would be left "scattered and unhoused".

But there are barriers that prevent Miriam, now twenty-five years old, from committing herself to Shatov. When she tries to tell him about her childhood garden memories, she finds that she cannot fully share her most private moments of transcendent joy.

Moreover, Miriam's suspicion of marriage has been confirmed since she learned that her sister Harriet and her husband, whose marriage she had respected, remain together only because of their love for their daughter. Miriam concludes that they found marriage a failure, it was a failure and that perhaps the freedom of London was a life in itself. More important, though, is the barrier of Michael's "otherness" which, to her mind, means that he is not English, he is Jewish, and he is male. Although Michael protests to Miriam that he is a "feminist", she cannot be convinced that he regards her as a fully equal partner in their relationship.

Both Shatov and Hypo Wilson, who have encouraged Miriam to write, create the rival that will ultimately win her commitment. Miriam discovers the pleasures of writing when she edits a lecture for an acquaintance and undertakes translations suggested by Shatov. She learns that time spent near the window in her room or stolen from her workdays at Wimpole Street creates a private world of intense life for her. After this discovery, personal relationships compete with Miriam's growing commitment to the writer's life. Unable to accept Michael as a lover or to let him go, Miriam reaches a deadlock. She speculates that the pursuit of her vision of joy must be undertaken alone.

Revolving Lights, continuing the exploration of Miriam's conflicts, is especially rich in interior monologue. Miriam attributes her current interest in socialist and revolutionary causes to her "masculine mind". Analyzing the poles of her divided self—female and male; bohemian and bourgeois; radical and conservative; the worldly, adventuresome—she sees her life as "the battlefield of her two natures," which stuggle to keep her adrift. She recalls telling Hypo Wilson when he recruited her for the Lycurgans [i.e., Fabians]. Miriam spends the four weeks of her summer holiday with the Wilsons, during which she discusses her growing body of published work with Hypo, who in fact intensifies Miriam's sense of her dual nature. He compliments the analytic ability, which she attributes to her "masculine mind,", while at the same time, he coyly coaxes her toward a love affair.

The Trap, in contrast to the interiority of *Revolving Lights,* is full of restless activity as Miriam tries to avoid dwelling on the conflicts troubling her life. She moves from Tansley Street to rooms in nearby Flaxman Court, shared with Miss Holland, a night-school teacher she has recently met at her club. She delights in catching glimpses of William Butler Yeats, who lives across the court. She is excited by reading Henry James's *The Ambassadors.* She pursues an active social life, inviting friends to her new rooms and hosting a dinner at her club for Michael Shatov, her new suitor Dr. Densley, and Dora and George Taylor, for whose journal she has been writing

DOROTHY RICHARDSON

---

articles on socialism. She cultivates her socialist acquaintances by attending a Lycurgan lecture and a formal Lycurgan evening party. Miriam is seen in a flurry of dramatized scenes, but in the end she is disillusioned with the social world, dissatisfied with her living arrangements, and oppressed by a sense of her youth passing. As she walks home from a party with Densley, Miriam realizes that they have no future. She sees her incompatibility with Densley as a final break with her past. As her future narrows, she feels trapped indeed.

TRANSITION, 1904–1907: OBERLAND (1927), DAWN'S LEFT HAND (1931), AND CLEAR HORIZON (1935)

By 1904 Richardson had fallen into a mood of listlessness that threatened to immobilize her. She was tired of her work and depressed with her living arrangements. When Mr. Badcock offered to finance a two-week holiday in Switzerland, she gladly accepted. She returned from her journey to the Swiss mountains temporarily refreshed. She was now able to make decisions and act on them. In summer 1905, as if determined to change her life by changing her scene, she moved from Endsleigh Street to Woburn Walk, a short distance away. In 1906 she began her year long affair with Wells. With his encouragement she began thinking of earning a livelihood by writing. She started writing reviews regularly for Charles Daniel's unconventional socialist magazines.

In 1907 Richardson's life was in transition. Although she was still working in Harley Street, she had established her credentials as a professional writer. Her personal life was complicated by three difficult relationships. Benjamin Grad still wanted to marry her, but Richardson's dependence on his intellectual companionship prevented her from giving him a definite refusal. Veronica Leslie-Jones, a twenty-one-year-old drama student involved in the suffragist movement, whom Richardson met in 1906, had attached herself possessively to Richardson. Distraught over the death of her married lover, Veronica became increasingly demanding emo-

tionally, insisting that she wanted to share her life completely with Richardson. As she became involved with Veronica, Richardson's liaison with Wells showed signs of breakage. She was increasingly critical of his scientific materialism and wary of his assertive personality. In the spring of 1907, when Richardson informed him she was pregnant, his need to dominate and control disturbed her when he assumed planning for her confinement and delivery. All of this tension came to a head when she suffered a miscarriage. She took a leave from her work and left London to recover from the physical and psychological breakdown that had been building for years. Before leaving London for an extended stay in Sussex, Richardson disentangled herself from Benjamin Grad and Veronica Leslie-Jones by bringing about their marriage; she also ended her affair with Wells.

The years 1904–1907 in Richardson's life are reflected in *Oberland, Dawn's Left Hand,* and *Clear Horizon. Oberland,* the most lyrically descriptive of the chapter-volumes, takes Miriam for a holiday in Switzerland, where distance from the conflicts in her London life leaves her open to the healing effects of nature. The golden rosy glow of sunlight, which usually accompanies images of transcendence for Miriam, draws her out of herself. Oberland marks a turning point in Miriam's pilgrimage because the memory of such scenes sustains her faith in finding harmony and peace.

Dawn's Left Hand brings a return to the complexities of London life left behind during Miriam's holiday. Hypo continues his seductive advances, and Miriam sidesteps Dr. Densley's intended marriage proposal. She has decided to leave the dismal atmosphere of Flaxman's Court and Miss Holland and return to Tansley Street. As she tries to achieve equilibrium, she is approached by an unknown young woman at her club whose charm prevents her from hearing a voice of warning within. Assuming the role of an adoring suppliant, Amabel pursues Miriam, who is soon involved in a relationship she finds more intimate than she has ever had with a man because there is no difference, no sexual barrier, to complete sharing of thought and emotion.

Miriam can describe her childhood joy in the flower- and bee-filled garden and feel Amabel's empathy and understanding. As Hypo tries to engage Miriam in the affair she has apparently agreed to, Miriam is distracted by thoughts of Amabel. Finally, perhaps the most oblique and least erotic seduction scene in literature takes place in Miriam's room during a visit to the Wilsons'. Miriam returns to London without the sense of romance she had felt with Michael Shatov but also without regret.

Clear Horizon begins with Miriam's recollection of an out-of-body experience she had had while writing to tell Hypo she is pregnant. If this experience, as Amabel interprets it, expresses the creative joy of carrying life, it is difficult to understand the coolness with which Miriam later represents her miscarriage. Perhaps Miriam's ecstatic experience is a symptom of the breakdown Dr. Densley diagnosed when he advised her to take a long rest. Unlike her earlier moments of transcendence, which evoked feelings of intense existence and harmony, this one implies dissociation that leaves her "hanging, suspended and motionless." In fact, in this chapter-volume Miriam disassociates herself from the relationships that connect her to London. She arranges a meeting between Amabel and Shatov in the hope of bringing about their marriage. She also arranges a meeting to introduce Amabel to Hypo, which ends with Amabel being sent home and Miriam walking away from Hypo, knowing that her life with him had ended. Miriam clears her horizon of all impediments, arranges an extended leave from the dental office, and plans her retreat from London.

MIDDLE YEARS, 1907–1915: DIMPLE HILL (1938) AND MARCH MOONLIGHT (1967)

Leaving London in 1907 Richardson sought peace first in the lovely coastal views among the downs and marshes of Sussex. Later she moved inland to stay on a fruit farm with a Quaker family, the Penroses, where she was drawn to the inner stillness of the Quaker way of life. Her writing took a new direction when, instead of a review, she sent Charles Daniel a personal essay

for the September issue of *Crank*. She wrote reviews for the November and December issues, but when she traveled to Vaud, Switzerland, to continue her recovery, she wrote a descriptive piece, "A Sussex Auction," based on memories of her experience at the farm, which she sent to the *Saturday Review*. It was published in June 1908.

On her return to England in the spring of 1908 Richardson formally resigned her position at the dental practice and went back to Penrose Farm. Thereafter she supported herself by writing. She contributed descriptive pieces to the *Saturday Review* until the middle of 1912; she also did proofreading for Wells and some translating. Beginning in 1911 she wrote articles and a monthly column for a dental magazine.

After Richardson left the farm in 1911 she stayed with friends, especially Jack and Beatrice Beresford. Jack, an aspiring novelist, encouraged her to write a novel. He introduced her to the north coast of Cornwall where artists and writers could live cheaply with a minimum of distractions. Richardson made several false starts on a novel, unhappy with the social realism in vogue. In fall 1912 the Beresfords gave her the use of a house they had rented in Cornwall. Alone there through the winter, she finished *Pointed Roofs* early in 1913.

Richardson returned to London, took a room in St. John's Wood, revised her manuscript, and sent it off to a publisher. When it was rejected, she put it away and resumed her journalism and translation. She also began two books inspired by her experience with the Quakers. In 1914 she published *The Quakers Past and Present* and an anthology from the writings of the founder of the Quakers, *Gleanings from the Work of George Fox*. When World War I broke out in August, Richardson was alarmed but optimistic that England would successfully resist "the desire for regimentation and domination" (Fromm, 1977, p. 77). When she returned to Cornwall to stay with the Beresfords in January 1915 Jack suggested that she send *Pointed Roofs* to Gerald Duckworth, the publisher for whom Edward Garnett, a friend of Beresfords, was the chief reader-editor. The manuscript was accepted and publication set for September.

Richardson's recovery of health and her commitment to writing are reflected in the last two chapter-volumes of *Pilgrimage, Dimple Hill,* published in 1938, and *March Moonlight,* published posthumously in 1967. In *Dimple Hill,* Miriam Henderson boards with the Rascorlas, a Quaker family living in Sussex. She finds contentment and security in the family setting and peace and spiritual renewal in the natural scenes that surround her. Richard, the oldest of the Rascorla brothers, is attracted to her, despite his mother's disapproval, and Alfred, the younger brother, often takes her along to the seaside town where he delivers fruit from the farm. She thrives in the affectionate company of Rachael Mary, the sister who wishes her part of the family and the Quaker community. Miriam's memories of her childhood are revived by a bed of delphiniums. Gazing at the deep-blue flowers, Miriam feels as if she had been on a journey. She understands her pilgrimage as both process and end, as ongoing and complete. When she settles a writing table into the little-used summerhouse at the farm, she reflects and finds happiness.

March Moonlight, the unfinished thirteenth chapter-volume found among Richardson's papers after her death, is perhaps the most modernist in its diary-like fragmentariness, its multiply embedded time frames, its selection and condensation of events and memories, and its merging of author and character, autobiography and fiction. Written for the most part in the first person and present tense, it projects through Miriam's consciousness a kaleidoscope of recollected scenes, beginning with the final stages of Miriam's recovery at her sister's suburban home following another trip to Switzerland. She recalls visiting Michael, Amabel, and their new son at their home outside London and unexpectedly encountering Hypo Wilson at a socialist meeting where both bade their farewell to political activism. Miriam accepts her past serenely and faces her future without apprehension. . At her writing table in her attic room she begins the story of the life she has created. Past and present,

author and character, memory and imagination collapse in the present moment that contains all.

YEARS OF FAME AND ECLIPSE, 1915–1938

When *Pointed Roofs* was published in 1915 Richardson was already at work on *Backwater,* to be published in 1916, and she would continue the chapter-volumes for the rest of her life. Although she had hoped to negotiate an agreement with Duckworth that would enable her to work on succeeding volumes without having to earn a living through journalism, she was unsuccessful. She therefore arranged to write a monthly column for the *Dental Record,* which she continued until 1919.

In 1915 Richardson moved to number 32, Queen's Terrace, in St. John's Wood, a semicircle of Regency houses occupied mostly by artists and sculptors. There she met Alan Odle, a tall, thin, otherworldly-looking artist, who dressed in an ancient black velvet coat and wore his long hair swathed around his head to reveal faunlike ears. His long, elegant fingers ended in tapered ink-stained nails. A little-known but professionally respected graphic artist whose grotesque, satiric pen-and-ink drawings were in the tradition of William Hogarth, William Blake, and Honoré Daumier, he spent his days drawing and his nights sipping absinthe at the Café Royal with a group of artists and writers. He was art editor of the *Gypsy,* a magazine edited by the poet Henry Savage that lasted for only two issues, and he depended on his father for a small allowance spent mostly on art supplies and absinthe. Richardson soon discovered his formal courtesy and his extensive reading, including the recently published *Pointed Roofs.*

Although impressed by his complete dedication to art, Richardson was alarmed by Odle's indifference to nutrition and his health in general, particularly when a cough he ignored persisted. She was concerned enough to give him a stove for his unheated studio bedroom during the winter of 1916–1917. He was grateful for her concern, grew to depend on it, and asked her to marry him.

DOROTHY RICHARDSON

Richardson apparently reached a decision while she was in Cornwall working on the difficult final chapter of *Honeycomb,* dealing with the suicide of Miriam's mother. Odle had written her that when he reported to his regiment after his conscription in July 1917 he was declared tubercular and warned that he could expect to live no more than six months if he remained in London. A specialist found X-rays inconclusive but advised him to follow a regimen of rest and a nutritional diet. Richardson returned to London in late July with the final chapter of *Honeycomb.* She and Alan Odle were married on August 29 at the registry office of St. Marylebone. Benjamin Grad provided Richardson's wedding band (Fromm, 1977, p. 108). Odle was twenty-nine and she was forty-four, although she gave her age as thirty-seven and apparently never revealed her real age to her husband.

As she began *The Tunnel,* concern for the effects of damp London winters on Alan's health, as well as her past experience in Cornwall, led to the establishment of a pattern that with a few exceptions the Odles followed until World War II made even limited residence in London impossible. They spent summers in Odle's Queen's Terrace rooms, rented a primitive bungalow or cottage in Cornwall where they worked from October through spring, and then took a brief holiday before returning to London. Odle, like Richardson, fell in love with the unspoiled beauty of the Cornish landscape; the sharp outlines of cliffs and trees appealed to his draftsman's eye. He soon exchanged his working days in Queen's Terrace and nights at the Café Royal for a new routine: drawing by the Cornish light at a cottage window while Richardson wrote at her table; taking long walks with her along the jagged coastline; and eating the regular meals she insisted upon. Richardson's reputation among writers and critics grew, and other artists recognized Odle as an outstanding draftsman and illustrator, but the couple never realized a living income from their highly regarded talent.

By 1919 Richardson had become "one of the most talked-about novelists of the day" (Fromm, 1977, p. 106). Her method of presenting her protagonist's experience exclusively from Miri-am's limited point of view drew inevitable comparisons with similarly autobiographical novels by James Joyce and Marcel Proust, whose groundbreaking works were written at about the same time as *Pointed Roofs.* Joyce's *A Portrait of the Artist as a Young Man* was published serially in 1914–1915 and Proust's *Swann's Way* appeared in 1913. Clearly a new direction in fiction was taking shape, and critics were trying to find a name for it.

In the April 1918 issue of the *Little Review* the novelist May Sinclair published a piece on Richardson's novels in which she adopted the term "stream of consciousness" from William James to describe Richardson's work. It was the first time the term had been used in a literary context, and Richardson later took issue with the description. But the term stuck and continued to be used to describe a distinctive quality of early modern fiction. The work of Joyce and Richardson, moreover, continued to appear before the public simultaneously. In June 1919 an installment of *Interim,* the first of Richardson's work to be serialized, appeared in the *Little Review,* in which excerpts from *Ulysses* had been running since April 1918. The January 1920 issue that was seized by the post office included an installment of *Interim* as well as part of Joyce's 'Cyclops' chapter.

Richardson caught the critical attention not only of May Sinclair but also of writers like Babette Deutsch, who compared the poetic rhythms of Richardson's prose with those of T. S. Eliot's poetry; H. G. Wells, who said that Richardson had "probably carried impressionism in fiction to its furthest limit"; and Randolphe Bourne, who called *Honeycomb* an "imagist novel" (Fromm, 1977, pp. 105–107). Other early reviewers of Richardson's work include Katherine Mansfield for the *Athenaeum* and Virginia Woolf for the *Times Literary Supplement.* Mansfield's review of *The Tunnel* conveys her reserved admiration for Richardson's ability to summon Miriam's mental life so completely "with nothing taken away from it—and nothing added" (p. 3). A later review of *Interim* notes that if all of Miriam's impressions are of "equal importance" to her, they are also of "equal unimportance" (p. 140). Richardson acknowledged her appreciation of Mansfield's wit, if not her sentiments: "[She is] as clever as old Nick. But a woman has a right to be, & I like her" (*Windows on Modernism,* p. 41n). Virginia Woolf, reviewing *The Tunnel,* appreciated that Richardson's method resulted from "a genuine discrepancy between what she has to say and the form provided by tradition for her to say it in" (p. 188). In her review of *Revolving Lights,* Woolf credited Richardson with developing "a sentence which we might call the psychological sentence of the feminine gender" (p. 191).

Although never a best-selling author, Richardson attracted enthusiastic and loyal readers, many of whom became her friends. Among them was Bryher, an aspiring writer and longtime partner of the poet H. D. The rebellious daughter of a millionaire shipping magnate and financier, Bryher, whose belief in *Pilgrimage* never faltered, became as close to a patron as Richardson ever had, offering loans and gifts when the Odles suffered their frequent periods of financial strain. Bryher generously provided the means for Richardson to relish the high point of her fame when, at her urging, the Odles spent the winter of 1923–1924 in Switzerland, capped by ten days in Paris, where writers and artists celebrated Richardson and her work. She was especially pleased when Ernest Hemingway, who had been invited to edit an issue of the *Transatlantic Review,* asked her for a contribution. After her return to London she sent him "In the Garden," a sketch based on her earliest memories of the garden at Abingdon.

But by the late 1920s Richardson's fame began to decline, although her energy and industry continued for many years. Writers who started with her on the "lonely track" of modernism that had become "a populous highway" had outpaced her, and her reputation suffered as a result of comparison with Joyce, Proust, and Virginia Woolf. Joyce had moved from autobiographical narrative to the epic and mythological themes of *Ulysses.* Much of Proust's work was now available in translation. Virginia Woolf, whose *The Voyage Out* had been published in the same year as *Pointed Roofs,* had achieved stunning effects in presenting the interior life in *Mrs. Dalloway* (1925) and *To the Lighthouse* (1927). Richard-

son's continuing focus on the consciousness of Miriam Henderson, although showing development in both the protagonist's maturity and the author's technique, did not keep pace with the ongoing experimentalism of her contemporaries. New chapter-volumes required readers to remember details about the previous experience of Miriam Henderson as *Pilgrimage* grew in length over more than two decades. Furthermore, the increasing gaps between the times represented in *Pilgrimage* and the publication of individual chapter-volumes made the novel and its heroine seem less than contemporary, especially to new readers. Many of the cultural changes that came in the aftermath of World War I were taken for granted by a new generation of women, and although *Pilgrimage* continued to offer a detailed historical record of the period from 1890 to World War I, the political, social, and economic issues that Miriam Henderson confronted seemed less urgent in the second quarter of the twentieth century.

Moreover, Richardson felt the pressure of managing her domestic life while reserving time for the project she had undertaken when she conceived of *Pilgrimage* as a sequence novel. Although marriage brought happiness and stability to her life, it made the isolation in which she wrote *Pointed Roofs* impossible. She assumed responsibility for her husband's health, for virtually all of the practical arrangements of their domestic life, and for providing income as Odle's prospects for sales and commissions dwindled. Odle had exhibited his drawings in 1920 at a one-man show in London, and in 1925, along with three other artists, he exhibited there again. Although his work attracted attention from the public and praise from critics, little of it sold. After anticipated contracts to illustrate *Candide* and works by Edgar Allan Poe failed to materialize, Odle dedicated himself to a lifelong project: the illustration of the works of François Rabelais, which, like *Pilgrimage,* was never completed. Among his few patrons was H. G. Wells, who purchased two drawings to hang above his writing desk.

While *Dawn's Left Hand,* the tenth chapter-volume of *Pilgrimage,* was in progress, Richardson was distracted by other projects to earn money. She had agreed to read proofs for a collected edition that Wells was preparing, expected to comprise more than twenty volumes. Editors were eager to have her work. In addition to the sketch for Hemingway, she wrote essays and reviews for *Vanity Fair* and for John Middleton Murray's *Adelphi,* including a review of Clive Bell's *Proust.* She published an excerpt from *Oberland,* which had been nominated for the French Femina Vie Heureuse Prize, in *Outlook.* "Journey to Paradise" was published in the *Fortnightly Review* in 1928. That year she wrote a series of essays for a monthly published by Charles Daniel, with whom she had begun her writing career. She was asked by the *Evening News* to respond to the novelist Storm Jameson's article "Bored Wives." Bryher solicited an article when she and her second husband, Kenneth Macpherson, began publishing a film magazine, *Close Up.* An avid cinema fan, Richardson wrote a series of twenty-one essays for *Close Up* between 1927 and 1933. She wrote "Ordeal," a short story, for *Window,* a new quarterly. And in 1930 she wrote *John Austen and the Inseparables,* a critical study on the art of the illustrator.

During the early 1930s Richardson, still in need of money, interrupted work on *Clear Horizon* and contracted to do several translations. She translated a biography of Madame du Barry and a German novel by Robert Neumann, *Die Macht,* which was eventually scrapped. To compensate for this loss of anticipated income, Bryher arranged for an annuity to guarantee Richardson an income for the next seven years. Richardson went on to translate Léon Pierre-Quint's critical biography *André Gide: His Life and Work* and Joseph Kastein's *Jews in Germany.* She resumed work on *Clear Horizon* but interrupted it when Wells asked her to do editorial work on the manuscript of his *Experiment in Autobiography.* She took on yet another translation, *Les Heures de silence,* about a sanatorium for tuberculars. The pressure of meeting deadlines and the stress of shifting from German to French and back again was draining Richardson's energy and creativity. She was on the point of exhaustion but dismissed her physical symptoms as the result of eyestrain and age.

The increasing gaps between new chapter-volumes and Richardson's advancing age suggested to both the public and publishers that *Pilgrimage* had run its course. At the urging of S. S. Koteliansky, the Russian émigré translator who was a friend of D. H. Lawrence and Katherine Mansfield, Richardson began negotiations for the reissue of *Pilgrimage.* Koteliansky, then a reader/adviser for the Cresset Press, thought it should be reissued in a uniform, compact edition of four volumes. After years of difficult negotiations with Duckworth and Knopf, Richardson's U.S. publisher, and a great deal of misunderstanding among the parties involved, the reissue was advertised—before the separate publication of *Clear Horizon*—as the "complete" novel in twelve parts. Richardson was prepared to give up the project because she did not foresee *Clear Horizon* as a conclusion of *Pilgrimage.* Finally *Clear Horizon* was published separately in 1935 by J. M. Dent and the Cresset Press as a first step toward the prospective collected edition, which a senior editor at Dent had suggested to Richardson might very well be her "final bid for fame" (*Windows on Modernism,* p. 187). The four-volume edition from Dent and Cresset, with one thousand sets to be distributed by Knopf, appeared in 1938. Initial sales were disappointing, and Richardson reconciled herself to the uncertain fate of any subsequent volumes she might write.

YEARS OF REFLECTION AND SILENCE, 1939–1957

In addition to failing health and the prospect that her life's work might not endure, the threat of nazism shadowed Richardson as World War II loomed. When the Odles made their annual trip to Cornwall in 1938 they had unknowingly left their rooms at Queen's Terrace for the last time, for the buildings were soon to be dismantled. They moved their belongings to storage and returned to London for the summer of 1939, but war broke out in September as they were again making their way west. When the evacuation and bombing of London made return impossible, they were happy to learn that Richardson had been granted a Civil List pension that would enable them to rent a small villa where they would remain until 1944. London, the city Richardson had known since she began her life there in 1895, would never be the same. In 1948 she wrote that she was glad Endsleigh Street had been spared destruction although number 7, her first London address, had suffered a direct hit by the bombing (*Windows on Modernism,* p. 587). As Cornwall became a haven for evacuees, war wives, and children sent out of harm's way as well as a temporary station for servicemen, the Odles, who had long distanced themselves from public affairs but were appalled by the persecution of the Jews and the aggression of Hitler, listened avidly to radio reports on the progress of the war. Alan volunteered for community war efforts, and U.S. servicemen on leave were invited to visit the Odles for coffee and conversation. What began as a stay in Cornwall for the duration of the war became permanent as Richardson found travel more difficult.

In 1944 Richardson resumed work on a thirteenth chapter-volume of *Pilgrimage,* abandoned during the war years. Never completed, it was published posthumously in 1967 as *March Moonlight* in the reissued Omnibus edition of *Pilgrimage.* Three short stories, "Excursion," "Visitor," and "Visit," based on early childhood memories, were published in 1945. Richardson was deeply affected to hear of the death of H. G. Wells in 1946.

Following the sudden death of Alan Odle during one of his routine walks to the village library in 1948, Richardson lived alone in Cornwall in increasing obscurity. Although she published a few pieces, kept up a lively correspondence, and continued work on *Pilgrimage,* she had become remote personally and professionally. After suffering a painful bout of shingles in 1954, she withdrew even more from social contacts. Her correspondence ceased, and her sister-in-law, Rose Odle, realized that she could no longer live on her own. She was removed, over her protests, to a nursing home outside London. As she resisted the invasion of her privacy and the thwarting of her will, her caregivers attributed her claim to be a writer to senile delusion. She

died at a nursing home in Beckenham in Kent on June 17, 1957.

Selected Bibliography

WORKS OF DOROTHY RICHARDSON

Pilgrimage. 4 vols. New York: Knopf, 1967. (The text of all complete editions is identical except for introductory material.)

Journey to Paradise: Short Stories and Autobiographical Sketches. Selected and introduced by Trudi Tate. London: Virago, 1989.

Windows on Modernism: Selected Letters of Dorothy Richardson. Edited by Gloria G. Fromm. Athens and London: University of Georgia Press, 1995.

CRITICAL AND BIOGRAPHICAL STUDIES

Blake, Caesar R. *Dorothy Richardson.* Ann Arbor: University of Michigan Press, 1960.

DuPlessis, Rachel Blau. *Writing Beyond the Ending.* Bloomington: Indiana University Press, 1985.

Edel, Leon. *The Modern Psychological Novel.* New York: Grosset & Dunlap, 1964.

Fleishman, Avrom. *Figures of Autobiography: The Language of Self-Writing in Victorian and Modern England.* Berkeley: University of California Press, 1983.

[Fromm], Gloria Glikin. "Dorothy M. Richardson: The Personal "Pilgrimage.' " *PMLA* 78:586–600 (December 1963).

Fromm, Gloria G. *Dorothy Richardson: A Biography.* Urbana, Chicago, and London: University of Illinois Press, 1977.

Gillespie, Diane F. "Dorothy Richardson (1873–1957)." In *The Gender of Modernism: A Critical Anthology.* Edited by Bonnie Kime Scott. Bloomington and Indianapolis: Indiana University Press, 1990. Pp. 393–435.

Hanscombe, Gillian E. *The Art of Life: Dorothy Richardson and the Development of Feminist Consciousness.* Athens: Ohio University Press, 1982.

Levy, Anita. "Gendered Labor, the Woman Writer and Dorothy Richardson." *NOVEL: A Forum on Fiction* 25, no. 1:50–70 (autumn 1991).

Mansfield, Katherine. *Novels and Novelists.* 1930. Edited by John Middleton Murray. Boston: Beacon, 1959.

Staley, Thomas F. *Dorothy Richardson.* Boston: Twayne, 1976.

Thomson, George H. "Dorothy Richardson's Foreword to

Pilgrimage." Twentieth Century Literature 42, no. 3:344–359 (autumn 1996).

———. *A Reader's Guide to Dorothy Richardson's Pilgrimage.* Number Eleven: 1880–1920 British Authors Series. Greensboro, N.C.: ELT Press, 1996.

———. *Notes on* Pilgrimage: *Dorothy Richardson Annotated.* Number Thirteen: 1880–1920 British Authors Series. Greensboro, N.C.: ELT Press, 1999.

Woolf, Virginia. *Women and Writing.* Edited by Michèle Barrett. New York: Harcourt, 1979.

MARY DARBY ROBINSON

(1758?–1800)

Ashley Cross

In *A Letter to the Women of England*, published under the pseudonym Anne Frances Randall in 1799, just a year before her death, Mary Robinson writes:

> The embargo on words, the enforcement of tacit submission, has been productive of consequences highly honourable to the woman of the present age. Since the sex have been condemned for exercising the powers of speech, they have successfully taken up the pen: and their writings exemplify both energy of mind, and capability of acquiring the most extensive knowledge. The press will be the monuments from which the genius of British women will rise to immortal celebrity: their works will, in proportion as their educations are liberal, from year to year, challenge an equal portion of fame, with the labours of their classical *male* contemporaries.
>
> (p. 91)

Letter reveals the blending of personal and literary concerns that was the hallmark of Robinson's writing. Emphasizing women's extensive textual production, Robinson's *Letter* set out to extol women's genius and to create a history of literary women that makes women writers the equals of men, but it is also an attempt to write herself into literary history. She speaks for women in general here, but her career clearly provides the exemplary case. As poetry editor of the *Morning Post,* Robinson was highly aware that popularity did not guarantee recognition as a writer of genius; even as she published more than seventy-four poems in the paper's pages in the last year of her life, engaged in a poetic exchange with Samuel Taylor Coleridge, and published her last volume of poems, *Lyrical Tales,* she was conscious that women writers, especially ones like herself and Mary Wollstonecraft whose lives did not fit proper models of femininity, were not being given the recognition they deserved. Up until about 1980, literary history confirmed her fears: Robinson was remembered mainly for her sexual history—her affair with the Prince of Wales—and not her literary history. But it is her literary history that is now beginning to ensure her an "equal portion of fame" with her contemporaries, both male and female.

Robinson was a major player in late-eighteenth-century culture and literary circles. If the sheer extent of her participation in all the major literary trends of her day is not enough to garner this fame, her metrical skill, her exploration of a poetics grounded in sensibility, and her performative subjectivity should mark her as an important figure in the development of romanticism. In the early part of her life, before she became paralyzed, she gained celebrity status for her acting career and her affair with the prince, who was then seventeen years old. Her beauty, her wit, and her sense of style made her the oft-emulated object of fashionable society gossip. Her popularity enhanced her publicity as a writer when she began to forge her new career as an author. Initially taken up with the Della Cruscan craze for erotic, ephemeral poetry, Robinson shaped herself into a poet of melancholy, meditative verse. She was "the chameleon poet" before John Keats entered the scene, and, like William Wordsworth, she saw poetry as "the spontaneous overflow of powerful feelings." She was, however, highly aware of the difference it made being female, and her writing continually draws attention to the constraints placed on women writers because of society's attitudes about women's intellect and sexuality. Like Mary Wollstonecraft, she argued for women's mental equality and equal education, but, unlike Wollstonecraft, she saw sensibility as a source, though a dangerous one, of women's strength and as the origin of poetic authority. She participated in several different literary circles of the day: her *Lyrical Tales* and her poetic exchange with Coleridge link her to the Lake Poets, Wordsworth, Coleridge, and Robert Southey; her friendship with William Godwin brought her into radical circles that included Mary Wollstonecraft, Mary Hays, Eliza Fenwick, and Samuel Jackson Pratt; her interest in the sonnet revival reveals a dialogue with Charlotte Smith and Anna Seward; her gothic novels suggest she should be read with Matthew Lewis and Ann Radcliffe. Charlotte Dacre, a poet and gothic novelist, was one of the few women writers to portray Robinson as her predecessor, though Robinson influenced many others. Little work has been done yet on Robinson's relation to the Shelleys and John Keats, but their writing reveals the influence of her imagery and form.

In a little more than ten years—the last years—of her life, Robinson published four collections of poems, a sonnet sequence, seven novels, two plays, a translation, at least six individually published long poems, three political essays, and innumerable poems for various newspapers. She also drafted her memoirs and arranged her collected works. Robinson wrote in all the dominant forms of her day—elegies and odes, Della Cruscan verse and Romantic lyrics, sonnets and occasional verse, gothic and epistolary novels. Many of her poems were written under a range of pseudonyms that allowed her to create what Judith Pascoe has called a "multiply-constituted female" self in contrast to the self-authorizing male Wordsworthian ego (Pascoe, 1995, p. 260). No less self-authorizing, Robinson's changing persona reveals a writer keenly attuned to the literary marketplace and her reading public, to whom she dedicated several of her volumes. She used the press to showcase her genius and exploited the public's hunger for the salacious details of her private life. Often accused of imitating other poets, Robinson saw herself as shaping current literary trends through a revisionary poetics that derived its strength from an intense identification with the other, be that another writer or an outcast. Such a poetics, grounded in the empathy of sensibility, opened the door for incisive social critique and for a continual exploration of loss. Robinson's writing reveals her lifelong concern for the suffering of others, women's rights and education, the dangers and strengths of sensibility, and the problem of social inequality. If *Letter* reveals an anxiety about reputation, it also reveals Robinson's literary authority. As Coleridge writes through the voice of Mount Skiddaw, in his poem "A Stranger Minstrel, written to Mrs. Robinson a few weeks before her Death," "many a stranger in my height / Hath sung to me her magic song, / Sending forth his extacy in her divinest melody" (*Selected Poems*, p. 379). At the end of the eighteenth century Robinson's "magic song" made her a writer worthy of emulation; in the twenty-first century her writing "should claim an equal portion of power in the TRIBUNAL of BRITISH LITERATURE" (*Letter*, p. 97).

MARY DARBY

Mary Robinson, née Darby, was born to Nicholas Darby and Hester Vanacott on November 27, in a cottage whose back wall pressed up to St. Augustine's monastery next to Bristol Minster. Whether she was born in 1758, as her gravestone and published memoirs specify; or in 1757 as Paula Byrne, one of her biographers, argues; or in 1756 as the marginal note in the baptismal register of St. Augustine implies, has not been definitively decided. The date hardly seems important to those interested in her short but intense literary career, but it would probably have been important to Robinson, who so carefully managed her image. Robinson describes the setting of her birth in her *Memoirs*, which she began in the last years of her life, "as a spot more calculated to inspire the soul with mournful meditation [than] can scarcely be found amidst the monuments of antiquity" (vol. 1, p. 3). Emphasizing the stormy night, she creates a gothic setting for her birth and a sorrowful and "Romantic" image for her authorial identity: "through life the tempest has followed my footsteps; and I have in vain looked for a short interval of repose from the perseverance of sorrow" (vol. 1, p. 4). Her *Memoirs* portray a young Robinson who was thoughtful, melancholy, and unattractive, even "swarthy," with eyes large in proportion to her face. Her first reading material was epitaphs inscribed on tombstones, and by the age of seven she was reciting the elegiac poetry of Alexander Pope, William Mason, John Gay, and George, Lord Lyttelton from memory. Though she later became renowned for her great beauty, her "too acute sensibility" (vol. 1, p. 12) became the source of her best poetry.

She may have had good reason to be so melancholy; prior to her stage debut at around age nineteen, her life was full of vicissitude. Born in America, Robinson's father was a merchant fisherman who spent most of his time traveling around Newfoundland. His marriage to her mother, a granddaughter of Catherine Seys with aristocratic bloodlines going back to John Locke, was a love match. As the middle of three surviving children, Robinson's childhood with her eldest brother, John, and her younger brother, George (there were two other children: a daughter, Elizabeth, died before she turned three and a son died at the age of six), was a happy, comfortable one under the care of an indulgent mother. Her father's decision, when she was nine years old, to leave his family to establish a whaling fishery on the coast of Labrador seemed precipitous. If the failure of his scheme was not enough to disrupt their home life, the fact of his taking a mistress with him was devastating. The family was forced to leave their home, and her parents' relationship never recovered. Robinson, perhaps, looking back from her own experience of love, saw her father as "held by a fatal fascination; he was a slave of a young and artful woman" (*Memoirs*, vol. 1, p. 31). Such "fatal" passion was to become one of her recurrent themes.

Despite the fact that her family, absent a father, moved from place to place, Robinson's mother managed to secure her daughter a good education. Before her father's departure Robinson attended Hannah More's boarding school, where she saw her first theatrical production, *King Lear*. In London, Robinson was placed at Meribah Lorrington's school for more than a year, where she received what Mary Wollstonecraft would call a "masculine education." As her writing shows, Robinson was classically educated; she learned Latin, German, and French in addition to the usual feminine accomplishments, and it was here that she learned to love books and began writing verse. After finances required removal from a third boarding school, Robinson's mother opened her own school and placed Robinson, at about age fourteen, in charge of English language, selecting readings for her students, and of the students' clothing—the combination clearly presaging her future. Again, circumstances worked against them: Robinson's father was horrified at being publicly exposed and closed the school after eight months.

Almost fifteen years old, Robinson's "early love for lyric harmony" had turned into "a fondness for the more sublime scenes of dramatic poetry" (vol. 1, p. 46). She had matured into a beauty and looked well beyond her age. An initial opportunity through an actor at Covent Garden dead-ended, but a friend of her mother's introduced Robinson to the magnificent David Garrick, then manager of the other major theater at the time, Drury Lane. As Byrne describes in her biography, *Perdita: The Literary, Theatrical, Scandalous Life of Mary Robinson* (2004), Garrick was a great supporter of theatrical women, and he was taken with Robinson's beauty, especially her "long, shapely legs ideal for the highly popular "breeches roles'" (p. 19) and her tone of voice, like that of Susannah Cibber. Garrick chose Robinson to play Cordelia to his Lear as her debut role; the choice itself shows his faith in Robinson. While Robinson's mother worried over "the perils, the temptations to which an unprotected girl would be exposed in so public a situation" (*Memoirs*, vol. 1, p. 50), Robinson, excited by the opportunity, worked extremely hard with Garrick, who "appeared to [her] as one who possessed more power, both to awe and to attract, than any man I ever met with" (vol. 1, p. 55). Garrick turned Robinson into an object of publicity; Robinson loved that "it was buzzed about that I was the juvenile pupil of Garrick,—the promised Cordelia" (vol. 1, p. 54).

MARY DARBY ROBINSON

MRS. ROBINSON, VIRTUOUS WIFE

The "buzz" around the beautiful Robinson drew suitors, first a captain who turned out to be married, and then a rich man, "old enough to be my grandfather" (*Memoirs,* vol. 1, p. 54). "The drama, the delightful drama" (vol. 1, p. 54) filled her head, but a young clerk working across the street named Thomas Robinson, who was to become her delinquent husband, began to court her. She had little interest in giving up her theatrical profession, but she came down with smallpox. Representing himself as a nephew and heir of a wealthy Welshman, Thomas besieged Robinson's mother with attention, attending first her ill son and then Robinson herself. In the *Memoirs,* Robinson emphasizes only her feelings of "gratitude" for Thomas, who "attended with the zeal of a brother" (vol. 1, p. 61). Pressed by her mother, Thomas, and her father's words, the almost sixteen-year-old Robinson allowed the banns to be published. Once done, however, Thomas' demand that they keep the relationship a secret revealed that he was less than he appeared: he still had three months to go to finish his clerkship and also had an obligation to another lady. Robinson was caught: the banns were published, but she did not want a clandestine marriage and did not want to give up her stage career. Nevertheless, under much pressure, instead of making her appearance as Cordelia, Mary Darby married Thomas Robinson on April 12, 1773, a marriage that was to create financial and social difficulties for the rest of her life. Still dreaming of her stage career, Robinson represents herself as an innocent who "only three months before...had dressed a doll" (vol. 1, p. 68) and only decided to marry to be able to live with her mother. "Dressed in the habit of a quaker," she emphasizes her "melancholy," "wretched," and precarious state as a just-married woman who must keep her marriage secret (vol. 1, pp. 70, 71, 72). On their return to London after a ten-day honeymoon, Robinson and her mother discovered that Mr. Robinson was not even a legitimate heir but an illegitimate son who had already come of age. Finally, however, a visit to Wales to see Thomas' "uncle," actually his father, Thomas Harris, not only made

the marriage public but seemed to secure a future estate, thanks to Mary's beauty. She could now make her debut in London society as a married woman.

Though she represents herself as "the victim of events" (vol. 1, p. 122), Robinson's entrance into the *ton* (London's high society) made a splash and reveals already her consciousness of the power of her beauty and a desire to set fashion trends. Throughout this early part of her marriage, Robinson documents her clothing and her ability to turn heads. Her first visit to the pleasure gardens of Ranelagh may be seen as representative. She comments on the plainness of her dress "a gown of light brown lustring with close round cuffs" when the fashion was to wear long ruffles) and dares to wear her hair without powder and only a "plain round cap and a white chip hat" when the fashion was to wear huge, towering headdresses (vol. 1, p. 95). Robinson was pregnant, but she dressed with care and attracted the gazes of many of the notorious rakes of the day, in particular Lord Lyttelton, who became her "*cavalier servante*" (vol. 1, p. 103). Lyttelton attached himself to the Robinsons, leading Thomas into nights of gambling, alcohol, and women and wooing Mary with gifts of poems. Even though Robinson blames Lyttelton for Thomas' decline, the gift of the poems of Anna Barbauld (then Miss Aikin) was to prove significant, as she "considered the woman who could invent such poetry, as the most to be envied of human creatures" (vol. 1, p. 102). Increasingly neglected, Robinson wrote verses. As Thomas became progressively involved in riotous living, Lyttelton, his supposed friend and partner-in-crime, revealed to Robinson that her husband had a mistress (Harriet Wilmot), hoping to force Robinson into an affair of revenge with him. Instead of giving in to his desires, however, Robinson jumped into a coach and rushed to confront Thomas' mistress, who, seeing the beautiful Robinson, promised never to receive Thomas again. But his infidelities did not decrease and his debt expanded, and Robinson was increasingly set upon by rakes, including one instance when the attentive George Fitzgerald tried to abduct her after an evening at Vauxhall. Though Robinson highlights her neglect and naïveté in the *Memoirs,* she also claims, "I was now known, by name, at every public place in and near the metropolis" (vol. 1, p. 128).

The money situation became so dire that another trip to Wales was needed. This time news of their situation preceded them and the Robinsons were mocked and ridiculed for their expensive lifestyle. The only saving grace for Robinson was the birth of her daughter Maria Elizabeth on October 18, 1774. Against custom and without much domestic training, Robinson nursed her daughter. When she was not available to care for her, her mother did. Maria would go on to be Robinson's main support throughout her life, but especially at the end. It was Maria who cared for Robinson as she was dying and who most likely finished her *Memoirs.* Maria published a single novel, *The Shrine of Bertha,* in 1794 to mixed reviews and much maternal pride and was instrumental in assuring the publication of Robinson's *Poetical Works* (1806). Several of Robinson's most moving poems are written to her daughter, whom she calls in an ode written on Maria's birthday in 1794 "sweet comfort of my days" (Brown Women Writers Project, *Poetical Works,* 1824, p. 93). Poems, like the two for Maria's birthdays, "Inscribed to Maria, My Beloved Daughter" (1793) and "Sonnet to my Beloved Daughter" (1791) reveal Robinson's talent for occasional verse and her protective affection for her daughter. Maria seems to have been the one constant in Robinson's life; her verse not only marks important occasions in Maria's life, like birthdays, inoculations, and the publication of Maria's novel, but it also presents Maria as an intelligent, centering force. In the 1794 ode Robinson writes:

Thou art more dear to me
Than sight, or sense, or vital air!
For every day I see
Presents thee with a mind more fair.
Rich pearl, in life's rude sea!

(p. 93)

On the Robinsons' return to London, Thomas was arrested for debt and eventually imprisoned in Fleet prison on May 3, 1775. Still loyal, Robinson and her daughter went with him for the fifteen months. Just before her husband's imprisonment, Robinson had been preparing her first book of poems for publication; she juggled her writing with caring for her daughter in "the mixed confusion of a study and a nursery" (*Memoirs,* vol. 1, p. 162), but she still managed to attend parties. In prison Robinson worked hard to care for and support their family, only venturing forth to obtain the patronage of Georgiana, duchess of Devonshire, while Thomas continued his profligate ways. Her first book of *Poems* appeared in summer 1775; in the *Memoirs* she describes them as "trifles" (vol. 1, p. 159) about which she is embarrassed in later life. They "sold but indifferently" (vol. 1, p. 168). Recalling the eighteenth-century graveyard poets Edward Young and Thomas Gray, these poems show Robinson's initial attempts to imitate dominant literary modes; the poems are well written but conventional. Robinson claims to have followed the "strict propriety of wedded life" (vol. 1, p. 181), and these poems fulfill that sense of propriety. Ironically these elegies, odes, ballads, and pastorals present a discontentment with fashionable life, as best seen in a "Letter to a Friend on Leaving Town." Here the speaker, in perfect iambic pentameter couplets, claims happily to flee the "giddy circle" that "no more, can please my sicken'd eye" (*Selected Poems,* p. 72) to lead a pure life in retirement. As she compares the "blithe maid," the pastoral shepherdess, with the "gay courtly dame," one sees already the social critic Robinson was to become as well as her Romantic leanings toward solitude. "The Linnet's Petition," a poem modeled after Anna Barbauld's "The Mouse's Petition" (Byrne, p. 59) reveals already Robinson's concern for those less fortunate than she and underscores her own captive state: the bird calls to Stella, "Ah! pity my unhappy fate, / And set a captive free, / So you may never feel the loss, / Of peace, or liberty" and Stella's response, to let the bird free, produces in her "strange extasy" (p. 71).

"Pastoral Stanzas. Written at Fifteen Years of Age" demonstrates her ability to write well-measured verse and reveals already her interest in challenging conventions and hierarchies. These lines use the pastoral's social critique to present a cutting indictment of society's inequities. Robinson claimed in her *Memoirs,* "were I to describe one half of what I suffered, during fifteen months captivity, the world would consider it as the invention of the novel" (vol. 1, p. 181); when she later turned to novel writing, readers were sure that the novels reflected her life. At this early point in her career, however, she chose to compose another poem, more pertinent to her current fate: *Captivity,* published with "Celadon and Lydia," a tale of marital betrayal, appeared in fall 1777, after the Robinsons' release, and was dedicated to the duchess of Devonshire. Written in heroic couplets, *Captivity* catalogs the misery caused by rank and inequity and expresses Robinson's compassion for the unfortunate, a prominent theme throughout her work. The poem begins with a concern that became another driving force of Robinson's later work: "Say, shall a Female's soaring breast aspire, / To boast what Genius only can acquire?" (p. 7). The poem's emphasis on the mind's freedom becomes a call to liberty that closes with her recognition that "Whate'er the Critics say,—the Tale is just" (p. 33).

PERDITA: FROM ACTRESS TO ROYAL CONSORT

Despite these forays into "literary labour" (*Memoirs,* vol. 1, p. 184), Robinson turned back to the stage in order to earn money. The actor William Brereton introduced her to Richard Brinsley Sheridan, now manager of Drury Lane and a playwright, best known for the scandalous *The Rivals* (1775), based on his elopement with Elizabeth Linley. The three decided on Juliet, and Robinson made her stage debut on December 10, 1776. The 1801 *Memoirs* abruptly end with Robinson, beautifully dressed (she describes her clothes in detail), facing her audience "with trembling limbs and fearful apprehension" (vol. 1, p. 192). Her debut was successful; she received "thundering applause [that] nearly over-powered all my faculties" (vol. 2, p. 1). The *Morning Post* wrote that "at present she discovers a theatrical genius in the rough" (cited in Byrne, p. 72).

Robinson went on to perform to great commendation for three additional seasons (1777–1778, 1778–1779, 1779–1780). Her roles were varied and numerous (she lists twenty-three different roles for the 1777–1778 season). To name just a few, she played Statira in Nathaniel Lee's *Alexander the Great* and Araminta in William Congreve's *The Old Bachelor,* two Restoration comedies; Amanda in Sheridan's *A Trip to Scarborough* and roles in several other Sheridan plays, including a comedy by his mother; Jacintha in Benjamin Hoadley's *The Suspicious Husband,* her first cross-dressed role; the lead role as Emily in Hannah Cowley's first play, "The Runaway," as well as the leading female roles in almost every Shakespeare play (Ophelia, Viola, Rosalind, Cordelia, Lady Anne, Lady Macbeth, Juliet, Imogen, Perdita). In her first season she performed the role of Fanny in George Colman's *The Clandestine Marriage* while she was pregnant. However, her second child, Sophia, baptized on May 24, 1777, died at the age of six weeks. During this second season Robinson also performed her benefit, a singular performance for which an actor was allowed to choose the play and keep the earnings, in the role of Lady Macbeth, but as usual the evening included a second play, this time called *The Lucky Escape,* a comical opera, by Mrs. Robinson. Her most celebrated, and most compromising, roles were the breeches roles: Jacintha, Rosalind, Viola, Imogen; two weeks after her performance as Jacintha, Robinson created a stir when she appeared offstage in public wearing breeches (Byrne, p. 79). Though Robinson was well paid for an actress of her day, she also had to face, as all actresses did, the connection between acting and sexual availability. She had managed until this point to maintain her reputation, but she was beset by offers of money and affection from many sides. As her popularity grew so did the gossip. It was rumored that she and Sheridan were more than friends. Then it was John Lade. But it was not until George, the Prince of Wales, came to see her performance of Perdita that Robinson yielded.

In her final season she played fifty-five nights (Byrne, p. 89). Her most famous and life-changing role came when she played Perdita in

Garrick's revision of *The Winter's Tale* at the royal command performance December 3, 1779. The prince was taken with her beauty; his flattering words "overwhelmed [her] with confusion" (*Memoirs,* vol. 2, p. 38); "just as the curtain was falling, [her] eyes met those of the Prince of Wales, and with a look that I *shall never forget,* he gently inclined his head a second time" (vol. 2, p. 39). The prince pursued Robinson by writing her love epistles addressed to Perdita and signed by Florizel. Eventually, after several clandestine meetings at Kew and the gift of a bejeweled miniature betokening his immutable love, the prince persuaded Robinson to leave her acting career; Robinson's portion of her *Memoirs* breaks off right before she succumbs.

Robinson's affair with the Prince of Wales was a turning point in her life. Ever after known as "the Perdita," she had given up her career to be the prince's consort. Significantly, her last stage performance was the breeches part in Lady Craven's *The Miniature Picture.* The affair made Robinson a celebrity, and while it lasted she reveled in it. Her new carriage even sported a design by John Keyes Sherwin that looked like the royal insignia (Byrne, p. 121). It was, unfortunately, a short-lived affair (it ended abruptly in December 1780 with a note from the prince saying, "we must meet no more," vol. 2, p. 72), as the prince took up with Elizabeth Armistead in under a year. Robinson was savvy enough to hold onto the £20,000 promissory note he had written her as well as his letters and the miniature. Shortly thereafter, she was able to negotiate, with the help of Lord Malden, for £5000 in exchange for the prince's love letters. These negotiations reveal a woman intent on saving her reputation; as Pascoe writes, "she was reluctant to have their relationship cast in mercenary rather than romantic terms" (Pascoe, 2000, p. 29). Later, in 1783, Charles James Fox, another of Robinson's lovers, was able to get her an annuity of £500 because of the promissory note.

In the early 1780s the press had a heyday with Robinson's reputation. *The Morning Post,* at the time pro-royalty, competed with the newly formed *Morning Herald,* a pro-theater paper, over representations of Robinson. Notices of her appearance, anecdotes, letters, puffs, smears, and speculations appeared almost daily in the papers. The textual production before and after Robinson's affair was immense. Poems like *The Poetic Epistle from Florizel to Perdita* (July 1781), caricatures like "Florizel and Perdita" (October 1783) and James Gillray's "The Thunderer" (August 1782), and fictional letters like *The Budget of Love; or, Letters Between Florizel and Perdita* (1781) and John "Jew" King's *Letters from Perdita to a Certain Israelite, and His Answers to Them* (1781) mocked Robinson for her ambition and her sexual proclivities. The public's seemingly insatiable desire for the juicy details of Robinson's life came to a head in the pornographic *Memoirs of Perdita* (1784), in which Robinson is portrayed again and again in compromising positions. According to her recent biographers, Robinson often fought back by puffing herself in the press. But she also fueled the demand by her later affairs with Lord Malden, Charles James Fox, Banastre Tarleton, and possibly Richard Brinsley Sheridan.

PORTRAIT OF A LADY: "LA BELLE ANGLOISE"

In 1781 Robinson made her first trip to the Continent to escape the frenzy. In Paris she was feted by the duke of Chartres and the duke of Lauzun, whom she later described for the *Monthly Magazine* (1800) and in her *Memoirs.* She depicts one party in particular where "every tree displayed the initials of *la belle Angloise*" (*Memoirs,* vol. 2, pp. 91–92), as she was nicknamed. But the highlight of her trip was her meeting with Marie Antoinette. Dressing herself carefully in an outfit from the queen's designer, Robinson attended the *grand couvert* at Versailles to see the queen. Separated by just a crimson cord, the two women gazed at one another's beauty. The queen borrowed Robinson's miniature of the Prince of Wales and returned "a purse, netted by [her own] hand" (vol. 2, p. 95). Robinson remembered this exchange and, despite her affinity for revolutionary ideals, sympathized with the queen. As Adriana Craciun writes in *Fatal Women of Romanticism* (2003), Robinson's portrayal of the queen "values both republican politics and *ancien ré-*

gime femininity" (p. 87). In *Impartial Reflections on the Present Situation of the Queen of France* (1791), Robinson went so far as to appeal to the National Assembly for the queen's release. In her "Monody to the Memory of the Late Queen of France" (December 1793), written shortly after the queen's execution, Robinson expresses her compassion for the "beauteous martyr" (*Poetical Works*, p. 36), whom she represents as a figure of maternal care, wedded virtue, and democratic generosity. Now destitute, "On a straw pallet, in a dungeon laid— / By all suspected, and by all betray'd!" (p. 34), the queen is the embodiment of kindness and gentle authority: "To rule she sought not; for obedience hung / On the soft accents of her tuneful tongue" (p. 37) and "by partaking, [she would] lessen every pain" (p. 36). Robinson's monody to the queen critiques the brutal, violent, and selfish direction the Revolution had taken, but she does so to uphold a greater liberty and genius that she felt crossed class boundaries and was embodied in Marie Antoinette. The queen was especially important for Robinson in 1793, the year of her mother's death. Her 1793 *Poems* included two more poems on the subject, a dramatic monologue that expresses "Marie Antoinette's Lamentation, in her Prison of the Temple" (March 8, 1793) and a "Fragment" that was published in the *Oracle*, supposedly written before the royals were executed.

Known for her wit, her beauty, and her large blue eyes, Robinson was highly aware of her public image, and between 1780 and 1782, while the press was gobbling up every gossipy detail about her life, Robinson sat for portraits with each of the most important painters of the age: George Romney, Thomas Gainsborough, and Joshua Reynolds. In addition, Robinson became a fashion icon, creating controversial trends that allowed women more freedom of movement and broke class boundaries. Fashionable hats, hoods, dresses, and handkerchiefs were named after her. Her most famous contribution to London society was the "Perdita chemise," a version of the nightgown-like muslin dress that Marie Antoinette had been wearing. If in France this dress had challenged court tradition, in London, Rob-

inson's style and visible body "blurr[ed] the distinction between ladies of virtue and the "impures'" (Byrne, pp. 190–192).

Robinson's friendship with Reynolds was close enough to inspire a 248-line poem on his death, "Monody to the Memory of Sir Joshua Reynolds" (1792), in which she portrays him as "Britain's Rafaelle" and herself as a painter of words, attempting to do in words ("Each feature mark'd the tenor of the mind!," p. 357) what he accomplished in visual art ("Where shall the Muse untrodden paths explore? / Where find a theme untry'd by thee before?," p. 360). Perhaps she was returning a favor. In an earlier poem, *Ainsi va la monde* (1791), a long revolutionary poem Robinson wrote in response to Robert Merry's *Laurel of Liberty* (350 lines in twelve hours! [Gristwood 2005, 247]), she digresses from praising Merry's poetic skill to compare Reynolds' artistic genius as he paints a beauty curiously like her in appearance. These two poems underscore Robinson's consciousness of the connection between artist and subject and the power of the portrait in late-eighteenth-century culture to shape public opinion. In fact, Reynolds' two portraits, in 1781 and 1783, hint at the transition in Robinson's life from object of beauty to artist, from visual object to writing subject. In the earlier one, titled *Portrait of a Lady*, Robinson, perhaps still mourning her affair with the prince, dressed in black with a large plumed hat, hands neatly folded, and head tilted, looks seductively and yet challengingly at her audience. In the later one, which was used as the preface to her 1791 *Poems*, the *Lyrical Tales*, and her posthumous poems (1806), Robinson, hatless and more casually dressed, gazes pensively, with eyes half closed, out to sea; she does not seem to care whether the audience responds to her beauty. Byrne links this image to Werther's "dejected Charlotte" and suggests it paves Robinson's way for her writing career (p. 218).

FATAL PASSION: BANASTRE TARLETON

It was at Reynolds' studio in January 1782, shortly after her return from Paris, that Robinson met Banastre Tarleton, who was to be a part of her life on and off for the next fifteen years. Tarleton was also a celebrity, having returned from the American Revolution as one of the few British heroes. Known as "Bloody Tarleton" or "Butcher Tarleton" for his ruthlessness in killing Americans and his surprise tactics, Tarleton had rapidly risen through the military ranks to become commander of the British Legion dragoons. As Reynolds' portrait makes clear, he was strikingly good-looking, shared Robinson's fashion sense, and carried a sign of his valor in his two missing fingers. His biographer, Robert Bass, writes of Tarleton and Robinson at this time: "At first Mary had been just another conquest. But as the months passed he found in her the fulfillment of his needs and fell passionately in love with her. He had the figure, the gallantry, and the elegant manners of the perfect soldier. She had the beauty, the wit, and the charm of the perfect actress. They were the handsomest couple in London" (p. 205). Robinson implicitly conveys her fascination with his military authority in her "Ode to Valour" (1791). Reynolds exhibited both their paintings in spring 1782 at the Royal Academy exhibition.

By the summer, Robinson and Tarleton were seen together everywhere, and Robinson's relationship with Malden had come to an end (he settled an annuity on her that she always had trouble getting). In 1783, however, Tarleton, facing large debts and increasingly badgered by his family to give up Robinson, departed for the Continent. With money in hand, Robinson chased him, unsuccessfully, to Dover; Tarleton had actually gone to Southampton, writing to his mother that he was finished with Robinson. Though it is unclear exactly what happened, the ride was to change her life forever. As Maria Elizabeth explains in the *Memoirs*, "an imprudent exposure to the night air in travelling, when, exhausted by fatigue and mental anxiety, she slept in a chaise with the windows open, brought on a fever, which confined her to her bed during six months" (vol. 2, pp. 95–96). Whether she suffered a "violent rheumatism" or a miscarriage, the end result was a progressive paralysis of her legs. "Thus, at four-and-twenty years of age, in the

pride of youth and the bloom of beauty, was this lovely and unfortunate woman reduced to a state of more than infantine helplessness" (vol. 2, p. 96). In France, Tarleton only found out about her illness several months after; when he returned to London in March, the pair was reunited. However, Robinson spent the rest of her life having to be carried from place to place; her ailing health required her often to seek respite at various resorts (Bath, Brighton, Spa, Aix la Chapelle, St. Amand). Her state and her relationship with Tarleton provoked an especially nasty cartoon, "Perdita on her last legs" (August 1784), which pictures Robinson prostituting herself on the street. However, perhaps more than anything, her disability shaped her compassion for those on the margins of society. It also heightened her sense of dependence on the vagaries of men.

Robinson's relationship with Tarleton was tumultuous, emotionally and financially. Their long affair was a public event, and Robinson's poetry, published as it was in the press, made sure that it remained public. She fed the public's desire to see her writing as a reflection of her life, even as she became a writer in her own right. Revealing the vicissitudes of her tenuous position, many of Robinson's poems and novels reflect on this "fatal passion" (*Selected Poems*, p. 133), as she describes it in "Stanzas, Written Between Dover and Calais, July 20, 1792," written as she left England because of her health but also to escape debt and Tarleton, whom she had discovered at the end of 1791 was having an affair, which she called a "Low Caprice" (Bass 312). In a letter to Richard Sheridan, 23 July 1792 (quoted in Byrne p. 282), Robinson claims she and Tarleton had "an irreproachable connection of more than *ten years*," but now declared she would not accept another favor from him. In "Stanzas, Written Between Dover and Calais," fearing the end of their relationship, Robinson extols her loyalty, acclaims her compassionate love, and stresses the depth of her loss:

I have lov'd thee! *Dearly* lov'd thee,
    Through an age of worldly woe!

How ungrateful I have prov'd thee,
    Let my mournful exile show!

(p. 134)

She claims "Nor could threats or fears alarm me, / Save the fear of *losing thee!*" (p. 134). Much of her poetry to Tarleton melodramatically expresses an ambivalent passion. Vacillating between joy and pain, Robinson reveals the danger of playing the role of wife but without the benefits. An early poem, "Lines to Him Who Will Understand Them" (October 1788), which fanned the Della Cruscan flames, similarly presents the end of their friendship as a "sweet delusion" and the beginning of an exile: "Where'er my lonely course I bend / Thy image shall my steps attend" (*Selected Poems*, p. 89). Poetry became for her a release from such debilitating passion, a way of sublimating her pain of rejection and defending her behavior.

From Calais, Robinson and her mother and daughter planned to travel to Spa, Flanders, for Robinson's health, but they never got there. While in Calais, Thomas Robinson appeared with the idea of presenting Maria Elizabeth to his wealthy Uncle William. Robinson did not want to part from her daughter, so she returned with them to London, on 2 September 1792, just before British subjects were placed under arrest in France. It turned out that the only grounds on which William would help Maria was her relinquishing her parents, which she refused. This incident is one of the last times that Robinson mentions Thomas in her *Memoirs,* though she stayed married to him, but separated, for the rest of her life (divorce was not a real option for women at the time). Little is known about Thomas Robinson's later life; Hester Davenport, one of Robinson's biographers, uncovered a Thomas Robinson, approximately the same age as Robinson's husband would have been, living in Datchet across the Thames from Old Windsor, where Robinson was buried, who died 30 July 1814 (p. 224). It was not, however, Thomas who mattered to Robinson. According to Byrne, Tarleton was in Paris at the time of Robinson's trip to Calais and may have traveled through Calais (Byrne, p. 285). By the end of September of that year, Robinson and Tarleton were again together.

Tarleton was and continued to be a major figure of Robinson's poetry, even after he married Susan Priscilla Bertie, a much younger woman and the illegitimate daughter of Robert Bertie, duke of Ancaster, on December 17, 1798, just a year and a half after his final separation from Robinson. In the summer of 1793, Tarleton's presence dominated Robinson's poetry, despite the death of her mother, who had been her constant companion. If in "Stanzas, written on the 14th of February to my once dear Valentine" (1793) she reproaches him for "seek[ing] some gaudier bower than mine" (*Poetical Works,* p. 322), in "Adieu to Fancy" (1793) she dismisses Fancy for the "tranquil scene, / The constant thought, the smile serene, /And know myself supremely blest!" (p. 327). If in "Stanzas Inscribed to a Once Dear Friend, When Confined by Severe Indisposition, in March 1793" the landscape reflects her concern and distance, in her response to his recovery the landscape glows with the possibility of "sweet discourses in our time to come" (p. 326). The vacillations of these poems, written as they were in such a brief span of time, reflect the volatility of Robinson's and Tarleton's relationship and highlight the precariousness of Robinson's position as a married woman living with a man who was not her husband. Though she increasingly differentiates herself from Tarleton's political views, writing poems explicitly against the slave trade at the end of her career ("The Negro Girl," *The Progress of Liberty*), Robinson also helped Tarleton write his parliamentary speeches for pro-slavery Liverpool and his *History of the Campaigns of 1780 and 1781.* Tarleton seems to have become entangled with her public's understanding of her as a writer. *Sappho and Phaon* (1796) asserted the moral authority of Sappho's responsiveness to Phaon as a source for poetry, but readers still read Sappho's obsession with Phaon as a reflection of Robinson and Tarleton's relationship. Reviews of *The False Friend* (1799) saw the novel as a tale of her own troubles, interpreting the libertine Treville as a figure for Tarleton, though the novel focuses primarily on Gertrude's mistaken obsession with her father. In addition to poems like "The Sorrows of Memory" (January 1798) and "To a False

Friend. In Imitation of Sappho" (September 1800), which address Tarleton directly, even poems not explicitly to Tarleton are haunted by his presence at the end of her life; poems like the "The Gamester" (January 1800) or "The Way to Keep Him" (May 1800) recall Tarleton's behavior in their social critique.

LAURA MARIA AND THE DELLA CRUSCANS

Tarleton's presence in Robinson's poetry, even as an absence, is not, however, defining of her oeuvre. Robinson spent the last ten to twelve years of her life reshaping herself into a woman of letters worthy of remembrance. In July 1786 while she was in Paris, much to Robinson's surprise, an obituary falsely announced her death. And though literally it was untrue, it perhaps marks the death of Perdita Robinson and the birth of Mary Robinson, author. The *Memoirs* mark the beginning of 1787, when she returned to London from the baths at St. Amand, Flanders, as "the commencement of her literary career" (vol. 2, p. 112). Because of the change in her body and thus in her status as a beautiful public object, Robinson turned increasingly to writing as a means of establishing her reputation. The *Memoirs* note that "the silence of a sick chamber prov[ed] favorable to the muse" (vol. 2, p. 116). Indeed, the last ten years of her life form the bulk of her oeuvre; as she was declining in health her pen ranged freely over a broad literary terrain. Not only did she take on different personas writing her newspaper poems, but she also changed poetic and novelistic styles over the course of these ten years. As Pascoe suggests, Robinson's "poetry serves as a kind of cultural barometer of aesthetic changes…. [Her] poems initiate or engage in her society's every literary preoccupation" (Pascoe, 2000, p. 20). The earlier part of Robinson's life had set the stage for her career as an author, and she played part after new part in her writing. Moreover, she often refers to her poems and novels as performances, and her novels are littered with references to the Shakespearean plays in which she performed.

At the end of the 1780s the re-publication of Robert Merry's sonnet to love from *The Florence Miscellany* (1785) created a new fashion for poetry of improvisation and ornament. Writing under pseudonyms, the Della Cruscans created a stir with their public amours. Robinson—as "Laura Maria"—triangulated the poetic romance between Robert Merry—as "Della Crusca"—and Hannah Cowley—as "Anna Matilda"—when Merry mistook Robinson's "Lines to Him Who Will Understand Them" as an address to him. This not only began Robinson's Della Cruscan phase, which culminated in two positively reviewed volumes of poems, in 1791 and 1793, but also commenced her career writing poetry under multiple pseudonyms (Laura Maria, Julia, Oberon, Daphne, Echo, Louisa, and later, Tabitha Bramble). Starting at the *World,* she soon became the *Oracle*'s resident poet; from there she went to the *Monthly Magazine,* and at the end of her life, she served as poetry editor of the *Morning Post.* In 1791 she published her quarto, pro-revolutionary poem *Ainsi va la monde. Impartial Reflections on the Present Situation of the Queen of France* followed shortly thereafter. Her first novel, *Vancenza; or, The Dangers of Credulity,* a gothic romance in the style of Ann Radcliffe, appeared at the beginning of 1792. Compared by reviewers to her well-recognized poetry and read through the lens of her affair with the prince, *Vancenza* was simultaneously praised for its elegant language and critiqued for being "too florid and too ornamental for prose" (*English Review* 20, 1792, p. 111). Set in fifteenth-century Spain, the novel's layered and convoluted romance plot explores the sexual dangers young, credulous women face; when the heroine, Elvira, a fifteen-year-old orphan, finally has cleared all the obstacles (mistaken identity, seduction, murder) to marrying the man she loves, Prince Almanza, he turns out to be her half-brother, the child of her mother's indiscretion. Robinson had been pleased with the six hundred subscribers to her poems, but she was elated with the fact that the first edition of her novel sold out within a day, with five more editions following shortly.

A review of Robinson's 1791 *Poems* found in *English Review* articulates through its critique several aspects of Robinson's verse at this time and more generally of Della Cruscan verse:

We cannot help regretting that the fair writer has too often imitated the new school of Poets, ...which sacrifices nature, simplicity, and passion, to luxuriant and ill-placed description, and to a load of imagery, and ornament of every kind. We are suffocated by the sweets of these poets, and dazzled by the glare of their tinsel. With them the rage of passion, the moanings of love, the scream of despair, all must be *pretty*.

(Pascoe, 2000, pp. 50–51)

Though the reviewer here denigrates the poetry as "tinsel," maligning its artificiality, he accurately highlights the highly ornamental and theatrical nature of the verse. The poetry's sweetness comes from its emphasis on adjectival phrases, its sensual imagery, and its emotional intensity. The Della Cruscans created a highly self-conscious, erotically charged poetic exchange in which each poet's responsiveness to the other revealed the writer's skill and sensibility. The poems are full of images that would become central to Romantic verse; lyres, nightingales, breezes all take center stage but in highly manicured landscapes, whose sensual surfaces appeal to emotion and not thought. In *Romantic Theatricality: Gender, Poetry and Spectatorship* (1997), Pascoe suggests such verse especially appealed to the reading public at this time, confronted as they were by daily accounts of the madness of King George III.

Robinson's 1791 and 1793 *Poems* are remarkable for their emotional extremes—from the sexual ecstasy of "Ode to Rapture" (1793) to the frenzied despair of "The Maniac"—and for their metrical and formal diversity—from the sonnet to the irregular ode, from the elegy to her own stanzaic experiments. The poems exhibit the Della Cruscan theatricality, ornate language, and emotional intensity, but her subject matter has a broader range. These include the sensual, microcosmic bowers of her "Fairy Poems," the solemn laments for lost genius in "Ode to the Harp of...Louisa" (1793) and "Monody to the Memory of Chatterton" (1791), her historically grounded and empathetic poems to Marie Antoinette, her concerns with social inequity in *Ainsi va la monde,* her tributes to public figures like the duchess of Devonshire, David Garrick, and John Taylor, and her more personal poems to her

daughter, Tarleton, and her recently deceased father. Given the number of poems that focus on the "doom'd victim of woe" ("To Cesario"), the figure of Goethe's Werther, to whom she addresses an elegy, perhaps best embodies the dominant mood.

Though both Coleridge and Wordsworth sought to differentiate themselves from the Della Cruscan style in different ways, Robinson's *Poems* are important precursors to their work and reveal Robinson's first attempts to define herself as an original poet. Robinson's interest in Chatterton, an interest she shared with many Romantic poets—in particular Coleridge, who may have had her poem in mind when he revised his own "Monody on the Death of Chatterton" for his 1796 poems—reveals her concern with creating a history of neglected poets and hints at her investment in a poetic practice like Chatterton's that involved imitating the styles of others. Her numerous occasional poems ("Lines Written..." "Stanzas on..."), which often evoke a sense of loss, usually in the frame of love, need to be read as precursors to Wordsworth's poems entitled, "Lines written..." in a particular spot (like Tintern Abbey), which seek to make "abundant recompense" for loss. Moreover, Robinson's "Ode to the Nightingale" (1791), one of two nightingale poems here, calls up Keats's later ode not only because of the title; while her bird does not provide even a momentary escape from bodiliness, like Keats's speaker hers returns "forlorn." In one of her best Della Cruscan poems, "Ode to Della Crusca" (1791), addressed to Robert Merry, Robinson represents her heart as an aeolian harp (though she doesn't call it that), as it "revibrates" to Robert Merry's "ever-witching song," "Till ev'ry nerve, with quiv'ring throb divine" (*Selected Poems,* p. 85). Claiming to praise Merry, she asserts her own sensibility as source of poetic authority. Both her odes to the muse in the 1791 *Poems* affirm this inspirational source; in both, she imagines her body as the medium of poetry, "extatic transport's wild excess" (p. 78), and the muse in her own image "whose soul like mine / Beams with poetic rays divine" (*Poetical Works,* p. 88). Combining reason and passion in these tributes, Robinson dedicates her mind and body to poetry.

Robinson later dismissed the Della Cruscan part of her career in her *Memoirs:* "dazzled by the false metaphors and rhapsodical extravagance of some contemporary writers, she suffered her judgment to be misled and her taste to be perverted" (vol. 2, p. 125). Her Della Cruscan "extravagance" haunted her reputation. Even with the publication of *Sappho and Phaon,* which she saw as a new direction, reviewers critiqued her connection to the Della Cruscan "imitators" (*Selected Poems,* p. 385). And the posthumous publication of *The Poetical Works of the Late Mrs. Mary Robinson* in 1806 elicited a similar rebuff. Until the 1980s it had been the tendency of twentieth-century critics to repeat the negative dismissals of Robinson's contemporaries. Della Cruscan verse, however, is part of a poetry of sensibility that was erased from the literary canon partly because of its feminine associations, a poetry that, as Jerome McGann argues in *The Poetics of Sensibility* (1996), was both the legacy of Enlightenment values and a shaping force of romanticism and modernism. Though Robinson may have wanted to downplay these affective associations, her position as a central figure in the Della Cruscan movement furthers her importance.

NOBODY'S BUSINESS: ROBINSON THE SOCIAL CRITIC

In 1793, as England began a war with France that was to last until 1815 when Napoleon was defeated, Robinson published, in addition to her *Poems, Sight, The Cavern of Woe,* and *Solitude,* her monody to the queen of France, and a satire of the *ton* on the model of Horace Juvenal, titled *Modern Manners.* "Sight" asserted an "aristocracy of genius" and was dedicated to John Taylor, who had become the *Morning Post* editor. As Byrne suggests, Robinson was "consciously positioning herself as an author of the marketplace, a meritocrat rather than a coterie writer relying on the patronage of the fashionable world" (p. 292), and her *Modern Manners* confirmed that, enraging the *ton.*

In spring 1794 her second novel, *The Widow; or, A Picture of Modern Times,* an epistolary bil-

dungsroman, was published, again offending the *ton,* especially the upper-class gambling ladies, whose dissipation she contrasts with the sentimental heroine, Julia St. Lawrence, a daughter of an American merchant and poet, like Robinson, and clearly an allusion to Rousseau's *Julie, La Nouvelle Heloise.* A "new species of woman" (*The Widow,* vol. 1, p.107), Julia's innocence, virtue, and unaffected nature contrast sharply with the other women, especially the nasty Mrs. Vernon. While they use their linguistic ability to manipulate and hurt others, Julia, disguised as a widow to protect herself, employs hers in writing melancholy poetry that shows her genius. Julia's compassion and situation provide the impetus for Lady Seymour's eventual transformation. Taking her critique of fashionable women a step farther, Robinson next wrote a play entitled *Nobody,* a comedy satirizing female gambling and aristocratic hypocrisy, starring the famous actress Dora Jordan. It played only for three nights and was withdrawn. Both the lead actress and author received hate mail, and the play was hissed, even, as noted in the *Memoirs,* "by women of distinguished rank" (vol. 2, p. 141). The attack on her play was only one of several that Robinson had to deal with in these years. Conservatives, like William Gifford in *The Baviad* (1791) and *The Maeviad* (1795) and Richard Polwhele in *The Unsex'd Females* (1798), were threatened by the Wollstonecraftian, outspoken woman and represented her and other women writers as "unsexed" and "unnatural" because of their profession of French values of equality and liberty.

The *Memoirs* gloss over the next four years, suggesting little of importance occurred except "indisposition and mental anxiety" (vol. 2, p. 143), but Robinson's immense textual production continued, despite the fact that she was still struggling financially. Her carriages were now a "necessary expense" (Byrne, p. 306) and her publications had not given her the returns she had hoped for, but she continued to write. By early 1795 Robinson was regularly contributing poems to the *Morning Post,* now under Daniel Stuart. A poem often cited to show Robinson's difference from the male Romantic poets because of its lack of a central subjective consciousness,

"January 1795" (*Selected Poems,* pp. 356–358) subtly registers her situation ("Genius, in a garret, starving," "Authors, who can't earn a dinner," and "Fools, the work of Genius scorning") and explicitly records her consciousness of social hierarchy ("Lords in ermine, beggars freezing; / Nobles, scarce the Wretched heeding"). Its list-like structure creates an impressionistic and satirical collage of late-eighteenth-century urban life in which "Poets, Painters, and Musicians; / Lawyers, Doctors, and Politicians; / Pamphlets, Newspapers, and Odes, / [all are] seeking Fame, by diff'rent roads" (pp. 356–357). In January 1796 her third novel appeared in print and its 750 copies sold out immediately. *Angelina,* a radical feminist novel about a father who tries to sell his daughter into marriage to a man who has deserted his older mistress (the eponymous character), articulates Robinson's concern with women's social position and might be read as a precursor to her *Letter.* Wollstonecraft, praising Robinson's "well-earned reputation" as a poet and novelist in her review in the *Analytical Review,* saw it as "breath[ing] a spirit of independence, and a dignified superiority to whatever is unessential to the true respectability and genuine excellence of human beings" (vol. 23, 1796, pp. 293–294).

THE ENGLISH SAPPHO: SAPPHO AND PHAON

In 1796 Robinson, who had been dubbed "The English Sappho" by the press, indicated her desire to take part in the sonnet revival that was taking place with her publication of *Sappho and Phaon, a Series of Legitimate Sonnets, with Thoughts on Poetical Subjects & Anecdotes of the Grecian Poetess.* For the second time in literary history, the sonnet became one of the dominant genres, and, as Daniel Robinson claims, it provided a common ground on which male and female poets could meet (p. 99). Mary Robinson here takes a seat with Charlotte Smith, Anna Seward, William Wordsworth, William Lisle Bowles, and Samuel Taylor Coleridge, but it was primarily women writers who revived the form. According to Daniel Robinson, "The sonnet claim is a bold statement of intellectual and poetic

superiority, an implicit act of self-canonization" (p. 99). Mary Robinson's sonnet sequence of forty-four "legitimate" Petrarchan sonnets was indeed a bold intervention into this debate, as she critiqued the contemporary interest in the English sonnet as a place for meditations on nature and reverted to the Renaissance conventions of Petrarch and Milton. Though she had earlier written a tributary "Sonnet to Mrs. Charlotte Smith, on Hearing that Her Son Was Wounded at the Siege of Dunkirk" (September 15, 1793), identifying with her as a mother and poet, Robinson's sequence—the first sonnet sequence since its initial heyday (Lady Mary Wroth's *Pamphilia to Amphilanthus* seems especially relevant)—not only shifted the formal discourse; it also revised the Petrarchan love exchange from the female poet/lover's perspective. In the *Poetics of Sensibility,* Jerome McGann interprets the volume as a defense of and manifesto for a poetry of sensibility grounded in feminine experience, a manifesto that put Robinson "at odds with the two dominant (and masculinist) theories of poetry articulated in the volatile 1790s," represented by Gifford's *Baviad* and Wordsworth's preface to *Lyrical Ballads* of 1800 (p. 98). *Sappho and Phaon* was praised for its melodious language, metrical accomplishment, and, ironically, the sonnets' chasteness.

The sonnet was an ideal form for Robinson, combining the lyrical emphasis on mood and demanding formal conventions, and a sequence in the voice of Sappho was an ideal, classical subject matter on which to stake her claims to poetic legitimacy. The poem combines two of her pseudonyms, Laura and Sappho, transforming the Petrarchan object of desire into a passionately feeling, sexually desiring individual and transforming autobiography into poetic philosophy. If later Robinson was to identify with Wollstonecraft, in *Sappho and Phaon* her emphasis on sensibility as a source of female authority differentiates her. In addition to the sonnets, the volume includes a preface that makes her case for the legitimate sonnet, argues for poetry's civilizing power, and critiques society's neglect of poetical genius, especially women; an address "To the Reader," which claims Sappho as the embodiment of "the human mind enlightened by the most exquisite talents, yet yielding to the destructive controul of ungovernable passions (*Selected Poems*, p. 149); and a biographical "Account of Sappho," which represents Sappho as a woman of genius.

Clearly identifying with Sappho as a woman, a poet with a gift for formal innovation, and a lover, Robinson's sonnets trace Sappho's desire for Phaon, from its initial awakening, through its fluctuations as she pursues the neglectful Phaon, up to the point of her final decision to kill herself. In the opening sonnet Robinson, speaking through Sappho, foregrounds the fact that these poems are as much about poetry as about love: "blest Poesy! with godlike pow'rs wert given / To calm the miseries of man" (p. 157). By sonnet 4, however, "Mute, on the ground [her] Lyre neglected lies, / The Muse forgot" (p. 159) because Phaon's presence distracts and disorders Sappho's senses. The sonnets pursue the contradictory extremes of Sappho's emotions in lines for and against reason, pursuing and reproaching Phaon. By the penultimate sonnet, Sappho gazes over the "dizzy precipice" hoping for

returning Reason's placid beam,
[...]
To calm rebellious Fancy's fev'rish dream;
  Then shall my Lyre disdain love's dread control,
And loftier passions, prompt the loftier theme!

(p. 179)

In the final sonnet, however, the Muse "droops," and "Reflection" takes over to contemplate "human destiny, / where gaudy buds and wounding thorns are twin'd" (p. 180); the reader is left with an apostrophe to the power of Virtue, here aligned with Sappho's poetic power and acute sensibility. If Robinson's sonnets reflect on the dangers of that sensibility, she also reveals it to be the source of poetic power, legitimizing herself as a poet and woman but also paying tribute to the genius of women poets.

FEMINIST NOVELIST, ROMANTIC POET

In the fall of 1795 Robinson wrote *The Sicilian Lover*, a blank-verse tragedy in Shakespearean

style, also about a father who sells his daughter into marriage; it was never staged but was put into print in early 1796 to prevent a forgery. Her fourth novel, *Hubert de Sevrac: A Romance of the Eighteenth Century*, noted as an imitation of Radcliffe's gothic romances by several reviewers and set during the French Revolution, came out at the end of that year. In the *Critical Review*, Coleridge suggested that the new vogue in literature was "real life and manners" and not this type of romance (vol. 23, 1798, p. 472), and Wollstonecraft criticized it for being too rapidly written; but the novel was well received. Its focus on a dispossessed French aristocrat who learns to believe in the values of liberty provides another example of Robinson's radical politics; its rushed quality, however, makes it a less pleasurable read than her other novels.

The year 1796 was also important because it marked the beginning of Robinson's friendship with William Godwin and her brief connection with Mary Wollstonecraft. Mary Shelley suggests that Robinson was, in Godwin's eyes, "the most beautiful woman he had ever seen, but though he admired her so greatly, their acquaintance scarcely attained an intimate friendship" (Cameron and Reiman, eds., vol. 1, p. 180). Though during his brief marriage with Wollstonecraft, Godwin withdrew from the friendship with Robinson, he became again an important friend and intellectual stimulant in the last year of her life and was one of two people to attend her funeral (the other was John Wolcot). Their friendship seems close enough, though, that their letters record a serious disagreement, and Godwin also describes her in his novel *Fleetwood* (Byrne, p. 298). Godwin introduced Robinson to Wollstonecraft, who introduced her to Mary Hays, another outspoken woman writer of the time. And it was in part through their connections and their shared radical sympathies that Robinson's literary circle was expanding.

As the 1790s were coming to a close, Robinson was working hard to change her reputation and to present herself as an author of substance. She had good reason to believe in herself as a writer, given her productivity and popularity. Despite the ending of her relationship with Tarle-

209

MARY DARBY ROBINSON

ton in spring 1797, she was publishing up to three poems a week, under various pseudonyms, for the *Morning Post.* German, French, and Irish editions of the majority of Robinson's novels were being published. During this time she developed a friendship and poetic correspondence with Coleridge that inspired her to write some of her finest poetry. Always receptive to others, Robinson responded to Coleridge with an eagerness that was both nurturing and competitive, praising and self-interested. In addition to their mutual professional interests, they shared an interest in opium-induced reverie (her "The Maniac"), parenting, metrical experimentation, and William Wordsworth. They wrote several poems explicitly addressed to one another, but many other poems suggest their shared concerns with poetic reputation and agency. Coleridge's "The Apotheosis; or, The Snow-drop" (3 January 1798) revises Robinson's "Ode to the Snow-drop" (December 26, 1797) by mingling her Della Cruscan language with imagery from his "Effusion XXXV" (1796), an early version of "The Eolian Harp." Her "To the Poet Coleridge" responds to Coleridge's "Kubla Khan," which Robinson read in manuscript, revising both its content and complex meter. The speaker of Robinson's poem traces with him his "NEW PARADISE extended" (*Selected Poems,* pp. 330–332) and hears, where Coleridge's speaker failed, his damsel with a dulcimer. Robinson also wrote an ode on the birth of Coleridge's son, Derwent. Coleridge's poems to Robinson include "Alcaeus to Sappho," a poem of Wordsworth's that he co-opted, and "A Stranger Minstrel," a tribute he wrote just before her death. Coleridge praised Robinson's metrical talent in particular, as he wrote on February 28, 1800, to Southey about "The Haunted Beach," a revision of Coleridge's *The Ancient Mariner:* "but the Metre—ay! that Woman has an Ear" (*Collected Letters,* vol. 1, p. 576). It was Coleridge who convinced Southey to include Robinson's poem "Jasper" in the *Annual Anthology.*

Between 1797 and 1799 Robinson published three more novels, her best three, in quick succession. As with her earlier novels, these express Robinson's interest in women's social position, the dangers of romance and sensibility,

abuses of power, equality among the classes, and her belief in the authority of genius. Robinson's novels, with their sensationalism and gothic trappings, their outlandish plots and overwrought protagonists (with the exception of Martha Morley) are everything that Jane Austen hated in the contemporary novel. They were often criticized for being mere imitations. And yet despite all this, they are wonderfully in tune with contemporary literary taste; they provide a powerful and pointed social critique, in particular of the dominant attitudes about women's sexuality; and their self-referentiality and their penchant for boundary crossing make them engaging to read. As she had written in *Captivity,* there is a sense of truth behind these outlandish events. Moreover, the novels reveal Robinson's masculine education; they are rife with literary allusions and philosophical references—the epigraphs alone mark an incredible reading knowledge—that reveal a writer well versed in the literary tradition and aware of her relationship to it. Their imitative nature demonstrates Robinson's brilliance in reinventing her career as an actor in these novel performances; in fact, this kind of revisionary method was a productive creative strategy.

Perhaps the figure that best embodies this is that of the "polygraph" who appears in her most fascinating novel, *Walsingham; or, The Pupil of Nature* (1797). Seemingly a marginal figure in the novel, the polygraph, a "fellow that ape[s] one's dress and manners as close as one's shadow" (*Walsingham,* 2003, p. 374), an impersonator, is a central figure for understanding the novel and Robinson's writing career because it draws attention to the performative nature of subjectivity. *Walsingham* is the story of a man, who, like Robinson, suffers from his sensibility. When he is disinherited because a son is born to his uncle and aunt, he becomes tormented by his jealousy for this son, who is the consummate gentleman. What Walsingham doesn't know is that Sidney's mother, Lady Aubrey and her servant, Mrs. Blagden, have transformed Sidney, born a girl, into a boy, a performance s/he sustains through the whole novel, unknown to all (including the readers) but the most intimate of her/his friends. Of course, Walsingham and Sidney plan to marry at the end. Sidney is the perfect mate because s/he is a masculinely educated woman; s/he bridges gender:

Sir Sidney was exactly the being whom Isabella had described—he was handsome, polite, accomplished, engaging, and unaffected. He sung, he danced, he played on the mandolin, and spoke the Italian and French languages with the fluency of a native. Yet these were not his only acquirements; he fenced like a professor of the science; painted with the correctness of an artist; was expert at all manly exercises; a delightful poet; and a fascinating companion.

(p. 129)

And Walsingham is his/her perfect mate because he is actually Robinson in drag, a Werther-like man of sensibility, a writer of poetry, and a victim of misjudgment. Rewriting Godwin's *Caleb Williams* from a feminist slant, Robinson thus creates what Julie Shaffer calls a "radical resistance to the ways in which societally-approved roles in the late eighteenth century proved limiting, especially for women" (p. 7).

Robinson returned to these limitations again in *The False Friend* (February 1799), another epistolary novel, which traces the heroine's fatal obsession with a man who turns out to be her father. Another exploration of the dangers of sensibility, *The False Friend* relentlessly traces the destructiveness of Gertrude's obsession, condensing its dangers into a symbolic moment when she touches the bust of Sappho, who represents both the literal and literary mothers from whom she is severed. Perhaps needing to distance herself from such despair, Robinson next produced *The Natural Daughter* (August 1799), her final and probably best novel (though the reviewers despised it), which offers an independent, rational Wollstonecraftian heroine. Set in 1792, this novel follows the perils of Martha Morley, clearly modeled on Robinson (she pursues an acting and then a writing career), who, at the risk of her reputation, protects an illegitimate child. Martha's intelligence is contrasted with her seemingly more proper but selfish sister, Julia, who eventually kills herself in Robespierre's bed. Here again Robinson chal-

lenges the social definition of what it means to be a respectable woman. As Sharon Setzer writes of this novel in the introduction to her 2003 edition, "Robinson complicates the easy equation between 'natural' and 'illegitimate' as well as the identification of her title character" (p. 29). A wonderful moment in the novel marks a change in Robinson's thinking about herself: When Martha is addressed as "one of the Julias or Sapphos of the present day" and then asked "Are you Anna Matilda, or Della Crusca, or Laura Maria?" she answers "I never wrote under either of those signatures" (pp. 234–235). Half jesting, half in earnest, Robinson here mocks her own literary pretensions, drawing attention to the many pseudonyms she used as well as her Della Cruscan history. Martha's rejection of these identities opens the door for Robinson's identity to come, that of Romantic poet.

In addition to her feminist novels, Robinson's *Letter* appeared in the spring of 1799, upholding Wollstonecraft's arguments for the masculine education of women but extending her philosophy farther into the literary realm to create a history of literary women founded on an aristocracy of genius. She also began working on a long poem entitled *The Progress of Liberty* and wrote a series of essays, called *The Sylphid,* for the *Morning Post.* These essays take Pope's character of the Sylph from *The Rape of the Lock* and use that figure to critique the various types of fashionable society, from the figure of the *demi-ton* lady to the man of fashion. At the end of 1799 Robinson replaced Robert Southey as poetry editor of the *Morning Post.* Given all this, it is no wonder that she was intermittently writing her memoirs during these years in an attempt to shape her earlier history. Published in 1801, this text shapes Robinson's intellectual and sexual history to cleanse her reputation and assert her original genius. She also began to collect her poems for publication.

LYRICAL TALES

If Robinson's novels remain unpolished gems, her final volume of poems is a finely cut diamond that showcases her real talent, poetry, and should have consolidated her reputation as a Romantic poet. The culmination of Robinson's poetic career, *Lyrical Tales* is a volume written in "the manner of Wordsworth's [and Coleridge's anonymously published] *Lyrical Ballads,*" as she described it in her inquiry letter to Longman and Rees, also the publishers of *Lyrical Ballads* (quoted in Byrne, p. 360). Dorothy Wordsworth notes that her brother was horrified enough by her imitative gesture to consider changing the title of the second edition of *Lyrical Ballads.* Here again Robinson uses imitation to her advantage, just as an actress makes new by her performance the Shakespeare scene that everyone knows. These poems are of course not imitations but repetitions and echoes of subject and form with a difference marked by Robinson's own concerns and poetic flair. In a review in the *Monthly Mirror,* October 1798, Della Cruscan poetry and the sonnet had been explicitly opposed to the poetry of *Lyrical Ballads.* Publishing these poems under her own name, Mrs. Mary Robinson, she was signaling her entrance into a new, more authentic realm of poetry and attempting to authorize both herself and the young poets of *Lyrical Ballads.*

Like *Lyrical Ballads,* Robinson's *Lyrical Tales* explores figures of social otherness and the effects of dispossession. Astoundingly metrically diverse, the volume includes two kinds of poems, a group of moralistic and ironically satirical tales written in the voice of Tabitha Bramble, an old spinster from Tobias Smollett's *The Expedition of Humphrey Clinker* (1771), and a group of poems each of which focuses on a single estranged figure. The overlaps between the two texts are numerous, from Robinson's revision of Wordsworth's "We Are Seven" in "All Alone" to her racializing of Wordsworth's "The Female Vagrant" and "Forsaken Indian Woman" in her "The Negro Girl" and "The Lascar." In each case, however, Robinson heightens the individual's sense of isolation and trauma. Again and again, individuals like the Negro Girl, the Lascar, Marguerite, Edmund, the Alien Boy, the poor singing Dame, and the Fugitive are made to feel their own otherness and their inability to control their surroundings. They turn to speech in self-defense,

but even these acts backfire upon them. Robinson, disabled and isolated at the end of her life, clearly identified her social and authorial position with these marginalized figures. As she writes in "The Lascar," "And who but such a wretch can tell, / The transports of the Indian boy?" (*Selected Poems,* p. 205).

More particularly, the two types of poems in Robinson's *Lyrical Tales,* though very different in nature, emphasize the dispossession of the female speaker and the dangers of romance, a theme throughout all of Robinson's writing. "Poor Marguerite," the story of a woman who, like Sappho and Robinson, has lost her lover and connection to the world, ends up a *"lifeless form"* (p. 255), dead on the beach. Though Marguerite is not a poet, she has the sensibility of one, and she sings "her Song" "with loud fantastic tone / ...her wild strain, sad—alone" (p. 253). Marguerite's fate—the dissociation of mind and body, form and content that the poem traces—reveals the results of thwarted creativity. The tales make even more explicit the dangerous entrapment of romance's conventions. Reminiscent of *The Canterbury Tales,* the moralistic endings of the tales conflict with the severe punishments that women receive in these poems for expressing their desires and asserting themselves. No one escapes: neither older women, like Granny Grey in her "Love Tale" and Deborah in "Deborah's Parrot, a Village Tale," who monitor the love lives of others because of their own unfulfilling realities, nor younger women, like Mistress Homespun in "The Mistletoe, a Christmas Tale" or Kate in "The Fortune-Teller, a Gypsy Tale," whose extramarital desires transgress social codes. Their attempts to control their own reputations and write their own stories incriminate them. Like Deborah, who is betrayed by her parrot, or Mistress Twyford in "The Confessor, a Sanctified Tale," who is betrayed by her parroting son, these women are continually forced, often physically, to see the dangers of speaking. As Lisa Vargo writes in "Tabitha Bramble and *The Lyrical Tales*" (2002), in these poems, "Robinson questions the transformative powers of nature and the imagination; she insists that desire and intolerance cannot so easily be extricated from social and material conditions" (p. 48). At the end of her life Robinson was especially aware of how these social and material conditions impinged on one's reputation.

In the last two years of her life Robinson's decline and financial struggles confined her to her house and to the solace of her intellectual abilities. In an oft-quoted letter to Jane Porter in September 1800, Robinson opined, "Oh! Heavens! If a select society could be formed,—a little colony of mental powers, a world of talents, drawn into a small but brilliant circle,—what a splendid sunshine would it display" (*Selected Poems*, pp. 43–44). But only a month before, she had written to Samuel Jackson Pratt commenting on the number of visitors—"charming literary characters—*authoresses*" (Cameron and Reiman, eds., vol. 1, p. 231)—she was receiving at her cottage at Englefield Green. This circle included the Porter sisters, John Flaxman, Godwin, Pratt, Eliza Fenwick, Elizabeth Gunning, John Wolcot, James Marshall, and Coleridge. By mid-September, however, Robinson was very ill, isolated, and impoverished, but she was still writing. In the final six months, in addition to finishing *Lyrical Tales,* she continued her editorial work for the *Morning Post;* she was working on a new novel entitled *Jasper;* she translated Joseph Hager's *Picture of Palermo* from the German in ten days; she published, in the *Morning Post,* "The Present State of the Manners, Society, Etc., Etc, of the Metropolis of England," a series of brilliant essays that capture both the limits and the wonders (in particular, women authors) of late-eighteenth-century urban culture; and she completed her arrangement of *The Poetical Works.*

An incredibly driven and charismatic woman, Robinson died of heart failure on December 26, 1800, at Englefield Green, near Old Windsor, attended only by her daughter and Elizabeth Weale, who remained Maria's companion for the rest of her life. Perhaps coming full circle, she was buried in Old Windsor Churchyard, near Windsor Castle, one of the prince's abodes; she was still in her early forties. One of her last poems, "Harvest Home," written for her epic work in progress *The Progress of Liberty* and a precursor to Keats's "To Autumn," provides a fitting final image. In these beautiful lines, Robinson, now in "the slow decline of Autumn," perhaps reflects metaphorically on the harvest of her poetic career:

Who has not seen the chearful HARVEST HOME!
Enliv'ning the scorch'd field, and greeting gay
The slow decline of Autumn? All around
The yellow sheaves, catching the burning beam,
Glow, golden-lustred; and the trembling stem
Of the slim oat, or azure corn-flow'r,
Waves on the hedge-rows shady …. Glowing scene!
Nature's long holiday! Luxuriant, rich,
In her proud progeny, she smiling marks
Their graces, now mature, and wonder-fraught!
(Selected Poems, p. 319)

EPILOGUE

Though Robinson hoped to "SNATCH A WREATH FROM BEYOND THE GRAVE" (*Memoirs,* vol. 1, p. 166) it has taken nearly two hundred years for her writing to be given the serious attention it deserves and for her to be seen as the gifted and important writer she is. The publication of three biographies in 2004 and 2005 as well as several monographs in which she is the central figure have begun to recover her critical role in the literary history of romanticism and women's writing. In fact, however, it might be argued that this recovery began even before Robinson's death with her commencement of her *Memoirs.* Ever attuned to the literary marketplace, Robinson was savvy enough to know that her place in literary history was not guaranteed and, given her history, would have to be fought for. Maria Elizabeth continued this recuperation with the publication of the *Memoirs* in 1801, the *Wild Wreath,* a miscellany of poems by Robinson and others in her circle, in 1804, and the *Poetical Works* in 1806. Maria was intent on focusing attention on Robinson's debilitated state at the end of her life in order to downplay Robinson's *corps* and to highlight instead her corpus. Of course, *corps* and corpus are inseparable in Robinson's oeuvre. But Robinson's sexual reputation continued to overshadow her literary one. Jane Porter, one of Robinson's closest friends at the end of her life, never dared to publish the memoirs she wrote about Robinson for fear of the taint they might cast on her character.

Until the end of the twentieth century Robinson's life overshadowed her remarkable literary achievements. During the Regency years, satires of the prince continued to recall Perdita as the prince's first mistress. While she clearly influenced the second-generation Romantic poets (the Shelleys, Keats, Felicia Hemans, Charlotte Dacre), male and female alike, the Victorian period all but forgot her in its concern with middle-class respectability. Though her metrical innovations haunt the writings of Laetitia Landon, Elizabeth Barrett, and Alfred, Lord Tennyson, as Stuart Curran has suggested, Robinson's poems and novels went out of print as literary tastes moved to the psychological complexities of the dramatic monologue and the realist novel. In the earlier part of the twentieth century a renewed interest in Robinson's story led to several romanticized and fictionalized biographies, including Stanley Makower's *Perdita: A Romance in Biography* (1908), E. Barrington's *The Exquisite Perdita* (1926), Marguerite Steen's *The Lost One: A Biography of Mary (Perdita) Robinson* (1937), Robert Bass's *The Green Dragoon: The Lives of Banastre Tarleton and Mary Robinson* (1957), and Jean Plaidy's *Perdita's Prince* (1969). It has been the job of late-twentieth- and early-twenty-first-century literary scholars and biographers to put her sensational life into perspective and to emphasize her central role in the shaping of British Romantic writing and eighteenth-century culture. Robinson's belief in the truth of her vision, her commitment to a literature grounded in sensibility and compassion for the other, her ability to change form and play new roles as literary and cultural fashions shifted, her political commitment to equality based on merit, and her pursuit of metrical innovation make her a central figure for any understanding of the late eighteenth century. As a woman writer, aware of literary history and her own reputation, Robinson challenges the very conventions of gender and genre that we have come to take for granted.

Selected Bibliography

WORKS OF MARY ROBINSON

POETRY

Poems by Mrs. Robinson. London: C. Parker, 1775.

Captivity, a Poem; and Celadon and Lydia, a Tale. London: T. Beckett, 1775.

Ainsi va la monde, a Poem Inscribed to Robert Merry. London: John Bell, 1790.

The Beauties of Mrs. Robinson. Selected and Arranged from Her Poetical Works. London: H. D. Symonds, 1791.

Poems by Mrs. Robinson. London: J. Bell, 1791.

Monody to the Memory of Sir Joshua Reynolds. London: J. Bell, 1792.

Poems by Mrs. Robinson. London: J. Evans and T. Becket, 1793.

Modern Manners; a Poem in Two Cantos. London: J. Evans, 1793.

Ode to the Harp of the Late Accomplished and Amiable Louisa Hanway. London: J. Bell, 1793.

Sight, The Cavern of Woe, and Solitude. London: Evans and Becket, 1793.

Monody to the Memory of the Late Queen of France. London: J. Evans, 1793.

Sappho and Phaon, in a Series of Legitimate Sonnets. London: Hookham and Carpenter, 1796.

Lyrical Tales. London: Longman and Rees, 1800.

The Mistletoe. A Christmas Tale. By Laura Maria. London: Laurie and Whittle, 1800.

The Progress of Liberty. Published in *Memoirs* (1801) and *Poetical Works* (1806).

FICTION

Vancenza; or, The Dangers of Credulity, a Moral Tale. 2 vols. London: J. Bell, 1972.

The Widow; or, A Picture of Modern Times. 2 vols. London: Hookham and Carpenter, 1794.

Angelina; a Novel. 3 vols. London: Hookham and Carpenter, 1796.

Hubert de Sevrac: A Romance of the Eighteenth Century. 3 vols. London: Hookham and Carpenter, 1796.

Walsingham; or, The Pupil of Nature. 4 vols. London: T. N. Longman, 1797.

The False Friend, a Domestic Story. 4 vols. London: Longman and Rees, 1799.

The Natural Daughter, with Portraits of the Leadenhead Family. 2 vols. London: Longman and Rees, 1799.

DRAMA

The Songs, Chorusses, etc. in *The Lucky Escape, a Comic Opera.* London, 1778.

Nobody. Unpublished. Staged at Drury Lane, 1794.

The Sicilian Lover: A Tragedy in Five Acts. London: Hookham and Carpenter, 1796.

NONFICTION PROSE AND TRANSLATION

Impartial Reflections on the Present Situation of the Queen of France, by a Friend to Humanity. London: John Bell, 1791.

A Letter to the Women of England, on the Injustice of Mental Subordination. By Anne Frances Randall. London: Longman and Rees, 1799. Reissued under Robinson's name as *Thoughts on the Condition of Women, and on the Injustice of Mental Subordination.* Joseph Hager's *Picture of Palermo.* Translated from the German. London: R. Phillips, 1800.

"Present State of the Manners, Society, etc. etc. of the Metropolis of England." *Morning Post* (August–November 1800).

Anecdotes of the Duke of Lauzun, the Duke of Chartres, and Marie Antoinette. *Monthly Magazine* (February–November 1800).

POSTHUMOUS COLLECTIONS

Memoirs of the Late Mrs. Robinson, Written by Herself. Edited by Maria E. Robinson. 4 vols. London: R. Phillips, 1801.

The Wild Wreath. Edited by Maria E. Robinson. London: R. Phillips, 1804. *The Poetical Works of the Late Mrs. Mary Robinson.* Edited by Maria E. Robinson. 3 vols. London: R. Phillips, 1806. (Reprinted in one volume in 1824.)

MODERN EDITIONS

Lyrical Tales. Facsimile edition. Introduction by Jonathan Wordsworth. Oxford: Oxford University Press, 1989; and an internet edition (http://digital.lib.ucdavis.edu/projects/bwrp/Works/RobiMLyric.htm).

Perdita: The Memoirs of Mary Robinson. Edited by M. J. Levy. London: Peter Owen, 1994; and an Internet edition (http://digital.library.upenn.edu/women/robinson/memoirs/memoirs.html).

Poems, 1791. Facsimile edition. Introduction by Jonathan Wordsworth. Oxford: Oxford University Press, 1994; and an Internet edition (http://digital.library.upenn.edu/women/robinson/1791/1791.html).

Poetical Works of the Late Mrs. Robinson. 1824. Brown University Women Writers Project. Providence, R.I., 1994; and a facsimile edition, introduction by Caroline

Franklin, London: Routledge/Thoemmes Press, 1996.

A Letter to the Women of England. Facsimile edition. Introduction by Jonathan Wordsworth. Oxford: Oxford University Press, 1998; and an Internet edition (http://www.rc.umd.edu/editions/robinson/).

Sappho and Phaon. Facsimile edition. Introduction by Jonathan Wordsworth. Oxford: Oxford University Press, 2000; a facsimile edition, introduction by Terence Hoagwood and Rebecca Jackson, Delmar, N.Y.: Scholar's Facsimiles and Reprints, 1995; and an Internet edition (http://etext.virginia.edu/britpo/sappho/sappho.html).

Selected Poems. Edited by Judith Pascoe. Peterborough, Ont.: Broadview, 2000.

A Letter to the Women of England and The Natural Daughter. Edited by Sharon Setzer. Peterborough, Ont.: Broadview, 2003.

Walsingham; or, The Pupil of Nature. Edited by Julie Shaffer. Peterborough, Ont.: Broadview, 2003; and a facsimile edition, introduction by Peter Garside, London: Routledge/Thoemmes, 1992.

The Wild Wreath. Internet edition (http://digital.lib.ucdavis.edu/projects/bwrp/Works/RobiMWildW.htm).

CRITICAL AND BIOGRAPHICAL STUDIES

Bass, Robert D. *The Green Dragoon: The Lives of Banastre Tarleton and Mary Robinson.* New York: Holt, 1957.

Bolton, Betsy. "Romancing the Stone: 'Perdita' Robinson in Wordsworth's London." *ELH* 64, no. 3:727–759 (fall 1997).

Byrne, Paula. *Perdita: The Literary, Theatrical, Scandalous Life of Mary Robinson.* New York: Random House, 2004.

Cameron, Kenneth Neill, and Donald Reiman, eds. *Shelley and His Circle.* Vol. 1. Cambridge, Mass.: Harvard University Press, 1961.

Coleridge, Samuel T. *The Collected Letters of Samuel Taylor Coleridge.* Edited by Earl Leslie Griggs. 6 vols. Oxford: Clarendon Press, 1956.

Craciun, Adriana. *Fatal Women of Romanticism.* Cambridge, Mass.: Cambridge University Press, 2003.

Craciun, Adriana, ed. "Present State of the Manners, Society, Etc. Etc. of the Metropolis of England." *PMLA: Publications of the Modern Language Association of America* 119, no. 1:103–107 (January 2004).

Cross, Ashley. "From *Lyrical Ballads* to *Lyrical Tales*: Mary Robinson's Reputation and the Problem of Literary Debt." *Studies in Romanticism* 40:571–605 (2001).

Curran, Stuart. "Mary Robinson's Lyrical Tales in Context." In *Re-visioning Romanticism: British Women Writers, 1776–1837.* Edited by Carol Shiner Wilson and Joel Haefner. Philadelphia: University of Pennsylvania Press, 1994. Pp. 17–35.

Davenport, Hester. *The Prince's Mistress: A Life of Mary Robinson.* Gloucestershire, U.K.: Sutton, 2004.

Fergus, J., and J. Thaddeus. "Women, Publishers, and

Money, 1790–1820." *Studies in Eighteenth-Century Culture* 17:191–207 (1987).

Fulford, Tim. "Mary Robinson and the Abyssinian Maid: Coleridge's Muses and Feminist Criticism." *Romanticism on the Net: An Electronic Journal Devoted to Romantic Studies* 13 (February 1999).

Gristwood, Sarah. *Perdita: Royal Mistress, Writer, Romantic.* London: Bantam, 2005.

Labbe, Jacqueline M. "Selling One's Sorrows: Charlotte Smith, Mary Robinson and the Marketing of Poetry." *Wordsworth Circle* 25, no. 2:68–71 (spring 1994).

Lee, Debbie. "The Wild Wreath: Cultivating a Poetic Circle for Mary Robinson." *Studies in the Literary Imagination* 30, no. 1:23–33 (1997).

Luther, Susan. "A Stranger Minstrel: Coleridge's Mrs. Robinson." *Studies in Romanticism* 33, no. 3: 391–409 (fall 1994).

McGann, Jerome. *The Poetics of Sensibility: A Revolution in Literary Style.* Oxford: Clarendon Press, 1996.

Mellor, Ann. "Making an Exhibition of Her Self: Mary 'Perdita' Robinson and Nineteenth-Century Scripts of Female Sexuality." *Nineteenth-Century Contexts* 22, no. 3:271–304 (2000).

Pascoe, Judith. "Mary Robinson and the Literary Marketplace." In *Romantic Women Writers: Voices and Countervoices.* Edited by Paula R. Feldman and Theresa M. Kelley. Hanover, N.H.: University Press of New England, 1995. Pp. 252–268.

———. *Romantic Theatricality: Gender, Poetry and Spectatorship.* Ithaca, N.Y.: Cornell University Press, 1997.

———. Introduction to *Mary Robinson: Selected Poems.* Peterborough, Ont.: Broadview, 2000.

Peterson, Linda H. "Becoming an Author: Mary Robinson's *Memoirs* and the Origins of the Woman Artist's Autobiography." In *Re-visioning Romanticism: British Women Writers, 1776–1837.* Edited by Carol Shiner Wilson and Joel Haefner. Philadelphia: University of Pennsylvania Press, 1994. Pp. 36–50.

Robinson, Daniel. "Reviving the Sonnet: Women Romantic Poets and the Sonnet Claim." *European Romantic Review* 6, no. 1:98–127 (summer 1995).

Setzer, Sharon. Introduction to *A Letter to the Women of England and The Natural Daughter.* Peterborough, Ont.: Broadview, 2003.

Shaffer, Julie. Introduction to *Walsingham; or, The Pupil of Nature.* Peterborough, Ont.: Broadview, 2003.

Ty, Eleanor. *Empowering the Feminine: The Narratives of Mary Robinson, Jane West, and Amelia Opie, 1796–1812.* Toronto: University of Toronto Press, 1998.

Vargo, Lisa. "Tabitha Bramble and the *Lyrical Tales.*" *Women's Writing* 9, no. 1:37–52 (2002).

Women's Writing 9, no. 1 (2002). Special issue on Mary Robinson edited by Jacqueline Labbe.

PETER SCUPHAM

(1933—)

Neil Powell

ONE OF PETER Scupham's many collections of poems is called, with characteristically wry humor, *Out Late* (1986): the title, though apt in itself, glances back to the fact that he was a late starter in his literary career, whose first book did not appear until 1972, when he was thirty-nine. This is something more than an interesting oddity. It means that there is no "early Scupham," no cringe-making juvenilia or brash youthful stuff which might prompt an Audenesque or Gravesian cull: his *Collected Poems* (2002; in citations hereafter referred to as *CP*), published to mark his seventieth birthday, contains—with only a few minor adjustments—every poem from all his previous collections. It also means that anything Scupham cares to tell us about his younger self, which is a good deal, is told from the perspective of recollected memory rather than fresh experience.

John Peter Scupham was born in Liverpool on February 24, 1933, the son of John Scupham and Dorothy Lacey, née Clark. He was educated at a variety of schools including the Perse, in Cambridge, and St. George's, in Harpenden; after National Service in the Royal Army Ordnance Corps, he went up to Emmanuel College, Cambridge, initially to read history but immediately switching to English; he graduated in 1957. That year, he married Carola Braunholtz: they had one daughter (Kate) and three sons (Toby, Giles, and Roger). He became a schoolteacher, first at Skegness Grammar School in Lincolnshire, and then, from 1961, at St. Christopher School, Letchworth, Hertfordshire, where he stayed until his retirement. On the surface this perhaps looks like a conventional enough life; but St. Christopher—international, vegetarian, "progressive," and with a then unconventional emphasis on the creative arts—was in fact an exceptional environment that suited Scupham's talents. There, with Margaret Steward, he established a highly successful drama department that eventually included a professionally equipped theater and, indeed, launched several professional theatrical careers. Meanwhile, not directly connected with the school but in much the same spirit of creativity, Scupham founded the Mandeville Press with John Mole, producing hand-set, illustrated limited editions of poetry from the cellar of his home in Hitchin. These activities resemble two panels of a triptych, in which writing and publishing his own poems formed the inescapable third.

As a teacher, he achieved a perfect balance of playfulness and scholarship which both entranced younger pupils and inspired those in their final years of secondary schooling, many of whom went on to study literature at university. When advised, on medical grounds, to reduce his teaching load and relinquish his post as head of English (which he did, in 1978), he devoted even more energy to directing plays and printing pamphlets, while taking on yet another role as a secondhand and antiquarian bookseller. In 1988, he retired from full-time teaching and moved with Margaret Steward to Old Hall, a sixteenth-century manor house in rural Norfolk, which they have gradually rescued from its semiderelict state (discovering some remarkable Tudor wall-paintings in the process) and where each summer they codirect an open-air Shakespeare production in the grounds. Scupham continues to run a catalogue book business—now named Mermaid Books, after the painted mermaids on the first-floor pediment at Old Hall—and, of course, to write.

PETER SCUPHAM

THE SMALL CONTAINERS *AND* THE SNOWING GLOBE

Scupham's first two collections, a substantial pamphlet titled *The Small Containers* and a hardback book titled *The Snowing Globe*, both appeared in 1972 under the auspices of Harry Chambers, the editor of the Manchester-based magazine *Phoenix* and of Peterloo Poets. These first collections strike a slightly different note from Scupham's subsequent work—they are seemingly light hearted and airily debonair, while the content is more straightforwardly drawn from material immediately to hand—yet the voice is an unmistakable one from the start. He opens, riskily, with a jaunty self-portrait in rhymed triplets called "Man on the Edge," placing himself strategically off center: if the poem evokes a distant recollection of E. M. Forster's famous description of C. P. Cavafy standing "at a slight angle to to the universe," it also offers more than a hint of Edward Lear in the tumbling procession of details. In the middle of the poem, these two elements fuse into something almost like a manifesto:

He laughs much, with what could nearly be innocence,
Tickling himself with feathers of nonsense;
His words all lean sideways, blown by his eloquence.
(CP, p. 3)

This sense of strategic lightness, of gravity made manageable, quickly becomes a trademark: "Be a pink bus-ticket used as a bookmark, / A maidenhair fern, pressed but eloquent," he advises in "Lessons in Survival" (*CP,* p. 36), as if part of the trick might be to encompass as much seriousness and eloquence as possible without getting above oneself. "If poetry is concerned with knowledge," he writes in the introduction to *The Small Containers,* "[W. H.] Auden is surely right when he calls it a game as well" (p. 6), and in a more recent prose self-portrait he recalls his childhood obsession with the nuts-and-bolts creative craftsmanship of Meccano model construction kits: "what better injunction can there be to a poet," he wonders, "than to make sure that his nuts are not tightened too much as he goes along, but are all tightened together at the last moment?" ("On Peter Scupham," p. 17). As

if to prove the connection between making things and making poems, the original dust jacket of *The Snowing Globe* has a photograph of a "spare parts" sculpture by Scupham, titled *Soldier,* put together out of odd bits and pieces. Scupham's method is always that of the poet as maker, and if that sounds an unfashionable formulation we might remind ourselves that T. S. Eliot called Ezra Pound *"il miglior fabbro"*—"the better craftsman."

The stuff of which the poems in the first two collections is made is often domestic, though not cozily so. Scupham charts the lives of small pets, from the moment they arrive in carrier bags until the moment when "Our serious children make gay funeral, / Huddled upon the decorated earth" (*CP,* p. 5); he watches his daughter draw "heraldic" fish on a blackboard (*CP,* p. 6); he visits the eye clinic and asks, "Is Purgatory like this?" (*CP,* p. 12). "Early Summer" is a time when "Small things get lost" and

The rambling bee, obtuse and hairy,
Unzips with his dull purr
The studious air
(CP, p. 23)

Even breakfast, in "Good Morning," is an assault course through the "inordinate chatter and pother of the world" (*CP,* p. 35). Comical, exasperating, and absurd, this contingent clutter is there to be wryly observed and then lightly batted away, like an insistent yet harmless insect. In "Arena," the poet's son watches puppets dancing and he asks his father how they work: "'By magic.' Then, corrective, the quick codicil: / 'By string.'" (p. 14). Scupham's poems, too, may be worked by string, but he can make it look like magic.

Love poems such as "Hungry" (*CP,* p. 40) and "Limbs" (*CP,* p. 41) have a physical urgency that later shades into something more carefully nuanced; while "A Wartime Childhood" (*CP,* pp. 25–28) is the prototype for Scupham's later retrospective sequences, here still buoyed up by fragments of chirpiness, as in "Oh, Mickey Mouse, you ruined man, / Your wrecked face bobs in the garden grass." We shall meet Peter Scupham in both these modes again.

PETER SCUPHAM

PREHISTORIES *AND* THE HINTERLAND

Although Scupham's poetic voice has not altered radically over the years—a consequence, arguably, of his relatively late start as a published writer—it is nevertheless possible to distinguish successive phases in his earlier books. In phase two, represented by *Prehistories* (1975) and *The Hinterland* (1977), the most notable tendency is for his area of interest to move outward and, as much to the point, downward. *Prehistories* opens magnificently, with a cluster of poems grounded in landscape: "West Country," "Public Footpath To," "Ploughland," and the sequence "Excavations." The gain is immediately evident, as his delight in verbal making locks onto imagery that is at once more solid and more expansive than previously. "Public Footpath To" is a perfect fusion of these apparent opposites:

Beyond the dented churns, the huddled farmyard,
Look, a green and lackadaisical finger
Reveals a hair-line fracture in the earth.

(CP, p. 49)

This opening exactly follows the eye's track, from the milk churns at the farmyard's edge through to the green fingerpost and the path it signals, which appears at this distance to be a fracture through the fields: the risky "lackadaisical" could appear fey in another writer's hands but here seems fully earned, consonant both with the skewed unsteadiness of the signpost (perhaps broken off, as in the title) and with the delight in language we have already come to expect from this poet. The whole poem is full of such felicities (for instance, "a church tower makes her slight invitation") and the ending—"one self-sufficient tractor / Dragging the sullen landscape down to earth"—exemplifies another trait of Scupham's, the telescoping of a literal and a figurative meaning into a single phrase. "Ploughland," too, is rich in linguistic twists which are both surprising and right—"knotted ploughland," "pawky hedgerows," "A shower of bells"—as well as passages such as this densely suggestive couplet, in which "rash," "rubricates," and "foundered" all resonate with powerful ambiguities: "A rash of brickwork rubricates their claim: / A foundered house, and a forgotten name" (*CP,* p. 50).

The deepening process in *Prehistories* is partly archaeological—the sequence called "Excavations" digs into a number of specific sites, including that of the poet's own home in Hitchin, and he describes the book's central theme as "our bond, strong though half-understood, with the stones and silences of periods before recorded history" ("Spring 1977: *The Hinterland*," p. 60)—and partly to do with less tangible, more ghostly aspects of the past. "Ghosts are a poet's working capital. / They hold their hands out from the further shore," he writes in a wonderfully memorable couplet from the book's title poem (*CP,* p. 83). But are they and do they? In fact, it takes a very particular sort of poet to attend so assiduously to the departed over the Styx: one who feels at least as at home in the past as in the present and who indeed makes no great distinction between the two; for Scupham has, he says, "always found ghosts, both real and imaginary, more substantial than human beings" ("On Peter Scupham," p. 17). Thus, a poem such as "Effacements" may seem at first reading to be a compacted example of the churchyard-visitation genre, like Philip Larkin's "Church Going" or "An Arundel Tomb'; but where Larkin seems excluded and baffled by the past, Scupham is perfectly at home, drawing obliquely on a nineteenth-century commonplace book and a passage from John Ruskin to people the unidentified Hertfordshire church of the poem. Finally, in a brilliant syntactical twist, the ghosts jump from noun to verb and the poem concludes with an appropriately grand Yeatsian cadence:

The last of day ghosts out a window; stains
The scarred porch wall, whose rough and honeyed
  weight
Glows from the shade: stones so intangible
A child might slip between them, bones and all.

(CP, p. 120)

In the ambitiously interlocking sequence of fifteen sonnets that gives its title to *The Hinterland* (*CP,* pp. 103–110), the ghosts are the dead of the Great War, viewed across the years from a heat wave at "The rim of summer, when great wars begin": some readers find these poems difficult, while others are rather oddly put off by the formal structure (each sonnet's last line becomes the opening line of the next, and the fourteen first/last lines stack up to make the fifteenth sonnet). But as long as one grasps the two fixed points within which the sequence oscillates— essentially, the summers of 1914 and 1975— much of the difficulty disappears; one needs also to see that the richness and density of language here belongs in the tradition of Wallace Stevens' "Sunday Morning" ("through a gauze-green skin / Cut sun lies lapidary on a book," for instance). Occasionally a line may seem too tightly packed, too loaded, such as "But there's a no-man's land where skull-talk goes," the awkwardness underlined by its structural recurrence in the sequence. Yet then one notices how deft it is in another way, as a Wordsworthian hinge, recalling "But there's a tree, of many, one" from the Immortality Ode (this is among the many poems that seem to glance over Scupham's shoulder here). The sequence and the summer heat wave both eventually end with "Diminished thunders, breaking in new rain," a poised image of rebirth subtly qualified by foreboding. "The Hinterland" is an engrossing sequence, of which a properly attentive close reading might easily occupy an essay of its own.

Of course, there are other sides to Scupham in *Prehistories* and *The Hinterland*. The former includes a series of love poems, first published in pamphlet form as *The Gift* in 1973. There are ghosts here, too—"We are the small ghosts of summer" (*CP*, p. 69)—as well as writing of a courtliness that is perfectly consonant with his distinctive voice: "I am most taken by this demure mood, lady: / The gentle voice with which you ease the air" (*CP*, p. 64). Elsewhere, he adopts a sturdy rhythmic vigor: in the opening lines of "Atlantic"—"There's loss in the Atlantic sky / Smoking her course from sea to sea" (*CP*, p. 100)—he could be John Masefield. And there is wry humor in the delightful "Answers to Correspondents: *Girls' Own,* 1881" (*CP*, pp. 97–99), which reworks a Victorian agony aunt's replies to her schoolgirl readers. They, too, are ghosts in their way.

SUMMER PALACES *AND* WINTER QUARTERS

Scupham is a poet who likes each individual collection to have its distinctive character and sense of cohesion—and one who hopes that these small edifices may, with luck, in turn form parts of a larger architectural whole: "It could be a Tower of Babel; it's not as tidy as a Palladian Villa. Let's say it's more like the rambling, half-tumbledown four-centuries-old house in which I live. Each book makes a kind of room" ("Writing the Poem," p. 22). *Summer Palaces* (1980) opens with poems in which half-neglected objects—a children's cart, a garden lantern—are transmogrified by their abandonment into more complex and interesting things; he is not much concerned with the new and the pristine. "The Cart" (*CP*, p. 123), in becoming "only a collection of leaves," has lost one identity and gained another; its somewhere has become a nowhere—"Is this, then, no-place?"—but that in turn is another somewhere. "Garden Lantern" (*CP*, pp. 125–126) teases a similar paradox: this source of light is now "A dull pavilion, mossed with verdigris, / Storing dark nonsense in its cavities." It is no accident that these poems are followed by a substantial group about theater, with its comparable transformations, its continual shifting between somewhere and nowhere, light and dark. Indeed, the very next poem, "Lighting Rehearsal" (*CP*, pp. 126–127), touches on both these ideas, "Until the darkness gathered in the wings / Lowers all colours": for even in Scupham's most brilliantly lit poems, there is always dark nonsense in the garden lantern and darkness in the wings. Here, of course, the lanterns are of an altogether brighter sort; and here, as elsewhere, Scupham's compacted language takes for granted some quite specialized information. A reader may stumble over "Fresnels and floods cool their bright hutches down," baffled both by sense and by cadence, unless he knows that a Fresnel is a hutch-shaped theater light, that its "s" is unsounded and that its stress falls on the second "e."

Theater is an art of transformation; Scupham re-transforms it into poetry. In "The Tragedy Of" and "The Comedy Of" (*CP*, pp. 130–133), two little sequences of three poems each, he deftly reinvents half a dozen Shakespeare plays; no characters are named, however, and the effect is of a distillation into something at once familiar and unparticularized, rich and strange. Then, in "Twelfth Night," which we will now naturally assume to be about Shakespeare's comedy, he once more stands expectation on its head by reflecting instead on an actual twelfth night, the bittersweet end of Christmas:

Our candles, lit, re-lit, have gone down now:
Only the tears, the veils, the hanging tree
Whose burning gauze thins out across the sky,
Whose brightness dies to image. And the snow.

(*CP*, p. 134)

Any lingering misapprehension, derived perhaps from a casual reading of his first two collections, that Scupham is a frivolous or a flippant poet will by now have been thoroughly dispelled. He chooses this moment to introduce another characteristic and progressively darkening mode (briefly prefigured in *The Snowing Globe*), in a retrospective sequence dealing with childhood, parents, the World War II—or some combination of these, for him, overlapping themes. In fact, the poems in "A Cambridgeshire Childhood" (*CP*, pp. 136–141) are strangely uninformative about the child himself: Scupham's method is to accumulate images and meditations on images, sometimes suppressing the links between them, rather than to dwell on the self which records them. It is hard to think of another writer in whose autobiographical poems the first person singular figures so seldom. The most direct piece in the sequence, and the darkest, is the sixth, about a mad neighbor who inhabits

A slattern house, reeking with dirt and music,
A compound of long grass, drawn round with wire,
A summer sky, aching with Cambridge blue—
These are the substances of her misery
Which forces through our bonded bricks and mortar.

(*CP*, p. 140)

Scupham recognizes the way in which "misery" turns to something concrete, a compound substance which can absorb almost anything into itself: thus, when her son visits, "the sobbing

furies / Thicken at night"; even "Our lives become a part / Of that insistent voice, those wavering grasses." Meanwhile, of course, it is wartime:

Low overhead the puddering doodlebugs
Comb the cold air, each weight of random pain
Clenched tight [...]

(*CP*, p. 140)

The notable intensity of this writing is paradoxically increased by that absurdly childish yet also ominous-sounding "puddering." Ultimately it is the poet's mother's "love" for her neighbor which "Betrays her to the ambulance, and asylum," another shrewd perception: the betrayal comes inevitably with the love.

Summer Palaces is a rich book, containing among much else the very different sequences "Megaliths and Water" (*CP*, pp. 145–148) and "Natura" (*CP*, pp. 154–161), but one other poem particularly needs comment as a kind of detached pendant to "A Cambridgeshire Childhood." This is "The Gatehouse" (*CP*, pp. 148–149). On one level it describes a childhood memory: of the railway-crossing gatehouse in Lincolnshire, near his grandparents' home. But this is layered with the exact time of the poem's composition, which happened late one evening while Scupham's son was playing Chopin,

And a grandfather whom he never knew
Plays Brahms and Schumann at the same keyboard—
Schiedmayer and Soehne, Stuttgart—
The old, stronger hands ghosting a ground-bass
Out of a life whose texture still eludes me,
Yet both hold up their candles to the night.

(*CP*, p. 149)

This grandfather is the "H. J. B." of the eponymous poem (*CP*, pp. 141–142) and of "Notes from a War Diary" (*CP*, pp. 198–203), from *Winter Quarters* (1983), where, German-born but Anglicized, he sardonically records the experience of fighting for England in the Great War. So "The Gatehouse" spreads out from the poet's own memory to embrace three other generations: his son, his son's grandparents, and his own grandparents. It is a rapt, mysterious piece of fewer than thirty lines; and it was completed in precisely the time his son continued to play the piano.

The counterpart to "A Cambridgeshire Childhood" in Scupham's next volume, *Winter Quarters,* is "Conscriptions: National Service 1952–1954" (*CP,* pp. 170–179): the point, one might too simply suggest, at which the boy becomes a man. National Service, Scupham told *PN Review* in 1984, "is a curious sort of time: it's time out of time, it's quite unlike anything else that happens in your life…a kind of comedy of pretended violence with, in my observation of other people in it, tragic elements" ("Lessons in Survival," p. 44). Although there are fleeting echoes of Henry Reed's Second World War sequence of poems "Lessons of the War" (1946)—especially in the opening of "Range": "Your weapons are given you to kill the enemy"—the most striking aspect of these poems is the way in which Scupham molds such intractable material to his own style. Anyone looking for the rough-and-ready treatment of National Service in 1950s fiction or drama (as in Arnold Wesker's 1962 play, *Chips with Everything*) will be disappointed; so will seekers after the autobiographical-confessional "I." That simply is not Scupham's method, and, in any case, one intended effect of army service is to subsume "I" into "we." So, in a vivid contraction from "Sunday," "We yawn our backs upon the iron bedsteads" while time seems to stand still:

A choleric sun, nailed to its meridian,
Bothers the lazy hours from slipping westward,
Idle on their afternoon parade.

(*CP,* p. 172)

This short stanza perfectly illustrates Scupham's skill: it is lucid and evocative, yet everything about it is subtly askew (the sun is neither choleric nor nailed; the hours neither lazy nor idle nor on parade; and nor do hours slip westward). It is, however, a technique which John Donne, with his own highly individual treatment of the sun, would surely have recognized and understood.

The tragic dimension of National Service emerges in two symmetrically placed poems, "Scapegoat" and "The Tents," the second and second-from-last poems in the "Conscriptions" sequence. The first describes the archetypal army misfit: "Nothing about you that will take a shine." Yet Scupham subtly realizes how such a person, like the hopeless last-to-be-picked member of a games team at school, is a sort of communal necessity:

You are our crying need,
The dregs and lees of our incompetence,
A dark difference, a blur on the sharp air

(*CP,* p. 171)

In "The Tents," he remembers sharing a tent with a soldier "who was giving every appearance of going quietly mad" and whose brother, it eventually emerged, had recently been hanged: "Night after night he picks a sentence over / Until we riddle out the half-told secret." Both these poems are unusual in Scupham's work of this period in their portrayal of strangers to whom he is connected only by briefly shared experience; and both are notable for their scrupulous balance of sympathy and detachment.

The theater poems in *Summer Palaces* also find their altered counterparts in *Winter Quarters:* a short sequence of five poems called "Transformation Scenes" (*CP,* pp. 182–186). These are about places which, while drama may produce an illusion of reality out of unreality (or magic out of string), produce unreality out of reality: the Quaker poet John Scott's eighteenth-century grotto at Ware, for example, or the fantastic Welsh village of "Portmeirion": "Such sprezzatura!" They are jaunty, high-spirited pieces, welcome diversions in a collection which often edges close to the troubled present: for instance, in "The Candles" (*CP,* pp. 207–208), which meditates on Ronald Reagan's instruction to light a candle for Poland, or in "Incident Room" (*CP,* pp. 204–205), where the discovery of a body in the soil beyond a garden turns an area of innocent childhood play into a crime scene. Darkness, as ever, lurks in the wings.

OUT LATE

Up to this point, Scupham's books seem to move forward in pairs: the overlapping domesticities of his first, nearly simultaneous collections; the wider, deeper views of landscape and history in *Prehistories* and *The Hinterland;* the explicitly matched titles of *Summer Palaces* and *Winter Quarters*. From here on, however, each collection has its own distinct flavor: in some cases, the books are so unified that they can be read almost as single sequences; in others, they are much more amorphous than their predecessors.

Out Late (1986) "throws the windows open onto darkness, visible and invisible, the mystery of things," says Scupham in his *PN Review* essay "Writing the Poem (p. 22). It begins with "Looking and Finding" (*CP,* p. 211), a compact, short-lined poem dedicated to Geoffrey Grigson, a writer much admired by Scupham; in fact, this poem is another of his sly manifestos. It is also another churchyard poem, and none the worse for that, even though Scupham wryly recalls Anthony Thwaite advising him: "Lay off the churchyards for a bit." Churchyards are, after all, places to find "cloudy ghosts and rain," "pocky stones, bare sky," "Green graves, cool meadow-sweet." Although, in these opening stanzas, Grigson is addressed as "you," this soon modulates to a "we" which spreads out to embrace all those who seriously embrace the vocation of poetry:

This is where we belong,
Who have inherited
The parish of the dead—

That dark substantial thing
Which hugs itself alone
In rubbled, brick, flint, bone,

And speaks with riddling tongue
Of what we were, and are:
Memorial, avatar.

(*CP,* p. 211)

One should note how "we belong" in "The parish of the dead," as if our (that is, the poet's) primary responsibility must be to keep open the channels of communication with the past; with "That dark substantial thing" we are back to darkness once again. There is an ambitious claim in the final lines, and a huge responsibility. And it is worth noting, too, that this quite modest-looking poem is tightly constructed: the first lines of each stanza are locked together by half-rhymes, the two

remaining lines fully rhyming with each other. Scupham knew better than to dedicate a shoddy piece of work to Grigson (who died in 1985, shortly before the publication of *Out Late*).

"Looking and Finding" is followed by a group of poems about gardens, although Scupham is less interested in the garden as carefully tended artifact than in processes of change, decay, and renewal. Thus, for example, "The Gardens" (pp. 211–212) explores the cycle which begins when a garden is dug up and divided; while "A Borderland" (pp. 215–216) is concerned with the hinterland at the margin of cultivation, where "childhood and the trees make their last stand / About the half-bricks and the foundered sheds" and beyond which is the wood "run by dogs— there it might start to snow." If the dichotomy between safe open space and wild wood reminds us partly of Kenneth Grahame's *The Wind in the Willows* (1908), it should still more powerfully suggest *A Midsummer Night's Dream;* and this is the starting point for the major sequence in *Out Late*.

During the 1970s and 1980s, drama at St. Christopher School flourished—largely thanks to the creative partnership of Margaret Steward and Peter Scupham—to such an extent that a touring company, made up of past and present students and called (with a properly Shakespearean neglect of the apostrophe) Phoebus Car, traveled to various venues with a new production after the end of each summer term. Many of Scupham's theater poems and sequences, including "A Midsummer Night's Dream" (*CP*, pp. 220–228), are rooted in these intense, rewarding experiences. Yet, as with the earlier and much more modest "The Tragedy Of" and "The Comedy Of," the texts are visited only fleetingly, as starting points for improvisation. His concern, as so often, is with transformation; or, more exactly, with the blurry transitions between one state and another. "I watched their waking from and waking to," he writes on the lovers (*CP*, p. 225); and, echoing this, in his epilogue: "I pray for amity and restoration, / Who have dreamed waking-thoughts, woken to dreams" (*CP*, p. 228). The ghosts are never far away.

None of Scupham's later collections is without poems of personal or ancestral memory. The

PETER SCUPHAM

memories may be transmitted through photographs, as in "A House of Geraniums" (*CP*, p. 237); or through recorded sound, as in "A Box of Ghosts" (*CP*, p. 232); or they may recall the child's archetypal fear of darkness, as in "Leave the Door Open" (*CP*, p. 231). In "The Plantations" (*CP*, p. 229) we revisit, not for the last time, the gatehouse at the railway crossing in Lincolnshire, but this time memory is blitzed by a strident intervention of the present: "A blue diesel shaking line and outline / On its mild swerve from nowhere to nowhere." The disruption unsettles not only the author but the reader, who will notice both the ambiguity of "line" (poem as well as railway) and the characteristic way in which the carefully realized location has—indeed, like a set in a play—nothing on either side of it, being between "nowhere" and "nowhere"; the poet who is so inclusive when threading together remembered details and their associations can be ruthless at exclusion, too.

Sensing perhaps that a contrastingly lighter note is needed, Scupham provides near the end of *Out Late* a series of brilliant literary parodies, "The Poets Call on the Goddess Echo" (*CP*, pp. 244–248). All of them are effective, and some are wickedly funny. Few readers would need convincing that "Deeply she slept, and far beyond my waking, / Upon a couch of snow, with more snow falling" is a lost couplet by John Crowe Ransom or that "i sing diminutives of i / (which is the wee of smallest small)" is the opening of a hitherto undiscovered poem by e. e. cummings. The plainest poets are the hardest to parody, but Scupham's Robert Frost has just the right tone of rumbling introspection:

It might have been right to go,
  It could have been wrong to come,
Though no one had let me know
  That the place was deaf, or dumb.

(p. 58)

And his John Betjeman catches precisely that writer's rather alarming chumminess with the Almighty:

Blessed bells of Great St Mary's,
  Hunting through the April air,

When He speaks among your tumult,
  Grant my name may find Him there.

(p. 61)

THE AIR SHOW

The Air Show (1988) is the most completely unified of all Scupham's collections and, partly for this reason, his own favorite among them. The linking theme is one that constantly preoccupies him: a childhood during the years surrounding and including the World War II. As with "The Hinterland," the self-referential difficulty of these poems will be eased if the reader can manage to hang on to a few navigational hints: in this case, three poems titled by addresses. These are: "1 Crich Circle, Littleover, Derby" (*CP*, pp. 259–260); "Woodlands, 7 Kilnwell Road, Market Rasen" (*CP*, p. 278); and "7 Newton Road, Harston, Cambridge" (*CP*, pp. 292–293). The first and last are houses where Scupham lived with his parents and sister (the book is dedicated "for Ann, who was there too"); the second is his grandparents' home in Lincolnshire. All the poems in the book are set in, nearby, or between these locations.

The air show itself is a multifaceted image: it is the airy space of childhood, where Scupham sees himself "Doing a hop-dance over a patch in my head / Which is called summer and grass" (*CP*, p. 257); an actual air show, where "A triplane bellies its fabric into the sunshine" (*CP*, p. 257); and the greater aerial adventure of the World War II itself. These three scales—childish, local, national—coexist and reinforce each other throughout the poems: thus, while "Good Flying Days" (*CP*, p. 280) turns out to be about nothing more warlike than kite flying, "Going Out: Lancasters, 1944" is about actual bombers, viewed against the elegiac backdrop of a Cambridgeshire garden:

"They're going out," she said.
  Together we watch them go,
The dark crossed on the dusk,
  The slow slide overhead

And the garden growing cold,
  Flowers bent into grey,
The fields of earth and sky
  Losing their strength to hold

224

The common lights of day
  Which warm our faces still.

(The Air Show, p. 36)

But there is also, inevitably, the overlapping of scales imposed by time and memory. In "Back," Scupham returns to "the land of was"—this is his earlier home in Derby—to find "The house was smaller, shrunken on the bone" and its present owner wondering whether it had always been haunted: "There's a ghost," the owner says,

I laughed: "Unless it's me…" and stared past him
To where some prying fiction of my past
Inked out the shadows in that upstairs room.

(CP, p. 256)

The irony, of course, is that Scupham *is* haunted by ghosts; but not that sort and not this one.

A further sense of superimposed perspectives comes from the contrast between the remembered things which were integral to his own childhood world—toys such as "The Spanish Train" (pp. 258–259), which he discusses in detail in "Writing the Poem," or the books recalled in "Children of Odin," "Jungle Book," and "Glory" (pp. 264–266)—and the adult objects of his grandparents' house, where "Grandad trims the gas lamp under his breath" while "Granny, bobbed with pearls / Loops her Waterman over the deckled paper" (*CP*, p. 268). Meanwhile, representing a world still further recessed into the past, "The papers are going their special kind of yellow / Up in the boxroom, which is made of dust" (*CP*, p. 271). This is a world in which, even to the child's perception, forms of words and habits of speech already seem dated and quaint, in a sometimes puzzling way: "Bother old Hitler," says his grandmother (*CP*, p. 273), using an unmistakably authentic grandmotherly idiom; while a garish postcard of Blackpool by night carries the printed statement, "This is a real photograph" (*CP*, p. 274), as indeed postcards once commonly did. The family portraits spread out in "Bigness on the Side of Good" (*CP*, pp. 275–276) to embrace, with wonderfully broad comic effect, Scupham's Uncle Tommy, who owned, among much else, "a monstrous pig," "As pink as Churchill wooffling

in his den, / All chubby-chopped, rooting for Victory." The child drapes the pig's backside with a Union Jack, which the pig subsequently devours, with disastrous consequences: "The pig died, surfeited by patriotism." Scupham knows how closely related the tragic and the ludicrous, the serious and the playful, usually are. His most compact and ingenious juxtaposition of war and game comes in the sestina "War Games" (*CP*, p. 289–290), where, through an additional twist of gamesmanship, each of the six phrases ending in "toys" is also a literary quotation: this may seem an intricate way to handle a poem about a child playing with lead soldiers on the carpet, yet the formal complexity deftly mirrors the formal complexity and even the high seriousness of the game.

Toward the end of *The Air Show*—and toward the end of the war itself—Scupham is twelve years old: "I am learning nothing at incredible speed, / Weltering in ink," (*CP*, p. 296) he writes, catching a sense of frustration familiar to many an intelligent adolescent. Soon the war itself will be the subject of memory—he is already collecting souvenirs, such as "a bit of shell, / A whorl of light I picked out of the gutter" (*CP*, p. 300)—although, in "V.E. Day" (*CP*, pp. 302–303), it is a far more ambiguous image that catches his attention. He notices how the celebratory flags have been "rubbed thin, / Bleaching in shut drawers, now unrolled / In blues, reds […]," "threadbare cotton to windy air." He sees precisely how the beginning of a new period, with "fresh light at the front door," is also necessarily the end of an old one: "a table-land of toys to be put away, / To wither and shrivel back to Homeric names." This is the moment at which the present melts into the past and becomes, as the final lines of "V.E. Day" so eloquently suggest, the stuff of future poetry:

Night, and the huge bombers lying cold to touch,
The bomb-bays empty under the perspex skull.
The pyres chill, that ate so fiercely, and so much,
The flags out heavily: the stripes charcoal, dull.
Ashes, ghosts, fables.

225

PETER SCUPHAM

WATCHING THE PERSEIDS

"Ashes, ghosts, fables," indeed: for in *Watching the Perseids* (1990), a group of poems about friends and relatives—they include Scupham's Aunt Marjorie and his Uncle Tommy (of the famous pig), as well as his father as a twelve-year-old lepidopterist—prefaces two major sequences in memory of his mother, who died at the end of 1987, and his father, who died early in 1990. A dispassionate though naive observer might think that these were occasions for which Scupham's poetic past had uniquely prepared him; except that no one is ever really prepared for them. As it happens, the two sequences are startlingly unalike and, in their different ways, profoundly surprising.

The first, "Young Ghost" (*CP*, pp. 318–329), seems at first glance the more characteristic: a cluster of memory poems moving in toward, and then away from, the deathbed at their center. It is typical of Scupham to begin with a journey, followed by arrival at a house; typical of him, also, to employ a wryly reversed perspective: "I see things out of the corner of their eyes / Glancing away from the huddle of the bed" ("Moving Round the House," *CP*, p. 319). The "things" may be evasive, but he is not: there is nothing sentimentally blurred about his vision, and the reader who expects soft-focused half-truths is in for a shock. Thus, "Old Hands" begins: "Old hands, burnt out, the sap fallen: tallons, / And a gold ring cutting closer to the bone" (*CP*, p. 320); to say less, or more, or other, would be an affront to honesty and accuracy. This is followed by "Christmas 1987," the most moving and uncompromisingly direct poem of the sequence, in which he tends his dying mother:

Once more I cover this nakedness which is my own,
Beyond shame, wasting, wanting; soon to be ash,
Pulling her nightdress down over the sharp bone
Which bites through the shocked absences of flesh.
(CP, p. 321)

Scupham has never written quite like this before; yet, precisely because he has been so often preoccupied as a poet by the complex transactions between past and present, this intimacy gains a peculiar force which it would have lacked in the

work of a more habitually intimate, confessional writer. Even here, he is alert to paradox: "I am becoming a ghost," (*CP*, p. 321) he unexpectedly writes, seeing himself blur and fade from his mother's point of view (rather than the other way around); while, in "The days are another way of spelling the night," "spelling" takes on the resonance of "magicking," hinting at the melting away of the known, physical world.

Always adept at contrasting textures, Scupham adds poems that recall younger images of his mother, of which one—"Dancing Shoes"—is a deliciously playful villanelle, ending:

The Charleston and the Foxtrot and the Blues—
The records end in blur and monotone.
At Time's *Excuse-me*—how could you refuse?
How long since you wore out your dancing shoes?
(CP, p. 325)

Nor does he spare himself some reflected irony. At the funeral, his casual clothes draw comment: "I hear my father drily say: 'Your mother / Would not have thought you out of character.'" (p. 324)

Yet "out of character" is what Scupham briefly seems to be in the opening poem, dated "November 24th, 1989," of the second sequence, "Dying" (*CP*, pp. 340–348):

My sister and brother-in-law think I should come
To see my father, who lies on his marriage-bed
Considering the seven ages of man.

This is a tone more conversational than any we have become accustomed to in his poetry (except, of course, in conversation), and it introduces, as only lightness can, material of great seriousness. "Time slips its moorings" while his father "eats little, / Sleeps to dream, and is pleased to see me": this is the moment when the son must "mother and father his childhood, / Fetch and carry, ease him out of tangles." "I would like to do justice to this mild, distinguished man," writes Scupham, and his unexpectedly appropriate method of doing so is to construct much of the sequence from his father's own words: learned, witty, and often aphoristic utterances, fragmented by age and illness. In the second poem, John Scupham remembers his "refined and educated" mother and his father "who was neither"; it was his mother's intellectual ambition, her "kind of heroism," which would push her children "as far up the educational ladder as they can go." John Scupham eventually became controller of educational broadcasting at the British Broadcasting Corporation, where his fine ambition—in his own words, from the third poem—

was to be able to talk
To the producer of each specialism
In his own language and on his own wavelength

and where, consequently, he met some of the greatest intellectuals of the age. In the fourth poem, he sends his son off to fetch books, with the pleasingly elliptical codicil: "And if you see a book that's not worth reading, / Pass it to me, and I won't read it." "26th December," in the fifth poem, is—for time has indeed slipped its moorings—an approximate Christmas:

He has put an occasion together in his head,
And, at some far, unguessable cost, watches
A candle in a lantern, swinging softly

They sing carols, eat and drink (although he merely "nibbles the air in a front of a petit-four"), do part of the *Spectator* quiz; by the end, "He is very tired now. He has managed it quite beautifully.'

This is the pivotal point in the sequence. In the sixth poem, John Scupham is genially disputing his son's identity ("Who do you say you are?"), and by the seventh he is, rather magnificently, beginning to recite the "History of the Scuphams" in epic verse. Yet, although he may be confident enough about where the Scuphams stood on the matter of Magna Carta in 1215, his sense of nearer chronology is crumbling away. Having asked, and been told, the time in the eighth poem, he replies: "Twenty to five? It can't be. / Do you mean twenty to five yesterday?" He is suffering from the kind of conceptual synaesthesia most of us know only fleetingly in dreams:

You say it's ten,
But by the amount of experience that's gone into it
It must be at least half-past four.

In the last poem, "January 10th, 1990," he can no longer speak and his eyes are constantly open;

his son reads to him from Wordsworth's "Prelude" and celebrates a midnight mass. He dies at three o'clock in the afternoon: "I glance to where he is quizzing his *Times* obituary. / Quietly, we continue our conversation."

"Young Ghost" and "Dying" dominate *Watching the Perseids,* and their concerns understandably spill over into many of the other poems. Between them comes "The Christmas Midnight," a sonnet sequence less elaborate than "The Hinterland," meditating on time, death, and mutability. A little later, there is "Watching the Perseids: Remembering the Dead," in which the meteors, "riding softly down," supply another image for "Life, set in its ways and constellations, / Which knows its magnitude, its name and status" (*CP*, p. 350). And immediately after "Dying" comes a more modest-looking poem, "Clearing," in which the poet visits his late parents' empty house. It is a kind of poem he has often written—about objects and their associations, in their spaces—but which here acquires a special resonance. These are its opening lines:

Four years ago, the house was waiting for them,
As cool and as convenient as light,
And each had eighty years to pack, unpack there,
To get things right,
As right as trivets, blackbirds, briar-roses,
Millennial stones and letters from old friends,
The winnowed books in which the past had printed
Beginnings, ends.

(*CP*, p. 349)

This is what Scupham once described as his "transparent" voice, a clear and eloquent counterpoise to the preceding sequence. In *Watching the Perseids* he successfully faces his greatest challenges: it is in many ways the most moving and impressive of all his books.

THE ARK

The Ark (1994) is the first of Scupham's collections to have been entirely written after his retirement from teaching and his move from Hitchin in Hertfordshire to South Burlingham in Norfolk. This makes a difference to the poems, although it isn't quite the one that usually comes with "retirement": in any case, he had never been the kind of teacher-poet who writes interminably about school life, except in the rather special field of dramatic productions—and these were to continue at Old Hall. No, the difference is deeper and less obvious than that: it lies in the fact that this writer whose poems had often colonized ancient places now had one of his own.

For a deceptively straightforward moment, the book's title seems to refer simply to the toy in the opening poem—"The boy on the floor is putting his ark to bed" (CP, p. 359)—though even this soon modulates into an image of the child's life, which must be steered to "its safe and certain loss"; death is seldom very far from birth in these poems, and in one ("First Things, Last Things") the two events are separated by a "long brocade of lies, / Truths, half-truths" (CP, p. 384), an image that seems to glance, bleakly and obliquely, toward Larkin's description of religion as a "vast moth-eaten musical brocade / Created to pretend we never die" in "Aubade" (Larkin, CP, p. 208). Yet the recurrent, ruminative gravity of theme implies that this ark is also, like the ark of the covenant, a storehouse of immutable truths. And it is thirdly—in "A Habitat" (CP, pp. 390–400), the longest of the four sequences in the collection—an image for the haunted, erratic sanctuary of his Norfolk manor house. Here, at least, in "All Roads Lead to It," we are in familiar if not altogether reassuring territory, as with baffled admiration he contemplates the building and its unknowable secrets:

Who bewildered those floors to sand,
Tumbled the tumbled brickwork? Who attended
To the long marriage of queen strut, king post,
Set swimming in the porch's pediment
A merman and a mermaid of white stucco
Who swing their lovely, rough-cut tails apart
And stare with chapped eyes at the east?

It is, he tells us, "A cock-eyed house, beset by open fields / And too much wind": a perfect symbol of his imaginative world, in its vulnerable antiquity, its combination of the elegant and the askew. This is a place where even mermaids have chapped eyes. The house is "full of awkward questions":

When the house was born, did it cry in the first wind
For its delivery from stone and clay,
Shaken, unhinged, gathering its baubles
To be the playthings of its own dark future?

In other hands, such speculations might turn to fey sentimentality; in Scupham's, such lightness is always tempered by his knowledge that the future is "dark" and that "Living here will be enough and more / To turn the hair white with grief." He likes it that way, which is just as well, since that's the way it is; and it is no great surprise to find the house invaded in the final poem, "Faces Come Thicker at Night," by ghosts, stars, and a dead white cat called Quince.

Other developments of Scupham's earlier modes in The Ark are both more quirky and more disturbing. For example, "Accident" (CP, pp. 360–365) is a set of deliberately floppy, gangling sonnets that begins and ends with a car crash; but its narrative terms are continually being questioned and renegotiated, rather in the manner of John Fowles's fiction, so that a glance at the driver's mirror discloses not the predictably retrospective view of the road but rather a view back over the poem itself to "A clumsy line break, / A repeated 'white' in the first section," while in the third sonnet the reader finds himself being abruptly interrogated about his acquisition of the book. Scupham's earlier language games were never quite as ferocious as this. "Nacht und Nebel" (CP, pp. 380–384) returns, more darkly than ever, to his preoccupation with hinterlands, borderlines: between seeing and unseeing (one section is set in Moorfields Eye Hospital) or between living and dying. Linking the themes, and running through the entire collection, is the metronomic presence of time: "Clocks are the unblinking eyes of time," he writes, while the final poem in the sequence focuses on the grim coincidence of "A child's case packed in an Auschwitz warehouse: "Jungkind, geboren 1933." My year."

After the two strongly unified collections, The Air Show and Watching the Perseids, which immediately preceded it, The Ark is a strikingly various book. Despite a summery Italian production of his favorite play, A Midsummer Night's Dream—"the performance, / As always, wrong in its open-air production" (*CP*, p. 368), he remarks, a bit grudgingly, though this wouldn't stop him putting one on at Old Hall—a wintry light predominates: in the beautifully titled "Light Frozen on the Oaks," he observes that "The sky, in all its graduals and ordinaries, / Promises no more than a midwinter pallor" (p. 389). In this context, consolations seem all the richer, more fully earned. "Cat on a Turkey Plate" has a huge ginger cat, "the Christmas Cat in his scallops of old china" (p. 370), presiding magnificently over the seasonal festivities. And "The Web" celebrates something Scupham has always treasured: the accidental pleasures of the imperfect. The web is broken, "hung about with rain," in a backyard

Where nothing seems to fit; just lies about—
That mountain-bike with rusty handlebars—
And nobody much in, and no one out [...]
(*CP*, p. 373)

The verse seems utterly relaxed, yet is perfectly held in place by syntactical balance, metrical stress, and rhyme. As for the web itself:

Clouds come, clouds go. They never look much
  wrong.
The fly gets framed, gets trussed. If there's a soul
The web is hung how something wants it hung
And would not be more perfect were it whole.
(*CP*, p. 373)

NIGHT WATCH

Scupham's last slim volume before the *Collected Poems* of 2002 was *Night Watch* (1999)—something of a ragbag of a book, as he might self-disparagingly say, rather than a themed or unified collection. But the increased diversity of a poet's later work is to be expected—the occasions of poetry change as a writer grows older—and several of the poems in *Night Watch* are, precisely, occasional: there is, for instance, an elegant "Epithalamion" to celebrate the marriage of his youngest son—"New foliage grows to a head on familial trees" (*CP*, p. 438)—as well as a "Song for Sophie: A Granddaughter, born 1998," a delightful reversion to the very lightest of his earlier styles as well as a perfect parody of Robert

Graves:

When you read these verses,
guess by words and spaces
what their wish might be,
thinking hard of postmen,
daisies, mice and milkmen—
packed tight with wishes
and saying just like me

each is special, singular,
together in their dancing,
in out, up down, sun, moon, star.
In a packet or a pocket
keep your wish a secret
and tell it just by being
exactly who you are.

(*CP*, p. 440)

Yet some family occasions are a good deal odder than this. "Family Reunion" (*CP*, pp. 414–416), a sort of pendant to the memorializing sequences in *Watching the Perseids,* is simultaneously among the funniest and the most touching of all Scupham's poems. In it, he finds himself in the half-dream world of a "puzzling room" which is also the familiar space of his own study: here he is visited by his dead parents, who "look as if they've chosen how to look, / deep in the prime of a late middle age." He worries about how they'll get home, advising them not to be "too late [...] the late departed." His father, as amiably cantankerous as when we last met him, retorts that this is "the sort of remark you'd expect from a minor poet"; and when his mother kindly observes, "Peter's books are so much neater than yours were, John," her husband replies, "That's because he never reads them." The poem is cast in the form of six free-flowing sonnets, and at this point Scupham comments, draping his outrageous joke over not just a line break but a sonnet break, "Chit-chat goes on // as if I'd written it myself." The real trouble, where dream logic cracks and falters, comes when Scupham asks if they've planned other excursions and his mother tells him: "We're on our way to visit Mother." But of course, to do this, "They'll have to change between the acts": they can hardly appear to her in their grumblesome middle age and Scupham wonders whether they'll be "Decked in sailor suits" instead. Eventually, smilingly, they depart:

"No handshake, kiss for mother; it's much too late now for seeing through each other."

"Family Reunion" is an excellent example of the poet reinventing and extending his territory: it is both utterly characteristic and quite unlike anything he has done before. *Night Watch* is rich in such poems. One direction takes Scupham into a new refinement of his "transparent" style, a poised laconic lyricism, in poems such as "A Slice of Cake" (*CP,* p. 413) or "Crossing the Peak" (*CP,* p. 417). Another produces a stunningly effective version of an old trick—the unexpectedly skewed perspective—in "Night Kitchen": the five stanzas comprise a snapshot of the kitchen, seen in immense and evocative detail, as lit by the headlamps of a car belonging to a burglar. Whether a crime actually takes place is unclear—we leave the intruder "bent on away, white gloves calming the wheel"—and unimportant, for what interests Scupham is the sense of a secret night scene surprised by an intruder:

Everything which happens happens in passing.
The kitchen drowses in light, that nervous stranger
coasting lost into a place of secrets.
Things here have made love to each other so often,
undressing each other's colours nightly,
that his embarrassment is hardly noticed
as the chair sleeps in the clock's arms,
what has been left out finds itself really in bed,
the cats and spoons grow desolate and cosy.
(*CP,* p. 427)

As so often with this writer, one wants to linger over small, astonishing details: the way in which the idea of the kitchen things "undressing each other's colours" so aptly invokes the actual process of darkness, perhaps glancing back to the Elizabethan poet Fulke Greville's equally magical "In night, when colours all to black are cast [… .]," the seemingly nonsensical yet precisely right image of the chair asleep "in the clock's arms"; the double surprise of the last line quoted, with its juxtaposed "cats and spoons" (both to be found in the kitchen at Old Hall), and, still more tellingly, "desolate and cosy."

The major sequence in *Night Watch* is "The Northern Line," subtitled (not, perhaps, quite straightforwardly) "End of Leave, 1950s" (*CP,* pp. 418–426). Though this clearly takes us back to Scupham's National Service days, it does so in a highly complex way, offering a ghost-train ride through the decade: thus, a compartment containing "the usual suspects of the time" is filled to more than its bursting point with "sixteen moustached poilus, eight horses / cut loose from Mark Gertler's roundabout"; in there too are Eccles, Bluebottle, and Moriarty (characters from BBC Radio's popular *Goon Show*), a gigantic doll, the actress Anna Neagle, and a Cameron Highlander. This is part nightmare, part *Alice in Wonderland.* The sequence is the most densely allusive in all Scupham's work, a patchwork of fragments evoking "the crossroads of a century"; it is also, though he might smile wryly at the thought, the most uncompromisingly modernist of his poems:

Hang on to that anthology, that Baudelaire
I've lent you, I'll expect to see them
back on my shelves when I get home.
Goodbye. "You, that way; we, this way."
(*CP,* p. 424)

The language could almost be Eliot's from *The Waste Land,* "mon semblable,—mon frère!"

A single poem in Scupham's *Collected Poems* was written after *Night Watch:* it comes at the start, as a dedication, and its stands in memory of his son Giles, who died in 2001. It is, as Robert Wells says in his long and thoughtful review of the *Collected Poems,* a poem "of extreme beauty":

Our love is a dark lantern; your secrets keep
Under this driftwood tree, dark brick, stiff clay,
And all the foreground speaks of distances.
Caught in your indirection, we lose our way
To find you again, alone and undispersed,
Briefly at home in colour, line, the light
Echoed by patched water. Then cloud and leaf
Turn in the loose wind, follow you out of sight.

CONCLUSION

The two commonest reservations some readers have about Peter Scupham's poetry can be briskly summarized and, perhaps, as briskly dismissed. One is that his fondness for odd and attractive words and expressions leads to a voice that is somehow unnatural or affected; yet reading him with any care will swiftly dispel this misapprehension and reveal a poetic voice which is both distinctive and utterly authentic. The other is that his concerns are in some way remote from the "real" contemporary world; but nothing could be more solidly real than the world in which he lives and which so firmly underpins his work—a world made of bricks and books, gardens and cats, enhanced by a dauntingly intense perception of the ways in which the present interacts with the past.

The claims one can make for Scupham are far from modest ones. There may be no other poet who has so finely evoked the experience of growing up in England in the 1930s and 1940s; who has so movingly and humorously memorialized his parents; or who has so fruitfully explored his cultural and intellectual landscape. He is a matchless conjuror of ghosts and memories, a beautifully eloquent love poet, and a wickedly funny parodist. He is a superb technician, not in any fussily sterile way, but in the proper sense of a master craftsman who knows that all art needs skillful making. In this essay we have been able only to examine a tiny sample of Scupham's *Collected Poems,* an inexhaustible book, sensibly arranged on a collection-by-collection basis, so that the individual rooms envisaged by the poet do indeed seem to be component parts of a greater building: this comprehensive volume is full of poems which repay rereading and provide a dizzyingly cumulative pleasure, and it belongs alongside the collected poems of Auden, say, or Graves.

All the same, Scupham is at present—so far as one can ever judge these things—undervalued and unfashionable. One might recall of F. R. Leavis's famous remark about a very different undervalued and unfashionable poet, George Crabbe. Crabbe, said Leavis, rather pompously, "was hardly at the fine point of consciousness in his time," to which C. H. Sisson justly replied: "What an excellent thing not to have been!" Scupham likewise may not be at the fine point of

consciousness in his time. He is much better than that.

Selected Bibliography

WORKS OF PETER SCUPHAM

EDITIONS
The Small Containers. Manchester, U.K.: Phoenix Pamphlet Poets, 1972.
The Snowing Globe. Manchester, U.K.: E. J. Morten, 1972.
The Gift. Richmond, U.K.: Keepsake Press, 1973.
Prehistories. London: Oxford University Press, 1975.
The Hinterland. Oxford: Oxford University Press, 1977.
Summer Palaces. Oxford: Oxford University Press, 1980.
Winter Quarters. Oxford: Oxford University Press, 1983.
Out Late. Oxford: Oxford University Press, 1986.
The Air Show. Oxford: Oxford University Press, 1988.
Selected Poems, 1972–1990. Oxford: Oxford University Press, 1990.
Watching the Perseids. Oxford: Oxford University Press, 1990.
The Ark. Oxford: Oxford University Press, 1994.
Night Watch. London: Anvil Press, 1999.
Collected Poems. Manchester, U.K.: Carcanet Press/Oxford Poets, 2002. (Page references in the text are to this edition.)

ESSAYS AND ARTICLES
"Spring 1977: *The Hinterland.*" In *Poetry Book Society: The First Twenty-five Years.* Edited by Eric W. White. London: Poetry Book Society, 1979. Pp. 60–61.
"On Peter Scupham." *Rialto* 46: 17–19 (2000).
"Writing the Poem." *PN Review,* no. 148: 21–27 (2002).
Peter Scupham's early manuscripts and papers are in the British Library; later manuscripts and papers are in the author's possession.

CRITICAL AND BIOGRAPHICAL STUDIES
"Lessons in Survival: A Conversation with Peter Scupham." *PN Review,* no. 37:42–45 (1984).
Powell, Neil. "Magic and String: The Poetry of Peter Scupham." *PN Review,* no. 1: 31–32 (1976).
———. "Mature Students: Peter Scupham and Andrew Waterman." In *British Poetry Since 1970: A Critical*

Survey. Edited by Peter Jones and Michael Schmidt. Manchester, U.K.: Carcanet Press, 1980. Pp. 131–137.

———. "Peter Scupham." In *Dictionary of Literary Biography.* Vol. 40, *Poets of Great Britain and Ireland Since 1960.* Edited by Vincent B. Sherry. Detroit: Gale, 1985. Pp. 509–516.

Stevenson, Anne. "Magic and String." *London Magazine,* April–May 2003, pp. 120–125.

Wells, Robert. "The Precise and the Mysterious." *PN Review,* no. 160: 32–37 (2004).

WILLIAM THOMAS STEAD

(1849–1912)

Michele Gemelos

IF DISTINCTIONS BETWEEN journalism and literature were, at one time, easy to draw, one general difference was that journalism concerned itself with the timely reporting of useful facts while most literature was considered to be work of the imagination designed to evoke emotional responses. Such distinctions did not rule out similarities: fundamentally, both journalism and literature both harness language and organize ideas in order to convey meaning, to have an "impact," and to increase awareness of diverse human experiences. In the nineteenth and early twentieth centuries, however, journalism and literature intersected and mingled, producing various hybrid writing styles and forms. Today these types of writing have paradoxical-sounding labels such as "literary journalism" and "creative nonfiction." For almost two centuries, journalism—in broadsheet or tabloid forms, whether objective or subjective, or for "highbrow" or "lowbrow" audiences—has challenged readers' expectations and literary conventions. In Victorian Britain, however, depending on one's political and aesthetic position, the similarities between literature and journalism were thought to have been either exploited or refined to develop these hybrid forms.

If there is greater acceptance and enthusiasm today for experimental and unconventional types of journalism, however, this can be seen as an outgrowth of the strenuous and often volatile debates that took place in nineteenth-century Britain. An important instigator of these debates was William Thomas Stead. One of the most influential and eccentric public figures of the Victorian and Edwardian period, Stead was a trailblazing journalist and author, a Liberal reform-minded editor, and experimental spiritualist. Journalism was Stead's "pulpit"; from the pages of noted publications such as the *North-*

ern Echo, the *Pall Mall Gazette* and the *Review of Reviews,* he preached for social and political reform, including the need for legislation against prostitution, the necessity of humanitarian intervention in overseas conflicts, women's suffrage, and pacifism. He did so imaginatively, emotionally, and with passionate but "virtuous" disregard for nineteenth-century conventions and mores. He disseminated stories of vice and corruption in the name of strengthening social virtue. Stead's allies—like his critics—were powerful, high-profile politicians, literary elites, radical reformers, and captains of industry. His reputation was sullied by rumors but also defended by devoted reformist friends such as Josephine Butler, Henry Edward Cardinal Manning, and Lord Ashley, earl of Shaftesbury.

Stead is often cited as the founder of English "New Journalism," a term describing the mid-nineteenth-century advent of sensational reportage and a stylistic precursor to modern-day tabloid journalism. "Founder" is a misnomer, though Stead was responsible for many innovations. The coinage of the term "New Journalism" and its association with Stead's work was courtesy of one of his staunchest critics, the English poet, essayist, and critic Matthew Arnold, with whom Stead clashed often but whose ideas about culture Stead freely adopted.

Through the newspapers presses, Stead published many of his own editorials, reviews, book-length nonfiction works, and historical fiction, as well as notable contributions by George Bernard Shaw and H. G. Wells, among other writers Stead championed. Prolific and polemical, Stead participated in many debates that arose from the expression of his radical beliefs and interests and from the revelation of his then-unconventional journalistic methods. His most significant contributions to British literary history, however, were the revolutions he led via the press, rather than any single work he penned. Though his successes were often punctuated by scandal and failure, his life, body of work, and even his extraordinary death exemplify his indefatigable idealism and literary experimentation in a period of great social and political upheaval.

EARLY LIFE AND EARLY CAREER

Stead's humble beginnings instilled in him the work ethic and sense of duty that steered his career. He was born in the village of Embleton, Northumbria, in England on July 5, 1849. His father, William, was a Congregational minister, and his mother, Isabella Jobson, was the daughter of a Yorkshire farmer. They had two daughters and four sons, including William Thomas, who would later be known as W. T. The family moved to Howden-on-Tyne, a village five miles from Newcastle-upon-Tyne, in 1850. Stead was educated at home until 1861, at which point he went to Silcoates School near Wakefield; at the time the school served as a boarding and day school for the sons of Congregational ministers. Stead's education—both informal and formal—emphasized religious devotion, moral rectitude, and social duty. As an independent-minded Christian Nonconformist, Stead immersed himself in the Bible as well as *Boys' Own Magazine.*

After only two years of formal schooling, Stead became a merchant's apprentice at a counting-house in Newcastle. By this time, he had, however, developed a passion for reading beyond scripture, penny papers, and periodicals. In the "countinghouse" years following his departure from Silcoates, Stead wrote essays for prize competitions in *Boys' Own Magazine,* and he wrote a winning biographical essay on the legendary Puritan solider and parliamentarian Oliver Cromwell. In the mid-nineteenth century, the reputation of Cromwell had been enhanced by the publication of the writer and historian Thomas Carlyle's *On Heroes, Hero-Worship, and the Heroic in History* (1841) and *Oliver Cromwell's Letters and Speeches* (1845), a biographical work that unconventionally and imaginatively "elucidates" its subject as a model of individual heroic leadership. Carlyle added commentary to the words of Cromwell presented in the work, thus producing a work of hagiography but also of social criticism. Accessing the life of Cromwell via Carlyle and others, Stead developed an appetite for imaginative historiography, hero worship, and prophetic "sage-writing"—all of which was in keeping with a Victorian sense of individual and social responsibility and models of Christian reform through the resuscitation of past ideals.

Indeed, his Cromwell essay won him a copy of *The Poetical Works of James Russell Lowell,* and the nineteenth-century American poet joined Stead's pantheon of writers and leaders from whom he gained inspiration from his journalistic career. Stead later revealed, in *James Russell Lowell: His Message and How It Helped Me* (1891) that the poetry volume was "the most precious of all my books" (p. 12). Lowell became a central figure in Stead's development as a writer with strong moral conviction. In the same book, Stead also commented that the "The Pious Editor's Creed" from Lowell's first series of *The Biglow Papers* (1848) presented the "great ideal of the editor as 'the Captain of our Exodus into the Canaan of a truer social order' [which] still glows like a pillar of fire amid the midnight gloom before the journalists of the world"(p. 11). Thus, in Cromwell, Lowell, and also in the Scottish essayist Thomas Carlyle, Stead had found apposite heroic models of leadership, whether political, moral, or literary.

The leaders and mentors to whom Stead was drawn were, to him, modern models of biblical prophets who proposed solutions—however radical, subjective, and sometimes unpopular—for social disunity and moral degeneration. Many of the ideas he accessed through his literary investigations were, however, at odds with each other, and many of his heroes were paradoxes themselves. For example, Carlyle became a "Tory" radical, while the "Brahmin" poet Lowell had led a privileged life that was hardly similar to that of a Northumbrian minister's son. But Stead's adoption of their ideas and ideals highlights the ways in which both he and his age were philosophically and politically paradoxical.

In Stead's time, the meaning of terms such as "radical," "conservative," and "liberal" were in flux; aspects of his ideas of progress were seen as both radical and conservative, and his proposals for social change often involved seemingly secular, sometimes immoral, and always surprising suggestions, especially in view of Stead's religiosity. In short, Stead was an idiosyncratic political thinker and a deeply religious but rebellious figure—not dissimilar to his Victorian contemporaries such as Alfred, Lord Tennyson and Charles Dickens. Rather than subscribing to a single mode of thought, area of interest, or style of expression, Stead reached across professed Victorian "oppositions" and divisions, preferring instead to fuse morals and aesthetic styles and vantage points in his writing and to apply his distinctive approaches to many political and literary subjects. This stylistic desire to unify and blend forms and styles can be read as part of a wider program of unification—of the English-speaking world, of liberal-minded republicans, or of democratic, peaceful nations. In Stead's view, these greater goals could be achieved through radical journalism.

However idiosyncratic he was, Stead was very much in touch with his times. Victorian modes of expression, and especially journalism, were challenged and revamped during the mid- to late nineteenth century, in centers as far apart as New York and London, St. Louis and Newcastle. The increased commodification of news is often thought to have begun with the abolition of taxes on newspapers in the nineteenth century: advertisement tax was abolished in 1853, the Stamp Act was repealed in 1855, and paper duty was abolished in 1861. This resulted in the proliferation of cheap, mass-circulation newspapers as well as innovative designs and layout. It was not long before Stead found the right outlet for his ideals and ideas. In 1870 the liberal daily newspaper the *Northern Echo* was founded in Darlington by John Copleston, who was also its first editor. Copleston's reactions to Stead's regular contributions were positive, and in April 1871, despite his lack of experience, Stead succeeded Copleston as editor, and thus became the youngest editor in England. Under Stead, the *Northern Echo* became the organ of William Ewart Gladstone's radical Liberalism. The paper opposed the Contagious Diseases Acts (of 1864, 1866, and 1869), spoke out against prostitution, advocated female suffrage and the improvement of working conditions, and also supported compulsory public education. Stead also used the *Northern Echo* to promote humanitarian interventionist British foreign policy, Irish home rule, and Anglo-American fraternity. During his time at the *Northern Echo* he became acquainted with his hero Carlyle, with whom he corresponded, and with the feminist advocate Josephine Butler. Stead also corresponded frequently with Gladstone on a variety of social issues.

Stead's social progressivism shaped his journalism, and a progressive approach to journalism affected its format. Throughout his career he professed a commitment to factual journalism and to improving literacy in Britain, reflected also in the goals of the Education Acts of the 1870s. Under Stead's leadership, the "provincial" paper was disseminated nationally by railroad, and it prospered. A 1952 volume by J. W. Robertson Scott—*The Life and Death of a Newspaper: An Account of the Temperaments, Perturbations, and Achievements of John Morley, W. T. Stead, E. T. Cook, Harry Cust, J. L. Garvin, and Three Other Editors of the "Pall Mall Gazette"*—quotes Stead's journal of July 4, 1875, in which he explains that the *Northern Echo*

> has the first position in the district. We now reach 13,000; we may reach 20,000. To address 20,000 people as the sole preacher is better than to be a tenth part of the preaching power on a journal with 200,000 circulation. There is no paper now in existence which can be to me what the Echo is. I have given it its character, its existence, its circulation. It is myself. Other papers could not bear my image and superscription so distinctly. I have more power and more influence here than on almost any other paper, for I work according to my inclinations and bias.
>
> (p. 103)

If his professional life represented dissent, radicalism, and progress, his private life appeared to be a portrait of constancy if not complete bliss. Stead married a childhood friend, Emma Lucy

WILLIAM THOMAS STEAD

Wilson (1849–1932) in 1873 and they had four sons—William Junior, Henry, Alfred, and Jack—and two daughters—Estelle and Pearl. Scott quotes Estelle's description of William and Emma's didactic parenting style:

> He read the *Spectator* to us on Sunday afternoons, ending up with the Bank Rate! My mother followed with stories. To ensure that we had been listening, each of us in turn had to fix on some name or episode mentioned; also after chapel at our meal we had to do the same, taking the sermon as our subject. It was a game very much in the manner of "Twenty Questions." Every morning each child had to bring to the breakfast table an interesting fact chosen out of the morning newspapers.
>
> (p. 220)

As in his own childhood, education of the Stead children began at home, though Estelle noted that her father had also been very athletic and sympathetic to society's less fortunate. She commented, however, on the strain that her father's work placed on family life:

> Though in many things my father and mother were not sympathetic, there was a strong bond between them, and I remember him saying that he would not have married anyone else…. My father was a demon for work. In the early morning, before going to the office, and after dinner at night, he would be writing.
>
> (p. 220)

Stead sensed that his ambition and "prophethood" had stalled in the years following his marriage. Yet his commitment to his profession did not diminish. He channeled his energies into the *Northern Echo* and hoped to attract the attention of leaders and men of influence outside his district.

THE NORTHERN ECHO AND STEAD'S ALLIANCE WITH GLADSTONE

In the late 1870s, Stead's newspaper devoted considerable column space to the advocacy of increased humanitarianism domestically and internationally. He published articles that supported English intervention in response to Ottoman atrocities against the Bulgarians (1876–1878), which Stead presented as an attack on fellow Christians. Stead gained support from Gladstone (1809–1898), who had at that time resigned from public office and from the Liberal party following the massive defeat in 1874. Stead was at the helm of public protests in the north of the country. Estelle W. Stead, in her 1913 memoir, *My Father: Personal and Spiritual Reminiscences,* quotes his description of himself, as he reflected in 1893: "When I was editing the *Northern Echo* I was a thorough-going Gladstonian of a very stalwart fighting kind, with a wholesome conviction that Tories were children of the Devil, and that the supreme duty of a Liberal journalist was to win as many seats as possible for the Liberal Party" (p. 92). Gladstone was a natural ally for Stead, as the former (as chancellor of the exchequer between 1859 and 1865) succeeded in abolishing the paper duty, which was one of the reforms that enabled the production of cheap newspapers. It was, however, the Bulgarian episode that cemented their alliance. The impact of the Bulgarian atrocities on British foreign policy is often amplified by historians and biographers sympathetic to Stead. Nevertheless, Stead's public profile was greatly enhanced by the episode, which illustrated the power of media sources and public opinion. Prime Minister Benjamin Disraeli was outspoken in his refusal to change the British policy of support for Turkey, citing national interests. Gladstone, then former prime minister, came out of retirement to oppose Disraeli and placed the Bulgarian atrocities at the center of his campaign, calling for military action on the basis of moral responsibility. His 1876 pamphlet on the subject, titled *Bulgarian Horrors and the Question of the East,* sold more than 200,000 copies.

Gladstone's eventual charismatic political resurrection came via the Midlothian county seat campaigns of 1879–1880 in southeast Scotland, which resulted in a massive victory for Gladstone and victory for the Liberals in the general election thanks in part to Stead's use of the *Northern Echo* as an organ for new Gladstonian "evangelical mass politics." However, Gladstone's speeches during the Midlothian campaigns were criticized by many Conservatives and by Queen Victoria directly.

Gladstone's platform was undoubtedly influenced by correspondence with Stead and Stead's leading articles in the *Echo*. Both men wanted to improve England's social and political outlook (due to the 1878 economic depression) as well as resuscitate their public image and careers. Fundamental to Stead's new vision of liberal politics was Gladstone's critique of "imperial overstretch," and he consequently called for increased national moral responsibility for the existing empire. Stead's association with Gladstone gave the northern journalist political gravitas and social status, while Stead raised Gladstone's public profile, thereby fostering mass appeal for a former prime minister whose public image and alliances in the Commons had been tarnished. Stead's accounts of this phase of his career—outlined in his notebooks—reveal his pride in having played a role and in establishing political ties. He even saw Gladstone's 1876 best-selling pamphlet as a direct response to a letter he had sent; Raymond Schults, in his 1972 study *Crusader in Babylon: W. T. Stead and the "Pall Mall Gazette,"* quotes a notebook entry dated January 14, 1877, in which Stead explained his involvement with the campaign in religious, albeit melodramatic, terms: "For the Bulgarian agitation was due to a Divine voice. I felt the clear call of God's voice, 'Arouse the nation or be damned.' If I did not do *all* I could, I would deserve damnation" (p. 12).

THE PALL MALL GAZETTE

Following Gladstone's victory in the general election, the new prime minister recommended Stead to the prolific Liberal writer and editor John Morley (1838–1923), later to be known as Viscount Morley of Blackburn, who invited Stead to work at the *Pall Mall Gazette* as an assistant editor. Despite Stead's dislike of London as a city, together with a dislike of the city's newspapers, he nevertheless accepted the post. Named by its proprietor George Murray Smith, who founded it in 1865, the *Pall Mall Gazette* was initially a conservative paper and took its name

from that of an imaginary newspaper invented by William Makepeace Thackeray and described in his 1850 novel *The History of Pendennis*. Morley edited the *Pall Mall Gazette*—and cemented its status as a Liberal party newspaper—from 1880 to 1883. Morley and Stead's professional relationship was later characterized in Stead's London *Times* obituary as "a union of classical severity with the rude vigor of a Goth" (cited in Schultz, p. 21). In his seminal work *On Compromise* (1874), Morley asserts the duty of the well-educated English speakers in curing societal ills through social prevention; the principles outlined in the essay were often cited in national debates concerning proper political conduct. Morley advocated moving slowly to realize social change and to convert theories into practice. Although Stead respected Morley's positions on duty and propriety, he was impatient and less controlled than his mentor—in short, a firebrand. His clash with Morley's noninterventionist attitude, for example, compelled Stead to support liberal humanitarian imperialism. Stead also asserted that Morley had less of an understanding of the general reader than he possessed himself, and he continued to produce his frenzied, impassioned hymns of social gospel from his position as assistant editor.

In Stead's words, Morley was "a great stickler for severity of style and restraint and sobriety of expression," and would return Stead's articles, remarking "No dithyrambs, *s'il vous plaît*" (Cited in Scott, p.67). Nevertheless, as a disciple of Morley, Stead did adopt Morley's fondness for literary allusion, for unifying literature and politics, and for leadership traits such as those displayed by the Puritan chiefs of England, whom Morley saw as true heroes for their sense of political and intellectual responsibility. Indeed, Morley's fusion of intellectualism and practical politics played an important role in Stead's formation of his literary and political program for journalism and is clearly observable in his later writings.

Proximity to power and influence and the possibility of promotion had ultimately convinced Stead to take the assistant editor post at the *Pall Mall Gazette* back in 1880. When Morley was elected member of Parliament for Newcastle-on-Tyne in February 1883 and subsequently appointed secretary of state for Ireland, Stead was promoted to acting editor of the *Pall Mall Gazette*—a post he gladly accepted. Not only had Morley's position in government and society widened Stead's political and journalistic access, but it also fed Stead's aspiration to shape political and literary practices in Britain.

From his position at the *Pall Mall Gazette,* Stead was relentless in his pursuit of readers and social reform, but he continued refashioning himself as a man of letters and as a defender of English-language culture. Under Stead's leadership, the *Pall Mall Gazette* continued to shed its Conservative reputation as a genteel digest or tame register of events. Stead furthered Morley's liberal program but made it an agent of direct action, compelling those in power to act with conscience and compassion where Britain's domestic and international interests were concerned. It also allowed Stead to experiment with the content of a daily newspaper, expanding the content to include candid social exposés, interviews, and gossip columns alongside cultural criticism and foreign policy editorials announcing Stead's recommendations on military operations and finance. Although Morley supported Stead's mission, he found the maverick editor's interest in vice and urban decay, fondness for interviews, and vision of Anglo-American fraternity troubling: on that final topic, Morley once wrote to Stead, "Your article tonight turned my hair grey" (quoted in Scott, p. 70).

Stead's subsequent projects unsettled his alliances with Morley and Gladstone but increased the impact of the *Pall Mall Gazette* and ultimately asserted Stead's independence and idiosyncrasy in letters and politics. Stead made substantial changes to the format of the newspaper, adding banner headlines and condensing features and interspersing them with illustrations and diagrams. Stead was criticized for the "Americanization" of the *Pall Mall Gazette* because of his interest in sensational stories and the dominance of the interview format. Nevertheless, members of the old guard saw that British standards in interviewing were high and "a vast improvement

over those of America" (cited in Schultz, pp. 64–65). Increased competition for readers from the middle and upper classes inspired many of these developments. From the late 1880s onward, Stead argued in favor of signed articles as a way of encouraging journalists to take responsibility for their work and a way of promoting Stead's concept of the journalist (or editor) as a heroic figure. It has been suggested that this can be seen as a defiant move; the expansion of the newspaper industry and periodical presses had depersonalized writers, so Stead's insistence on names was a way of combating this.

Stead's career and his brand of journalism evolved during his time at the *Pall Mall Gazette*. He criticized and chronicled transformations in politics and in the press in an era of increased competition for readers. Through its publication of letters and leading articles, for example, the *Pall Mall Gazette* reflected debates about government intervention to combat crime and hostility toward foreigners and the poor in London. The publication of the Reverend Andrew Mearns's *The Bitter Cry of Outcast London* (1883) was the first instance of the success of Stead's plan to campaign for social change through the evening paper. Based on a Nonconformist pamphlet, Mearns's work exposed conditions of life in the slums and resulted in an investigation by a royal commission that called for construction of low-income housing.

After this victory for his brand of journalism, Stead turned his missionary zeal to the crisis over Anglo-Egyptian rule in the Sudan. On January 9, 1884, Stead published an exclusive interview with General Charles George Gordon in the *Pall Mall Gazette,* in an article titled "Chinese Gordon on the Soudan," which featured the popular hero's position on the crisis. Gordon represented many of Stead's Christian and social ideals, and thus he was added to Stead's Victorian pantheon. Gordon had served in the Crimean War and in China in 1864, earning the nickname "Chinese Gordon" for having ended the Taiping Rebellion. He returned to Gravesend in southeast England and became involved in local housing and education reform and other benevolent work that allied him to figures such as "General" William Booth of the Salvation Army, who would play a role in Stead's progressivism. From 1874 Gordon commanded troops in the Sudan and oversaw the opening of Egypt under orders of the khedive (the viceroy of the sultan of Turkey). From 1877 to 1880 Gordon was the British governor of the Sudan. In 1880 he was appointed as the private secretary to the viceroy of India. In the decade preceding his death, Gordon supported "native rule" for many African and Asian nations as well as for Ireland—a position that made him unpopular among politicians in Britain.

After featuring Gordon in the *Pall Mall Gazette,* Stead called for Gordon's dispatch to rescue the English garrisons in Anglo-Egyptian Sudan that were under attack by the charismatic Muslim leader Muhammad Ahmad, who claimed to be the messianic redeemer prophesied in Islam and was thus known as "the Mahdi." The revolt's religious dimension increased Stead's vociferousness about the need for intervention. Despite the government's reluctance to intercede in Sudan, Gordon was nonetheless dispatched to Khartoum in 1884; there he was subsequently besieged, captured, and killed two days before a relief expedition arrived in January 1885. The presentation of Gordon as Victorian martyr in the popular press amplified public grief and indignation, and the Sudan crisis led to the defeat of the Gladstone administration. Following these events, the paper under Stead's direction was characterized, fittingly, in letters to the *Northern Echo* as "wild, hysterical, bloodthirsty" and the "worst of Jingo prints, the reckless and blustering *Pall Mall Gazette* (cited in Schults, p. 78). In 1885 Gladstone resigned after the government's budget was defeated. However, in February 1886, aged seventy-six, Gladstone became prime minister for the third time. His Irish home rule bill was defeated, and he lost the July 1886 general election held in July 1886.

Stead's ability to use the *Pall Mall Gazette* for the furthering of his political agenda resulted in subsequent influential social and political campaigns—two of which resulted in questionable victories for his moral rectitude. For instance, Stead's 1884 series in the *Gazette* titled "The

Truth About the Navy" played upon the notion that naval superiority was important both emotionally and politically to the country. Although Stead's campaign was not based entirely on facts, it resulted in excessive and adverse naval spending on the part of the government.

THE "MAIDEN TRIBUTE" CAMPAIGN

The full extent of Stead's influence over governmental policy, however, was illustrated dramatically in his campaign against prostitution—"white slavery"—in London. Supported by his fellow activists Josephine Butler and William and Catherine Booth of the Salvation Army, Stead set out to expose the inner workings of white slavery networks in the nation's capital as well as the institutional blindness to it. Stead posed as a trader and purchased a young girl named Eliza Armstrong, who underwent procedures that prepared her for export. Using an allusion to the Greek mythological tale of the maiden sacrifice in tribute to King Minos of Crete, Stead's "The Maiden Tribute of Modern Babylon" featured in the *Pall Mall Gazette* as a four-part series on July 6, 7, 8, and 10 of 1885 presenting a "report of a secret commission." It chronicled Stead's findings and the "preface" to his findings makes clear his call for reform:

> If Chivalry is extinct and Christianity is effete, there is still another great enthusiasm to which we may with confidence appeal. The future belongs to the combined forces of Democracy and Socialism, which when united are irresistible. Divided on many points they will combine in protesting against the continued immolation of the daughters of the people as a sacrifice to the vices of the rich.
>
> (p. 1)

Crowds clamored for copies of the articles and were shocked by the details and methods used to obtain them. The London daily press called the investigation indecent and Stead's punishment inevitable. His allies spoke out: Millicent Garrett Fawcett, Cardinal Manning, Lord Shaftesbury, and the Bishop of London all supported his crusade. Stead was nevertheless put on trial, found guilty of reckless endangerment, and sent to Holloway prison for three months, mainly on the grounds of not receiving permission to purchase the child from both of her parents. Following Stead's earlier controversial campaigns, the "Maiden Tribute" campaign and the revelation of his journalistic methods cemented Stead's reputation as the unscrupulous representative of New Journalism. Stead's action also undoubtedly furthered the passage of the Criminal Law Amendment Act of 1885, which raised the age of consent to sixteen, and helped bring about the repeal of the Contagious Diseases Act in 1886.

Despite the "Maiden Tribute" scandal and prison sentence, Stead returned to journalism after his imprisonment with a renewed sense of determination. His new brand of journalism had engaged with the public mood. A type of reactive moral panic had been exacerbated by public perception that the Liberal government's legislations and policies concerning crime and disorder at home and rebellion throughout the empire were weak in contrast with its dynamic rhetoric. In terms of international relations, Stead used the *Pall Mall Gazette* and subsequent publications to air controversial views about the British involvement in Southern Africa. The *Pall Mall Gazette* featured opinions that reflected what Stead believed to be the loss of trust between the public and its elected officials, whether on the issue of home rule for Ireland, women's suffrage, free trade, or arbitration for peaceful resolution of conflicts. For Stead, the social contract between newspapers and their readers was far more important than citizens' contract with their government and laws.

Stead's journalism was not only reactionary; Frederic Whyte, in his 1925 *Life of W. T. Stead*, quotes one admirer of Stead's work who wrote: "This 'New Journalism' is very English and the fact explains its popularity. The proudest boast of the Englishman is that he says what he means and is prepared to accept the consequences of his saying" (vol. 1, p. 237). This reaction portrays Stead's project as a bold, brave, and populist alternative to impotent political rhetoric. Stead's new brand of journalism sought to identify with

its readership, and in turn, Stead also hoped to shape how the readership defined itself.

THE "NEW JOURNALISM": ARNOLD'S CRITICISM

Stead's unconventional and sensational editorial style coupled with his belief in the effectiveness of newspapers as agents for reform were hallmarks of what Matthew Arnold termed the "New Journalism" in 1887. Although the style had been a feature of daily journalism for a number of years, and was thus hardly "new," Arnold obliquely named Stead as the "clever and energetic" inventor of "New Journalism" in an article titled "Up to Easter" that appeared in the May 1887 edition of *The Nineteenth Century*. While Arnold praised "New Journalism" as being "full of ability, novelty, variety, sensation, sympathy, generous instincts" he also points out that

> its one great fault is that it is feather-brained. It throws out assertions at a venture because it wishes them true; does not correct either them or itself, if they are false; and to get at the state of things as they truly are seems to feel no concern whatever.
>
> Well, the democracy, with abundance of life, movement, sympathy, good instincts, is disposed to be, like this journalism, feather-brained; just as the upper class is disposed to be selfish in its politics, and the middle class narrow.... The democracy is by its nature feather-brained; the English nation is not; and the democracy will in England work itself, probably, at last clear. But at present, even here, in England, and above all in those industrial centres where it is most left to itself, and least in contact with other classes, it is disposed to be feather-brained.

Arnold's essay takes issue with the revolutionary undertones of liberal rhetoric espoused by Gladstone and his supporters, distinguishing it from "lawful political agitation." He also expressed concern about new voters' ability to make reasonable decisions in a climate of press-induced passion for change. In Arnold's view, Stead's journalism encouraged oversimplified and knee-jerk reactionary opinions, and a deterioration of objectivity is the dangerous result that Arnold predicts will come from Stead's championing of sensation. Arnold hoped that journalism could be protected from the corrosive effects of public taste and preserved as a realm for true "criticism."

Stead's production of "culture" differed from Arnold's concept of culture as seriousness and perfection. Although both men saw culture in moral terms, Stead's belief that culture should act as a social adhesive gave his cultural product—journalism—a edge that Arnold interpreted as imperfect, immoral, and lacking sobriety. Stead provoked Arnold with the sensationalism of his work and his celebrity, regardless of his intentions.

AFTER THE FALL FROM PALL MALL: THE REVIEW OF REVIEWS

Ultimately Stead's maverick approach to investigative journalism made his position at the *Pall Mall Gazette* impossible to maintain. His final years at the paper were spent writing about his idea of "government by journalism," but the newspaper's proprietor was unwilling to support Stead's continuous campaigning. Stead resigned in 1890 and founded the monthly international journal *Review of Reviews*. An American *Review of Reviews* and an Australasian *Review of Reviews* were founded in 1891 and 1892 respectively. The *Review of Reviews* came to represent what Stead wanted to achieve in letters, politics, and civic culture. As the *Review of Reviews* editor, Stead wanted to distinguish himself and his publication. In *The Life of W. T. Stead*, Frederic Whyte reprints the impressions of an American journalist upon meeting Stead in London in late 1892, which paint a larger-than-life portrait:

He is more like an electric dynamo in clothes than any man I know. He talks like lightning, and a blaze of intellectual sparks follow his words. He looks more like a practical American Methodist preacher than a London *littérateur*. He is plain in his dress and habits. His soft brown hat is crushed in at top, and his snuff-coloured suit of business clothes looked as though their owner had been on a roughing tour and had just got home. He talks more like an American than an Englishman. He has no cockneyisms or anglicisms in his conversation.... He

laughs easily, and tells a story as well as he writes it.

(vol. 2, pp. 54–55)

In the shadow of publications such as the daily *Pall Mall Gazette* and the weekly *Tit-Bits* (launched in 1881), the *Review* distinguished itself as an encyclopedic monthly with a democratic sweep yet devoted to cultural commentary. In nineteenth-century Britain "monthlies" positioned themselves as less ephemeral than the dailies, and in the *Review*, Stead paraphrased Matthew Arnold's definition of "culture" as "knowing the best thoughts of the best men upon the subjects that come before us." It placed political pamphlets, reportage, and fiction side by side; the fiction was historical, however, and featured veiled contemporary figures battling for social and political justice.

For the *Review's* core material Stead looked to the working and lower classes of Britain and America for consumable stories of hardship, misfortune, and vice as well as including the works of established writers. The "programme" Stead set out for the *Review* on page 14 of the magazine's first issue in January 1890 also established it as a synoptic guide to contemporary English-language periodicals in both Britain and America. Fashioned as a digest of the monthlies, *Review* had four standard features. Each number included a survey of domestic and foreign current affairs; a catalog of recently published titles of books and parliamentary "bluebooks"; a condensed "best foreign novel of the month"; and a character sketch of a person who had recently "figured conspicuously...written with sympathy and with a sincere desire to present the individual as he seems to himself in his best moments." Although the *Review's* included stories of hardship and vice, its main editorial aims were "to enable the busiest and poorest in the community to know the best thoughts of the wisest; to follow with intelligent interest the movement of contemporary history; and to understand something of the real character of the men and women who rank among the living forces of our time."

Yet the content and style of the *Review* emphasizes Stead's competing interest in entertainment, particularly in storytelling. In many of his pieces, Stead's attention often moves away from the scaffold of facts and figures to concentrate on revealing aspects of characters and their motivations. In his agenda for the *Review*, he stated that "if a strange true story of real life or a really good original tale should offer it will not be refused," and it would replace the monthly condensed foreign novel. The *Review Christmas Annuals* promised its readers a volume of historical fiction, but they tended to vary in topic and style, as the following selection of titles illustrates: *Real Ghost Stories* (1891); *Two and Two Make Four: A Story Based on the Liberator Building Society Frauds* (1893); *The Splendid Paupers: A Tale of Coming Plutocracy* (1894); and *Mr. Carnegie's Conundrum: £40,000,000, What Shall I Do With It?* (1900).

Stead produced another annual in 1903 titled *"In Our Midst": The Letters of Callicrates to Dione, Queen of the Xanthians, Concerning England and the English*. This work was more explicit in its combination of fiction and history and is an example of Stead's literary shift from reporting and exposé writing to more imaginative forms. It is a "state of England" report that uses the device of the Christian reformer in Africa to investigate and scrutinize English life.

Stead had already produced two volumes scrutinizing the state of city life in the United States. Like his mentor Morley, whose visit to the United States in 1867 transformed his own views on immigration and British rule in Ireland, Stead too found that travel generated ideas about governance and identity. He embarked on his first two trips to the country in order to investigate the municipal politics of Chicago and then New York City. Each trip resulted in a book published through the *Review: If Christ Came to Chicago! A Plea for the Union of All Who Love in the Service of All Who Suffer* (1894) and *Satan's Invisible World Displayed; or, Despairing Democracy: A Study of Greater New York* (1897), which appeared as the 1898 *Review* Christmas annual.

Stead did not intend to wholeheartedly assail Chicago—and the book includes sympathetic passages about Chicagoans—but the reception of the text by locals was mixed, often expressing impatient and critical views based on his outsider status rather than his revelations. As Stead wrote in the preface to the British edition:

It is perhaps hardly necessary for me to say more than a word in presenting this book to the readers in the Old World. Nothing can be further from the mark than to represent it as an attack upon Chicago.... That my picture of Chicago as it is fairly represents the city of the World's Fair is not denied by any of the Chicago newspapers.... What they say is not that I have overcoloured the facts or exaggerated the evil. Their criticism is just the reverse. They say that everything I have written is so familiar to everybody in Chicago as not to be worth printing. If by "everybody" they mean everybody who has paid any attention to politics in Chicago, I would admit the justice of that objection. But as comparatively few persons outside the party wirepullers concern themselves much with politics, I venture to believe that I have not wasted my time in putting on record what I saw and heard in the future capital of the United States....

I published a British Edition, not so much to satisfy the natural curiosity of Englishmen, Scotchmen and Irishmen about the city of the World's Fair, as to suggest to readers on this side of the Atlantic the inquiry which proved so profoundly inspiring in Chicago. "If Christ came to London," to Edinburgh, to Liverpool, or to any of our great cities, the last thing His visit would encourage would be a Pharisaic exultation over the shortcomings of any other city. The problems dealt with in this book confront citizens everywhere, and I venture to believe that the solution is everywhere to be sought in the same lines... . The suggestion "If Christ came" seems to me destined to be the watchword of a revival of Civic Religion, the signs of which are not lacking either in the American Republic or in the British Empire.

(pp. v-vii)

Stead's involvement with local reform deepened his involvement with his subject—he became more than just a British observer of American life. After observing "the rapidly unfolding drama of civic life in the great city which has already secured an all but unquestioned primacy among capitals of the New World" (p. viii), Stead chose to elaborate on the facts by collecting upstanding citizens' opinions and less respectable residents' views of Chicago, and the resulting condensation of these impressions is this volume.

The two figures that embodied the struggles Stead witnessed were the "tramp" (or unemployed drifter persecuted by the police) and the child prostitutes, forced into ignominy by poverty. As a counterpoint to the profiles of the underclass, Stead presents the figure of Jesus Christ as "the most majestic and the most pathetic of all the conceptions which Man has formed of God," explaining that "the fascination of the popular conception of the Christ is His intense humanness" (p. x). His narrative of vice is tempered by his assertion that compassion through the eyes of a "Citizen Christ" is necessary.

For his study of New York, Stead avoided creating a "If Christ came to" narrative, but Stead does revisit aspects of *Chicago* in *Satan's Invisible World Displayed*. He was still concerned with the city's leadership, and he draws heavily from models of leadership in literature, including reference to Carlyle and Lowell. Ultimately Stead's recommendation for New York is for the city's journalists and editors to promote "government by newspaper"—and he reasserts the importance of the bond between the reading public and journalism.

In control of his own publication and with new-found stability, Stead launched other publishing projects supported by the *Review*. In 1895 he began publishing monthly editions of children's books in a series called "Books for the Bairns"; his daughter Estelle called it "the genuine result of his affection for children" (quoted in Scott, p. 220). The series included versions of fairy tales, Greek mythology, and English classics. He also published "penny" editions of poetry and classic novels in series that ran from 1895–1898. Among the seventy-one poets featured in "penny" series were John Milton, Lord Byron, William Wordsworth, Henry Wadsworth Longfellow, Walt Whitman and Alfred, Lord Tennyson. The series published a total of 127 novels, ranging from Nathaniel Hawthorne's *The Scarlet Letter* (from 1850) and Victor Hugo's *Les Miserables* (1862) to the bizarre archaeological mystery *The Incubated Girl* (1896) by Fred Thomas Jane. Stead's dissemination of a wider variety of texts—written by him and written by others—was motivated by his belief that vibrant and diverse literary culture would combat ignorance and inspire readers to counteract negative social forces.

MISCELLANEA: SPIRITUALISM AND ODD COUPLES

Over the years Stead developed friendships and associations that often raised eyebrows but that always underscored his open-mindedness and desire to unite disparate ideas, feelings, and people. Stead's interest in psychic communication was as strong as his interest in print communications. He became involved in "automatic writing"—the unconscious or subconscious recording of messages—and other spiritualist activities such as séances in the 1890s. He edited a psychic journal called *Borderland* from 1893 to 1897. In 1898 he published *Letters from Julia; or, Light from the Borderland*, a selection of messages he claimed to have received by automatic writing from the spirit of an American woman he had met named Julia Ames and who died in 1891. Estelle Stead, in her 1913 reminiscence, recalled her father's words, reflecting on the journal's four-year run and on his commitment to spiritualism:

> The four volumes of *Borderland* are interesting and useful contributions to psychic study. No doubt faults can be found with their contents, no matter what stand-point we take…. One thing only am I more absolutely convinced of than ever, and that is that the ordinary limited materialism of man, and of the world on which he lives, is absolutely inadequate to account for what we know to be happening all the time.
>
> (pp. 214–215)

In 1909 he established "Julia's Bureau," where inquirers could obtain information about the spirit world from a group of resident mediums. Unfortunately, his involvement with these activities alienated many of his allies and called his authority into question.

Among his other surprising involvements were friendships with the captain of industry Andrew Carnegie and the imperial entrepreneur and statesman Cecil John Rhodes. The radical spiritualist Stead befriended Carnegie, the agnostic American industrialist and multimillionaire known as the "Steel King of America," through his connections at the *Pall Mall Gazette*. Carnegie and Stead were united in their desire for Anglo-American unity, and both were extremely devoted to transatlantic journalism as a way of disseminating these ideas, though Carnegie's writings on the subjects were oddly, ferociously, patriotic, pro-American, and hypercritical of British society. Stead also saw Carnegie as a potential investor for fledgling publications, but Carnegie refused to get involved. Carnegie took particular exception to Stead's critiques of Chicago and New York; Joseph Wall, in a summer 1993 article for the journal *NewsStead*, quotes a letter from Carnegie to Stead dated January 7, 1898: "Well, these titles, 'Christ in Chicago'—'Invisible Satan in New York' render it impossible that what you write under them can ever have weight. I wish you would consult me about the title of your next work" (p. 4).

Cecil Rhodes and Stead had also built a friendship around the idea of political and cultural fraternity; they, too, shared a dream of an Anglo-Saxon, English-speaking imperial fraternity that would strengthen imperial power and concentrate on its ability to improve life in the colonies. Stead had been influential in helping Rhodes manage his philanthropy and reputation in Britain, and he had been named an executor of Rhodes's will. However, Rhodes's business ambitions and political practices were viewed by Stead with great concern. Their versions of imperialism had diverged by the end of the 1890s: Stead had become devoted to international peace movements and had formed a "Stop the War" committee in response to British involvement in the Second Boer War (1899–1902). Stead's pro-Boer views led to the disintegration of his friendship with Rhodes. The unpopularity of Stead's pacifist views also affected the circulation of the *Review of Reviews* in this period.

A MAIDEN BUT FINAL VOYAGE

At the turn of the century, the internationalist and pacifist Stead had lost favor with the British public for opposing the British position in the Boer War. He remained a highly regarded peace activist, however, and he was nominated for the Nobel Peace Prize in 1901 for his work in international arbitration, his attendance at peace conferences in 1899, and for the publication of his journal *War Against War*. He was subsequently nominated for the Nobel Prize in 1902, 1908, 1909, and posthumously in 1912.

Stead's last trip to the United States was at the invitation of President William Howard Taft in 1912; he was to speak at the "Great Men and Religion Forward Movement" at Carnegie Hall in New York City. Stead was one of hundreds who died, however, aboard the *Titanic* after it struck an iceberg and sank during its maiden voyage to New York in April 1912. The historian Steven Biel notes that immediately after the disaster, newspapers on both sides of the Atlantic presented the deceased first-class male passengers as "Anglo-Saxon" heroes who sacrificed themselves so that the few lifeboats available could be used to save women and children. Colonel John Jacob Astor, the businessman Benjamin Guggenheim, and Stead were presented in such light. Biel also cites an excerpt from a contemporaneous folk song that presents the men as

Giving life to rescue others
Lab'ring hard 'mid frenzied throngs.
Saving children, wives and mothers.

(p. 46)

Stead's role during the disaster has never been verified, but his reputation as the champion of the downtrodden and as a beacon of moral rectitude was cemented by the hero worship and mythology surrounding his tragic and mysterious death.

The moral and social dilemmas highlighted by his journalism also remained. Stead occupied a sometimes awkward position as both an activist and man of letters, and he negotiated the line between rectitude and immorality with great difficulty at times. The impulse behind his campaigns and writings often led Stead to create works that also crossed the accepted boundaries between conventional fiction and nonfiction. Despite his devotion to realism and facts, he often created imaginative versions of crimes, conflicts, and crises that used sensational language and shocking detail to entice readers. His beliefs, rather than impartial investigations, often determined his recommendations for social reform. Nevertheless, Stead remains a fascinating figure thanks to his passionate convictions, his radical suggestions, and his innovations in journalism. He was a maverick who redefined the role of newspapers and journalism in modern society; for him, social justice had to be served by the press.

Stead's career caught the attention of several contemporary writers. George Meredith reportedly intended to portray Stead as a character in a novel to be titled "The Journalist." James Joyce's socialist-feminist character McCann in *Stephen Hero* (1944)—a novel that Joyce first worked on in 1904–1906, before completely revising it into *A Portrait of the Artist as a Young Man* (1916)—is described in a loaded pun as a "steadfast reader of the *Review of Reviews*." The novelist and critic Rose Macaulay's satire on the modern press, *Potterism* (1920), mentions a journalist-author who penned "that gushing and hysterical book *In Darkest Christendom and a Way Out*"—a satirical barb at the 1890 collaboration between Stead and General Booth of the Salvation Army titled *In Darkest England and the Way Out*. Stead's friendships with industrialists and imperialists, his popularization of literature, and his philanthropic agenda also irritated Joseph Conrad, who found journalism in general "fatuous" and Stead's worldview dangerous. Stead's influence stretched to continental Europe as well; the French impressionist writer Jean Giraudoux's *Eglantine* (1927) built on Stead's idea of historical figures (for example, Moses, Socrates, Jesus Christ) visiting and reforming American cities. More recently, Stead featured as a character in act 2 of Tom Stoppard's play *The Invention of Love* (1997), in which Stead discusses his impact on Victorian morality circa 1885.

For better or for worse, Stead's legacy can be evidenced most clearly in the passionate investigative journalism on display today in a wide variety of American and British periodicals and daily newspapers.

Selected Bibliography

WORKS OF WILLIAM THOMAS STEAD

SOCIAL AND POLITICAL JOURNALISM

The Truth About the Navy. Pall Mall Gazette Extra 12. London: 1884.

The Armstrong Case: Mr. Stead's Defence in Full. London: H. Vickers, 1885.

The Maiden Tribute of Modern Babylon: The Complete Exposé by the "Pall Mall Gazette" of the Illicit Traffic in Children. Philadelphia: International Publishing, 1885.

The Maiden Tribute of Modern Babylon: The Report of the "Pall Mall Gazette" Secret Commission. London: Pall Mall Gazette, 1885. (Articles from July 6, 7, 8, and 10, 1885, collected and reprinted.)

"We bid you be of Hope," Preface to *The Maiden Tribute of Modern Babylon Pall Mall Gazette,* July 6 1885, No. 6336 Vol XLII, p. 1.

"Government by Journalism." *Contemporary Review* 49: 654–674 (1886).

The Truth About Russia. London: Cassell, 1888.

In Darkest England and the Way Out. With William Booth. London: International Headquarters of the Salvation Army, 1890.

If Christ Came to Chicago! A Plea for the Union of All Who Love in the Service of All Who Suffer. London: Review of Reviews Office, 1894.

Her Majesty the Queen: Studies of the Sovereign and the Reign: A Memorial Volume of the Great Jubilee. London: Review of Reviews Office, 1897.

Satan's Invisible World Displayed; or, Despairing Democracy: A Study of Greater New York. London: Review of Reviews Office, 1898.

Shall I Slay My Brother Boer? London: Review of Reviews Office, 1899; reprint, 1900.

The United States of Europe on the Eve of the Parliament of Peace. London: Review of Reviews Office, 1899.

Mr. Carnegie's Conundrum: £40,000,000, What Shall I Do With It? London: Review of Reviews Office, 1900.

Coming Men on Coming Questions. Edited by Stead. London: Review of Reviews Office, 1905.

The M.P. for Russia: Reminiscences and Correspondence of Madam Olga Novikov. Edited by Stead. 2 vols. London: Andrew Melrose, 1909; New York: Putnam's, 1909.

SELECTED FICTION

Two and Two Make Four: A Story Based on the Liberator Building Society Frauds. London: Review of Reviews

Office, 1893. (Christmas stories.)

"I Wish I Were King"; or, Harry's Dream: A Fairy Tale of the Coronation. Books for the Bairns, no. 76. London: Office for the Books for the Bairns, 1902.

"In Our Midst": The Letters of Callicrates to Dione, Queen of the Xanthians, Concerning England and the English, Anno Domini 1902. London: Review of Reviews Office, 1903. (Historical fiction.)

Here Am I, Send Me. London: Review of Reviews Office, 1905. (Religious fiction.)

OTHER WORKS

James Russell Lowell: His Message and How It Helped Me. London: John Haddon, 1891.

Real Ghost Stories. London: Review of Reviews Office, 1891. (Spiritualist writings.)

Borderland. Vols. 1–4. London: Horace Marshall, 1893–1897. (Quarterly periodical.)

Letters from Julia; or, Light from the Borderland. London: Grant Richards, 1898.

The Bairn's Bible: An Introduction to the Study of the Old Book. Books for the Bairns, no. 59. London: Review of Reviews Office, 1900.

The Last Will and Testament of Cecil John Rhodes, with Elucidatory Notes to Which Are Added Some Chapters Describing the Political and Religious Ideas of the Testator. London: Review of Reviews Office, 1902.

CRITICAL AND BIOGRAPHICAL STUDIES

Baylen, Joseph O. "W. T. Stead and the Boer Wars." *Canadian Historical Review* 40:304–314 (1959).

———. "A Victorian's 'Crusade' in Chicago, 1893–94." *Journal of American History* 51, no. 3;418–434 (December 1964).

———. "The 'New Journalism' in Late Victorian Britain." *Australian Journal of Politics and History* 18:367–385 (December 1972).

———. "W. T. Stead as Publisher and Editor of the *Review of Reviews.*" *Victorian Periodicals Newsletter* 12:70–83 (1979).

———. "Politics and the 'New Journalism.'" *Victorian Periodicals Review* 20, no. 4:126-141 (winter 1987).

———. "Stead's Publishing House." In *British Literary Publishing Houses, 1881–1965.* Dictionary of Literary Biography, Vol. 112. Edited by J. Ross and P. J. Anderson. Detroit: Thomson Gale Research, 1991. Pp. 266–271.

———. "W. T. Stead: A Christ in Chicago." *British Journalism Review* 3:57–61 (1992).

Biel, Steven. *Down with the Old Canoe: A Cultural History of the "Titanic" Disaster.* New York: Norton, 1997.

Eckley, Grace, ed. *NewsStead,* nos. 1–25 (1992–2004); the journal of the W. T. Stead Memorial Society. "Journalism That Made History: A Stead Bibliography," *NewsStead,* no 19:19–36 (fall 2001), is a comprehensive bibliography that includes work for the *Pall Mall Gazette.* (The journal was discontinued with no. 25; information on how to obtain back copies is available at http://www.newsstead.itgo.com/newssteadpage.html.)

Jones, Victor Pierce. *Saint or Sensationalist? The Story of W. T. Stead, 1849–1912.* Chicester, U.K.: Gooday, 1988.

Plowden, Alison. *The Case of Eliza Armstrong: A Child of Thirteen Bought for £5.* London: BBC Books, 1974.

Schults, Raymond L. *Crusader in Babylon: W. T. Stead and the "Pall Mall Gazette."* Lincoln: University of Nebraska Press, 1972.

Stead, Estelle Wilson. *My Father: Personal and Spiritual Reminiscences.* London: Thomas Nelson, 1913.

Terrot, Charles. *The Maiden Tribute: A Study of the White Slave Traffic of the Nineteenth Century.* London: Frederick Muller, 1954.

Wall, Joseph. "The Odd Couple: Andrew Carnegie and W. T. Stead." *NewsStead,* no. 2:4 (summer 1993).

Whyte, Frederic. *The Life of W. T. Stead.* 2 vols. London: Cape, 1925.

ON "NEW JOURNALISM" AND THE BRITISH PRESS

For a concise history of the British newspapers since 1620, see http://www.bl.uk/collections/britnews.html.

Arnold, Matthew. "Up to Easter." *Nineteenth Century,* May 1887, pp. 629–643. (Available at http://www.attackingthedevil.co.uk/related/easter.php.)

Brake, Laurel, B. Bell, and David Finkelstein, eds. *Nineteenth-Century Media and the Construction of Identities.* New York: Palgrave, 2000.

Codell, Julie F., ed. *Imperial Co-Histories: National Identities and the British Colonial Press.* Cranbury, N.J.: Fairleigh Dickinson University Press, 2003.

Griffiths, Dennis, ed. *The Encyclopedia of the British Press, 1492–1992.* London: Macmillan, 1992.

Jackson, Kate. *George Newnes and the New Journalism in Britain, 1880–1910.* Aldershot, U.K.: Ashgate, 2001.

Jones, Aled. *Powers of the Press: Newspapers, Power, and the Public in Nineteenth-Century England.* Aldershot, U.K.: Scolar Press, 1996.

———, and Lionel Madden. *Investigating Victorian Journalism.* New York: St. Martin's, 1990.

Linton, David, and Ray Boston, eds. *The Newspaper Press in Britain: An Annotated Bibliography.* London and New York: Mansell, 1987.

Scott, J. W. Robertson. *The Life and Death of a Newspaper: An Account of the Temperaments, Perturbations, and Achievements of John Morley, W. T. Stead, E. T. Cook,*

WILLIAM THOMAS STEAD

Harry Cust, J. L. Garvin, and Three Other Editors of the "Pall Mall Gazette." London: Methuen, 1952.

Wiener, Joel H., ed. *Innovators and Preachers: The Role of the Editor in Victorian England.* Westport, Conn.: Greenwood Press, 1985.

———. *Papers for the Millions: The New Journalism in Britain, 1850s to 1914.* New York and Westport, Conn.: Greenwood Press, 1988.

EDWARD UPWARD

(1903—)

Robert Sullivan

EDWARD UPWARD WAS, for a time, one of the most influential literary figures in England. At times referred to as "the English Kafka," he was a major influence on those writers collectively known as the "Auden Generation," members of which included Auden himself, Stephen Spender, and Christopher Isherwood. These writers eagerly awaited any new Upward composition that circulated in manuscript, just as they sought Upward's criticism of their own writing. However, unlike these contemporaries who flirted with communism for a short time, Upward fully immersed himself in the Communist cause and for decades this led to an irreparable breach between his political work and his creative writing. Indeed, it stopped him from writing altogether and he published nothing for approximately twenty-five years. Extraordinarily, Upward has made a phoenix-like reappearance. The reissuing of some of his earlier writings and several new story collections, by the Enitharmon Press, makes a reassessment of Upward's contribution to twentieth-century English literature all the more urgent.

Edward Upward was born on September 3rd, 1903 in Romford, Essex, England. His grandfather was of Dissenter stock and his father, a professed atheist, was a doctor. He had two brothers, one of whom spent most of his lifetime in a mental institution suffering from bouts of insanity, a fate that threatens more than a few of Upward's fictional characters. His father, who knew W. H. Auden's father at university, was an easy going man, but Upward's mother, as he remembered her, was "very socially conscious"; so much so that she insisted Edward attend a public school, Repton, rather than the local school that the father and son preferred. At Repton, Edward formed a strong friendship with Christopher Isherwood, a bond that would last

until Isherwood's death in 1986. More than likely, the two boys came together in friendship because they were both rebels and both strongly disapproved of their mothers. While at school, they invented the fictional village of Mortmere and it is no coincidence that such nomenclature echoes the French for "dead mother." Throughout his writing career, Isherwood would send all his manuscripts to Upward for final approval; moreover, having been to preparatory school with Auden, Isherwood introduced Upward to the poet and to other well-known figures of the nineteen-thirties such as the poet Stephen Spender and John Lehmann, who was an editor of the Hogarth Press run by Virginia and Leonard Woolf. It was this press that was to publish Upward's first major work, *Journey to the Border* (1938). Both Isherwood and Upward went to Corpus Christi College, Cambridge, within a year of one another where they continued their friendship and literary collaboration. They wrote more episodes of the scatological and macabre stories set in Mortmere, peopling the village with all sorts of caricatured types. While at Cambridge, Upward also won the Chancellor's Medal for Poetry.

Unlike Isherwood, who had private funds and was able to pursue his literary career without working, as soon as Upward left Cambridge in 1926 he took positions teaching at preparatory schools in Cornwall and Scotland. During this time, he wrote *The Railway Accident,* the last, longest, and most famous Mortmere tale. He finished the story in 1928 but withheld publication until 1948, and only then released it in an expurgated version under Isherwood's (he wrote the Introduction) chosen pseudonym, "Alan Chalmers." Between its composition and publication, the story was circulated widely among Upward's and Isherwood's acquaintances. Auden is reported to have been able to quote large tracts of it, including a sanitized incident in which a male character is raped by three choir boys. By 1932, Upward had found a permanent position at Alleyn's School, a minor public school in Dulwich, London. He would remain in this post, eventually becoming Head of English, until his retirement thirty years later in 1961. Many of his experiences teaching found their way into his fiction, most especially his long trilogy *The Spiral Ascent,* which is a thinly disguised autobiography. Upward is on record as to how he conducted his political work in the evenings much as the schoolmaster, Alan Sebrill, does in the trilogy. It was certainly very unusual to have someone as left-wing as Upward teach at an English public school. In 1932, he took a tour of the Soviet Union and shortly thereafter joined the Communist Party of Great Britain (C.P.G.B.). It was at the local branch of the C.P.G.B that he met his wife Hilda Percival, also a teacher, and they were married in 1936. Both of them were very active in the Party while holding down teaching jobs. Hilda died in 1995 The couple had two children, Christopher and Kathy, both linguists. Christopher suffered from multiple sclerosis and died in 2002.

During the World War II, Upward was a volunteer in the auxiliary fire service. Shortly after the war, in 1948, he and his wife Hilda resigned from the C.P.G.B. because they believed that the Party had become un-Leninist and anti-revolutionary. During these years, from just before the war until the nineteen-fifties, when he began work on his trilogy, Upward fell silent. He was undergoing severe anxiety and depression as he tried to reconcile his political work, his job as a schoolmaster and his faltering creative work. As described in the semi-autobiographical *The Spiral Ascent,* even taking a year's sabbatical from teaching did not solve his problems and they resulted in what can only be described as a nervous breakdown. Extraordinary as it seems, especially given his output in his retirement years, Upward published nothing of substance between *Journey to the Border* (1938) and the first volume of the trilogy *In the Thirties* (1962). The second volume, *The Rotten Elements,* appeared in 1969, and the third, *No Home But the Struggle,* in 1977.

After his retirement in 1961, Upward lived at the family home on the Isle of Wight and produced all his late work from this base. This includes the short-story collections *The Night Walk and Other Stories* (1987), *An Unmentionable Man* (1994), *The Scenic Railway* (1997), *The Coming Day and Other Stories* (2000), as well as two memoirs of Isherwood and Auden. There remains unpublished multiple manuscripts of poems, plays, essays, and fiction, as well as scores of private diaries, all housed at the archive in the British Library and which Upward prefers kept from publicity until after his death. He has reached the ripe old age of one-hundred-and-two and, apparently, still tries to write something everyday. While there is as yet no biography, a fairly full picture of Upward's life can be constructed by reading his trilogy along with the two "auto-biographical fictions," *Lions and Shadows* and *Christopher and his Kind,* by his friend Christopher Isherwood in which Upward appears as the "character" Allen Chalmers.

THE EARLY WRITINGS

Although Edward Upward had won the Chancellor's Medal for Poetry at Cambridge and in his youth considered himself primarily a poet, little or none of his poetry survives in print. In their bibliography, Munton and Young list poems that were published in Upward's public-school journal *The Reptonian* and others (many under pseudonyms) in various ephemeral periodicals, but none of these have been collected. Around 1922, while at Corpus Christi College, Cambridge, Upward turned to prose and seemingly wrote no more poetry (he certainly did not publish any) for the rest of his long life. The reasons for this are uncertain, but the collaboration with Isherwood on the Mortmere stories may have deflected his interests away from "serious" poetry, though he did contribute a few satiric verse pieces to the Mortmere collection. Two other factors are relevant in assessing the reasons for his turning toward prose. First, as Upward fictionalizes in the trilogy and as Isherwood corroborates in *Lions and Shadows* (see especially page 94), Upward's attending the lectures of I.

EDWARD UPWARD

A. Richards while at Cambridge had a devastating influence on his commitment to poetry. Richards, who appears under the fictional name "B.K. Wilshaw" in *The Spiral Ascent,* maintained that poetry is essentially non-referential, is purely emotional, and thus can have no bearing on "reality." Upward is on record as saying that such a position was a major factor in "putting a stop" to his writing poetry. Second, another factor might have been the negative comments apparently made about his poetry by W.H. Auden when Isherwood brought the two together in a Soho restaurant in 1927. Whatever the reasons, for the next sixty years, Upward would publish nothing but prose.

MORTMERE

In *Lions and Shadows,* Isherwood describes in some detail his and Upward's friendship while at Cambridge and how they formed what amounted to a secret society of two, as well as how they set themselves against what they called the "poshocracy," or establishment, and how they set about lampooning it in their Mortmere stories. The two principal narrators are Hynd and Starn (sometimes amalgamated to "Hearn"), while the "Laily Worm" is the personage who represents all that the two friends abhor, the "symbol of the Public school social-team-spirit" (*The Mortmere Stories,* p. 35). One of Upward's poetic contributions that still survives, "Tale of a Scholar," sets out not only to "lampoon the Worm, but to give vent to [their] opinion of the whole academic tradition" (p. 36). It also captures Upward's jaundiced opinion of the university and Cambridge in general. Written in the style of Pope, the following lines give the flavor:

Morning, a garish half-light filtering down
Through interminable fog, wakens the town
With draymen's brawls and muted echo of hoofs
And aqueous flares that star the salesmen's booths
Where draper bows or butcher flings his slops
Or, stooping stiff and decorous and drab,
The aproned poulterer sluices his blood-streaked slab.
Always in Cambridge town it seems to me
Morning's like midnight in a cemetery.
* * *

[Laily] loathed pure history worse than cleanliness,
But loved competitive exams and prizes
And all rewards the History Board devises—
High marks and hinted praise, promises muttered
To those who know which side their bread is buttered.
Honours he relished, yet found joy no less
In others' failure than in his success,
And gave God thanks that in exams at least
One does not lose by stinking like a beast,
And that the kind examiners subtract
No marks for sweating like a sexual act;
(*Mortmere,* p. 36, 37)

Among other pieces, Upward contributed a story, that is now lost, about a brothel for necrophiliacs. Isherwood's "The Horror in the Tower," reprinted in the Enitharmon Press edition, is a Poe-like tale about a decadent aristocratic family with an unusual penchant for their unsuspecting visitor's excrement. Starn, the narrator, relates the "secret" to his friend Hynd: "The secret of the tower was, as I suspected, a small chamber, situated just below the water-closet and entered by a secret door... It was here that Kester and his ancestor Barsac had come night after night, obeying the promptings of that terrible mania. It was here that they had enjoyed their loathsome and solitary feasts" (*Mortmere,* p. 63).

The Railway Accident, the longest of these stories and the last that Upward was to write, has survived in an expurgated version and has been reprinted many times. It was written in 1928 while Upward was working as a private tutor in Lockerbie, Scotland, an experience that he would draw on for *Journey to the Border,* arguably his best work of fiction. A kind of farewell to Mortmere, the first half of *The Railway Accident* is a surreal telling of a train journey through the English countryside: a terrain at once easily recognizable—"the first gasometers, restful, solemn like stumps of semi-amputated breasts, curved past the window in frost-bright air" (p. 130)—yet somehow estranged due to the first-person narrator Hearn's peculiar vision, as if Kafka had set one of his allegories in an English pastoral landscape. Hearn shares a compartment with Gustave Shreeve, Headmaster of Frisbald College, a Mortmere landmark, and both are traveling to Mortmere to attend the Rector's Treasure Hunt. We learn from their conversation that there are two trains, an express and a local, both going to Mortmere and that timing is critical if both trains are not to end up on the same track. There is much foreshadowing of a catastrophe, including talk of a previous accident under mysterious circumstances on the same line. Inevitably, as if by fate, the two trains collide, the express running into the back of the slower train from which Hearn and Shreeve have narrowly escaped:

> The express had taken the points. Booster-fitted, excessively rolling, the racing Mogul engine rounded the curve, bounded into the rear of the carriage we had left. Coaches mounted like viciously copulating bulls, telescoped like ventilator hatches. Nostril gaps in a tunnel clogged with wreckage instantly flamed. A faint jet of blood sprayed from a vacant window... Tall rag-feathered birds with corrugated red wattles limped from holes among the rocks.
>
> (*Mortmere*, p. 150–151)

The scene shifts abruptly after the accident, if indeed it was an accident rather than one of Hearn's hallucinations, to the village of Mortmere itself, a very strange "English" village indeed, at least as Hearn sees it: "Snakes hung from the elm branches; pigeons rose from black curtains of leaves, startled by the engine of the car. The river coiled through the woods, avoiding boles of pine and willow. Across the waters of the sun-white marshes alligator fishermen punted their craft" (p. 152).

The Treasure Hunt turns nasty and there is much violent behavior. No doubt the rape scene from the uncensored version was from one of the scenes where Anthony Belmare is roughed-up by Ernie Travers, Boy Radnor, and Tod Erswell. Recrimination follows recrimination between Gustave Shreeve and Mr. Wheery until one of the party suggests a duel. Toy pistols are produced by Miss Belmare, but one of them turns out to be real and Wheery is shot in the groin and permanently maimed. The story closes a few sentences later with the news that "Harold Wrygrave has been arrested on a charge of train wrecking" (p. 159).

STORIES OF CONVERSION

After his tour of the Soviet Union in 1932, Upward began to turn more and more toward Marxism, as evidenced by some of his stories during these years. He published two stories in the anthology *New Country* (1933) that document his new interest in bringing his writing into line with his new outlook. The very short "Sunday" concerns an unnamed narrator (the point of view shifts from first person, through third, and closes with the second person) who comes to consciousness of the dying culture that is unconsciously lived during the week, a week of "drudgery and servility." He begins to realize on his way to lunch that he has a choice of either a crippling neurosis that will come with accepting the status quo or the sanity that will come with trying to change it. Essentially a story of conversion, it closes with the narrator deciding to join the Communist Party: "He will go to the small club behind the Geisha Café. He will ask whether there is a meeting tonight... He will have to prove himself, to prove that he isn't a mere neurotic, an untrustworthy freak. It will take time. But it is the only hope. He will at least have made a start" (*The Railway Accident and Other Stories*, p. 84).

"The Colleagues," also published in *New Country*, introduces a setting and theme that Upward would return to in his lengthier fictions, the English Public School and the hypocrisy of the schoolmaster-protagonist who is obliged to uphold a system he inherently abhors. The colleagues in question are Lloyd, a priggish master and disciplinarian who is absolutely comfortable with his position, and the "new man," Mitchell, who becomes conscious of his hypocrisy and false consciousness. His choice he believes is a "romantic" opposition or an acceptance of the school apparatus as it stands. As the narrative draws to a close, Mitchell watches Lloyd playing rugby, a perfectly ordinary sight, but not as Mitchell sees it: "There are no other witnesses. If there were they would have nothing to report except that a young preparatory schoolmaster has kicked a football. I have seen a horror which no one else here would have been privileged to see. For an instant I must have been authentically insane" (p, 78). This vision of an ordinary world, of what Isherwood and Upward had derisively called the "symbol of the Public school social-team-spirit," transmogrified by the peculiar insight of a protagonist looks back to Mortmere, but also forward to Upward's most sustained treatment of insanity and conversion.

JOURNEY TO THE BORDER

Written under the working title of "The Border Line," *Journey to the Border* is perhaps Upward's best fiction. Somewhere between novel and novella (135 pages in the recent Enitharmon edition), it allows for the kind of concentrated prose normally associated with the short story. The fact that the action takes place in less than twenty-four hours magnifies this intensity. It resembles his previous longest fiction, *The Railway Accident,* in its use of a traditional English setting, only to defamiliarize the setting through the vision of a deranged consciousness. The "journey" of the title describes the narrator's passage from the edge of insanity to the potential haven of political commitment, and it could be said to describe Upward's own journey during these years from neurotic indecision to committed Marxist.

The novel opens with an unnamed private tutor who is employed in a large country house debating with himself as to why he should accompany his employer Mr. Parkin to a local race-meeting, since this is really not part of his duties. The tutor sees himself as a willing participant in his own servitude, a "lackey" to the landed gentry who realizes his weakness and today resolves to make some gesture of rebellion, if only he can summon up the courage. From the very beginning, the narrative is constructed upon a division, a split, between the chronic intensity of the tutor's inner turmoil and what seems like everyday action and conversation. Indeed, the novel could be said to dramatize the fight for integrity in at least two senses of that term: the tutor struggles to overcome a disintegrating sense of self and achieve a sense of self-worth and at the same time, he fights to come to terms with "reality" and his aberrant vision of it. Early in the

novel, he experiments with the idea that since "reality" is constructed by human beings he could therefore change his reality and his "serfdom":

> The tutor must kill thinking and he must really kill feeling, which still lingered on in spite of his first attempt to kill it. Because if he killed thinking and feeling he would automatically destroy the world of his serfdom, the only knowable world, which after all was nothing more than an evil decoration created by thinking and feeling...
>
> * * *
>
> Thinking and feeling had been poisoned and had in turn poisoned sight and touch and hearing. And thinking and feeling could not be killed... But couldn't they be changed, couldn't they be healed, drained of their poison? If they could then the whole world would be changed. Because the whole world was a world created by human thinking and feeling and seeing and touching and hearing.
>
> (*Journey to the Border,* p. 30, 31)

The notion that the world, or "reality," might be changed by an individual consciousness only leads the tutor to the border of insanity. Eventually he realizes, in true Marxist fashion, that the consciousness of human beings is formed by social relations, and it is only by changing these relations that the "world" can be changed and thus the tutor's plight of serfdom. Later in the novel, we learn that the tutor has a political conscience but seems to have repressed it in order to be subservient to his employer, and this is a contributing factor in his instability. A young lady at the races puts it like this: "The strange thing about you is that you see quite clearly what is wrong with the system under which you are living. More clearly than I do. But you take no action. You are content to hate and despise your life" (p. 62). A little earlier, the tutor had projected such self-loathing onto a clowning tipster at the racetrack who he imagines has singled him out for ridicule: "I'm telling you for your own good. Wake up and be a man. Be human. You're British aren't you? Then learn to take reasonable risks and don't always be worrying about the safety of your own skin" (p. 57). As the tutor descends into a kind of hallucinatory hell he "witnesses" a proto-fascist cell led by the Master of Fox Hounds, one of whose henchmen is Tod Ewan, a brutish and racist colonist home on leave from Nigeria. In his solipsistic hell, the tutor sees Tod grow menacingly in stature: "Not only Tod's face but his body grew bigger. He was taller and his shoulders were broader, than before" (p. 73). At what the tutor perceives as a fascist rally, it is the same Tod who, Mussolini-like, gives a provocative speech against international Jewry and the International Workers' Movement: "Broad-backed and stiff, fists on hips, elbows jutting sideways like the heavy handles of a fat earthenware jug" (p. 90).

As he descends into the nadir of his despair, the tutor imagines an Orwellian future without hope: "Horror of the future alone supported him, kept his consciousness alive. He would be gassed, bayoneted in the groin, slowly burned, his eyeballs punctured by wire barbs. Yet it was not the thought of these physical agonies that really horrified him…[but] the other slower horrors which he *was* able to imagine…The death of all poetry, of all love, of all happiness" (p. 105,). Escaping from the race-meeting's marquee, he at first contemplates suicide, then enters a state of temporary paralysis, unable to move. He imagines that a voice speaks to him out of the trees, but comes to realize that this is his alter-ego urging him toward a "rational" solution to his problems. There is only one way to preserve his sanity and regain his integrity: by getting in touch as soon as possible with the "Internationalist Movement for Working-Class Power" (p. 116). The tutor has always known this but could not bring such knowledge to consciousness. Now he could: "He would get in touch. Then he would walk back to the house, and the next morning he would ·begin tutoring again, but with a difference… His decision to join [the movement] would not make life easier for him. But at least he would have come down to earth, out of the cloud of his irresponsible fantasies; would have begun to live" (p. 135). As his most extensive work of fiction clearly shows, Edward Upward's decision to join the Communist Party of Great Britain during the time he was writing this novel would not "make life easier" for him either.

THE SPIRAL ASCENT

Upward's trilogy stands as a vast textual monument to his long struggle both as a writer and a politically committed human being. Indeed, it this very struggle that the three semi-autobiographical novels dramatize: how can Alan Sebrill, Upward's alter-ego, continue to write poetry, or as he rather abstractly puts it, live the "poetic life," while at the same time engaging in left-wing political action? More to the point, how can he write the kind of poetry that would serve the cause yet at the same time preserve his integrity as a poet? This was a common dilemma for young writers in the nineteen-thirties as social conditions worsened and the rise of fascism threatened another world war. Like other writers during the decade, Alan Sebrill realizes very early in the trilogy that he could not superimpose a Marxist stance on his poetry, but rather he must first become a Marxist in his life. Upward had predicted Alan Sebrill's dilemma as early as 1937 in his essay "A Marxist Interpretation of Literature":

> A writer today who wishes to produce his best work that he is capable of producing, must first of all become a socialist in his practical life, must go over to the progressive side of the class conflict… He is aware that it will involve him in extra work other than imaginative writing…He is aware also that this work may in certain circumstances stop him writing altogether, that he may be required to sacrifice life itself in the cause of the workers.
> (Day Lewis, *The Mind in Chains*, p. 52–53)

Just as the journey motif was crucial to his earlier fiction, it is most relevant to the trilogy as wellA much more extensive fiction, the trilogy traces both the spiritual journey of Alan Sebrill (Bunyan was a favorite of Upward's from an early age), as well as being a historical journey through a great deal of the twentieth-century. The three novels chronicle more than thirty years of political history, and if one includes the pre-World War memories of Alan's schooldays as recounted in the third volume, the trilogy spans some sixty years from around 1910 to 1970. In many senses an Everyman, Alan either witnesses or remembers the First World War, the General Strike, the rise of Fascism, the Spanish Civil War, the World War II, Vietnam and the anti-war movement, the Cold War, and the emergence of the C.N.D. (Campaign Against Nuclear Disarmament), in which, during his retirement, Alan plays a part. The first two volumes, *In the Thirties* and *The Rotten Elements,* are predominantly chronological, expressing as they do, one man's life as it coincides with twentieth century history. The third volume, *No Home But the Struggle,* mainly concerned with memory and the recovery of the past, suitably oscillates between the "now" of the narrative and past events. The peculiar blending of massive historical fact narrated in an ultra-realist manner, interfused with continuous subjective self-analysis (Alan Sebrill is a chronic self-analyzer), is unique in twentieth century British fiction. There are few other fictions in the British tradition that attempt such an historical sweep while fusing such with a poetic consciousness. Thus, it is no coincidence that, given Upward's renunciation of the modernist experiment (he has Alan Sebrill denounce the ways of modernism in the trilogy), that one has to look back to the nineteenth century for anything like *The Spiral Ascent.* Whatever its status may be in any future estimation of twentieth century British literature, *The Spiral Ascent* remains the spinal cord, as it were, of Edward Upward's oeuvre. Upward has described its grand scheme in an "Author's Note":

> The trilogy as a whole has the form of two inter-linked dialectical triads. In volumes 1 & 2 the "political life" supersedes the "poetic life" and is in its turn superseded by the "new poetic life", that is to say Alan Sebrill comes back to the "poetic life" on a higher level; and in volumes 2 & 3 the "new poetic life" supersedes the "political life" and is in its turn superseded by the "new political life", that is to say he comes back at last to the "political life" on a higher level. There is a spiral ascent in his development.

The title of the first volume, *In the Thirties,* is descriptive in that it recounts a decade in the life of its protagonist but also serves as a typological marker, alluding as it does to many of the com-

mon anxieties of that decade. Alan Sebrill is at once an individual with poetic aspirations and an Everyman who witnesses and endures much of the political turmoil and ideological warfare of those years. Above all, Alan suffers the pangs of a conscience that seeks an equilibrium between political and social responsibility and his desire to lead the "poetic life." The novel begins with Alan's arrival on "the island" (the actual Isle of Wight) at the invitation of his erstwhile university friend Richard Marple (Upward's fictional name for Christopher Isherwood). Alan arrives feeling buoyant about the long poem he hopes to write as he and Richard live on the island and devote their time to writing. Early in the novel, the two friends walk together and, much like Stephen Dedalus in Joyce's *A Portrait of the Artist as a Young Man,* they indulge themselves in the "magic of words": "They spoke geological words—more for the sound and poetic suggestiveness than for scientific meaning—such as sandrock, the Perna Bed, mud-flows, blue slipper, the Gault, the crackers." (*The Spiral Ascent,* p. 10–11, henceforth abbreviated *SA*). They go to dances together and watch the young people dancing what they poetically associate with the dance of a doomed class, a dance of death.

After Richard abruptly announces that he wants to leave for London (eventually we learn this was so that he could meet "a boy"), Alan takes up with one of the local girls, Peg, but after a brief sexual encounter she decides to return to her fiancé in London. Now alone, unable to write, Alan contemplates taking up a full-time teaching position if "some headmaster or board of governors could be gulled by his academic qualifications or, more likely, by his classy public-school education into offering him a teaching post" (*SA,* p. 33). But he considers such a move beneath him, a kind of slavery; so now, his poetry failed, abandoned by his friend Richard, turned down by his lover Peg, Alan contemplates suicide and walks to one of the cliffs on the island reciting to himself some verses from "Othello." He then turns his mind to religion, but rejects this possible solution as "anti-progressive." Then, in a significant association of ideas—given the numerous testaments from the 1930s about the "quasi-religious" motives of joining the workers' movement and/or the Communist Party—Alan decides to put his "faith" in Marxism. Before he could approach the Party, he would need time to study the Marxist classics: "Above all he needed plenty of time to build up his courage again, to purge off the sick demoralization which had come over him during the last two months" (*SA,* p. 43). Thus the first chapter of the novel ends with a determined Alan Sebrill vowing to leave the island, find a job as a schoolmaster and, in due course, approach the Communist Party to become a member. Eventually, when he feels the time is right, he is voted unanimously into the Party by members of his local branch. The second chapter of *In the Thirties* closes on a proleptically ironic note:

> "A day of bliss," he thought as he stood waiting for the tram that would take him back to the hotel. At last he had emerged from the quag of self-questioning. He knew how he must live and die. He saw now what it meant to be a Communist. A mere change of heart, a mere revolution in the soul, would not make a Communist. Only constant political action could do that. If he lived his external life rightly, kept unfailingly in touch with the Party and worked for it, there would be no need to worry about his soul or his poetry.
>
> (*SA,* p. 69).

As the remaining seven-hundred-plus pages of the trilogy testify, this is hardly the end of Alan Sebrill's "self-questioning" and only the beginning of the internecine struggle between his political work and his poetry. Much of the rest of *In the Thirties* is taken up with Alan's quotidian duties as a schoolmaster, interspersed with his participation in various Party activities and, chronically, his continuing desire to live the "poetic life," a mode of existence that is constantly invoked as a binary opposite to his prosaic everyday life. Alan meets Elsie Hutchinson, a schoolteacher, while attending meetings of his local branch of the Communist Party, and he is attracted to her in what he terms a "purely animal" way. Alan's upper-middle-class intentions toward Elsie are ambiguous to say the least and are connected to his residual bourgeois desire to lead the "poetic life" (the very vagueness of this term might help explain the impossibility of ever achieving it) and what Elsie represents—working-class mediocrity. To marry Elsie would be tantamount to marrying the Party and the working class, and this was a desirable outcome for many upper-middle-class individuals in the 1930s, as many fictions, biographies, and autobiographies of the period testify. For Alan, this would mean becoming accustomed to a prosaic life in a petite-bourgeois maisonette that he detests, to a woman he does not, and thinks he *could* not, love. Indeed, he more than once thinks to himself how physically repulsive Elsie is, and it is in the maisonette that they are thinking of renting that all of Alan's misgivings about the prospective misery of his future overwhelms him:

> A misery rose in him at the thought of how he had betrayed her [Alan has just told her that he cannot marry her], of how he was injuring her. But at the same time a fear was in him that he might weaken, might retract what he had said, might betray the poetic life. He was impelled to add something outrageous, something that he would not be able to go back on and that she could never forgive. He said, "Oh Elsie, you are so ugly."
>
> (*SA,* p. 214).

However, Alan tells himself that a marriage with Elsie would be politically and physically suitable, and eventually he confesses to himself "he was lucky to have married her," and how he "must put a stop to his endless bourgeois whining, to his miserable fussing about his own happiness" (p. 251). By the novel's end (it is historically marked as "two months after Munich"), Alan and Elsie are not only married but also have a child and Alan's admiration for his wife has grown into love. The novel closes with Alan and Elsie on a ramble in the country with fellow Party members. Alan has a kind of epiphany that brings him back to the novel's beginning and his hopes of living the poetic life on the island with Richard, but he soon realizes that he would have to cure himself of such "illusions." It was not the proper time: "The poetic life was the finest life. No other, not even the Party life, could compare with it. But it could not be lived now... There was only one way towards it, and that was the way of constant political effort, of Communist struggle for a struggleless world in which poetic living would at last become actual" (p. 282) Thus the first volume of the "dialectical triad" closes with a recognition of the necessity for the eclipse of poetry in the interest of politics.

Despite the extensive tracts of political debate and ideological wrangling, the first volume of *The Spiral Ascent* is counterbalanced by a lyricism that all but disappears in *The Rotten Elements*. This is no doubt part of Upward's grand dialectical design, in which the poetic succumbs to the political only for the two antithetical components to become a synthesized unity in *No Home But the Struggle,* the final volume. In 1969, when it appeared as a single volume, *The Rotten Elements,* was subtitled "A Novel of Fact," not only hinting at its autobiographical strain (Upward, like his alter-ego, Alan Sebrill, left the Communist Party in 1948 because of what he understood as its un-Leninist revisionism), but also giving an historically accurate picture of left-wing politics in Britain just after the World War II. In an "Author's Note," Upward explains: "The phrase 'rotten elements' was sometimes used in the party to refer to members who deviated seriously from the correct party line" (p. 284).

When we meet Alan and Elsie at the beginning of this novel, they have just embarked on a campaign to educate their local branch members in Leninist revolutionary communism, especially the tenets of his *State and Revolution,* as a countermeasure to the Party's executive branch's deviation from this line. Their personal "deviation" from the "correct party line" eventually results in Elsie tearing up her Party card and both of them leaving the branch before their inevitable expulsion. Despite the recurrence of the motif of yearning for the "poetic life" that runs through all three volumes, *The Rotten Elements,* (as its original subtitle implied) is much more concerned with a factual account of communist politics. Much of the novel reads less like a dramatic fiction than a series of summaries of political positions and/or conversations that rehearse Marxist philosophy. It seems as if every conversation turns into a Hegelian account of thesis and antithesis, even in the most domestic of settings, as when, for example, Alan and Elsie are in the kitchen making the family meal and discussing the pros and cons of bourgeois versus communist morality (pp. 414–416). Even in the most intimate of places, Alan and Elsie find themselves inclined to discuss Party business and its deviation from Leninist revolutionary socialism. At the beginning of Chapter 3, they lie in bed unable to sleep because of the controversy at their local Branch over the publication of the book *Britain's Way Forward* by the leader of the British Communist Party that they see as reactionary. Eventually, they escape their political duties through coitus and move into a realm that transcends all the pressing worries of the moment. It is one of the very few instances of genuine intimacy and contentment in this volume: "He moved away with her away from themselves and far away from any thought of tomorrow's meeting, away from his identity as a Party member, as a schoolmaster, as a father and a husband... Away from his class origin, his nationality, his epoch, away from Elsie as an individual person. This act linked him with men and women of every race all over the world, in the past as well as in the present" (p. 331).

Alan Sebrill's estrangement from the Party he had joined in order to preserve his mental stability leads to a kind of relapse. To make matters worse, even after taking a year's leave of absence from his school, he has still not managed to complete the long poem he had been working on for years. Bereft now of both of his political commitment to the Party and the concomitant inability to write, Alan is faced with a total mental breakdown. He turns to Wordsworth (a figure who is to become more inspirational in the third volume), particularly that poet's disillusionment with the French Revolution as expressed in his long poem *The Excursion.* By the novel's end, Alan has regained his mental equilibrium and believes that he has worked out a methodology for sustaining both his political and poetic life *outside* the Party. *The Rotten Elements* closes on a hopeful and resilient note, but the "home" (both literal and metaphysical) that Alan has found for himself would not be as free from adversity as the title of the final volume indicates.

EDWARD UPWARD

No Home but the Struggle, the third volume of the trilogy, is dedicated to Upward's son Christopher (no doubt named after Isherwood) and his daughter Kathy, and to "both their families." This personal dedication is, in many ways, a reflection of the change in register Upward adopts for this novel. If the major influences of the first two volumes are Marx and Lenin, respectively, the presences that hover over the final volume are those of Wordsworth and Bunyan, alongside a certain amount of Proustian reflection. The very first word of this volume is the personal pronoun and it opens up a narrative bent on recovering the past, from Alan Sebrill's childhood during the World War I to the 1970s. This reflection is meant to help capture a poetic sensibility that Alan feels he lost due to his political engagement. The narrative opens with Alan remarking on how "now," after his retirement from teaching, he could devote himself to writing poetry in his inherited house on the Isle of Wight: "I have arrived home for good at last. There will never again be a morning now when I have to say to myself here: 'Tomorrow I must return to London and to my job as a teacher.' Until I die or until I am kept in bed by a serious illness I shall be able every day after breakfast to come into this pleasant white and yellow room... and every day I shall be free to write poetry" (p. 503). These words of Alan Sebrill's could easily be attributed to Edward Upward, living on the Isle of Wight, and writing all his late work there.

Political animal that he is, Alan is unable to relinquish political and/or socialist activity altogether, so he decides to join the island branch of the Campaign for Nuclear Disarmament (CND). He is able to assuage his political conscience in this way while at the same time holding the belief that, unlike the utter impasse between his writing and his Party work dramatized in the previous volumes, such action would not hinder his creativity. Most of the early chapters consist of a willed reflection on his childhood now that he is living in his parents' and grandparents' house, in which most of the events have taken place: he remembers his brother Hugh's games; the mostly negative aspects of his preparatory and public schools;

and Christine, his first love and begetter of the young Sebrill's first poem. Many of these chapters are reminiscences of a time pre-World War I when Sebrill was at "Marchfield," his preparatory school (563ff.) and later when he attended "Rugonstead," his public school. These latter sections of the novel dealing with Alan's public schooldays (606ff.) are, over and above their fictional function, extremely interesting social texts, shedding light on the mores of the English public school system just before and after the Great War. Contained in these pages are an intriguing account of the "fagging" system, as well as latent and full-blown homosexuality—the young Sebrill has a "poetic love" for a fellow pupil, but is "saved" by his heterosexual love for Christine Dunbar. There is in these pages a peculiar fusion of Wordsworthian emotion recollected in tranquility and a Proustian search for the essence of childhood, all in the service of inducing poetic labor. Unfortunately, much of the writing reads too much like many self-help books that are meant to aid aspiring writers, rather dramatic renderings of consciousness: time and time again the narrator Alan Sebrill admonishes himself to remember this, or "let me think" of that as he negotiates between past and present. The following is one of many, many instances:

> I broke out of that mood [neurotic despondency] by remembering how at my Prep. School my imagination developed in spite of all the constrictions and distortions which might have stunted its growth there... Let me think how it survived and developed during my time as a boy at my "Public" school... I have walked past the newsagents and now I am walking past the Gas showrooms too. The bills can be paid tomorrow... But if I were to turn back immediately and go into the Gas showrooms I might risk losing my hold on a remembrance which began to come to me a moment before I passed the newsagents."
>
> (p. 603).

There is something unsettling about the banality of this kind of discourse in what is supposed to be a dramatic fiction.

Eventually, Alan bids his memory to revisit his Cambridge University days and his friendship with Richard Marple (Isherwood). There is much in these pages (672ff.) that sheds light on their friendship and Upward and Isherwood's invention of the fictional Mortmere, including discussion of some of the macabre tales. Many of these "fictional" details are in fact biographical, as Isherwood's various autobiographical writings attest, and much of this section of the trilogy is as valuable for the thoughts and compositions of Edward Upward as for Alan Sebrill. For example, when Alan recounts his tutoring job at a country house in the North of England, secured for him by "Rabbitarse and String" (Isherwood's sobriquet for an academic employment agency), his description of the household (pp. 754–59) replicates much of the detail of Upward's novel *Journey to the Border,* which, in turn, is based on Upward's own experience of such a position. As if to confirm this, Alan Sebrill describes in these pages his new penchant for surrealist narrative and a revival at this time (c. 1928) of his interest in socialism, the very ingredients of Upward's novel, and of Upward's experience at this time.

The final pages of *No Home But the Struggle* approach a kind of summary of Alan Sebrill's life long struggle to reconcile his art with his political conscience. The narrative returns to the beginning, to the early pages of the trilogy when Alan arrived on the island to meet Richard with the hope of living the poetic life. As this novel closes, bringing the long trilogy to an end, Alan believes he has reached a compromise, or, in terms of the trilogy's scheme, a synthesis between politics and creative writing. On the one hand he recognizes the need to engage in politics, but on the other hand he recognizes the need not to let this engagement prevent him from writing: "I shall make my main contribution to the struggle in the way I am best fitted to make it, though poetic creation, unless political circumstances arise in which the interests of the struggle absolutely require me to do otherwise. I shall live the new political life" (p. 787). And so the lengthy narrative closes, with Alan Sebrill sitting on his veranda on the Isle of Wight with a "completed poem in [his] notebook on the small table beside [his] chair." That Edward Upward continued his struggle well into his old age is

evidenced by the large number of stories he wrote from this very same island.

THE STORY COLLECTIONS

The identifiable themes that cut across the short-story volumes could be described collectively as a concern with politics with a small "p," the politics of everyday life, rather than the grand sweep of politics and history as in the trilogy. Most of these stories are concerned with the quotidian vicissitudes of older people as they try to cope with illness, the grief of losing a life-long partner, and with loneliness in old age. However, woven within the fabric of these domestic tales there is usually a social text as well, whether it be hospital closures due to economic pressures, the effects of capitalist industrialism on the eco-system, or the threat of a resurgence of fascism in Europe due to unemployment. As he wrote in old age—Upward was approaching one-hundred-years old when some of these stories were published—many of these concerns are Edward Upward's own, as is the relationship of art to politics, the recurrent rehearsal of Upward's position as a Marxist and how this has affected his writing.

"The Procession" is a crucial story in this vein. The narrative tells of an old artist who imagines he sees his own funeral procession. This leads him to reflect on his career and to project his concerns and criticisms onto two friends who have been conjured up for the occasion. In response to one of them as to why he has abandoned the kind of "realistic fantasy" he had became famous for in his earlier years, the old painter replies: "I couldn't have gone on in my earlier style however much I'd wanted to. I couldn't have ignored how shallow and false it was as a response to the real horrors of the contemporary external world" (*The Night Walk and Other Stories,* p. 16). The other figure, whom the old artist greatly admires, offers a stylistic compromise suggesting that the artist might have achieved a more successful aesthetic had he been able to "meld" the earlier mode of realistic fantasy with the later naturalistic approach. The story ends with a self-reflexive comment on the narrative itself and suggests what is to be

Upward's chosen method in these later writings: "This was not a dream. I have invented it, with help from an actual nightmare I had in bed at home several years ago. It is a fantasy, and not even a realistic one. Yet it may convince me I can after all tell the truth about reality in a style that comes more readily to me than naturalism" (p. 18).

This aesthetic, proclaiming to be able to access "the truth about reality" through fantasy and/or dream (essentially an allegorical aesthetic) rather than a purely naturalistic approach, marks a distinction in Upward's oeuvre between a narrative such as *The Railway Accident,* for example, and that of *The Spiral Ascen*t, which is written almost entirely in a naturalistic mode. It also marks a division in the later stories, some of them employing dream like narratives while others are of a solely naturalistic bent. Moreover, regardless of Upward's intention, there are few of these stories (*The Scenic Railway* may be one of the exceptions) that are able to get at "the truth about reality" through fantasy as successfully as did *Journey to the Border.* In that fiction, there is a kind of organic, even if deranged, "vision" that inhabits the narrative and creates a whole, if bizarre, world. In many of the later stories, the dream serves for the most part as a frame for the usually episodic narrative that follows, seemingly only there to allow for the illogicality of time and place associated with dream.

The collection *The Night Walk and Other Stories* (1987) sets the tone and style for the other volumes that were to follow, in that it includes a mixture of dream like verisimilitude (the title story for example) and other stories of a naturalistic kind. Of the latter, two are of particular interest. "Her Day" is a narrative about the burial of a wife and mother whose "belief in the rightness of upper-class attitudes" and her "constant criticisms of the weaknesses of her husband and her sons" (*Night Walk,* p. 6) recall similar attitudes Upward has ascribed to his own mother. "The White-Pinafored Black Cat" is a beautifully rendered naturalistic tale of old age and loneliness and is perhaps the most successful story in the volume. A woman left alone after her brother dies finds solace in imaginary conversations with her cat Abigail. She rehearses her past, notably her missed opportunity to marry after the person she loves dies in the Great War, and also her present fears about her failing health. When she tells the cat that her recently modified will makes the provision to have Abigail "put down" when she dies, the cat disappears. As the story closes, Esther realizes that "there was nothing ahead for her now except aging and aloneness and illness and death" (p. 122). "At the Ferry Inn" is worth noting in that it records what seems to have been an imaginary attempt on Upward's part to heal a rift between him and W. H. Auden. It tells of a meeting between two old poet friends who have been estranged since the 'thirties, much as Upward and Auden had been due to the latter's adoption of what Upward had thought was "reactionary politics." They discuss writing at the Ferry Inn by the boat dock on the island where Arnold Olney is now living. Arnold (the Upward figure) defends his politics and recent writing against Walter's (the Auden figure) accusations that he has renounced his radical political stance as evidenced by his latest book, remarking that it is not a move away from Marxist-Leninism even if he now admits to his disillusionment with Stalinist communism. Eventually, Walter excuses himself to go to the toilet and he disappears. His old friend sees him on the ferry going back to the mainland, taking him "still further from Arnold," symbolizing perhaps their irreconcilable differences.

The title of Upward's next published volume, *An Unmentionable Man,* says much about its contents. In a series of sequentially interlinked stories, Upward's alter-ego the "elderly writer Stephen Highwood," has a series of dreams as he lies in his hospital bed. In these dreams, Highwood meets in episodic fashion some of his old friends as he seeks to understand both his neglect as a writer and, again, to defend his political position. In the title story, one of Stephen's "formerly close friends" refers to his "naïve and now completely out of date left-wing views that have always been so evident in [his] writings" (*An Unmentionable Man,* p. 15). In another episode in this dream like picaresque journey, a young man admires his work, but this only reminds Stephen that "all his books were out of print, and nearly all of them unobtainable in the majority of public libraries..." (p. 17). The young man, Paul Irlam, takes Stephen on a strange tour of the dreamscape in which the story is set that includes a visit to the gallery and workshop of The Excrementalists, a group of painters whose medium needs no further explanation. As with all these sequential stories, the narrative closes with Stephen Highwood back in his hospital bed attended by his wife and the doctor who is treating him. The next story has Stephen lunching with a prospective publisher who wonders why Highwood has not been able to publish his recent writings. This is because, Stephen explains, he writes about "unmentionable things," such as the "root cause of the horrific suffering of so many millions of our fellow human beings in the present day world [because of] the imperialist capitalist system" (p. 34). Here, as elsewhere in this volume, the didactic purpose eclipses much of the fictional art.

The final story, "With Alan to the Fair," is paradigmatic in its use of dream as an appendage to account for unlikely events rather than as a medium that the narrative inhabits. In this sense, this story and others like it resemble Hawthorne's "Young Goodman Brown" rather than, say, Upward's own *The Railway Accident* or *Journey to the Border*. Alan Sebrill gets up before his wife (we are led to believe) so that he might go to the Seaside Summer Fair. During his day, he encounters many bizarre happenings: Lara, an old love, not only propositions him but forces herself on him in one of the fair's tents. He then enters the "Oxbridge" tent and runs into a bookish person who it turns out had reviewed very negatively one of Alan's books, remarking that Alan's poems would never have been heard of but for "the boosting they got from [his] Public School Pals" (p. 95). This is an allusion to accusations concerning Upward's own work. As if to confirm the autobiographical strain, Upward has Alan agree that "politics weakened [his] poetry and finally stopped [him] writing it for some years. But this was because the Party line [he] loyally followed went rotten" (p. 100). After believing himself the victim of a fascist bomb,

he is finally awakened by his wife, who says, "You are going to be very late for the Fair" (p. 102). It had been a dream after all!

The title story in *The Scenic Railway* collection tells the story of a day in the life, or indeed a life in a day, of the aging Leslie Brellis (an anagram of Sebrill) who has volunteered to drive a group of disabled people to an amusement park. The highlight of the trip is an excursion on a small train that is shaped in the form of a dragon that passes on its route artificial scenery consisting of cardboard constructions. Shortly after the train starts on its short journey, the magical mystery tour becomes a magical memory tour as Leslie's imagination transforms the passing scenery into various historical landscapes. He witnesses the famous Christmas Day truce between the lines of the German and British armies during the Great War, a day the opposing sides came together to play football. He "sees" the vast vista of the Ukraine, remembered from a visit to the Soviet Union in 1932 (about the same time that Edward Upward had made such a visit). He also witnesses a commemoration marking the Battle of Jarama, fought during the Spanish Civil War, during which the British section of the International Brigade was cut to ribbons defending the road to Madrid. When the little train arrives at its destination, Leslie sees a tree that functions somewhat like a Proustian madeleine, taking him back to his youth and childhood. The world-historical events witnessed on the train are now transformed into a more personal and nostalgic desire to revisit his past: "His imagination became even more strongly alive than when he had watched the artificial scenery from the dragon train, and the scene he began to imagine now [the landscape of his past] was so vivid that it completely replaced in his consciousness the real sycamore and the real valley" (*The Scenic Railway*, p. 22). The narrative now makes a great imaginative leap and Leslie finds himself back in his home town "half a century afterwards." He lingers a while outside his first love Isabelle's house and finally reaches his own home where his parents (in reality long dead) are pleased to see him. The story closes with Leslie settling down in his old armchair, "more and more deeply, downwards into its safety" (p. 29). The final word of this story, "safety," may very well suggest how Leslie Brellis has found refuge from all his personal worries, as well as those woes that have afflicted twentieth-century history, by regressing to a time of innocence and parental protection.

Two other stories in this volume return to the recurrent theme of the concerns of growing old and dependent, and, most fearful of all, the necessity of having to live in "a home for old people." In "Investigation After Midnight," the insomniac Alan Sebrill awakens from a disturbing dream and begins to rehearse its manifest content in order that he might discover its etiology. In the dream, a group of fascist-like bullies burst into his house and proceed to evict him and his wife Elsie, presumably, Alan believes, so that they may turn their home into yet another residence for old and infirm people. It might well have been that Alan's unconscious had been working over in dream-form some remarks he had made to his wife during the day: "'The big danger for us in this town,' I said, 'is the spreading of these profit-making homes at such a rate that we may wake up one morning to discover that our house with ourselves inside it has been swallowed up into one of them'" (p. 36). In "Emily and Oswin," a wealthy widow reads in the local newspaper that the neglected and aging poet, Oswin Walden, is now living in a home for old people and she decides to rescue him from such a fate. After a brief affair and a trip to France, Emily arranges to finance a house for Oswin, thus making him independent. Unaware of the irony of the reversed gender-roles in his situation, the left-wing Oswin is cognizant of the fact that "if it hadn't been for the help of a member of the upper-middle class he might have remained in Sundown House and have become slowly insane" (p. 93).

Finally, something must be said of Upward's latest volume of stories, *The Coming Day and Other Stories* (2000), the title story of which (described as a novella in the table of contents) accentuates many of the weaknesses of some of these later writings. At some seventy pages, this episodic tale relates the picaresque adventures of

one Cedric Durcombe, "a schoolmaster who was known to have visited the Soviet Union," and who has escaped (or is dreaming that he has escaped) a nursing home for old people. His many adventures, including an erotic one with the exotically named Zaniah, a revolutionary who happens to be a "gerontophile," are only tenuously related and at times totter on the edge of farce. The random incidents are connected by some very flimsy connective tissue such as, "Well, where are we going now?" with a typical response being, "Is it to be a random ramble again?" (p. 51). The unbelievable narrative—unbelievable as a dream is "unbelievable," yet here presented as verisimilitude—ends with Zaniah joining a band of "professional revolutionaries" and arranging for Cedric to go to a "safe house." The narrative ends thus: "She bent forward to kiss him, and tears streamed over both their faces" (p. 72). Another story in this volume, "The Serial Dreamer," concerns a man who dreams he meets his dead wife acting as a voluntary nurse in a twenty-first century revolutionary war only to wake up and remember that he is still in the "dreadful reality of the twentieth-century" and that his wife is indeed dead: "His friends would continue to invite him out to evening meals, and while he was with them he would show his gratitude by being as cheerful as he could be. Then he would return to his own lonely house" (p. 109).

The title of this late story could very well serve as a general description of Edward Upward's long career, his "serial" commitment to narrative experiment and his recurrent "dreaming" of a more just and equable world.

Selected Bibliography

WORKS OF EDWARD UPWARD

"Sketch for a Marxist Interpretation of Literature." In Cecil Day Lewis, (ed.) *The Mind in Chains: Socialism and the Cultural Revolution.* London: Frederick Muller Ltd., 1938, pp. 40-55.
Journey to the Border. With an Introduction by Stephen

Spender. London: Enitharmon Press, 1994. (First published by The Hogarth Press, 1938.)

The Spiral Ascent London: William Heinemann Ltd., 1977. Published serially as: *In the Thirties* 1962, *The Rotten Elements,* 1969, *No Home but the Struggle,* 1977.)

The Railway Accident and Other Stories. Harmondsworth: Penguin Books, 1972. (Heinemann 1969).

The Night Walk and Other Stories. London: Heinemann, 1987.

An Unmentionable Man. Introduced by Frank Kermode. London: Enitharmon Press, 1994

Isherwood, Christopher, and Edward Upward. *The Mortmere Stories.* Introduction by Katherine Bucknell. London: Enitharmon Press, 1994.

Christopher Isherwood: Notes in Remembrance of a Friendship. London: Enitharmon Press, 1996.

The Scenic Railway. London: Enitharmon Press, 1997.

Remembering the Earlier Auden. London: Enitharmon Press, 1998.

The Coming Day and Other Stories. London: Enitharmon Press, 2000.

A Renegade in Springtime. London: Enitharmon Press, 2003. ...I heard with the tremor of excitement that an entomologist feels at the news of an unknown butterfly sighted in the depths of the forest, that behind Auden and Spender and Isherwood stood the even more legendary figure of an unknown writer, Edward Upward.—John Lehmann

CRITICAL AND BIOGRAPHICAL STUDIES

Barley, Tony. "'A Narrow Strictness': Political Constraints in Edward Upward's *The Rotten Elements.*" In *Literature and History,* vol. 6, no. 1: (Spring, 1997), pp. 63–79.

Bergonzi, B. *Reading the Thirties.* Pittsburgh: University of Pittsburgh Press, 1978.

Bucknell, Katherine, and Nicholas Jenkins, eds. *W. H. Auden: "The Language of Learning and the Language of Love.* Oxford: Clarendon Press, 1994.

Carpenter, Humphrey. *W. H. Auden: A Biography.* Boston:

Houghton Mifflin, 1981.

——. *Christopher and His Kind.* New York: Farrar, Straus and Giroux, 1976.

Isherwood, Christopher. *Lions and Shadows.* New York: New Directions Publishing Co., 1977.

Johnstone, Richard. *The Will to Believe: Novelists of the Thirties.* Oxford University Press, 1982.

Kamenka, Eugene. Ed. *The Portable Karl Marx.* New York: Penguin Books, 1984.

Kermode, Frank. *History and Value.* Oxford: Oxford University Press, 1988.

Lehmann, John. *In My Own Time.* Boston, Toronto: Little, Brown and Company, 1969.

——. *Thrown to the Woolfs.* New York: Holt, Rinehart and Winston, 1979.

——. *Christopher Isherwood: A Personal Memoir.* New York: Henry Holt and Company, 1987.

Roberts, Michael, Ed. *New Country*: Prose and Poetry by the authors of *New Signatures.* London: The Hogarth Press, 1933.

Spender, S. *The Destructive Element.*

——. *World Within World.* London: Faber and Faber, 1997. (first published 1951.)

BIBLIOGRAPHIES

Alan Walker's bibliography supplements the Munton/Young compilation: Munton, Alan and Alan Young. (Compilers) *Seven Writers of the English Left: A Bibliography of Literature and Politics, 1916–1980.* New York and London: Garland Publishing, 1981. Walker, Alan. *Edward Upward: A Bibliography 1920–2000.* London: Enitharmon Press, 2000.

ARCHIVAL MATERIAL

Upward's papers are housed in The British Library and are being catalogued by Ms. Sally Brown, Curator of Modern Literary Manuscripts. The archive includes numerous unpublished plays, essays, fiction, and over seventy volumes of private diaries.

KEITH WATERHOUSE

(1929—)

Fred Bilson

KEITH WATERHOUSE HAS been a successful and prolific novelist, playwright, and columnist since the sixties, with a reputation for good sense. He was born in conditions of desperate poverty in industrial South Yorkshire and had very little formal education. Despite his beginnings and owing entirely to his facility as a writer, he became a Fleet Street reporter in his twenties and wrote two definitive novels describing life in his native Leeds. He appears to occupy the sort of position once held by another writer from the same region, J. B. Priestley.

LIFE

Keith Waterhouse, the youngest of five children, was born in the working-class district of Hunslet, Leeds, Yorkshire, in the industrial North of England on February 6, 1929. His father, Ernest Waterhouse, was a costermonger; he sold fruit and vegetables from a handcart in the street. A heavy drinker, Ernest Waterhouse died in 1932. In an interview with Nicholas Wroe, Waterhouse recalled that his father's total estate was a brown suit and a halfpenny left in the pocket. Despite having her property seized for debt, his mother gave the family stability. Her encouragement of Keith (she bought him exercise books when she found he wanted to write) was not really based upon understanding. "She knew I was different, and she encouraged this difference without quite knowing what it was. For instance, she got me into school a year early, aged four, because I wouldn't stop reading" ("A Legend in his Lunchtime" *The Guardian,* Saturday April 14, 2001).

Waterhouse did not pass the examination to go to a grammar school, (which would have prepared him to go to University) and instead attended a commercial school. In 1944, during World War

II, he left school at age fifteen because the family needed the money he could earn. He had always worked hard, "I had at least five paper rounds, I sold firewood and I had a window-cleaning round, ground floor only because I didn't have a ladder. As a schoolboy, I was in fact earning at my height more than I earned in my first job" ("A Legend in his Lunchtime," *The Guardian,* Saturday April 14, 2001). It was also at age fifteen that he made his first sale to a London magazine as a writer.

He had a number of jobs around Leeds that included working for a shoe-mender and for a firm of undertakers. At age eighteen, in 1947, he was conscripted into the Royal Air Force; after his two-year service ended he became a journalist in Leeds, then moved to London in 1951 at the age of twenty-two. From that time forward he was a prolific and popular journalist on Fleet Street with a regular column first in the *Daily Mirror* and, beginning in 1986, in the *Daily Mail.* Both were populist newspapers that required a light and easy style. In addition, he was a novelist, dramatist and script writer for film and television, producing both original work and adaptations.

CHARACTERISTICS AS A WRITER

When he first began writing, Waterhouse's model was P. G. Wodehouse and the form he generally uses in his fiction is derived from Wodehouse. There is a first-person narrator, who allows the reader to eavesdrop if he wishes, but the intention of the narration is closer to a diary or a memoir; it is basically self-addressed to the narrator. This allows for the possibility of dramatic irony; often in Waterhouse's writing the narrator finds himself the victim of some scheming which has been implied in the narrative, but not fully recognized.

As in Wodehouse's writing, the fictions are distinguished by careful variation in and placing of individual language forms. Characters are distinguished by language use; this effect, seen in Wodehouse's Wooster and Jeeves, is mirrored particularly in *Billy Liar.* Often the language is aphoristic and the work of both authors is characterized by memorable one-liners.

THERE IS A HAPPY LAND *(1957)*, BILLY LIAR *(1959)*

Waterhouse's first novel *There is a Happy Land* is about childhood, and centers on a schoolboy growing up in West Yorkshire. He followed it up with *Billy Liar,* that describes a day in the life of Billy Fisher, a young man in the fictitious Yorkshire town of Stradhoughton,The two novels deal with the difficulty of coming to terms with a world where adult values dominate and the power of the child's imagination, an imagination that persists in Billy as a young man.

THERE IS A HAPPY LAND *(1957)*

There is a Happy Land was written during a newspaper strike, when Waterhouse was able to give it his full attention, and the care shows in the polishing of the text and its attention to detail. For example, the time in which it is set is never actually stated, but we can deduce it from two apparently incidental details, typical of the accuracy of Waterhouse's recall. People can buy as much candy as they want (p. 24) and the children's comic, *The Dandy,* comes out every week, not once every two weeks (p. 19). Both these facts place the action before 1940. The setting is the area where Waterhouse grew up in Leeds. The central narrator is a boy of about nine or ten, not named.

The first chapter suggests that this will be a conventional boyhood friendship tale. In a welter of noise and game playing, the boy is walking home with his friend, Ted Patterson: "It was bet-

ter than Christmas, the way we rolled off down the road, shouting and bawling and pretending to limp as though we had cork legs like Mr Bailey" (*There is a Happy Land,* p. 5). The surroundings are described through the acute and prurient eye of the preadolescent boy. A woman reproves them: "She was sitting in an armchair near their gate with all her big fat legs showing. There was a big furniture van...and all carpets in the road and that" (p. 5). The phrase "and that" neatly catches the loss of interest as the end of their? attention span is reached. The boys go off singing parodies of Christmas carols even though "It was in the middle of July and right hot" (p. 6).

Christmas is at the top of the boys' minds because Ted's mother is to take them to a pantomime. Pantomimes are shows for children based on fairy tales that usually open just after Christmas, but at the time *There is a Happy Land* was written the runs were often extended well into the spring or summer as audiences grew smaller.

Ted proposes a game. "Have we to talk in Arjy Barjy?" he says in Yorkshire dialect, meaning "Shall we talk in Arjy Barjy?" Arjy Barjy is a form of Pig Latin—"You had to put 'arj' in the middle of each word and if you could speak it fast you were right good" (p. 6). They practice it for a while but it is noticeable that all they talk about is using Arjy Barjy itself. They discuss using Arjy Barjy, not because they have any secrets to hide, but because they want to have something secret. The Yorkshire phrase suggests that the games they play are imposed upon children—they are compulsory.

They continue on toward home. Passing the library suggests a game of silly book titles (*Smashed Windows,* by Eva Brick). Another game demonstrates the workings of child logic. "Ted was frightened to go in because he'd got mud all over his stockings so we squatted down at the edge of the road and started flattening tar bubbles." Of course the game has rules: "You couldn't get up, but you could lean out as far as you wanted" (p. 7). The sticks they are using lead to a sequence of rapidly changing games (fencing, Robin Hood) and the boy is just about to knock Ted's stick away when a bike comes "pelting down the street swerving so that it wouldn't run into us" (p. 8). Ted's stick goes through the spokes of the bike's wheel and the bloke on it is nearly unseated. This is the character the boys will later call him—Uncle Mad. "We stood there, waiting for him to play pop with us. He didn't say anything, though...He just looked at us, winked and made this noise out of the side of his mouth. 'Grr-quack.' I can't do it, because it's not a noise that anything makes" (pp. 8–9). They go off home, making this noise. "Ted never knew when to stop and he started going "Grr-quack" at all the blinking rotten neighbours. *He* was all right, because he lived further down the street from us, and they didn't know him. Anyway, Mrs. Theaker saw us and said we were cheeky, and she knew his mother so he stopped after that" (pp. 9–10). Ted gets tar on his trousers from the boy's stick. "Just as we were going in their gate he said: 'If my mother wants to know how I got all this tar on, it was your stick that did it, not mine.' Just like him, blames it all on to me. Pinches my stick off me then says it was all my fault. He was my nest friend, was Ted, but I hated him sometimes. He was all right but he was awkward in lots of ways" (p. 10).

They part on a quarrelsome note—they fight and bite each other. After they part, the boy plans revenge on Ted: "imagining me getting drowned saving Theaker's dog in Park Lake and him being sorry. No, this is it—saving *him* from being drowned and walking away without speaking after I had got him out" (p. 16). As the games change rapidly, so does the script that the children write for the dramas they imagine could enter their lives and readjust the unfairness that exists. Coming to his home the boy finds a furniture van unloading at the house next door. "I imagined me getting run over with this van and having my legs off, and Ted mocking me and spitting at me, and me just watching him with tears in my eyes because I couldn't move" (p. 16).

The woman moving in is Mrs. Longbottom, the woman he and Ted had shouted at earlier in the day. She and the boy's Aunty Betty are talking about the man on the bike that the boys had seen earlier. "'I think he's a bit simple...' the woman said... 'He's not simple, he's blinking crackers,' I said" (p. 17). This utterance simply attracts the women's attention, and he is once more accused of shouting at Mrs. Longbottom. "I started crying. I went 'I wasn't shouting at all, and I'm off to run away!' "He hides in a big hole he has been digging and imagines "my Aunty Betty finding my dead body in the morning" (p. 18).

The opening "It was better than Christmas" suggests that Waterhouse is inviting direct comparison with a slightly earlier work about boyhood, Dylan Thomas's *A Child's Christmas in Wales*, which appeared in 1955. It was a reading of Dylan Thomas that convinced Waterhouse of the possibility of writing about childhood (Wroe, "A Legend in his Lunchtime"). However, Thomas employs a totally different technique than Waterhouse, by looking back on childhood from later life, being ironic and even arch about it. Furthermore, Thomas describes a rosier, less confrontational child-adult relationship in a safer, more middle-class, world than Waterhouse's Yorkshire. He inclines to the sentimental, where Waterhouse is clear-sighted and astringent. Life in working-class Northern England in the 1930s and 1940s was limited in a number of ways and, other than fantasy, there was no escape for a boy.

In Waterhouse's world, boys do not, in fact, have friends in the adult sense—people they choose to be with because of some shared interest. Friends are the children who live near you of whom your parents approve; the unsuitable are doomed with some phrase as "I don't want you playing with that one." As a result of the arbitrary nature of the relationship, the temperature of encounter varies; as the boy puts it, "Next day I thought I might as well go down past Ted's so that if he was in their garden, well, I could walk straight past him without speaking. Wanted to have a squint at him anyway, just in case he'd got blood poisoning in his leg where I'd bitten him" (p. 19). Adult power is absolute and arbitrary. Adults report to each other and constitute a monolith of authority. Aunty Betty immediately accepts Mrs. Longbottom's story of being shouted at in the street. She responds, "I'm going to get him sent away if he doesn't stop calling after people" (p. 16). It is the fact that there is no gradation of response that, for example, led Ted to play in the tar rather than go home covered in mud; all bad behavior is equally bad.

The adult world gives inappropriate clues to behavior. Mrs. Patterson takes the two boys to the pantomime and they become excited at the clowning on stage. When one of the clowns enters on a bicycle, the boys begin imitating Uncle Mad, and eventually become so noisy that they are asked to leave the theater. It is a curious fact that the action on stage can become hysterical, but the audience must, by social convention, restrict themselves to polite laughter. "We followed after [Mrs. Patterson] going: 'What's up? What have *we* done?' to each other" (p. 94).

Mrs. Patterson had intended to take the two boys to the feast, which is a carnival, but as Ted is in disgrace, the boy goes on his own. Waterhouse's description of this carnival and the boy's feelings is graphic. The boy is hurt by the suggestion he has been cheating on a roll-the-penny game when he is actually skilled at it. He uses up too much of the money he has (and there is a lot of penny-counting) on a single ride, then bitterly regrets it when the ride is over. While at the Feast he sees Uncle Mad paying for rides for Raymond Garnett, one of the boys at his school, and later sees them walking hand-in-hand (pp. 89–93). At school a few days later, there is a great fuss: "Don't ask me why, but there was blue murder at school...over Raymond Garnett letting Uncle Mad pay for him at the Feast" (p. 113). All the boys who have been at the Feast are interrogated. Had they let anyone pay for them? Had anyone given them money? The boy confesses he was given a dinner plate by a lady who had won it as a prize. The incident is baffling; Uncle Mad is a child-molester, but the adult world responds to this by imposing prohibitions on the children without explanation. They are not to go with strangers or take money from them, and that is another rule like not playing in the tar or making a noise in the theater. It does not stop the boy going to Uncle Mad's house, though.

The boy is humiliated when he becomes involved in a fight with Raymond, who has the reputation of being soft, but who wins hands down. By one of the great laws of children, he is left to face this humiliation on his own (pp. 116–121). Prohibitions apply to relationships with girls too. Boys are not to take girls into the local rhubarb fields (West Yorkshire grows more rhubarb than anywhere else on earth) but such relationships are fraught anyway. The boy forms a friendship with Marion Longbottom, the daughter of the woman who had moved in next door, that continues off and on until Marion finally humiliates him. The boy was in the habit of making magazines out of pieces of paper he stole from his Aunt Betty, and offered to show one to Marion. When he catches up with her, she is with her friends and scorns his offer to lend it to her.

> I said, "Don't you want it?" She said: "Want what, don't know what you're on about." I said: "That film book, thought you *wanted* it." None of the other three lasses said anything. They were all too busy trying to keep their faces straight. "Not mine," said Marion and I knew she didn't want my film book any more...I called out "Have I to call for you tonight?"...one of the other lasses ...said: "Says you needn't bother."
>
> (pp. 159–160)

Waterhouse narrates this incident in the style of a film or theater script that concentrates on external behavior and does not directly show interior feeling. All we have is dialogue and stage directions, and it is to a script that the boy turns next. He looks at his film book with the stuck-on photograph of a cowboy peeling off and sees how untidy it is (p. 140). It is a dramatic symbol of the disintegration of the relationship with Marion, and suggests strongly that future success will depend on producing an offering with more quality.

Chapter 18 begins "The next night Marion Longbottom got lost." "I didn't know where Marion was, and I didn't blinking well care," the boy says (p. 166). He describes the search for the girl and then describes how he found her, where

KEITH WATERHOUSE

he expected her to be, on a ledge in the local quarry.

> Marion was lying there, lying up against the side of the bushes. She lay with her head back over a stone. Her mouth and eyes were open, and there was dried blood on her face. She wore the velvet dress that I liked so much...I shouted "Mister! Mister! She's down here" ...and then the policeman came... I felt proud and happy and sad and sick, all at the same time.
>
> (p. 174)

The remainder of the narrative fails to confirm the boy's belief that he had found Marion. In the school yard "I found a quiet group of kids all standing round Raymond Garnett. He had fainted during assembly that morning—he was *always* blinking fainting... I didn't like the way Raymond was getting all the kids round him when it was *me* who found Marion..." (p. 177).

But the other children refuse to accept the claim. It was the policeman who found Marion, and one of them jeers, "Bet you knew just where to look, didn't you?" (p. 155). Furthermore, when the boy later goes to look for Marion's grave, he cannot find it. What is left is an insoluble problem, because there is nothing in the narrative to resolve it. Is the boy making up the story of his finding Marion? Is he making up the whole narrative of Marion's death, as he had earlier made up fantasies of his own death? Is there, in child thinking, that clear cut between truth and fantasy that we pretend exists in adult thinking?

Early in the novel, the boy finds himself in the street that is for once quiet. Marion is busy in the background. "It made me feel sad like you get back from church on Sunday nights and the house is all quiet with reading." He notices a kid with one of his legs in irons walking towards him:

> We didn't know him but he was singing to himself. "There is a happy land, far far away / Where they have bread and jam three times a day. / Just one big fam-i-lee, / Eggs and bacon they don't see." I had never heard these words before... They sounded ghostly and mournful, and even though it was hot I shivered as he sang the last lines "Get no sugar in their tea,/ Three times a day." The kid walked past

us without speaking, without even looking at us, and limped off...

(pp. 37–8)

The lyricism of this moment depends on a complex reading of the song. Originally it had been a children's hymn: "There is a happy land, far, far away, / Where saints in glory stand, bright, bright as day." Parodied in the form given here, it had been sung by soldiers in World War I and its appearance here reminds us (as does the strange boy's leg iron) of the suffering of that war, and the nearness of World War II that lies just ahead of the children. But it is also a paean to the loss of childhood, and the feeling of sadness that this summer must end. Childhood will soon be the happy land far, far away. In view of the heartache, Waterhouse narrates we may wonder why this land should be happy. The answer lies in the book's ending:

> It began to get cold, and I started thinking of a fire at home and the comics and new cake and that... I reached our house and the lights were on. Through the window I could see Aunty Betty peering out at the rain. She saw me and beckoned for me to come in. She was smiling, in a way. It began to rain faster. I rubbed a hand over my eyes and ran indoors.
>
> (p. 189–190)

However qualified the welcome, this is a warm, safe place. In a way.

BILLY LIAR *(1959)*

Like *There is a Happy Land*, *Billy Liar* was written in another period of leisure at a time when Waterhouse was enjoying a respite from day-to-day newspaper work. It is the story of a young man living in Stradhoughton, a fictitious Yorkshire town, bound to it by upbringing and family ties and desperate to escape to London.

Characteristically, Billy Fisher is a creative liar whose fictions mire him in ever greater complications. For example, he is engaged to one girl and proposes to another, who demands a ring. To solve this problem, he recovers the ring he has given to the first girl on the (quite untrue) grounds that it requires mending and gives it to the second girl. He thus builds a situation which will involve him in the wrath of both girls and he worries intensely about this. When the crisis comes and the two girls meet, Billy will increase the complication of the lies. It is in part the managing of this increasing mound of lies that gives the book its comic tone. This technique, of course, derives from P. G. Wodehouse; compare Wooster's involving himself in similar farragoes. The origin of this trait lies in the imaginative life of the boy narrator in *There is a Happy Land.* It coexists with a great deal of creativity and wit in the thinking of Billy Fisher.

The book opens with Billy still in bed: "Lying in bed, I abandoned the facts again and was back in Ambrosia." (*Billy Liar,* p. 5). This becomes the first of the Ambrosia monologues that are a feature of the book. They are set in an alternate world in which Billy is a hero (military or political or both) and are powerfully satiric, especially of the British tradition of understatement in dealing with war. At one point Billy looks sideways at the tradition in the British army where a regiment is awarded some trivial honor (a badge, a nickname, or the right to ride a horse into a church, for example) because of some act of heroism. "It is often wondered how the left-handed salute, peculiar to Ambrosia originated. Accounts differ, but the most widely-accepted explanation is that of the seven men who survived the battle of Wakefield all, by an amazing coincidence, had lost their right arms" (p. 36). The phrase "Accounts differ" is particularly telling here, thumbprinting the narrative style adopted by this school of military historians.

The Ambrosia monologues are carefully scripted, and absorb a great deal of Billy's creative imagination. Their day-to-day function is explained thus:

> I had two kinds of thinking and I had names for them, applied first jocularly and then mechanically... No. 1 thinking was voluntary, but No. 2 thinking was not; it concerned itself with obsessional speculations about the scope... of disease..., the probable consequences of misdemeanours, and the solu-

tion to desperate problems, such as what one would do... [if one had] a firework jammed in one's ear by mischievous boys.

> (p. 15)

So No. 2 thinking has its origins in the fears of childhood (like the fear of the firework in the ear) and goes on to include all the misdemeanors of the adult (of which we will learn more); No. 1 thinking is the escape from and the transformation of these fears.

The name "Ambrosia" has been misleading. It happens to be (both now and at the time Waterhouse wrote the book) the brand name is sold in the United Kingdom. This leads readers to suppose that Billy intends Ambrosia to be soft, childlike, like a comfort food. In fact ambrosia is the food of the gods in Homer and confers immortality.

One of the deep, unmentioned fears of Billy's generation is that of compulsory service in the army—and those who go into the army sometimes die or get wounded. Billy's own father suggests military service will be a cure for Billy's problems: "'He wants to get into t' bloody army, that's what he wants to do,' he said" (p. 83). He is using "wants" here in the Yorkshire sense of "needs" rather than "wishes to," but in a sense the latter meaning is present as well. Billy may wish to get into the army to prove he can survive, since a major component in Ambrosia is surviving war, the archetype for all survivals.

Functionally, Billy sets off for "the fast excursion to Ambrosia" (p. 15) when No. 2 thinking becomes repellent; but he also sometimes does so when he feels he has achieved something, passed some boundary, as at the end of the novel.

The boy that narrates *There is a Happy Land* had difficulty internalizing a coherent moral stance because of the contradictory input and lack of coherence in the behavior of adults. It was much the same with Billy, who has a family, whose behavior, as expressed in their talk, is utterly predictable but who claim absolute moral authority over him.

His mother spends the morning nagging at Billy to get up, in stock and regularly repeated phrases "that graduated from 'Are you awake, Billy?' to 'It's a quarter past nine, and you can stay in bed all day for all I care,' meaning twenty to nine and time to get up" (p. 6). His grandmother always refers to everyone in the third person. Objecting to the raincoat Billy wears in place of a dressing gown, she says (or rather "chip[s] in"):

"He wants to burn that raincoat, then he'll have to get dressed of a morning." ...Doing the usual decoding, I gathered ...that he who should do the burning was the old man, and that he who would have to get dressed of a morning was me. "I gather," I began, "that he who should burn the raincoat—" but the old man interrupted: "And what bloody time did you get in *last* night? If you can call it last night. This bloody morning, more like."

(pp. 9–10)

Later, his mother "took over... *What were you doing down Foley Bottoms at nine o'clock last night?*" For a moment, we are back in the rhubarb fields. The answer is Billy had been with Rita, the second fiancée, rather than Barbara, the first. "I wondered how she had managed to get her hands on so many facts without actually hiring detectives" (p. 10).

He tries to tell them the significant fact that he has been offered a job in London as a scriptwriter for Danny Boon, a well-known comedian:

Old Man: "What bloody job?" Mother: "How do you mean, you've been offered it?" Gran: "What's he talking about..." I had often likened the conversation at Hillcrest to the route of the old No. 14 tram [street car]. Even when completely new subjects were being discussed, the talk rattled on along the familiar track ... culminating at the terminus of the old man's wrath

(p. 12)

At this point in the narration there is a significant aside: "I had taken him some material-including my 'thick as lead' catchline which Boon now uses all the time" (p. 13). In narrative terms, we have here a gap between the time of narrating and the earlier time of narrated events (all the rest of the book, in fact), with a suggestion that at the time of narrating, Billy is making it as a scriptwriter.

The letter from Danny Boon reads:

Dear Mr Fisher Many thanks for script and gags, I can use some of the gags and pay accordingly. As for staff job, well I regret to tell you, I do not have "staff" beside my manager, but several of the boys do work for me, you might be interested in this. Why not call in for a chat next time you are in London? Best of luck and keep writing, Danny Boon

(p. 86)

Although this letter (interestingly rather illiterate) says "I do not have staff" and therefore constitutes a refusal of a regular job, it also points out that Boon employs writers on a freelance basis. So Billy's claim that he has been "offered a job" is actually substantially true; he has been offered the sort of employment customary in freelance work. He knows that in the England of the time, he will easily find regular employment in London to support himself while he builds his writing skills. Later, when people in the town jeer at his claim to have an offer of a job, it may be that they are riding the No. 14 tram.

Billy carries around (or hides at home in his Guilt Box) a weight of guilt. First, there is a pile of calendars advertising the funeral parlor where he works. He should have posted them just before Christmas (it is now September) but he kept the postage money and didn't post them. He makes feeble efforts to dispose of these calendars in a way that only increases the chance of detection. Secondly, he carries a letter that his mother had written to a radio record request program, *Housewives' Choice* (which actually existed). She had given it to him to post (one wonders why, given her picture of him—absence of mind? a vestigial belief in him?) He has been too ashamed to post it, because it is "full of mistakes":

Dear Sir, just a few lines to let you know how much I enjoy Housewife's "Choice" every day, ...could you play (Just a Song at Twilight) for me though I don't suppose you get time to play everyone that writes to you, but this is my "favourite song" ...Yours respectfully (Mrs) N. Fisher

(p. 19)

The other items in the box include postcards from a girl called Liz. "They were matter-of –fact little notes full of tediously interesting details about the things she had seen in...places where whatever urge possessing her had taken her; but at least they were literate. I felt mildly peculiar to be treasuring love-letters for their grammar, but there was nothing else I could treasure them for" (p. 20). This is the first reference to Liz, and there is something grown-up and honest in Billy's feelings here.

A man can only have one reputation in a small town, as he can only have one reputation in a family, and Billy, as the spiritual descendent of the boy who claimed to have found Marion's body, has the reputation of a liar, even among his friends. Or rather, his allies. So, when he leaves home and moves about Stradhoughton, he is careful to keep those he is deceiving apart.

His first call is to Shadrack and Duxbury, the funeral parlor where he works. Here he spends time with his ally, Arthur, devising comic routines and mocking the accent and backward-looking nostalgia of Councillor Duxbury. They share the office with another clerk they dislike, Stamp. The use of Arthur's given name and Stamp's surname is indicative. They go to coffee at a cafe where Rita, the second fiancée, works. In the churchyard, Billy meets Barbara, the first fiancée. Each fiancée in her own way is a grotesque. A second visit to Shadrack and Duxbury leads to a pivotal meeting with Shadrack. He refuses to accept Billy's letter of resignation, which would enable him to go to London, until the matter of the calendars and the postage book is cleared up. After lunch at home, Billy goes for a walk in which he meets Duxbury and listens to his reminiscences; Duxbury however is concerned as a councilor to further the destruction of the buildings in the town that he claims to love.

A visit to the local cemetery with Barbara results in the failure of an attempted seduction. It is followed by a return visit to the café to meet Rita, and then by a call at the XL Disc bar, where Billy finally encounters Liz. Liz is a free spirit; she is the girl whose postcards he kept because they were literate.

His evening begins with a visit to a pub where Billy does a stand-up comic routine that is a flop, as usual. He has a need to court humiliation in this way. It is here that he is finally dubbed Billy Liar, after a publication that is sold around the pubs. *Billy's Weekly Liar,* (which was an actual publication) is a mock-newspaper full of gags and comic routines- the sort of thing that Billy aspires to write.

He agrees to escort Rita and Barbara to the Roxy, a dance hall, where everyone finally meets up. Liz, Barbara and Rita are there; Arthur and Stamp; even Shadrack. Billy is paged on the public phone. All the complications caused by his lying to Barbara and Rita and to his employers suddenly come together to face Billy, but he simply escapes them and walks out with Liz. They make love, and he asks her to marry him. She agrees, but refuses to come to London with him.

He returns home to find his father has been paging him at the Roxy; his grandmother is seriously ill in the hospital. He takes a taxi there, but she dies just after midnight. Billy has his suitcase, determined to go to London that night. His mother makes a direct appeal to him "We need you at home lad" (p. 174).

Billy goes to the station and buys a ticket to London but he does not get on the train. Instead, he sets off toward home, acting an Ambrosia encounter, rather than giving it in speech. At the War Memorial he gives the left-hand salute "head erect, shoulders back..." then "I dropped into a normal step and began the slow walk home" (p. 191). The novel ends on the same note as *There is a Happy Land.*

Many readers see Billy's return as a failure of nerve. For example, the blurb on the Penguin cover tells the reader exactly what to think using the phrase, "His bang of revolt peters out in an adolescent whimper." Certainly his longing to go to London runs deep; even his Yorkshire dialect is breaking down. At the pub his stand-up routine got the bird because he let slip the London expression, "Nark it," for the local "Give over" into the routine. He is, for a second, a Londoner asking his audience to hold off their persecution of his performance.

Other interpretations of his staying at home are possible. He may well be responding to his mother's appeal; he may wish to face down Shadrack before leaving, to demonstrate to Liz that he can stop lying. Again, as in the story of

Marion Longbottom, no resolution of these open possibilities is present in the text.

BILLY LIAR AND JAMES JOYCE

The action of *Billy Liar* falls into three parts. In Chapter 1, Billy hangs around at home making a slow breakfast, in no rush to go into town. Chapters 2 to 11 narrate a series of encounters in Stradhoughton during a morning, afternoon, and evening. Chapters 12 to 14 narrate the events that lead to his returning home well after midnight. If this outline suggests the structure of an earlier, greater comic novel, it is probably intended. The structure derives from James Joyce's *Ulysses* and represents a Telemachiad. Telemachus in Homer was the son of Ulysses who wanted to leave home in search of his father; in Joyce Telemachus is represented by Stephen Daedalus, Joyce's depiction of himself; he finds his father in Leopold Bloom. As Telemachus, Billy wants to leave home and seek a substitute father ("Boon" is close enough to "Bloom," after all) and is prevented from leaving by loyalty to his mother, Penelope.

There is not, of course, a slavish following of Joyce. This is not pastiche. Rather, both the writing and the reader's enjoyment of it are enriched by the Joycean touches. In terms of the narrative, Homeric figures often lie behind the people Billy meets; Billy himself describes his first fiancée, Barbara, as the Witch, reminding us of Joyce's (and Homer's) Circe, who has the power of turning men into hogs. There are also direct quotations. Liz suggests Nausicaa; Homer's Nausicaa is introduced playing with a ball, Liz is seen working with records, "discs," similar round objects to the ball. When Billy tells Liz he loves her, "I knelt down on the grass and reached my arm up to her," (p. 149) in the gesture Ulysses made to Nausicaa.

Additionally, Waterhouse has Joycean "epiphanies." Sometimes, in Homer, a god will take on the shape of one of the people in the action to address another character, and it is only afterwards that the person visited will realize he has spoken to a god. So Councilor Duxbury (Nestor) offers Billy a sudden clear piece of advice, "'...talk as thi mother and father brought thee up to talk, then. Ah've had no education... but that's no reason for thee to copy the way *I* talk.' He spoke sharply but kindly in a voice of authority with some kind of infinite wisdom behind it, and at that moment I felt genuinely ashamed" (p. 93). There is a similar epiphany in Billy's encounter with his mother at the hospital, when she tells him "we need you at home, lad" (p. 177).

In terms of language, Waterhouse opens up for the reader's inspection the interior monologues that Billy indulges in, and introduces other texts (letters, advertisements, pieces of scripts, songs, and stand-up comic routines) to vary and defocus the underlying narrative line. At one point Billy experiments with using words not as tokens with meaning but as tranches of sound; "the words degenerating into ape-like sounds... increasing in absurdity until I was completely incoherent... 'A man can lose himself in London...Loo-hoo-hoose himself. Loooooooose himself. Himself. Him, himmmmnnn, himnnn, himself' ... and going through all the Joycean variations" (pp. 67–68).

LATER NOVELS

Much of Waterhouse's later work is farcical, reminiscent of the work of Tom Sharpe. Interesting adulteries with no commitment to either wife or mistress, office intrigues, and saloon bar jokes at the expense of political correctness characterize such works as *Billy Liar on the Moon* and *Unsweet Charity*. They usually climax with some carnival of chaos, such as an opening ceremony for a charity week that ends with a stand-up fight.

Of greater achievement are novels like *Our Song* which relates the obsession of a man for a younger woman, who is subtly drawn. *Good Grief* is the story of a woman left widowed by a Fleet Street editor who has suggested before he died that she keep a diary to help cope with her grief. Gradually, she uncovers the lies he told her; she was a second wife and he had told her that his first wife and daughter did not miss him when he left them. She finds a letter written by the stepdaughter at the time which pleads with him to return. In the end, she refuses the offer of a séance with him and cries "Get a death!" to him. There are several subtle and varied new relationships formed in her widowhood, with the stepdaughter, with old colleagues of her husband, and with new acquaintances.

ADAPTATION

Willis Hall (born April 6, 1929—died March 7, 2005) was born in the same district of Leeds as Waterhouse and they attended the same schools and youth club, where they began writing together. Hall's first great success was a play, *The Long and the Short and the Tall,* produced at Edinburgh in 1958.

In the professional career of Waterhouse and Hall they made a number of adaptations of works from novel to stage or film. Their first considerable success was a film-script based on Mary Hayley Bell's novel *Whistle Down the Wind.* A family of three children growing up in Surrey discover a hobo sleeping in the barn and ask him who he is. Bewildered and shocked, the hobo says "Jesus Christ." The children take this literally and decide the hobo is in fact Jesus, so they protect him and bring him food. Gradually, the other children in the village are allowed to visit Jesus. But, in truth, Jesus is an escaped murderer. When the police catch up with him, he gives himself up without any fuss rather than endanger the children. He has in fact been redeemed by their adoration, making the novel an interesting essay on the nature of religious faith.

Bryan Forbes, the director, was an established movie actor, but had not previously directed. He decided to move the locale of the film to the North of England and commissioned a script from Waterhouse and Hall. and bid them to "make it more Northern." They set it in rural North Lancashire, one of the most remote areas of England; unlike West Yorkshire it has no industries and unlike Surrey it has no middle-class suburbs so the naivety of the children is thus more explicable.

The film catches the contrast between the restrictive, regulated life of rural society and the freedom offered to the children outside the home within their own group. (The phrase "whistle down the wind" comes from falconry and means "fly free"). Perhaps its greatest achievement is to take the children's belief that the hobo is Jesus totally on its own terms, without any irony. The children's game is the structure of *Whistle Down the Wind,* which makes it one of the great documents of childhood in film, on a par with Rene Clement's *Les Jeux Interdits (Secret Games)* (1952) or Victor Erice's later *El Espiritu de la Colmena (The Spirit of the Beehive)* (1973). All these films share a totally nonironic commitment to the imaginative world of the children they depict, in a manner reminiscent of Waterhouse's novel *There is a Happy Land.*

Waterhouse and Hall followed up the success of this first adaptation by writing a script for *Billy Liar;* they would later adapt it as a play and later again another pair of writers would turn it into a musical.

BILLY LIAR, *THE FILM (1963)*

The problems in the adaptation began almost at once. The film opens with opening, credit scenes showing streets in various parts of Britain (both working class and suburban) during the broadcast of *Housewives, Choice.* We see women running from their own houses to bang on the front doors of neighbors whose names have just been read out to make sure they are listening. This contextualizes the Fishers as typical, by placing Mrs. Fisher as one of millions who send in requests to the program.

The breakfast scene that opens the film proper loses the edge it has in the novel. Billy is played as a broadly clownish figure by Tom Courtenay with more than a touch of the persona of Norman Wisdom, a contemporary film clown who specialized in sad-sack roles, with ill-fitting clothes and gauche mannerisms. The novel uses the inner monologue of Billy to point out the monotony of life in the family, the fact that there could be no new experience in the face of the inability to vary their language shown by his parents and grandmother. All this is lost. Deciding against voice-over, Waterhouse and Hall use instead an intercut fantasy shot of Billy using a spray machine gun to blast away those who annoy him; the No. 14 tram now stops at Billy's anger. The Ambrosia scenes represent a succession of military parades and open-air rallies; their only function is to place Billy at the center of attention of crowds of people.

It has been suggested above that the novel leaves two interesting points open. The first is the question of whether Billy's belief that he could make a living script writing in London was practical or not. The second is the question of whether Billy's decision not to take the London train represents running away from a chance to make good, or accepting the responsibilities of clearing up the mess at Shadrack and Duxbury and supporting his mother following his grandmother's death. The film closes both of these open questions.

Danny Boon is introduced in person; he is in Stradhoughton to open a supermarket. Billy exposes himself to humiliation to introduce himself to Boon in his hotel. Boon makes it clear that there is not much hope of Billy's working for him; only as a sop does he suggest Billy might send in some more material. His claim not to employ anyone is made while he is surrounded by minders and personal assistants. The scene has the effect of diminishing our faith in Billy. It is reminiscent of the sort of situation that Norman Wisdom regularly encounters in his films and comes near to sharing Wisdom's failure as a comic actor, which derives from the fact that he tries to make the audience feel sorry for him.

Without the constraint of the interior monologues, the narrative line breaks down and Billy becomes merely an eccentric, whom nobody understands, the archetype of the teenager. Much of the interest shifts to Liz, played by Julie Christie. In the interval between the writing of the book and the making of the film, life had become much freer and relaxed. Liz represents the spirit of the late sixties. Content within her own style, warm and friendly, she moves through the film like the future. In a splendid scene, she knocks on a shop window to attract someone she knows. The camera films from the inside and the outside of the window alternately in such a way that we can never hear what the two characters are saying, but we can see them talking. Despite the lack of speech, we know exactly what is being said. It is a classic example of film at its best, and demonstrates that those who wish to communicate always will.

In the film, rather than insisting that she is going to Doncaster, Liz invites Billy to go to London with her. He buys a ticket and joins her on the train, then. becomes increasingly uncomfortable and insists he should buy some drinks for the journey. Billy goes to buy two cartons of milk and deliberately delays until the train departs then runs onto the platform and throws the cartons after the train in pretended rage. We see Liz looking out wistfully from the train window, still hoping he will join her, but she has put his suitcase on the platform. Billy has finally become what everyone calls him, a liar who deceives himself about his own wishes and motivations.

If this suggests that the film is coarser in tone and narratively more restricted than the book, it must also be said that the script does not disappoint. The film was a success and where *Whistle down the Wind* made reputations for Bryan Forbes and Alan Bates, *Billy Liar* made reputations for John Schlesinger and Julie Christie. Waterhouse and Hall were established as lucky writers, whose work was welcomed by professionals and the public alike.

LATER PLAYS

Two of Waterhouse's later plays *Mr. and Mrs. Nobody* and *Jeffrey Bernard is Unwell* were West End successes. They are both adaptations; the first is a two-hander, the second a one-man show, each with a small supporting cast. The plays consider the limits of the comic approach to life.

MR. AND MRS. NOBODY
(FIRST PRODUCTION 1986)

The minor classic, *The Diary of a Nobody,* written by George and Weedon Grossmith and illustrated by Weedon Grossmith, first appeared in 1892. The book has always been enormously popular with English readers and has never been out of print. It was the product of collaboration between the two brothers. George (1847–1912) was one of the most celebrated performers in the Savoy productions of the operas of Gilbert and Sullivan; his brother Weedon (1854–1919) was trained as an artist, but had no success painting and switched to the theater, where he was an actor, a manager and a playwright. They collaborated on a series of sketches in *Punch* which formed the basis of the book.

The humor is quiet and understated in a totally English way. The "nobody" is a clerk in the city of London, Charles Pooter, who lives in the suburb of Holloway (about five miles from the City) with his wife Carrie. The action is episodic. Friends, especially Gowing and Cummings, call; there are teas and encounters with tradesmen and servants; there is a ball given by the Lord Mayor of London, where the local paper misspells the Pooters' name on the guest list. Charles improves the home by buying tins of red varnish and painting everything—furniture, the backs of books, the bath. Finally, the paint comes off while he is in the bath and he ends up "looking like a second Marat, as I remember him at Madame Tussaud's" (*Jeffrey Bernard is Unwell and Other Plays*, p. 84).

Waterhouse wrote "[an] impertinent but affectionate pastiche" called *Mrs. Pooter's Diary* (p. 7) which represented a diary kept by Carrie. When he decided to to write the play, Waterhouse intercut the Grossmith original with his own work. In the resultant scenes, Carrie is aware of Charles's diary while he is unaware of hers. While they carry on their writing ignoring each other, Carrie sometimes reacts to deflate Charles. Charles is notoriously partial to his own jokes. At one point, Cummings drops in and leaves almost at once; Gowing then arrives. Charlie says:

> 'Doesn't it seem odd that Gowing's always coming and Cummings always going?"
>
> (*While* CHARLES *is convulsed in silent laughter,* CARRIE *notes the joke as she remembers it.*)

> CARRIE: 'Doesn't it seem odd that one of you is always arriving while the other is always leaving?'
> (p. 84)

There is a serious point being made here. Carrie is driven to silent fury by Charles's entire approach. He fails to mend the window sashes or the bells in the house, but spends time painting flowerpots and bricks. The climax comes over the question of the house itself.

Carrie loathes the house in Holloway. It is right on the railway line and smoke and noise (brilliantly represented onstage in the West End production) fill the sitting room. Carrie negotiates to move to Peckham, but at the last moment a telegram arrives from Charles at work saying that his employer has bought the house and presented it to them. Carrie weeps; she is trapped in this house she hates. Charles takes her tears for tears of joy. "Dear, good Charlie. I shall make the best of this misfortune and make The Laurels as pretty a little home as it can be" she writes in her last diary entry (p. 121).

There is a point where amiability and good humor fail. Perceptiveness counts, too. Charles never sees what he has done. (*They embrace each other,* CARRIE *weeping again as the curtain falls.*) (p.122)

JEFFREY BERNARD IS UNWELL *(FIRST PRO-DUCTION 1989)*

Jeffrey Bernard (1932–1997) was a supreme raconteur who wrote a column called "Low Life" for the *Spectator* magazine from 1978 on, and the play is based on this column, which didn't always appear. Sometimes he was too drunk to produce anything and the paper printed the explanation "Jeffrey Bernard is Unwell." At least once there was a variant. "Jeffrey Bernard's column does not appear his week, as it is remarkably similar to that which he wrote last week." (p. 41). The column was dubbed by a friend "a suicide note in weekly instalments."

Bernard was well known around Soho for his refusal to live conventionally. Waterhouse

KEITH WATERHOUSE

describes him as "in his mid-fifties still moving…in the same raffish circles that most of us make a strategic withdrawal from in our late twenties or early thirties as marriages and mortgages close in. Jeff I saw as the eternal truant." (p. 8). He was celebrated as a hard drinker, but that in itself would not make him of interest. Summing it up, Waterhouse writes "It is a play about friendship, about failure, about coming to terms with life. Rambling it is—deliberately, following the haphazard pattern of Jeff's ramshackle career" (p. 13). The success of the play does not depend on knowing the people who are the subjects of Bernard's anecdotes. Anecdotes survive as miniature treatments of human behaviour if they have any value in themselves, and Bernard is a symbolic type. He first arrives in Soho at the age of fourteen, when it is the haunt of "Dylan Thomas, Francis Bacon, Lucien Freud…French Vera, No Knickers Joyce" (p. 37) and he decides that this is where he will spend his life. It is an existential choice and he takes the consequences of his choice.

Waterhouse found the structure of the play by remembering an anecdote about another friend who once got locked in a club after it closed. He has Bernard locked in The Coach and Horses, his favourite Soho pub, overnight. He desperately tries to phone the landlord, the notoriously surly Norman Balon, who also found fame partly as a result of the play. While Jeff tries to reach Balon he reminisces. A group of four actors play the roles of those he meets, providing a series of varied vignettes.

The play was first produced in 1989 with Peter O'Toole in the title role, and there is an available filmed record of his performance on stage. When it was revived with Tom Conti in 2006, Michael Billington in a *Guardian* review expressed surprise: "…something in the climate has changed. In a world that oscillates uneasily between moral puritanism and sanctioned hedonism, Jeffrey Bernard now seems less a defiant nonconformist than a dated anachronism" (*The Guardian*, 2006) Billington wonders why it was revived at all. The answer that made the boldest claim would be that Jeff is like Falstaff: "not only witty in myself, but the cause that wit is in other men." (Henry IV Part 2, Act 1 scene 2) this gives *Jeffrey Bernard is Unwell* lasting value.

The play opens with the reading of a poem to Jeff by Elizabeth Smart, originally published in the *Spectator*: "My dear Jeff / I can't say enough / how much I admire / the way you have / conducted your entire / life, and the way you have / used your marvellous Muse…"

> (*Her voice fades as we lose the spot. Darkness. Pause. Then a groan, a stirring, and the sound of a head hitting a piece of furniture.*)

JEFF: Shit!

> (*…blundering about…he switches on a single wall light. He is in his shirtsleeves and has been using his jacket for a pillow…he looks at the pub clock.*)

Five in the morning. Mark you, that's pub time. It's only ten to really.

(pp. 1–2)

This is a strong introduction. There is the contrast between idealism of the poem and the reality of the Coach and Horses, and the optimistic grasping for the best of the habitual drunk ("It's only ten to really.")

> (*He is about to pour himself a large vodka when he pauses and cries feebly.*)

Help! (*Pouring the vodka*) …So nobody can say I didn't try to get out.

(p. 2)

But now that the situation is established, it is up to Jeff to prove he has a "marvellous Muse." A series of anecdotes follow linked to the theme of waking up in the wrong place. There was a bloke who woke up at dawn in the back stalls of a cinema in Dover. "All he could remember was a poster for *High Noon* in the foyer and the fact that he'd got married…the previous day…He's divorced now. He can't even bring his ex-wife's name to mind, but he does remain a very great fan of Gary Cooper" (p. 2). This takes him to waking up in a field while working on the *Sporting Life* and being fired from the *Sporting Life*.

One of the supporting cast now reads the letter of dismissal while Jeff intercuts the story of the occasion which brought on the editor's wrath— being too drunk to make a speech at a formal dinner on behalf of the paper, since he had been drinking all day because of nerves. He concludes after the reading: "Some people are in the habit of writing angry letters to the press.... The Press is in the habit of writing angry letters to me" (p. 3). He follows up with an angry letter from Miles Kington of *Punch* and one from Michael Molly of the *Daily Mirror*:

> JEFF: One day I was asked to write my autobiography and I put a letter in the *Spectator* asking if anyone could tell me what I was doing between 1960 and 1974.

> MOLLY: ...On a certain evening in September 1969 you rang my mother to inform her that you were going to murder her only son. If you would like further information I can put you in touch with many people who have enjoyed similar bizarre experiences in your company...
>
> (p. 3)

This is the other side; many people have suffered from Jeff's actions, from those who have had their furniture set on fire by Jeff's careless smoking habits to women who have tried to love him. Trying to call Norman again, he says:

> Come on Norman, some of us have got homes to go to...Though now I come to think about it, some of us haven't. (He ...brings out a suitcase and a couple of carrier bags stuffed with possessions) Women again. Why haven't they got labels on their heads saying "Danger. Government health warning: women can seriously damage your brains...current account, confidence, razor blades and good standing among your friends"? ...This was a throwing out job. At least I was allowed access to my worldly goods.
>
> (pp. 9–10)

The first act ends with another reading by Elizabeth Smart:

> "It's terrible to think that dear Elizabeth got me my first job in journalism...Until then I was a reason-

ably happy, sane stage hand. She's dead now...God forgive you and rest in peace, Elizabeth. And if anyone writes to tell me you only get out of life what you put into it, I might just kill them."
>
> (p. 21)

He falls asleep remembering a less complimentary poem by one of his mistresses and smoking a cigarette.

Act Two is darker. We find Jeff has set the sofa on fire as he slept and is putting it out with an old pair of cricket flannels and a soda siphon. "This—is going to do—my reputation—no good—whatsoever. Such as it is. How absurd" (p. 23). His reflections on the absurd remind him of an old drinking companion, Eva Johansen, who had died after setting fire to her bed and who wrote to Jeff a few months before her death, "So I have no flat, no job, no lover, no income and...no prospects. Even my cat has left me. I keep...expecting fear and all I'm getting is exhilaration...there's nothing more they can do to me." (p. 24) Finding a biscuit tin, he tries a trick with an egg, a glass of water, and the biscuit tin "that Keith Waterhouse used to do...You need a good unsteady hand... (*He does the egg trick which, it is to be hoped, works*) I wish I hadn't done that." [*If it doesn't work, and the egg should be hard-boiled just in case:* Sorry about that Norman.] (pp. 24–25)

But the anecdotes in Act Two begin to center on those friends who have already died, and the shaking caused by drink is more evident. Norman's arrival at the end of the play comes as a relief. It is almost intolerable for Jeff to be locked in the pub, spinning his life into anecdotes for the audience. He stirs as he sees a shadow flit past the window... "Come on Godot!... (*To himself softly*)And life does go on, whatever proof there may be to the contrary... Come on Norman!" (p. 37)

Creative writing always comes at a cost. Bernard paid in terms of debt, ill health and failed relationships. Like Eva Johansen, he often found himself with nothing. For all his talent, he never had a staff appointment for a paper; he always faced the insecurity of the freelance.

REPUTATION

In 2003, Waterhouse produced a novel, *Palace Pier,* whose central character, Murray Gibbs, looks back to the sixties when he wrote a first novel that had no success and a second that was rejected as being too much like Kingsley Amis' *Lucky Jim.* After that Gibbs, unlike Waterhouse, stopped writing. Waterhouse's first two novels are certainly among his best work. They do not attract the readership they deserve, perhaps, because they are strongly regional in character and uncompromisingly working-class. It is this that distinguishes *Billy Liar* from *Lucky Jim,* as well as the fact that its humor is more subtle and varied Waterhouse remains a writer of limpid clarity, with a genuine vision of modern English life.

Selected Bibliography

WORKS OF KEITH WATERHOUSE

NOVELS

There is a Happy Land. London: Michael Joseph, 1957.

Billy Liar. London: Michael Joseph, 1959.

Jubb. London: Michael Joseph, 1963.

The Bucket Shop. London: Michael Joseph, 1968.

Billy Liar on the Moon. London: Michael Joseph, 1975.

Office Life. London: Michael Joseph, 1978.

In the Mood. London: Michael Joseph, 1983.

Mrs Pooter's Diary. London: Michael Joseph, 1983.

Thinks. London: Michael Joseph, 1984.

The Collected Letters of a Nobody: including Mr Pooter's Advice to his Son. London: Michael Joseph, 1986.

Our song. London: Hodder and Stoughton, 1988.

Bimbo. London: Hodder & Stoughton, 1990.

Unsweet Charity. London: Hodder & Stoughton, 1992.

Good Grief. London: Hodder & Stoughton, 1997.

Soho, or, Alex in Wonderland. London: Hodder & Stoughton, 2001.

Palace Pier. London: Hodder & Stoughton, 2003.

PLAYS

Billy Liar. London: Michael Joseph, 1960.

Celebration. London: Michael Joseph, 1961.

All Things Bright and Beautiful. London: Michael Joseph, 1963.

England, Our England. A revue. Book and lyrics by Keith Waterhouse and Willis Hall. Music by Dudley Moore. London, Evans Plays, 1963.

Say Who You Are: A comedy. London: Evans Plays, 1966.

Who's Who? A comedy. London: Waterhall Productions, 1972.

Saturday, Sunday, Monday, a play by Eduardo de Filippo, adapted by Keith Waterhouse and Willis Hall. New York, London : Samuel French, 1974; London Heinemann 1974.

Children's Day: a play. New York, London, Samuel French, 1975.

The Card. Musical in two acts. Music and lyrics by Tony Hatch and Jackie Trent. Book by Keith Waterhouse and Willis Hall. Adapted from the novel by Arnold Bennett. London : Josef Weinberger, 1976.

Filumena: a play by Eduardo de Filippo, adapted by Keith Waterhouse and Willis Hall. London : French, 1978.

Whoops-a-daisy. London: French, 1978.

Jeffrey Bernard is Unwell: a play. New York, London: Samuel French, 1991.

ARTICLES

Wroe, Nicholas "A Legend in his Lunchtime", *The Guardian,* Saturday April 14 2001. www.guardian.co.uk/Archive/Article/0,4273,4170219,00.html

JOHN WYNDHAM

(1903–1969)

Fred Bilson

In 1951 John Wyndham was one of a hundred competent, undistinguished science fiction hacks. He was forty-eight years old, had volunteered for active service in World War II despite his age, and had no settled occupation. What he did then was to reinvent himself as a writer, change the tone of his writing completely, and produce in *The Day of the Triffids* one of the most successful books of the postwar period. From then on he was to enjoy a career as one of the most widely read authors of his day.

LIFE

John Wyndham was born John Wyndham Parkes Lucas Beynon Harris on July 10, 1903, in Knowle, Warwickshire, England. His father, George Beynon Harris, was a barrister from South Wales. Gertrude Parkes, Wyndham's mother, was the daughter of an ironmaster. Wyndham and his younger brother, Vivian Parkes Lucas Beynon Harris (1906–1987), were very close all their lives. Until 1911 the family lived in Edgbaston, one of the most prosperous areas of Birmingham. At this point the parents separated and Mrs. Harris and the children moved from place to place. However, the boys' childhood was not unhappy.

Wyndham left Bedales School in Petersfield, Hampshire, at age eighteen and then studied farming. He also started to train as a lawyer and tried advertising before turning to writing in 1925, and from 1930 until World War II in 1939 he wrote science fiction stories, mostly for the U.S. market; he also published in England. He wrote under a variety of pen names, generally selecting two of his given names. A number of novels, including one detective novel, were published before World War II.

During the war he worked censoring mail, but in 1944 he took part in the invasion of Normandy as a corporal cipher operator in the Royal Corps of Signals. After the war, his brother, Vivian, who had studied at the Royal Academy of Dramatic Art and become an actor, turned to writing and between 1948 and 1951 produced four moderately successful thrillers. It was possibly this that inspired Wyndham to change his approach to writing, abandoning the harder science of the earlier fiction in favor of a more approachable narrative style, which made his work more accessible to a readership that did not generally take in science fiction. He described his approach as "logical fantasy"; in this, ordinary people are forced to cope with the logical consequences of some change in the environment, generally cataclysmic. In 1951 *Collier's* magazine in the United States serialized *The Revolt of the Triffids*, which appeared as a novel under Wyndham's preferred title *The Day of the Triffids*. It was the first of a succession of significant novels.

He lived quietly in Petersfield, Hampshire, shunning publicity, and died on March 11, 1969.

EARLY FICTION: "WORLDS TO BARTER" (1931)

Even at school Wyndham had been able to write with facility, and it is evident from this early published story (under the name John Beynon Harris in *Wonder Stories,* May 1931) that he had mastered the techniques necessary for success in science fiction: he shows lightness of touch, manages the use of double-narrator structures to control the strangeness of incidents, and suggests the world in which scientists live rather than expounding scientific theory. Appearance rather than motivation marks the characters; the author writes as though scripting for the illustrator. The story begins:

> Outside the tall laboratory windows, the Sun shone brightly on the gardens ...that kind of June morning when everything seems for the best.... Professor Lestrange and myself...had already been working for three and a half severely practical hours. Lestrange, in that year 1945, was not unlike the photographs, taken ten years later, that now adorn the text-books.
>
> (*Sleepers of Mars*, p. 61)

The function of the first narrator, Harry Wright, assistant to Lestrange, is to present as normal what is outside the experience of the reader—the world of fourteen years in the future. This normality is about to be disrupted. There is a terrific crash, then

> half way up the room...lay a piece of machinery. A few feet from it sprawled the figure of a man.... For a few seconds he gazed about...then alarm seized him. "Quick!" he said. "Some string. Quick!"
>
> (p. 62)

The stranger loops the string over a lever on the machine, and gives "a jerky pull.... There was no machine" (p. 62).

Science fiction is strongly intertextual; writers regularly borrow from other writers. The machine on which the man has arrived, a rickety framework with a few simple dials and levers and a habit of simply disappearing from sight, echoes H. G. Wells's description of the time machine in the story of the same name. The reader recognizes it at once for what it is and understands that the only explanation for the man's presence is that he has come from the future.

However, by a conventional irony of the genre, Lestrange and Wright find it difficult to believe Jon Lestrange, their visitor. Wyndham handles the encounter with a lightness of touch, exemplified by the fact that the first thing Jon asks for after a journey of two hundred years is some string. He happens to have arrived a few years earlier than he had calculated and baffles Lestrange by hailing him as the inventor of the Lestrange battery, the only source of power in his world, and telling Harry that his rescue of

Professor Lestrange was an act of real bravery. Since both these references are to events still in their future, they baffle the Professor and Harry. The mystery is increased by the fact that the visitor does not reveal his identity at this point.

The story now moves to an internal narrative told by Jon about the world of 2145. Invaders have arrived in this world, but they are not aliens; they are our own descendants from half a million years in the future, transformed by evolution. They communicate by pure thought. Because the world of their time is dying, they propose that they should take over the earth of 2145 and ship the current population into their time. Meeting with a refusal, they arrange a demonstration of their power. They turn off the power in the Lestrange batteries. Jon's account is graphic.

> I was in the city; the roar of the city's life rose through my open windows. One moment, busy hubbub and bright lights; the next, silence and darkness. It was a quiet...during which men died; during which cages dropped down mines...surgeons cut too deep.
>
> From below there came a scream, and, as if at that signal, a murmuring rose; the voice of the crowd growing louder and louder, wilder and wilder.
>
> (p. 80–81)

Jon and his lover Mary escape on two time machines, but she alters the setting by accident and is lost. The story ends with another arrival in the laboratory. It is Mary. Some patron saint has guided her, Jon says; she has only altered the setting by six hours.

He turns to the professor. "If you please, great-great-great-grandfather...I should like another piece of string" (p. 88).

The dichotomy in this story between the light, easy outer narrative and the dark inner narrative is at the heart of much of Wyndham. One the one hand, science fiction was optimistic—it looked at a future of Lestrange batteries providing cheap power for everyone. On the other hand, there was the profoundly pessimistic acceptance of the possibility of sudden disaster, of immediate, total, and irreversible catastrophe.

JOHN WYNDHAM

WYNDHAM AND H. G. WELLS

Criticism of Wyndham tends to tackle the change of direction that led to the success of *The Day of the Triffids* in terms of decisions by the writer himself, but another question that arises is why there should suddenly be a large market for science fiction for the first time since H. G. Wells's classic "scientific romances" fifty years before. Wells was both a scientist and a socialist; he believed science would bring immense benefits to a society that was socialist and therefore pacifist. His science fiction is an allegory of living with these two beliefs—science and socialism—in a society blinded by religion and militarism. Though Wyndham is no socialist, he stands shoulder to shoulder with Wells in the belief that we live within a social world; the characters of both writers respond to the challenges posed by external situation rather than existing in the world of the inner life. Wells offered ideas to a late-Victorian, early-Edwardian public faced with scientific challenges, the threat of war, labor unrest at home, and possible civil war in Ireland. His message was that history could be understood and changed. He offered characters formed by their schooling, their work experience, their disappointments and dreams—for example, the title characters of *Kipps: The Story of a Simple Soul* (1905) and *The History of Mr. Polly* (1910). When Wyndham wrote *The Day of the Triffids* in 1951, World War II was just over; World War III might be only weeks away. In Britain middle-class values seemed under threat from the welfare state. Consciously or unconsciously, Wyndham responded to the anxiety created by these external conditions.

The irony is that Wyndham, for all his devotion to Wells, shares almost none of his values. He is a libertarian rather than a socialist, pessimistic about progress, pessimistic about society as a collective. His work constantly subverts Wells, as we shall see, by deliberately reversing the drive of Wells's work. Wyndham is a more controlled stylist than Wells; above all, he has no time for Wells's comic touches, which he generally avoids imitating.

THE DAY OF THE TRIFFIDS *(1951)*

The novel represents Wyndham's reinvention of himself and his writing. What is striking about *The Day of the Triffids* is the way in which the scientific element in the book is backgrounded in favor of the human interest of the story of Bill Masen and Josella Payton and the development of their relationship. Wyndham handles the disaster and its consequences by looking at it through the eyes of two middle-class English lovers and a small group of their acquaintances, none of whom is presented as a comic character. Furthermore, they are all intelligent and introspective and capable of self-expression; they analyze the situation they find and respond to it by changes in their behavior. They disagree about what survival requires and how to attain it; they change their views as the situation develops.

Chapter 1 ("The End Begins") opens with Bill Masen waking up in a hospital with a feeling of unease. "When a day that you happen to know is Wednesday starts off by sounding like Sunday, there is something seriously wrong somewhere" (p. 1). It is eight o'clock, and no one comes to take off the bandage that covers his whole head, including his eyes. It is part of the treatment for an accident that might have blinded him. "The way I came to miss the end of the world—well, the end of the world as I had known it for nearly thirty years—was sheer accident, like a lot of survival when you come to think of it" (p. 1), and it was due entirely to the bandages. This is the morning they are due to come off.

The previous night (Tuesday, May 7) there had been a sensational display in the sky caused by comet debris that produced intense green flashes. It had stirred great excitement, and everybody who could had watched. Masen, of course, had missed it. He had regretted this: "it helped to impress on me what it is to be sightless. I got round to feeling that if the treatment had not been successful, I'd rather end the whole thing than go on that way" (p. 5).

When no one comes to take the bandages off, he removes them himself and explores the hospital. He is aware of a vague sound of voices, of the noise of shuffling movement, and of screams from the street outside. The first person he meets is a doctor, "but it was curious he should be crouching against a wall and feeling his way along" (p. 10). There is nothing to show he is blind. "His eyes were wide open and apparently looking straight at me." Masen takes Dr. Soames to his room, where the phone turns out to be dead. "Slowly his expression changed. The irritability and the harassed lines faded away. He looked simply tired." He asks Masen where the window is. "Before I had realized what he was doing he had launched himself full at it and crashed through.... I didn't look to see. After all, it was the fifth floor" (p. 11).

Needing a drink, Masen leaves the hospital and stops in at a pub called the Alamein Arms. The blind landlord is desperately drunk on gin instead of the whisky he has been searching for; Masen finds the whisky bottle and hands it to him. The landlord puts together the pieces of the puzzle; it is the comet debris that has blinded everyone. The landlord says that when his wife discovered that both she and the children were blind, she had gassed herself and them; he will do the same when he has worked up a little courage. Masen drinks up a couple of brandies and goes "out into the silent street" (p. 16).

Chapter 2 ("The Coming of the Triffids") takes the narrative back in time to relate the first appearance of the triffid, the plant whose sting had landed Masen in the hospital. Its origins (both geographic and biological) are unknown, but it first comes to attention when an adventurer called Palanguez shows a sample of its oil to a representative of a company producing edible oils. Heavily bribed, he smuggles a box of triffid seed out of the Soviet Union, but the plane in which he is escaping with the seed is shot down and the seed is accidentally broadcast all over the world. Triffids begin to grow everywhere. Masen places the triffid in a technology pushed to the extreme to feed the world's growing population, a world habituated to risk taking. For example, although the triffid has a devastatingly dangerous sting, the practice of docking the stingers is abandoned in order to increase productivity. Triffids (which eat carrion) also develop the ability to walk and ap-

pear to communicate with each other. Masen becomes fascinated by triffids and goes to work with them. He is stung several times—the last occasion is the one that hospitalizes him. The world's habituation to risk taking is also seen in the use of orbital satellites to carry weapon systems, including nuclear and biological weapons; Masen will suggest that the green flashes were not comet dust but a malfunctioning weapon system.

The narrative now resumes on May 8. Masen wanders about London with no definite plan, hungry but unwilling to take food from a shop. "I was not yet ready to admit, after nearly thirty years of a reasonably right-respecting existence...that things had changed in any fundamental way. There was too a feeling that as long as I remained my normal self, things might...return to *their* normal" (p. 41). He finds a delicatessen whose window has been smashed by a taxi, takes food, and leaves money.

Blinded people are finding unblinded helpers (sometimes small children) to help them select items from the shops. But this process has an ugly side. Masen rescues an unblinded girl from a blinded man who has secured her with a cord. The girl, Josella Playton, has avoided being blinded because she was asleep, heavily sedated, at the time of the comet display; she has left her blinded father at home, and she and Masen commandeer an automobile to get her back to her house. Here Masen is stung by a triffid, but the injury is comparatively minor. He destroys the triffid and finds the poison sac empty. At the house they find that all the members of the household have been killed by triffids that have escaped from a nearby park; normally they have been kept shackled, but they have managed to free themselves. Masen and Josella return to central London, take clothes and triffid guns from shops, and spend the night in a luxury flat (except that it has no hot water). In the night they see a light shining in the sky like a beacon. They become lovers.

The light is shining from the tower at the Senate House of London University. The next day Masen and Josella drive to the entrance to find a crowd of several hundred blinded people there led by an unblinded man (his name is Coker, we later discover, and he had been hiding from the police in a cellar at the time of the blinding; he is a labor agitator). Coker is quarreling with those on duty at the gate. They should be helping the blinded to find food until someone arrives to clear up the mess, he says. Those on duty refuse and disperse the crowd by firing a gun over their heads. Josella says, "He was right." Masen replies, "He was right.... And yet he was quite wrong too...there is no 'they' to come to clear up this mess.... Either we can set out to save what can be saved from the wreck ... or we can devote ourselves to stretching the lives of these people a little longer. That is the most objective view I can take" (p. 85).

They are welcomed at the university and join a group of about thirty-five people (of whom twenty-eight are unblinded). The organizer of the group, Michael Beadley, sends them off to scrounge for supplies. The plan is to leave London the following day. A conference is held that evening to lay down the rules for survival: isolation in a large house in the country for at least a year, till it is safe to forage again. Any woman who comes must be prepared to have children. Each man must have three wives—two unsighted.

Coker sets off a fire alarm during the night and captures both Masen and Josella, who are separated and forced to be the eyes for a group of blinded people, tied to two of them who act as guards. They scour a given area of London for food and live in one of the hotels. After a few days the blinded begin to fall ill and to die of a plague. Others fall victim to the triffids. Coker's plan has clearly failed. A blinded girl of about eighteen offers herself to Masen if he will stay with her and her family. He refuses, and they die of the plague—when the girl falls ill, Masen finds her a poison to end her suffering. "So futile and it might all have been so different," she says as she dies. He reflects, "There was a thing that made it still more futile—I wondered how many would have said 'Take me with you,' where she had said, 'Stay with us.' And I never even knew her name" (p. 126).

Masen finds that Josella has disappeared. He checks at the university, finds an address chalked on a wall (TEYNSHAM MANOR, TEYNSHAM, nr DEVIZES, WILTS). He sets off for this address and on the way picks up Coker. They arrive at the manor, each with a truckload of supplies, to find it is being run by Miss Durrant, one of the original party from the university, as a Christian community, supporting many blinded people. She has only five sighted helpers. Michael Beadley and his party have left to set up a community elsewhere, unable to accept Miss Durrant's regime. Masen and Coker set off to find Beadley but are deliberately misdirected by Miss Durrant, who wants to put them into a position where they must return to Teynsham. After a wild-goose chase, during which they join up with another group of survivors, Croker suggests they return to Teynsham and try to help there. He has already restored the electricity supply during his previous visit. Masen decides, however, to look for Josella, following her to a place she had mentioned in north Surrey. On his way (alone for the first time), he becomes prey to despair. He finds in one village a young sighted girl, Susan, whose brother Tommy has just been killed by a triffid. "Will we bury him—like the puppies?" she asks. "In all that overwhelming disaster that was the only grave I dug—and it was a very small one" (p. 180).

Finally reunited with Josella at a farm called Shirning, Masen finds he cannot set off for Teynsham at once. One of the group at the farm is recovering from a triffid sting and one is expecting a baby, which arrives safely. Three weeks later Masen drives to Teynsham but finds the plague has hit it, and those who have not died have evacuated it. A notice pinned to the door has been torn away.

Masen and Josella live for several years on the farm, and their son David is born safely, but it becomes clear that they are losing the battle against the triffids. They are saved by the appearance of a helicopter. The pilot comes from the community led by Beadley, of which Croker and other survivors from Teynsham are members. They now number some three hundred and have taken over the Isle of Wight, which they have cleared of triffids. Before Masen and Josella can join him, they are visited by Torrence, who is building a militaristic mini-state, with the unsighted as slaves; he insists at gunpoint that they join his scheme. They pretend to agree and get Torrence and his men drunk at dinner. At night they sneak out of the house, get into a vehicle, and then crash through the gates of the farm. Torrence and his men try to follow, but Masen has put honey in their gas tanks. The engines stall and Torrence is at the mercy of the triffids, who come in through the gates Masen has broken down in his escape.

So Masen, Josella, and their son come to the Isle of Wight, from which one day they expect to embark on the "great crusade to drive the triffids back and back and [wipe] them from the land they have usurped" (p. 233).

STRUCTURE OF THE DAY OF THE TRIFFIDS

The novel opens with Bill Masen lying helpless on a hospital bed, with a bandage bound around his eyes, listening to vague and incomprehensible sounds. Yesterday he had been the only unsighted man in a hospital full of sighted people; today he is the only sighted man in a hospital full of the unsighted. It is a powerful and emblematic image that most readers never forget; it brings home how sudden, complete, and irreversible the effect of the comet has been.

The image is reminiscent of the beginning of Book 1 of Jonathan Swift's *Gulliver's Travels* (1726). Gulliver lies helpless on the shore of Lilliput, bound hand and foot and similarly hearing vague and incomprehensible human voices.

The problem for the writer in both these cases is that, with an initial image that so strongly encapsulates the entire situation, it is difficult to drive a narrative line forward from that point. In Swift's case he must answer the obvious questions. Who has done this? Why? In effect, the answers constitute the entire narrative of Book 1. Swift's narrative consists of a series of Gulliver's encounters with the Lilliputians, but it is progressive because the hatred and fear the Lilliputians feel for Gulliver grow until he must escape, first to the neighboring island of Blefuscu

and then to the outside world, following the chance discovery of a longboat from the ship on which he had been wrecked.

Gulliver's Travels is an important book for two reasons. Both in the story of Lilliput in Book I and in later adventures in the other three Books, there are two features that make the reading enjoyable and profitable. The first is that Swift is always intellectually engaged with the model he has created; he delights in working out what Gulliver must observe in a world of people only six inches tall (a seamstress sewing with a needle and thread invisible to Gulliver, for example). The reader participates in this as an intellectual game, and writers can develop it; T. H. White wrote a children's novel, *Mistress Masham's Repose* (1946), that carried on the Lilliput game by considering the life led by a group of Lilliputians brought to England.

The second factor that gives Swift's work consequence is its satiric purpose. Gulliver in part represents Swift himself as he had been ten years before he wrote the book: a frequenter of the court of the stubborn and stupid Queen Anne, who appears as a Lilliputian. Swift had felt himself frustrated in his pursuit of promotion in the Church by the actions of small men. What better revenge than to shrink them to six-inch size and expose their triviality?

Wyndham, like Swift, has created an engaging model. What would a sighted man see or do in a world of the unsighted? That model is clear in the London scenes, in vignettes such as when Masen meets a man who has been blind since long before the comet. When Masen explains the situation, the man gives "a short, bitter laugh," says "They'll be needing all their damned patronage for them selves now," and goes off "with an exaggerated air of independence" (p. 43). On a more general level, Wyndham represents well the way in which Masen brings himself to start looting.

The scenes outside London are less achieved. Wyndham seems concerned with telling a tale of migration and settlement and does not always follow through the logic of the situation he has created. For example, he has Masen go off to London after four years at Shirning. Masen is indispensable to Shirning, but he sets off alone—in a truck that has not been professionally serviced in four years through an England occupied by crazed humans and starving triffids—to pick up some "scarce necessity" (p. 198). Sometimes, though, Wyndham remembers the essentials, such as when Mason offers a cigarette to Josella six years after their arrival at Shirning: "I opened a vacuum-packed tin of cigarettes and lit one for each of us" (p. 211). But in the country scenes this is a rare moment of engagement with the model. It is possible that the London episodes are stronger because they represent the sort of scenes Wyndham had witnessed during the war; the death of Dr. Soames reads very like descriptions of the way that badly wounded men die. Further, the management of the narrative is often disrupted by an intrusive sentimentality, as in the account of the unnamed girl who dies of plague because she will not leave her parents (p. 126) or the burial of Tommy (p. 180).

The triffids, too, are puzzling. Before the comet they are kept tethered and fed; afterward they free themselves and kill humans and animals for food. Yet in the country scenes they mill around the settlements, sometimes for years, trying to get at the humans, expending energy but not having any obvious source of food, in defiance of the laws of metabolism. Predators that wipe out all their prey die of hunger. There is a paradox here; Wyndham seems to believe that nature favors the ruthless (the triffids). It doesn't: it favors those species that find a suitable niche to occupy. And the triffids have not done that.

These objections are small in scale but cumulatively significant. Unfortunately, in many ways *The Day of the Triffids* is not good science fiction. Despite this, it has inspired a sequel. Simon Clark's *The Night of the Triffids* (2001) is set thirty years after the blinding and centers on David Masen, who has become a pilot and visits a New York City of some thirty thousand people.

If *The Day of the Triffids* is nothing more than a "cosy catastrophe," then it is of course simply a catharsis for the nuclear dread experienced universally between 1945 and the Cuban missile crisis of October 1962, after which it seemed unlikely that a nuclear war would ever happen. Deeper interpretations have been attempted.

WYNDHAM AND ORWELL

Coincidentally, Wyndham and George Orwell were born in the same year, 1903, and their best-known works appeared very close to each other, *Nineteen Eighty-four* in 1949 and *The Day of the Triffids* in 1951. L. J. Hurst, in two provocative and stimulating articles, has discussed similarities in structure and theme in the two works. His view in "'We Are the Dead': *The Day of the Triffids* and *Nineteen Eighty-four*" (1986) is bleak: "The main theme that is never discussed by critics of either book is, quite simply, permanent horror...both *Nineteen Eighty-four* and [*The*] *Day of the Triffids* are about an eternity of irrecoverable pain.... Furthermore, the two authors are not religious. Their eternity of pain is on this physical earth.... The novels are about immediate suffering but they premise this going on forever." Given this approach, Hurst will have nothing to do with the notion of the "cosy catastrophe," and his analysis of *The Day of the Triffids* is consequently sharper.

Each of the works underwent a change of title (from the working *Last Man in Europe* to *Nineteen Eighty-four* and from *The Revolt of the Triffids* in *Collier's* to *The Day of the Triffids*); in each case what is emphasized in the change is a sense of historic time. (Additionally, the titles are disorienting. Why not "1984"? Is this number more than a date? What is a triffid and why should it have a day?)

Hurst notes that the action of *The Day of the Triffids* is set some years forward of 1951 (Masen is thirty years old and cannot remember World War II), and the world that is being lost is the one created by victory in that war. The references to the war are that "Montgomery's likeness is on the signboard of the Alamein Arms, and the title of chapter 1, "The End Begins," follows Churchill's speech of November 10th, 1942— *"This is not the end. It is not the beginning of the end. But it is, perhaps, the end of the beginning."* Ironically, Masen's experiences mark the end of the normality that the end of that beginning brought. (There is one additional irony. May 8, the day the blinding is discovered, was the date on which the war in Europe came to an end in 1945).

In "Remembrance of Things to Come: *Nineteen Eighty-four* and *The Day of the Triffidsx Again*," (1998), Hurst, reporting research by David Ketterer, refers to the opening paragraphs of the two novels. Orwell originally wrote, "It was a cold, blowy day in early April, and a million radios were striking thirteen." Later revision gave the famous "It was a bright cold day in April, and the clocks were striking thirteen." "Thirteen," with its suggestion of bad luck, is retained. Wyndham originally wrote, "On the day when the Great Calamity put an end to the world I had known for almost 30 years, I happened to be in bed with a bandage all around my head and over my eyes. Just a matter of luck, like most survival." He moves in his revision much closer to Orwell. "When a day that you happen to know is Wednesday starts off by sounding like Sunday, there is something seriously wrong somewhere." As Hurst says, "just as Wyndham later removed the big adjectives—'Great Calamity'...so Orwell removed the large scale—'a million radios,' leaving both authors with a much more specific text. And the specifics of the text are time in its different formulations—'day,' 'April,' 'thirteen,' 'day,' 'Wednesday,' 'Sunday,' 'moment.'"

THE DAY OF THE TRIFFIDS*AS A STATE-OF-ENGLAND NOVEL*

When an author describes the overthrow of a social order, we may ask how far he welcomes that overthrow. How far does it appear from the fiction that Wyndham would have welcomed the end of the postwar consensus that dominated Britain in 1951? In "Five English Disaster Novels, 1951–1972" (2005) Nick Hubble suggests that "The frequent repetition of the formula over the ...twenty years [following 1951] suggests that the production of such cosy catastrophes...came to constitute a...rite of passage for any...science fiction writer...." He suggests "The reason why [the collapse of an ordered middle class] was so attractive to a middle-class readership is because the order being overthrown

by Wyndham's triffids was not their own but that of the Welfare State and collectivised social democracy...." Unlike the order of Wells's England, it was not long established but very recent.

Hubble does not see these "cosy catastrophes," of which Wyndham's was the first to appear, as "simply reflecting cold-war anxieties." On the contrary, the collapse of civilization is "overdetermined." Wyndham has the blinding, the triffids, and the plague, and this overdetermination enables the genre, by facing the destruction of all society, to critique both the British complacency summed up in the myth of "the spirit of the Blitz" and concepts of civilization as a whole.

Following Hubble, then, we can see what lies behind Masen's impatience with Coker's attempts to sustain the unsighted. Coker represents to the middle-class readership what they would have seen as the waste of effort and taxpayers' money on such enterprises as socialized medicine and universally available university education.

The myth of the Blitz demonstrates itself in the belief that Britain "stood alone" during the war and that there was an overriding social solidarity. Coker expresses this when he believes someone will be along to help, as someone always turned up after a bombing raid. Solidarity meant you both gave and got help. The helpers who turned up in World War II were of course the Americans, and throughout *The Day of the Triffids* a constant hope is expressed that they will do so again. Britishness is both independent and dependent (especially on the United States).

Through Masen, Wyndham rejects all this. Coker might have succeeded in feeding his unsighted dependents until some reordering of society occurred had the blinding been only a single disaster, but he fails because he is beaten by the plague and the triffids. But Hubble points out that the experience of sustaining Coker's blinded "[goes] a long way to cure the prejudicial attitudes Bill [Masen] had directed against women and the working class earlier" and that Coker is "a hybrid...of lower class origins and progressive education—identical to [the experience] of Wells."

For Wyndham the situation demonstrates the validity of what Hubble accurately characterizes as his "social Darwinism." This combines with a libertarianism that rejoices in the collapse of bureaucracy. In South Wales there are larger communities of sighted people because so many miners were down in the pits at the time of the comet dust, but they resist Beadley's invitations to join his group. They have made "sorts of tribal communities, and resent the idea of any organisation except the minimum they've set up for themselves" (*The Day of the Triffids,* p. 218).

From the point of view of anyone from South Wales, this is an odd passage. The miners had been passionate supporters of the Labour government of 1945–1951 and were totally collectivist in their approach. Wyndham is comforting the middle classes here; the Welsh may be a bit stubborn and awkward, but at heart they are quite sound, and the devotion of the working class to the Left will turn out to be a passing fancy. There was a great deal of this sort of thinking at the time.

Hubble analyzes in detail the gap between Masen and Josella, who seek survival on an individual basis and are libertarian in approach, with that of Beadley, who has notions of preserving the race. "We aren't out to reconstruct, we want something new and better," says the pilot who invites them to join the community on the Isle of Wight. If people cannot take to that, they must move on, to one of the Channel Islands (p. 220). The end of the novel, with its Churchillian call to a crusade against the triffids is to Hubble the promise to the middle-class readership that one day they will finally "establish a new society."

SUBVERTING H. G. WELLS: "THE COUNTRY OF THE BLIND" *(1911) AND* IN THE DAYS OF THE COMET *(1906)*

The famous Wells short story "The Country of the Blind" describes how a man climbing in the Andes comes to a valley that has been cut off centuries ago by a geological upheaval. Gradually, over generations, the people cut off there become blind, but they have time to build a technology that enables them to live (e.g., patterns in the brick edgings to the pathways and specially constructed ovens that the blind can light, but which are shielded and will not burn them as they cook. They also have a series of explanations of life (it is good to work in the cold and sleep in the hot of the day). At first the visitor thinks he will be at an advantage there; "In the country of the blind, the one-eyed man is king," he tells himself in the words of an old proverb. But he has nothing the people need. When he tells them of seeing, they think he is mad. He falls in love with a local girl; he will be allowed to stay if a surgeon cuts out the things he calls eyes. In the end he sets off back up the mountain and dies on the climb. The story ends with a poetic description of the beauty of the universe, of crystals and lichens.

Wyndham's novel is a subversion of Wells's short story. Because Wyndham's blinding is a sudden catastrophe rather than Wells's slow one, society has no time to adjust. In fact, there is no longer any society to contain this adjustment.

In London, Masen and Josella discuss safety. He says,

> "Make it a rule not to talk to anyone and nobody's going to guess that you can see... "In the country of the blind, the one-eyed man is king.'" "Oh, yes, Wells said that, didn't he? Only in the story it turned out not to be true." "The crux of the difference lies in what you mean by the word 'country'—patria in the original... '*Caecorum in patria luscus rex imperat omnis'* ...But there's no organized patria, no state, here—only chaos. Wells imagined a people who had adapted themselves to blindness. I don't think that is going to happen here—I don't see how it can."
>
> (p. 66)

The subversion is encapsulated in the fact that in Wyndham's world, the one-eyed man really is king. That is only common sense, a great middle-class virtue. Note that Wyndham flatters his audience by giving the Latin without translating it or pointing out that it is verse. "A classical gentleman called Fullonius said it first; it's all anyone seems to know about him," Masen explains.

Wells's novel *In the Days of the Comet* describes how the world passes within the tail of a comet, as a result of which everyone is rendered unconscious. When they wake they are changed: they are generous in spirit, embrace socialism, and reject the values of late Victorian life, holding fests called Beltanes at which they burn unwanted books and ugly furniture. In part the story is satirical, mocking the easy socialism of William Morris in *News from Nowhere* (1891), which came without real struggle, but Wells did believe that socialism might come suddenly. For Wyndham, if anything comes suddenly it won't be welcome.

WYNDHAM AND "SURVIVAL" (1952)

This Wyndham story, collected in *The Seeds of Time* (1956), looks rather like a tongue-in-cheek reflection by the author on the debate within *The Day of the Triffids*. Alice is the only woman on a shuttle to Mars, whose propellant system fails. The ship goes into orbit around Mars and awaits rescue. After many months food runs out and cannibalism begins. The survivors draw lots to see who will die first. Alice refuses to take part in the draw, since she is pregnant and represents two lives. Besides, the world press is aware of her situation; she is the story, and she hints that she had better be found on the ship when rescue arrives.

The action resumes some time later when the rescue vessel arrives. Members of the boarding party are baffled to see, floating in the air, a human bone cracked open. They hear the sound of singing (as Masen had several times in London). It is Alice, singing "Rock a Bye Baby" to her child. "Her eyes brightened.... She slid her right hand under the pillow and drew it out holding a pistol.... 'Look, baby,' she said. "Look there! Food! Lovely food...'"(*The Seeds of Time*, p. 95).

Wyndham describes himself here as "us[ing] the pattern of the English short story in its heyday" (*The Seeds of Time*, p. 8). Such a pattern creates a narrative that culminates in an ending that provides closure by either confirming or subverting the narrative line. Some very short stories of this kind are jokes, which classically achieve such closure. It is possible to read this ending as comic, but the ending has a non-comic reading too. The experience of surviving has made Alice nonhuman, and this in turn means that she cannot recognize her rescuers as human. Sometimes survival is bought at too high a price.

TROUBLE WITH CHILDREN: THE CHRYSALIDS (1955) AND THE MIDWICH CUCKOOS (1957)

In Wyndham, relationships between husbands and wives are often warm and understanding, but relationships with children are problematical. There is a strand in Wyndham criticism that attempts to locate this disjunction in Wyndham's own childhood, but science fiction is among the least autobiographical of genres and Wyndham never directly handles his own personal experience of family life. Some authors (Charles Dickens or Dennis Potter, for example) deliberately foreground the unhappiness of their childhood, but there is no textual evidence that Wyndham's experience lies behind his treatment of the monster children of these two novels, and it is probably unproductive to see them as allegorical of the dysfunctional family.

Our children menace us, thinks Wyndham. They contain the potential for new growth and new ideas that we cannot understand. The ghost of those super-evolved monsters from that early story "Worlds to Barter" returned to haunt him in the 1950s.

The Chrysalids begins with a young boy's dream. "When I was quite small I would often dream of a city—which was strange because it began before I even knew what a city was" (p. 5). In the dream he sees the curve of a bay with boats and at night lights in the air and on the water. He asks his sister where the city might be. "[She] told me there was no such place, not now." It might be a dream of long ago, "the wonderful world that the Old People had lived in; as it had been before God sent Tribulation."

On his sister's advice David conceals his dreams from other people. "People in our district had a very sharp eye for the odd...so that even my left-handedness caused slight disapproval." He also does not mention "the curious understanding I had with my cousin Rosalind, and that would certainly have led us into very grave trouble—if anyone had happened to believe me" (p. 6). But he remains a normal boy until the day he meets Sophie. She is not from his community, but he meets her regularly. One day she falls and twists her ankle. David removes her shoe and sees that she has six toes. He escorts her back to her home and agrees to keep her secret.

David's understanding with Rosalind is that he can talk to her through "thought shapes" when she is some distance away. His Uncle Axel discovers this and urges David to keep it secret. As they grow up to young adulthood, David and Rosalind come to know other telepaths. Uncle Axel acts as a protective force for David and the other telepaths, who eventually number eight, even going so far as to kill a man who marries one of their number and beats the secret out of her.

Gradually we learn that we are in the distant future, many years after a nuclear holocaust, when the society of Waknuk in Labrador, Canada, is dominated by a religion that compounds evangelical Christianity with a crusade against all deviations from the norm that arise by genetic mutation, destroying crops and livestock that have not bred true and driving those like Sophie out into the Fringes; in time she and her family will have to escape to the Fringes when her secret becomes known.

This is the way Wyndham tells his story. A publisher's summary, however, reverses the flow, opening with "a community where the chances of breeding true are less than 50 percent and deviations are rooted out and destroyed. The narrator...is David who can communicate...by means of "thought shapes."'" If Wyndham had told the story that way, the reader's sympathies might be differently distributed. As it is, David is our standard of judgment, and his views seem closer to our views, despite the fact that he is an oddity. For example, when he visits Sophie's house, "the room seemed the better, too, for not having groups of words hanging on the wall for people to point to in disapproval. Instead it had several drawings of horses" (p. 11). So when in David's home we see the texts "BLESSED IS THE NORM," and "WATCH THOU FOR THE MUTANT," we feel closer to David because we share his distaste for the texts.

David is a mutant, of course; he has a trait that has developed as a result of genetic mutation, but that does not mean he is more evolved. Wyndham is referring here to what in evolutionary theory is called "pre-adaptation." It is not necessary for a mutation to confer an advantage as long as it does not confer a disadvantage. In that case it may stay in a species for generations until eventually it becomes useful and confers an advantage—webbed fingers become wings, for example.

Had this been all, David and Rosalind might have lived out their lives quietly as prosperous farmers, shielded by Uncle Axel. But David's sister is born with an even greater power. She can transmit agony very loudly, so that the telepaths can hear her clearly. She is distressed by the fact that her pony is attacked by a lion, and she transmits pain. All the telepaths come to help her. A man nearby asks how they knew she was in trouble. They claim to have heard her, but he has heard nothing. In this way their secret is discovered, and they are forced to flee into the Fringes. A battle takes place between the deviants who live in the Fringes and a posse from Waknuk.

The children become aware of messages from other telepaths, the Sealanders who live in New Zealand and who can hear Petra. They need Petra's telepathic ability and send a flying machine to help them. The Sealanders arrive in time to interrupt the battle and spray all present with a sort of plastic web. The children are released and taken to New Zealand, to the city of David's dream. All the telepaths, the young adults and the child Petra, are released from the web, but everyone else is left to die. The Sealander woman who leads the expedition makes a long apologia for this, but in the end, she says, higher species must replace earlier ones. The death has been mercifully quick.

In *The Midwich Cuckoos* (1957) an alien force impregnates all the women in an English village. The children that are born are superintelligent yet insistent on their own way, and in the end they have to be destroyed. Other clutches of cuckoos have been born elsewhere in the world. Whatever the purpose of the alien intelligence behind them, it takes no account of our needs. Of all Wyndham's work, it is the closest to approaching paranoia.

Apart from *The Day of the Triffids*, this was the only one of Wyndham's works to be filmed; the 1960 film's title *Village of the Damned* invites us to ask whether it is the children or the parents who are damned. The children in the film are alike; all are blond and beautiful, paradoxically both typically English and reminiscent of the Hitler Youth.

In each of these novels, one seen through the eyes of the children, one through the eyes of the troubled parents, we see the children as somehow in touch with a next stage of existence that will displace us. The children are a Trojan horse that introduces danger to the citadel. In fact, of course, generation by generation that is what children do. They have new knowledge and experience that we cannot understand; they share a secret conversation we cannot overhear. Yet for Wyndham there remains a puzzle, almost as if he were asking, why does life brush us aside, tie us up in the Sealanders' web, and leave us for dead? Why too do we respond by becoming dogmatic and creating a world like Waknuk, full of restriction and prohibition?

TROUBLE WITH LICHEN *(1960)*

Aldiss describes this novel as "rich in ideas" (p. 294), and the ideas are among those that interested H. G. Wells. Like Wells's *The World of William Clissold* (1926), it considers what it is to be a scientist and how a scientist might exercise power; like his *Ann Veronica* (1909) it centers upon a young woman who looks for freedom and feminine power in a world dominated by men and women who submit themselves to male power; above all, like his *The Food of the Gods* (1904) it depicts the ability of scientific discovery to change society irrevocably. Interestingly, on this occasion there is little subversion of Wells's values. Rather, *Trouble with Lichen* brings forward to today's society the interests Wyndham and Wells share, so that, for example, the novel regrets the loss of impetus in the development of women's emancipation since the period of the suffragettes.

Trouble with Lichen opens with a prologue set at the funeral of Diana Brackley, which is attended by numbers of sorrowing women. Not since the funeral of Emily Wilding Davison in 1913 has London witnessed such a tribute to a woman by women, a newspaper reports. (Emily Wilding Davison was the suffragette who died when she threw herself under the king's horse at the Epsom Derby.)

The narrative proper begins with Diana as a brilliant high school student, who is clever enough to have won a scholarship to Cambridge and also has impeccable taste in dress. Wyndham has her encounter some of the models for female behavior available fifty years after Emily Wilding Davison's death. These include her teachers, clever women responsible for her success but living through their pupils. Diana asks one of them, "Why is it that mothers will think it so much more respectable to be bedworthy rather than brainy?" Miss Benbow says "judicially," "I would substitute 'comprehensible' for "respectable.'" Diana can see that, despite her mother's attempt to be proud of Diana's success, she would almost wish her to fail and prove to be no better than herself (p. 13).

In fact her mother's comment to her father is the middle-class regretful "I simply don't know where she gets it from." "Well, it isn't from me," he responds, and she suggests it may be down to her aunt, who had been a suffragette in 1912 or 1913. He also reveals that Diana's grandfather had left her forty thousand pounds, which she cannot touch until she is twenty-five. In this narrative, the family functions as a device for restricting the choices available to its children and for filtering out such dangerous trends to female freedom as those represented by the suffragette aunt (pp. 14–18).

At Cambridge, Diana switches from chemistry to biochemistry, under the influence of a lecture from Francis Saxover, director of a research center called Darr House. After her degree she goes to work at Darr House, despite Saxover's reluctance to employ a woman so attractive and likely to prove disruptive to his male workers.

Here he reproves her one day for leaving a saucer of milk out for the cat overnight. They notice something odd about the curdled milk, and it is this that leads to their interest in the lichen that had contaminated the milk. Perhaps there might be an antibiotic there.

Saxover's wife falls ill and dies, and Diana befriends his daughter, Zephanie. It is some time before Diana asks him if there was any thing interesting about the lichen-tainted sample. No, he replies, it is not an antibiotic. This reply strikes her as indirect and evasive, so she continues work on the lichen independently. Eventually she discovers what it is that Saxover has suppressed, and this leads to a moral crisis. One the one hand, knowledge must not be suppressed; on the other hand, she is obliged to communicate her results to Saxover. But she realizes he must know the truth about the lichen, and she cannot see what to do if he continues to refuse to make the truth public.

Her crisis is resolved by a conversation with Zephanie, who had reported to her teacher Diana's disappointment with the fact that women had achieved so little after the gaining of the vote by the suffragettes. Her teacher had agreed but said there was so much to fight against, and life was so short. Instantly Diana sees what she must do and leaves Darr House, taking her results and samples with her.

If this first part deals skillfully with the question of what it is to be a scientist and with the question of the degree of freedom available to a woman in current society, the remainder of the book deals with the question of what use a scientist can make of new knowledge. Part 2 opens fourteen years later. The lichen turns out to have yielded not an antibiotic but what Saxover calls an anti-gerone, which slows down human metabolism and delays aging. This is what Saxover and Diana have independently discovered. One further complication is that supplies are limited—the lichen grows only in one part of northern China.

Saxover's approach is at the micro level. He tells his children, Paul and Zephanie, that he has for some time been implanting both himself and them with the anti-gerone and consequently they

can expect to live for two hundred years. His dilemma is that he can no longer keep this fact secret; they will soon notice. But the first result is that Paul feels he must tell his wife, a truly awful woman who uses the word "darling" "edge uppermost" (p. 75). She of course demands an implant, but rather than retaining it she sells it; the secret is ceasing to be a secret.

Diana has chosen another path and is working at the macro level. Through a company she owns called Nefertiti, which provides beauty advice and treatment, she has aimed both to increase the power and confidence of individual women and to provide them with anti-gerone injections (which of course constitute an effective beauty treatment). Her plan is twofold. First, she intends to advantage women over men by extending their lives, and secondly, she aims to create in the population a group of people who will eventually discover that they have an extended life span and that the problems arising from overpopulation will not occur some years in the future after their deaths but will occur within their own lifetime. This will increase the motivation to solve these problems.

Eventually the secret becomes public knowledge. Diana has manipulated the process knowing that when public demand for anti-gerone becomes intense, an effort to find alternative anti-gerones, parallel to the creation of alternative antibiotics, will be inevitable. Even the announcement that the Chinese have plowed up the whole area where the original lichen was found cannot stop the process.

Wyndham considers in detail the way in which Diana manipulates public opinion through the press and the ruthless measures taken by other companies to secure the secret. In the end they destroy Darr House and compel Diana for her own safety to fake her own murder. She ends the book living quietly as Mrs. Ingles, using her name from a brief marriage, and preparing to marry Francis Saxover.

In many ways this is Wyndham's most achieved novel, having more of the features of general fiction rather than of genre fiction, with characters who take on a life of their own rather than representing an editorial voice and with double plotlines centering on Diana and Saxover that meet up at the end.

REPUTATION

Wyndham used to tell the tale of how in a pub he heard "two gardeners discussing their weeds over a pint of beer; one said "There's one by my tool shed—a great monster. I reckon it's a triffid'" (Aldiss, p. 293). He had introduced a new word into the language, and for a few years he gave expression to the fears and determination of his readers.

His kind of science fiction is not much read or written nowadays. Other models have taken its place and explore the inner world of sensation rather than social preoccupations. But he retains his attraction for many, who find themselves, like Aldiss, for all his cavils, using words like "magic" and "beautifully realised" (p. 294) to describe Wyndham's best fiction.

Selected Bibliography

WORKS OF JOHN WYNDHAM

NOVELS

The Day of the Triffids. New York: Doubleday, 1951; London: Michael Joseph, 1951; London: Penguin, 1954; Penguin Classics, 2000.

The Kraken Wakes. New York: Ballantine, 1953; London: Michael Joseph, 1953.

The Chrysalids. New York: Ballantine, 1955; London: Michael Joseph, 1955; London: Penguin, 1958.

The Midwich Cuckoos. London: Michael Joseph, 1957.

Trouble with Lichen. New York: Ballantine, 1960; London: Michael Joseph, 1960; London: Penguin, 1963, reprinted 1965.

Chocky. New York: Ballantine, 1968; London: Michael Joseph, 1968; London: Penguin, 1970.

Web. London: Michael Joseph, 1979.

SHORT STORY COLLECTIONS

The Seeds of Time. London: Michael Joseph, 1956; London: Penguin, 1959, reprinted 1971.

Consider Her Ways. London: Michael Joseph, 1961; London, Penguin, 1965.

Sleepers of Mars (as John Beynon Harris). London: Hodder/Coronet, 1973.

ARCHIVE

Liverpool University Library, England, holds the archives of both John Wyndham and his brother Vivian Harris. For details visit the archive's website (www.liv.ac.uk/~asawyer/wyndham.html).

CRITICAL AND BIOGRAPHICAL STUDIES

Aldiss, Brian. *Billion Year Spree: The History of Science Fiction*. London: Weidenfeld and Nicholson, 1973.

Hubble, Nick. "Five English Disaster Novels, 1951–1972." *Foundation: The International Review of Science Fiction* 95: 89–103 (autumn 2005).

Hurst, L. J. " "We Are the Dead': *The Day of the Triffids* and *Nineteen Eighty-four*." *Vector: The Critical Journal of the British Science Fiction Association* 133 (August–September 1986). (*http://www.rbd26.dial.pipex.com/*).

———. "Remembrance of Things to Come: Nineteen Eighty-four and The Day of the Triffids Again." *Vector: The Critical Journal of the British Science Fiction Association* 201 (September–October 1998). (*dialspace.dial.pipex.com/l.j.hurst/firstpar.htm*).

Ketterer, David. "John Wyndham: The Facts of Life Sextet." In *A Companion to Science Fiction*. Edited by David Seed. Oxford: Blackwell, 2005.

Parrinder, Patrick. "The Ruined Futures of British Science Fiction." In *On Modern British Fiction*. Edited by Zachary Leader. Oxford: Oxford University Press, 2002. Pp. 209–223.

MASTER INDEX

The following index covers the entire British Writers series through Supplement XIII. All references include volume numbers in boldface roman numerals followed by page numbers within that volume. Subjects of articles are indicated by boldface type.

"Affliction" (Herbert), **II:** 125, 127; **Retro. Supp. II:** 179
"Affliction" (Vaughan), **II:** 187–188
Affliction (Weldon), **Supp. IV:** 531, 532–533
"Affliction of Childhood, The" (De Quincey), **IV:** 152–153, 154
"Afon Rhiw" (Thomas), **Supp. XII:** 290
African Elegy, An (Okri), **Supp. V:** 359
"African Socialism: Utopian or Scientific?" (Armah), **Supp. X:** 2
African Stories (Lessing), **Supp. I:** 240, 243
African Witch, The (Cary), **VII:** 186
"After a Childhood away from Ireland" (Boland), **Supp. V:** 36
"After a Death" (Stevenson), **Supp. VI:** 254
"After a Journey" (Hardy), **VI:** 18; **Retro. Supp. I:** 118
"After an Operation" (Jennings), **Supp. V:** 214
"After a Romantic Day" (Hardy), **Retro. Supp. I:** 118
After Bakhtin (The Art of Fiction: Illustrated from Classic and Modern Texts) (Lodge), **Supp. IV:** 366–367
"After Civilization" (Carpenter), **Supp. XIII:** 38
"After Closing Time" (Dunn), **Supp. X:** 69
"After Dunkirk" (Lewis), **VII:** 445
"After Eden" (MacCaig), **Supp. VI:** 187
After Hannibal (Unsworth), **Supp. VII:** 357, 365–366
"After Her Death" (Stevenson), **Supp. VI:** 254
After Julius (Howard), **Supp. XI:** 138, 139, 142–144, 145, 147, 148
After Leaving Mr. Mackenzie (Rhys), **Supp. II:** 388, **392–394**, 400
"After Long Ages" (Carpenter), **Supp. XIII:** 38
"After Long Silence" (Yeats), **VI:** 212inline"After Lucretius" (Burnside), **Supp. XIII:** 26
After Magritte (Stoppard), **Supp. I:** 443, 444–445, 447, 451; **Retro. Supp. II:** 346–347
After Many a Summer (Huxley), **VII:** xviii, 205
"After Rain" (Thomas), **Supp. III:** 406
After Rain (Trevor), **Supp. IV:** 505
After Strange Gods (Eliot), **VI:** 207; **VII:** 153
After the Ark (Jennings), **Supp. V:** 217
After the Ball (Coward), **Supp. II:** 155
After the Dance (Rattigan), **Supp. VII:** 310–311, 312, 318
After the Death of Don Juan (Warner), **Supp. VII:** 376, 377
"After the funeral" (Thomas), **Supp. I:** 176, 177
"After the Irish of Aodghan O'Rathaille" (Boland), **Supp. V:** 36
"After the Swim" (Dutton), **Supp. XII:** 93
"After the Vision" (Warner), **Supp. XI:** 298
"After the War" (Dunn), **Supp. X:** 70–71

"After Viking" (Burnside), **Supp. XIII:** 14
After–Dinner Joke, The (Churchill), **Supp. IV:** 181
"Afterflu Afterlife, The" (Ewart), **Supp. VII:** 42–43
Aftermath, The (Churchill), **VI:** 359
"Afternoon" (Conn), **Supp. XIII:** 71
"Afternoon Dancing" (Trevor), **Supp. IV:** 503–504
"Afternoon in Florence" (Jennings), **Supp. V:** 210
Afternoon Men (Powell), **VII:** 343–345
Afternoon Off (Bennett), **VIII:** 27
"Afternoon Visit" (Conn), **Supp. XIII:** 74
"Afternoons" (Larkin), **Supp. I:** 281
"Afterthought, An" (Rossetti), **V:** 258
"Afterwards" (Hardy), **VI:** 13, 19; **Retro. Supp. I:** 119
Against a Dark Background (Banks), **Supp. XI:** 1, 12–13
"Against Absence" (Suckling), **II:** 227
"Against Coupling" (Adcock), **Supp. XII:** 5
"Against Dryness" (Murdoch), **Supp. I:** 216, 218, 219, 221
Against Entropy (Frayn), see *Towards the End of Morning*
"Against Fruition" (Cowley), **II:** 197
"Against Fruition" (Suckling), **II:** 227
Against Hasty Credence (Henryson), **Supp. VII:** 146, 147
Against Religion (Wilson), **Supp. VI:** 297, **305–306,** 309
"Against Romanticism" (Amis), **Supp. II:** 3
"Against the Sun" (Dutton), **Supp. XII:** 88, 94
Against Venomous Tongues (Skelton), **I:** 90
Agamemnon (Seneca), **II:** 71
Agamemnon (Thomson), **Supp. III:** 411, 424
Agamemnon, a Tragedy Taken from Aeschylus (FitzGerald), **IV:** 349, 353
Agamemnon of Aeschylus, The (tr. Browning), **IV:** 358–359, 374
Agamemnon of Aeschylus, The (tr. MacNeice), **VII:** 408–409
Agate, James, **Supp. II:** 143, 147
Age of Anxiety, The (Auden), **VII:** 379, 388, 389–390; **Supp. IV:** 100; **Retro. Supp. I:** 11
Age of Bronze, The (Byron), **IV:** xviii, 193
Age of Indiscretion, The (Davis), **V:** 394
Age of Iron (Coetzee), **Supp. VI:** 76, **85**
Age of Longing, The (Koestler), **Supp. I:** 25, 27, 28, 31–32, 35
Age of Reason, The (Hope), **Supp. VII:** 164
Age of Shakespeare, The (Swinburne), **V:** 333
Age of the Rainmakers, The (Harris), **Supp. V:** 132
Agents and Patients (Powell), **VII:** 345–346
Aglaura (Suckling), **II:** 226, 238

Agnes Grey (Brontë), **V:** xx, 129–130, 132, 134–135, 140–141, 153; **Supp. IV:** 239; **Retro. Supp. I:** 52, 54–55
"Agnes Lahens" (Moore), **VI:** 98
Agnostic's Apology, An (Stephen), **VI:** 289
"Agonies of Writing a Musical Comedy" (Wodehouse), **Supp. III:** 451
"Agnus Dei" (Nye), **Supp. X:** 202
Ah, But Your Land Is Beautiful (Paton), **Supp. II:** **353–355**
"Ah, what avails the sceptred race" (Landor), **IV:** 88
"Ahoy, Sailor Boy!" (Coppard), **VIII:** 97
Aids to Reflection (Coleridge), **IV:** 53, 56
Aiken, Conrad, **VII:** 149, 179; **Supp. III:** 270
Aimed at Nobody (Graham), **Supp. VII:** 106
Ainger, Alfred, **IV:** 254, 267
Ainsi va la monde (Robinson), **Supp. XIII:** 202, 205
"Air and Angels" (MacCaig), **Supp. VI:** 185
"Air" (Traherne), **Supp. XI:** 267
"Air Disaster, The" (Ballard), **Supp. V:** 33
Air Show, The (Scupham), **Supp. XIII:** 224–225
"Aire and Angels" (Donne), **II:** 197
Airship, The (Caudwell), **Supp. IX:** 35
"Aisling" (Muldoon), **Supp. IV:** 418–419
"Aisling Hat, The" (McGuckian), **Supp. V:** 286, 288, 289
Aissa Saved (Cary), **VII:** 185
"Akbar's Bridge" (Kipling), **VI:** 201
Akerman, Rudolph, **V:** 111
Akhenaten Adventure, The (Kerr), **Supp. XII:** 198
Akhmatova, Anna, **Supp. IV:** 480, 494
"Al Som de l'Escalina" (Eliot), **VII:** 152
Alaham (Greville), **Supp. XI:** 110, 120
Alamanni, Luigi, **I:** 110–111
Alamein to Zem–Zem (Douglas), **VII:** xxii, 441
Alarcos (Disraeli), **IV:** 306, 308
Alaric at Rome (Arnold), **V:** 216
"Alas, Poor Bollington!" (Coppard), **VIII:** 94–95
"Alaska" (Armitage), **VIII:** 5
Alastor (Shelley), **III:** 330, 338; **IV:** xvii, 195, 198, 208, 217; **Retro. Supp. I:** 247
"Albergo Empedocle" (Forster), **VI:** 399, 412
Albert's Bridge (Stoppard), **Supp. I:** 439, 445
Albigenses, The (Maturin), **VIII:** 201, 207, 208
"Albinus and Rosemund" (Gower), **I:** 53–54
Albion! Albion! (Hill, R.), **Supp. IX:** 111
"Albion & Marina" (Brontë), **V:** 110
Albion and Albanius (Dryden), **II:** 305
Album Verses (Lamb), **IV:** 83, 85
Alcazar (Peele), *see Battle of Alcazar, The*
Alcestis (Euripides), **IV:** 358

Beaconsfield, Lord, *see* Disraeli, Benjamin

"Bear in Mind" (Cameron), **Supp. IX:** 29

Beardsley, Aubrey, **V:** 318n, 412, 413

"Beast in the Jungle, The" (James), **VI:** 55, 64, 69

Beastly tales from Here and There (Seth), **Supp. X:** 287–288

Beasts and Super-Beasts (Saki), **Supp. VI:** 245, 251

Beasts' Confession to the Priest, The (Swift), **III:** 36

Beasts Royal (O'Brian), **Supp. XII:** 249

Beatrice (Haggard), **Supp. III:** 213

Beattie, James, **IV:** 198

Beatty, David, **VI:** 351

Beau Austin (Stevenson), **V:** 396

Beauchamp's Career (Meredith), **V:** xxiv, 225, 228–230, 231, 234

Beaumont, Francis, **II: 42–67,** 79, 82, 87

Beaumont, Joseph, **II:** 180

Beaumont, Sir George, **IV:** 3, 12, 21, 22

Beauties and Furies, The (Stead), **Supp. IV:** 463–464

Beauties of English Poesy, The (ed. Goldsmith), **III:** 191

"Beautiful Lofty Things" (Yeats), **VI:** 216; **Retro. Supp. I:** 337

"Beautiful Sea, The" (Powys), **VIII:** 251

Beautiful Visit, The (Howard), **Supp. XI:** 137–138, 140–141, 148–149

"Beautiful Young Nymph Going to Bed, A" (Swift), **III:** 32, 36; **VI:** 256

"Beauty" (Thomas), **Supp. III:** 401–402

"Beauty and Duty" (Carpenter), **Supp. XIII:** 46

Beauty and the Beast (Hughes), **Supp. I:** 347

Beauty in a Trance, **II:** 100

Beauty Queen of Leenane, The (McDonagh), **Supp. XII:** 233, 234, 235–236, 238, 239, 241

Beautyful Ones Are Not Yet Born, The (Armah), **Supp. X:** 1–6, 12–13

Beauvoir, Simone de, **Supp. IV:** 232

Beaux' Stratagem, The (Farquhar), **II:** 334, 353, 359–360, 362, 364

"Beaver Ridge" (Fallon), **Supp. XII:** 113–114

"Because of the Dollars" (Conrad), **VI:** 148

"Because the pleasure-bird whistles" (Thomas), **Supp. I:** 176

Becket (Tennyson), **IV:** 328, 338

Beckett, Samuel, **Supp. I: 43–64;** **Supp. IV:** 99, 106, 116, 180, 281, 284, 412, 429; **Retro. Supp. I: 17–32**

Beckford, William, **III:** 327–329, 345; **IV:** xv, 230

Bed Among the Lentils (Bennett), **VIII:** 27–28

"Bedbug, The" (Harrison), **Supp. V:** 151

Beddoes, Thomas, **V:** 330

Beddoes, Thomas Lovell, **Supp. XI: 17–32**

Bedford-Row Conspiracy, The (Thackeray), **V:** 21, 37

"Bedroom Eyes of Mrs. Vansittart, The" (Trevor), **Supp. IV:** 500

Bedroom Farce (Ayckbourn), **Supp. V:** 3, 12, 13, 14

Beds in the East (Burgess), **Supp. I:** 187

Bedtime Story (O'Casey), **VII:** 12

"Bedtime Story for my Son" (Redgrove), **Supp. VI: 227–228,** 236

Bee (periodical), **III:** 40, 179

Bee Hunter: Adventures of Beowulf (Nye), **Supp. X:** 193, 195

"Bee Orchd at Hodbarrow" (Nicholson), **Supp. VI:** 218

"Beechen Vigil" (Day Lewis), **Supp. III:** 121

Beechen Vigil and Other Poems (Day Lewis), **Supp. III:** 117, 120–121

"Beehive Cell" (Murphy), **Supp. V:** 329

Beekeepers, The (Redgrove), **Supp. VI:** 231

"Beeny Cliff" (Hardy), **Retro. Supp. I:** 118

Beerbohm, Max, **V:** 252, 390; **VI:** 365, 366; **Supp. II: 43–59,** 156

"Before Action" (Hodgson), **VI:** 422

"Before Dark" (Conn), **Supp. XIII:** 75

Before Dawn (Rattigan), **Supp. VII:** 315

"Before Her Portrait in Youth" (Thompson), **V:** 442

"Before I knocked" (Thomas), **Supp. I:** 175

Before She Met Me (Barnes), **Supp. IV:** 65, 67–68

"Before Sleep" (Kinsella), **Supp. V:** 263

Before the Knowledge of Evil (Braddon), **VIII:** 36

"Before the Mirror" (Swinburne), **V:** 320

"Before the Party" (Maugham), **VI:** 370

Beggars (Davies), **Supp. XI:** 87, 88

Beggars Banquet (Rankin), **Supp. X:** 245–246, 253, 257

Beggar's Bush (Beaumont, Fletcher, Massinger), **II:** 66

Beggar's Opera, The (Gay), **III:** 54, 55, **61–64,** 65–67; **Supp. III:** 195; **Retro. Supp. I:** 80

"Beggar's Soliloquy, The" (Meredith), **V:** 220

Begin Here: A War-Time Essay (Sayers), **Supp. III:** 336

"Beginning, The" (Brooke), **Supp. III:** 52

Beginning of Spring, The (Fitzgerald), **Supp. V:** 98, 106

"Beginnings of Love, The" (Carpenter), **Supp. XIII:** 42

Behan, Brendan, **Supp. II: 61–76**

Behind the Green Curtains (O'Casey), **VII:** 11

Behn, Aphra, **Supp. III: 19–33**

"Behold, Love, thy power how she despiseth" (Wyatt), **I:** 109

"Being Boring" (Cope), **VIII:** 80

"Being Stolen From" (Trevor), **Supp. IV:** 504

"Being Treated, to Ellinda" (Lovelace), **II:** 231–232

"Beldonald Holbein, The" (James), **VI:** 69

"Beleaguered City, A" (Oliphant), **Supp. X:** 220

Belfast Confetti (Carson), **Supp. XIII:** 53, 54, 57–59

"Belfast vs. Dublin" (Boland), **Supp. V:** 36

"Belief" (Dutton), **Supp. XII:** 96

Belief and Creativity (Golding), **Supp. I:** 88

Belief in Immortality and Worship of the Dead, The (Frazer), **Supp. III:** 176

Believe As You List (Massinger), **Supp. XI:** 185

Belin, Mrs., **II:** 305

Belinda (Edgeworth), **Supp. III: 157–158,** 162

Belinda, An April Folly (Milne), **Supp. V:** 298–299

Bell, Acton, pseud. of Anne Brontë

Bell, Clive, **V:** 345

Bell, Currer, pseud. of Charlotte Brontë

Bell, Ellis, pseud. of Emily Brontë

Bell, Julian, **Supp. III:** 120

Bell, Quentin, **VII:** 35; **Retro. Supp. I:** 305

Bell, Robert, **I:** 98

Bell, Vanessa, **VI:** 118

Bell, The (Murdoch), **Supp. I:** 222, 223–224, 226, 228–229

"Bell of Aragon, The" (Collins), **III:** 163

"Bell Ringer, The" (Jennings), **Supp. V:** 218

"Belladonna" (Nye), **Supp. X:** 198

Bellamira; or, The Mistress (Sedley), **II:** 263

Belle Assemblée, La (tr. Haywood), **Supp. XII:** 135

"Belle Heaulmière" (tr. Swinburne), **V:** 327

"Belle of the Ball-Room" (Praed), **V:** 14

Belloc, Hilaire, **VI:** 246, 320, 335, 337, 340, 447; **VII:** xiii; **Supp. IV:** 201

Belloc, Mrs. Lowndes, **Supp. II:** 135

Bellow, Saul, **Supp. IV:** 26, 27, 42, 234

Bells and Pomegranates (Browning), **IV:** 356, 373–374

Belmonte, Thomas, **Supp. IV:** 15

Below Loughrigg (Adcock), **Supp. XII:** 6

Belsey, Catherine, **Supp. IV:** 164

Belton Estate, The (Trollope), **V:** 100, 101

"Bench of Desolation, The" (James), **VI:** 69

Bend for Home, The (Healy), **Supp. IX:** 95, 96, 98–100, 101, 103, 106

Bend in the River, A (Naipaul), **Supp. I:** 393, **397–399,** 401

Bender, T. K., **V:** 364–365, 382

Bending of the Bough, The (Moore), **VI:** 87, 95–96, 98

Benedict, Ruth, **Supp. III:** 186

Benjamin, Walter, **Supp. IV:** 82, 87, 88, 91

Benlowes, Edward, **II:** 123

Benn, Gotfried, **Supp. IV:** 411

"Bennelong" (Wallace-Crabbe), **VIII:** 319–320

Bennett, Alan, **VIII: 19–34**

Bennett, Arnold, **VI:** xi, xii, xiii, 226, 233n, **247–268,** 275; **VII:** xiv, xxi; **Supp. III:** 324, 325; **Supp. IV:** 229, 230–231, 233, 239, 241, 249, 252;

"Ex–Queen Among the Astronomers, The" (Adcock), **Supp. XII:** 7

"Exstasie, The" (Donne), **II:** 197; **Retro. Supp. II:** 88

"Extempore Effusion on the Death of the Ettrick Shepherd" (Wordsworth), **IV:** 73

Extending the Territory (Jennings), **Supp. V:** 216

Extravagant Strangers: A Literature of Belonging (ed. Phillips), **Supp. V:** 380

Extravagaria (tr. Reid), **Supp. VII:** 332

Exultations (Pound), **Supp. III:** 398

Eye for an Eye, An (Trollope), **V:** 102

Eye in the Door, The (Barker), **Supp. IV:** 45, 46, 57, 59–61

"Eye of Allah, The" (Kipling), **VI:** 169, 190–191

Eye of the Hurricane, The (Adcock), **Supp. XII:** 1, 4

Eye of the Scarecrow, The (Harris), **Supp. V:** 136–137, 139, 140

Eye of the Storm, The (White), **Supp. I:** 132, 146–147

Eye to Eye (Fallon), **Supp. XII:** 105, 110–112, 114

Eyeless in Gaza (Huxley), **II:** 173; **VII:** 204–205

"Eyes and Tears" (Marvell), **II:** 209, 211

Eyes of Asia, The (Kipling), **VI:** 204

"Eyewitness" (Armitage), **VIII:** 4

Eyrbyggja saga, **VIII:** 235, 239, 240

Ezra Pound and His Work (Ackroyd), **Supp. VI:** 4

"Ezra Pound in Pisa" (Davie), **Supp. VI:** 110, 113

Ezra Pound: Poet as Sculptor (Davie), **Supp. VI:** 115

Faber Book of Contemporary Irish Poetry, The (ed. Muldoon), **Supp. IV:** 409, 410–411, 422, 424

Faber Book of Pop, The (ed. Kureishi and Savage), **Supp. XI:** 159

Faber Book of Sonnets (ed. Nye), **Supp. X:** 193

Faber Book of Twentieth–Century Women's Poetry, The (ed. Adcock), **Supp. XII:** 2

"Faber Melancholy, A" (Dunn), **Supp. X:** 70

Fabian Essays in Socialism (Shaw), **VI:** 129

Fabian Freeway (Martin), **VI:** 242

Fabian Society, **Supp. IV:** 233

"Fable" (Golding), **Supp. I:** 67, 83

"Fable of the Widow and Her Cat, A" (Swift), **III:** 27, 31

Fables (Dryden), **II:** 293, 301, 304; **III:** 40; **IV:** 287

Fables (Gay), **III:** 59, 67

Fables (Powys). See *No Painted Plumage*

Fables (Stevenson), **V:** 396

"Fables, The" (Malouf), **Supp. XII:** 220

Façade (Sitwell and Walton), **VII:** xv, xvii, 128, 130, 131n, 132

"Face of an Old Highland Woman" (Smith, I. C.), **Supp. IX:** 213

Face of the Deep, The (Rossetti), **V:** 260

Face to Face: Short Stories (Gordimer), **Supp. II:** 226

"Faces" (Conn), **Supp. XIII:** 79

"Faces, The" (James), **VI:** 69

"Faces Come Thicker at Night" (Scupham), **Supp. XIII:** 228

Facial Justice (Hartley), **Supp. VII:** 131

Facilitators, The (Redgrove), **Supp. VI:** 231

"Facing the Pacific at Night" (Hart), **Supp. XI:** 129

"Factory–Owner, The" (Plomer), **Supp. XI:** 213

Fadiman, Clifton, **Supp. IV:** 460

Faerie Queene, The (Spenser), **I:** 121, 123, 124, **131–141,** 266; **II:** 50; **IV:** 59, 198, 213; **V:** 142

"Faery Song, A" (Yeats), **VI:** 211

"Faeth Fiadha: The Breastplate of Saint Patrick" (Kinsella), **Supp. V:** 264

"Fafaia" (Brooke), **Supp. III:** 55–56

"Fag Hags" (Maitland), **Supp. XI:** 174

Fagrskinna, **VIII:** 242

"Failed Mystic" (MacCaig), **Supp. VI:** 188, 194

"Failure, A" (Thackeray), **V:** 18

Fair Haven, The (Butler), **Supp. II:** 99, **101–103,** 104, 117

"Fair Ines" (Hood), **IV:** 255

Fair Jilt, The; or, The Amours of Prince Tarquin and Miranda (Behn), **Supp. III:** 29, 31–32

Fair Maid of the Inn, The (Ford, Massinger, Webster), **II:** 66, 69, 83, 85

Fair Margaret (Haggard), **Supp. III:** 214

Fair Quarrel, A (Middleton and Rowley), **II:** 1, 3, 21

"Fair Singer, The" (Marvell), **II:** 211

Fairfield, Cicely, *see* West, Rebecca

Fairly Dangerous Thing, A (Hill, R.), **Supp. IX:**111, 114

Fairly Honourable Defeat, A (Murdoch), **Supp. I:** 226, 227, 228, 232–233

Fairy and Folk Tales of the Irish Peasantry (ed. Yeats), **VI:** 222

Fairy Caravan, The (Potter), **Supp. III:** 291, 303–304, 305, 306, 307

Fairy Knight, The (Dekker and Ford), **II:** 89, 100

"Fairy Poems" (Robinson), **Supp. XIII:** 206

"Faith" (Burnside), **Supp. XIII:** 21

"Faith" (Herbert), **II:** 127

Faith Healer (Friel), **Supp. V:** 123

"Faith Healing" (Larkin), **Supp. I:** 280–281, 282, 285

"Faith on Trial, A" (Meredith), **V:** 222

Faithful Fictions: The Catholic Novel in British Literature (Woodman), **Supp. IV:** 364

Faithful Friends, The, **II:** 67

Faithful Narrative of . . . Habbakkuk Hilding, A (Smollett), **III:** 158

Faithful Shepherdess, The (Fletcher), **II:** 45, 46, 49–52, 53, 62, 65, 82

"Faithfulness of GOD in the Promises, The" (Blake), **III:** 300

"Faithless Nelly Gray" (Hood), **IV:** 257

"Faithless Sally Brown" (Hood), **IV:** 257

Faiz, Faiz Ahmad, **Supp. IV:** 434

"Falk" (Conrad), **VI:** 148

Falkner (Shelley), **Supp. III:** 371

"Fall in Ghosts" (Blunden), **Supp. XI:** 45

"Fall of a Sparrow" (Stallworthy), **Supp. X:** 294

Fall of Hyperion, The (Keats), **IV:** xi, 211–213, 220, **227–231,** 234, 235

Fall of Kelvin Walker, The (Gray, A.), **Supp. IX:** 80, 85, 89

Fall of Princes, The (Lydgate), **I:** 57, 58, 59, 64

Fall of Robespierre, The (Coleridge and Southey), **IV:** 55

"Fall of Rome, The" (Auden), **Retro. Supp. I:** 11

"Fall of the House of Usher, The" (Poe), **III:** 339

"Fall of the West, The" (Wallace–Crabbe), **VIII:** 321

Fallen Angels (Coward), **Supp. II:** 141, 145

Fallen Leaves, The (Collins), **Supp. VI:** 93, 102

"Fallen Majesty" (Yeats), **VI:** 216

"Fallen Yew, A" (Thompson), **V:** 442

Falling (Howard), **Supp. XI:** 142, 144–145

Falling into Language (Wallace–Crabbe), **VIII:** 323

Falling Out of Love and Other Poems, A (Sillitoe), **Supp. V:** 424

Fallon, Peter, **Supp. XII: 101–116**

"Fallow Deer at the Lonely House, The" (Hardy), **Retro. Supp. I:** 119

Fallowell, Duncan, **Supp. IV:** 173

"Falls" (Ewart), **Supp. VII:** 39

Falls, The (Rankin), **Supp. X:** 245

False Alarm, The (Johnson), **III:** 121

False Friend, The (Robinson), **Supp. XIII:** 204, 211

False Friend, The (Vanbrugh), **II:** 325, 333, 336

"False Morality of the Lady Novelists, The" (Greg), **V:** 7

False One, The (Fletcher and Massinger), **II:** 43, 66

"False though she be to me and love" (Congreve), **II:** 269

Falstaff (Nye), **Supp. X:** 193, 195

Fame's Memoriall; or, The Earle of Devonshire Deceased (Ford), **II:** 100

Familiar and Courtly Letters Written by Monsieur Voiture (ed. Boyer), **II:** 352, 364

"Familiar Endeavours" (Wallace–Crabbe), **VIII:** 317

Familiar Letters (Richardson), **III:** 81, 83, 92

Familiar Letters (Rochester), **II:** 270

Familiar Studies of Men and Books (Stevenson), **V:** 395; **Retro. Supp. I:** 262–263

Familiar Tree, A (Stallworthy), **Supp. X:** 294, 297–298, 302

"Joachim du Bellay" (Pater), **V:** 344

Joan and Peter (Wells), **VI:** 240

Joan of Arc (Southey), **IV:** 59, 60, 63–64, 71

Joannis Miltonii Pro se defensio . . . (Milton), **II:** 176

Job (biblical book), **III:** 307

Jocasta (Gascoigne), **I:** 215–216

Jocelyn (Galsworthy), **VI:** 277

"Jochanan Hakkadosh" (Browning), **IV:** 365

Jocoseria (Browning), **IV:** 359, 374

"Joe Soap" (Motion), **Supp. VII:** 260–261, 262

Joe's Ark (Potter, D.), **Supp. X:** 229, 237–240

"Johann Joachim Quantz's Five Lessons" (Graham), **Supp. VII:** 116

"Johannes Agricola in Meditation" (Browning), **IV:** 360

Johannes Secundus, **II:** 108

John Austen and the Inseparables (Richardson), **Supp. XIII:** 191

"John Betjeman's Brighton" (Ewart), **Supp. VII:** 37

John Bull's Other Island (Shaw), **VI:** 112, **113–115; Retro. Supp. II:** 320–321

John Caldigate (Trollope), **V:** 102

"John Clare" (Cope), **VIII:** 82

John Clare: Poems, Chiefly from Manuscript (Clare), **Supp. XI:** 36, 63

John Clare by Himself (Clare), **Supp. XI:** 51

"John Fletcher" (Swinburne), **V:** 332

John Gabriel Borkman (Ibsen), **VI:** 110

"John Galsworthy" (Lawrence), **VI:** 275–276, 290

John Galsworthy (Mottram), **VI:** 271, 275, 290

"John Galsworthy, An Appreciation" (Conrad), **VI:** 290

"John Gilpin" (Cowper), **III:** 212, 220

John Keats: A Reassessment (ed. Muir), **IV:** 219, 227, 236

John Keats: His Like and Writings (Bush), **IV:** 224, 236

John Knox (Muir), **Supp. VI:** 198

"John Knox" (Smith, I. C.), **Supp. IX:** 211–212

"John Logie Baird" (Crawford), **Supp. XI:** 71

John M. Synge (Masefield), **VI:** 317

John Marchmont's Legacy (Braddon), **VIII:** 44, 46

"John Norton" (Moore), **VI:** 98

"John of the Cross" (Jennings), **Supp. V:** 207

"John Ruskin" (Proust), **V:** 183

John Ruskin: The Portrait of a Prophet (Quennell), **V:** 185

John Sherman and Dhoya (Yeats), **VI:** 221

John Thomas and Lady Jane (Lawrence), **VII:** 111–112

John Woodvil (Lamb), **IV:** 78–79, 85

Johnnie Sahib (Scott), **Supp. I:** 259, 261

Johnno (Malouf), **Supp. XII:** 221–222

Johnny I Hardly Knew You (O'Brien), **Supp. V:** 338, 339

Johnny in the Clouds (Rattigan), see *Way to the Stars, The*

Johnson, Edgar, **IV:** 27, 40; **V:** 60, 72

Johnson, James, **III:** 320, 322

Johnson, Joseph, **Retro. Supp. I:** 37

Johnson, Lionel, **VI:** 3, 210, 211

Johnson, Samuel, **III:** 54, 96, **107–123,** 127, 151, 275; **IV:** xiv, xv, 27, 31, 34, 88n, 101, 138, 268, 299; **V:** 9, 281, 287; **VI:** 363; **Retro. Supp. I: 137–150;** and Boswell, **III:** 234, 235, 238, 239, 243–249; and Collins, **III:** 160, 163, 164, 171, 173; and Crabbe, **III:** 280–282; and Goldsmith, **III:** 177, 180, 181, 189; dictionary, **III:** 113–116; **V:** 281, 434; literary criticism, **I:** 326; **II:** 123, 173, 197, 200, 259, 263, 293, 301, 347; **III:** 11, 88, 94, 139, 257, 275; **IV:** 101; on Addison and Steele, **III:** 39, 42, 44, 49, 51; **Supp. IV:** 271

Johnson, W. E., **Supp. II:** 406

Johnson over Jordan (Priestley), **VII:** 226–227

"Joker, The" (Wallace–Crabbe), **VIII:** 315–316

"Joker as Told" (Murray), **Supp. VII:** 279

Joking Apart (Ayckbourn), **Supp. V:** 3, 9, 13, 14

Jolly Beggars, The (Burns), **III:** 319–320

"Jolly Corner, The" (James), **Retro. Supp. I:** 2

Jonah Who Will Be 25 in the Year 2000 (film), **Supp. IV:** 79

Jonathan Swift (Stephen), **V:** 289

Jonathan Wild (Fielding), **III:** 99, 103, 105, 150; **Retro. Supp. I:** 80–81, 90

Jones, David, **VI:** xvi, 436, 437–439, **Supp. VII: 167–182**

Jones, Henry Arthur, **VI:** 367, 376

Jones, Henry Festing, **Supp. II:** 103–104, 112, 114, 117, 118

Jonestown (Harris), **Supp. V:** 144–145

Jonson, Ben, **I:** 228, 234–235, 270, **335–351; II:** 3, 4, 24, 25, 27, 28, 30, 45, 47, 48, 55, 65, 79, 87, 104, 108, 110, 111n, 115, 118, 141, 199, 221–223; **IV:** 35, 327; **V:** 46, 56; **Supp. IV:** 256; **Retro. Supp. I: 151–167**

Jonsonus Virbius (Digby), **Retro. Supp. I:** 166

Jonsonus Virbius (King), **Supp. VI:** 157

Joseph Andrews (Fielding), **III:** 94, 95, 96, 99–100, 101, 105; **Retro. Supp. I:** 80, 83–86

Joseph Banks: A Life (O'Brian), **Supp. XII:** 257–258

Joseph Conrad (Baines), **VI:** 133–134

Joseph Conrad (Ford), **VI:** 321, 322

Joseph Conrad (Walpole), **VI:** 149

Joseph Conrad: A Personal Reminiscence (Ford), **VI:** 149

Joseph Conrad: The Modern Imagination (Cox), **VI:** 149

Joseph Conrad and Charles Darwin: The Influence of Scientific Thought on Conrad's Fiction (O'Hanlon), **Supp. XI:** 195

"Joseph Grimaldi" (Hood), **IV:** 267

"Joseph Yates' Temptation" (Gissing), **V:** 437

Journal (Mansfield), **VII:** 181, 182

Journal, 1825–32 (Scott), **IV:** 39

Journal and Letters of Fanny Burney, The (eds. Hemlow et al.), **Supp. III:** 63

Journal of Bridget Hitler, The (Bainbridge), **Supp. VI:** 22

Journal of a Dublin Lady, The (Swift), **III:** 35

Journal of a Landscape Painter in Corsica (Lear), **V:** 87

Journal of a Tour in Scotland in 1819 (Southey), **IV:** 71

Journal of a Tour in the Netherlands in the Autumn of 1815 (Southey), **IV:** 71

Journal of a Tour to the Hebrides, The (Boswell), **III:** 117, 234n, 235, 243, 245, 248, 249

Journal of a Voyage to Lisbon, The (Fielding), **III:** 104, 105

Journal of Beatrix Potter from 1881 to 1897, The (ed. Linder), **Supp. III: 292–295**

"Journal of My Jaunt, Harvest 1762" (Boswell), **III:** 241–242

Journal of Researches into the Geology and Natural History of the various countries visited by HMS Beagle (Darwin), **Supp. VII:** 18–19

Journal of the Plague Year, A (Defoe), **III:** 5–6, 8, 13; **Retro. Supp. I:** 63, 73–74

Journal to Eliza, The (Sterne), **III:** 125, 126, 132, 135

Journal to Stella (Swift), **II:** 335; **III:** 32–33, 34; **Retro. Supp. I:** 274

Journalism (Mahon), **Supp. VI:** 166

Journalism for Women: A Practical Guide (Bennett), **VI:** 264, 266

Journals and Papers of Gerard Manley Hopkins, The (ed. House and Storey), **V:** 362, 363, 371, 378–379, 381

Journals 1939–1983 (Spender), **Supp. II:** 481, 487, 490, 493

Journals of a Landscape Painter in Albania etc. (Lear), **V:** 77, 79–80, 87

Journals of a Landscape Painter in Southern Calabria . . . (Lear), **V:** 77, 79, 87

Journals of a Residence in Portugal, 1800–1801, and a Visit to France, 1838 (Southey), **IV:** 71

Journals of Arnold Bennett (Bennett), **VI:** 265, 267

"Journals of Progress" (Durrell), **Supp. I:** 124

"Journey, The" (Boland), **Supp. V:** 41

"Journey Back, The" (Muir), **Supp. VI:** 207

Journey Continued (Paton), **Supp. II:** 356, 359

Journey from Cornhill to Grand Cairo, A (Thackeray), *see Notes of a Journey from Cornhill to Grand Cairo*

Journey from This World to the Next (Fielding), **Retro. Supp. I:** 80

Journey into Fear (Ambler), **Supp. IV:** 11–12

"Journey of John Gilpin, The" (Cowper), *see* AJohn Gilpin"

"Journey of the Magi, The" (Eliot), **VII:** 152

Journey Through France (Piozzi), **III:** 134

Journey to a War (Auden and Isherwood), **VII:** 312; **Retro. Supp. I:** 9

Journey to Armenia (Mandelstam), **Supp. IV:** 163, 170

"Journey to Bruges, The" (Mansfield), **VII:** 172

Journey to Ithaca (Desai), **Supp. V:** 56, 66, 73–74

Journey to London, A (Vanbrugh), **II:** 326, 333–334, 336

Journey to Oxiana (Byron), **Supp. IV:** 157, 170

Journey to Paradise (Richardson), **Supp. XIII:** 180, 181

"Journey to Paradise" (Richardson), **Supp. XIII:** 180, 191

Journey to the Border (Upward), **Supp. XIII:** 250, 251, 253–254, 259, 260

Journey to the Hebrides (Johnson), **IV:** 281

Journey to the Western Islands of Scotland, A (Johnson), **III:** 117, 121; **Retro. Supp. I:** 143

Journey Without Maps (Greene), **Supp. I:** 9; **Retro. Supp. II:** 153

"Journeying North" (Conn), **Supp. XIII:** 72–73

Journeys (Morris, J.), **Supp. X:** 172, 183

Journeys and Places (Muir), **Supp. VI:** 204, **205–206**

Journeys in Persia and Kurdistan (Bird), **Supp. X:** 31

Jovial Crew, A (Brome **Supp. X:** 49, 55–59, 62–63

Jowett, Benjamin, **V:** 278, 284, 285, 312, 338, 400

"Joy" (Dutton), **Supp. XII:** 94

Joy (Galsworthy), **VI:** 269, 285

"Joy Gordon" (Redgrove), **Supp. VI:** 236

Joyce (Oliphant), **Supp. X:** 218

Joyce, James, **IV:** 189; **V:** xxv, 41; **VII:** xii, xiv, 18, **41–58; VII:** 54–58; **Supp. I:** 43, 196–197; **Supp. II:** 74, 88, 327, 332, 338, 420, 525; **Supp. III:** 108; **Supp. IV:** 27, 233, 234, 363, 364, 365, 371, 390, 395, 396, 407, 411, 424, 426, 427, 500, 514; **Retro. Supp. I:** 18, 19, **169–182**

Joyce, Jeremiah, **V:** 174*n*

"Jubilate Matteo" (Ewart), **Supp. VII:** 44

"Judas Tree, The" (Welch), **Supp. IX:** 269

Jude the Obscure (Hardy), **VI:** 4, 5, 7, 8, 9; **Supp. IV:** 116; **Retro. Supp. I:** 110, 116

"Judge, The" (Crawford), **Supp. XI:** 75–76

Judge, The (West), **Supp. III:** 441, 442

"Judge's House, The" (Stoker), **Supp. III:** 382

"Judge Chutney's Final Summary" (Armitage), **VIII:** 6

Judgement of Martin Bucer . . . , The (Milton), **II:** 175

Judgement of Paris, The (Congreve), **II:** 347, 350

Judgement in Stone, A (Rendell), **Supp. IX:** 192, 194–195

Judge's Wife, The (Churchill), **Supp. IV:** 181

"Judging Distances" (Reed), **VII:** 422

Judgment on Deltchev (Ambler), **Supp. IV:** 4, 12–13, 21

Judith, **Supp. VI:** 29; **Retro. Supp. II:** 305, 306

Judith (Bennett), **VI:** 267

"Judith" (Coppard), **VIII:** 96

Judith (Giraudoux), **Supp. III:** 195

"Judkin of the Parcels" (Saki), **Supp. VI:** 245

Jugement du roi de Behaingne, **I:** 32

"Juggling Jerry" (Meredith), **V:** 220

"Julia" (Brontë), **V:** 122, 151

Julia and the Bazooka and Other Stories (Kavan), **Supp. VII:** 202, 205, 214

"Julia Bride" (James), **VI:** 67, 69

"Julia's Churching; or, Purification" (Herrick), **II:** 112

"Julian and Maddalo" (Shelley), **IV:** 182, 201–202; **Retro. Supp. I:** 251

"Julian M. & A. G. Rochelle" (Brontë), **V:** 133

Julian of Norwich, **I:** 20; **Retro. Supp. II:** 303; **Supp. XII:** 149–166

Julius Caesar (Shakespeare), **I:** 313, 314–315

"July Evening" (MacCaig), **Supp. VI:** 187, 194

"July Storm" (Healy), **Supp. IX:** 106

July's People (Gordimer), **Supp. II:** 231, 238–239, 241

Jumpers (Stoppard), **Supp. I:** 438, 444, 445–447, 451; **Retro. Supp. II:** 347–349

Jump-to-Glory Jane (Meredith), **V:** 234

"June Bracken and Heather" (Tennyson), **IV:** 336

"June the 30th, 1934" (Lowry), **Supp. III:** 285

"June to December" (Cope), **VIII:** 72

Jung, Carl, **Supp. IV:** 1, 4–5, 6, 10–11, 12, 19, 493

"Jungle, The" (Lewis), **VII:** 447

"Jungle Book" (Scupham), **Supp. XIII:** 225

Jungle Books, The (Kipling), **VI:** 188, 199

Juniper Tree, The (Comyns), **VIII:** 53, 63–64, 65

Junius Manuscript, **Retro. Supp. II:** 298–299, 301

Junk Mail (Self), **Supp. V:** 406–407

"Junkie" (Morgan, E.), **Supp. IX:** 164

Juno and the Paycock (O'Casey), **VII:** xviii, 4–5, 6, 11

Juno in Arcadia (Brome), **Supp. X:** 52

Jure Divino (Defoe), **III:** 4, 13

"Jury, The" (Hart), **Supp. XI:** 125

Jusserand, Jean, **I:** 98

Just Between Ourselves (Ayckbourn), **Supp. V:** 3, 13

Just So Stories for Little Children (Kipling), **VI:** 188, 204

Just Vengeance, The (Sayers), **Supp. III:** 336, 350

Justice (Galsworthy), **VI:** xiii, 269, 273–274, 286–287

Justine (Durrell), **Supp. I:** 104, 105, 106

Juvenal, **II:** 30, 292, 347, 348; **III:** 42; **IV:** 188

Juvenilia 1 (Nye), **Supp. X:** 192, 194, 196–200, 202–203, 205

Juvenilia 2 (Nye), **Supp. X:** 192–194, 197–200, 204–205

"Kabla–Khun" (Dunn), **Supp. X:** 79

Kaeti and Company (Roberts, K.), **Supp. X:** 273

Kaeti on Tour (Roberts, K.), **Supp. X:** 273

Kafka, Franz, **III:** 340, 345; **Supp. IV:** 1, 199, 407, 439

Kafka's Dick (Bennett), **VIII:** 29–30

"Kail and Callaloo" (Kay), **Supp. XIII:** 108

Kain, Saul, pseud. of Siegfried Sassoon

Kaisers of Carnuntum, The (Harrison), **Supp. V:** 164

Kakutani, Michiko, **Supp. IV:** 304

Kalendarium Hortense (Evelyn), **II:** 287

Kallman, Chester, **Supp. IV:** 422, 424; **Retro. Supp. I:** 9–10, 13

Kama Sutra, **Supp. IV:** 493

Kane, Sarah, **VIII:** 147–161

Kangaroo (Lawrence), **VII:** 90, **107–109,** 119

Kant, Immanuel, **IV:** xiv, 50, 52, 145

Kanthapura (Rao), **Supp. V:** 56

"Karain: A Memory" (Conrad), **VI:** 148

Karaoke (Potter, D.), **Supp. X:** 228, 240–241

Karl, Frederick R., **VI:** 135, 149

Karl–Ludwig's Window, (Saki), **Supp. VI:** 250

"Karshish" (Browning), **IV:** 357, 360, 363

Katchen's Caprices (Trollope), **V:** 101

"Kate's Garden" (Burnside), **Supp. XIII:** 29

"Kathe Kollwitz" (Rukeyser), **Supp. V:** 261

Katherine Mansfield (Alpers), **VII:** 183

Kathleen and Frank (Isherwood), **VII:** 316–317

Kathleen Listens In (O'Casey), **VII:** 12

"Kathleen ny Houlahan" (Mangan), **Supp. XIII:** 127

"Katina" (Dahl), **Supp. IV:** 210

Kavan, Anna, **Supp. VII:** 201–215

Kavanagh, Julia, **IV:** 108, 122

Kavanagh, Dan, pseud. of Julian Barnes

Kavanagh, Patrick, **Supp. IV:** 409, 410, 412, 428, 542; **Supp. VII:** 183–199; **Retro. Supp. I:** 126

Kay, Jackie, **Supp. XIII:** 99–111

Kazin, Alfred, **Supp. IV:** 460

Keats, John, **II:** 102, 122, 192, 200; **III:** 174, 337, 338; **IV:** viii–xii, 81, 95, 129, 178, 196, 198, 204–205, **211–237,** 255, 284, 316, 323, 332, 349, 355; **V:** 173, 361, 401, 403; **Supp. I:**

Lee), **V:** 290

Lives of the Novelists (Scott), **III:** 146n; **IV:** 38, 39

Lives of the Poets, The (Johnson), *see Lives of the English Poets, The*

Lives of the English Saints (Newman), **Supp. VII:** 296

Livia (Durrell), **Supp. I:** 118, 119

Living (Green), **Supp. II:** 251–253

Living and the Dead, The (White), **Supp. I:** 129, 130, 134

Living in America (Stevenson), **Supp. VI: 254–256**

"Living in Time" (Reid), **Supp. VII:** 329

Living Novel, The (Pritchett), **IV:** 306

Living Nowhere (Burnside), **Supp. XIII:** 23, 25, 30

Living Principle, The (Leaves), **VII:** 237

Living Quarters (Friel), **Supp. V:** 122

Living Room, The (Greene), **Supp. I:** 13; **Retro. Supp. II:** 161–162

Living Together (Ayckbourn), **Supp. V:** 2, 5

Living Torch, The (Russell), **VIII:** 277, 286, 290, 292

"Livings" (Larkin), **Supp. I:** 277, 282

Livingstone's Companions (Gordimer), **Supp. II:** 229, 233

Liza of Lambeth (Maugham), **VI:** 364–365

Liza's England (Barker), *see Century's Daughter, The*

"Lizbie Brown" (Hardy), **Retro. Supp. I:** 110

"Lizzie Leigh" (Gaskell), **V:** 3, 15

Ljósvetninga saga, **VIII:** 242

"Llanrhaeadr ym Mochnant" (Thomas), **Supp. XII:** 285

Lloyd, Charles, **IV:** 78

Lloyd George, David, **VI:** 264, 340, 352, 353; **VII:** 2

Loaves and Fishes (Brown), **Supp. VI:** 65, 71

"Lob"(Thomas), **Supp. III:** 394, 405

Lobo, Jeronimo, **III:** 107, 112

Local Habitation (Nicholson), **Supp. VI:** 213, **217–218**

Locations (Morris, J.), **Supp. X:** 172, 183

"Loch Ness Monster's Song, The" (Morgan, E.), **Supp. IX:** 162–163, 169

"Loch Roe" (MacCaig), **Supp. VI:** 182

"Loch Sionascaig" (MacCaig), **Supp. VI:** 195

"Lock, The" (Coppard), **VIII:** 88

"Lock the Door, Lariston" (Hogg), **Supp. X:** 110

"Lock up, fair lids, The treasure of my heart" (Sidney), **I:** 169

Locke, John, **III:** 22; **IV:** 169; **Supp. III:** 33, 233

Lockhart, J. G., **IV:** 27, 30, 34, 36, 38, 39, 294; **V:** 140

"Locksley Hall" (Tennyson), **IV:** 325, 333, 334–335

"Locksley Hall Sixty Years After" (Tennyson), **IV:** 328, 338

Locust Room, The (Burnside), **Supp. XIII:** 23, 29–30

"Locust Songs" (Hill), **Supp. V:** 187

Lodge, David, **Supp. II:** 9, 10; **Supp. IV:** 102, 139, **363–387**, 546; **Retro. Supp. I:** 217

Lodge, Thomas, **I:** 306, 312

"Lodging for the Night, A" (Stevenson), **V:** 384, 395

"Lodging House Fire, The" (Davies), **Supp. XI:** 94–95

"Lodgings for the Night" (Caudwell), **Supp. IX:** 35, 37

Lodore (Shelley), **Supp. III:** 371, 372

Loftis, John, **III:** 255, 271

"Lofty in the Palais de Danse" (Gunn), **Supp. IV:** 258

"Lofty Sky, The" (Thomas), **Supp. III:** 401

Logan, Annie R. M., **VI:** 23

Logan Stone (Thomas), **Supp. IV:** 490

"Logan Stone" (Thomas), **Supp. IV:** 491, 492

"Loganair" (Crawford), **Supp. XI:** 75

"Logic of Dreams" (Fuller), **Supp. VII:** 74

Logic of Political Economy, The (De Quincey), **IV:** 155

"Logical Ballad of Home Rule, A" (Swinburne), **V:** 332

"Logos" (Hughes), **Supp. I:** 350

Loiners, The (Harrison), **Supp. V:** 149, 150–151

"Lois the Witch" (Gaskell), **V:** 15

Loitering with Intent (Spark), **Supp. I:** 204, 212, 213

Lokasenna, **VIII:** 230, 241

Lolita (Nabokov), **Supp. IV:** 26, 30

Lolly Willowes (Warner), **Supp. VII:** 370, 373–374, 375, 381

Lombroso, Cesare, **V:** 272

Londinium Redivivum (Evelyn), **II:** 287

"London" (Blake), **III:** 294, 295

"London" (Johnson), **III:** 57, 108, 114, 121; **Retro. Supp. I:** 137

London (Russell), **Supp. IV:** 126

London Assurance (Boucicault), **V:** 415

"London by Lamplight" (Meredith), **V:** 219

London Fields (Amis), **Supp. IV:** 26, 27, 35–37

"London hast thou accusèd me" (Surrey), **I:** 113, 116

London Journal 1762–1763 (Boswell), **III:** 239, 240, 242

London Kills Me: Three Screenplays and Four Essays (Kureishi), **Supp. XI:** 156–157, 159, 161

London Lickpenny (Ackroyd), **Supp. VI:** 3

London Life, A (James), **VI:** 67, 69

London Magazine (periodical), **III:** 263; **IV:** xviii, 252, 253, 257, 260; **V:** 386

London Mercury (periodical), **VII:** 211

London Pride (Braddon), **VIII:** 49

"London Revisited" (Beerbohm), **Supp. II:** 52

"London Snow" (Bridges), **VI:** 78

London Spy (periodical), **III:** 41

London Street Games (Douglas), **VI:** 304, 305

London: The Biography (Ackroyd), **Supp. VI:** 13

London to Ladysmith via Pretoria (Churchill), **VI:** 351

London Tradesmen (Trollope), **V:** 102

London Zoo (Sisson), **Supp. XI:** 249

"Londoner" (Adcock), **Supp. XII:** 8

Londoners (Ewart), **Supp. VII:** 38

"Lone Voices" (Amis), **Supp. II:** 11

"Loneliest Mountain, The" (Davies), **Supp. XI:** 100

"Loneliness" (Auden), **Retro. Supp. I:** 13

"Loneliness" (Behan), **Supp. II:** 64

"Loneliness of the Long–Distance Runner, The" (Sillitoe), **Supp. V:** 409, 410, 413, 419–421

Lonely Girl, The (O'Brien), **Supp. V:** 334, 336–337

"Lonely Lady, The" (Powys), **VIII:** 254, 258

Lonely Londoners, The (Selvon), **Supp. IV:** 445

"Lonely Love" (Blunden), **Supp. XI:** 46–47

Lonely Passion of Judith Hearne, The (Moore, B.), **Supp. IX:** 141, 142, 143, 144, 146

Lonely Unicorn, The (Waugh), **Supp. VI:** 270

Lonesome West, The (McDonagh), **Supp. XII:** 233, 235, 236–237, 238, 239, 245

"Long ages past" (Owen), **VI:** 448

"Long Ago" (Dunn), **Supp. X:** 80

Long Day Wanes, The (Burgess), *see Malayan trilogy*

Long Kill, The (Hill, R.), **Supp. IX:** 119

Long River, The (Smith, I. C.), **Supp. IX:** 211

"Long Story, A" (Gray), **III:** 140

Long View, The (Howard), **Supp. XI:** 135, 138–139

"Longes MACnUSNIG: The Exile of the Sons of Usnech and The Exile of Fergus and The Death of the Sons of Usnech and of Deidre" (Kinsella), **Supp. V:** 264

Longest Day, The (Clough), **V:** 170

Longest Journey, The (Forster), **VI:** 398, **401–403**, 407; **Retro. Supp. II:** 136, 139–141

"Long–Legged Fly" (Yeats), **Retro. Supp. I:** 337

Longley, Michael, **VIII: 163–178; Supp. IV:** 412

"Longstaff's Marriage" (James), **VI:** 69

Lonsdale, R., **III:** 142n, 144

"Look" (Motion), **Supp. VII:** 259

Look After Lulu (Coward), **Supp. II:** 155

Look at All Those Roses (Bowen), **Supp. II:** 92–93

Look at Me (Brookner), **Supp. IV:** 125–126

"Look at the Children" (Graham), **Supp. VII:** 116

"Look at the Cloud His Evening Playing Cards" (Graham), **Supp. VII:** 116

Look Back in Anger (Osborne), **Supp. I:** 329, **330–332**, 338; **Supp. II:** 4, 70,

"Man with Night Sweats, The" (Gunn), **Supp. IV:** 276–277

Man with Night Sweats, The (Gunn), **Supp. IV:** 255, 257, 274–278

"Man with the Dog, The" (Jhabvala), **Supp. V:** 236

"Man with the Twisted Lip, The" (Doyle), **Supp. II:** 171

Man Within, The (Greene), **Supp. I:** 2; **Retro. Supp. II:** 152

"Man Without a Temperament, The" (Mansfield), **VII:** 174, 177

"Mana Aboda" (Hulme), **Supp. VI:** 136

Manalive (Chesterton), **VI:** 340

Mañanas de abril y mayo (Calderón), **II:** 312n

Manchester Enthusiasts, The (Arden and D'Arcy), **Supp. II:** 39

"Manchester Marriage, The" (Gaskell), **V:** 6n, 14, 15

Manciple's Prologue, The (Chaucer), **I:** 24

Manciple's Tale, The (Chaucer), **I:** 55

"Mandela" (Motion), **Supp. VII:** 266

Mandelbaum Gate, The (Spark), **Supp. I:** 206–208, 213

Mandelstam, Osip, **Supp. IV:** 163, 493

"Mandrake" (Burnside), **Supp. XIII:** 23

Manet, Edouard, **Supp. IV:** 480

Manfred (Byron), **III:** 338; **IV:** xvii, 172, 173, 177, 178–182, 192

Mangan, James Clarence, **Supp. XIII:** 113–130

Mangan Inheritance, The (Moore), **Supp. IX** 144, 148, 150–151, 153

Manhatten '45 (Morris, J.), **Supp. X:** 182

"Manhole 69" (Ballard), **Supp. V:** 21

"Maniac, The" (Robinson), **Supp. XIII:** 206, 210

"Manifesto" (Morgan, E.), **Supp. IX:** 163

Manifold, John, **VII:** 422, 426–427

Manin and the Venetian Revolution of 1848 (Trevelyan), **VI:** 389

Mankind in the Making (Wells), **VI:** 227, 236

Manly, J. M., **I:** 1

"Man–Man" (Naipaul), **Supp. I:** 385

Mann, Thomas, **II:** 97; **III:** 344; **Supp. IV:** 397

Manner of the World Nowadays, The (Skelton), **I:** 89

Mannerly Margery Milk and Ale (Skelton), **I:** 83

Manners, Mrs. Horace, pseud. of Algernon Charles Swinburne

"Manners, The" (Collins), **III:** 161, 162, 166, 171

Manning, Cardinal, **V:** 181

Manoeuvring (Edgeworth), **Supp. III:** 158

"Manor Farm, The" (Thomas), **Supp. III:** 399, 405

"Mans medley" (Herbert), **Retro. Supp. II:** 181–182

Manservant and Maidservant (Compton–Burnett), **VII:** 62, 63, 67

Mansfield, Katherine, **IV:** 106; **VI:** 375; **VII:** xv, xvii, 171–184, 314; list of short stories, **VII:** 183–184

Mansfield Park (Austen), **IV:** xvii, 102–103, 108, 109, 111, 112, 115–119, 122; **Retro. Supp. II:** 9–11

Mantissa (Fowles), **Supp. I:** 308–309, 310

Manto, Saadat Hasan, **Supp. IV:** 440

Mantz, Ruth, **VII:** 176

Manuel (Maturin), **VIII:** 207, 208

"Manus Animam Pinxit" (Thompson), **V:** 442

Many Dimensions (Williams, C. W. S.), **Supp. IX:** 281

Manzoni, Alessandro, **III:** 334

"Map, The" (Hart), **Supp. XI:** 130

Map, Walter, **I:** 35

Map of Love, The (Thomas), **Supp. I:** 176–177, 180

"Map of the City, A" (Gunn), **Supp. IV:** 262, 274

Map of the World, A (Hare), **Supp. IV:** 282, 288–289, 293

Map of Verona, A (Reed), **VII:** 423

Mapp Showing . . . Salvation and Damnation, A (Bunyan), **II:** 253

Mappings (Seth), **Supp. X:** 279–280

Mapplethorpe, Robert, **Supp. IV:** 170, 273

Mara, Bernard, *see* Moore, Brian

Marble Faun, The (Hawthorne), **VI:** 27

March of Literature, The (Ford), **VI:** 321, 322, 324

March Violets (Kerr), **Supp. XII:** 187, 188–189

"Marchese Pallavicini and Walter Landor" (Landor), **IV:** 90

March Moonlight (Richardson), **Supp. XIII:** 181, 188, 192

Marching Soldier (Cary), **VII:** 186

"Marching to Zion" (Coppard), **VIII:** 91–92

"Marchioness of Stonehenge, The" (Hardy), **VI:** 22

Marconi's Cottage (McGuckian), **Supp. V:** 284, 286–287

Marcus, Jane, **Retro. Supp. I:** 306

Marcus, S., **V:** 46, 73

Marfan (Reading), **VIII:** 262, 274–275

Margaret Drabble: Puritanism and Permissiveness (Myer), **Supp. IV:** 233

Margaret Ogilvy (Barrie), **Supp. III:** 3

Margin Released (Priestley), **VII:** 209, 210, 211

"Margins" (Conn), **Supp. XIII:** 72

Margoliouth, H. M., **II:** 214n, 219

Mari Magno (Clough), **V:** 159, 168

Maria; or, The Wrongs of Woman (Wollstonecraft), **Supp. III:** 466, 476–480

"Mariana" (Tennyson), **IV:** 329, 331

"Mariana in the South" (Tennyson), **IV:** 329, 331

Mariani, Paul L., **V:** 373n, 378, 382

Marianne Thornton (Forster), **VI:** 397, 411

Marie (Haggard), **Supp. III:** 214

"Marie Antoinette's Lamentation, in her Prison of the Temple" (Robinson), **Supp. XIII:** 202

Marinetti, Filippo T., **Supp. III:** 396

"Marina" (Eliot), **Retro. Supp. II:** 130

"Marine Lament" (Cameron), **Supp. IX:** 19

"Mariner's Compass, The" (Armitage), **VIII:** 11

Marino, Giambattista, **II:** 180, 183

Marino Faliero (Swinburne), **V:** 332

Marino Faliero, Doge of Venice (Byron), **IV:** xviii, 178–179, 193

Marion Fay (Trollope), **V:** 102

Marionette, The (Muir), **Supp. VI:** 198, 203–204

Marius the Epicurean (Pater), **V:** xxv, 339, 348, 349–351, 354, 355, 356, 411

Marjorie, **VI:** 249; pseud. of Arnold Bennett

"Mark of the Beast, The" (Kipling), **VI:** 183, 193

Mark of the Warrior, The (Scott), **Supp. I:** 263

Mark Only (Powys), **VIII:** 250–251

Markandaya, Kamala, **Supp. IV:** 440

"Markers" (Thomas), **Supp. XII:** 290

"Market at Turk" (Gunn), **Supp. IV:** 260–261

Market Bell, The (Powys), **VIII:** 251, 258

Market of Seleukia, The (Morris, J.), **Supp. X:** 175

"Market Square" (Milne), **Supp. V:** 302

Markey, Constance, **Supp. IV:** 347, 360

Markham, Robert, **Supp. II:** 12; pseud. of Kingsley Amis

"Markheim" (Stevenson), **V:** 395; **Retro. Supp. I:** 267

Marking Time (Howard), **Supp. XI:** 145, 146, 147, 148

"Mark–2 Wife, The" (Trevor), **Supp. IV:** 503

Marlborough: His Life and Times (Churchill), **VI:** 354–355

Marlowe, Christopher, **I:** 212, 228–229, 275–294, 336; **II:** 69, 138; **III:** 344; **IV:** 255, 327; **Supp. IV:** 197; **Retro. Supp. I:** 199–213

Marlowe and His Circle (Boas), **I:** 275, 293

Marlowe and the Early Shakespeare (Wilson), **I:** 286

Marmion (Scott), **IV:** xvi, 29, 30, 38, 129

Marmor Norfolciense (Johnson), **III:** 121; **Retro. Supp. I:** 141

Marquise, The (Coward), **Supp. II:** 146

"Marriage, A" (Thomas), **Supp. XII:** 290

Marriage A–la–Mode (Dryden), **II:** 293, 296, 305

"Marriage in a Free Society" (Carpenter), **Supp. XIII:** 41, 42

Marriage of Heaven and Hell, The (Blake), **III:** 289, 297–298, 304, 307; **V:** xv, 329–330, 331; **Supp. IV:** 448; **Retro. Supp. I:** 38–39

Marriage of Mona Lisa, The (Swinburne), **V:** 333

"Marriage of Tirzah and Ahirad, The" (Macaulay), **IV:** 283

Marriages Between Zones Three, Four and Five, The (Lessing), **Supp. I:** 251

Married Life (Bennett), *see Plain Man and His Wife, The*

Married Man, The (Lawrence), **VII:** 120

"Memorial for the City" (Auden), **VII:** 388, 393; **Retro. Supp. I:** 8
Memorials of a Tour on the Continent (Wordsworth), **IV:** 24–25
Memorials of Edward Burne–Jones (Burne–Jones), **V:** 295–296, 306
"Memorials of Gormandising" (Thackeray), **V:** 23, 24, 38
Memorials of Thomas Hood (Hood and Broderip), **IV:** 251, 261, 267
Memorials of Two Sisters, Susanna and Catherine Winkworth (ed. Shaen), **V:** 149
Memories and Adventures (Doyle), **Supp. II:** 159
Memories and Hallucinations (Thomas), **Supp. IV:** 479, 480, 482, 483, 484, 486
Memories and Portraits (Stevenson), **V:** 390, 395
"Memories of a Catholic Childhood" (Lodge), **Supp. IV:** 363–364
"Memories of a Working Women's Guild" (Woolf), **Retro. Supp. I:** 311
Memories of the Space Age (Ballard), **Supp. V:** 24
"Memories of the Space Age" (Ballard), **Supp. V:** 33
Memories of Vailiona (Osborne and Strong), **V:** 393, 397
"Memories of Youghal" (Trevor), **Supp. IV:** 501
"Memory, A" (Brooke), **Supp. III:** 55
"Memory and Imagination&rdqo; (Dunn), **Supp. X:** 77
"Memory Man" (Ewart), **Supp. VII:** 41
Memory of Ben Jonson Revived by the Friends of the Muses, The (Digby), **Retro. Supp. I:** 166
"Memory Unsettled" (Gunn), **Supp. IV:** 277
"Men and Their Boring Arguments" (Cope), **VIII:** 78
Men and Wives (Compton–Burnett), **VII:** 64, 65, 66–67
Men and Women (Browning), **IV:** xiii, xxi, 357, 363, 374; **Retro. Supp. II:** 26, 27–28
Men at Arms (Waugh), **VII:** 304; *see also Sword of Honour* trilogy
Men Like Gods (Wells), **VI:** 226 240 244; **VII:** 204
Men on Women on Men (Ayckbourn), **Supp. V:** 3
"Men Sign the Sea" (Graham), **Supp. VII:** 110
"Men Who March Away" (Hardy), **VI:** 415, 421; **Retro. Supp. I:** 120
"Men With Coats Thrashing" (Lowry), **Supp. III:** 283
Men Without Art (Lewis), **VII:** 72, 76
"Menace, The" (du Maurier), **Supp. III:** 139
"Menace, The" (Gunn), **Supp. IV:** 261
Menand, Louis, **Supp. IV:** 305
Mendelson, Edward, **Retro. Supp. I:** 12
"Menelaus and Helen" (Brooke), **Supp. III:** 52
Menaphon (Greene), **I:** 165; **VIII:** 135, 138–139, 143

Mencius on the Mind (Richards), **Supp. II:** 421
Men-of-War: Life in Nelson's Navy (O'Brian), **Supp. XII:** 255
Men's Wives (Thackeray), **V:** 23, 35, 38
"Mental Cases" (Owen), **VI:** 456, 457
Mental Efficiency (Bennett), **VI:** 250, 266
Merchant of Venice, The (Shakespeare), **I:** 310
Merchant's Tale, The (Chaucer), **I:** 36, 41–42
Mercian Hymns (Hill), **Supp. V:** 187, 189, 194–196
Mercier and Camier (Beckett), **Supp. I:** 50–51; **Retro. Supp. I:** 21
"Mercury and the Elephant" (Finch), **Supp. IX:** 71–72
"Mercy" (Collins), **III:** 166
Mercy Boys, The (Burnside), **Supp. XIII:** 28
Mer de Glace (Meale and Malouf), **Supp. XII:** 218
Mere Accident, A (Moore), **VI:** 86, 91
Mere Christianity (Lewis), **Supp. III:** 248
"Mere Interlude, A" (Hardy), **VI:** 22
Meredith (Sassoon), **V:** 219, 234
Meredith, George, **II:** 104, 342, 345; **IV:** 160; **V:** x, xviii, xxii–xxvi, **219–234,** 244, 432; **VI:** 2
Meredith, H. O., **VI:** 399
Meredith et la France (Mackay), **V:** 223, 234
"Meredithian Sonnets" (Fuller), **Supp. VII:** 74
Meres, Francis, **I:** 212, 234, 296, 307
Merie Tales, The, **I:** 83, 93
Meriton, George, **II:** 340
Merkin, Daphne, **Supp. IV:** 145–146
Merleau–Ponty, Maurice, **Supp. IV:** 79, 88
Merlin (Nye), **Supp. X:** 195
"Merlin and the Gleam" (Tennyson), **IV:** 329
Mermaid, Dragon, Fiend (Graves), **VII:** 264
Merope (Arnold), **V:** 209, 216
"Merry Beggars, The" (Brome), **Supp. X:** 55
Merry England (periodical), **V:** 440
Merry Jests of George Peele, The, **I:** 194
Merry Men, and Other Tales and Fables, The (Stevenson), **V:** 395; **Retro. Supp. I:** 267
Merry Wives of Windsor, The (Shakespeare), **I:** 295, 311; **III:** 117
Merry–Go–Round, The (Lawrence), **VII:** 120
Merry–Go–Round, The (Maugham), **VI:** 372
Mescellanies (Fielding), **Retro. Supp. I:** 80
Meschonnic, Henri, **Supp. IV:** 115
Mespoulet, M., **V:** 266
"Message, The" (Donne), **Retro. Supp. II:** 90
"Message, The" (Russell), **VIII:** 280–281
"Message Clear" (Morgan, E.), **Supp. IX:** 165

"Message from Mars, The" (Ballard), **Supp. V:** 33
Messages (Fernandez), **V:** 225–226
"Messdick" (Ross), **VII:** 433
Messenger, The (Kinsella), **Supp. V:** 269–270
"M. E. T." (Thomas), **Supp. III:** 401
"Metamorphoses" (Malouf), **Supp. XII:** 220
Metamorphoses (Ovid), **III:** 54; **V:** 321; **Retro. Supp. II:** 36, 215
Metamorphoses (Sisson), **Supp. XI:** 249
Metamorphosis (Kafka), **III:** 340, 345
Metamorphosis of Pygmalion's Image (Marston), **I:** 238; **II:** 25, 40
"Metaphor Now Standing at Platform 8, The" (Armitage), **VIII:** 5–6
"Metaphorical Gymnasia" (Dutton), **Supp. XII:** 97
Metaphysical Lyrics and Poems of the Seventeenth Century (Grierson), **Retro. Supp. II:** 173
Metempsycosis: Poêma Satyricon (Donne), **Retro. Supp. II:** 94
"Methinks the poor Town has been troubled too long" (Dorset), **II:** 262
"Method. For Rongald Gaskell" (Davie), **Supp. VI:** 106
Metrical Tales and Other Poems (Southey), **IV:** 71
Metroland (Barnes), **Supp. IV:** 65, 66–67, 71, 76
Mew, Charlotte, **Supp. V:** 97, 98–99
Meynell, Wilfred, **V:** 440, 451
MF (Burgess), **Supp. I:** 197
"Mianserin Sonnets" (Fuller), **Supp. VII:** 79
Micah Clark (Doyle), **Supp. II:** 159, 163
"Michael" (Wordsworth), **IV:** 8, 18–19
Michael and Mary (Milne), **Supp. V:** 299
Michael Robartes and the Dancer (Yeats), **VI:** 217; **Retro. Supp. I:** 331–333
"Michael X and the Black Power Killings in Trinidad" (Naipaul), **Supp. I:** 396
Michaelmas Term (Middleton), **II:** 3, 4, 21
Michelet, Jules, **V:** 346
Microcosmography (Earle), **IV:** 286
Micro–Cynicon, Six Snarling Satires (Middleton), **II:** 2–3
Midas (Lyly), **I:** 198, 202, 203
"Middle Age" (Dunn), **Supp. X:** 80
Middle Age of Mrs Eliot, The (Wilson), **Supp. I:** 160–161
Middle Ground, The (Drabble), **Supp. IV:** 230, 231, 234, 246–247, 248
Middle Mist, The (Renault), see *Friendly Young Ladies, The*
"Middle of a War" (Fuller), **VII:** 429; **Supp. VII:** 69
Middle Passage, The (Naipaul), **Supp. I:** 386, 390–391, 393, 403
"Middle–Sea and Lear–Sea" (Jones), **Supp. VII:** 176
Middle Years, The (James), **VI:** 65, 69
"Middle Years, The" (Ewart), **Supp. VII:** 39
"Middle Years, The" (James), **VI:** 69

(Wordsworth), **II:** 189, 200; **IV:** xvi, 21, 22

"Ode on a Distant Prospect of Eton College" (Gray), **III:** 137, 144

"Ode on a Grecian Urn" (Keats), **III:** 174, 337; **IV:** 222–223, 225, 226; **Supp. V:** 38; **Retro. Supp. I:** 195–196

"Ode on Indolence" (Keats), **IV:** 221, 225–226

"Ode on Melancholy" (Keats), **III:** 337; **IV:** 224–225

"Ode on Mrs. Arabella Hunt Singing" (Congreve), **II:** 348

Ode, on the Death of Mr. Henry Purcell, An (Dryden), **II:** 304

"Ode on the Death of Mr. Thomson" (Collins), **III:** 163, 175

"Ode on the Death of Sir H. Morison" (Jonson), **II:** 199

Ode on the Death of the Duke of Wellington (Tennyson), **II:** 200; **IV:** 338

Ode on the Departing Year (Coleridge), **IV:** 55

Ode on the Installation of . . . Prince Albert as Chancellor of . . . Cambridge (Wordsworth), **IV:** 25

"Ode on the Insurrection at Candia" (Swinburne), **V:** 313

"Ode on the Morning of Christ's Nativity" (Milton), **Retro. Supp. II:** 272

"Ode on the Pleasure Arising from Vicissitude" (Gray), **III:** 141, 145

"Ode on the Popular Superstitions of the Highlands of Scotland" (Collins), **III:** 163, 171–173, 175

Ode on the Proclamation of the French Republic (Swinburne), **V:** 332

"Ode on the Spring" (Gray), **III:** 137, 295

"Ode Performed in the Senate House at Cambridge" (Gray), **III:** 145

Ode Prefixed to S. Harrison's Arches of Triumph . . . (Webster), **II:** 85

"Ode to a Lady on the Death of Colonel Ross" (Collins), **III:** 162

"Ode to a Nightingale" (Keats), **II:** 122; **IV:** 212, 221, 222–223, 224, 226; **Retro. Supp. I:** 195–196

"Ode to Apollo" (Keats), **IV:** 221, 227

"Ode to Delia Crusca" (Robinson), **Supp. XIII:** 206

"Ode to Duty" (Wordsworth), **II:** 303

"Ode to Evening" (Blunden), **Supp. XI:** 43

"Ode to Evening" (Collins), **III:** 166, 173; **IV:** 227

"Ode to Fear" (Collins), see "Fear"

Ode to Himself (Jonson), **I:** 336

Ode to Independence (Smollett), **III:** 158

"Ode to John Warner" (Auden), **Retro. Supp. I:** 8

"Ode to Liberty" (Shelley), **IV:** 203

"Ode to Master Endymion Porter, Upon his Brothers Death, An" (Herrick), **II:** 112

"Ode to May" (Keats), **IV:** 221, 222

Ode to Mazzini (Swinburne), **V:** 333

"Ode to Memory" (Tennyson), **IV:** 329

"Ode to Mr. Congreve" (Swift), **III:** 30

"Ode to Naples" (Shelley), **II:** 200; **IV:** 195

Ode to Napoleon Buonaparte (Byron), **IV:** 192

"Ode to Pity" (Collins), **III:** 164

"Ode to Psyche" (Keats), **IV:** 221–222

"Ode to Rae Wilson" (Hood), **IV:** 261, 262–263

"Ode to Rapture" (Robinson), **Supp. XIII:** 206

"Ode to Sir William Temple" (Swift), **III:** 30

"Ode to Sorrow" (Keats), **IV:** 216, 224

"Ode to the Harp of...Louisa" (Robinson), **Supp. XIII:** 206

"Ode to the Moon" (Hood), **IV:** 255

"Ode to the Nightingale" (Robinson), **Supp. XIII:** 206

"Ode to the Setting Sun" (Thompson), **V:** 448, 449

"Ode to the Snowdrop" (Robinson), **Supp. XIII:** 210

"Ode to the West Wind" (Shelley), **II:** 200; **IV:** xviii, 198, 203

Ode to Tragedy, An (Boswell), **III:** 247

"Ode upon Dr. Harvey" (Cowley), **II:** 196, 198

"Ode: Written at the Beginning of the Year 1746" (Collins), **III:** 169

Odes (Gray), **III:** 145

Odes and Addresses to Great People (Hood and Reynolds), **IV:** 253, 257, 267

Odes in Contribution to the Song of French History (Meredith), **V:** 223, 234

Odes on Several Descriptive and Allegorical Subjects (Collins), **III:** 162, 163, 165–166, 175

Odes on the Comic Spirit (Meredith), **V:** 234

Odes to . . . the Emperor of Russia, and . . . the King of Prussia (Southey), **IV:** 71

Odette d'Antrevernes (Firbank), **Supp. II:** 199, 201, 205–206

"Odour, The" (Traherne), **Supp. XI:** 269

"Odour of Chrysanthemums" (Lawrence), **VII:** 114; **Retro. Supp. II:** 232–233

"Odysseus of Hermes" (Gunn), **Supp. IV:** 275

Odyssey (Homer), **Supp. IV:** 234, 267, 428

Odyssey (tr. Cowper), **III:** 220

"Odyssey" (Longley), **VIII:** 167

Odyssey (tr. Pope), **III:** 70, 77

Odyssey, The (Butler translation), **Supp. II:** 114, 115

Odyssey of Homer, The (Lawrence translation), **Supp. II:** 283, 294

Odyssey of Homer, done into English Verse, The (Morris), **V:** 306

Oedipus Tyrannus; or, Swellfoot the Tyrant (Shelley), **IV:** 208

Of Ancient and Modern Learning (Temple), **III:** 23

"Of Commerce and Society: The Death of Shelley" (Hill), **Supp. V:** 186

"Of Democritus and Heraclitus" (Montaigne), **III:** 39

"Of Discourse" (Cornwallis), **III:** 39–40

"Of Divine Love" (Waller), **II:** 235

Of Dramatick Poesie, An Essay (Dryden), see Essay of Dramatick Poesy

Of Education (Milton), **II:** 162–163, 175

"Of Eloquence" (Goldsmith), **III:** 186

"Of English Verse" (Waller), **II:** 233–234

"Of Essay Writing" (Hume), **Supp. III:** 231–232

"Of Greatness" (Cowley), **III:** 40

Of Human Bondage (Maugham), **VI:** xiii, 365, 373–374

Of Justification by Imputed Righteousness (Bunyan), **II:** 253

"Of Liberty" (Cowley), **II:** 198

Of Liberty and Loyalty (Swinburne), **V:** 333

Of Liberty and Servitude (tr. Evelyn), **II:** 287

Of Magnanimity and Chastity (Traherne), **II:** 202

"Of Masques" (Bacon), **I:** 268

"Of My Self" (Cowley), **II:** 195

"Of Nature: Laud and Plaint" (Thompson), **V:** 443

"Of Only a Single Poem" (Dutton), **Supp. XII:** 95, 96

"Of Pacchiarotto" (Browning), **IV:** 366

"Of Plants" (Cowley), **Supp. III:** 36

"Of Pleasing" (Congreve), **II:** 349

"Of Poetry" (Temple), **III:** 23, 190

Of Prelatical Episcopacy . . . (Milton), **II:** 175

Of Reformation Touching Church Discipline in England (Milton), **II:** 162, 175

"Of Silence and the Air" (Pitter), **Supp. XIII:** 141–142

Of Style (Hughes), **III:** 40

Of the Characters of Women (Pope), see Moral Essays

Of the Friendship of Amis and Amile, Done into English (Morris), **V:** 306

Of the House of the Forest of Lebanon (Bunyan), **II:** 253

Of the Knowledge of Ourselves and of God (Julian of Norwich), **Supp. XII:** 155

Of the Lady Mary (Waller), **II:** 238

Of the Law and a Christian (Bunyan), **II:** 253

Of the Laws of Ecclesiastical Polity (Hooker), **I:** 176, 179–190

Of the Trinity and a Christian (Bunyan), **II:** 253

"Of the Uncomplicated Dairy Girl" (Smith, I. C.), **Supp. IX:** 216

Of the Use of Riches, an Epistle to . . . Bathurst (Pope), see Moral Essays

Of True Greatness (Fielding), **III:** 105

Of True Religion, Haeresie, Schism, Toleration, . . . (Milton), **II:** 176

"Of White Hairs and Cricket" (Mistry), **Supp. X:** 140–141

Off Colour (Kay), **Supp. XIII:** 101, 108

"Off the Map" (Malouf), **Supp. XII:** 220

"Offa's Leechdom" (Hill), **Supp. V:** 194

"Offa's Second Defence of the English People" (Hill), **Supp. V:** 195

Offer of the Clarendon Trustees, The (Carroll), **V:** 274

"Office for the Dead" (Kinsella), **Supp. V:** 263

"Office Friendships" (Ewart), **Supp. VII:** 39

"Office Girl" (Hart), **Supp. XI:** 123

Office Suite (Bennett), **VIII:** 27

Officers and Gentlemen (Waugh), **VII:** 302, 304; *see also* Sword of Honour trilogy

"Officers Mess" (Ewarts), **VII:** 423; **Supp. VII:** 37

Offshore (Fitzgerald), **Supp. V:** 96, 97, 98, 102

"Oflag Night Piece: Colditz" (Riviere), **VII:** 424

Ogden, C. K., **Supp. II:** 405, 406, 407–408, 409, 410, 411, 422, 424

Ogg, David, **II:** 243

O'Grady, Standish James, **Supp. V:** 36

"Oh, dreadful is the check—intense the agony" (Brontë), **V:** 116

"Oh, Madam" (Bowen), **Supp. II:** 92–93

"Oh! That 'Twere Possible" (Tennyson), **IV:** 330, 332

Oh What a Lovely War (musical), **VI:** 436

O'Hanlon, Redmond, **Supp. XI:** 195–208

Ohio Impromptu (Beckett), **Supp. I:** 61

"O'Hussey's Ode to the Maguire" (Mangan), **Supp. XIII:** 118

Okri, Ben, **Supp. V:** 347–362

Óláfs saga helga, **VIII:** 242

"Olalla" (Stevenson), **V:** 395

"Old, The" (Hart), **Supp. XI:** 123

"Old Aberdeen" (Kay), **Supp. XIII:** 108

Old Adam, The (Bennett), *see Regent, The*

"Old Andrey's Experience as a Musician" (Hardy), **VI:** 22

"Old Atheist Pauses by the Sea, An" (Kinsella), **Supp. V:** 261

Old Batchelour, The (Congreve), **II:** 338, 340–341, 349

"Old Benchers of the Inner Temple, The" (Lamb), **IV:** 74

Old Boys, The (Trevor), **Supp. IV:** 505–506, 507, 517

Old Calabria (Douglas), **VI:** 294, 295–296, 297, 298, 299, 305

"Old Chartist, The" (Meredith), **V:** 220

"Old Chief Mshlanga, The" (Lessing), **Supp. I:** 242

"Old China" (Lamb), **IV:** 82

"Old Church Tower and the Garden Wall, The" (Brontë), **V:** 134

"Old Colonial Boy, The" (Carson), **Supp. XIII:** 54

"Old Crofter" (MacCaig), **Supp. VI:** 192

Old Country, The (Bennett), **VIII:** 30

Old Curiosity Shop, The (Dickens), **V:** xx, 42, 53, 71

Old Debauchees, The (Fielding), **III:** 105

Old Devils, The (Amis), **Supp. II:** 3, 18–19; **Supp. IV:** 37

"Old Dispensary" (Murphy), **Supp. V:** 329

Old English (Galsworthy), **VI:** 275, 284

Old English Baron, The (Reeve), **III:** 345

"Old Familiar Faces, The" (Lamb), **IV:** 78

"Old Folks at Home" (Highsmith), **Supp. V:** 180

"Old Fools, The" (Larkin), **Supp. I:** 282–283, 285

Old Fortunatus (Dekker), **II:** 71, 89

"Old Francis" (Kelman), **Supp. V:** 249

Old French Romances, Done into English (Morris), **V:** 306

"Old Friend, The" (Cornford), **VIII:** 106

Old Gang and the New Gang, The (Lewis), **VII:** 83

"Old Garbo" (Thomas), **Supp. I:** 181

Old Glory: An American Voyage (Raban), **Supp. XI:** 227, 232–235

"Old Hands" (Scupham), **Supp. XIII:** 226

"Old Harry" (Kinsella), **Supp. V:** 261

"Old Holborn" (Kelman), **Supp. V:** 256

"Old Homes" (Blunden), **Supp. XI:** 34, 44

"Old House" (Redgrove), **Supp. VI:** 228

Old Huntsman, The (Sassoon), **VI:** 423, 430, 453

"Old John's Place" (Lessing), **Supp. I:** 240

Old Joiner of Aldgate, The (Chapman), **I:** 234, 244

"Old Lady" (Smith, I. C.), **Supp. IX:** 221

Old Lady Shows Her Medals, The (Barrie), **Supp. III:** 6, 9, 16

Old Law, The (Massinger, Middleton, Rowley), **II:** 21; **Supp. XI:** 182

Old Lights for New Chancels (Betjeman), **VII:** 361, 367, 368

"Old Main Street, Holborn Hill, Millom" (Nicholson), **Supp. VI:** 216–217

"Old Man" (Jennings), **Supp. V:** 210

"Old Man" (Thomas), **Supp. III:** 402

"Old Man, The" (du Maurier), **Supp. III:** 142–143

"Old Man and the Sea, The" (Morgan, E.), **Supp. IX:** 164

Old Man of the Mountains, The (Nicholson), **Supp. VI:** 220–221, 222

Old Man Taught Wisdom, An (Fielding), **III:** 105

Old Man's Love, An (Trollope), **V:** 102

"Old Meg" (Gunn), **Supp. IV:** 276

Old Men at the Zoo, The (Wilson), **Supp. I:** 154, 161

Old Mrs. Chundle (Hardy), **VI:** 20

Old Mortality (Scott), **IV:** 33, 39

Old Negatives (Gray, A.), **Supp. IX:** 91–92

Old Norse Literature, **VIII:** 227–244

"Old Nurse's Story, The" (Gaskell), **V:** 14, 15

Old Possum's Book of Practical Cats (Eliot), **VII:** 167

Old Pub Near the Angel, An (Kelman), **Supp. V:** 242, 244, 245

"Old Pub Near the Angel, An" (Kelman), **Supp. V:** 245

Old Reliable, The (Wodehouse), **Supp. III:** 451

Old Times (Pinter), **Supp. I:** 376–377

"Old Tongue" (Kay), **Supp. XIII:** 108

"Old Toy, The" (Fuller), **Supp. VII:** 79

"Old Vicarage, Grantchester, The" (Brooke), **Supp. III:** 47, 50, 54

Old Whig (periodical), **III:** 51, 53

Old Wife's Tale, The (Peele), **I:** 206–208

Old Wives' Tale, The (Bennett), **VI:** xiii, 247, 249, 250, 251, **254–257**

"Old Woman" (Smith, I. C.), **Supp. IX:** 211, 213

"Old Woman, An" (Sitwell), **VII:** 135–136

"Old Woman and Her Cat, An" (Lessing), **Supp. I:** 253–254

"Old Woman in Spring, The" (Cornford), **VIII:** 112

"Old Woman of Berkeley, The" (Southey), **IV:** 67

"Old Woman Speaks of the Moon, An" (Pitter), **Supp. XIII:** 142

"Old Women, The" (Brown), **Supp. VI:** 71

"Old Women without Gardens" (Dunn), **Supp. X:** 67

"Oldest Place, The" (Kinsella), **Supp. V:** 268

Oldham, John, **II:** 259

Oley, Barnabas, **II:** 141; **Retro. Supp. II:** 170–171

"Olga" (Blackwood), **Supp. IX:** 12

Oliphant, Margaret, **Supp. X:** 209–225

"Olive and Camilla" (Coppard), **VIII:** 96

Oliver, H. J., **I:** 281

"Oliver Cromwell and Walter Noble" (Landor), **IV:** 92

Oliver Cromwell's Letters and Speeches (Carlyle), **IV:** 240, 244, 246, 249, 250, 342

Oliver Newman (Southey), **IV:** 71

"Oliver Plunkett" (Longley), **VIII:** 173

Oliver Twist (Dickens), **V:** xix, 42, 47–50, 51, 55, 56, 66, 71

Olney Hymns (Cowper), **III:** 210, 211, 220

Olor Iscanus . . . (Vaughan), **II:** 185, 201

Olympia (Manet), **Supp. IV:** 480

O'Malley, Mary, **Supp. IV:** 181

Oman, Sir Charles, **VI:** 387

Omega Workshop, **VI:** 118

Omen, The (film), **III:** 343, 345

Omniana; or, Horae otiosiores (Southey and Coleridge), **IV:** 71

"On a Brede of Divers Colours Woven by Four Ladies" (Waller), **II:** 233

On a Calm Shore (Cornford), **VIII:** 113–114

"On a Chalk Mark on the Door" (Thackeray), **V:** 34

On a Chinese Screen (Maugham), **VI:** 371

"On a Croft by the Kirkaig" (MacCaig), **Supp. VI:** 194

"On a Dead Child" (Bridges), **VI:** 77–78

"On a Drop of Dew" (Marvell), **II:** 211

"On a Girdle" (Waller), **II:** 235

"On a Joke I Once Heard from the Late Thomas Hood" (Thackeray), **IV:** 251–252

"On a Midsummer Eve" (Hardy), **Retro. Supp. I:** 119

"On a Mourner" (Tennyson), **IV:** 332

V: xvi, xx–xxi; **VI:** 371
"Poem" (Cornford), **Supp. XIII:** 91–92
"Poem" (Welch), **Supp. IX:** 269–270
"Poem About a Ball in the Nineteenth Century" (Empson), **Supp. II:** 180–181, 183
"Poem about Poems About Vietnam, A" (Stallworthy), **Supp. X:** 294–295, 302
"Poem as Abstract" (Davie), **Supp. VI:** 106
"Poem by the Boy Outside the Fire Station" (Armitage), **VIII:** 4
"Poem Composed in Santa Barbara" (Cope), **VIII:** 78
"Poem from the North," (Keyes), **VII:** 439
"Poem for My Father" (Reid), **Supp. VII:** 325
"Poem in October" (Thomas), **Supp. I:** 177, 178–179
Poem in St. James's Park, A (Waller), **II:** 238
"Poem in Seven Books, A" (Blake), **Retro. Supp. I:** 37
"Poem in Winter" (Jennings), **Supp. V:** 213–214
"Poem of Lewis" (Smith, I. C.), **Supp. IX:** 211
"Poem of the Midway" (Thomas), **Supp. IV:** 493
"Poem on His Birthday" (Thomas), **Supp. I:** 179
Poem on the Late Civil War, A (Cowley), **II:** 202
"Poem on the Theme of Humour, A" (Cope), **VIII:** 81
Poem Sacred to the Memory of Sir Isaac Newton, A (Thomson), **Supp. III:** 411, 418–419
"Poem Upon the Death of O. C., A" (Marvell), **II:** 205, 211
"Poem with the Answer, A" (Suckling), **II:** 228
Poemata et Epigrammata, . . . (Crashaw), **II:** 201
Poemata et inscriptiones (Landor), **IV:** 100
Poems [1853] (Arnold), **V:** xxi, 165, 209, 216
Poems [1854] (Arnold), **V:** 216
Poems [1855] (Arnold), **V:** 216
Poems [1857] (Arnold), **V:** 216
Poems (Bridges), **VI:** 83
Poems (Brooke), **Supp. III:** 51–53
Poems [1844] (Browning), **IV:** xx, 311, 313–314, 321, 356
Poems [1850] (Browning), **IV:** 311, 321
Poems (Byron), **IV:** 192
Poems (Carew), **II:** 238
Poems (Caudwell), **Supp. IX:** 33, 35
Poems (Clough), **V:** 170
Poems (Cornford), **VIII:** 102, 103
Poems (Cowley), **II:** 194, 198, 199, 202
Poems (Crabbe), **III:** 286
Poems (Eliot), **VII:** 146, 150
Poems (Empson), **Supp. II:** 180
Poems (Gay), **III:** 55
Poems (Golding), **Supp. I:** 66
"Poems, 1912–13" (Hardy), **Retro. Supp. I:** 117

Poems (Hood), **IV:** 252, 261, 266
Poems (Jennings), **Supp. V:** 208
Poems (Keats), **IV:** xvii, 211, 213–214, 216, 235; **Retro. Supp. I:** 183, 187–188
Poems (Kinsella), **Supp. V:** 260
Poems (Lovell and Southey), **IV:** 71
Poems (Meredith), **V:** xxi, 219, 234
Poems (Robinson), **Supp. XIII:** 199, 202, 205, 206, 207
Poems (C. Rossetti), **V:** 260
Poems [1870] (D. G. Rossetti), **V:** xxiii, 237, 238, 245
Poems [1873] (D. G. Rossetti), **V:** 245
Poems [1881] (D. G. Rossetti), **V:** 238, 245
Poems (Ruskin), **V:** 184
Poems (Sassoon), **VI:** 429
Poems (Southey), **IV:** 71
Poems (Spender), **Supp. II:** 483, 486–487
Poems [1833] (Tennyson), **IV:** 326, 329, 338
Poems [1842] (Tennyson), **IV:** xx, 326, 333–334, 335, 338
Poems (Thompson), **V:** 439, 451
Poems (Waller), **II:** 238
Poems (Wilde), **V:** 401–402, 419; **Retro. Supp. II:** 361–362
Poems, The (Landor), **IV:** xvi, 99
Poems, The (Swift), **III:** 15n, 35
Poems, The (Thomas), **Supp. I:** 170
Poems Against Economics (Murray), **Supp. VII:** 270, 273–275
Poems and Ballads (Swinburne), **V:** xxiii, 309, 310, 313, **314–321,** 327, 330, 332
"Poems and Ballads of Goethe" (Clough), **V:** 170
Poems and Ballads: Second Series (Swinburne), **V:** xxiv, 314, 327, 332
Poems and Ballads: Third Series (Swinburne), **V:** 332
Poems and Letters of Bernard Barton (ed. FitzGerald), **IV:** 343–344, 353
Poems and Lyrics of the Joy of Earth (Meredith), **V:** 221, 224, 234
Poems and Melodramas (Davie), **Supp. VI:** 113
Poems and Metrical Tales (Southey), **IV:** 71
Poems and Prose Remains of A. H. Clough, The (ed. Clough and Symonds), **V:** 159, 170
Poems and Songs, The (Burns), **III:** 310n, 322
Poems and Songs (Ewart), **Supp. VII:** 34, 36–37
Poems and Translations (Kinsella), **Supp. V:** 264
Poems Before Congress (Browning), **IV:** 312, 315, 321
Poems by Alfred, Lord Tennyson (Lear), **V:** 78, 87
Poems by Currer, Ellis and Acton Bell (Brontës), **V:** xx, 131–134, 151
Poems by John Clare (Clare), **Supp. XI:** 63
Poems by the Author of the Growth of Love (Bridges), **VI:** 83
Poems by the Way (Morris), **V:** 306

Poems by Two Brothers (Tennyson and Tennyson), **IV:** 337–338
Poems, Centuries, and Three Thanksgivings (Traherne), **Supp. XI:** 263–264, 265, 266, 267, 268, 269, 270, 271, 272, 273, 274, 275, 276, 278
Poems Chiefly in the Scottish Dialect (Burns), **III:** 315
Poems, Chiefly Lyrical (Tennyson), **IV:** xix, 326, 329, 331, 338
Poems Chiefly of Early and Late Years (Wordsworth), **IV:** xx, 25
Poems, Descriptive of Rural Life and Scenery (Clare), **Supp. XI:** 49, 54–55
Poems, Elegies, Paradoxes, and Sonnets (King), **Supp. VI:** 162
"Poems for Angus" (MacCaig), **Supp. VI:** 193
Poems for Donalda (Smith, I. C.), **Supp. IX:** 217
Poems for Young Ladies (Goldsmith), **III:** 191
Poems from Centre City (Kinsella), **Supp. V:** 272
Poems from the Arabic and Persian (Landor), **IV:** 99
Poems from the Russian (Cornford), **VIII:** 110–111
Poems from Villon, and Other Fragments (Swinburne), **V:** 333
Poems in Prose (Wilde), **Retro. Supp. II:** 371
Poems, in Two Volumes (Wordsworth), **IV:** 22, 24
Poems 1926–1966 (Pitter), **Supp. XIII:** 136, 145–146
Poems, 1930 (Auden), **VII:** xix
Poems 1938–1945 (Graves), **VII:** 267–268
Poems, 1943–1947 (Day Lewis), **Supp. III:** 118, 128
Poems 1950 (Bunting), **Supp. VII:** 5, 13
Poems 1960–2000 (Adcock), **Supp. XII:** 2, 11, 13, 14–15
Poems 1962–1978 (Mahon), **Supp. VI:** 173–174
Poems of Conformity (Williams, C. W. S.), **Supp. IX:** 274
Poems of Dedication (Spender), **Supp. II:** 489, 490
Poems of Edmund Blunden, The (Blunden), **Supp. XI:** 36, 37, 44
Poems of Felicity (Traherne), **II:** 191, 202; **Supp. XI:** 266
Poems of Henry Vaughan, Silurist, The (ed. Chambers), **II:** 187
Poems of John Keats, The (ed. Allott), **IV:** 223n 224, 234–235
"Poems of 1912–13" (Hardy), **VI:** 14
Poems of Ossian, The (Macpherson), **III:** 336; **VIII:** 180, 181, 182, 183, 184, 185, 187, 188, 190, 191, 192, 193, 194
Poems of the War and After (Brittain), **Supp. X:** 41
Poems of William Dunbar, The (Dunbar), **VIII:** 118–119
Poems of Wit and Humour (Hood), **IV:** 257, 266
Poems on His Domestic Circumstances (Byron), **IV:** 192

Shadow of Cain, The (Sitwell), **VII:** xvii, 137
Shadow of Dante, A (Rossetti), **V:** 253n
Shadow of Hiroshima, The (Harrison), **Supp. V:** 164
Shadow of Night (Chapman), **I:** 234, 237
Shadow of the Glen, The (Synge), **VI:** 308, 309, 310, 316
Shadow of the Sun, The (Byatt), **Supp. IV:** 140, 141, 142–143, 147, 148, 149, 155
Shadow Play (Coward), **Supp. II:** 152–153
"Shadow Suite" (Brathwaite), **Supp. XII:** 35
Shadow–Line, The: A Confession (Conrad), **VI:** 135, 146–147, 148
"Shadows" (Lawrence), **VII:** 119
"Shadows in the Water" (Traherne), **II:** 192; **Supp. XI:** 269
Shadows of Ecstasy (Williams, C. W. S.), **Supp. IX:** 279–280
Shadows of the Evening (Coward), **Supp. II:** 156
Shadowy Waters, The (Yeats), **VI:** 218, 222
Shadwell, Thomas, **I:** 327; **II:** 305, 359
"Shadwell Stair" (Owen), **VI:** 451
Shaffer, Anthony, **Supp. I:** 313
Shaffer, Peter, **Supp. I:** 313–328
Shaftesbury, earl of, **Supp. III:** 424
Shaftesbury, seventh earl of, **IV:** 62
Shaftesbury, third earl of, **III:** 44, 46, 198
Shahnameh (Persian epic), **Supp. IV:** 439
Shakes Versus Shav (Shaw), **VI:** 130
Shakespear, Olivia, **VI:** 210, 212, 214
Shakespeare, William, **I:** 188, **295–334; II:** 87, 221, 281, 302; **III:** 115–117; **IV:** 149, 232, 352; **V:** 41, 328; and Collins, **IV:** 165, 165n, 170; and Jonson, **I:** 335–337, **II:** 281; **Retro. Supp. I:** 158, 165; and Kyd, **I:** 228–229; and Marlowe, **I:** 275–279, 286; and Middleton, **IV:** 79–80; and Webster, **II:** 71–72, 74–75, 79; influence on English literature, **II:** 29, 42–43, 47, 48, 54–55, 79, 82, 84; **III:** 115–116, 167n; **IV:** 35, 51–52; **V:** 405; **Supp. I:** 196, 227; **Supp. II:** 193, 194; **Supp. IV:** 158, 171, 283, 558
Shakespeare (Swinburne), **V:** 333
"Shakespeare and Stage Costume" (Wilde), **V:** 407
Shakespeare and the Allegory of Evil (Spivack), **I:** 214
Shakespeare and the Goddess of Complete Being (Hughes), **Retro. Supp. II:** 202
Shakespeare and the Idea of the Play (Righter), **I:** 224
"Shakespeare and the Stoicism of Seneca" (Eliot), **I:** 275
"Shakespeare as a Man" (Stephen), **V:** 287
Shakespeare Wallah (Jhabvala), **Supp. V:** 237–238
Shakespeare's Sonnets Reconsidered (Butler), **Supp. II:** 116
Shall I Call Thee Bard: A Portrait of Jason Strugnell (Cope), **VIII:** 69

Shall We Join the Ladies? (Barrie), **Supp. III:** 6, 9, 16–17
Shaman (Raine), **Supp. XIII:** 173
"Shamdev; The Wolf–Boy" (Chatwin), **Supp. IV:** 157
Shame (Rushdie), **Supp. IV:** 116, 433, 436, 440, 443, 444–445, 448, 449
Shamela (Fielding), **III:** 84, 98, 105; **Retro. Supp. I:** 80; **Retro. Supp. I:** 82–83
Shamrock Tea (Carson), **Supp. XIII:** 63–65
Shape of Things to Come, The (Wells), **VI:** 228, 241
"Shape–Changer, The" (Wallace–Crabbe), **VIII:** 318–319
"Shapes and Shadows" (Mahon), **Supp. VI:** 178
SHAR: Hurricane Poem (Brathwaite), **Supp. XII:** 35–36
Sharawaggi: Poems in Scots (Crawford and Herbert), **Supp. XI:** 67–71, 72
Shards of Memory (Jhabvala), **Supp. V:** 233, 234–235
"Shark! Shark!" (Kay), **Supp. XIII:** 109
"Sharp Trajectories" (Davie), **Supp. VI:** 116
Sharp, William, **IV:** 370
Sharpeville Sequence (Bond), **Supp. I:** 429
Sharrock, Roger, **II:** 246, 254
Shaving of Shagpat, The (Meredith), **V:** 225, 234
Shaw, George Bernard, **III:** 263; **V:** xxii, xxv, xxvi, 284, 301, 305–306, 423, 433; **VI:** viii, ix, xiv–xv, **101–132,** 147, 343; **Supp. II:** 24, 45, 51, 54, 55, 117–118, 288, 296–297; **Supp. III:** 6; **Supp. IV:** 233, 288, 292; **Retro. Supp. II:** 309–325
Shaw Gives Himself Away: An Autobiographical Miscellany (Shaw), **VI:** 129
Shaw–Stewart, Patrick, **VI:** 418–419, 420
She (Haggard), **Supp. III:** 211, 212, 213, 219–222, 223–227
She Stoops to Conquer (Goldsmith), **II:** 362; **III:** 177, 181, 183, 188, 191, 256
She Wou'd if She Cou'd (Etherege), **II:** 266, 268, 271
Sheaf of Verses, A (Hall), **Supp. VI:** 119
"Sheep" (Hughes), **Retro. Supp. II:** 209
Sheep and the Dog, The (Henryson), **Supp. VII:** 136, 138–139, 141
"Sheepdog Trials in Hyde Park" (Day Lewis), **Supp. III:** 130
"Sheer Edge" (Malouf), **Supp. XII:** 219
"She's all my fancy painted him" (Carroll), **V:** 264
Shelf Life (Powell), **Supp. IV:** 258
"Shell" (Kay), **Supp. XIII:** 102, 109
Shelley, Mary Wollstonecraft, **III:** **329–331,** 336, 341, 342, 345; **IV:** xv, xvi, xvii, 118, 197, 201, 202, 203; **Supp. III:** **355–373,** 385; **Supp. IV:** 546; **Retro. Supp. I:** 246
Shelley, Percy Bysshe, **II:** 102, 200; **III:** 329, 330, 333, 336–338; **IV:** vii–xii, 63, 132 158–159, 161, 163, 164, 168–169, l72, 176–179, 182, **195–210,** 217, 234, 281, 299, 349, 354, 357, 366,

372; **V:** 214, 330, 401, 403; **VI:** 453; **Supp. III:** 355, 357–358, 364–365, 370; **Supp. IV:** 468; **Retro. Supp. I:** **243–257**
Shelley (Swinburne), **V:** 333
Shelley (Thompson), **V:** 450, 451
Shelley: A Life Story (Blunden), **IV:** 210
Shelley and Keats as They Struck Their Contemporaries (Blunden), **IV:** 210
Shelley's Idols of the Cave (Butler), **IV:** 210
"Shelley's Skylark" (Hardy), **Retro. Supp. I:** 119
Shells by a Stream (Blunden), **Supp. XI:** 37
Shelmalier (McGuckian), **Supp. V:** 280, 290–292
"Shelmalier" (McGuckian), **Supp. V:** 291
Shelter, The (Phillips), **Supp. V:** 380
Sheol (Raine), **Supp. XIII:** 173
Shepheardes Calendar (Spenser), *see Shepherd's Calendar, The*
Shepheard's Oracles, The (Quarles), **II:** 139
Shepherd, Ettrick, *see* Hogg, James
Shepherd, and Other Poems of Peace and War, The (Blunden), **Supp. XI:** 36, 42
"Shepherd and the Nymph, The" (Landor), **IV:** 96
Shepherd of the Giant Mountains, The (tr. Smedley), **V:** 265
"Shepherd's Brow, The" (Hopkins), **V:** 376, 378n
Shepherd's Calendar, The (Spenser), **I:** 97, 121, 123, 124–128, 162
Shepherd's Calendar, The; with Village Stories, and Other Poems (Clare), **Supp. XI:** 59
"Shepherd's Carol" (Nicholson), **Supp. VI:** 214–215
Shepherd's Life, A (Hudson), **V:** 429
Shepherd's Week, The (Gay), **III:** 55, 56, 67
Sheppey (Maugham), **VI:** 377
Sherburn, George, **III:** 73, 78
Sheridan, Richard Brinsley, **II:** 334, 336; **III:** 32, 97, 101, 252–271
Sheridan, Susan, **Supp. IV:** 459
Sherlock Holmes and the Limehouse Horror (Pullman), **Supp. XIII:** 151
"Sherthursdaye and Venus Day" (Jones), **Supp. VII:** 177
Shewan, R., **V:** 409n, 421
Shewing of a Vision, The (Julian of Norwich), **Supp. XII:** 155
Shewings of the Lady Julian, The (Julian of Norwich), **Supp. XII:** 155
Shewing–Up of Blanco Posnet, The: A Sermon in Crude Melodrama (Shaw), **VI:** 115, 117, 124, 129
"Shian Bay" (Graham), **Supp. VII:** 110–111
"Shield of Achilles, The" (Auden), **VII:** 388, 390–391, 397–398; **Retro. Supp. I:** 10
Shikasta (Lessing), **Supp. I:** 250, 251, 252, 253
Shining, The (King), **III:** 345
"Shining Gift, The" (Wallace–Crabbe), **VIII:** 323

South African Winter (Morris, J.), **Supp. X:** 175

"South African Writers and English Readers" (Plomer), **Supp. XI:** 209

South Sea Bubble (Coward), **Supp. II:** 155

South Seas, The (Stevenson), **V:** 396

South Wind (Douglas), **VI:** 293, 294, 300–302, 304, 305; **VII:** 200

Southam, Brian Charles, **IV:** xi, xiii, xxv, 122, 124, 337

Southern, Thomas, **II:** 305

"Southern Night, A" (Arnold), **V:** 210

Southerne, Thomas, **Supp. III:** 34–35

Southey, Cuthbert, **IV:** 62, 72

Southey, Robert, **III:** 276, 335; **IV:** viii–ix, xiv, xvii, 43, 45, 52, **58–72,** 85, 88, 89, 92, 102, 128, 129, 162, 168, 184–187, 270, 276, 280; **V:** xx, 105, 121; **Supp. IV:** 425, 426–427

"Southey and Landor" (Landor), **IV:** 93

"Southey and Porson" (Landor), **IV:** 93, 97

"Southey's *Colloquies*" (Macaulay), **IV:** 280

Southey's Common–place Book (ed. Warter), **IV:** 71

"South–Sea House, The" (Lamb), **IV:** 81–82

"South–Wester The" (Meredith), **V:** 223

Souvenirs (Fuller), **Supp. VII:** 67, 81

Sovereign Remedy, A (Steel), **Supp. XII:** 274–275

Sovereignty of Good, The (Murdoch), **Supp. I:** 217–218, 225

"Soviet Myth and Reality" (Koestler), **Supp. I:** 27

"Sow's Ear, The" (Sisson), **Supp. XI:** 258

Space Vampires (Wilson), **III:** 341

"Space–ship, The" (Smith, I. C.), **Supp. IX:** 216

Spain (Morris, J.), **Supp. X:** 176, 178–179

"Spain 1937" (Auden), **VII:** 384; **Retro. Supp. I:** 8

Spanbroekmolen (Roberts, K.), **Supp. X:** 274–275

Spanish Curate, The (Fletcher and Massinger), **II:** 66

Spanish Fryar, The; or, The Double Discovery (Dryden), **II:** 305

Spanish Gipsy, The (Middleton and Rowley), **II:** 100

Spanish Gypsy, The (Eliot), **V:** 198, 200

"Spanish Maids in England, The" (Cornford), **VIII:** 112–113

"Spanish Military Nun, The" (De Quincey), **IV:** 149

"Spanish Oranges" (Dunn), **Supp. X:** 80

Spanish Tragedy, The (Kyd), **I:** 212, 213, 218, 220, **221–229; II:** 25, 28–29, 69

"Spanish Train, The" (Scupham), **Supp. XIII:** 225

Spanish Virgin and Other Stories, The (Pritchett), **Supp. III:** 316, 317

Spanner and Pen (Fuller), **Supp. VII:** 67, 68, 74, 81

Sparagus Garden, The (Brome), **Supp. X:** 52, 61–62

"Spared" (Cope), **VIII:** 84

Spark, Muriel, **Supp. I:** 199–214; **Supp. IV:** 100, 234

"Sparrow" (MacCaig), **Supp. VI:** 192

Sparrow, John, **VI:** xv, xxxiv; **VII:** 355, 363

Sparrow, The (Ayckbourn), **Supp. V:** 2

"Spate in Winter Midnight" (MacCaig), **Supp. VI:** 187

"Spätlese, The" (Hope), **Supp. VII:** 157

Speak, Parrot (Skelton), **I:** 83, 90–91

Speak for England, Arthur (Bennett), **VIII:** 22–25

"Speak to Me" (Tennyson), **IV:** 332

Speaker (periodical), **VI:** 87, 335

Speaker of Mandarin (Rendell), **Supp. IX:** 192, 198

"Speaking a Foreign Language" (Reid), **Supp. VII:** 330

Speaking Likeneness (Rossetti), **V:** 260

Speaking Stones, The (Fallon), **Supp. XII:** 104–105, 114

"Speaking Stones, The" (Fallon), **Supp. XII:** 104

"Special Type, The" (James), **VI:** 69

"Specimen of an Induction to a Poem" (Keats), **IV:** 214

Specimens of English Dramatic Poets (Lamb), **IV:** xvi 79, 85

Specimens of German Romance (Carlyle), **IV:** 250

Specimens of Modern Poets: The Heptalogia . . . (Swinburne), **V:** 332

Speckled Bird, The (Yeats), **VI:** 222; **Retro. Supp. I:** 326

Spectator (periodical), **III:** 39, 41, 44, **46–50,** 52, 53; **V:** 86, 238; **VI:** 87; **Supp. IV:** 121

Spectatorial Essays (Strachey), **Supp. II:** 497, 502

"Spectre of the Real, The" (Hardy), **VI:** 20

Speculations (Hulme), **Supp. VI:** 134, 140

Speculative Instruments (Richards), **Supp. I:** 426

Speculum hominis (Gower), **I:** 48

Speculum meditantis (Gower), **I:** 48

Speculum Principis (Skelton), **I:** 84

Spedding, James, **I:** 257n, 259, 264, 324

Speech Against Prelates Innovations (Waller), **II:** 238

Speech . . . Against Warren Hastings (Sheridan), **III:** 270

Speech . . . for the Better Security of the Independence of Parliament (Burke), **III:** 205

Speech, 4 July 1643 (Waller), **II:** 238

Speech . . . in Bristol upon . . . His Parliamentary Conduct, A (Burke), **III:** 205

Speech on American Taxation (Burke), **III:** 205

Speech . . . on Mr. Fox's East India Bill (Burke), **III:** 205

Speech on Moving His Resolutions for Conciliation with the Colonies (Burke), **III:** 205

Speech on Parliamentary Reform (Macaulay), **IV:** 274

Speech on the Anatomy Bill (Macaulay), **IV:** 277

Speech on the Army Estimates (Burke), **III:** 205

Speech on the Edinburgh Election (Macaulay), **IV:** 274

Speech on the People's Charter (Macaulay), **IV:** 274

Speech on the Ten Hours Bill (Macaulay), **IV:** 276–277

Speech Relative to the Nabob of Arcot's Debts (Burke), **III:** 205

Speech to the Electors of Bristol (Burke), **III:** 205

Speeches on Parliamentary Reform (Disraeli), **IV:** 308

Speeches on the Conservative Policy of the Last Thirty Years (Disraeli), **IV:** 308

Speeches, Parliamentary and Miscellaneous (Macaulay), **IV:** 291

Speedy Post, A (Webster), **II:** 69, 85

Spell, The (Hollinghurst), **Supp. X:** 120, 132–134

Spell, The: An Extravaganza (Brontë), **V:** 151

Spell for Green Corn, A (Brown), **Supp. VI:** **72–73**

Spell of Words, A (Jennings), **Supp. V:** 219

"Spelt from Sybil's Leaves" (Hopkins), **V:** 372–373

Spence, Joseph, **II:** 261; **III:** 69, 86n

Spencer, Baldwin, **Supp. III:** 187–188

Spencer, Herbert, **V:** 182, 189, 284

Spender, Stephen, **VII:** 153, 382, 410; **Supp. II:** 481–495; **Supp. III:** 103, 117, 119; **Supp. IV:** 95

Spengler, Osvald, **Supp. IV:** 1, 3, 10, 11, 12, 17

Spenser, Edmund, **I:** 121–144, 146; **II:** 50, 302; **III:** 167n; **IV:** 59, 61, 93, 205; **V:** 318

Sphinx (Thomas), **Supp. IV:** 485

"Sphinx, The" (Rossetti), **V:** 241

Sphinx, The (Wilde), **V:** 409–410, 415, 419; **Retro. Supp. II:** 371

"Sphinx; or, Science" (Bacon), **I:** 267

"Spider, The" (Nye), **Supp. X:** 205

Spider (Weldon), **Supp. IV:** 521

Spielmann, M. H., **V:** 137, 152

Spiess, Johann, **III:** 344

Spingarn, J. E., **II:** 256n

"Spinoza" (Hart), **Supp. XI:** 123

"Spinster Sweet–Arts, The" (Tennyson), **IV:** 327

"Spiral, The" (Reid), **Supp. VII:** 330

Spiral Ascent, The (Upward), **Supp. XIII:** 250, 251, 254–259, 260

Spire, The (Golding), **Supp. I:** 67, **79–81,** 83; **Retro. Supp. I:** 99–100

"Spirit, The" (Traherne), **Supp. XI:** 267

"Spirit Dolls, The" (McGuckian), **Supp. V:** 292

"Spirit is Too Blunt an Instrument, The" (Stevenson), **Supp. VI:** 256

Spirit Level, The (Heaney), **Retro. Supp. I:** 132–133

Spirit Machines (Crawford), **Supp. XI:** 67, 76–79

Tale of Pigling Bland, The (Potter), **Supp. III:** 288–289, 290, 291, 304
Tale of Rosamund Gray and Old Blind Margaret, A (Lamb), **IV:** 79, 85
Tale of Samuel Whiskers, The (Potter), **Supp. III:** 290, 297, 301, 305
Tale of Sir Gareth of Orkeney that was called Bewmaynes, The (Malory), **I:** 72, 73; **Retro. Supp. II:** 243, 247
Tale of Sir Lancelot and Queen Guinevere (Malory), **Retro. Supp. II:** 243, 244
Tale of Sir Thopas, The (Chaucer), **I:** 67, 71
"Tale of Society As It Is, A" (Shelley), **Retro. Supp. I:** 245
Tale of Squirrel Nutkin, The (Potter), **Supp. III:** 288, 290, 301
Tale of the House of the Wolflings, A (Morris), **V:** 302, 306
Tale of the Noble King Arthur that was Emperor himself through Dignity of his Hands (Malory), **I:** 69, 72, 77–79
Tale of the Pie and the Patty–Pan, The (Potter), **Supp. III:** 290, 299
Tale of the Sankgreal, The (Malory), **I:** 69; **Retro. Supp. II:** 248–249
Tale of the Sea, A (Conrad), **VI:** 148
Tale of Timmy Tiptoes, The (Potter), **Supp. III:** 290
"Tale of Tod Lapraik, The" (Stevenson), **Retro. Supp. I:** 267
Tale of Tom Kitten, The (Potter), **Supp. III:** 290, 299, 300, 302, 303
Tale of Two Bad Mice, The (Potter), **Supp. III:** 290, 300–301
Tale of Two Cities, A (Dickens), **V:** xxii, 41, 42, 57, 63, 66, 72
"Talent and Friendship" (Kinsella), **Supp. V:** 270
Talent to Annoy, A (Mitford), **Supp. X:** 163
Talented Mr. Ripley, The (Highsmith), **Supp. V:** 170
Tales (Crabbe), **III:** 278, 285, 286; *see also Tales in Verse; Tales of the Hall; Posthumous Tales*
"Tales" (Dickens), **V:** 46
Tales and Sketches (Disraeli), **IV:** 308
Tales from a Troubled Land (Paton), **Supp. II: 344–345,** 348, 354
Tales from Angria (Brontë), **V:** 151
Tales from Ovid (Hughes), **Retro. Supp. II:** 202, 214–216
Tales from Shakespeare (Lamb and Lamb), **IV:** xvi, 80, 85
Tales I Tell My Mother (ed. Fairbairns et al.), **Supp. XI:** 163, 164, 175
Tales I Told My Mother (Nye), **Supp. X:** 195
Tales in Verse (Crabbe), **III:** 275, 278, 279, 281, 286
Tales of a Grandfather (Scott), **IV:** 38
Tales of All Countries (Trollope), **V:** 101
Tales of Good and Evil (Gogol), **III:** 345
Tales of Hearsay (Conrad), **VI:** 148
Tales of Hoffmann (Hoffmann), **III:** 334, 345
Tales of Mean Streets (Morrison), **VI:** 365
Tales of My Landlord (Scott), **IV:** 39

Tales of Natural and Unnatural Catastrophes (Highsmith), **Supp. V:** 179
Tales of St. Austin's (Wodehouse), **Supp. III:** 449–450
Tales of Sir Gareth (Malory), **I:** 68
Tales of the Crusaders (Scott), **IV:** 39
Tales of the Five Towns (Bennett), **VI:** 253
Tales of the Hall (Crabbe), **III:** 278, 285, 286; **V:** xvii, 6
"Tales of the Islanders" (Brontë), **V:** 107, 114, 135
Tales of the Punjab (Steel), **Supp. XII:** 266
Tales of the Tides, and Other Stories (Steel), **Supp. XII:** 275
Tales of Three Cities (James), **VI:** 67
Tales of Unrest (Conrad), **VI:** 148
Talfourd, Field, **IV:** 311
Taliesin (Nye), **Supp. X:** 193
"Taliessin on the Death of Virgil" (Williams, C. W. S.), 283
"Taliessin Returns to Logres" (Williams, C. W. S.), **Supp. IX:** 282
Taliessin Through Logres (Williams, C. W. S.), **Supp. IX:** 282–283
Talisman, The (Scott), **IV:** 39
"Tall Story, A" (Burnside), **Supp. XIII:** 18
Talk Magazine, **Supp. XIII:** 174
Talk Stories (Kincaid), **Supp. VII:** 217, 231
Talkies (Crawford), **Supp. XI:** 67, 72–74
Talking Bronco (Campbell), **Supp. III:** 119
Talking Heads (Bennett), **VIII:** 27–28
Talking It Over (Barnes), **Supp. IV:** 65, 67, 68, 72–74
Talking of Jane Austen (Kaye–Smith and Stern), **IV:** 123
"Talking to Myself" (Auden), **Retro. Supp. I:** 13
"Tam o' Shanter" (Burns), **III:** 320
Tamburlaine the Great (Marlowe), **I:** 212, 243, 276, 278, 279–280, **281–282; II:** 69, 305
Tamburlaine, Part 2 (Marlowe), **I:** 281–282, 283
"Tamer and Hawk" (Gunn), **Supp. IV:** 258
Taming of the Shrew, The (Shakespeare), **I:** 298, 302, 303, 327; **II:** 68
Tamworth Reading Room, The (Newman), **Supp. VII:** 294
Tancred (Disraeli), **IV:** 294, 297, 300, 302–303, 307, 308
Tancred and Gismund (Wilmot), **I:** 216
Tancred and Sigismunda (Thomson), **Supp. III:** 411, 423, 424
Tangier Papers of Samuel Pepys, The (ed. Chappell), **II:** 288
Tangled Tale, A (Carroll), **V:** 273
"Tannahill" (Dunn), **Supp. X:** 74–75
Tanner, Alain, **Supp. IV:** 79, 95
Tanner, J. R., **II:** 288
Tanner, Tony, **VI:** xxxiv
Tannhäuser and Other Poems (Clarke), **V:** 318n
"Tano" (Brathwaite), **Supp. XII:** 39
Tao of Pooh, The (Hoff), **Supp. V:** 311

"Tapestry Moths" (Redgrove), **Supp. VI:** 235–236
"Tapestry Trees" (Morris), **V:** 304–305
"Tardy Spring" (Meredith), **V:** 223
Tares (Thomas), **Supp. XII:** 284
Tarr (Lewis), **VII:** xv, 72
"Tarry delight, so seldom met" (Housman), **VI:** 161
Tarry Flynn (Kavanagh), **Supp. VII:** 186, 194–195, 199
Task, The (Cowper), **III:** 208, **212–217,** 220; **IV:** xv, 184
"Task, The" (Nye), **Supp. X:** 205
Tasso, Torquato, **II:** 49; **III:** 171
"Taste" (Dahl), **Supp. IV:** 215, 217
Taste and Remember (Plomer), **Supp. XI:** 214, 222
Taste for Death, A (James), **Supp. IV:** 320, 330–331
Taste of Honey, A (Rattigan), **Supp. VII:** 320
"Taste of the Fruit, The" (Plomer), **Supp. XI:** 214
Tate, Nahum, **I:** 327; **II:** 305
Tatler (periodical), **II:** 339; **III:** 18, 29, 30, 35, 39, **41–45,** 46, 51, 52, 53
Tausk, Victor, **Supp. IV:** 493
Tawney, R. H., **I:** 253
Tax Inspector, The (Carey), **Supp. XII:** 51, 54, 59–60, 62
Taxation No Tyranny (Johnson), **III:** 121; **Retro. Supp. I:** 142–143
"Taxonomy" (Burnside), **Supp. XIII:** 25
Taylor, A. L., **V:** 270, 272, 274
Taylor, A. J. P., **IV:** 290, 303
Taylor, Henry, **IV:** 62n
Taylor, Jeremy, **Supp. IV:** 163
Taylor, John, **IV:** 231, 233, 253
Taylor, Mary, **V:** 117
Taylor, Thomas, **III:** 291
Taylor, Tom, **V:** 330
Te of Piglet, The (Hoff), **Supp. V:** 311
"Tea"(Saki), **Supp. VI:** 244
Tea Party (Pinter), **Supp. I:** 375
"Tea with an Artist" (Rhys), **Supp. II:** 390
"Tea with Mrs. Bittell" (Pritchett), **Supp. III:** 328–329
"Teachers" (Dunn), **Supp. X:** 82
"Teacher's Tale, The" (Cope), **VIII:** 83
Teapots and Quails (Lear), **V:** 87
"Tear" (Kinsella), **Supp. V:** 274
"Teare, The" (Crashaw), **II:** 183
"Tears" (Thomas), **VI:** 424
"Tears" (Vaughan), **II:** 187
"Tears are Salt" (Smith, I. C.), **Supp. IX:** 217–218
"Tears, Idle Tears" (Hough), **IV:** 323n, 339
"Tears, Idle Tears" (Tennyson), **IV:** 329–330, 334
"'Tears, Idle Tears' Again" (Spitzer), **IV:** 323n, 339
Tears of Amaryllis for Amyntas, The: A Pastoral. (Congreve), **II:** 350
Tears of Peace, The (Chapman), **I:** 240–241
"Teasers, The" (Empson), **Supp. II:** 190
Tea–Table (periodical), **III:** 50

"Tony Kytes, The Arch–Deceiver" (Hardy), **VI:** 22

"Tony White's Cottage" (Murphy), **Supp. V:** 328

"Too Dearly Bought" (Gissing), **V:** 437

Too Good to Be True (Shaw), **VI:** 125, 127, 129

"Too Late" (Browning), **V:** 366, 369

Too Late the Phalarope (Paton), **Supp. II:** 341, **351–353**

Too Many Husbands (Maugham), **VI:** 368–369

"Too Much" (Muir), **Supp. VI:** 207

"Toot Baldon" (Motion), **Supp. VII:** 253

Tooth and Nail (Rankin), see *Wolfman*

Top Girls (Churchill), **Supp. IV:** 179, 183, 189–191, 198

Topkapi (film), **Supp. IV:** 4

"Torridge" (Trevor), **Supp. IV:** 501

"Tortoise and the Hare, The" (Dahl), **Supp. IV:** 226

Tortoises (Lawrence), **VII:** 118

Tortoises, Terrapins and Turtles (Sowerby and Lear), **V:** 76, 87

"Torturer's Apprenticeship, The" (Murray), **Supp. VII:** 280

"Tory Prime Minister, Maggie May . . . , A" (Rushdie), **Supp. IV:** 456

Totemism (Frazer), **Supp. III:** 171

"Totentanz" (Wilson), **Supp. I:** 155, 156, 157

Tottel's Miscellany, **I:** 97–98, 114

Touch (Gunn), **Supp. IV:** 257, 264, 265–266

"Touch" (Gunn), **Supp. IV:** 265–266

Touch and Go (Lawrence), **VII:** 120, 121

Touch of Love, A (screenplay, Drabble), **Supp. IV:** 230

Touch of Mistletoe, A (Comyns), **VIII:** 54–55, 56, 58–59, 65

Tour Thro' the Whole Island of Great Britain (Defoe), **III:** 5, 13; **Retro. Supp. I:** 75–76

Tour to the Hebrides, A (Boswell), *see Journal of a Tour to the Hebrides*

Tourneur, Cyril, **II:** 24, 33, **36–41,** 70, 72, 85, 97

Toward Reality (Berger), *see Permanent Red: Essays in Seeing*

"Toward the Imminent Days" (Murray), **Supp. VII:** 274

"Towards an Artless Society" (Lewis), **VII:** 76

Towards Democracy (Carpenter), **Supp. XIII:** 36, 37–40

"Towards Democracy" (Carpenter), **Supp. XIII:** 37–38

Towards the End of Morning (Frayn), **Supp. VII:** 53–54, 65

Towards the Human (Smith, I. C.), **Supp. IX:** 209

Towards the Mountain (Paton), **Supp. II:** 346, 347, 351, 359

Towards Zero (Christie), **Supp. II:** 132, 134

Tower, The (Fry), **Supp. III:** 194, 195

Tower, The (Yeats), **VI:** 207, 216, 220; **Retro. Supp. I:** 333–335

Towers of Silence, The (Scott), **Supp. I:** 267–268

Town (periodical), **V:** 22

"Town and Country" (Brooke), **VI:** 420

"Town Betrayed, The" (Muir), **Supp. VI:** 206

Townley plays, **I:** 20

Townsend, Aurelian, **II:** 222, 237

Townsend Warner, George, **VI:** 485

Town–Talk (periodical), **III:** 50, 53

"Trace Elements" (Wallace–Crabbe), **VIII:** 323

"Track 12" (Ballard), **Supp. V:** 21

Trackers of Oxyrhyncus, The (Harrison), **Supp. V:** 163, 164

Tract 90 (Newman), see *Remarks on Certain Passages of the 39 Articles*

"Tractor" (Hughes), **Retro. Supp. II:** 211

Tracts for the Times (Newman), **Supp. VII:** 291, 293

"Traction–Engine, The" (Auden), **Retro. Supp. I:** 3

"Trade" (Carpenter), **Supp. XIII:** 40

"Tradition and the Individual Talent" (Eliot), **VII:** 155, 156, 163, 164

"Tradition of Eighteen Hundred and Four, A" (Hardy), **VI:** 22

Tradition of Women's Fiction, The (Drabble), **Supp. IV:** 231

Tradition, the Writer and Society (Harris), **Supp. V:** 145, 146

"Traditional Prize Country Pigs" (Cope), **VIII:** 82–83

"Traditions, Voyages" (Wallace–Crabbe), **VIII:** 318

Traffics and Discoveries (Kipling), **VI:** 204

"Tragedy and the Essay, The" (Brontë), **V:** 135

"Tragedy Of, The" (Scupham), **Supp. XIII:** 220–221, 223

Tragedy of Brennoralt, The (Suckling), **II:** 226

Tragedy of Byron, The (Chapman), **I:** 233, 234, 241*n*, 251

Tragedy of Count Alarcos, The (Disraeli), **IV:** 306, 308

Tragedy of Doctor Faustus, The (Marlowe), **Retro. Supp. I:** 200, 207–208

"Tragedy of Error, A" (James), **VI:** 25

Tragedy of Sir John Van Olden Barnavelt, The (Fletcher and Massinger), **II:** 66

Tragedy of Sophonisba, The (Thomson), **Supp. III:** 411, 422, 423, 424

Tragedy of the Duchess of Malfi, The (Webster), *see Duchess of Malfi, The*

Tragedy of Tragedies; or, The Life . . . of Tom Thumb, The (Fielding), *see Tom Thumb*

"Tragedy of Two Ambitions, A" (Hardy), **VI:** 22

Tragic Comedians, The (Meredith), **V:** 228, 234

Tragic History of Romeus and Juliet, The (Brooke), **I:** 305–306

Tragic Muse, The (James), **VI:** 39, **43–55,** 67

"Tragic Theatre, The" (Yeats), **VI:** 218

Tragical History of Doctor Faustus, The (Hope), **Supp. VII:** 160–161

Tragical History of Dr. Faustus, The (Marlowe), **III:** 344

Traherne, Thomas, **II:** 123, **189–194, 201–203**; **Supp. XI:** 263–280

Trail of the Dinosaur, The (Koestler), **Supp. I:** 32, 33, 36, 37

Traill, H. D., **III:** 80

Train of Powder, A (West), **Supp. III:** 439–440

Trained for Genius (Goldring), **VI:** 333

Traité du poeme épique (Le Bossu), **III:** 103

Traitor's Blood (Hill, R.), **Supp. IX:** 117

"Trampwoman's Tragedy, The" (Hardy), **VI:** 15; **Retro. Supp. I:** 120

Transatlantic Review (periodical), **VI:** 324; **Supp. XIII:** 190

Transatlantic Sketches (James), **VI:** 67

"Transfiguration, The" (Muir), **Supp. VI:** 207

"Transformation" (Carpenter), **Supp. XIII:** 47

"Transformation Scenes" (Scupham), **Supp. XIII:** 222

Transformed Metamorphosis, The (Tourneur), **II:** 37, 41

"Transients and Residents" (Gunn), **Supp. IV:** 271, 273

transition (quarterly periodical), **Supp. I:** 43*n*

Transitional Poem (Day Lewis), **Supp. III:** 117, 121–123

"Translation of Poetry, The" (Morgan, E.), **Supp. IX:** 168–169

Translations (Friel), **Supp. V:** 123–124

Translations and Tomfooleries (Shaw), **VI:** 129

"Translations from the Early Irish" (Kinsella), **Supp. V:** 264

Translations of the Natural World (Murray), **Supp. VII:** 281–282

"Transparencies" (Stevenson), **Supp. VI:** 262

"Transvaal Morning, A" (Plomer), **Supp. XI:** 214

Trap, The (Richardson), **Supp. XIII:** 184–186

Traps (Churchill), **Supp. IV:** 179, 180, 183–184, 188, 198

Traulus (Swift), **III:** 36

Travelers (Jhabvala), **Supp. V:** 230

"Traveling to My Second Marriage on the Day of the First Moonshot" (Nye), **Supp. X:** 202

"Traveller" (Kinsella), **Supp. V:** 263

Traveller, The (Goldsmith), **III:** 177, 179, 180, 185–186, 191; **Retro. Supp. I:** 149

"Traveller, The" (Stevenson), **Supp. VI:** 254, 265

"Travelling" (Healy), **Supp. IX:** 106

Travelling Behind Glass (Stevenson), **Supp. VI:** 256–257

"Travelling Behind Glass" (Stevenson), **Supp. VI:** 257, 261

"Travelling Companion, The" (Kinsella), **Supp. V:** 261

"Travelling Companions" (James), **VI:** 25, 69